The History of
Post-War Southeast Asia

JOHN F. CADY

THE HISTORY OF
POST-WAR SOUTHEAST ASIA

OHIO UNIVERSITY PRESS / Athens, Ohio

PREFACE

This historical survey of postwar Southeast Asia is intended for both students and general readers who are seriously interested in the subject. It does not presume to be a specialized study of the process of political decolonization per se, nor an exposition of the economic problems of underdeveloped areas, nor a study of the complicated process of modernization, however defined. The preparation of such monographic analyses can better be left to specialists in their several disciplines. It is nevertheless apparent that if historical developments are to be understood they must be viewed in the broad context of attendant circumstances, political, economic, and social. A balanced historical treatment can provide a useful setting within which more analytical studies can be profitably considered.

Even when reduced to the simpler dimensions of a straight-forward narrative approach, the task is a difficult one. Few students can claim expert historical knowledge covering all of the political units of Southeast Asia, not to mention acquaintance with associated disciplines. The sheer abundance of monographic works covering the many facets of postwar Southeast Asia poses a formidable task of sifting and evaluation. Some may even question whether the quarter-century that has elapsed since the expulsion of the Japanese invaders and liquidation of the colonial presence can provide a sufficient time perspective in which to assess what has happened in the area. The varied story does not lend itself to easy generalizations. It is complicated by the

v

emergence of differing kinds of internal tensions within the several countries, coupled with friction between contiguous states over issues that are rooted in precolonial patterns of friction. Furthermore, the region has been caught up since 1949 in the turmoil of world power rivalries.

A single-author approach does afford certain inherent advantages, especially in the perception of similarities and differences within the several developing situations, which is not easily achieved in multiple-authored accounts. The total area needs to be brought into focus. Any particular interpretation of events can be, admittedly, only approximately correct, since the complete evidence is never in and consensus cannot be assumed. But the task of trying to explain what has happened in postwar Southeast Asia cannot be indefinitely postponed. The painful, two-decade-long American involvement in the affairs of former French Indochina has demonstrated the tragic mistakes arising from dubious premises, false analogies, and the general lack of basic understanding at high government levels concerning Southeast Asia generally. Professional scholarship must face its serious responsibilities in this connection.

The preparation of this study was initiated during the course of an eighteen-month assignment to the Faculty of History at Thammasat University in Bangkok under appointment by the Rockefeller Foundation. It was completed following my return to Ohio University, with the help of a sabbatical leave. Acknowledgement is hereby made of the generous and understanding assistance afforded by the Rockefeller Foundation in providing me opportunity to visit again most of the countries of the area. The distribution of space allocations to the various countries of the region has been made roughly in accordance with the importance of the role that a given unit has played in the story and assessment of the significance of events with which it has been associated. I assume full responsibility for both factual content and the interpretations herein advanced.

The book is dedicated to the well-being of the hundreds of students of Southeast Asian countries whom I have been privileged to know during the course of the last thirty-eight years.

John F. Cady
Ohio University

TABLE OF CONTENTS

INTRODUCTION

A brief descriptive introduction to Southeast Asia and its people will assist uninitiated readers who have had limited acquaintance with the affairs of prewar Southeast Asia. The region is vast, being bounded along its exterior perimeter by a 5,000-mile, semicircular arc extending from the Tibetan borders of northern Burma southward around Sumatra, eastward to the Moluccas, and thence northward to the top of the Philippines. It included in 1945 some 160 million people, and by the mid-sixties the number had grown to 220 million. Almost half of the total population reside in the Indonesian islands, with two-thirds of these crowded into Java and adjacent Madura, only 7 percent of the total area. Four second-level states, roughly equal in size, match Indonesia in total population namely the Philippines, Vietnam, Thailand, and Burma. Smaller populations were found in Malaya and Singapore (8 million), Cambodia (5.7 million), Laos (2.5 million), plus several hundred thousand in British Borneo. The indigenous population of Southeast Asia descended from Malay and Mongoloid ancestors who migrated to the area millennia ago. In the extensive mountain areas of Burma, Laos, Vietnam, and interior island sections, widely variant cultural and linguistic differences still persist, spanning virtually the total civilizing process. Aside from Java, the major population concentrations are found presently in the Red River delta of Tonkin, the lower Mekong Valley of Cambodia and Cochin-China, the southern reaches of the Chao Phraya Menam (river) of Thailand, and in Lower Burma's vast delta plain.

During colonial times, large numbers of coastal Chinese migrated to Southeast Asia. They managed in time to take over most urban trading activities plus skilled labor and craftsmanship roles. Malaya's population became some 37 percent Chinese, and that of Singapore island around 75 percent. They settled in substantial numbers in all commercial centers, with the single exception of northern Vietnam, where effective local competition offered them less opportunity for advancement. In the 1960s the overseas Chinese came to number more than 12 million.

Around two million Indian settlers, most of them transients, settled in British Burma and Malaya-Singapore after 1880. Many of them were brought in as members of recruited labor service groups, who returned home with their savings after several years' residence. Despite the large numbers who departed annually, Rangoon became largely an Indian city during the interwar decades. In Penang and Singapore, as well, Indians were the common laborers and shopkeepers. They dominated the transportation services and port facilities and also invaded the professions of moneylending, law, and medicine. Indian immigrants provided workers for the rubber plantations of Malaya and Singapore. The mass of Asian immigrants functioned economically in between the European colonial elite and the indigenous population. Thus in modern times as in its historical beginnings, Southeast Asia was influenced by neighboring China and India.

The material resources of Southeast Asia contributed to its increasing importance as a world trading and investment center during the early twentieth century. The seven to eight million tons of surplus rice exported annually from the ports of Burma, Thailand, and southern Indochina during the interwar years were matched in volume by no other region of the world. The Malayan peninsula and neighboring Indonesian islands also produced much of the world's tin and natural rubber. Oil was available in central Burma, in southern Sumatra, and along the upper Borneo coasts, while valuable timber resources were accessible in Burma, Thailand, North Borneo, and the Philippines. Southeast

Asia also produced much of the world's supply of pepper and spices, plus sugar, tobacco, kapok, and hemp. High quality coal was available in northern Vietnam, and a variety of valuable minerals were found in Burma. Most of these natural resources were developed by alien entrepreneurs after 1885 and prior to 1929. Western capital investments were particularly heavy in mills needed to process local production and in the development of various aspects of the economic infrastructure, such as irrigation controls, transportation and communication services, port facilities, and urban development in general.

The colonial legacy had both positive and negative aspects. Economic development activities greatly increased the volume of trade, expanded opportunities for employment, and thus gradually raised popular living standards generally, even though wage scales for unorganized laborers remained abysmally low. Once colonial controls were fully established around 1900 (Siam was the only exception), peace and order were maintained both within the several units and throughout the region. Epidemic diseases were curbed, and medical services became more generally available. Educational facilities were also expanded and modernized, especially for selected elite groups whose sons could aspire to attractive governmental employment.

The negative impacts of colonial rule were largely political and cultural. They included the discrediting of the indigenous symbols of governmental authority and the disruption of traditional patterns of social control. The forced pace of centralized governmental administration required the implementation of unfamiliar legal codes and court procedures, the detailed assessment of all land for taxation purposes, and the multiplication of other services generally associated with a capital investment economy. Such changes placed foreigners in complete control of all colonialized areas and left the mass of the indigenous population socially disrupted as well as politically helpless. The people could neither influence governmental policy nor participate meaningfully in the advantages to be derived from the colonizing process. The usual colonial-ruler tactic of divide and rule was generally effective, mainly because the various uncoordinated expressions of nationalist sentiment did not agree on their definition of objectives or the methods for realizing political ends.

Historical trends within Southeast Asia during the course of the first four decades of the twentieth century were also influenced by important events in the outside world, which provided a context for efforts at revolutionary change. The first important event was the defeat of Russia by Asian Japan in 1905. This was followed by the collapse of imperial rule in China in 1911 and the emergence during the 1920s of the anti-Western Kuomintang movement. Following World War I came the Communist party triumph in Russia, the appearance of fascism in Italy, and the emergence of the Congress party movement in India. The world depression struck from 1929 to 1933, dealing a staggering blow to the prestige of capitalism in general and to Western-type democracy in particular. Rebellions—all badly coordinated, highly confused, and generally ineffective—flared in Burma, Vietnam, and Java. The depression led to Hitler's rise to power in Germany, an event that altered the entire political context of Western Europe.

Meanwhile, the emerging pattern of gradual progress toward self-government, as attempted in the Philippines and Burma and tentatively in the Javan Volksraad Council, seemed to have little relevance to ending colonialism and the associated domination of Southeast Asia's economy and society by aliens. French Socialist party reform leadership exerted by Premier Reynaud in the twenties and Leon Blum in the late thirties collapsed in the face of vigorous French-resident opposition in Cochin-China. French repression forced Vietnamese nationalism underground, where it became dominated by the Indochina Communist party, organized in 1930.

The demand for change became increasingly insistent with the outbreak of World War II in 1939, followed by the aggressive Asian stance assumed by Japanese militarists. Hitler's conquests in Western Europe greatly weakened the colonial rulers of Southeast Asia and diverted

American attention thus facilitating Japan's conquest of Southeast Asia in 1942. Apart from that catalytic event, the colonial system might well have survived for several decades longer. The French, as of 1939, were still in effective control of Indochina; the Dutch continued to enjoy the assistance of the priyayi elite in administering Java and had the cooperation of local sultans in the Outer Islands. In 1941 British Malaya was showing only the first evidences of anticolonial sentiment. Even in Burma, the so-called Freedom Bloc, including Ba Maw and the Thakins, had been effectively suppressed by U Saw's indigenous government. Anticolonialism everywhere was still largely negative, widely fragmented, and thus subject even during wartime to a considerable degree of Japanese manipulation. Tokyo's initial goal of a Greater East Asia Coprosperity Sphere, with Japan as leader, persisted well into 1944. Even when the Japanese, in the face of impending defeat, decided in 1945 to encourage nationalist aspirations for independence, the response was often varied and ill defined.

The Japanese conquest facilitated the emergence of national leadership but created serious problems as well. Changes in the psychological milieu involved both immediate and long-term implications. The demoralizing anarchy of wartime spawned lawlessness and violence, so that long submerged domestic tensions came to the surface and gradually took on new dimensions. Difficulties of maintaining internal order multiplied, while closer contacts within the region and with outside power groupings complicated the developing situation.

Policy options became confusingly varied and deceptively broad. The new nationalist leadership was bent on achieving both political and economic independence, which involved the elimination of alien control, but the path was far from clear. Population pressures generally vetoed the possibility of returning to traditional precolonial patterns of government and livelihood. The alternative aspirations of the educated indigenous leadership to appropriate the technological assets of the West were also beyond early

realization, due mainly to deficiencies of material resources and the lack of necessary training and administrative experience. Because of the political confusion that
attended the enforced departure of alien entrepreneurs,
such countries as Burma, Indonesia, and most of French
Indochina found it very difficult to recover from wartime
losses, both economic and governmental.

The obverse side of the postwar problem was that the
peoples newly freed from colonial tutelage were understandably concerned to revitalize valued aspects of their
traditional cultures. This was especially the case in situations where recovery of national identity was involved.
Such efforts usually diverted attention from concern for
political and economic progress. Ingrained habits of social
deference and the observance of religious and ethical
norms, including traditions and taboos, tended to get in
the way of rational planning. Within the broad pattern here
suggested, circumstances differed widely from country
to country, as will become apparent. Partly because drastic
alteration in the basic cultural dimension is virtually impossible to measure in the short run, this study will focus
attention primarily on attempted adjustments in the spheres
of government and economics.

I

THE IMPACT OF WORLD WAR II

The Wartime Occupation

Japan's conquest and occupation of Southeast Asia from 1942 to 1945 produced both immediate and long-term effects. The myth of Western invincibility was permanently shattered, and Asia for the Asiatics became the universally accepted goal. The devastating psychological impact resulting from Japan's spectacular elimination of colonial controls left many observers dazed and incredulous. Among the first to recover their aplomb were the younger nationalists, many of whom were participating politically or militarily in public affairs for the first time. They assumed in many instances an assertiveness and self-confidence not justified by their capacities and experience. Toward the end of the occupation, the Japanese propaganda deliberately stimulated expressions of popular opposition to any restoration of colonial control, thus encouraging aggressive action by such youthful nationalists.

Since the peoples of Southeast Asia all suffered dire physical privations during the course of the occupation, popular hostility to the Japanese forces was almost universal. The Japanese appropriated whatever resources they needed, particularly food and transportation facilities, often without compensation. When they did offer payment, their newly printed currency notes, either local in character or in yen, were not matched by any purchasable consumer imports from Japan. Surplus rice could not be exported nor even transported to scarcity areas within the same country for lack of facilities. Enormous stretches of paddy land remained uncultivated and reverted to semijungle. All categories of manufactured goods, especially cloth, were in very short supply, so that prices multiplied some tenfold. To the imposition of forced labor for military construction was added the calculated barbarities of the Military Police (Kempetai), in wanton violation of social and cultural sensitivities.

Labored efforts made by trained Japanese liaison officers to identify religiously with Muslims in Indonesia, with Buddhists in Burma, or with Christians in the Philippines were everywhere unconvincing. Similarly, the persistent efforts of Tokyo to popularize the Greater East Asia Coprosperity Sphere slogan enlisted few converts. Japanese language training was pushed, and officially sponsored delegations from all occupied countries were sent to visit Japan. Nippon's "new order" promised at most the forbidding prospect of Southeast Asian political and economic subordination to a technologically dominant Asian power. Victims of Japanese mistreatment affirmed, after the war, that whereas the Europeans had appropriated their wealth, the Asian occupation forces had sucked the marrow of their bones. The possibility of regional domination by an Asian power was made more forbidding by the misconduct of demoralized Chinese troops in Upper Burma during their 1942 withdrawal. A similarly negative example was set by Kuomintang forces sent into upper Indochina by the victorious Allies in 1945 to take the surrender of the Japanese. If independent Southeast Asian countries should require some measure of security protection in the future, they would, without exception, prefer not to obtain it from powerful Asian neighbors.

For a number of reasons, partly political and partly economic, the prestige of Soviet Russia was widely acclaimed among Southeast Asian nationalists at the end of the war. In contrast to the defeated forces of Western Europe, Russian armies had thrown back the Nazi invaders. Among the victorious Allied nations, furthermore, the USSR alone advocated in unqualified fashion the ending of colonial rule. On this issue United States policy equivocated out of deference to the sensitivities of European allies. Experience seemed thus to authenticate in some measure the Communist accusation that Western capitalism and colonialism were closely allied. The Soviet Union also afforded for many a demonstration of industrial progress and national strength achieved quickly by a previously backward nation through planned development under governmental auspices. The leadership of many of the newly emerging states aspired to similar accomplishment. Wartime hardships had also underscored the necessity of outgrowing a colonialized economy that produced mainly food and raw materials for export to industrially advanced countries, who could provide the needed consumer goods in return.

Planned economic development seemed to afford both a short-cut path to self-sufficiency and the means of liquidating the dominant economic roles previously played by the Western entrepreneurs and by alien Chinese and Indian residents. National economic expectations were raised unduly high by the theoretical prospect of indigenous enjoyment of the total profits that had been realized in prewar times by aliens from the exploitation of colonial resources. Postwar economic planning usually ran aground on social and cultural barriers, plus an accumulation of political and administrative deficiencies. The mirage of Soviet-style planned economic development was, at best, highly deceptive.

Although some individual members of Japanese-sponsored puppet regimes gained ruling experience during the course of the occupation, the war period contributed little to governmental progress in general. French colonial administrators in Indochina continued to carry out their routine duties down to the spring of 1945. The princely facades at Hué, Phnom Penh, and Luang Prabang were kept in place. The Japanophile government of Thailand's Marshal Pibun Songgram, which was almost as antagonistic to Chinese residents as were the invaders, initially took on a measure of arrogance. This mood waned after mid-1944, when the civilian-controlled Free Thai faction took over from the military. Even so, governmental authority in Siam remained a monopoly of the same restricted ruling class elite that had been dominant before the war.

Elsewhere in Southeast Asia wartime conditions afforded little opportunity for political experimentation. The Japanese-sponsored regime of *Adhipati* (chief of state) Dr. Ba Maw in Burma, for example, actually regressed measurably in the direction of a revival of ancient court ritual. The Malay sultans continued to function as titular rulers throughout the wartime period, although they commanded diminishing popular respect. Four sultanates were transferred temporarily to Thai control, and the rest of Malaya was administered under a Japanese military command centering in Sumatra. The occupation forces took such brutal vengeance on the Chinese civilian residents of Malaya and Singapore that a Chinese resistance movement, Communist directed, took to the jungle out of sheer desperation. Indonesia was divided arbitrarily into three separate military administrative districts, west, central, and east. Indigenous prisoners previously incarcerated by the Dutch were liberated and belatedly encouraged to express their nationalist aspirations. A substantial fragment of the Indonesian nationalist movement operated underground.

Filipino resistance to the Japanese persisted in remote areas of the Islands throughout the war, but Tokyo had no difficulty enlisting self-seeking politicians and bureaucrats to perform necessary governmental functions. President Laurel declared war on the United States in 1943. The Philippines and Burma suffered extensive physical damage during both the Japanese conquest and withdrawal, but political prospects differed. In contrast with the Philippines, where the pre-war constitution of 1936 survived intact, the returning British Governor for Burma

4

was directed to set aside the pre-war constitutional system for an indefinite period pending economic recovery.

Continuity of Governmental Institutions: Thailand

Postwar Southeast Asian countries can be divided into two main groups, according to the degree of continuity they maintained with respect to prewar governmental institutions. The five states that registered comparatively little change, namely Thailand, Malaya, Cambodia, Laos, and the Philippines, can conveniently be considered first.

When the Japanese made their initial move into Southeast Asia, in 1940–41, the government of Siam was administered by two principal elements, the Cabinet and the nonpolitical bureaucracy. Cabinet posts were controlled by representatives of the reforming "promoter" group, both military and civilian, who had brought an end to royal absolutism in 1932. The career civil service still retained its prestige deriving from long association with royal authority. Although the promoter faction tried to establish a superficial democratic façade, only half of the Legislative Assembly was elected, and most of its members had no political affiliation, since party organizations were not permitted. Virtually all Assembly members were therefore subject to persuasion, intimidation, or bribery by the ruling clique. In 1937 the elite military faction assumed control under the nationalistic Colonel Pibun Songgram. Pibun changed the name of the country from Siam to Thailand in 1939, a move reflecting his irredentist ambitions to recover Thai-inhabited border lands and those lost during the preceding century to British and French colonial authorities. Pibun's principal civilian rival, lawyer Luang Pridi Phanomyong, resigned from the cabinet in late 1941, protesting Pibun's failure to oppose the Japanese invasion.

In 1940 Pibun took advantage of the collapse of French power in Europe to take over by force two enclaves on the right bank of the upper Mekong River, which the French

5

had seized in 1904 and 1907. French colonial troops were able to stage only token resistance, and the cession of territory was subsequently formalized under Japanese "mediation." Pibun later enlisted Japanese support, in August 1941, for his claim to Cambodia's Battambang Province plus cis-Mekong Laotian territories located near the Cambodian border. Following the Japanese invasion in early December, Pibun signed a hastily prepared Japanese alliance on December 21. He declared war on both Great Britain and the United States in January, alleging that Britain had failed to aid Siam in 1893 and that the United States had failed to deliver military aircraft already paid for by Bangkok.

Pibun's alliance with Japan entailed numerous advantages. Siam was spared Japanese interference with its internal administration, plus exemption from destructive bombing attacks and other acts of war. Bangkok was not required to provide forced labor for Japanese projects, including the Railway of Death, which victimized so many conscripted Burmese and European prisoners of war. In August 1943 Pibun annexed, with Japanese support, four border states of Malaya, two neighboring Shan states of Burma, plus the Cambodian province of Siem Reap, the seat of the ancient capital of Angkor. He also responded to Japanese encouragement to intensify persecution of resident Chinese in educational and economic spheres.

Pibun's close association with the overassertive and distrusted Japanese occupation forces proved his political undoing. Price inflation, shortage of consumer goods, and loss of face, plus Japanese monopoly of the use of transportation facilities, were major grievances. Official corruption also attained a new peak within Pibun's wartime regime. The exercise of public power in Thailand degenerated into a scramble for personal enrichment within a jungle of bureaucratic factions. By mid-1944 the fading of Japan's cause in the Pacific area contributed to Pibun's outright displacement. Pibun proposed at the time to shift Thailand's capital northward to a more secure base from which to defend his power against an eventual enemy, whether Allied or Japanese. The Assembly's rejection of the proposal on August 2, 1944, signaled the downfall of his already discredited regime. Pibun's civilian rival, Pridi Phanomyong, stepped into the vacant role of political leader and undertook a discreet reorientation of foreign policy. (Since his resignation as minister of finance in December 1941, in protest to Pibun's refusal to resist Japanese entry, Pridi had filled the innocuous post of regent to the absent king.)

A primary preoccupation was launching the Free Thai movement in cooperation with Ambassador Seni Promoj at Washington, who had disowned Pibun's January 1942 declaration of war. In 1943 Seni was afforded access by American authorities to blocked Thai funds, which he used in cooperation with Pridi's agents to establish the Free Thai radio network. Representatives of the American Office of Strategic Services, smuggled into various alien internment camps of Bangkok, eventually managed to establish short-wave radio communication with Lord Mountbatten's headquarters at Kandy, Ceylon.

As Premier of the new civilian government of July 1944, Pridi installed the clever **Khuang Aphaiwong**, who parried questions raised by Japanese military spokesmen concerning the new regime. By early 1945 the Free Thai leadership was committed to provide a fifty-thousand-man army to aid the Allies by attacking the Japanese rear at the appropriate time. Whether or not a military effort of such magnitude could really have been launched will never be known. Positive evidence is lacking that Pibun's army-officer faction, still very much in evidence at Bangkok, was fully committed to or even aware of such a program. Washington nevertheless accepted in good faith the Free Thai offer of cooperation and elected to ignore Pibun's declaration of war.

Following Japan's surrender, the Bangkok government was obliged to deal initially with the British-officered Southeast Asian Command rather than with the American forces operating in the Pacific theater. London's policy of treating Siam as an enemy nation did not lack some

7

justification. Pibun had facilitated the Japanese invasion of both Burma and Malaya. He had publicly aligned himself with Tokyo and had declared war against the United Kingdom with no provocation. Bangkok was also a passive partner to the atrocious tactics of Japanese officers directing the construction of the railway leading to the Burma border. In London's view, Siam was legally liable for damages arising from her conduct. Bangkok must therefore submit to temporary Allied control of Siam's foreign trade, cooperate in the repatriation of Japanese troops, and help reduce the influence of hostile elements presumably still present within the Siamese army. British policy conceivably could have had a salutary effect in curbing the power of the military in Siam, just as the U.S. role did in postwar Japan, thus assisting the eventual triumph of constitutional democracy.

Washington took a different view of the peace-making problem at Bangkok. The admittedly hostile Pibun faction had been displaced in 1944 by Pridi's Free Thai group, which had afforded substantial evidence of willingness to support the Allied cause. Pridi changed the name back to Siam, accepted Allied demands to restore all territorial acquisitions obtained with the aid of Japan, and offered to relieve the distress of neighbor wartime victims by providing food and other needs. Ambassador Seni Promoj was brought back to Bangkok in September 1945, to supervise the peace negotiations on a short-term assignment as Prime Minister, despite his remote princely rank. At one crucial point in the late 1945 parleys, the American Secretary of State threatened by trans-Atlantic phone to disown the proposed punitive British peace terms as being excessively harsh. Siam was the only country within the region where the newly organized State Department's policy division for Southeast Asia was free of the veto of senior European desk officers who customarily gave low priority to emerging nationalist aspirations. Washington argued that if the civilian-Assembly-based government headed by Pridi's Free Thai were punished for actions taken by Pibun's ousted military clique, the Allied contribution to the cause of democratic government would be nil. The United States subsequently granted Siam some ten million dollars for railway restoration, afforded access to surplus military supplies, and supported Siam's international recognition via United Nations membership.

The peace treaty with Britain and India required Siam's restoration of all territorial annexations made since 1940, a pledge not to construct a canal across the Kra isthmus without prior British and Indian consent, plus pledges of economic and trade assistance. Some one and a half million tons of rice were to be supplied gratis by Siam to needy neighbors and accumulated tin, tea, and rubber sold at below world market prices. Only a fraction of the gift rice was ever actually delivered. The British treaty was signed on January 1, 1946, and the distressed Seni Promoj resigned as Prime Minister shortly thereafter.

Although forced to return French Indochina territories, Pridi's policy with respect to the revived French colonial presence continued to be sharply hostile. In 1945–46 Bangkok provided asylum for the anti-French Lao Issara (Free Lao) exiles from Vientiane, who were protesting the restoration of French colonial rule. King Norodom Sihanouk of Cambodia also found temporary refuge in Bangkok during the course of his prolonged negotiations for a French pledge of independence for Cambodia. Some 50,000 Vietnamese refugees from French rule were allowed to settle down in northeastern Siam, from which group both recruits and supplies were provided, with Pridi's connivance, for the use of the Vietminh rebel forces. Domestically, Pridi amended the Constitution in 1946 to bar army officers from holding political posts and undertook otherwise to buttress the power of the elected Parliament in support of his civilian regime. He seems to have contemplated making Siam the champion of both nationalism and liberal government in postwar noncolonial Southeast Asia.

Thailand's performance during the course of the East Asian War and its immediate aftermath can be characterized as a demonstration of *realpolitik*. The country

9

emerged militarily unscathed from the ordeal that had engulfed most of Eastern Asia. Siam itself suffered no net territorial losses or revolutionary upheaval, emerging under a government opposed to militarism and championing freedom and unity among emerging nations of the region. Political power remained concentrated within ruling circles in which the army clique still controlled the means of physical coercion. The thwarting of Pridi's commendable hopes belongs to a later discussion of the functioning of democratic institutions in postwar Southeast Asia.

The Postwar Philippines

For the Philippines as for Thailand, the Japanese occupation did little to alter the traditional social basis and composition of the ruling class. The Constitution of 1936 carried over with little significant change. Japan found politicans willing to collaborate during the course of the war, but Tokyo's promise of freedom from American rule carried little appeal with the people. Anti-Japanese guerrilla units operated throughout the war in many parts of the Islands. What the Free Thai movement promised in the way of eventual collaboration with the Allied forces during the final stages of the war, the Filipino resistance maintained throughout the struggle. Filipino ruling circles, with American backing, managed to avoid sharing postwar power with popular elements identified with the guerrilla nationalist operations. Because independence was already promised for 1946, no nationalist independence struggle ensued as was the case in Indonesia or Vietnam. Politically dominant economic groups who had a stake in the status quo readily cooperated with the returning American forces without incurring any stigma of national betrayal. When political stability was restored, the same landlord-supported oligarchy was again in charge.

Not every Filipino could join the rebels in the hills, so that wartime political alignments became blurred. The vulnerable urban population had to conform outwardly and

some found cooperation profitable. Associate Justice José P. Laurel, for example, accepted the Japan-offered post of President, while Manuel Roxas served under Laurel as minister without portfolio charged with the procurement of rice for the occupation forces. Most officials stayed at their posts ostensibly as a means of avoiding anarchy. The same excuse was not valid for the near 50 percent of the members of Congress who accepted membership in the Japanese-appointed National Assembly of the "Republic" in October 1943. Some of the apparent collaborators, such as Roxas, played both sides of the street by communicating in clandestine fashion with General MacArthur's returning forces.

Although some change in Filipino political leadership appeared to be in prospect at the end of the war, none was actually forthcoming. The initially contemplated punishment of enemy collaborators, which could have altered materially the character of the political elite, simply failed to come off. Not a single important personage was convicted by the special People's Court established for the purpose. The returning Americans in April 1945 promptly "liberated" Roxas, MacArthur's friend, and a year later he became the successful American-supported candidate for the Presidency against the prewar Vice-President, Sergio Osmeña. Roxas accepted the constitutional alteration according parity to American investors in developing Filipino resources, a concession that was the price exacted by Washington for postwar financial assistance. José Laurel took temporary refuge in Japan in 1945, but unlike Burma's *Adhipati* Ba Maw, he was able to return to active politics in Manila a few years later, as a Nacionalista critic of the pro-American Roxas. Laurel came very near being elected president as his party's candidate in 1949. With Roxas elevated to the presidency and Laurel permitted free political activity, little ground remained on which to raise charges of pro-Japanese collaboration as a political or legal issue. The resumption of "politics as usual" may have contributed to governmental stability in the Philippines, but it also added to the de-

11

moralization of governmental services and incurred grave political liabilities for the long run.

The problem of growing corruption stemmed in part from the enormously expanded temptations afforded by American aid policies. In prewar times, United States standards of official performance, legally enforceable, had kept nepotism and graft under some measure of control, while the disciplined advocacy of the nationalist cause generated its own restraints on misconduct. The war experience itself had made cheating something of a patriotic duty as well as a family asset. Ethical standards of conduct applied primarily in any case within the family and kinship groups, which provided basic personal security and jobs. Opportunities for personal aggrandizement at the expense of the public interest multiplied enormously after the war in connection with the disposition of military stockpiles, claims for bogus war damages, and applications for guerrilla back pay.

After July 1946, when complete independence removed all American restraints, official corruption proliferated. It involved, among other things, dishonesty in election-cost declarations and official expense accounts, plus connivance with smugglers and quota juggling. Elected officials could sell their votes, collect from application recipients, forge useful vouchers and income reports, and receive salary kickbacks from official appointees and contributions from recipients of government contracts. Popular indignation was muted because private ethical standards tended to support the practice of seeking family advantage at public expense. Most officials were guilty at some point, differing only in the degree of their dishonest involvement.[1] The underlying foundations of political administration were thus rendered treacherously unstable.

Malaya's Wartime Experience

Japanese policy with regard to occupied Malaya reflected Tokyo's complete lack of regard for expressions

of Malay nationalism. Similarly, the retiring British rulers themselves had felt no compulsion in 1941 to take nationalist sentiment into account. The fledgling anti-British Union of Malay Youth, founded in 1937 and outlawed in 1940, had favored political union with an independent Indonesia. The Japanese released the youthful Union leaders from jail to form the People's Association of Peninsular Indonesia, but the association was generally detested by both Malay and the slightly less numerous Chinese residents. The Japanese later, as indicated above, assigned four northern sultanates to Thailand and associated the rest of Malaya administratively with neighboring Sumatra.

Most of the 2.4 million Chinese residents of pre-war Malaya were little interested in Malayan nationalism. After 1939 politically active Chinese had generally adopted a pro-British stance, and even the Communist elements fell in line after Hitler attacked Russia in 1940. Threatened with massacre and extortion at the hands of the Japanese, many Chinese fled to the fringes of the malarial jungle, where they resorted to subsistence agriculture as a means of survival. The all-Chinese, Communist-led Malayan Peoples Anti-Japanese Army, which initiated organized rebellion in 1943, numbered only six thousand men, who were dependent on support from less active countrymen. British Force 136 flew in arms and agents from India. Such forces managed to disrupt Japan's military transportation, but they were too weak to constitute a significant military factor. Even so, Britons connected with the resistance efforts in wartime Malaya were understandably appreciative of the heroic efforts of Chinese allies. Some Chinese renegades turned informers for personal profit, while the regular Malayan police normally did the bidding of the Japanese.

Malaya's Indian population of seven hundred and fifty thousand fared slightly better than did the Chinese. An estimated sixty thousand unemployed estate laborers were drafted for a variety of forced labor projects, including building the railway of death in Siam. Only one in three survived the Siam ordeal. Disease also took a heavy toll among destitute Indian residents. On the other hand, the Japanese enlisted the support of politically conscious Indians by sponsoring the Azad Hind (Free India) organization and the so-called Indian Independence Army. Resident Indian businessmen were blackmailed to finance the movement. Both groups eventually transferred headquarters to Burma in late 1943 under the leadership of Subhas Chandra Bose.

Because all inhabitants of Malaya suffered from food shortages, collapse of trade, and soaring prices, the population welcomed the return of British forces as a deliverance from three years of political and economic distress. Even so, the political climate was radically altered, and reconciliation locally was far from easy. During the several weeks interim period between the surrender of Japan and the arrival of the British occupation forces, clashes between feuding Chinese and Malays became widespread. The returning British authorities had to screen and retrain the demoralized Malayan police before they could be used effectively in restoring order. Factional rivalry persisted for several years while authorities attempted to find a compromise solution for difficult constitutional and communal problems. The details of this story will be covered in a later chapter.

Cambodia at the End of the War

The virtual absence of overt anticolonial sentiment in prewar Cambodia can be attributed to historic factors. Cambodia traditionally had been a political pawn between rival contestants. The original French assertion of protector status at Phnom Penh in 1867 had entailed an acknowledgment of Bangkok's counterclaim to the border provinces of Battambang and Siem Reap. These areas the French subsequently reclaimed for Cambodia in 1909. Although the power of the Cambodian monarchy was heavily compromised at the time of King Norodom's death in 1904, the traditional governmental façade long survived as a symbol of popular allegiance and respect.

The French interfered little in cultural and religious affairs and customarily employed the more industrious Vietnamese in plantation development. By 1941 Cambodia had developed neither a malcontent nationalist leadership nor issues around which popular unrest could easily crystalize.[2]

The Japanese occupation subjected Cambodia's deeply ingrained respect for French authority to a severe buffeting. The ground invasion of Thailand in 1941–42 came via Cambodia. In 1943 came the aforementioned cession of the frontier provinces Battambang and Siem Reap back to Thailand, a move that exposed completely the impotence of the hitherto protective French role. In March 1945 Japan abruptly cancelled French colonial authority, imprisoned all resident French officials, and prompted King Norodom Sihanouk to declare Cambodia's "independence." To counter governmental efforts to reestablish the traditional system of divine monarchy, the Japanese brought back Son Ngoc Thanh, an anti-French editor, from his wartime exile in Japan. Son was assigned the role of foreign minister covering little more than relations between Phnom Penh and Tokyo. He assembled a limited youthful following who advocated independence from France and an end to monarchy, goals pictured as a kind of magical solvent for all political and economic problems. In opposition to Son's policy, the royal court preferred the prospect of eventual French return and a gradual approach to independence.

On the eve of the Japanese surrender in mid-August 1945, Son Ngoc Thanh assumed the post of prime minister from the despondent king and proceeded to arrest all of his pro-French Cabinet associates. When internal tensions generated clashes between resident Vietnamese and Cambodians, the king threatened to abdicate. Son's final act as premier, taken just prior to the Allied return in October 1945, was to stage a French-style plebiscite registering general approval of his policies. He was arrested a short time thereafter by British occupation authorities, who were accompanied by French officers. Although Son

15

was later convicted of treason and exiled to France, the still-active proponents of his anti-French policy enjoyed covert support from both Pridi Phanamyong's Free Thai regime at Bangkok and from Vietminh partisans in Vietnam. Son was destined to return in 1972 following Sihanouk's expulsion. Despite the apparent acquiescence of the court, the returning French were not able to restore the traditional security of their colonial protectorate. The train of events transpiring outside Cambodia were beyond Phnom Penh's control.

Sihanouk's compromise agreement with Paris representatives, reached in January 1946, decreed that Cambodia should become an "autonomous state within the Indochina Federation of the French Union," whatever that might mean. The Allied peace treaties meanwhile obliged Siam to return Cambodian border territories seized during the war. French authorities resumed essential policing powers and foreign policy control. Important items of future governmental responsibility were theoretically assigned to the new Indochinese Federation, in process of organization. Political opposition to the French in Cambodia was not united and therefore proved amenable to manipulation. French control continued to operate on a de facto basis until 1953.[3]

In Cambodia as elsewhere, the wartime experience made a new order necessary, but it was a long time maturing. Two considerations would be determinative. One was the desirability of exploiting continuing popular respect for royal authority; the other was the importance of maintaining the territorial boundaries with Thailand, now that border provinces were recovered. A third factor related to the country's eventual involvement in the Vietnamese War.

Laos after the War

The principal effect of the wartime undermining of French prestige in Laos was to precipitate an orgy of princely feuding. For the most part, the people lacked any

16

sense of national identity, and few of them were not directly involved in the personal rivalries that developed within elite ranks. Following the forced cession of the cis-Mekong province of Samaboury to Japan-supported Thailand in early 1941, the French authorities undertook to strengthen the position of King Sisavang Vong at Luang Prabang. They defined more clearly the extent of his territorial authority and permitted for the first time his establishment of a royal cabinet covering virtually all aspects of government. The cabinet and king exercised little initiatory power, functioning mainly to administer policy decisions determined elsewhere. As prime minister of the new government and as the newly appointed viceroy, Prince Phetsarath, the ambitious half-brother of the king, took over the number one post. Feuding developed shortly thereafter with the eldest son of the king, Prince Savang, who saw in Phetsarath a rival to his succession claims.

Princely feuding came to an inevitable crisis after the Japanese in 1945 expelled all French officials and required the king to declare Laos independent of French control. Following the Japanese surrender, Premier Phetsarath assumed an openly anti-French stance, declaring himself in favor of national unification. The king and crown prince, acting in cooperation with the hereditary governor of Champassak province, Prince Boun Oum, favored the alternative policy of restored French rule and preservation of the traditional feudal structure. Utilizing the support of the occupying Kuomintang Chinese forces who were assigned to take the surrender of the Japanese, Phetsarath and friends managed in the fall of 1945 to form their own Lao Issara government and to declare the traditional ruler deposed in favor of a constitutional monarchy. Unable to stem the advance of returning French forces, the Lao Issara government and its several princely supporters fled to Bangkok in April 1946.

Another royal half-brother, Prince Souphanouvong, a French-educated engineer with Hanoi family connections, acted for a time as titular foreign minister of the ephemeral Lao Issara government. Until hospitalized by a minor wound, Souphanouvong participated in the Vietminh-sponsored guerrilla efforts to resist French reentry into central Laos. His eventual move to join the exiles in Bangkok added another dimension to the royal feuding. Prince Phetsarath opposed Vietminh activity in Laos, while Souphanouvong favored it.

While the frustrated Lao Issara faction of royal elite sat out the next three years in Bangkok, the royalist pro-French faction in Laos encountered difficulties of its own. A modus vivendi with the French was fashioned in August 1946, which led to the drafting of a constitution in May 1947. In order to include the southern Laotian state of Champassak within the unified arrangement, the French designated Prince Boun Oum as the permanent inspector general of the kingdom and president of the upper house of the legislature. This move also assured the Francophile prince an important role in designating royal successors.

Most of the Bangkok exiles returned to Laos in 1949, following French recognition of Laotian "independence" as an associated state within the French Union. For several years thereafter, little change occurred. French residents were still subject only to the jurisdiction of their own courts, and the command of the Laotian army as well as the direction of foreign policy were in French hands. Many of the returnees were assigned important posts in the merging state government. Among the few important figures who refused to return to Vientiane following the dissolution of the Lao Issara were Princes Phetsarath and Souphanouvong, both of whom continued to be adamantly anti-French. Phetsarath was refused pardon by the king, while Souphanouvong in cooperation with the Vietminh helped organize the Pathet Lao (Lao Country) movement to contest the French presence in Laos. It was part of the continuity of political tradition in Laos that all factions and cliques were headed by princes. Such personal rivalries contributed nothing to political or economic progress. Emerging postwar Laos was far from being a nation state.

18

Burma's Wartime Revolution

Burma's Anti-Fascist People's Freedom League (AFPFL) was nurtured within the very cradle of the Japanese-sponsored government of the Anglophobe *Adhipati* Dr. Ba Maw. During the early thirties, Ba Maw had headed one of the factions of the boycotting General Council of Burmese Associations. He had been minister of education during the student strike of 1936, and as Burma's first premier, in 1937–38, had initiated important reform proposals covering land alienation, tenancy, and agricultural credit. After being forced out of office by political rivals, he joined the Thakins as leader of the Freedom Bloc in 1939 and suffered arrest in 1940. Ba Maw escaped from an Upper Burma jail during the course of the Japanese conquest and was installed by the invaders as *adhipati* in August 1942. The two principal Anti-Fascist conspirators, Thakins Aung San and Than Tun (related by marriage), served respectively as Ba Maw's minister of war and commander of the national army and as minister of agriculture and of transportation. Than Tun became Communist oriented during the course of the war. Most of the Thakins connected with the wartime government (Mya and Nu in particular) respected Ba Maw's efforts to establish a semblance of independence for Burma, to preserve its territorial integrity, and to protect the population, including minority elements, from abuse by the occupying Japanese forces. The *adhipati* on his part was not unaware of the Anti-Fascist League's efforts to establish contacts with the British authorities in India (a policy he emphatically disapproved), but he did not expose the conspirators to the Japanese.

What ruined Ba Maw's political standing with the people of Burma generally was his identification with Tokyo's self-proclaimed mission to free Asia from European imperialism to the advantage of Japan. Despite his corrosive relations with the local Japanese army commanders in Burma, which became so bitter at one point that they made

19

an abortive attempt to assassinate him, Ba Maw maintained to the very end his close relations with the Tokyo authorities. He actually journeyed to Japan during the final desperate year of the war to help fan the *kamikazi* spirit of fanatical resistance to the American attack. At the end of the war, he sought refuge in Japan. Whether he was motivated primarily by his Anglophobia, by his close identification with the Bengali revolutionary Subhas Chandra Bose as head of the Azad Hind from 1943 to 1945, or by personal vanity and ambition (he assumed the title of *Mingyi*, or Great Prince), Ba Maw lost rapport with the Burmese people. His government's recruitment of some sixty-five thousand forced laborers for building the Burma section of the Railway of Death from Siam was the most memorable offense, for which he later apologized.[4] Politically, he was more fanatic than statesman, and he burned too many bridges behind him to be able to retrace his steps. His political career ended, therefore, with his flight to Japan.

In contrast to Dr. Ba Maw, his youthful Thakin associates displayed adaptable tactics combined with a singleness of political purpose that elevated them by 1945 to the level of undisputed leaders of the nationalist cause. They completely outflanked the elite prewar political leadership, some of whom had fled to India with Governor Sir Reginald Dorman-Smith. A substantial number of the older generation of educated Burman leaders found places in postwar law courts, in cultural agencies, and in education, but they could not challenge the political influence of the Thakin element. The *pongyi* (great glory) monks who had been active in the prewar anti-Separation movement and in boycotting dyarchy elections were also politically emasculated. Having mistakenly regarded the Japanese as liberators and fellow Buddhists in 1942, they later suffered extreme personal abuse at Japanese hands. Even the sincerely Buddhist Thakin Nu denounced political involvement on the part of the *pongyis*. The Thakin leadership in general was secularist in viewpoint, and a substantial portion was Marxist in orientation. Than Tun emerged as the acknowledged Communist leader.

20

The recapture of central Burma and the port of Rangoon by Imperial British forces, including large Indian and African contingents, in May 1945 was substantially assisted by elements of Aung San's Burma National Army. Starting in late March, in cooperation with the British-organized Force 136, they struck the Japanese forces in the rear, especially in the areas of Toungoo and Pegu. What had previously been a stubborn Japanese retreat averaging a few miles a day became a hurried withdrawal. The Japanese evacuated Rangoon by the end of April, just prior to the beginning of the monsoon season. Lord Louis Mountbatten, acting as supreme allied commander, concluded that enlisting the aid of the Burmese forces was essential to the timely capture of Rangoon and the continuing campaign. But in elevating the AFPFL forces to the level of allies, he precipitated opposition from both London and Dorman-Smith's government-in-exile at Simla. Mountbatten respected the nationalist aspirations espoused by Aung San and Than Tun and put the Thakin leaders in a favored political position as compared to Dorman-Smith's associates. Rising nationalist support for the AFPFL movement reduced substantially the relative influence of the minority Marxist element within the total alignment. In October 1945 a serious crisis developed, when the returning governor elected to deny the bona fide status of AFPFL leaders as nationalist spokesmen. The resulting situation will be considered in Chapter II.

The Japanese Impact on Java

Political protest in prewar colonial Indonesia had difficulty finding expression. Engineer Sukarno's Indonesian Nationalist Party (PNI), organized in 1927, became active in 1929, but its leaders suffered police detention later in the same year. Several years later, a moderate Democratic Socialist party emerged, led by two European-educated Sumatrans, Sjahrir and Hatta, who similarly found their way to penal camps in 1934. Because political aspirations were permitted local expression only within

21

the circumscribed limits of the indirectly elected Volksraad Assembly, the popular roots of both the PNI and the Socialists remained shallow. Since cautious Dutch reforming efforts were unrelated to Indonesian cultural traditions or political aspirations, the popular response that they generated was disappointingly meager. As of 1941, the Netherlands Indies was still being run very largely by the Dutch, with indigenous elements denied participation in the formulation of political or economic decisions.[5]

The Japanese occupation forces apparently contemplated the indefinite occupation of the vast and resource-rich Indonesian domain, and therefore did not consider it necessary or advisable at first to encourage expressions of political nationalism. Japan's propaganda objective was designed to shatter Dutch prestige and that of the traditional *priyayi* (elite) hierarchy of officials, so long associated with colonial rule. Europeans everywhere in Indonesia were taken into custody and publicly humiliated. Every grievance of which the Indonesians were conscious was laid at the door of the allegedly greedy and heretical Dutch, a tactic calculated to help make impossible any permanent re-establishment of colonial control. Japanese naval administration of the highly disparate eastern islands region of Indonesia refrained from stressing political indoctrination at any time.

Positive efforts of the Japanese to enlist Indonesian acceptance and cooperation were concentrated in the Java section via the newly formed Islamic Council, or MIAI. The council included at first the actively modernist Muhammadijah group, the more conservative Nahdatul Ulama organization, and remnants of the one-time politically important Sarekat Islam. Posing as the friend of Asian Muslims, the Japanese enlisted the cooperation of the hundreds of Islamic scribes associated with the broadly inclusive MIAI Council. Council groups numbering several score persons were assembled one after another to be told about Japan's pro-Islamic objectives and the intrinsic merits of the Greater East Asia Coprosperity Sphere. The effort was moderately effective at the outset, but it ran aground by late 1943. Mounting popular resentment against Japanese requisitions of labor and food undercut the propaganda drive. The MIAI also demanded that the allegedly friendly Japanese should subsidize the projected Islamic revival and assist the Council's relief efforts.

The second move of the Japanese was to sponsor the organization of the so-called Masjumi Party, or Consultative Council of Indonesian Muslims. The Masjumi did not include fanatical elements of the MIAI and functioned essentially as a Muslim political organization. Some of the scribes who continued to give credence to Japan's pretensions were later joined by various orthodox trading groups seeking access to travel and trading permits available only from the Japanese. The Masjumi influence did not extend to the irreconcilable West Javanese Darul-Islam advocates of an Islamic state. The effectiveness of Masjumi's influence within Java tended to decline progressively with growing anti-Japanese feeling.[6]

Meanwhile, in the spring of 1943, the Japanese initiated formation of a secular political organization known as Putera, (Indonesian Nationalist Party) headed by popular nationalist personalities, Sukarno and Hatta. Taking advantage of Putera's limited measure of autonomy, Sukarno maintained secret relations with the nationalist underground led by Sutan Sjahrir. Putera undertook to assist the nearly prostrate economy by recruiting an emergency labor force. It also enlisted under officers of its own choosing an auxiliary Peta (Avengers of the Country) army dedicated to oppose any eventual Dutch efforts to return. Putera lasted for less than a year, while the Peta youth militia carried on somewhat longer. Sukarno and Hatta took on a new role in March 1944 as leaders of an ephemeral People's Loyalty Organization. The fall of Tojo's government in mid-1944 brought a vague promise from Tokyo of future Javanese independence plus some religious concessions corresponding to earlier MIAI demands.

Finally in March 1945 Tokyo made the first significant Japanese move in the direction of independence by asking

Sukarno and Hatta, as heads of a representative committee of nationalists drawn from Java and nearby Madura, to devise a formula for political cooperation. The resulting *Pantja Sila* (five principles) statement was a platitudinous affirmation of nationalism, internationalism, representative government, social justice, and faith in God. The formula lacked both vitality and popular appeal, but it was the first overt indigenous move not predicated on Indonesian subservience to Japan as "Leader, Protector, and Light of Asia." A student conference held in June demanded outright independence. Student militants virtually dictated Sukarno's and Hatta's subsequent declaration of independence, issued by the Independence Preparatory Committee on August 17, 1945.

Indonesia's secular nationalist leadership, both above and underground, supported by *Peta* militia and student pressure, dominated the early postwar political scene. The prevailing viewpoint was radically modernist, for the temporary Japanese presence had stimulated the desire for change. Cultural inhibitions were bypassed. Modern music and painting gained popularity alongside Western literature and political ideas. English emerged as the new second language, displacing Dutch and supplementing the Malay-Indonesian *lingua franca*. Youth groups repudiated the traditional respect and homage due to traditional (*adat*) aristocracy and Muslim scribes. The initial mood of youthful pride and idealism was vibrantly real, to be recalled by Indonesian spokesmen later with a sense of nostalgia.[7] Aspirations for progressive change were nevertheless deceptive, because the innovations proposed were themselves divergent and fragmented. *Adat* traditions and religious partisanship simply refused to die, so that any basic transformation of the Indonesian scene would inevitably take time.

Beneath the froth of political excitement, Indonesians experienced dire suffering during the years of imposed Japanese rule. The recruitment of forced laborers from Java alone numbered an estimated three hundred thousand men, many of whom never returned. The army requi-

24

sitioned 70 percent of Java's food production, thus reducing the crowded island population to near starvation. Urban migrants returned to their original villages, where traditional and community ties facilitated survival. Whatever popular satisfaction was generated by the humiliation of the Dutch was far exceeded by popular hatred and distrust of the offending Japanese. And yet at the end of the ordeal, Europeans who emerged from the concentration camps encountered a bewildering different atmosphere. Former Indonesian employees and associates discarded their previous attitude of deference and subordination in a remarkable psychological transformation. The wartime experience made impossible any reversion to the older colonial order of relationships.[8]

For the resident Chinese in Indonesia as elsewhere in Southeast Asia, Japanese control spelled persecution. Adult Chinese were assessed a one hundred dollar registration fee plus irregular monetary levies from time to time. Not until near the end of the occupation, and then only out of deference to the wishes of the cooperating Wang Ching-wei regime at Nanking, did local Japanese commanders undertake to protect resident Chinese from thievery and abuse at the hands of lawless Indonesian elements.

At the outset, leadership within the nationalist movement was firmly lodged with Sukarno and Hatta, who assumed the posts of president and vice-president, respectively, of the "Independent Republic" in August, 1945. In November, 1945, the Japanophile Premier Subarjo gave way by agreement to the leader of the anti-Japanese underground organization, Sutan Sjahrir, a Democratic Socialist, and to Sjarifuddin, who later turned Communist. Meanwhile, President Sukarno's nationalist followers elicited support from civil servants and administrators throughout Java. The rival Masjumi Muslim party commanded a large following among the religiously-oriented trading community (*santri*) outside of Java. Nationalist leadership remained for the better part of a decade in the hands of these two groups.[9]

25

Vietnam during Wartime

Because French repression of political reform efforts forced all opposition underground, prewar political protests in Vietnam were fragmented and weak despite widespread discontent. A Vietnamese Nationalist party, fashioned during the late twenties on the Kuomintang model, was virtually destroyed in 1930 following an abortive coup staged along the Chinese border. A similar organization was destined to reappear in 1945, again under Kuomintang auspices, as the Dong Minh Hoi. A more deeply committed revolutionary organization appeared in 1930–31 at Hong Kong, where the long-time Vietnamese exile to Europe, Nguyen Ai-Quoc, formed the Indochina Communist party (ICP) by uniting three rival factions. The organizer had spent his early adult years, from 1914 to 1922, in London and Paris. He was associated for a time with the French Socialist party but turned revolutionary Marxist in 1920, after the Third Communist Internationale assumed an unequivocal anti-imperialist stance. He changed his name at this juncture from Nguyen Van Tranh to Nguyen Ai-Quoc (the patriot), and shifted his residence to Moscow in 1922. He assumed a leading role in the East Asian branch of the Comintern and accompanied the Michael Borodin mission to Canton in 1925. There he organized the Association of Annamite Youth (Thanh Nein). Although obliged to return to Moscow at the time of Borodin's expulsion from China in 1927, he was back in Hong Kong in 1930–31, when the ICP was launched.

Communist-style rebellion fared no better in Vietnam than had the Kuomintang effort. Strikes in plantations and factories were initiated in 1931; the French authorities countered with mass arrests and the execution of a number of captured rebel leaders. Nguyen Ai-Quoc escaped to Hong Kong, where he was detained by British police authorities at the request of the French. He was eventually released in 1933 for lack of incriminating evidence. After a brief residence in England, he returned to the vicinity of Vietnam, spending a considerable period of time in

Thailand. The ICP was only one of several underground nationalist movements in prewar Vietnam. It was challenged in Cochin-China by a more radical Trotskyite organization that refused to abide by the Popular Front tactic advocated by Moscow following the development of the Hitler threat in Europe. The Trotskyites won a Saigon city council election in 1939, only to be firmly suppressed by the French police. The ICP meanwhile, shifted its headquarters to South China.[10]

French Indochina was first subjected to Japanese military pressure in June 1940, immediately following Hitler's invasion of France. The first demand concerned closing the Hanoi-Kunming railway to the Kuomintang supply traffic to Kweichow and Yunnan Provinces. In August and September of 1940 the Japanese took over the Tonkin portion of the railway and also closed adjacent airports, while conceding for the time being legal French sovereignty over Indochina. Subsequent demands made in mid-July 1941 forced the unhappy French authorities to permit Japanese troop movements within Cochin-China, including access to strategic roadways, railways, port facilities, and airfields. In the stormy final round of negotiations held in December 1941, following the Pearl Harbor incident, France was also obliged to grant full Japanese access to desired economic resources and to provide the services of French administrators and technicians where needed, including the use of some 50,000 tons of river and coastal shipping. Otherwise governmental administration continued in French hands and under the French flag throughout most of the war. The forty-thousand resident French nationals were spared much of the harsh treatment imposed on other captured colons throughout Southeast Asia.[11]

The stubborn but futile efforts of the French authorities to generate indigenous hostility toward the Japanese and to salvage a modicum of influence while conforming to Japanese requirements contributed important consequences for the post-war period. As a result, virtually all expressions of Vietnamese nationalism became simultaneously anti-French and anti-Japanese. French forces, including Vietnamese contingents, had put down an initial anticolonial rebellion staged by the Communists in November 1940. Colonial authorities maintained thereafter a comprehensive police and intelligence check covering all potentially dissident elements. The situation afforded no opportunity for the development of anything comparable to the Free Thai movement at Bangkok or the AFPFL in Burma. Also ruled out was the possibility of meaningful collaboration between the fragmented above and underground nationalist agencies, as occurred in Java, or the pro-American and anti-Japanese guerrilla resistance of the Filipinos. The French enlisted some Vietnamese civilian and military cooperation in their effort to bolster authority, but the cost was heavy in terms of vetoing any future modulation to self-rule sponsored by a genuine nationalist movement independent of Communist instigation. The equivocal postwar French proposal of federalized self-government within an ill-defined French union carried no nationalist appeal.

The wartime colonial governor, Admiral Decoux, cooperated scarcely at all with the Free French emissaries who reached the Tonkin-China frontier in 1942 and later established a mission in Chungking. It was not until July 1944 that the mission established regular radio contacts with a retired French general in Hanoi, Mordant. Governor Decoux resented the presumption of the Free French, but his own efforts to sustain the national spirit by promoting sports, vernacular songs, flag ceremonies, and boy scout activities aroused little positive response. Decoux refused to react affirmatively to an Allied proposal, advanced in late 1944, to attempt a direct anti-Japanese attack from Manila along the northern Annamese coast. The overseas operation would have been basically American, but its success required both French and Vietnamese cooperation on land. Governor Decoux refused to provide the essential information covering the disposition of Japanese forces in coastal areas of concern.

Invasion plans were carried forward in Washington to the point of preparing comprehensive maps of the upper

Annamese coasts, including photographs of feasible landing beaches, and profile drawings identifying important landmarks. It was in connection with preparations for this prospective military venture into Annam that American intelligence agents in China enlisted the assistance of Vietnam's widely acclaimed nationalist leader and also head of the Indochinese Communist party, Nguyen Ai-Quoc, who had previously been released from a Chinese jail in early 1943. His change of name to Ho Chi Minh provided a semblance of disguise. U.S. intelligence agents in 1944–45 facilitated Ho's entry into northern Tonkin, providing arms, radio equipment, and other supplies. The flat refusal of the French colonial authorities to cooperate with this contingent anti-Japanese invasion effort contributed substantially to President Roosevelt's strong reservations to the restoration of French Colonial control in Vietnam. Following Japan's March 9 cancellation of French colonial authority, a State Department staff suggestion to the president that U.S. Indochina policy might need clarification elicited no White House response. The failing president died in April.

The denouement of French resistance efforts within Indochina followed Japan's assumption of full control on March 9, 1945. Because the timing was their own, the Japanese were able within twenty-four hours to disarm most of the French garrisons and cut off the escape of the remainder. The single exception was a 6,000-man force, largely Vietnamese but under French command, which staged a successful retreat up the Black River valley to the China border.[12] Emperor Bao Dai was influenced by the Japanese at this juncture to announce the abolition of the French protectorate and to proclaim Vietnam's right to independence. A pro-Japanese government was assembled by Bao Dai,[13] headed by Prime Minister Tran Trong Kim. The Tran government disappeared in early August 1945, just before Bao Dai's own abdication on August 25.

Ho Chi Minh's Vietnamese Independence League, or Vietminh, had been organized by the Central Committee of the Indochina Communist party in May 1941. Its primary purpose was to unite all elements of the Vietnamese population behind a program of national liberation. Its declared policies were therefore broadly nationalist, playing down for the time being all distinctively Communist methods and objectives. By late 1943 the Vietminh propaganda had attracted considerable favorable acceptance within Vietnam, but it was not until December 1944, after Ho had contacted the Americans, that the National Liberation Army was initiated. Starting with a mere handful of recruits and fewer guns, the army increased to a force of 1,000 by March 1945, when the Japanese pushed the French out; it numbered an estimated 5,000 by August.[14]

Technically and in terms of formal sponsorship, the Vietminh effort was part of the larger Kuomintang projection into Tonkin, although the actual cooperation of the two groups was minimal. It was the U.S. involvement with this officially China-sponsored effort that prompted the decision at Potsdam to entrust to Chinese forces the task of taking the surrender of the Japanese in northern Vietnam. The principal Chinese-backed component of the joint intelligence and subversionary operation was called the Dong Minh Hoi. This group was quite as strongly anti-French as was the Vietminh, but it was largely under Kuomintang control. The Vietminh, not the Dong Minh Hoi, commanded major popular enthusiasm and support within Vietnam.

Acting quickly at the time of the Japanese surrender, the Vietminh, on August 13, convened a congress at Hanoi, which elected Ho Chi Minh chairman of its National Liberation Committee. The objective was to confront both the Chinese and the returning French with a *fait accompli*. From the first, the Committee included non-Communists, and their number was subsequently raised to a majority of the membership. Ho's second move was to force Emperor Bao Dai to abdicate on August 25 while offering him the face-saving post of supreme political adviser of the Committee government. On the occasion of the formal proclamation of the Independent Republic of Vietnam at Hanoi on September 2, an estimated half-million people attended the ceremonies.

The aims of the new state were cautiously stated. It would cultivate friendly relations with the victorious Allies (especially the Americans) and promote the enjoyment of democratic rights. Communal lands would be redistributed, but no comprehensive land policy was defined. The new government was widely accepted as the de facto authority in the central and northern sections of the country. Its acceptance in the South, where Trotskyite opposition persisted and rival religious sects had appeared, was less extensive.[15] Omitted throughout these preliminary moves by the Vietminh was any reference whatever to the rival China-sponsored provisional government under the direction of the Dong Minh Hoi.

In direct contrast to the strongly anti-French trend throughout the North was the action taken by the Allied occupation forces in the South, commanded by British General Gracey. Upon his arrival at Saigon on September 13, 1945, he rebuffed a welcoming group from the Liberation Committee and proceeded to release and arm captive French. With British cooperation, the rearmed French proceeded to take over Saigon, thus precipitating widespread civil war. In opposition to Gracey's pro-French policy, the Chinese occupation forces in the north provided credits to Hanoi for the purchase of Chinese guns plus access to military stocks left behind by both the French and Japanese. In order to make the Liberation Committee government more acceptable to all the Allies, the Indochina Communist party formally disbanded on November 11, becoming the Association for Marxist Studies. At the same time, non-Communists and China-sponsored groups were guaranteed substantial representation in the Republic's legislature, which was subsequently selected on January 6, 1946. This election coincided with the retirement of British forces from the South and the completion of the French take-over in Cochin-China by Admiral Thierry d'Argenlieu, the new commissioner.[16]

The initial political stage of the contest for control of Vietnam thus came to an end with anti-Chinese agreement reached between Ho's government and the French on March 6, 1946. In order to rid north Vietnam of the hopelessly undisciplined Chinese occupation forces, Ho agreed that French troops could enter Tonkin so as to be in a position to negotiate legally for the Chinese withdrawal. It was a heavy price for the nationalists to pay, and Ho needed all of his personal prestige to justify the action. The French in return declared the emergent Democratic Republic to be a free, self-governing state "belonging to the Indo-Chinese Federation and the French Union." A referendum was promised, to determine whether all three sections of Vietnam should be included in the Federation and when France should withdraw her troops. The Viet Minh thus cooperated with the French to eliminate surviving pro-Chinese nationalists in the north following withdrawal of Chinese forces in June, 1946.[17] The subsequent efforts of the French and the Viet Minh to arrange the boundaries and to define the powers the new state would enjoy belong to a later phase of the struggle for independence.

1. See Onfre Di Corpuz, *The Philippines* (Englewood Cliffs, N. J., 1965), pp. 78-79.

2. Roger M. Smith, "Cambodia," in George M. Kahin, ed., *Governments and Politics of Southeast Asia* (Ithaca, 1964).

3. *Ibid.*, pp. 605-08.

4. Ba Maw, *Breakthrough in Burma* (New Haven, 1969), pp, 292-97.

5. Harry Benda, "The Pattern of Administrative Reforms in the Closing Years of Dutch Rule in Indonesia," *Journal of Asian Studies* 25 (August, 1960): 589-605.

6. Clifford Geertz, *The Religion of Java* (Glencoe, Ill., 1960), pp. 142-47.

7. James H, Mysbergh, "The Indonesian Elite," *Far Eastern Survey* 26 (March, 1957): 38-42.

8. W. F. Wertheim, *Indonesian Society in Transition* (The Hague, 1959), 305-313.

9. Robert Van Neil, "The Course of Indonesian History," in Ruth McVey, ed., *Indonesia* (New Haven, 1963), pp. 302-08.

10. Roy Jumper and Marjorie Weiner Normand, "Vietnam," in Kahin, *op. cit.*, pp. 389-90.

11. Donald Lancaster, *The Emancipation of French Indochina* (London, 1961), pp. 91-96.

12. *Ibid.*, pp. 101-106, 111.

13. Jean Chesneaux, *Contribution a l'histoire de la Vietnamienne* (Paris, 1955), pp. 228-33.

14. Jumper and Normand, *op. cit*, pp. 390-91.

15. *Ibid.*, pp. 390-92.

16. *Ibid.*, p. 393; Bernard Fall, "The Road to Socialism in North Vietnam," in Doak Barnett, ed., *Communist Strategies in Asia* (New York, 1963), pp. 202-06.

17. Lancaster, *op cit.*, pp. 166-67.

II

INDEPENDENCE PROB-
LEMS IN BURMA,
INDONESIA AND
VIETNAM

Initial Allied Policy with Respect to Colonial Restoration

The three countries of Southeast Asia where revolutionary leadership emerged during the course of the war, namely Burma, Indonesia, and Vietnam, were all subjected theoretically to the same Allied policy with respect to the takeover of power from the Japanese. With the exception of northern Vietnam, where Nationalist Chinese troops were assigned control, the three nations were entrusted to Lord Louis Mountbatten's Supreme Allied Command for Southeast Asia (SACSEA) for postwar occupation. His basic policy, as demonstrated in Burma prior to Tokyo's capitulation, was to put military considerations ahead of those relating to the eventual restoration of colonial rule. Thus the British Empire forces of Generals Christison and Gracey, sent to Indonesia and Cochin-China respectively, were under Mountbatten's orders to take the Japanese surrender and to establish order, but not to take sides in emerging controversies between returning colonial authorities and their nationalist opponents.

In Burma, Mountbatten's June 1945 policy of soliciting

the cooperation of leaders of the nationalist Anti-Fascist League was buttressed by compelling military considerations relating to the prospective use of the country as a base for continuing Allied operations eastward. This consideration no longer applied following the overall surrender of the Japanese. Even so, the general policy of Allied nonparticipation in essentially colonial controversies continued in force. In actual situations, the line proved hard to draw. The sheer numerical inadequacy of the available British forces assigned to both Christison and Gracey forced them on several occasions to enlist the aid of the surrendered Japanese forces to maintain even a semblance of order. Other occasions developed in time when they found it convenient to use available Dutch and French assistance in seeming violation of Mountbatten's policy. When the eventual withdrawal of British troops occurred, events outran such theoretical policy considerations.

The diverging policies of the British, French, and Dutch colonialists developed within differing world contexts. Britain's decision to grant independence to Burma was an almost inevitable consequence of London's determination to withdraw from India. The latter action undermined the manpower and military base that had so long undergirded England's role in Southeast Asia, and especially in Burma. Under the circumstances, Premier Attlee accepted Burma's claim to independence with sound sense and good grace. The returning French, by contrast, faced in Indochina a highly complicated situation, which they endeavored to exploit for both economic and political ends. Paris authorities had compelling reasons of state to avoid as long as possible any withdrawal from Southeast Asia, since such a move would inevitably set up a chain reaction throughout French colonial holdings in Africa. The eventual result for Vietnam was the capture of the nationalist cause by Communist leadership and the precipitation of a prolonged and devastating war.

For the harried Dutch, victimized as they had been by the Germans in Europe and by the Japanese in Asia, voluntary withdrawal from Indonesia was almost unthinkable. Re-establishing some kind of colonial establishment was for them a psychological as well as an economic necessity. Their return was not opposed by the peoples of the Eastern Islands, and Dutch leaders believed that a firm stand in Java and Sumatra might force the entire region back into line. A pattern of gradual movement toward self-government could then eventually be resumed. Events proved otherwise. The stubborn Dutch were ousted in 1949 under pressure of nationalist and world opinion, with the Communists playing a negligible role.

British Policy in Postwar Burma

The official statement of postwar British policy for Burma was set forth in a white paper released by London in late May 1945. Reflecting the views of British businessmen who had been active in Burma before the war, the policy affirmed that the country's shattered economy would have to be restored before any serious consideration could properly be given to reviving the prewar constitution. For the time being, the Governor's Cabinet and Advisory Council would be responsible only to him. Meanwhile, economic restoration would be entrusted to experienced British technicians and businessmen functioning within a modified colonial system of government. The white paper suggested that the recovery process might require as long as three years, after which the 1935 Constitution could be restored, enabling Burma to resume its interrupted progress toward complete self-government.

During the seven months of Governor Dorman-Smith's postwar administration, starting in October 1945, little progress was made toward realizing the objectives set forth in the white paper. He refused to accept as bona fide nationalist spokesmen the leaders of the AFPFL, who on their part would not agree to cooperate under the regressive political timetable set forth in the White Paper. Meanwhile Lord Mountbatten, as commander of the Imperial Army in Burma, denied to civilian officials the use of most of the available military transport, ostensibly because the U.S. lend-lease agreement restricted the use

35

of nonsurplus U.S. vehicles to military purposes. A basic question was the wisdom or feasibility of using Indian and African forces, which made up a large fraction of the occupation army, to crush a possible Burmese nationalist rebellion. Mountbatten's tentative answer was no.

The turning point came in April 1946, when Premier Attlee vetoed Dorman-Smith's proposal to arrest Aung San on criminal charges. The governor returned to England, presumably for health reasons, but was later replaced by Sir Hubert Rance, a protégé of Lord Mountbatten. When faced with a many-sided strike on his arrival in August 1946, Sir Hubert selected a new government drawn largely from the ranks of the AFPFL. Meanwhile, Premier Attlee's decision to accord independence to India paved the way for negotiations with Aung San's Burmese nationalist delegation at London in January 1947. The final steps in the transfer of power, accomplished under a constitution of Burma's own devising, belong to a later aspect of the story.

Postwar Dutch Policy

Postwar relations between the Dutch colonialists and the Indonesian nationalists developed within a context radically different than that prevailing in Burma. Whereas the victorious British forces were already in full control of Burma before the Japanese surrendered in mid-August 1945, no Dutch army was available to be sent to Indonesia for several months thereafter. The Allied occupation forces of General Sir Philip Christison reached Jakarta only around the end of September. The Dutch encountered difficulty in finding ships to transport expatriates and available troops—including a superb body of Dutch marines trained during the war in America's Chesapeake Bay area—to Java.

Christison's orders were to take the surrender of the Japanese and to maintain order until the legal Dutch authorities could arrive. He found on landing that a nationalist administration, headed by Sukarno and Hatta and enjoying wide popular support, was already functioning in many parts of Java and Sumatra. The principal evidences of disorder at the time involved clashes between Indonesian nationalist partisans and scattered Japanese units who refused to turn over their arms to any except Christison's forces. Because Christison was unable to control so huge a population and area, he used Japanese units to preserve order in remote regions. Disorders of another kind erupted when the Allied commander released from concentration camps a large body of Dutch colons. The latter were completely unprepared psychologically or in terms of their personal interests to adjust to a situation so radically different from what they had known before the war. The problems of the occupation forces were somewhat less difficult in Sumatra than in Java. Australian forces, which took the surrender of Japanese in the Eastern Islands, encountered no comparable trouble.

The official Dutch point of view was that the extravagant expressions of Indonesian nationalism that they encountered were the artificial creation of Japanese enemies and could therefore be brushed aside. Indonesian efforts to counter this view included the elevation of anti-Japanese underground leaders such as Sjahrir and Sjarifuddin to high positions in the government. The cabinet of November 1945, headed by Socialist Sutan Sjahrir, contained a large percentage of intellectuals and left-of-center politicians and was not popularly rooted. The two nationalist groupings that carried over from the war period, the Masjumi and the PNI coalitions, cultivated the support of scattered guerrilla units. It was convenient under the circumstances for such nationalist factions to leave to Sjahrir and his associates the difficult and thankless task of trying to come to terms with the Dutch. During 1946 the Dutch authorities managed to recover effective control over urban centers generally and throughout most of the Outer Islands, where they organized local governmental units. The two police actions by which the Dutch attempted to assert control will be considered in a later connection.

The French Point of View

The considerable number of French officials and the 1,400 European prisoners of war whom General Gracey released upon his arrival at Saigon in September 1945 were highly assertive. They were also better informed concerning the postwar situation than were the long-isolated Dutch internees of Java. Gracey subjected them to minimal restraints. General Leclerc's French troops began arriving in early October. The French also enlisted the support of trained Vietnamese troops who had collaborated with the colonial authorities during the course of the Japanese occupation. The several anti-Communist sect groups— Catholic, Cao Dai, and Hoa Hao—held aloof from the Vietminh partisans, who were themselves less extremely Francophobic than were the Saigon Trotskyites. Even though Ho Chi Minh was widely popular personally, the South Vietnamese generally did not welcome the presumption of northern leadership. Profiting from their enjoyment of direct British support, to which SACSEA's Lord Mountbatten gave reluctant approval, the French forces flatly rejected the claims asserted by the Vietminh Executive Committee at Saigon and proceeded to establish their own control throughout Cochin-China. The developing guerrilla resistance was widespread but uncoordinated. The French also moved into Cambodia and Laos with little British assistance and eventually into northern Annam and Tonkin, with the qualified consent of the Vietminh as indicated in Chapter I.

The major problem of French policy was to define the actual meaning of Vietnam's promised membership in the proposed Indochina Federation as part of an eventual French Union. Unfortunately, Paris was governed by short-lived governments, none of which possessed the authority or the inclination to rule on the question. An official conference convened at Dalat in South Vietnam in April and May 1946 but registered no progress. At Saigon on May 31, French Commissioner Admiral Thierry d'Argenlieu declared unilaterally that the colony of Cochin-China must continue indefinitely under French control and not be subject to the referendum previously promised in the March 6 agreement with Ho Chi Minh. Throughout the course of the negotiations of 1945-46, the French treated Ho Chi Minh as a bona fide nationalist leader rather than as a Communist conspirator, while insisting also that their arrangements with him were exclusively the concern of France.

Following the abortive Dalat Conference, the Vietminh leadership decided to seek agreement by conducting direct negotiations in France. A broadly representative delegation departed for France in early June.[1] Ho's Communist associate Pham Van Dong was titular chairman, but several leading spokesmen of the delegation were non-Communists. The originally nominated chairman, Foreign Minister Nguyen Tuong Tam, a member of the older Nationalist Quoc Don Dang Party of the 1920s, was more anti-French than Ho and had refused to attend. The participating minister of national defense had at one time been leader of the Vietnamese youth organization. His assisting vice-minister was an Oxford-trained mathematician who had previously been head of the boy scouts. Other academicians included a French-trained engineer, a specialist in French language and literature, an Orientalist connected with the French École Française in Hanoi, and two trained economists. Also formally associated with the Fountainebleau delegation was a leader of the Catholic youth group in Tonkin and a royalist scientist, cousin of former Emperor Bao Dai, who was at the time director of research on cancer at the Radium Institute in Paris. A future South Vietnamese ambassador to Washington, Vu Van Thai, was also present at Fountainebleau. The group was predominantly youthful, ardently nationalistic, and far from uniform ideologically. Some of the non-Communists were more anti-French than Ho himself.

On his arrival at Paris, Ho was treated with respect as a Socialist chief of state. He was provided a residence near the Étoile, received by the Paris City Council, and invited to place a wreath on the tomb of the unknown soldier. On the opening day of the Conference, the Viet-minh flag, red background with a gold star, was raised alongside the Tricolor. Actual negotiations were eventually opened on July 5 at Fountainebleau, but with only minor French officials in attendance. Very little was accomplished. Ho himself spent most of the ensuing three months in Paris, conferring with friends of the political Left, who held out some prospect that they might gain increased representation in the elections scheduled for that fall. At the conclusion of the abortive Fountainebleau meeting, Ho signed, on his own personal initiative, the *modus vivendi* agreement of September 22, which included substantial concessions to the continued French presence. It accorded preferred status to French advisors in both economic and cultural affairs and stipulated that currency, customs collections, and property rights would continue unchanged, pending resumption of negotiations in January 1947; meanwhile, the political affiliations of individuals should not constitute grounds for persecution by either side.

Ho returned to Haiphong aboard a French war vessel, arriving two weeks later than the rest of the delegation. French concessions had been minimal. Paris made no move to repudiate Commissioner d'Argenlieu's action of May 31 reserving Cochin-China for the French and acquiesced in the proceedings of his second Dalat Conference held on August 1, where representatives of all sections of Indochina except North Vietnam were in attendance. Nothing came from the *modus vivendi*, except that rebel groups gained time for preparations.

The leadership of the Hanoi government in early 1946 was broadly nationalist, but the Communist members were the only closely knit group. Ho's immediate associates included two former history teachers, Pham Van Dong as minister of finance and General Vo Nguyen Giap, head of the army. Truong Chinh was the leading expert on Marxist orthodoxy, and Le Duan, a Southerner, occupied a top party position. Tran Van Giau was leader of the Communist Committee for the South, but the ruthless methods he had employed against the Trotskyites had offended many. Although Ho himself as nationalist champion towered above the Communist party in popular appeal, his central core of disciplined party followers was closely knit and fanatically loyal.[2]

Nationalist Protagonists in Indonesia

In comparison with the internationalist Ho Chi Minh, Indonesia's nationalist leader Sukarno was parochially Javanese. His engineering training was at Bandung Technical College. Sukarno was an orator rather than a thinker, a charismatic personality in the messianic tradition rather than a fashioner of tactics and programs. His popularity owed much to his having been singled out for imprisonment by the Dutch during most of the period from 1929 to 1942. As organizer of the Nationalist Party (PNI) in the later twenties, Sukarno had attracted wide respect from intellectuals and members of the Volksraad, and from the masses of Central and Eastern Java. After being released from prison by the Japanese invaders in 1942, he permitted himself to be exploited by the occupying authorities, although he insisted later that his wartime activities were essentially nationalist and traditionalist in tone. In any case, he came to symbolize not the hated Japanese yoke, as Dr. Ba Maw had done in Burma, but rather the longings of his Indonesian countrymen for freedom.

The Western ideals of nationalism, government by consent, and social justice, which Sukarno espoused so volubly, were for the most part platitudes divorced from any institutional means of realization. More basic was his embodiment of the values and mystical symbolism of indigenous Javanese culture. He attempted, for example, to apply on a national basis the traditional ritual of spirit propitiation, the *slametan* of the Javanese village, as a means of achieving mutual cooperation and reconciliation (*gotong rojong*) between highly disparate political factions not really susceptible to such influences. Sukarno's dislike of Muslim

41

partisanship derived in part from his concern for consensus and in part from his own secularist and nationalist point of view.

Second and third to Sukarno in the hierarchy of the Indonesian national leadership, but differently oriented and far inferior in popular appeal, were Mohammed Hatta and Sutan Sjahrir. Both men were Dutch-educated intellectuals. Sjahrir was the younger and brighter of the two; he was Socialist in point of view and lacked Hatta's Islamic orientation. Upon their return from Europe in 1932, the two collaborated in organizing the Marxist-oriented National Education Club. Rejecting Sukarno's oratorical appeal to the masses as a kind of emerging messiah, which made him highly vulnerable to police suppression, Sjahrir and Hatta undertook to enlist and train a cadre of followers that might be capable of continuing its political maturation regardless of the fate of the leaders. Their personal participation in the club was cut short by imprisonment in 1934, but the Socialist party training program persisted within a limited circle.

When Sjahrir and Hatta were released from prison by the Japanese in 1942, Hatta associated himself with Sukarno in the aboveground nationalist movement, while Sjahrir elected to go underground. Hatta and his aides functioned as liaison, providing funds and information to four important underground groups, of which Sjahrir's was one. The suspicious Japanese afforded Hatta much less public exposure than they gave Sukarno; they even contemplated imprisoning Hatta at one time. He was, in any case, incapable of rivaling Sukarno as a popular personality. Sjahrir was able to attract a following of students and intellectuals, but not mass popularity. He also lacked Sukarno's imposing personal presence.

The fourth-ranking member of the Indonesian nationalist hierarchy was Amir Sjarifuddin. His Marxist commitment lay considerably to the left of Sjahrir's. He nevertheless commanded sufficient respect to elicit Dutch cooperation in establishing an underground organization just prior to the arrival of the Japanese in 1942. His group, like Sjahrir's, maintained liaison with Hatta. Marked by the Japanese as anti-Fascist and therefore hostile, Sjarifuddin was arrested by the military police in early 1943 and barely escaped execution at their hands. Following the return of the Dutch, Sjahrir and Sjarifuddin were brought in to replace Japan-selected Subarjo to head the nationalist cabinet. The move was designed as a rejoinder to the Dutch allegation that the independence movement was nothing more than a Japanese-initiated conspiracy.[3]

Burma's AFPFL Leadership

As previously indicated, Burma's postwar political elite was drawn almost entirely from the limited circle of the Thakin student movement, which got its important political start in the University strike of 1936. The president of the strike-sponsoring Rangoon University Student Union and senior member of the Thakin group was U Nu, an able speaker and dedicated nationalist. He was in 1936 reading for a postgraduate degree in law, having taught school briefly prior to returning to the University under a headmaster named U Thant. Nu was a would-be playwright and something of a Buddhist mystic, a personality capable of establishing rapport with villagers as well as with students. In 1939 Nu had allied himself with ex-Premier Ba Maw in the Freedom Bloc demand for independence, and like Ba Maw had suffered imprisonment for subversive utterances prior to the Japanese invasion. In the wartime government, Nu filled the nonfunctional post of foreign minister. He acted as cover for the developing anti-Japanese preparations of his fellow Thakins in the emerging Anti-Fascist League, but without direct personal participation in their plans.

Although Nu was widely respected as a nationalist leader, few anticipated that he would distinguish himself as a participant in the postwar nationalist government. He fled to Moulmein with Ba Maw in April 1945 and took no active part in the early Burmese negotiations with the British. His first important role was to preside over the sessions of the

43

Constitutional Assembly in the late spring and early summer of 1947. It was the assassination that July of Thakins Aung San and Mya, the two ranking members of the Thakin coterie, that elevated the unaggressive Nu to leadership. Nu completed the independence preparations and became the first prime minister of the new Burma Union on January 4, 1948.

Burma's authentic national hero, Thakin Aung San, had been the undergraduate secretary of the University Student Union during the 1936 strike. Although he demonstrated no unusual intellectual capacity, he was both courageous and daring and noted for his personal integrity and dedication. He led the first group of Burma exiles who fled the country in 1940 and established contact with the Japanese. He returned covertly during the following year to recruit other members of the "Thirty Hero" group. Aung San contributed substantially to restoring order in the delta following the Japanese conquest by cultivating the confidence of Karen partisans, and later assumed the leading role in hastening the Japanese withdrawal in 1945.[4] As a secularist, Aung San opposed the political activities of the Buddhist monks, along with other perversions of the faith. He also challenged ethnic and religious antagonisms generally, boasting that the Thakin movement was the only non-racial, non-religious enterprise in all of Burma's political history. He argued that the state must undertake to be religiously neutral.[5]

Aung San's contribution to Burma's independence effort during the postwar negotiations with the British authorities was very substantial. He ended almost single-handedly a dangerous strike situation that developed shortly after Governor Rance's arrival in September 1946. A month later he obliged his Communist-oriented colleague, Than Tun, to withdraw peacefully from the AFPFL, and then in January 1947 led the Burmese nationalist delegation to London for final negotiations with Premier Attlee on the terms of independence. Following his return to Burma, he again quieted the revolutionary ferment that had built up against the possibility of failure in the London negotiations. In the spring of 1947 he utilized his enormous personal influence in working out acceptable compromises with the Shan, Karen, Kachin,

44

and Chin minority peoples. He contributed to Burma's withdrawal from the Commonwealth connection, more from concern to be completely free from the Indian connection than from the British. The constitution for independent Burma was virtually completed at the time of Aung San's tragic assassination on July 19, 1947. His ablest lieutenant, Thakin Mya, died on the same occasion, and both were sorely missed in subsequent years.

Another Thakin leader of political stature was the previously mentioned Than Tun, who became the White Flag (Stalinist) Communist leader. He served ably as a cabinet minister under *Adhipati* Ba Maw during the war. Many who knew Than Tun rated his capacity for personal daring, his nationalist commitment, and his dedication to convictions on a par with Aung San's. He broke with Nu's government in early 1948, on the grounds that Burma's real emancipation demanded class struggle, and maintained his Communist rebellion for more than a score of years thereafter. One is tempted to speculate whether the rift would ever have occurred if Aung San had survived, for the two men respected each other.

Premier Nu's closest associates in the independent government, Thakins Kyaw Nyein, Ba Swe, and Shu Maung, were also drawn from the student strike personnel of 1936, but only the last (as Boh Ne Win) was destined to attain national leadership. The intelligent, administratively experienced Dr. Ba Maw was unable to recover political prominence. Nor was it possible for many better-educated Burmans from the prewar civil service to find any leadership role in the changed political milieu. Burma was probably the loser for their exclusion.

Deferred Concern over Southeast Asian Independence

Whereas London's not-ungenerous grant of independence to Burma developed in the context of the loss of Britain's two-century-old imperial base in India, Dutch and French policy makers faced no such immediate pressure to withdraw from Indonesia and Vietnam. Nor did either of the two super powers, the United States and the Soviet Union, see fit at the outset to force the issue. During the immediate postwar years, world attention was focused on the possibility that the Western European democracies, all verging on economic collapse, would succumb politically to Communist domination. Senior State Department officials attached little importance to the gathering crisis in Indonesia and Vietnam. European desk officers refused to embarrass their relations with resident Dutch and French ambassadors by raising the anticolonial issue. Down to late 1947, Moscow also gave priority to European considerations by refraining from encouraging colonial rebellions that might embarrass the election prospects of Communist parties of Western Europe. Because Soviet military preponderance in Eastern Europe was balanced at the time only by America's sole possession of the atom bomb, the prevention of possible Communist takeover by elections in Western Europe turned very largely on the prospects for prompt economic recovery.

The success of America's Marshall Plan assistance program for Europe, initiated in mid-1947, ended any serious Communist political threat to Western Europe but ushered in an ominous era for Southeast Asia. The abrupt shift of Cominform objectives in late 1947 to the deliberate fomenting of overt rebellion by responsive party agencies in a number of Southeast Asian countries will be discussed in a later chapter. It is significant to note at this juncture that by 1948-49 the combination of the rising tide of Communism in China and Soviet-instigated rebellion in other areas of Eastern Asia, including the Korean war of 1950, made very difficult any objective assessment by Washington of the merits of the Communist-led nationalist cause in Vietnam in particular. The Cold War confrontation came to occupy the center of the diplomatic stage.

The Dutch Exit from Indonesia

The story of the elimination of Dutch control from Indonesia has been explored in admirable detail elsewhere[6] and needs only summary treatment here in the general context of independence problems. For more than a year, the returning Dutch colonial authorities, left to their own devices, refused to concede that the "Fascist" Sukarno was qualified to speak for the Indonesian people. In mid-1946, the Dutch governor-general, Hubertus Van Mook, began to organize autonomous "states" among the more receptive Island peoples residing outside of Java and Sumatra, in accordance with a plan drawn up at a conference held in the Celebes. Colonialists argued with some justification that the recovery of prosperity within Indonesia was conditioned on the restoration of Dutch rule. Sjahrir's de facto government, on the other hand, faced militant nationalist opposition to any kind of negotiation. Tensions reached a near breaking point in July 1946, when an abortive coup attempt was staged by the unorthodox Communist leader, Tan Malaka. At the end of November 1946 continuing pressure exerted by the withdrawing British forces produced a semblance of negotiation. The resulting Linggajadti Agreement recognized the Republican Government in Sumatra and Java as a de facto authority with whom the Dutch agreed to negotiate concerning the eventual establishment of a sovereign federated Indonesia. Sjahrir had to take most of the blame for this vaguely defined agreement and was accordingly driven from office in June 1947.

The ensuing Dutch police action against Republic-held territory in late July 1947 was something of a *fait accompli*. A substantial portion of the available 150,000 Dutch troops was used to seize control of strategic food and plantation areas. The action was challenged in tentative fashion by the United Nations Security Council, which set up a Good Offices Commission to supervise a ceasefire and to encourage a resumption of negotiations. The subsequent Renville Agreement of January 1948 conceded much to the Dutch and was so unsatisfactory to Indonesian nationalists that the signatory government of Sjarifuddin was displaced. The successor Hatta Cabinet, backed by the Masjumi Muslims and the Nationalist PNI followers of Sukarno, also attracted the support of Sjahrir. Sjarifuddin, by contrast, threw in his lot with the pro-Communist labor groups and the demobilized army personnel.

47

Civil war in Java threatened for a time. Hatta's nationalist government put down the ill-timed Communist Madiun Rebellion of September 1948, led by Sjarifuddin and Musso, the latter recently returned following a long residence in Moscow. Musso was killed, and Sjarifuddin was later executed. The exhausting military effort reduced the anti-Dutch capabilities of the Republican regime to guerrilla-level operations only. The stage was therefore set for an all-out Dutch effort at the end of 1948 to recover full control. Inability of the Republic to deal with urgent social and economic problems had already contributed to some dissillusionment and bitterness.[7] Nationalist resistance proved unable to withstand the impact of the second Dutch police action, so that the fate of the nationalist cause became largely dependent on outside assistance.

The seizure by Dutch forces of the Republican capital of Jogjakarta, capturing both Sukarno and Hatta, aroused widespread concern throughout the world. As one expression of protest, Pandit Nehru assembled a conference at New Delhi of representatives of Asian and African states. The gesture was fraught with ominous propaganda overtones. American policy, at this juncture, could not acquiesce in the Dutch destruction of the Hatta government, which had itself crushed the Communist Madiun Rebellion only a few months before, and at a time when Mao Tse-tung's armies were overrunning China. Washington therefore threatened to suspend Marshall Plan aid to the Netherlands unless Indonesian independence was conceded.

The Republic of the United States of Indonesia was eventually fashioned at a roundtable conference held at the Hague from August to November 1949. The plan associated fifteen Outer Island states, all Dutch sponsored, with the dominant Republican unit of Java and Sumatra in a federated system that permitted varying degrees of self-government. The proposed federation plan had much to be said for it administratively, but nationalists denounced it as a nefarious scheme to preserve Dutch economic control. Treaty references to the prospective Netherland-Indonesian Union and to guarantees for Dutch property and personnel were openly challenged, along with Indonesia's assumption of some four billion

48

guilders in debts. The federation scheme died in August 1950. Except for the unresolved status of Western Irian in New Guinea, a sovereign Indonesia emerged completely free of alien control.

Governmental Problems of Independent Indonesia

President Sukarno posed as a kind of presiding genius over the revolutionary undertaking, which had enlisted the courage and self-sacrifice of many nationalist participants. All were newcomers to power. Sukarno himself was administratively inexperienced and entertained little awareness of essential political or economic objectives. He was also unwilling to accept any substantial personal responsibility for conducting the routine business of government.[8] The new military and bureaucratic elite associated with Sukarno were drawn mainly from the families of former minor colonial officials. Most of them had acquired a smattering of Dutch education but had little administrative experience. The group was incapable of developing any close identification with the mass worker and peasant population, especially among the non-Javanese. They were in some respects as alien as the Dutch had been. Once the excitement of revolutionary activity had died down, patriotic fervor and devotion tended to give way to disillusionment and self-seeking. Idealism evaporated in a milieu of personal rivalries and administrative ineptitude. The basic disease of incompetence and declining morale proved not to be curable by Sukarno's subsequent efforts to fan the flames of revolutionary zeal.[9]

Political sentiment tended to fragment along social and cultural lines. The ancient *adat* tradition opposed both Muslim and Christian norms. Traditionally prestigious *priyayi* lost out to salary-conscious bureaucrats. Outer Islanders resented Javanese control, while anti-Chinese sentiment was latent everywhere. Islamic modernists vied with orthodox Muslims; *santri* traders opposed *slametan* spirit-propitiating villagers. Even the Leftist *Partai Murba* of Tan Malaka and Adam Malik opposed the orthodox Communist PKI.

Another problem was bureaucratic blight. The size of the bureaucracy in Indonesia began to multiply beyond all bounds of effective utilization. White-collar jobs, long denied Indonesians under Dutch rule, carried exaggerated implications of social status, so that civil service candidates became legion. The attractiveness of government service reflected the lack of employment opportunities in business, which still functioned largely under Chinese and Dutch control. To accommodate the horde of applicants, older services were enlarged and new agencies were created, ostensibly to deal with welfare needs. Political rivalry aggravated the problem of overstaffing, since loyal partisans were usually accommodated in those governmental agencies that happened to be under a particular party's control. Conversely, aspiring bureaucrats tended to join those parties that might be able to obtain promotions for them.[10] Government employment thus developed into a system of outdoor relief for the politically minded.

Because partisan and revolutionary spirit tended to be rated ahead of administrative performance, the recurring political crises paralyzed decision making. Both morale and efficiency also suffered from the practice of regarding diplomas and seniority, in preference to job performance, as bases for promotion. Government offices closed at two to give incumbents an opportunity to earn supplemental incomes needed to cover price-inflated costs. In the emerging new order, Western dress, the possession of a brief case or fountain pen, or familiarity with a European language were significant social assets. The use of Javanese as a lingua franca tended to decline in favor of Indonesian-Malay, partly because of objection to inferior-superior vocabulary usages, which traditional Javanese custom required. In Java as elsewhere, social status continued to be important, but the normative criteria were changing.[11]

Issues in the Vietnamese War

The primary objectives of the Vietminh leadership at the outbreak of the long war with France were twofold. The first was to exclude the French military presence from all of

Indochina, including Cambodia and Laos as well as Tonkin, Annam, and Cochin-China. This concern found expression in the early support accorded by the Vietminh to Son Ngoc Thanh's faction in Cambodia and to Prince Souphanouvong's Pathet Lao insurgents in Laos. A second major objective was to unify Vietnam as an independent and sovereign state. An economically viable Vietnam must include both the population heartland of Tonkin and the distant Mekong Delta region with its rice surplus, plus the arc of French-developed plantations neighboring to Saigon. The Annam littoral would connect the two. Realization of these basic goals demanded that the Vietminh movement attract nationalists of all political views in support of the independence struggle. The most serious problem developed in faction-ridden Cochin-China, where the Vietminh leader, Tran Van Giau, had suppressed the rival Trotskyite party in September 1945 and reportedly caused the death of several leaders of the opposing Cao Dai and Hoa Hao religious sects. Generally speaking, however, Ho Chi Minh became the symbol of the freedom struggle throughout all regions of Vietnam. The exceptions included the French-trained army officers, some Catholic partisans, and others who shared a tangible personal stake in the continued French presence.

Although observing Frenchmen recognized that postwar Indochina would have to undergo significant governmental changes, the Paris authorities and those in Saigon were unable to clarify the vague formula of a Federation of Indochina states within the framework of a prospective French Union. French patriotism and pride of cultural superiority became heavily involved at Paris. The Saigon colons were also keenly aware of their enormous economic stake in urban real estate, plantations, business and banking resources, and government jobs that had survived the wartime ordeal. Beyond Vietnam was the fate of a vast French empire in Africa.

The immediate circumstances attending the outbreak of strife in Tonkin in late 1946 were incidental to the basic refusal of French authorities to make significant concessions to the nationalist demand for independence and unification. A quarrel involving actions by French customs officials at

51

Haiphong in October led to naval and air bombardment. General Giap's army, numbering several tens of thousands, withdrew northward from the Red River delta to prepared impregnable bases in the neighboring hills, from which they could threaten French control.[12]

French opinion in Europe was understandably confused over the issues involved in the emerging conflict. Admiral d'Argenlieu declared that France must defend itself against attacks launched by a Communist conspiracy intent on seizing illegal control. In actuality, no Communist conspiracy was involved. The Vietminh-led nationalists received no support at the time from the politically cautious French Communist party and no encouragement from Moscow. French intransigence drove most of the moderate anti-Communists into Ho's camp.[13] The increasingly Marxist flavor of the insurgency was not sufficiently offensive to influence the Vietnamese generally to scuttle their desire for independence. Despite the small number of Vietnamese forces, their lack of arms and other military supplies, and French control of major population centers, the insurgency proved much stronger than the French had anticipated. In the persons of Ho Chi Minh and Vo Nguyen Giap, the nationalist cause enjoyed dedicated leadership that could generate strong psychological motivation and morale focusing against the common French enemy.[14]

Peacemaking Efforts and the Enlistment of Bao Dai

In March 1947 Emile Bollaert replaced the discredited d'Argenlieu as high commissioner for Indochina. Bollaert enjoyed little freedom of maneuver in his efforts to find a settlement with the Vietminh. He was a compromise selection at best, and his instructions reflected lack of awareness at Paris of political realities in Vietnam. His initial proposal to reopen negotiations with the Vietminh on the basis of an offer of complete self-government, qualified only by continuance of the French economic and advisory roles, aroused virulent hostility within French circles in Saigon and was eventually vetoed by Paris. Forbidden to use the magic word "independence" or to make any forthright commitment such as Premier Attlee had done for Burma, Bollaert's apparent equivocation bred distrust and fear, which ensured the indefinite continuation of civil war backed by the popular will. As the months wore on, the initial support of France's presence, even by subsidized Cao Dai and Hoa Hao sect leaders, gradually faded.

In a near desperate effort to enlist some nationalist anti-Communist support for the French cause, Bollaert decided shortly after his arrival to ask former Emperor Bao Dai to abandon his exile in France and to return as titular head of a native government centering at Dalat in southern Annam. Bao Dai responded initially by inviting various anti-Communist leaders, some pro-French and others pro-nationalist, to meet him at Hong Kong to help formulate proposals for an honorable and lasting peace. Negotiations made little headway, partly because the prince tried to act as a kind of mediator and refused to accept any personal responsibility. Following a specially arranged meeting in Hong Kong in December 1947, Bollaert and Bao Dai published a joint declaration that completely sidestepped the basic issues of independence and unification of Vietnam. The accompanying secret protocol actually limited Bao Dai's authority over military and diplomatic matters and refused to include Cochin-China within his jurisdiction or to permit the Vietminh to be a party to the peace negotiations.

The longer the negotiations continued, the more hopeless Bollaert's situation became. When Bao Dai visited Europe in early 1948, political forces were still clashing within France. Influential Leftist leaders favored negotiating with the Vietminh,[15] while Rightist elements balked at any offer of independence and demanded priority guarantees for French colons. When the former emperor returned to Hong Kong in March 1948, he learned that the previously pro-French Cao Dai spokesman now demanded full dominion status, including economic, military, and diplomatic autonomy. Meanwhile the American ambassador in France had informed Bao Dai that American support of Vietnam's political aspirations might be more readily available if the request could come from an indigenous non-Communist government.

53

After his unsuccessful effort to persuade the Catholic nationalist, Ngo Dinh Diem, to head the provisional government of the Cochin-China state, Bollaert had to settle for the colorless General Xuan. On June 5, 1948, the two agreed to safeguard French interests within Cochin-China and to give continued preference to French political and technical advisers. Meanwhile, Xuan's supposed authority was ignored by both French residents and civil servants generally. In August 1948 a new Paris government approved the June 5 agreement, but only "in principle." Bollaert thereupon refused to treat further with Xuan until the still-reluctant Bao Dai resumed the post of emperor. Bao Dai then decided to remain in France until the independence of Vietnam, including Cochin-China, was guaranteed and until America would pledge support for his proposed regime. Meanwhile, Vietminh propaganda made the most of the alleged perfidy of the French and their colonial "puppets," while the Communist segment of the nationalist forces strengthened its control over both the army and the party structure.[16]

The discouraged Bollaert gave up his frustrating task in September 1948, to be replaced in October by Leon Pignon. The eventual agreement between Pignon and Bao Dai for the "independence" of Vietnam as finally signed on March 8, 1949, was far from clear. Defense arrangements and foreign relations, together with financial and customs control, were left in French hands; French citizens still enjoyed special legal status; nationalization of businesses or properties could be done only with consent of the French government. The promised inclusion of Cochin-China within the new state was still made conditional on the consent of the population of the area, plus approval of the proposal by the French Assembly and prior arrangements to safeguard French interests. Bao Dai finally left France for Dalat on April 25, 1949, only after a special unofficial vote of Paris Assembly delegates approved the qualified inclusion of Cochin-China within his domain.

The futility of the long and torturous French negotiations with Bao Dai, extending over some two years, was underscored by his complete lack of both personal prestige and authority except among tribal peoples in the mountains. He was unable to make his political influence felt, and even opponents of the Vietminh regarded him as a French stooge.[17] Meanwhile, the French army in Indochina—composed of some one hundred thousand men drawn mainly from Foreign Legion and African troops—failed to establish any effective control outside the principal cities and along major lines of communication.

Conclusions

The dismal record of French negotiations with the Vietnamese nationalists contributed to the internationalization of the problem and to eventual American involvement. This story will be considered in the broad context of the cold war, which will be discussed in the next chapter. It remains to summarize the conclusions to be drawn from the comparison of British, Dutch, and French postwar relations with their respective colonial wards.

The Burma revolution produced a new political elite who were youthful, inexperienced, and often parochial. Few of the AFPFL leadership had studied or travelled abroad. They preferred democratic institutions, but were also socialistically inclined. The violence that was spared down to 1948 by reason of Aung San's respected leadership and Britain's agreed withdrawal, was destined to engulf the new state on the morrow of independence. Dissident Communist revolutionaries, who had been denied by Nu's negotiated settlement their expected opportunity to seize control, combined with restive veterans, disappointed in their lack of participation in the new government, to start the rebellion. During the course of the struggle, ethnic minority elements attempted to seize power in particular areas. The economic recovery languished. British technicians and firms were obliged to leave before the economic base of war-ravaged Burma was even partially restored. Popular hostility to the presence of the Indian minority also tended to take precedence over more rational approaches to economic development.

Indonesia's revolution was similar to Burma's in that a

young and inexperienced national leadership assumed control. Individually the top echelon of the new Javanese and Minangkabau elite was somewhat more mature and better educated than were their Burman counterparts. Sukarno was more sophisticated than Nu, Sjahrir better educated than the Socialist Kyaw Nyein, and Tan Malaka, Musso, and Sjarifuddin more intimately aware of the character of the world Communist movement than was Burma's Than Tun.

Burma's potential advantage in the area of trained leadership lay with the prewar adult generation, which unfortunately was denied any real opportunity to participate politically in postwar affairs. Indonesia had no adult-trained group to match the prewar promoters of Burma's General Council of Burmese Associations. British-trained judges of the higher courts of law and some Burman parliamentary leaders of the dyarchy and 1935 constitutions were still available. Democratic institutions survived for more than a decade in Burma, whereas they barely got under way at all in post-independence Indonesia.

Burma did not share Java's population problem and was spared the extreme cultural and economic divergencies found in the Outer Islands of Indonesia. On the other hand, the Chinese minority problem in the Indies was somewhat less volatile and demanding than was the almost psychopathic determination of the Burmese to be rid of resident Indians. In both countries the army represented a kind of residuum of disciplined power due to come to the surface in the late fifties, although under widely varying circumstances.

Vietnam differed from the other two mainly in the presence of the towering personality of Ho Chi Minh, who combined the roles of nationalist hero and experienced Communist organizer. Repressive French police policies both before the war and during the Japanese occupation ensured that much of the nationalist unrest would gravitate toward Ho's Communist leadership. French Indochina had experienced no twentieth-century welfare effort comparable to the Dutch Ethical Policy, no Sarekat Islam movement, and no Volksraad, inadequate as these Dutch experiments had proved to be. On the other hand, world opinion did not erupt to condemn the French efforts at colonial reconquest, as it did for the Dutch police action of 1948–49. This was partly because France was crucially important in Europe during the immediate postwar period and partly due to American hostility toward the Communist leadership of Vietminh movement. The wartime collapse of French authority and prestige, Bao Dai's abandonment of the imperial court at Hué in August 1945, and the collapse of the mandarinate system, contributed to the almost universal demand to be rid of French control.

The anti-French nationalist struggle of the Vietnamese, starting in December 1946, was destined to continue for seven and one-half years. Once the common enemy was eliminated in 1954, South Vietnam, in particular, became fragmented politically into scores of factional groups that could not be mutually reconciled or made to cooperate. The situation was rendered more difficult by the enforced re-settlement of Catholic refugees from the north. The post-Geneva South Vietnamese state faced in aggravated form the handicaps of inexperienced leadership, aborted economic recovery and development, and unbridged social and cultural cleavages.

1. Lancaster, *The Emancipation*. pp. 124-37.

2. Ellen Hammer, *The Struggle for Vietnam* (Stanford, 1954), pp. 166-67.

3. Kahin, *Nationalism and Revolution* pp. 90-94, 104-8, 123-26.

4. Ba Maw, *Breakthrough*. The author cites a letter allegedly sent him by Aung San, suggesting that the latter's forces did little or nothing to challenge the retreating Japanese forces at Prome.

5. Fred R. von der Mehden, *Religion and Nationalism in Southeast Asia; Burma, Indonesia, the Philippines* (Madison, 1963), pp. 81-82.

6. Kahin, *op. cit.*, pp. 90-94, 107-8, 125-26.

7. Van Niel, in Ruth McVey, ed., *Indonesia*, pp. 302-8.

8. Rupert Emerson, *Representative Government in Southeast Asia* (Cambridge, 1955), pp. 24-40.

9. Mysbergh in *Far Eastern Survey*, 26 (1951): 38-40.

10. Selosoemardjan, *Social Change in Jogjakarta* (Ithaca, 1962), pp. 106-11.

11. *Ibid.*, pp. 111-21, 125-29, 136-37.

12. Lancaster, *op. cit.*, 11. 142-49, 163-69; also Jean Lacouture, *Ho Chi Minh* (New York, 1968) p. 101.

13. Philippe Devilliers, *Vietnamese Nationalism and French Policies* (New York, 1953), pp. 199-220.

14. Bernard Fall, *Le Viet Minh* (Paris, 1960), pp. 181-90.

15. It was not until May 4, 1948, that the five Communist party ministers resigned from the Ramadier Cabinet.

16. Devilliers, *op. cit.*, pp. 220-37; Lancaster, *op. cit.*, pp. 181-88.

17. Lancaster, pp. 188-95. The agreement concluded on March 8, 1949, was not formally ratified by the French Chambers until early 1950.

III

REVOLUTIONS, COMMU-
NIST AND OTHER-
WISE

The rash of revolutions that characterized the history of Southeast Asia from 1948 to 1951 were probably more than coincidental. They all owed something to policy decisions made by the Soviet-dominated Cominform, even though local factors were everywhere relevant. Direct instigation is evident in the origins of the 1948 rebellions of Burma, Malaya, and Indonesia, while Moscow's encouragement of overt revolution was also reflected in the revival of Hukbalahap violence in Luzon and within the pro-Communist Pathet Lao movement in Laos. In the broader Asian context, the more aggressive Soviet line found expression in a complete shakeup of the Communist party leadership in India in 1948 and subsequently in the outbreak of the Korean war in 1950. Mao Tse-tung's takeover in China in 1948–49 also changed the context within which Asian Communist parties operated, but Red China played no significant role in Southeast Asia prior to 1953. Most of the Communist rebellions were short-lived because they were based on doctrinaire considerations and on dubious expectations that did not correspond with political realities. The very impracticability of these moves supports the conclusion that they related to superficial Soviet tactical preferences.

Evolution of Soviet Policy in Southeast Asia, to 1947

Successive phases of developing Soviet policy with respect to Southeast Asia during the course of the 1940s can be identified. At the outbreak of World War II and continuing to the occasion of Hitler's invasion of Russia in June 1941, Moscow characterized the European contest as an "imperialistic war," one to be sabotaged by all loyal Communists living in colonial countries. After June 1941 the contest became overnight a "people's struggle against fascist tyranny." This change of Soviet tactics was reflected immediately in Malaya and India, where previously antagonistic Communist elements began collaborating with British colonial authorities. The trend was intensified, albeit unevenly, when allegedly "fascist" Japan invaded Southeast Asia. The eventual titles of Burma's Anti-Fascist League, the Malay People's Anti-Japanese Army (MPAJA) and the Hukbalahap People's Anti-Japanese Army in the Philippines all reflected borrowings from Communist terminology.

The successive changes in official Communist policy that occurred following the end of the war were also significant. From 1945 to late 1947, Cominform policy for colonial regions advocated United Front collaboration with bourgeois nationalists in support of freedom from imperialist-capitalist rule. This tactic was influenced by Moscow's concentration on the attractive prospect of Communist election victories in Western European countries and the need to avoid jeopardizing such prospects by instigating overt rebellion prematurely. For example, the French Communist party, as previously indicated, contributed little or no support to the Vietminh rebellion of 1946-47. The Dutch Communists elected to back the Linggadjati Agreement of late 1946 and offered only mild verbal support to the eventual goal of Indonesian independence.

Within Burma, the orthodox Communists under Than Tun continued to cooperate with Burmese nationalists down to late 1947. This was in spite of the fact that Than Tun was forced to surrender his secretaryship of the Anti-Fascist League and his Council membership by October 1946, and to submit to his party's exclusion from the AFPFL. He supported the Aung San-Attlee agreement of January 1947 and encouraged members of his party to participate in the Constituent Assembly elections and in the Assembly's subsequent deliberations. Following the assassination of Aung San by U Saw's agents in July 1947, Than Tun stood firmly behind Premier Nu and Governor Rance. It was not until the concluding months of 1947 that a serious rift opened between the Communists and the Socialist core of the AFPFL. It was in March 1948 that the open break with Nu occurred.

The timing was much the same in Malaya. Here the heirs of the wartime Chinese MPAJA organization got involved in labor union rivalries and other intraethnic feuding at the expense of discipline and morale. Chinese disillusionment with the futile United Front approach coincided in early 1948 with dissatisfaction over the Federation constitution and receipt of the news of a shift in Cominform policy. In Indonesia, the Communist PKI functioned down to 1948 as the left wing of the nationalist coalition headed by Premiers Sjahrir and his associate, Sjarifuddin. The latter was driven from power in early 1948 following his negotiation of the Renville Agreement. He later joined hands with the Communist Musso, instigator of the Madiun Rebellion.

Marxist ideology appealed inherently to many types of postwar Southeast Asian nationalist leaders, but except in Vietnam, the several Communist parties could advance no genuine claim to nationalist leadership. One did not have to be a doctrinaire Marxist to work for independence or even for the nationalization of alien capital holdings. State-planned economic modernization under elite indigenous control was convenient because it did not entail the difficult task of enlisting the political participation of the population as a whole. Problems of economic independence and political stability were obviously destined to plague the emerging governments for many years. Moscow was mistaken in expecting that rebellions initiated against such nationalist leaders as Nu, Sukarno, Hatta, Roxas, and the varied ethnic elites of Malaya could successfully establish Communist governments.

The New Soviet Line, 1947–48

Western Europe's remarkably rapid economic recovery following the initiation of Marshall Plan aid in the latter half of 1947 contributed substantially to Soviet abandonment of the United Front policy in colonial areas. The interpretation of Marxism presented for the approval of the Comintern by Zhadonov in September 1947 revived the Hobson-Leninist view that imperialism was the final stage of capitalist development. Theoretically, income from colonial investments provided the essential prop for faltering economies in the metropole countries. In the context of this doctrinaire interpretation, liberation from capitalism was unlikely to occur as long as colonial investment holdings remained unliquidated. Struggles for people's liberation therefore became a condition for realizing world Communist ends.

The initial transmission of this new Communist policy to party sessions held in India in December 1947 aroused sharply negative protests from the party secretary, P. C. Joshi, who was also editor of the *People's Age*. When asked to denounce Pandit Nehru as a Fascist reactionary comparable to Chiang Kai-shek and as one who had betrayed India's national revolution, Joshi flatly refused to comply. He was accordingly forced to surrender his secretaryship, his editorship, and eventually his place in the Politbureau. Even so, the adaptable new leader, Renadive, was himself incapable of instigating any rebellion against Nehru's newly independent government.

Wider transmission of the Cominform's new policy orientation was made by European spokesmen attending the Southeast Asia Democratic Youth Conference held at Calcutta in February 1948, under the sponsorship of the Communist World Federation of Trade Unions. The exhortations to challenge the newly emerging nationalist regimes aroused varying responses. The Vietminh, for example, had already been conducting its anti-French struggle for more than a year without benefit of Soviet encouragement. Its Calcutta spokesman was quite ready to settle for as much independence as Premier Nu's Burma had just received. The Filipino Youth delegate, who was not a member of the Hukbalahap peasant-oriented movement, rejected the Cominform's proposed denunciation of the allegedly fraudulent independent government of President Roxas.[1] The quarrel between the Communist Huk leader, Luis Taruc, and the Manila authorities clearly preceded the change of Moscow's policy and the Calcutta Conference. Settlement of the Luzon rebellion seemed to be possible following the death of anti-Huk President Roxas in the spring of 1948. It was following the failure of Manila's peace negotiations in August 1948 that Taruc announced openly his affiliation with Communist party and his espousal of radical political aims in addition to his previous demands for agrarian reforms.[2]

The Outbreak of Successive Rebellions

Burma. The early 1948 decision of the Burmese Communist leaders in attendance at the Calcutta meeting, Goshal and Than Tun, to embark on rebellion was reached with some reluctance at a peasants' rally held in mid-March at Pyinmana in central Burma. Several Yugoslav spokesmen participated in the sessions. A possible break had been brewing for several months. A Communist quarrel with the Socialist core of the AFPFL had developed following the October 1947 Nu-Attlee agreement, which had included substantial concessions to the British. Burma then agreed to pay provident and retirement fund obligations to former colonial employees, to employ a British unit to train the new Burma army and to grant access to Burma's airfields and seaports in times of crisis. Than Tun also advocated the expropriation of landlord holdings by the Peoples Courts without compensation. The Communists and the AFPFL Socialists were also contesting control of the labor unions.

63

Presumably the most important reason for Than Tun's discontent was the fact that the Attlee agreements of 1947 had denied his Communist following their expected opportunity to modulate from anticipated violent revolution to full Communist control. Even so, no indication of Communist intention to initiate overt rebellion was in evidence during the January 4, 1948, independence celebration, which occurred directly prior to the Calcutta conference. The Pyinmana peasants' meeting of mid-March was followed by an attempted trade union rally at Rangoon on March 27, which actually attracted only Indian workers. When the police moved in tardily to curb such Communist activities, the party leadership escaped to Pyinmana. The revolution started immediately thereafter.

Malaya. The new Cominform policy was communicated to the MPAJA by the Australian Communist Lawrence Sharkey during his two-weeks visit to Malaya, while en route home from Calcutta. Preparations for the shift to overt rebellion were interrupted by repressive police action. An initial reform move was to purge the thieving Communist party secretary and to oust his fumbling Chinese associates from control of the organization. Calcutta conference spokesmen also demanded more serious effort to develop mass support on an interracial basis. Intraparty strife included feuding between leadership and worker groups, and the tension was aggravated when British authorities began arresting all union leaders who had court records as law violators. Singapore's trade unions staged an abortive general strike in April 1948, which was followed by equally ineffective efforts to launch mass political protests. Police suppression of union activity strengthened the influence of extremist elements.

The hurried precipitation of armed Communist rebellion came in June 1948, before party plans were fully completed. Once started, the rebels reverted to their wartime jungle-centered tactics for lack of alternatives. Contemporaneous developments within China were marginally relevant to the decision, but communications from the Calcutta meeting were the immediately influencing factors.

REVOLUTIONS, COMMUNIST AND OTHERWISE

Cominform influence on the Malayan Communist party outweighed that of Mao Tse-tung in early 1948. The so-called Malayan Emergency rebellion was destined to embarrass British authorities during the course of the ensuing decade, but it fitted rather badly into Cominform objectives per se. The rising was essentially Chinese opposition to British authority, rather than any nationalist demand for independence or a popular upsurge protesting economic exploitation.[3]

Java. The contemporaneous Madiun Rebellion in Java, in September and October 1948, was prompted not by any direct receipt of the news of the proceedings of the Calcutta Conference, but rather by the return from Moscow in August of the long-absent Indonesian Communist spokesman, Musso. He was accompanied by Suripno, the recalled Leftist Indonesian diplomatic agent assigned to Eastern Europe, who had previously signed irregular consular exchange agreements with the Russians and the Czechs. When Premier Hatta refused to heed Musso's initial urgings to follow an extreme anti-Dutch line corresponding to Cominform demands, the Moscow returnees took over Communist party (PKI) leadership. The reorganized Politbureau, with the names of Suripno and Sjarifuddin added, thereupon broke with Hatta and initiated the rebellion at Madiun in mid-September 1948. Within two months time, Indonesian forces drove Musso's followers into the mountains and captured the ringleaders. A contributing factor to Musso's lack of success in attracting a following was Hatta's release of the Trotskyite Tan Malaka, head of the· *Partai Murba* (Proletarian party), an action that split the Communist ranks.[4]

After an abortive effort to foment labor union strikes, the discredited and decapitated PKI was reduced for several years to the tactic of buying time for recuperation by backing President Sukarno in his struggle against their common enemies, the Socialist party and the Masjumi. Substantial Communist party recovery was realized by 1952, and by 1955 the PKI managed to score impressively in the first general elections. Dedicated effort on the part of cadres to educate a worker-peasant following in support of broadly socialistic ends, raised party membership by the late fifties to one and a half million. The associated Labor Union Federation counted an estimated additional 2.7 million followers. This success was tempered by the handicap of having to operate within the protective shadow of Sukarno himself, a tactic that limited the party's political initiative.[5] The story was associated with Sukarno's Guided Democracy scheme, to be examined in a later chapter.

Revolution in Burma, 1948-51

The center of the Communist rebellion in Burma, once it got under way in the spring of 1948, was located along the northern edge of the Pegu Yomas, extending westward from the upper Sittang Valley into the oil field region and over to the right bank of the Irrawaddy River. Proximity to mountain jungle areas made the government's task of cornering the insurgents exceedingly difficult. Long after the coordinated rebellion in Lower Burma collapsed in 1950-51, portions of central Burma remained under Than Tun's control. The Communist movement itself developed little popular appeal in the total national scene.

The revolutionary situation that developed in the spring of 1948 took on more ominous overtones when a disgruntled majority element of the People's Volunteer Organization (PVO) moved to join the Communists. The PVO had been organized by Thakin Aung San in 1946 as a kind of local veterans' militia. Unrest stemmed from a decline of discipline within the PVO ranks following the death of Aung San in July 1947. Veteran hostility also developed to Socialist elements within the AFPFL, who tried to absorb the PVO into the party apparatus. Rebel leadership in 1948 derived mainly from ex-guerrilla PVO personnel who had been omitted from the five activated Burman regiments. Although generously represented in the Constituent Assembly, not a single representative of the PVO was included in Premier Nu's first cabinet, mainly because the ex-guerrillas lacked educational and administrative experience.

During April and May of 1948, Nu undertook to appease the malcontent veteran faction. Noting their ostensible acceptance of several items of Communist ideology, he even went so far in early June as to issue a "Leftist Unity Front" pronouncement prepared for him by a non-rebelling Communist. This ill-conceived move caused a mild furor, both domestically and among resident legations. Despite such efforts at accomodation, a majority faction of the PVO joined the insurrection in mid-1948, concentrating their efforts in the lower Irrawaddy basin but also linking up tenuously with Communist strongholds in central Burma. A third dissident faction, centering around a fanatical Trotskyite Communist group, operated in the Arakan district near the Pakistani border, collaborating with a rebellious Muslim *Mujahid* (crusader) movement challenging Burmese-Buddhist control in Arakan.

In July 1948 the discouraged Nu announced his intention to resign as Prime Minister. The move threatened the disintegration of his cabinet and precipitated an ominous scramble for power. In August, two of the army's five regular Burman battalions mutinied. Fortunately they were widely separated geographically and unable to join forces. Nu finally agreed to return to his post as premier when a conservative faction, led by Ba Maw and Thakin Ba Sein, offered their services to save the nation. Nu reorganized his cabinet in September, including in it several non-Leftist members, and inaugurated a series of counterrevolutionary measures. He appealed for popular support and exhorted the civil service to eschew politics and stay at their posts.

The gloom was intensified in January 1949 by the outbreak of a Karen rebellion. It was sponsored by the Karen National Defense Organization (KNDO) and enjoyed the support of professionally trained Karen elements of the army. The Karen dissidents were encouraged in their move by some British sympathizers, who shared the Karen complaint that Premier Attlee had let the Karens down, despite their proved loyalty, when he acceded to nationalist demands. Some Karen leaders sensed the opportunity, afforded

67

by the growing strife between rival Burman groups, to create a Karen-Mon state comprising, they hoped, some thirteen districts of Lower Burma. Nu's conciliatory offers fell far short of meeting these extreme demands.

Karen rebels were able to occupy the Moulmein sector of Tenasserim, to take up a strong position at Insein only a dozen miles north of Rangoon, and to control the middle Sittang Valley around Toungoo and the area around Prome. The serious Karen threat to Rangoon afforded time for the Communist dissidents in central Burma to consolidate their control. The only encouraging sign for the government in early 1949 was that some of the PVO dissidents and Burman army mutineers forgot their alleged grievances against Nu's government and rallied to oppose the Karen threat.

The rebellions faded in 1950–51 almost as rapidly as they had developed in 1948–49. By wide use of air transportation facilities, Nu and his agents maintained effective contact with peripheral regions of the Union. They managed to keep the allegiance of important Kachin and Chin elements of the regular army and gained the backing of the newly formed United Hill People's Congress. Taking advantage of his government's access to sources of aid from overseas, Nu obtained needed arms from the United Kingdom. Socialist leaders of the AFPFL who had resigned from the Cabinet in early 1949, presumably abandoning the sinking ship, returned to the government in 1950 and 1951. Nu was able to stage nationwide elections in June 1951, which strengthened his hand considerably. He emerged from the ordeal as a truly national figure. No other politician could match his rapport with the people, which was subsequently fortified by his vigorous advocacy of a traditionalist Buddhist revival.

Revival of the Hukbalahap Rebellion in the Philippines

The Communist-directed Hukbalahap rebellion in central Luzon Island, which began in desultory fashion in 1946 and was revived in 1948, was mainly a projection of the anti-

Japanese and antilandlord resistance effort of the war period. Its political roots ran deep in the soil of peasant discontent. The conviction was widely entertained that no real amelioration of tenancy grievances could be expected from the politico-landlord oligarchy, which controlled both Filipino party machines. Peasant complaints related to high rental charges and the virtual impossibility of achieving cultivator ownership. During the preliminary American occupation period, the Huk leader Luis Taruc suffered arrest and repression at the hands of landlord and U.S. forces. Released in 1946, Taruc and a number of his followers were elected to the Philippines Congress only to be later excluded from membership by President Roxas in 1947 as part of his anti-Huk repression campaign. Following President Roxas' death from a heart attack in April 1948, the succeeding president, Quirino, tried in vain to work out a settlement. At the very end of the deadline date, on August 31, Luis Taruc announced that he was a Communist and revived the rebellion in serious fashion. The date is suggestively close to Musso's comparable action.

Following the scandalously violent and dishonest Philippines general election of 1949, an increasing number of Filipino observers shared with peasant rebels a disillusionment with democratic reform efforts. The rebellion spread into the Visayan Islands of the central Philippines. By 1950 the Huk authorities of central Luzon began collecting taxes and performing other governmental duties. Wealthy Chinese were persuaded to contribute to the cause. Communist leaders boasted that all of the island republic would be theirs by 1951.

But while Communist leadership could exploit peasant grievances, the problems were demonstrably subject to correction by measures less extreme than Marxist revolution. Affairs took a dramatic turn for the better after Ramon Magsaysay was made minister of defense by President Quirino and assigned to the task of dealing with the Huks. Beginning in 1950, he punished rural officials who abused their authority and also rewarded and protected peasants who cooperated with the police and the military. Huks who

69

surrendered were pardoned and provided access to farm lands newly opened in sparsely settled Mindanao. The government supplied loans, schools, roads, water supplies, and health facilities. When Magsaysay himself ran for the presidency in 1953, he won in a landslide. At the time of his tragic death in an airplane accident in 1956, the Huk rebellion had ended, and popular faith in the democratic approach had measurably revived. Social grievances of the Filipino people, particularly the peasants, were by no means ended, however. Much of the agrarian reform legislation that had been enacted—particularly provision for land purchase and redistribution—was opposed by the conservative politicians who still controlled the party machines. Trouble was destined to revive a decade later, again with Communist overtones, but the problems were capable of domestic political solution.

The differences between the several Communist-sponsored rebellions in Indonesia, Burma, and the Philippines derived in large measure from radical variations of context. The 1947 socialistic constitution of Premier Nu's Burma government was explicitly pledged to the liquidation of large landlord holdings and to gradual modulation toward cultivator ownership. Indian moneylender titles had already disappeared. Than Tun's People's Court technique held little attraction in areas where family holdings continued to be the rule. The Communist rebellion in Burma was essentially a bid for political power, not the outcome of any pent-up peasant unrest and frustration, as was the case in Luzon. Both rebellions ran counter to majority commitments to nationalist political ends. Communist revival in Java was subsequently possible only because party leaders were willing to come to terms with Sukarno's nationalist leadership.

Moscow's presumed objective of late 1947 to wreck the capitalist economies of Western Europe by removing the colonialist props failed completely of realization. Soviet interests actually profited very little from the rash of Communist-instigated violence that erupted in Southeast Asia from 1948 to 1951.

Malayan Constitutional Problems and Politics

Britain's initial postwar scheme for recasting the government of Malaya contemplated the virtual emasculation of the powers of the nine hereditary sultans, except in religious matters, by the establishment of a centrally administered Malayan Union. Singapore alone was to be omitted. During the war, the Sultans had done little to counter the activities of the occupying Japanese forces, while Chinese rebel elements had afforded genuine assistance to the Allied cause. The proposed constitutional scheme would accord citizenship status on equal terms to all persons born in Malaya and to most immigrants with ten years residency. At the outset, the incumbent sultans were powerless to reject the postwar treaty agreements which were presented for their several signatures by London emissary, Sir Harold MacMichael, in later 1945. MacMichael was empowered to recommend the removal of any sultan whose wartime record suggested that he was unworthy of trust.

The Union proposal, published in London in early 1946 and officially promulgated at Kuala Lumpur in April, vested extensive powers in a British governor who would be responsible to the Crown. The several state councils, operating under the chairmanship of British residents, would deal only with such matters as the central government might assign to them. The new arrangement was intended to facilitate a gradual transition from the multiracial state to full nationhood to be realized as soon as circumstances permitted.

The Union Constitution attracted widespread opposition. Malays denounced it as a betrayal of the inherent rights of the indigenous inhabitants and for its prospective assignment of political influence to alien elements who already dominated the economy. Chinese and Indian opponents, on the other hand, criticized the new constitution for not providing immediately some measure of self-government and for London's arbitrary exclusion of Singapore. Lacking defenders in Malaya and arousing virulent protests from both Malayans and their former civil service friends resident in Britain, the Union constitution was stillborn, but it did elicit the first vigorous expression of Malay nationalism.

The alternative Federation Constitution, almost two years in preparation, ostensibly restored the legal sovereignty of the sultans and their British advisers. A British high commissioner at the center, assisted by appointive legislative and executive councils would exercise substantive power. The councils included official and nonofficial categories, with Malays accorded a bare majority in the legislative unit. Second generation Indians and Chinese were granted full citizenship rights, but in their several states of residency rather than on a national basis. The high commissioner was explicitly charged to safeguard the special status of the Malays and the undefined "legitimate interests" of non-Malays. Full self-rule would await the emergence of national unity and the restoration of order.[6]

London's actions took inadequate account of the dynamics of emerging political activity in both Malaya and Singapore. The occupying Japanese had done little to encourage nationalism during the course of the occupation. As happened in Indonesia, they released several imprisoned nationalists, especially those connected with the Singapore Malay Union (SMU), who had advocated independence during the prewar decades. They also sponsored the Malayan version of the militant Indonesian Peta group. Other similarities with Japanese policy in Indonesia were indicated when both the SMU survivors and Peta leaders were influenced to champion the idea of a Pan-Malay Empire (*Indonesia Raya*) very late in the period of occupation. Such Japanese-sponsored movements lacked popular roots and promptly collapsed on the arrival of postwar British forces. The idea of *Indonesia Raya* survived within some circles of strongly anti-Chinese Malays, and it was later destined to become a factor in Sukarno's ill-starred Confrontation move in 1963–66.[7]

Within the Malay community as a whole, political pressures tended to be low keyed despite the loud outcry in 1946–48 over the original Union Constitution. The average Malay peasant or fisherman was politically inert and tenaciously committed to a life style sharply at variance with the competitively acquisitive concerns of the alien Chinese and Indians. Except for students who aspired to enter the civil service, educational endeavor was peripheral to indigenous values. Malay language schools were poor in quality, and the few high schools within the system afforded very inadequate preparation for university attendance. Those who gained entrance usually avoided technical subjects in favor of religious studies. Political loyalty among Malays was primarily provincial and parochial, confined to allegiance to the several sultans, to particular states, and to the Islamic hierarchy. Assimilation with non-Malays was blocked by religious and racial prejudices, each reenforcing the other. Politically aware Malays, largely Western educated, were pleased with the Federation Constitution of 1948 and cooperated with the United Malays National Organization (UMNO), which had championed its adoption. The new order afforded essential guarantees for the survival of the sultans' authority, accorded virtual Malayan monopoly of civil service employment, and promoted their preferential access to commercial licenses and scholarships.[8]

The first articulate postwar demand for independence came from the self-styled Malayan Democratic Union (MDU), composed for the most part of frustrated professionals, including many teachers. They advocated an early end of colonial rule, the inclusion of Singapore within Malaya, westernized education conducted along noncommunal lines, and equality of legal and political rights for all elements of the population. At first the MDU attracted few Malay followers and was also too mild to win over the alien Chinese or Indians. In an attempt to broaden its impact, the Union leadership, in 1947, helped organize the All Malayan Council of Joint Action (AMCJA), in a vain effort to block the implementation of the Federation proposal. The Joint Action group formulated an alternative constitution granting automatic citizenship to most Malaya-born Chinese and to eight-year resident immigrants. Its proposals would still guarantee for the first ten years a 55 percent

73

Malay majority in the Legislative Assembly. It would also abolish the sultans' prerogative, remove Islam from state control, and give the Upper Chamber (Council of Races) a suspensive veto over discriminatory legislation. Communist elements in time took advantage of their opportunity to infiltrate the AMCJA, so that the organization tended to become increasingly radical in its policies and Chinese in its membership. All Malays withdrew from the MDU in early 1948, and it died in June of the same year following the outbreak of the Communist rebellion.[9] Radicalism among Malays shifted thereafter to the far Right, becoming increasingly religiously oriented and strongly anti-Chinese. Meanwhile the East Asian context of Malayan politics changed by reason of the independence of India, Pakistan, and Burma, the withdrawal of the Dutch from Indonesia, and the prospective victory of the Communists in China.

The Chinese population of postwar Malaya and Singapore had been obliged to adjust to an entirely different political climate. The occupying Japanese had executed some twenty-five thousand Kuomintang supporters and had subjected all well-to-do Chinese to personal harassment and monetary exactions. A particular casualty was the anachronistic Straits Chinese British Association, whose desired continuation of the colonial connection became hopelessly out of date. The more youthful postwar Chinese leadership wanted Singapore included in the constitutional system along with a definite move toward independence. An essential corollary demand was equality of citizenship rights. This group rejected the traditional Chinese tactic of avoidance of governmental activity. With British rule discredited and personal return to China out of the question for most resident Chinese, they felt obliged to confront the broader Malayan constituency. If political equality were denied, some were ready to resort to other political tactics, including assassination, boycotts, strikes, and intimidation of more cautious opponents within the Chinese community itself. The youthful leadership had not lost the ingrained sense of Chinese cultural superiority, but it was anti-religious and less subject to the influence of the traditional Secret Society hierarchies and to linguistic factionalism. The alien community generally was still vastly superior to the Malays in educational preparation, in business acumen, and in per-capita income.[10] The problems of adjustment to eventual independence would not be easy to solve.

The Communist Movement in Malaya and Singapore

Although the anti-Japanese Communist Party was prestigious and well organized when it emerged from the Malay jungle at the end of the war, it progressed very little in the immediate postwar years. Following the "popular front" tactic advocated by the Cominform down to 1948, the party directed its principal efforts toward infiltration of trade union groups within Singapore and of the so-called Democratic Union, as previously indicated. Leaders paid less attention to issues than to promotional tactics. The latter included resort to extortion and intimidation, practices carried over from the war experiences, plus the provocation of politically motivated strikes. The authorities countered by increased police surveillance, by raiding union and party headquarters, and by enforced registration of trade union officials.

As previously indicated, a Communist party shake-up ensued in early 1948, when word came through via the Calcutta Youth Conference that overt rebellion against imperialism in general was Moscow's new order of the day. The disreputable secretary-general, Loi Tak, thereupon decamped with large amounts of party funds rather than face the disciplined rigors of rebellion. Australia's Communist leader Sharkey talked with Malayan representatives both at the Calcutta meeting and subsequently in Singapore, indicating that revolutionary measures were required. The new secretary-general, Chin Peng, initiated in April a program of increasing violence, arson, and antigovernment strikes. Governmental outlawry of the infiltrated Labor Federation in June, forced a premature Communist re-

75

tirement to the jungle. The outbreak of full rebellion in July cut the ground from under Chinese critics of the new Federation Constitution, introducing a prolonged moratorium on such political activity. [11]

The size of the Chinese Communist guerrilla force was severely limited from the outset by the scarcity of weapons, munitions, and supplies. It enjoyed little outside support. The body reached a peak strength of some eight thousand in 1951. Then rebels obtained funds by blackmailing wealthy Chinese businessmen, by looting vulnerable plantation establishments, and by intimidating peasant villages located on the jungle frontier. The Peking government apparently gave no substantive support because it was concerned at the time with more urgent problems in Korea. The principal Communist assassination victims were fellow Chinese, including especially Kuomintang enemies, who had also been outlawed by the government in 1949. British personnel were attacked wherever they were found exposed. The British high commissioner, Sir Henry Gurney, was himself the victim of an ambush in 1951. Victims also included Asian foremen (usually Chinese) of rubber plantations. Two-thirds of the total of 1200 victims were Chinese, and only 4 percent were British.

The determined British effort to crush the rebellion was conducted by empire forces under the eventual command of Sir Gerald Templer, who succeeded Gurney as high commissioner. At first thousands of suspected village collaborators were detained by the police, and some offenders were repatriated to China. More effective were the later efforts to isolate terrorist groups and to deny them access to reinforcements, food, and other supplies. A major long-term undertaking was the resettlement of some 500,000 peasant Chinese living on the edges of the jungle into some 550 newly constructed village sites. The settlers were accorded protection against molestation and access to new land, plus water supplies, schools, and electricity. The outcome was long in doubt, for the guerrillas were hard to corner. Full recovery depended upon the government's enlistment of positive political cooperation by means of sustained efforts to contribute to popular needs and upon the achievement of some kind of relaxation of communal tensions. As the country eventually moved toward independence in 1957, the rebellion effort withered away.

The so-called Emergency Crisis dampened virtually all political activity for approximately two years. The key United Malay National Organization (UMNO) which had been formed in 1948 by Dato Onn bin Ja'afar, the minister of justice of Johore state, assumed a neutral stance. As the sponsor of the revised Federation Agreement, the UMNO attracted wide recognition among Malays. Because the Communist Chinese leaders themselves wanted to attract some measure of indigenous tolerance in their attack on British rule, the UMNO was spared direct denunciation. Although opposed to the rebellion, the latter at first adopted a nonbelligerent stance.[12] Changes occurred in 1951–52, when Dato Onn began to espouse the goal of complete independence within ten years. Hoping to attract some Chinese adherents to his cause, he proposed the granting of full citizen rights to all second-generation Chinese and increased eligibility for first-generation immigrants. When he began to encounter Malayan objections, he resigned from the allegedly procolonialist UMNO and started his rival Independence of Malaya party (IMP), hoping thereby to capture both nationalist support and, possibly, a Chinese following. Actually, Dato Onn overreached himself badly. He discovered that his qualified noncommunal approach carried no conviction with the aliens and no appeal for the Malays. His anti-British sentiments were not widely shared, for independence would obviously involve dangers without some modification of communal tensions.

Following Dato Onn's resignation in 1951, the leadership of the UMNO was assumed by the British-educated Tengku Abdul Rahman, a younger son of the sultan of Kedah. In an effort to find some way to counter the appeal of Dato Onn's new Independence party in the local Kuala Lumpur elections of 1952, Tengku worked out an ad hoc plan of cooperation with Tan Cheng-lock, head of the Malayan

Chinese Association (MCA) and a political rival of Dato Onn. The organization of the MCA had been sponsored in 1949 by High Commissioner Malcolm MacDonald in an effort to reduce the appeal of the Communists among the Chinese inhabitants by encouraging counteraction on the part of responsible elements of that community. The MCA represented the influential and wealthy Chinese. In order to provide funds for the MCA, the government in October 1952 legalized the operation of a charitable lottery as a means of providing relief funds for destitute Chinese otherwise likely to cooperate with the rebels. Intended at the outset as a nonpolitical organization, the MCA would provide the non-Communist Chinese with a stake in the suppression of the rebellion and an avenue for constructive social endeavor. The agreement between the Tengku and Tan Cheng-lock was reached only some five weeks before the impending 1952 elections. Both parties would support jointly selected candidates across communal lines, the majority of whom were Malays. The nationwide electoral victory of the allied groups discredited Dato Onn's opportunism and launched the MCA as a political organization in alliance with the UMNO. Cheng-lock began distributing lottery earnings to benefit destitute Malays as well as Chinese. Dato Onn was subsequently defeated in his own state of Johore in 1953. Thereafter, the officially sponsored Negara party became the principal rival of the Alliance.

Tan Cheng-lock continued his cautious bargaining efforts both at Kuala Lumpur and at London. In 1953, colonial authorities conceded that Chinese candidates for the civil service could begin to share appointment with Malays on a minimal one-to-four basis. In 1955, London accepted the further MCA demand that the new Legislative Council should contain an elected majority of fifty-two in a total of ninety-eight seats.[13] In preparation for the elections of 1955, the directors of the Alliance party made independence the overriding issue and nominated nationwide candidates on an agreed ethnic-ratio basis of thirty-five Malays, to fifteen Chinese, to two Indians, all of whom would be accorded Alliance support in single-member districts. The arrangement was realistic politically, and the outcome was astonishingly successful. Alliance candidates captured all but one of the fifty-two elected seats and attracted nineteen supporters elsewhere in the Assembly. The single loss was to a Pan Islamic party candidate running in a strongly Malay constituency. A semblance of political stability was thus achieved and a long step taken toward complete independence and ending of the rebellion.

Independence came in 1957, and the Emergency was completely terminated by July 1960. Meanwhile the nonrebel Communist leader Chin Peng tried in vain to salvage a meaningful political role for his fading party following.[14] Political manipulation and projected economic reforms contributed quite as much to eventual pacification as had military and police suppression. The psychological lift derived from the Alliance experiment was particularly important. The later history of independent Malaysia will be considered in a subsequent chapter.

Interpretation of the Malayan Communist Movement

A perceptive analysis of testimony garnered from surrendered Communist participants in the Malayan rebellion has contributed a valuable new dimension to the episode.[15] Most of the surrendered youth who were interviewed ranged from ages twenty to twenty-three. They were drawn as a rule not from peasant or worker families, but from teenage rebel groups who had broken with traditional ties and with such apolitical organizations as secret societies or trade unions. Their primary objective was to find opportunity for social mobility commensurate with their educational achievement and personal sophistication. Only a peasant mentality, they reasoned, would give precedence to such traditional virtues as patience, diligence, and industry. Rebel recruits were interested in career prospects, in finding release from the frustration of inactivity, and in the possible achievement of personal dignity through peer-group participation in the worldwide Communist revolution. Disciplined exposure to the regimen of self-accusation and cleansing from bourgeois errors might conceivably contribute significance to an otherwise discouraging personal and social environment. Such persons were little interested in religion, ethics, or philosophical problems, and equally contemptuous of poetry and literature. A majority of them prized shrewdness over intellectual acumen, and skillful employment of violence over idealistic concerns.

The identifiable misgivings that led the defectors to abandon the rebellion were equally significant. They stemmed primarily from personal disillusionment and from revulsion against some of the demands connected with Communist activities. Their world became in time oppressively impersonal; checking up on others left them no friends in whom to confide. Many disliked doing housekeeping chores at camp, as well as the perennial task of collecting material support by threat and terrorism, and their exposure to endless indoctrination sessions in Communist theory and in praise of the role of the Soviet Union in the world. Was their losing cause worth continuing self-sacrifice? Ideals completely evaporated when corrupted leadership succumbed to predatory selfishness. Most of the defectors who emerged from the jungle during the fifties were hostile to Communism and disillusioned with political activity generally and in social concerns in particular. They conceded, however, that leaving the party had been both difficult and dangerous.

Conclusions

The evidence presented in Pye's study as cited above and others concerning the revolutionary upheavals in Southeast Asia suggests that Communist rebellion was essentially a social and political phenomenon associated with the achievement of independence. It was usually not directly attributable to poverty per se or to frustrated nationalist aspirations. To urbanized persons caught in the confusions of an erratically changing world, Communism seemed to offer a kind of psychological haven. Marxism provided a face-saving explanation for discouraging situations, coupled with a disciplined plan of corrective activity operating on a worldwide scale. Countermeasures to such Communist drift must be undertaken mainly at the political level rather than through relief of physical distress or by police repression. Feasible patterns of political behavior appropriate to dealing with social problems had to be devised. The limited appeal of fanatical Communism in Malaya was effectively countered by substituting alternative ideas and organizational forms more positive in character and less costly than frustrated violence. Genuinely constructive activities capable of satisfying widely shared concerns usually had little relevance to world revolution and endless class struggle. What was needed to balance the inarticulate clamor, the unsure convictions, and the general feeling of insecurity associated with rapid change, was the promotion of social innovations capable of satisfying personal problems and group needs.

The Communist-instigated risings of 1948–51 in Southeast Asia, historically considered, were both illtimed and ineffective. In most situations, the articulate non-Communist elite still maintained a measure of faith in alternative social innovations and nonrevolutionary means of implementing political change. Nu's appeal was thus stronger than Than Tun's; Magsaysay won out over Luis Taruc; Hatta overcame Musso. The Alliance party compromise triumphed over the forlorn jungle-based Communist guerrillas. Real threats would arise in the future, when the Burmese would lose faith in both democracy and in Ne Win's arbitrary military authority, however patriotic; when Sukarno's guided democracy or army repression in Indonesia threatened to close the door to institutional adjustment; when Malaya's Chinese minority in 1969 would despair of achieving political equality; when oligarchic army rule and martial law under Sarit and Thanom in Thailand would run roughshod over personal liberties and constitutional guarantees; when French colonial intransigence or American obsession with the cold war would block

Vietnamese nationalist aspirations; when corruption and political excesses in the Philippines undermined the integrity of democratic procedures. All of these situations call for further explanation.

A variety of inter-state crises were also destined in time to become factors of genuine social peril. Intraregional rivalries over Malaysia's creation, conflicting claims to Sabah, Cambodia's fear of Thailand, and revival of centuries-old rivalry between north and south Vietnam, these would constitute essential aspects of the problem of peace and cooperation within Southeast Asia. By comparison, the fumbling machinations of world communism after 1948 constituted a provocative element, but certainly not the most decisive issue in the continuing problem of revolutionary adjustment to independent status. The emerging situation could not be understood, much less solved, by American application of the Cold-War dichotomy.

1. See Ruth McVey, *The Calcutta Conference and the Southeast Asia Communist Rebellion* (Ithaca, 1958).

2. David Wurfel, "The Philippines," in George M. Kahin, ed., *Governments and Politics of Southeast Asia* (Ithaca, 1964), pp. 698-99.

3. Virginia Thompson and Richard Adloff, *The Left Wing in Southeast Asia* (New York, 1950), pp. 141-62; Lucian Pye, *Guerrilla Communism in Malaysia: Its Social and Political Meaning* (Princeton University, 1956), pp. 103-8.

4. Thompson and Adloff, *op. cit.*, pp. 181-86.

5. Ruth McVey, "Indonesian Communism Under Guided Democracy," in Doak Barnett, ed., *Communist Strategies in Asia* (New York, 1963), pp. 148-55.

6. See D. G. E. Hall, *A History of Southeast Asia* (London, 1968), pp. 834-37.

7. Gordan P. Means, *Malaysian Politics* (London, 1970). pp. 44-49, 81-86.

8. *Ibid.*, pp. 17-23.

9. *Ibid.*, pp. 87-95.

10. *Ibid.*, pp. 29-33, 44-50.

11. *Ibid.*, pp. 70-77.

12. *Ibid.*, pp. 75-77.

13. *Ibid.*, pp. 120-27, 132-37, 143-48.

14. *Ibid.*, pp. 161-67, 280.

15. Pye, *op. cit.*, pp. 103-108.

IV

POSTWAR THAILAND, TO
THE RETIREMENT OF
PIBUN

The Continuing Vitality of Tradition

By reason of Thailand's prewar avoidance of European colonial rule and its exemption from the devastation during World War II, the country's deep-rooted political and social institutions survived the ordeal. Cohesive village communities retained their capacity to resist arbitrarily imposed regimentation, partly because both society and governmental agencies valued the principles of voluntary cooperation and reciprocity. Continued popular acceptance of status gradations also assisted in negating any overt challenge to the traditional order. The prevailing ethnic and cultural homogeneity re-enforced villager attachment to community and family, to Buddhism, and to the symbols of governmental authority. Prestigious village elders and family patrons helped in the enforcement of customary law, in the maintenance of essential commercial relationships, and in temple administration. The accepted norm of good manners underscored the obligation to avoid direct personal confrontation and giving of offense. Preserving face and personal dignity thus took precedence over the aggressive promotion of personal interests. Acceptable jobs were expected to afford some opportunity for having fun (*sanug*). On the negative side, traditional social factors added to the difficulty of generating any sustained endeavor to pursue innovative objectives; within the context of accepted norms, however, the Thai social system continued to function with vigor.

At the governmental level, Thai society included relatively few persons who were inclined to assume any overtly antagonistic or revolutionary stance. The custom was to treat agencies of government with the same formal deference traditionally accorded to royal authority, so long as customary rights were respected. Unpalatable demands of officials were usually ignored rather than challenged directly. In reciprocation, government agencies tended not to execute unpleasant assignments too rigidly. Higher-echelon officials avoided scolding their inefficient subordinates, while the latter refrained from disclosing the shortcomings or irregularities in the conduct of their superiors. In this world of Buddhist impermanence, it was better to coexist under muted tensions rather than precipitate the violence that would attend an open break. Postwar rulers in Thailand, whatever their political persuasion, took full advantage of the aura of sanctity surrounding both the monarchial tradition and the national Buddhist identity.

Thailand also differed from much of the rest of postwar Southeast Asia in that the enhanced sense of national identity had little relevance to resistance to colonial rule. Except for inveterate hostility to the traditional Burmese enemy, there were no expressions of hostility to foreigners. The several million resident Chinese centering in Bangkok were less alien in Thailand than were their fellow countrymen in other countries of Southeast Asia. Unlike the revolutionary regimes that emerged in Burma, Indonesia, and Vietnam, Bangkok's postwar rulers did not face the necessity of legitimatizing their authority on the basis of critically evaluated performance. Holding elections and devising new constitutions were designed more for the purpose of impressing world opinion than for authenticating authority domestically. Few Thai citizens developed any deep-seated attachment to the principles of representative democracy, whether theoretical or pragmatic.

This is not to suggest that the word "democracy" was a forbidden word in describing the Thai government. By dint of sheer affirmation and rote memorization, Bangkok University students persisted into the late sixties in describing their government as a democracy. The promoters of the antiroyalist coup of 1932 had affirmed that sovereign power was vested in the people, even though the actual control was clearly elitist and the bureaucracy continued to function under the traditional royal mandate. Partly to keep the term "democracy" current, successive constitutions and elections provided a convenient façade behind which to legitimatize the usurpation of power by successive coup leaders. Democracy continued to be a good word; even during the decade of 1958–68, when the Thai constitution was suspended under martial law, the approved copybook description of the government as a democracy remained unchanged, with no regard to the meaning of the term or to the actual locus of political control.

The Postwar Free Thai Government

For approximately two years, postwar Bangkok witnessed an attempt to substitute civilian rule for that of the military. The lawyer leader of the Free Thai movement, Luang Pridi Phanomyong, had taken over from Marshal Pibun, as previously detailed, in July 1944. The army leadership was further discredited by the defeat of Japan, and Pibun was made temporarily liable for trial as a war criminal. Two royalist-oriented civilian politicians—the affable Khuang Aphaiwong and the former ambassador to the United States, Mom Seni Pramoj—took turns filling the role of premier under Pridi's tutelage at the war's end. The Free Thai civilian government was united only in its repudiation of Pibun personally and in its affirmation that the army should be divorced from politics; its members were otherwise disparate. Pridi himself was a quasi socialist and strongly anticolonialist. His postwar coalition included some naval and civil service personnel, support from proroyalists, and limited popular backing.

Following his conclusion of peace negotiations with the British in early January 1946, Seni Pramoj joined hands with Khuang Aphaiwong in sponsoring the Democrat party, a moderately liberal proroyalist group that successfully contested the elections held in late January. Khuang took over as premier temporarily. The Democrats advocated qualified cabinet responsibility to the partly elected lower house, coupled with reduced powers for the appointed Senate. They also envisioned the revitalization of monarchial influence as a stabilizing factor to counter the popular elements aligned with Pridi. Pridi, by contrast, favored a more thoroughgoing liberalization of electoral and governmental procedures as a means of widening his political base.

In March 1946, Pridi pushed Khuang aside and assumed the premiership himself in a move to implement several reform proposals. As defined in Pridi's revised constitution of May 1946, a fully elected lower house was empowered to select the upper chamber, thus facilitating the exclusion of both royalist supporters and army leaders. Pridi enjoyed an enthusiastic but poorly organized student following. He also sustained his anti-imperialist reputation of prewar days by assisting anti-French nationalist proponents in neighboring Laos, Cambodia, and Vietnam.

As an expression of liberal tendencies and as a conciliatory gesture toward the army, the civilian Bangkok authorities approved the Supreme Court's March 1946 action of refusing to try General Pibun as a war criminal and releasing him from jail. The potential threat of a military coup was discounted at the time in view of Pridi's proposed constitutional revisions, based on civilian control, and also by reason of his close relations as regent with the youthful King Ananda. The teen-age king returned in December 1945 from his wartime domicile in Switzerland for a visit to Bangkok, in the company of his mother and younger brother. His most important assignments prior to returning to school in Switzerland were to learn something about his future duties as king and to approve Pridi's new constitution.

The prospect of establishing civilian dominance over

army rule was dimmed by several negative factors. The civilian faction itself was divided, with the Khuang-Seni group favoring a reassertion of royalist influence and the selection of a kind of elder-statesman senate. The strongly entrenched civil service faction also preferred to regard itself as serving under royal authorization rather than at the whim of a cabinet government based on theoretical popular sovereignty and election credentials. The civil service bureaucracy, furthermore, was alone competent to handle routine administrative duties and was therefore in a favorable position to come to terms with either a military or a civilian cabinet. The fairly wide urban and student support enjoyed by Pridi personally lacked disciplined and articulate leadership or popular connections. Pridi himself was too Westernized and too socialistically inclined to establish intimate rapport with the traditionalist village constituency. Whatever chance of survival civilian rule may have enjoyed was seriously compromised by developments following King Ananda's tragic death in early June 1946.

King Ananda's Death and the Downfall of Pridi

King Ananda died in bed of a bullet wound in the temple in early June, 1946, on the very eve of his planned return to Europe. He had approved Pridi's new constitution only the day before. Inconclusive evidence suggested the likely possibility of royal suicide, apparently arising from mental stress on Ananda's part over the traditional role expected of the king. The subsequent trial of the accused assassins produced evidence that Ananda had also, at one time, contemplated abdication. Prince Mahidol, the deceased father of the king, was a Westernized man of liberal convictions, trained as physician, who had never anticipated during his lifetime the prospect of kingship for himself or his sons.

Because Pridi's role as regent entailed direct responsibility for the orientation program and, presumably, the safety of the young king, the Free Thai premier was vulnerable to criticism for the sad event. He was not accused at that time of instigating the king's death, for he could

87

realize no possible advantage from it. But Pridi had arranged for the prince's return to Bangkok and had attempted to acquaint him with his future duties as ruler. What happened to the king was therefore his affair.

As head of the government, Premier Pridi provided from the outset full support for the police investigation of the circumstances attending the king's death. But the evidence turned up was meager. Political opponents of Pridi, especially the recently freed Pibun and the army clique, thereupon initiated a politically motivated effort to pin responsibility on the Free Thai leader. Since most Thais found the idea of royal suicide unthinkable because it compromised the prestige of the sacrosanct monarchy, and since no plausible alternative explanation was forthcoming, the embarrassed Pridi felt obliged to resign as premier in August 1946. His Free Thai government managed to carry on for another year despite army opposition, under the leadership of a retired admiral, Thamrong Nawasarat, whose regime in time became very corrupt.

The eventual army coup of November, 1947, was designed ostensibly to restore the honor of the army and honesty in the government. The coup was occasioned by Thamrong's attempt to economize by cutting appropriations for the army. It was a bloodless affair and enjoyed the support of the proroyalist Democrat party. Pridi narrowly avoided capture by fleeing down the river, with the assistance of representatives of the British embassy. He proceeded first to Singapore and later took up residence in China. His followers within the Assembly were either jailed or driven into hiding. On two subsequent occasions, in 1949 and 1951, Pridi's civilian supporters, acting in collusion with some naval officers, made efforts to recover control, but the opposing army and air force contingents proved too strong. During the initial five months of control by the coup group, Pibun covered up the fact of army dominance by installing the accomodating Khuang Aphaiwong as the new premier, even permitting the Democrat party to win a majority in the Assembly elections of January, 1948. The charade ended in April 1948, when Pibun pushed Khuang aside by means of a mere radio announcement. The army leader allied himself with two ambitious army Colonels, Phao Sriyanon and Sarit Thanarat,[2] whose roles will be considered later.

The Trial of Ananda's Alleged Assassins

Pibun's relentless feuding against the exiled Pridi was carried on via the trial of three arrested suspects in the death of King Ananda. The trial began in September 1948 and continued for more than seven years. Two of the three defendants, Butra and Nai Chit, were court pages who had been posted outside the bedchamber of the king at the time of his death; the third was a former private secretary of the monarch, one Chaleo, who had previously been designated as a senator by Pridi. Chaleo was presumed to have been hostile to Ananda because of his dismissal as secretary and was alleged to have been in communication with Pridi's naval friend, Lieutenant Vacharachi, who had fled in the company of the Free Thai leader in November 1947. Vacharachi was also reported to have been seen in the vicinity of the palace before and following the alleged assassination, while Butra and Nai Chit were accused of having permitted the lieutenant or his assassin agents to enter the bedchamber. But the presence and identification of Vacharachi at the palace was supported by no tangible evidence, and naval partisans friendly to Pridi challenged the antagonistic allegations advanced by the pro-army prosecutors.

Naval resentment found expression in the two previously mentioned abortive coups in 1949 and 1951. The three-day naval effort in June, 1951, was precipitated by Pibun's reduction of the navy's budget by a staggering 75 percent. On this occasion, the rebels actually held Pibun captive temporarily aboard the battleship Sri-Ayuthia in the river off Bangkok. When the ship was sunk by air force bombs, the premier escaped by swimming ashore. These developments were all effectively exploited by Pibun, who argued, quite inconclusively, that Pridi and the navy were both hostile to royalty.

The original hearings and successive reviews of the court findings, down to the final execution of all three defendants, continued until February 1955. Political overtones were in evidence throughout the course of the trials, although a labored effort was made by the judges to establish a strictly legal case. The unpalatable possibility of suicide had to be rejected arbitrarily if the army's political objectives were to be served. The revolver (Ananda's own) and the bullet found imbedded in the mattress were exhaustively examined, as were the king's posture on the bed and the direction of firing by the assumed assassin. Meanwhile, the accused were imprisoned under heavy duress, including persistent efforts by the police to extort confessions from them.

The original two and one-half years of hearings included the testimony of more than 120 witnesses. The judges produced a 50,000-word document reviewing every aspect of the findings. The first verdict dismissed the charges against Chaleo, whose presence on the scene was never established, and also against Butra, but Nai Chit was judged guilty. The court review of Nai Chit's conviction, lasting some three years, included a revival of the charges against the two previously acquitted defendants.[3]

The two politicians who profited most politically from the prolonged tensions that attended the course of the trial were Pibun and Phao, now police general. The accused Butra was convicted at the end of the first appeals session in December 1953, while Chaleo was similarly condemned following a final appeal to the high level Dikka Court in October 1954. Four months of futile appeals for mercy ensued before the final execution of all three victims in February 1955. The trial served as an example of the army's willingness to exploit legal processes to serve political ends, and their efforts to exploit the aura of royalty for personal advantage. Meanwhile, in 1950, King Ananda's younger brother, Prince Bhumiphon Adunyadet, returned to Bangkok from Switzerland to assume the throne.

Following his tarnished legal victory over Pridi and his friends, Prime Minister Pibun embarked on a world tour.

He was the recipient of numerous public honors, including the Legion of Merit decoration in Washington, ostensibly in recognition of his strongly anti-Communist stance at the time. Upon his return to Bangkok, he found himself beset by mounting political difficulties. Hoping to enlist further American support as a champion of democracy and freedom of speech, he set up an experimental speaker's corner on Bangkok's central market grounds. He enlisted General Phao's support for a time, but the embarrassing project was quickly abandoned.

The Political Policies of Premier Pibun

Governmental changes initiated by Pibun's military junta after 1948 rejected the democratic pattern proposed by both the Free Thai and the Democrat parties. At the outset, Pibun replaced Pridi's Assembly-elected Senate with 100 appointed members and then proceeded to ignore the Assembly itself. He nevertheless maintained a measure of accomodation with the proroyalist Democrat party until early 1949. When the Democrat leaders, Seni Pramoj and Khuang Aphaiwong, were given an opportunity to serve in the constitutional revision process in January 1949, they deliberately championed a genuinely democratic constitution. The proposal would have made the cabinet responsible to the lower house of the Parliament, which would be elected by universal adult suffrage. Princes would have been permitted participation in both the royally appointed Senate and in the Privy Council. The proposal died aborning. Pibun's own new constitution, promulgated in March 1949, removed from Assembly control all executive authority, including policing and court functions and allocation of budgeted funds. Under official pressure, legislative approval could be solicited for the ratification of executive decisions and emergency ordinances. Newly established governmental economic agencies, functioning as autonomous legal corporations, were empowered to define their own policy objectives and to allocate whatever funds were made available to them.[4]

Elections continued to be held every other year down to 1957, but democracy withered away. In the 1949 elections, the army party resorted to widespread bribery and defeated all of the Democrat party candidates. Instead of the mere five Assembly seats they had won in 1947, the army group came up with seventy-five. In 1951 the ruling group split, permitting the army and the Democrat party, in alliance with Pibun, to recover temporary control of both houses of Parliament. Generals Phao and Sarit thereupon staged a counter coup in November 1951, cutting off all army co-operation with the Democrats and revising the constitution in 1952. The lower house was made only half elective, while the Senate was put entirely under army control. Pibun kept his titular role as premier down to 1955, when Ananda's murder trial ended, but real power was in other hands. He tried in vain after 1955 to attract liberal support by encouraging public political discussion, as previously indicated. His governing role during the final two years of his faltering premiership, 1955–57, amounted to little more than a cover for actual domination by the corrupt Phin-Phao military clique.[5]

Because elected elements of the government were denied opportunity to enlist the backing of organized constituencies, all political initiative rested with the wielders of military power. Political competition within government circles usually took the form of contests for the more attractive positions and for available funds. The rules of the game apparently forbade the complete exclusion of subordinate army factions. The navy was wholly excluded. The controlling group placed its own candidates in the most desirable strategic positions, while losers were relegated to less attractive government posts.[6] Elections under the 1952 constitution were invariably marred by corrupt manipulation. Their only positive effects were to give opportunity for the emergence of political leadership at provincial levels and to afford popular experience in conducting election contests.[7]

In such areas as education and economic opportunity, Pibun resorted to discriminatory treatment of the alien Chinese. In 1948 he reduced the annual Chinese immigration quota from the previous level of 10,000 to a mere 200 per year. Another aspect of his nationalist emphasis was to change the country's name back to Thailand in 1949, thus reviving the wartime idea of irredentist frontier claims. After 1950 he buttressed his anti-Chinese domestic policies by taking an increasingly anti-Peking stance. He supported the United Nations in the Korean War, and also the anti-Communist Emergency measures of the neighboring Malayan government.[8] As a means of enlisting both French and American support, he approved the revived Bao Dai regime in Vietnam. His "Un-Thai Activities Act" of 1952, copied from Washington, permitted the arbitrary arrest, as alleged Communist subversives, of virtually all open critics of his military regime. His pro-American posture earned substantial rewards, including American grants for military assistance, education, health, and agricultural development. These funds helped double the budget of the Bangkok government from 1950 to 1952.

Pibun's pro-American and anti-Communist policy became even more pronounced following the end of the Korean War in 1953 and the French military debacle at Dienbienphu in 1954. Thailand joined the SEATO alliance in 1954 and permitted the establishment of SEATO headquarters at Bangkok. Thereafter all opposition to conservative army rule could be denounced as Communist inspired. By the time Pibun retired in 1957, American military assistance, totalling some 138 million dollars, had served to fortify the power of the ruling army clique to the point where it was unassailable by civilian or naval rivals. Pibun's characteristic anti-Peking stance was qualified for a short time only, following the Bandung Conference of early 1955, when Chou En-lai undertook a rapprochement with China's southeastern neighbors.

Economic Recovery Policies in Postwar Thailand

Thailand's problems of economic recovery after the war, although formidable and politically involved, were nevertheless manageable. The immediate need was to make good the

93

cumulative deficit in consumer goods requirements. A nine-million-dollar credit remaining to Thailand's account in the United States was utilized for this purpose, and sixteen million pounds sterling of blocked currency was released in London. Indian authorities contributed a loan of fifty million rupees, and America advanced a similar sum for the purchase of needed war surplus supplies.

As a means of partial avoidance of punitive British treaty demands to compensate for Thailand's wartime collusion with Japan, Bangkok offered to provide gratis up to 1.5 million tons of Thai rice to meet urgent regional food needs. The delivery system was vastly complicated. The rice was to be obtained on the initiative of the International Emergency Food Agency operating from Washington. A Singapore committee of the agency worked through the Combined Siam Rice Commission in Bangkok in cooperation with a local consortium of British firms known as the Siamese Rice Agency. The latter obtained the grain through the Thai government's Rice Bureau, which alone dealt with the local Chinese compradors. In actuality, the Chinese merchants of Bangkok utilized their own marketing facilities to evade the elaborate control system and delivered most of their rice surpluses to cooperating countrymen overseas. Eventually, in 1947, the Combined Rice Commission departed from Bangkok, and the government's own Rice Bureau assumed monopoly control over all rice exports.

Only a small fraction of the promised 1.5 million tons was ever delivered. Whatever expectation the British might have entertained in 1945–46 of recovering their substantial prewar influence over Thailand's economy was also effectively thwarted. In 1949 Thailand ended its financial dependence on the sterling bloc and associated itself with the International Monetary Fund and the International Bank for Reconstruction and Development.[9]

Although Thailand restored prewar levels of economic output as early as 1947, gains were painfully slow for a decade thereafter. Pibun's initial moves were more negative than positive. His effort to curb the domination of Thailand's economy by the resident Chinese business community was pursued vigorously after 1948. He required resident Chinese to pay a periodic 400-*baht* poll tax or an annual 200-*baht* immigration fee. Pibun also interfered with the operation of Chinese language schools and challenged the alien community's virtual monopoly of vocational opportunities outside government employ. In 1948, for example, he sponsored the War Veterans' Organization, utilizing both private and public funds, ostensibly for the purpose of creating business opportunities for retired soldiers. The main tangible result was to widen the patronage of the army command and to enrich army politicians.[10] By assuming a strong anti-Communist stance after 1949, Pibun also exploited the friction that developed within the resident Chinese community between Kuomintang and Communist partisans in rival guilds, incipient trade union organizations, and chambers of commerce. Business interests were vulnerable, with the result that wealthy Chinese found it expedient to come to terms with the ruling army elite.

The ending of the Korean War in 1953–54 and the consequent abrupt decline of the world price of rice created an annual payments deficit for Thailand amounting to some 800 million *baht* (40 million U.S. dollars). It also entailed large losses for the government's rice sales monopoly agency. In 1955, when the agency found itself unable to market the current crop, the rice was turned over for distribution to local Chinese merchants, who paid the Department of External Trade a premium over domestic prices. Import restrictions were also imposed, and the International Monetary Fund was asked to advise Bangkok on trade-policy, marketing, and budgetary problems. Negotiation of a World Bank loan for railways, harbors, and other development purposes helped make good the $200-million trade imbalance. The use of accumulated currency reserves enabled the government to sustain the free market value of the *baht*. The task of maintaining orderly finances was further assisted in 1956 by improved accounting and budgeting procedures and by collection of trade statistics. In that year, one-sixth of the budget was covered by overseas loans, including the 1.5-billion-yen settlement of Japan's wartime obligations.[11]

The premier's positive economic tactics included the

95

launching of an ambitious program of state-sponsored public corporations covering a large variety of industrial activities. Approximately 140 such projects were eventually undertaken. Because most of them were badly administered, they operated at a chronic deficit.[12] The manufacture of cigarettes was one of the few to prove profitable, mainly because the process was simple and a local market was assured. Although experienced Chinese managers were sometimes employed for efficiency purposes, government-recruited personnel became heavily involved in the direction of such state enterprises.

Pibun's policy of state-sponsored enterprises owed more to the traditional practices of royal monopoly than to the socialist ideology Pridi had previously advocated. Pibun and his principal collaborator, General Phao of the police, headed the new National Development Corporation. Subordinate organizations included a Trade Monopolies Agency, a Ministry of Industrial Factory Development, and a Military Industry Department within the Defense Ministry. Influential officials often received gratis shares of stock in the several government enterprises, while the lower-level administrative bureaucracies took advantage of opportunities afforded by the burgeoning system to supplement their meager salaries. In the resulting conspiracy of connivance, government officials found it neither effective nor prudent to elicit public discussion of the growing miasma of corruption. Only occasionally did some strategically placed accounting personnel in the Budget Bureau (who preferred to remain anonymous) take advantage of the visits of international agency teams to expose some of the more flagrant practices.[13] Absent from the Bangkok political scene was any open discussion of the political or ethical implications of such practices.[14]

It was only a matter of time before elite Thai officials and the Chinese business community entered into collusion. In the absence of any effective legal means of protecting their interests, the Chinese community came to terms with the government. The resulting accomodation usually took the form of asking Thai political personalities to accept membership on the boards of directors of Chinese firms,[15] coupled with a modest grant of stock to compensate them for their services. Such practices were destined to be greatly expanded under Marshal Sarit after 1958, when the persecution of the Chinese business community was gradually abandoned.[16] The struggling state enterprises were also gradually liquidated. Business began to improve, and despite the widespread corruption, essential routine government operations were sustained and services were performed.

During the first half of the fifties, Thailand's foreign trade volume expanded substantially, due mainly to rising prices that attended the outbreak of the Korean War in June 1950. The Bank of Thailand was able to set up its own foreign exchange market, build up its foreign currency holdings, and resume regular payments on overseas debt obligations. The profits realized from the increased world demand for rice, rubber, and tin not only erased budgetary deficits, but also increased the volume of consumer goods imports. The conservative fiscal policies pursued by the Bank were designed primarily to strengthen Thailand's credit status, while tending to discourage expenditures on internal economic development.[17] But substantial help also came from the outside, partly as a result of Pibun's strong anti-Communist posture and Thailand's participation in the Korean War. The first substantial American grant—$24.4 million—helped build the Chainat irrigation dam facility in Central Thailand and to improve railway, port, and electrical generating capacity. Much more was to come later.

Modulation from Pibun to Sarit, 1954–57

The principal contest for governmental control after 1954 developed between General Phao's military police, numbering some forty-three thousand men, and the army itself, headed by General Sarit Thanarat.[18] Premier Pibun remained titular head of the government, but he lacked access to comparable sources of armed support. The shifting locus of power went far to explain Pibun's feigned enthusiasm, following his return from Britain and America in mid-1955, for political freedom and democracy. He advocated excluding the army from political activity and barring government officials from economic connections. As an ostensible act of good faith, Pibun resigned his own post as inspector-general of the armed forces and sold his stock in private companies. He even dispensed for a time with armed escorts and began to drive his own car. Newspaper censorship was lifted, and regular press conferences were held at which government officials were required to be present to answer questions. For a time, as previously mentioned, Pibun afforded opportunity for free discussion of public questions on the central market Pramane Grounds. He legalized political parties in September 1955, reduced the voting age to twenty, and eliminated earlier educational requirements.

While General Phao was absent in Washington negotiating a loan, Pibun took over the Ministry of Interior, demoting Phao's supporters and forbidding all police involvement in commercial ventures. He even exposed some of the general's dubious operations in the opium trade racket in North Thailand, where police had collected rewards ranging up to one million dollars for repeated capture of the same opium without arresting or convicting a single smuggler.[19]

Upon his return General Phao pretended for a time to go along with Pibun's democratic reform efforts by appearing on the Pramane Grounds. He even sponsored the Local Government Act of 1955, which authorized locally chosen councils, capable of sharing policy making and fiscal controls, at provincial and municipal levels. But half of the council members were to be nominated by the presiding provincial governors (Phao's own appointees), and half were elected by local parties that he hoped to develop into a mass following. Phao's decentralization proposal was a patent political fraud. The 120 municipal councils were permitted no real control over policy decisions, personnel, or monetary allocations.[20]

The simulated democratic revival effort of Pibun and Phao ended in early 1956. The Hyde Park-type discussions were closed down by General Phao's own police in February. Several cabinet ministers, as well as influential members of the Assembly, had been embarrassed by sensational exposés of their misconduct. Constructive efforts to move toward responsible government ran completely aground in late 1956, when police and the military suppressed all criticism on allegations that it was designed to foment rebellion.

Pibun had obviously overplayed his hand. Washington's aid to Thailand was conditioned more on the need to contain alleged Communist threats than on concern to support his opportunistic advocacy of democracy. Nor did Pibun's ostentatious liberalism arouse any supporting response within Thailand. Meanwhile, General Sarit denounced Pibun's reform proposals as a move to make the country into an American colony and protégé in the cold war and questioned the wisdom of continued acceptance of American aid.[21] Seeing his own political survival at stake, Pibun reacted to Sarit's criticism by temporarily playing up to Peking, following Chou En-lai's demonstration of conciliation at the previous Bandung Conference. In 1956 Pibun halted the persecution of pro-Communist Chinese in Thailand, initiated trade with mainland China, and permitted Thai tourists to visit China.[22]

In the general elections staged in February 1957, Pibun and Phao joined forces in a last desperate effort to retain power. Their official party enlisted civil-servant and police support for its candidates, resorted to ballot stuffing and voter intimidation, and engaged in open bribery up to an estimated sum of 120 million *bahts.* Khuang's Democrat party staged a dignified and effective protest campaign in Bangkok, only to be robbed of victory by open fraud. A score of opposition groups denounced government corruption, the SEATO alliance, and various other U.S. connections. Kukrit Pramoj, Seni's journalist brother and editor of Bangkok's *Siam Rath* newspaper, denounced the government's victory as criminally dishonest, while university students joined in the growing protest.

The principal gainer from the election scandal was Field

99

Marshal Sarit Thanarat, who elected to ride the wave of anti-American and antigovernment feeling. He repudiated his official party affiliations, while keeping his army command intact and refusing to resign any of his private commercial connections, as he was ordered to do by Pibun. He attacked both SEATO and American colonialism, and even talked of seeking accomodation with the Soviet Union or Peking, as a means of vindicating Thailand's national independence. His eventual coup, staged on September 17, 1957, was undertaken allegedly in the interest of peace, order, and the welfare of the Thai people. It ended for more than a decade any serious attempt to revive democratic rule.[23]

Popular revulsion had contributed substantially to ending the domination of Marshal Pibun and General Phao, only to play into the hands of a still more arbitrary army dictatorship. The story of the domination of General Sarit and his followers over the ensuing sixteen years will be covered in a subsequent chapter.

1. David Wilson, *Politics in Thailand* (Ithaca, 1962), pp. 57-71.

2. *Ibid.*, pp. 114-15.

3. Rayne Krueger, *The Devil's Discuss* (London, 1964), pp. 121-25, 180-85, 236-40.

4. Wilson, *op. cit.*, pp. 212-17. See also Fred Riggs, *Thailand: Modernization of a Bureaucratic Polity* (Honolulu, 1966), pp. 165-66.

5. Wilson, *op. cit.*, pp. 26-30.

6. Riggs, *op. cit.*, pp. 316-26.

7. Wilson, *op. cit.*, pp. 256-61.

8. Donald E. Nuechterlein. *Thailand and the Struggle for Southeast Asia* (Ithaca, 1965), pp. 100-7, 188-20.

9. T. H. Silcock, ed., *Thailand, Social and Economic Studies in Development* (Canberra, 1967), pp. 7-9.

10. Frank C. Darling, *Thailand and the United States* (Washington, 1965), pp. 69-90.

11. Silcock, *op. cit.*, pp. 17-20.

12. *Ibid.*, pp. 10-17.

13. *Ibid.*, pp. 90-98. Beginning in the middle fifties, top personnel in the Thai Government were assigned blocks of stock and directorships in companies, often numbering from twenty to twenty-five firms.

14. Gunnar Myrdal, *Asian Drama: An Inquiry into the Poverty of Nations*, 3 vols. (New York, 1968), 2: pp. 840-42.

15. Silcock, *op. cit.*, pp. 7-9; K. H. Silvert, ed., *Expectant Peoples, Nationalism and Development* (New York, 1963), pp. 191-95.

16. Darling, *op. cit.*, pp. 69-90.
17. Silvert, *op. cit.*, pp. 191-95.
18. Darling, *op. cit.*, pp. 97-114.
19. *Ibid.*, pp. 138-46; see also Germaine Krull and Dorothea Melcher, *Bangkok, Siam's City of Angels* (London, 1964), pp. 111, 170.
20. Riggs, *op. cit.*, pp. 188-96.
21. Darling, *op. cit.*, pp. 148-53.
22. Nuechterlein, *op. cit.*, pp. 124-29.
23. Darling, *op. cit.*, pp. 153-56.

V

THE POSTWAR
PHILIPPINES

Aspects of the Governing Tradition

Filipinos differed from other peoples of Southeast Asia in their governing traditions and by reason of geographic location and historical experiences. The widely dispersed peoples of the Islands developed no indigenous political-cultural center such as Java provided for Indonesia; they developed no sense of national identity and no centralized governmental institutions. The Philippines were located outside the periphery of Indianized Southeast Asia and borrowed little from the more proximate but highly sophisticated Chinese civilization. They spoke no common language and invented no writing medium. Adaptations from continental patterns of art, religion, and architecture were few. Three centuries of Spanish rule served to increase the disparity between Filipinos and their Southeast Asian cousins. The European rulers left an indelible religious impression that provided some basis for national identity, but the islanders generated little indigenous capacity for self-expression or self-rule.

The experience of American control during the first four decades of the twentieth century opened new opportunities politically and culturally. An educated, nonclerical elite minority emerged, including landlords, professional men, lawyers and judges, and politicians, who assumed leadership governmentally as well as socially. As the champions of independence, they consolidated their postwar control of both the Nacionalista and Liberal parties. They were essentially self-serving, little interested in reforming the pattern of land distribution, improving administrative efficiency, or promoting a more equitable distribution of wealth or opportunity.

The contrast between the postwar Philippines governmental system and that of Thailand is striking. In the immediate post-war period, neither of the two countries endured any substantive change in the locus of power, but the indigenously developed conservative tradition of Siam was far more deeply rooted than were comparable patterns in the Islands. A basic difference was the absence in the Philippines of any concept of kingly sovereignty that could serve as a buttressing sanction to governmental authority.

This idea persisted in Siam despite the actual emasculation of royal authority after 1932. The holding of elections served different purposes in the two countries. In the Philippines, the four-year elections determined the personnel of the emerging ruling coterie of politicians, whereas in Bangkok, elections provided a kind of legitimatizing façade for the perpetrators of successive military coups. The absence of any military tradition within the Islands was fortified not only by the continuing American security presence in the country, but also by the borrowing of the American constitutional tradition of the supremacy of the civilian authorities. Freedom to criticize governmental leadership and performance vocally or in the press was conspicuously lacking in Bangkok, whereas in Manila it assumed at times the dimensions of political and psychological frenzy. Denunciations tended to increase in intensity because political results were never commensurate with the emotional energy expended. The exercise of criticism reached the point of diminishing returns and was therefore not destined to persist indefinitely. Elections decisions, no matter how vigorously contested, afforded for Filipinos no realistic prospect of altering prevailing policies or improving administrative functioning of what was essentially a self-serving governmental system.

The Commonwealth constitution, which was drafted by

103

the Filipinos themselves in the mid-thirties, carried over with few alterations into the independence period. It borrowed heavily from the pattern of government of the United States, except that it was unitary rather than federal in character. The four-year presidency was not dependent on continuing Congressional support, thus leaving the chief executive in a position to exercise leadership. The 24 senators were elected for six-year terms, with one-third of the membership renewable every two years. The 120-member legislature was elected simultaneously with the president and for the same four-year term. An independent hierarchy of courts, American style, was empowered to interpret the constitution, to protect the civil rights of citizens, to adjudicate cases brought to it on appeal, and to maintain the supremacy of civilian authority over the military. Special courts were subsequently provided for the settlement of agrarian and industrial relations problems.[1] In the political system of the Philippines, the rival parties tended to attract opportunist followers who, like the leaders, usually lacked dedication to any precise political philosophy. Politicians were drawn from the well-to-do social leadership, with little chance for the intrusion of other elements of the population. Party cadres centered around *politicos*, who were perennial candidates for election but were committed to few issues.

The party in power enjoyed an enormous advantage during election contests because of its control of patronage, public funds, and special favors. The incumbent leadership was vulnerable, none the less, because everyone could not be satisfied. Disgruntled party factions readily defected to the opposition, which could always attack the group in power on grounds of corruption. Such defections from party affiliations carried no onus of disloyalty or stigma of betrayal.[2] Elections were conducted with the enthusiasm of a national fiesta, accompanied by lavish distribution of favors and sporadic outbreaks of violence. The winners spent much of their time in office recovering campaign costs by more or less irregular methods, a practice the public generally took for granted. The actual policies of successive regimes will be described following an examination of postwar economic problems.

Economic Crisis and the Need for Reforms

Postwar economic conditions in the Philippines suffered at the outset, quite paradoxically, from a surfeit of American financial assistance, coupled with official abuse of power. The Congressional Trade Act of 1946 set forth the economic terms under which independence was granted but did not guarantee effective utilization of American contributions for the realization of long term objectives. Philippines free trade with the United States was permitted until 1954, after which date an annual increment of 5 per cent of the currently operative tariff rates on particular items would be added until full duties would be in effect by 1973. Limited annual quotas for the sale of sugar, coconut oil, and hemp cordage in America were provided. The law prohibited tariffs on exports and fixed the peso-dollar ratio at two to one. The Philippines government was obliged, in return, to accord to American investors full parity with Filipinos in the exploitation of the natural resources of the islands. In actuality, the new republic was somewhat less than fully independent economically.

Favored officials profited from American largess in a number of ways. Cheating developed in the collection of dollar compensation for private property losses caused by the war, involving some $620 million. Some $120 million were collected for public properties destroyed, and another $100 million (conservatively estimated) in transferred wartime surpluses. Disability pension payments, veterans' back pay, and other GI benefits added another $124 million annually for a full decade. Over the initial five-year period, pay arrears totalled $473 million. The United States Treasury also covered the first year's deficit of the Roxas government and returned to Manila some $90 million in excise collections from Philippines imports.[3] If they had

105

been properly husbanded, those funds could have provided a substantial basis for economic recovery. Unfortunately, however, they were largely dissipated in an orgy of improvidence and corruption—which included the launching of some thirty government corporations, designed ostensibly to Filipinize the economy against the dual threats of Chinese and American domination.

The aura of seeming prosperity, accompanied as it was by a decline in the wartime consumer price index by some 50 per cent from 1945 to 1950, was highly deceptive. During the four-year period prior to 1950, governmental deficits totalled 461 million pesos, due in large measure to the government's refusal to tax the holders of new wealth and its failure to collect those obligations that were legally due. By 1950, government bonds found no ready market; funds were lacking to pay the civil service, army, and school teachers; the Huk rebels seemed about to achieve victory by default. Graft centered mainly in surplus property sales, in the blackmail of Chinese refugees and businessmen, and in the widespread avoidance of existing exchange and import controls.[4]

The basic causes of corruption in the Philippines were of long standing. The political and economic elite of both parties habitually put personal and family interests first. The Congress refused to approve tax revenue increments, land tenure reforms, and minimum wage requirements. Even when passed, reform measures were frequently poorly implemented. Tenant farmers thus had ample reason to discount the government's declared benevolent intentions. They also resented having inexperienced government "experts" lecture them about soils, water supply, seed procurement, or widely advertised experiments in gardening and orchard innovations.[5] Skepticism regarding the government's good faith became virtually universal following the fraudulent election campaign of 1949.

The Bell Report of 1950

The abrupt decline of foreign exchange holdings during 1949 from $420 million to $160 million forced the imposition of emergency controls over exchange and imports. The arrival of the American Survey Mission, headed by Daniel Bell, in June 1950 coincided with the outbreak of the Korean War, which added urgency to the need to salvage the dismal financial situation.[6] Filipinos resented the fact that the uninvited Bell Mission was exclusively an American affair. Many anticipated that the report would be a humiliating indictment of prevailing corruption and maladministration. Others complained that Washington was according favored treatment to former enemy Japan.[7] The Bell Mission constituted a sobering and salutary, if somewhat painful experience.

The Mission's report revealed that the islands had failed to restore prewar levels of production despite the availability of ample funds and a 25 percent increase of population. Disparity of income between employer and employee, landowner and tenant farmer, had actually widened since the end of the war, and little had been done to diversify the economy or to improve productive efficiency. Tax revenues were woefully inadequate, as were wage standards for both agriculture and industry. Land redistribution objectives were not being pursued, and the official rule guaranteeing 70 per cent of agricultural income to the tenant cultivator was widely ignored. The report directed some of its most biting criticism toward abuses found in the thirty-odd government corporations designed to eliminate alien control of the economy. They were denounced for mismanagement, corruption, and political favoritism and as the greatest single threat to implementing a sound reform program.

The positive recommendations of the report were equally incisive. The government was exhorted to provide such public services as private enterprises could not furnish, especially in terms of improved methods of cultivation, land improvement and resettlement, health and educational needs, transportation, and expansion of fishing and forestry. It recommended that industrial development efforts be placed under the direction of a Philippines Development Corporation, to be assisted by a supervisory United States Technical Mission. Stress should be placed on developing

107

small-scale privately operated projects, depending on available managerial experience, labor, and marketing opportunities. Revenues could be increased 60 per cent by taxing the sale of luxury items, corporation and private incomes, and estates and gifts. Local revenues could benefit by introducing more realistic property assessments. Another major recommendation was to improve wages by setting minimum standards of three to four pesos daily.

The report recommended finally that United States assistance grants of $250 million annually over a five-year period be made conditional on Philippines acceptance of the Mission's recommendations, coupled with appropriate supporting legislation. Executive agreement to implement the report was reached in November 1950, but it was six months later before the requisite legislation governing taxes and wages was approved by the reluctant Philippines Congress. Washington's initial grants, made in April 1951, were assigned to meet agricultural and health needs, the development of textile and cotton industries, and a survey of fuel and transportation facilities.[8]

American aid and the accompanying reform measures were generally responsible for Manila's weathering of the economic storm of the early fifties. The Korean War period and Magsaysay's successful handling of the Hukbalahap peasant disaffection also helped, as did strong bipartisan citizen support for reform. Within two years, Philippines tax receipts doubled, minimum wages for urban industry and agricultural labor were made operative, annual budgets were balanced, and export earnings improved. Magsaysay's election as president in 1953 revived public confidence in the integrity of the government.[9]

Economic Development Efforts of the 1950s

Filipino economic development efforts generated a plethora of agencies that were designed to implement the program and were financed in large measure by American grants. One of the most successful was the Rehabilitation and Resettlement Administration, devoted to the opening of new lands for agricultural development in the southern islands, particularly in Mindanao. Less could be claimed for the work of the new Court of Agrarian Relations, the Agricultural Tenancy Commission, and the Corporate Credit and Finance Administration, all dedicated to ameliorating peasant poverty. Agencies concerned with the industrial side of development plans included the Rehabilitation Finance Corporation, dating from 1946; the Industrial Guarantee Loan Fund of 1952; and the Development Bank of 1958. To encourage approved industrial projects, the government offered after 1953 a five-year tax remission that tapered off during the succeeding four years, plus customs dues protection against foreign competition and special allocations of foreign exchange.[10]

Under such artificial stimulation, total industrial output expanded impressively, even though many new business ventures proved highly inefficient. Once the initial protective regulations had lapsed, industrial producers usually found it impossible to compete in terms of price with similar items available abroad. The capacity of projected cement plants far exceeded maximum needs. Locally produced fertilizers found few peasant purchasers, partly for lack of funds and partly because cooperative agricultural agencies were permitted under law to import what they needed duty free. Monetary reserves began to dwindle and domestic prices to rise. Commercial efficiency was not aided by politically motivated efforts to bar resident Chinese from business participation.[11]

The industrial expansionist boom reached an early peak in 1956 as a result of the annual quarter-billion-dollar aid grants from the United States, which continued in reduced amounts beyond the promised five-year period. Another contributing factor was the receipt in 1956 of Japanese Reparations Treaty payments totalling $550 million outright in goods and services, plus additional loan funds of $250 million. Such economic stimulation resulted in the elevation of total output by 1958 to a level some 50 percent above prewar standards, and this despite the continued stagnation of the agricultural sector.[12] Philippine iron exports to Japan increased rapidly during the 1950s, and by 1958 coconut products constituted 40 percent of the country's exports.

But the encouraging GNP figures were deceptive. Domestic capital for industrial development was inadequate, and efforts to diversify production for export purposes faltered badly. The government's initiation and operation of industrial ventures ran aground on nepotism and inefficiency, aggravated by strikes and wastage of public funds. Officials became heavily involved personally in the rice trade, coal mines, hotels, banking and insurance, cement, steel, textiles, and paper manufacture. The volume of processed staples, such as sugar and cordage, remained below prewar levels. Few of the more than eight hundred "new and necessary" industries initiated under government encouragement extended output beyond domestic market needs, or proved able to function profitably after their tax exemption privileges expired.[13]

Agricultural Problems

Economic "progress" achieved during the fifties had little relevance to the agricultural sector in general and to the tenant farmer in particular. The blight of tenancy and technological stagnation depressed rural incomes to around one-fourth that enjoyed by the nonpeasant population. The only agricultural sector that kept pace with expanding industrial output was the coconut plantation.

Problems were manifold. Much of the arable land was poor because of silting from floods. Rural labor was badly utilized and largely underemployed, forcing most tenants to live little above the subsistence level. Meanwhile the politically dominant landlord aristocracy effectively blocked authorized efforts at land redistribution. The limited funds provided by the Congress for such purposes were absorbed in high administrative costs and chronic default by peasants on payments due. In the original law, landlords could retain up to 300 hectares (later reduced in 1963 to 185 acres) of contiguous cultivable lands. Narrow separating strips could be sold legally as a means of evading this regulation, but the necessary purchase funds were not usually available to the peasants in any case.[14] Attempts to implement legislation intended to facilitate tenant purchase of the land they currently cultivated ran completely aground.

Both vindictive and legal methods were used effectively to block enforcement of the alternative share-cropper tenancy law of 1954. The law provided that a tenant could, at his own option and prior to any given crop season, give notice to his landlord that he wanted to become a leasee instead of a mere renter of the land. The terms of such a lease would call for the payment of a fixed annual rental equal to only 25 percent of the value of the average crop yields over the previous three years, less some operating expenses. Traditional share-cropper obligations ranged upward from the landlord's legal claim of 30 percent of the crop, to the customary level of 50 percent. Tenants also had to pay exorbitant interest rates on short-term crop loans (often at the rate of 200 percent per annum) and could be ejected if they resisted the owner's authority.

The usual response of landlords to lease applicants was to bring civil suit against the prospective leasee for alleged violation of the preceding tenancy contract. The lawsuit was expensive, and the tenant could be evicted barring presentation of an effective legal defense. The peasant was thus effectively intimidated in most cases. When free legal counsel was eventually provided for the peasant, the landlords' tactics shifted to criminal suits, for which counsel was also required. As mere tenants, the peasants could acquire no stake in land improvements that they themselves initiated, while the owners refused as a rule to finance improvement measures calculated to augment tenant earnings. Courts and police usually cooperated with the politically influential landlord group.[15]

The succession of presidential incumbents from Magsaysay on made little appreciable difference. Magsaysay himself was well intentioned, but he was unable to wrest control from dominant elements within his own ruling party who were hostile to his reform objectives. Following his death in an airplane crash, Magsaysay's weak successor, Vice President Garcia, managed to win election as president in his own right in 1957. In 1960 Garcia vetoed an important antigraft bill, on the ground that its application would be excessively harsh on the relatives of high officials who might be involved. Garcia's vice president, Macapagal, shifted to the Liberal party and won election on his proclaimed concern for official integrity and land reform. Liberal party control within the legislature was achieved during his administration only by soliciting opposition defections at a considerable price. During his early incumbency, Macapagal did indeed sponsor a number of well-intentioned reform measures designed to correct the maldistribution of landed wealth, but he accomplished very little in their implementation.[16]

A new land purchase law of 1963, for example, reduced the landlord's reserved holding to 185 acres, as indicated above, while another law was intended to improve wages by facilitating labor union organization. Enforcement failed in part because the legislature did not provide requisite funds to implement the measures. In only twelve of the Republic's sixty-five provinces did the Congress take the required initial legal step of defining the so-called land-reform area. Macapagal spent virtually the entire final year of his incumbency conducting his re-election campaign and neglecting his presidential duties. Smuggling became rampant, and revenue deficiencies were aggravated by pork-barrel appropriations and overt looting of the treasury by the president himself during the course of the campaign.[17] Ferdinand Marcos and the Nacionalista party won the 1965 election.

The Political Malady

The malady of the Philippines government was essentially political. The cost of electioneering ran exorbitantly high.

The first cost was the candidate's personal deposit into the party treasury. Competition for places on the ticket involved the enlistment of convention delegate support. Donations were solicited from business interests by promising favored access to government-dispensed trade licenses and contracts. The estimated total election expenditures in 1961 was equivalent to some 13 per cent of the total national budget for the year.[18] Roast-pig feasts in the barrios were not cheap, and direct vote buying was even more expensive. But candidates could not afford to lose. Election costs borne by individual candidates had to be recouped somehow by officeholders.

The political outcome was highly unsatisfactory. Neither workers nor peasants were sufficiently well organized to generate the political pressure needed to obtain an affirmative congressional or executive response to their grievances. The reform-motivated minority in the Congress was powerless to force the hands of the reactionary leadership, which controlled both major parties. The political situation did not require the ruling elite to take serious account of the wishes of the disorganized peasantry, the generally inarticulate middle class, or the fledgling labor organizations of the Manila area.

The presidential system placed a heavy burden on the chief executive in terms of the conduct of routine administration, the implementation of legislative enactments, the exercise of party control, and the conduct of elections. The president was powerful only so long as he played the political game according to the prevailing rules. He controlled the appointment of officials in the chartered cities of the several provinces, along with local tax collectors, assessors, and auditors of accounts. His budgetary powers were extensive, even though his legislative influence was limited. He could issue emergency decrees relating to critical situations of local tension and economic crisis, subject only to subsequent legislative review.[19]

In most of the islands, economic gains did not keep pace with the rapidly expanding population. (Population growth between 1948 and 1960 was estimated to be more than forty percent.) One exception was Mindanao, where numbers doubled but where new opportunities for timber, rubber, abaca (hemp), and food production were made available by government efforts to relieve general peasant distress. Even so the influx of Christian migrants into previously dominant Muslim areas of the island precipitated violent conflict subsequently. The Greater Manila area, including satellite cities, came to include some 2.1 million people by 1960. Here urban amenities (such as water, electricity, paving, and refuse collection) failed to keep pace with public needs. By 1960, manufacturing activity comprised only 18 percent of the total output, and these operations were confined in large measure to the assembly of foreign-produced parts (electrical items and car equipment).[20] The number of trained workers and technicians, however, more than kept pace with expanding employment opportunities in all categories, and educated youths crowded into the expanding bureaucracy.[21]

The Retail Trade Nationalization Law, aimed ostensibly at reducing Chinese control, actually gave "dummy front" Filipinos an opportunity to find lucrative employment and for politicians to collect bribes from illegal Chinese firms.[22] Under the circumstances economic expansion, to be socially effective, had to be of such magnitude that tensions derived from gross inequalities of wealth and income could be submerged in the total gain.

Efforts to Cure Political Ills

Repeated efforts of reform-minded Filipino leaders to abolish or at least qualify the dominance of the two-party oligarchy were largely abortive. Reformist concern found early expression in the "Magsaysay for President" movement of 1953, which survived his death. The same group helped elect at least one Progressive party senator in 1957 and later cooperated with the so-called Grand Alliance party, which helped bring the supposedly liberal Macapagal to the presidency in 1961. Not only did Macapagal fail to implement approved reform legislation; he also raised the dubious Sabah claim issue in North Borneo, and generally placed politics ahead of his official duties.

Reforming religious agencies included the Manila Citizens for Good Government, sponsored by Catholic lay leaders, and the somewhat opportunistic Iglesio ni Kristi, a politically oriented anti-Catholic, anti-landlord brotherhood centering in Luzon. Neither group generated adequate funds or an effective political organization. Wealthy contributors frequently found that their interests were better served by cultivating both of the regular parties.[23] The National Movement for Free Elections, dating from Magsaysay's era, was measurably effective for a time in preventing gross election frauds, but it exercised little long-term influence. Following Macapagal's abdication of his responsibilities in 1965, few accepted at face value President Marcos' promises to accept responsibility for promoting general economic well-being and social ends. Growing pessimism was reflected in the exodus of many educated Filipinos, seeking to escape their social frustrations.[24]

Actually, the political and social traditions of the Islands provided no feasible alternative to the American pattern of parties and elections, however much abused. Military rule seemed remote, mainly because the defense of the Islands still lay in American hands.[25] The revolutionary Hukbalahap unrest in central Luzon's Panpanga province was more peasant oriented than Communist in character and also carried limited linguistic and geographical appeal. A subsequent revival of Huk activity in 1967 reflected the government's continuing failure to meet peasant needs for schools, roads, and market facilities. Aside from radical Huk followers, most Filipinos were unready to surrender political freedoms, even though abused, in favor of rigidly imposed Communist discipline. The revived Huk movement actually drew financial support from adjacent town officials and from brothel owners enjoying GI patronage at Angeles City, near Clarke Field.[26]

The Manila daily press exhibited a continuing exercise in self-flagellation. News stories that appeared on two days in October, 1968, picked at random, will suffice to illustrate the phenomenon. For example, the complete failure of the Filipino performers in the Olympic games recently staged in Mexico elicited the acid comment that three officials—not counting accompanying wives—participated in the junket for every one athlete. "Who paid the travelling expenses?" the papers asked. Discipline among the athletes was described as completely lacking, and politics allegedly had affected their selection. One columnist commented:

> The difficulty is that Filipinos are burdened with a sense of grandeur. . . . When will Filipinos ever learn that athletic competition . . . cannot be won in the same way that political office is won? . . . Unless they give proper answers to these questions, the Filipinos will continue to make fools of themselves for all the world to see. . . . We have to remove politics from sports or we will never amount to anything.[27]

The same two papers, the Manila *Chronicle* and *Times*, contained additional allegations. Rural electrification efforts of the government were being grossly mishandled; customs officials at the port of Cebu were hamstrung in their efforts to curb smuggling by interference from Manila agencies and members of the Congress; a number of Internal Revenue Bureau officials had allegedly been suspended for dishonesty and neglect of duty. Even more disturbing was the accompanying charge that officials of the Philippines Public School Teachers Association could not account for some seventy thousand pesos of expenditures and were therefore under suspicion of gross mismanagement, if not graft and corruption. Such newspaper charges of official malfeasance frequently provided tangible ways to supplement the reporter's income, while successful libel suits were virtually unknown in the Islands.[28]

Philippine Identity and Antialien Sentiment

Sympathetic observers of the Philippines scene questioned whether democracy, as practiced in the Islands, could really become an effective instrument for meeting the country's needs. Independence had been rather cheaply won. The process had entailed no sacrificial mobilization of nationalist determination and unity, and the process had generated correspondingly little confidence in the patriotic concern of the eventual recipients of power. Popular disillusionment with the resulting democratic system and the associated emergence of anti-American sentiment were rooted in a variety of psychological considerations.

Nationally conscious Filipinos wanted to be something more than a reflected image of the West, perennially dependent on outside assistance for commercial prosperity and military security. The long process of weaning the Islands from the United States, and the American-imposed regulations connected with it, were viewed by some as derogatory to national pride. Others criticized America's allegedly overgenerous treatment of its defeated World War II enemy, Japan—especially in economic assistance and in the administration of military bases—, ignoring the "debt of honor" owing to Filipino allies. There developed a growing concern among Filipinos, especially following Manila's participation in the Bandung Conference of 1955, to establish a national identity as an Asian state. The proficiency of most educated Filipinos in American English, although obviously advantageous for interisland and international communication, tended to underscore their sense of cultural subservience. The Philippines lacked an indigenous national language and literature of its own.[29]

Most of the approximately five thousand American civilian residents in the Islands were connected with business. They represented major firms that were exercising treaty investment rights under the parity terms set forth in 1946. From the outset, these firms had been able to enlist substantial support from Filipino sugar interests and others who profited from favored access to American markets. The importance of such considerations decreased in time, and Washington's direct financial assistance ceased after 1959, when the Bell agreement payments were completed. Friction developed thereafter with regard to American jurisdictional rights over a number of defense installations and their operating personnel. On occasion Filipino pilferers were shot by American guards.[30] The Manila treasury benefited—as did localities adjacent to base installations—from expenditures of American service personnel. Also profitable was the participation of Filipino volunteers in American intervention in the Indochina war. A medical unit operated in Laos, and a twelve-hundred-man construction contingent (selected from twenty times that number of volunteers) was assigned to South Vietnam. The total situation nevertheless carried implications of subservience. The American role fell somewhat short of the requirement of the Filipino social code that a well-mannered patron should take into sympathetic consideration not only the client's deserts, but also his susceptibilities with respect to preserving dignity and face.[31]

The options open to Manila and Washington were progressively limited, as relations continued to deteriorate. If American associations were severed, the Islanders faced the discouraging alternatives of attempting to achieve economic security and cooperation with feeble and often jealous neighbors in Southeast Asia, or seeking a working accord with China or Japan. The basic problem here as elsewhere in Southeast Asia could not be comprehended within the oversimplified dichotomy of the Cold War. If America's ideological stake in the successful operation of Philippines democracy was to be safeguarded, the underlying political, economic, and psychological factors responsible for the frustrated Filipino mood had to be dealt with. In the face of the continuing abuse of political power and the erosion of cohesive religious and kinship traditions, America's repeated affirmation of faith in democracy was hardly sufficient. There was still a remote prospect that a politically active middle class would emerge and ally with peasant leadership to challenge the dominant wealthy elite. Freedom of political expression alone counted for little in correcting governmental performance, even if carried to the level of violent protest.

Responsible Filipino leaders themselves were aware that considerations of defense, trade outlets, and investment needs made any abrupt repudiation of U.S. connections inadvisable. But political leaders both within and outside the government could realize cheap political capital by denouncing the American role and alleging that Washington was responsible for perpetuating oligarchic rule. Consumer groups challenged in court the existing trade regulations, which denied the public free access to cheaper overseas goods. Most of the existing treaties governing American investments and trading rights would be up for renegotiation in 1973, but that was a long time to wait.[32] Mutual trust continued to erode in the context of differing premises and diverging interests.

No Filipino group was more determined to eliminate the American presence than was the Manila Chamber of Commerce. Its determination to end both American and Chinese business competition carried political as well as economic implications. The emerging Filipino business community aspired to become strong enough to challenge the virtual political monopoly of the wealthy landlord class. Business interests could then opt for land reform objectives and, with peasant cooperation, conceivably achieve an election victory. But how many would credit the sincerity of such reform pretensions?

The principal problem with the Chinese in the Philippines was domestic in character. Resident Chinese merchants bore the brunt of accelerated nationalist efforts to control trade. Many of them were involved in smuggling operations from Hong Kong and in finding ways to bypass restrictive laws respecting domestic retail trade. Wealthy merchants were regularly squeezed by both political parties for political contributions. The resident Chinese disliked discriminatory decrees, interference with their educational activities and book distribution, and the laws prohibiting alien land ownership, but they were otherwise apolitical. They commonly accepted Christianization as an aid to marrying Filipinas, in whose names property holdings could legally be placed. Progressive assimilation of the economically useful Chinese element into the Filipino population would presumably serve national ends.[33]

119

Opposition to increased Japanese participation in the economy was reflected in the tardy use of funds made available from Japanese treaty reparations and loans, dating from 1956. A full decade later, some $250 million of the reparations were still unused, as was approximately four-fifths of the promised $250 million in loans. (Portions of the reparation funds to be devoted to highway construction were finally utilized in 1968.) One of the reasons for the long delay was the refusal of the Manila government to ratify the proposed comprehensive commercial treaty. In the meantime, the authorities issued special permits to facilitate the entry of Japanese businessmen connected with aid programs as well as private business. Such permits enabled them to gain access to local banks, rent offices, and acquire tax liability exemptions. Despite these difficulties, trade with Japan expanded steadily. As of 1967, the value of imports from Japan was second only to those from the United States, and by a steadily dwindling margin at that. From the Philippines Japan bought minerals, timber, copra, and fibers in return for consumer manufactures and capital equipment, with only a slight trade balance in Japan's favor.[34]

Problems of Regional Relations

After 1962, Filipino leaders made a persistent effort to draw closer to their Southeast Asian neighbors. They participated in a succession of organizational meetings with Indonesia, Malaysia, and Thailand having to do with regional cooperation in a variety of situations. A primary consideration was to enhance national prestige and an Asian identity. It was within this psychological context that authorities in Manila advanced a dubious claim to former British protectorate holdings in north Borneo's Sabah. In June 1962 President Macapagal proposed to London that the prospective transfer of Sabah to Malaysia should properly become the subject of direct negotiations. He affirmed that the Philippines' claim to residual sovereignty over the former domain of the Sultan of Sulu was "soundly based on law and justice." He also projected a vague Association for Southeast Asia (ASA) scheme, which would unite the Philippines with Indonesia, Thailand, and Malaysia as a regional cultural, economic, and political agency to promote freedom, progress, and peace. He otherwise disclaimed any thought of hampering the formation of the proposed Malaysian Federation, then under consideration.

Macapagal's suggestions probably had more relevance to national pride and to his personal interests than to any serious expectation of territorial aggrandisement. The legal basis of the Philippines claim to Sabah related to a transaction consummated in 1878 between Baron Overbeck, a trader adventurer in North Borneo who had tenuous British connections, and the last titular sultan of Sulu, Esmail Kiram. Overbeck agreed to pay an annual lease or rental fee for the privilege of trading within the vaguely defined region over which the sultan claimed jurisdiction. The obligation was taken over by Dent and Company of Hong Kong shortly thereafter and subsequently by the North Borneo Company, which, down to World War II, administered North Borneo as a colonial unit extending far beyond any boundary claims previously affirmed by Sultan Esmail.

When the British in 1946 asserted a formal protectorate over all of North Borneo, extending southwestward to Sarawak, they elicited no protest whatever from the newly independent Philippines government. But in early 1962, when news of the proposed Malaysian Federation emerged, several of the surviving relatives of Esmail Kiram selected a nephew of the last Sulu sultan to pose as his ostensible successor, and he promptly ceded the Kiram Corporation's residual Sabah claims over to the Philippines government in return for promised support from Macapagal. Neither Spain nor the United States had even laid claim to the territory administered by the North Borneo Company, nor had Manila done so during the first sixteen years of Philippine independence. But with the final exit of the Western imperialists, the situation was presumed to revert to the pre-1878 status quo.[35]

The British government's reactions to Manila's several proposals for negotiations were understandably negative. London first indicated that any public debate over conflicting North Borneo claims would entail disruptive repercussions that could seriously impair the capacity of the peoples of the region to decide their own future and to resist the Communist threat. For the Philippines, Sabah was important as a bothersome smuggling center and as a future source of timber, minerals, and possibly oil. When the request for negotiations was repeated, Britain asked the Manila spokesman to explain precisely what he wanted to talk about and why. Filipinos resented London's brusque refusal to treat their claims with respect and were also angry with the American press for not taking them seriously.

Several efforts were made to save face. The Manila press suggested that a plebiscite might resolve the problem, if accompanied by a satisfactory monetary settlement of the claims of the sultan's heirs.[36] In July, 1963, an effort was made to paper over regional differences when Macapagal's vague Maphilindo (Malaya - Philippines - Indonesia) Confederation agreement was projected at Manila. On August 5, the Philippines government requested formally that the International Court of Justice adjudicate the conflicting Sabah claims, but to no avail. In mid-September Sabah was duly incorporated into the Malaysian Federation. For two years thereafter the Indonesian Konfrontasi challenge to Malaysia occupied center stage, during which time Marcos succeeded Macapagal as president of the Philippines in 1965.

The early actions of the new president suggested that he was ready to forget the Sabah dispute if a face-saving device could be found. His foreign minister participated actively in the ASA (Thailand, Philippines, and Malaysia) sessions of 1966, where a number of interregional cooperative measures were proposed. These included the possible cancellation òf visa requirements, multilateral trade agreements, cooperation in scientific research, lower rates for press communications, and integration of telecommunication, aviation, and shipping services. When in 1967 ASA was expanded into the Association of Southeast Asian Nations

(ASEAN, with Indonesia and Singapore added), Philippines representatives again played a promoting role. This action was widely interpreted as implying reconciliation with Kuala Lumpur over Sabah. Marcos also negotiated an antismuggling treaty with Malaysia involving the coast of northeastern Borneo.

Then in April 1968 came the enigmatic Corregidor incident, which opened Sabah's Pandora's box, apparently to the great embarrassment of President Marcos. A group of Muslim guerrilla recruits were being trained on Corregidor Island in Manila Bay, presumably for infiltration purposes and possibly as a means of influencing Malaysian acceptance of World Court jurisdiction over the Sabah dispute. Mutiny developed within the group, and one Jibin Arula escaped execution only by swimming to Cavite, where he made contact with an opposition Liberal party politician. Manila's faltering attempts to pass off what had been going on at Corregidor as an effort to prevent violations of the undetermined Sabah boundary were widely discounted. The incident created such excitement that Marcos felt obliged to revive Macapagal's nearly forgotten title claim.

When representatives of the Philippines and Malaysian governments met in Bangkok in May 1968 to discuss the question, the Malaysian spokesmen showed no concern for working out a face-saving formula for the Marcos regime, declaring flatly that the Filipinos had presented no concrete evidence to support their position.[37] Malaysian spokesmen pointed to the fact that in the Sabah elections held in 1967, not a single candidate advocated union with either Indonesia or with the Philippines. Meanwhile the Kuala Lumpur authorities had located a dubious claimant of their own as the heir to the sultanate of Sulu. The Sabah issue was eventually overshadowed by the Filipino election contest of 1969.[38]

The First Marcos Administration

One of the valued compensations of the Philippines elective routine was that different faces appeared every four years, so that a new start could be attempted. Filipinos were

123

thus spared the indefinite tenure of a Sukarno, a Diem, a Pibun, or a Ne Win.

Marcos shifted to the Nacionalista party and won the presidency in 1965 as an advocate of land reform and economic development. He undertook within the first year of his administration to establish price incentives for increased output of rice and corn, and he enacted laws against smuggling that made the possession of smuggled goods a criminal offense. He eased bank credits, refinanced the faltering state textile industry, and expanded road construction and irrigation development. Otherwise the new president undertook to retrench government expenditures, improve tax collections, and facilitate cargo handling at various leading ports. Funds realized from new loans went for improved water facilities, better sewage disposal, bridges, and highways. These ambitious efforts ran aground within the first year because of the refusal of his own Nacionalista party to vote the needed tax increases and to expand the borrowing program commensurate to the needs.[39]

During the latter half of 1966, President Marcos made state visits to both the United States and Japan. He hoped to attract private investments in the dimension of $500 million from each country, plus additional economic aid. One of the reasons that a Filipino construction battalion was sent to South Vietnam and a medical team to Laos was to facilitate the receipt of additional American aid for road construction in the Philippines. Unlike Japan, Taiwan, and Singapore, Manila profited little from America's purchase of supplies for the Vietnam war. Substantial gains were registered in corn output, in copper exports, and in textile production, but otherwise all major construction programs were running far behind schedule: airport expansion by 95 percent, bridges by 90 percent, school construction by 80 percent, and roads by 75 percent. By the end of 1966, Marcos realized that large additional funds could not be attracted from abroad. In mid-1968, efforts to conclude the comprehensive commercial treaty with Japan were again frustrated by politically motivated restrictions on alien entry, vocations, and capital ownership.[40] Meanwhile,

124

the president's initial success in curbing smuggling by 40 percent had faded to a negligible level.

In the generally successful mid-term Senate elections (Marcos candidates won six of eight seats), the president staked his political future on expanded promotion of infrastructure development: roads, bridges, flood-control, schools, and electrical power facilities. The election contests were marred by some one hundred politically-motivated assassinations, with the Nacionalista majority of the Congress exploiting the allocation of construction projects as pork barrel largess for selected constituencies and as avenues for personal graft. The irresponsible mayor of Manila, Antonio J. Villegas, bankrupted the city's treasury with a plethora of street construction. To counter such lavish election expenses, Marcos, in February, 1968, had to negotiate a Central Bank Loan to meet the city's payroll. A profitless feud developed between the president and the mayor.[41]

Some progress was made in the area of agricultural reform, despite the lack of landlord and politician cooperation. Sharecropper relief was assisted by a private Catholic-oriented group known as the Free Farmers Association, which provided legal counsel for would-be leaseholders. Under the leadership of a former Ateneo law professor, the Association enlisted the membership of some one hundred thousand peasants, who could command the services of six full-time lawyers and nine part-time legal experts to contest the diversionary suits brought by landlords. Even so, by 1969, some fifteen years after the reform legislation had become law, only sixty-four hundred sharecroppers had been able to exercise their legal option to become registered leaseholders. Leaders of the Free Farmers Association were nevertheless convinced that the leasehold approach was more promising than efforts to promote outright cultivator purchase.

In early 1968, Marcos made a dramatic move to finance the purchase and distribution of large landed estates to tenant farmers with money obtained from the sale of choice government-owned building sites in the Greater Manila area. But the total sum of one hundred million pesos realized in this fashion provided only a start. In April, a formal ceremony involving the minister of land reform and the governor of the province was staged some one hundred miles north of Manila, and certificates of land ownership were distributed to fifty farmers. By early 1968, only ten thousand acres of agricultural land in Luzon had been transferred to cultivator ownership.[42]

The goal of cultivator ownership was actually set back by the development of miracle rice (IR-8) by the International Rice Institute of Luzon in 1967-68. The new strain of rice could produce five or six times more output per unit of land, but it required expert handling and several times the capital outlay needed for traditional cultivation. Spraying by plane and harvesting by tractor were beyond the capabilities of the peasants. Large producers argued the necessity of employing such advanced methods if the islands were to achieve food sufficiency and insisted that the size of the landlord's cultivation allocations should be correspondingly enlarged. The prevailing 90 percent tenancy rate in the rebel Huk stronghold of Pampanga province was not improved by the planting of miracle rice. Although the new rice was less popular with consumers, the cumulative surplus tended to depress the market price of rice everywhere. Capitalism thus invaded the agricultural sector in a new dimension, and it was the wealthy landlord who reaped the benefit.

Agricultural statistics for the Philippines from 1965 to 1968 nevertheless looked very good. Rice imports declined from 30 million bushels in 1965, to 5.7 million in 1966, and to an actual surplus for export in 1967-68. The shift represented an annual savings of some $50 million in foreign exchange, which was otherwise heavily in deficit in 1967 (to the extent of $80 million). In 1968, additional foreign trade gains were made in timber, sugar, and pineapple sales abroad. Improvements in mining output were also in prospect in 1960, when German firms began exploring for nickle, iron, cobalt in northern Mindanao.[43] The essential fact remained that economic growth was passing the peasant by, while population pressures continued to raise land prices to forbiddingly high levels.

Corruption, Crime, and Rebellion

Despite the moderately successful efforts of President Marcos to improve economic conditions and thus make a case for his reelection in 1969, the political climate—particularly in Luzon—failed to improve. An observer noted as of late 1967: "Graft and corruption . . . still corrode . . . every level of the Philippine government. Law-enforcement agencies are politically ridden and apparently unable to cope with crime." Increasing gang warfare in Manila involved little or no ideological content; it simply reflected the breakdown of police restraint. The general relaxation of social controls evident in urban lawlessness was generally acknowledged and publicly deplored.[44] A widely publicized incident in 1968 involved the police hiring of a known thug to kill a wealthy Manila Chinese, only to have the assassin apprehended on the spot by a policeman not privy to the arrangement. To ensure that the assassin would not talk, a superior police officer who was in on the plot pushed the arresting officer aside and shot the murderer outright. Overheard shortly thereafter was this comment by a lecturer at Ateneo University: "When are the Filipino people going to develop some dignity and conscience by improving the present disreputable system of government?"

In 1965 peasant frustration over the failure of the government to implement agrarian reform produced a revival of the Huk rebellion in central Luzon. The movement differed substantially from that of the early fifties. Communist instigation and exploitation were minor factors compared to cumulative peasant resentment. The new Huk leader, Sumulong (otherwise known as Faustino del Mundo), was not a doctrinaire Communist, and his youthful second in command, a law student, was no Marxist at all. Destitute peasant rebels outnumbered both reformers and bandits. Their

127

violent tactics were selectively applied, calculated to establish a rival local government of their own, following the pattern long pursued by the Vietcong. The victims included non-cooperating mayors and former Huk partisans who had turned informers. Some eighty-three mayors and other officials were liquidated in a single year.

Overt Huk belligerents numbered only about five hundred in 1965 and less than a thousand by 1967. But, with villager connivance, the movement functioned as an invisible government. The rebels usually did not interfere with barrios controlled under the Land Reform Authority or with other areas where civic action reform efforts were reasonably effective. In controlled areas they operated stores, transportation facilities, real estate transfers, lending agencies, tax collections, and lotteries. The Communist minority among the Huks was reportedly pro-Peking, and the Huk tactics in some respects were akin to those used in South Vietnam. The movement as a whole sought constitutional remedies wherever redress seemed possible.[45]

The revival of Huk resistance to governmental authority in Central Luzon at first attracted a wide measure of public toleration, if not popular sympathy. Support for the peasants was widespread, and local officials often found it convenient to connive at Huk operations as just another facet of a widely irregular governmental system. In some places, Huk representatives suppressed thievery and protected farmers from landlord harassment, Robin Hood fashion. One observer declared that Huk justice "was faster, surer, and even more just than the peasant can get out of the government." Huk tax collections, amounting to an estimated $400,000 to $500,000 were utilized to finance government activities and also to pay the wages of guerrilla recruits. United States jeeps and even guns were acquired via cooperating sources connected with nearby Clarke Field, along with considerable income from entertainment services provided for American service personnel. In some of the government-held towns, the regular police collaborated on occasion with the colorful Faustino del Mundo.[46]

The more doctrinaire Filipino Marxist leadership, on

the other hand, was reportedly much more concerned with educational changes and the overthrow of the total economic establishment than with specific reform efforts conducted at the village level. The peasant Huk recruits, by comparison, followed a tactic not designed to lead to any frontal attack on the establishment per se. José Maria Sison, the Communist leader, enjoyed a substantial student following, and his associate José Drokno was dedicated to ending United States influence generally, as well as challenging the persistence of the so-called semifeudal mentality. Even so, the two Josés were by no means in full agreement between themselves.[47]

Reform Efforts of the Church and Students

Far more relevant to the Filipino milieu than any advocacy of revolutionary Marxist redress was the growing minority demand on the part of professors and students, liberal Catholic laymen, and the parish priests that the Church hierarchy itself must challenge directly the immorality of continuing official dishonesty and peasant exploitation. The leader of the Free Farmers Federation and one-time dean of the law school at Ateneo University, Jeremias Montemayor, argued that only concerned churchmen could reverse the tide, which was moving toward violent revolution. He proposed, albeit without effect, that priests withhold communion from those landowners who continued to prevent peasants from shifting to leasehold farming.

One of the few liberal bishops, Mariano Gaviola, who headed the Catholic Welfare Organization, made a frequent point of quoting Pope John XXIII as an advocate of Christian social reform. Former Senator Raul Manglapus, a leader of the Christian Social Movement, became concerned particularly with helping to elect liberal delegates to the constitutional convention that was scheduled to convene in 1971. Manglapus cited thirteenth century canon law to support his contention that promoting a more equitable distribution of wealth was a Christian objective.

129

Student demonstration critics were more direct. They frequently denounced the reactionary archbishop of Manila, Rufino Cardinal Santos, and called on the liberal-minded Vatican to remove him from office. They also advocated the total involvement of the church in the solution of social problems, in particular its alignment with exploited peasants. The Church not only charged fees to poor people for administering the sacraments, but was itself a large landowner. The palaces and air-conditioned cars of the clerical hierarchy attracted sharp criticism as did their lavish state dinners. The response from the Church leadership was disappointingly qualified. Only nine of the sixty-eight Filipino bishops could be characterized as liberal, and even these hesitated to break with their wealthy landlord supporters. Somewhat more encouraging was the generally positive response from the four thousand parish priests, who were much closer to the people—even to the point of sharing their poverty.[48] Optimistic observers hoped that an application of Christian ethics, plus active clerical support of already-legislated land reforms might work to redeem the demoralized democratic process and make possible the avoidance of violent revolution. The situation at the end of the first Marcos administration was at best a race against time.

The Elections of 1969

Superficially, the election year of 1969 resembled in its political and economic contours that of 1965. In the latter year, President Macapagal, while struggling to attain re-election, had been obliged to restrict financial credits and government expenditures in an effort to curb inflationary trends. At the end of 1968, the Marcos regime faced a similar dilemma. Interest rates on safe loans rose from the 7 to 8 percent of 1965, to levels of from 10 to 14 percent in 1967–68, which meant that little money was available for new development projects.[49] Marcos' overliberal spending on roads, schools, and other infrastructure facilities had been curtailed because of the refusal of Congress to levy new taxes. The $51-million balance of payments surplus available at the end of 1967 was transformed by August 1968 into a $45-million deficit. The required imposition of imports curbs in early 1969, combined as in 1965 with exchange controls, had the same depressing economic effect. The gross national production increment of 6.3 percent for 1968 (up from 5.6 percent for 1967) was poorly distributed at best, and the rate tapered off in the year-end decline. More austerity was to be the rule in 1969.[50]

Nor was the social unrest and the crime situation of 1969 greatly different from that of 1965. The treasury was being robbed by tax evasion and by official misappropriation of funds. Increased smuggling was aggravated by Malaysia's cancellation of the previously negotiated agreement to curb illegal trading activities originating from the disputed Sabah territory. For most of the population, the rise in living costs in 1967–68 more than absorbed any income gains. Agricultural reform still lagged badly, and peasants realized no gains from miracle rice. The vast disparity between the wealthy and the poor bred corruption on the one hand and violence on the other. By 1969 the murder rate in the Islands was up to thirty-nine per thousand, and an irregular Huk administration was replacing legal authority in parts of central Luzon.[51] The situation was somber.

Electioneering began months before the legal starting time in July (120 days before the election date). Since Marcos was almost sure to be the Nacionalista candidate, his principal rival in the party, with the prestigious name of Genaro Magsaysay (the brother of Ramon), defected to the opposition Liberals. He eventually became their vice-presidential candidate, but the party was itself torn by rivalry for the presidential nomination. The several contestants included members of the younger generation of famous political families, such as Osmeña, Roxas, Aquino, and Macapagal himself. New names were Villareal and Villaneuva. In the end, Roxas, president of the Liberal party, and Manila's mayor Villegas backed the candidacy of Osmeña,

131

a Cebuan businessman, who was duly nominated in July. Meanwhile, the serious legislative affairs of the Congress (taxes, budget, tariff changes, and land reform implementation) were neglected amid a welter of political controversy.[52]

The emerging election issues were mainly personal. Opponents of Marcos demanded his impeachment before a congressional judicial committee on the customary allegations of graft and mishandling of state funds. Marcos responded by reviving a pending lawsuit against Osmeña for the latter's one-time involvement in irregular contracts. Few were interested in the actual merits of the allegations made by the two sides; senatorial speeches denouncing graft and public swindle reportedly aroused more popular boredom than active concern. Some of the evidence brought to light regarding smuggling operations came close to incriminating members of the president's own personal entourage. Much gossip also developed over how Marcos and his beautiful wife, Imelda, had managed to grow so wealthy in four short years. To these criticisms were added complaints about the rising crime rate, plus the revival of the Huk rebellion and terrorism. Sabah did not emerge as an important campaign issue, nor was there any marked difference between the candidates with respect to continued cooperation with the United States in Eastern Asia.

Once both candidates had been selected in July, the immediate prognostication favored Marcos. His Nacionalista party had suffered fewer defections and less internal strife than had the Liberals, and it was better organized and financed. The president's distribution of some twenty thousand checks to as many village chiefs, each in the amount of two thousand pesos (five hundred dollars), ostensibly intended for local development projects, also helped get out the Nacionalista vote. In Marcos' favor were his record of road construction, his efforts at land reform, and the country's achievement of surplus rice production.

Osmeña, on his side, could count on the support of his large Cebuaño constituency. His claims that a businessman in the office of president would apply better administrative methods and thus reduce the dimension of economic problems was for many not particularly reassuring. The outcome of the election, as usual, turned on which party could register the most supporters and see that they got to the polls on election day. Armed bands had been employed for such purposes in the past, and the average value of the purchased vote had been around ten dollars.[53] Marcos won by a wide margin, to become the only Filipino president to achieve re-election. The disturbing events of his second administration will be covered in the concluding chapter.

As a major urban center, Manila in 1969 maintained its own peculiar identity. It rivalled Singpore and Bangkok in the volume of its automobile traffic and other evidences of modernity; it was less Oriental and more American in dress and manners, more outspokenly raucous in its political and press activity. But the principal monument of the country's past was still the ruins of the Spanish fort opposite from the Manila Hotel, skirted by a golf course and adjacent to the newly built public park surrounding the venerated statue of José Rizal. With all the changes which had transpired since 1945, much remained the same, despite evidences of political and cultural maturity. Any realistic yardstick for progress had to be at least a generation long, not merely from administration to administration. In any case, the future of the Filipinos was their own to determine.

1. Clifford Geertz, ed., *Old Societies and New States* (Glencoe, Ill., 1964), pp. 4-9.

2. Edward A. Shils, "On the Comparative Study of New States" in Geertz, *op. cit.*, 21-26.

3. Frank H. Golay, *The Philippines: Public Policy and National Economic Development* (Ithaca, 1961), pp. 62-64.

4. *Ibid.*, pp. 67-74, 88.

5. Joseph E. Spencer, *Land and People in the Philippines* (Berkeley, 1954), 214-15.

6. Golay, *op. cit.*, 76-79.

7. Shirley Jenkins, *American Economic Policy Toward the Philippines* (Stanford, 1954), pp. 15-17.

8. *Ibid.*, pp. 153-61.

9. Golay, *op. cit.*, pp. 78-89.

POSTWAR SOUTHEAST ASIA: INDEPENDENCE PROBLEMS

POST

POSTWAR SOUTHEAST ASIA: INDEPENDENCE PROBLEMS

POSTWAR SOUTHEAST ASIA: INDEPENDENCE PROBLEMS

10. *Ibid.*, pp. 89-99, 245-54.
11. B. Ronquillo "System Under Strain," *Far Eastern Economic Review*, April 17, 1969, pp. 204-06 (hereafter cited *FEER*).
12. Golay, *op. cit.*, pp. 46-54; Onofre D. Corpuz, *The Philippines* (Englewood Cliffs, N.J., 1965), pp. 11-13.
13. Golay, *op. cit.*, pp. 94-99, 101-08, 241-54, 344-45.
14. *Ibid.*, pp. 266-92.
15. Charles Mohr, "Philippines Lags on Land Reform", *New York Times*, August 8, 1969.
16. *Ibid.*
17. Corpuz, *op. cit.*, 130-39.
18. R. S. Milne, "Political Finance in Southeast Asia", *Pacific Affairs*, 41 (1968-69), 491-510.
19. Rupert Emerson, *Representative Government in Southeast Asia* (Cambridge, 1955), pp. 108-12.
20. Corpuz, *op. cit.*, pp. 11-13.
21. Golay, *op. cit.*, pp. viii, 3-4.
22. Albert Ravenholt, "The Spoils of Nationalism: the Philippines" in K. H. Silvert, ed., *Expectant Peoples: Nationalism and Development* (New York, 1963), pp. 185-91.
23. Corpuz, *op. cit.*, pp. 112-124.
24. Justus M. van der Kroef, "Patterns of Cultural Conflict in Philippine Life", *Pacific Affairs*, 39 (1966-67), 326-28.
25. *New York Times*, November 2, 1965.
26. Corpuz, *op. cit.*, pp. 107-12; *FEER*, December 28, 1967, pp. 576-77.
27. *Manila Chronicle*, October 17, 1968; *Manila Times*, October 18, 1968.
28. *Ibid.*
29. Silvert, *op. cit.*, pp. 191-95.
30. Golay, *op. cit.*, pp. 23-27.
31. David Wurfel, "The Process of Decolonization" in Frank Golay, *The United States and the Philippines* (Ithaca, 1966).
32. Corpuz, *op. cit.*, pp. 68-76.
33. The American Assembly, *Philippine-American Relations* (New York, Columbia University, 1966).
34. *FEER*, August 22, 1968, pp. 355-58; January 9, 1969, p. 40.
35. *New York Times*, June 23 and July 16, 1962.
36. *FEER*, August 11, 1966, pp. 277-79.
37. *Ibid.*, August 15, 1968, pp. 326-27; *New York Times*, January 20, 1967.
38. *FEER, 1968 Yearbook*, pp. 279-281.
39. *Ibid.*, March 14, 1967, p. 486; Jean Grossholtz, "The Philippines: Mid-term Doldrums for Marcos," *Asian Survey*, 8 (Jan., 1968), 52-57.
40. *FEER, 1968 Yearbook*, pp. 279-81.
42. *New York Times*, April 1, 1968.
43. *FEER*, April 3, 1969, pp. 43-44.
44. Anthony Polosky, "Murder in Manila", *FEER*, November 30, 1967, pp. 409-10.
45. Bernadino Ronquillo, "Reformers or Revolutionaries", *FEER*, September 1, 1966, pp. 405-406; Frances L. Starner, "Report from Arayat", *FEER*, October 21, 1967, pp. 144-49.
46. *New York Times*, April 17, 1965.
47. *FEER*. October 20, 1968, pp. 192-194.
48. Charles Mohr, "Filipinos Hopeful Church Will lead the Way to Much-needed Social Reform", *New York Times*, August 6, 1969; also *FEER*, June 26, 1969, pp. 660-62.

134

49. Mohr, "Manila Politics", *New York Times*, June 27, 1969.

50. Maximo V. Soliven, "Lagging Projects Need Aid Infusion," *New York Times*, January 20, 1967.

51. *FEER*, June 26, 1969; p. 696; *ibid.*, September 18, 1969. p. 683; *ibid.*, September 25, 1969, pp. 813-14.

52. *Ibid.*, May 1, 1969, p. 282, and May 15, 1969, p. 367.

53. Mohr, "Manila Politics", *New York Times*, June 27, 1969.

VI

MALAYSIA AND SINGAPORE

Economic Recovery in Malaya

The prompt economic recovery achieved by Malaya and Singapore from the blight of wartime stagnation owed much to the survival of prewar productive facilities and to the absence of nationalist upheaval. War-damaged transportation was quickly restored, and tin dredges were replaced at recoverable cost. The extensive rubber plantations' trees were several years older, but still healthy and productive. Replanting operations were undertaken without undue delay. British standards of disciplined administrative performance were gradually restored, and the training routines for Malayan civil service replacements were revived. Police and courts started functioning, and tax collections were resumed. The symbol of traditional sultanate authority was reaffirmed by the Federation Agreement of 1948, and a national hero figure emerged in the early fifties in the person of Tengku (Prince) Abdul Rahman. He was the British-educated leader of the United Malay National Organization (UMNO), a loyal Muslim who had adopted several Chinese orphan children, and a man sufficiently cosmopolitan to maintain cordial relations with leaders of the non-Malay community. Despite attempted sabotage of economic activities by Communist Chinese rebels, their operations interfered little with the recovery processes already under way by 1948.

136

The British-directed government got into the recovery act in a positive way in the early fifties. The Industrial Development Authority undertook to encourage rural Malays to participate in such enterprises as cooperative rice mills, small-scale rubber processing, and fishing boat construction and repair. A move was made to establish a system of national schools emphasizing a common core curriculum tailored to meet the educational needs of the Malays. A ruling made in 1953 accorded to Chinese and Indians qualified citizenship rights and permitted their participation on a one-to-four basis in routine civil service posts previously reserved for Malays. The withdrawal of British personnel and the absence of technically trained Malays to fill upper-level posts in the service permitted Indian and Chinese job candidates to acquire a somewhat larger measure of participation, thus improving the competence of the service.

By 1954-55, economic prospects were enhanced by the declining incidence of rebellion and the development of cooperative political effort through the Alliance party coalition. Abdul Rahman's UMNO cooperated with both the Malayan Chinese Association (MCA) and the Malayan Indian Congress (MIC) to provide a *modus operandi* that continued to be effective despite the fact that communal hostility underlay the deceptively calm political surface.

The persisting rifts within Malayan society, essentially ethnic and religious but also coupled with economic rivalry, proved in the end too wide to bridge. Intermarriage between Muslim Malays and nonbelievers was virtually impossible, so that normal methods of social assimilation were vetoed. The economic contest was highly unequal. The fiercely competitive attitude of the immigrant Chinese, conditioned to thrift and industry by the problem of sheer survival, was alien to the nonaggressive Malays, who were correspondingly ill adapted by tradition to disciplined roles in trade or industry. Malay's 37 percent Chinese population could neither be denied economic opportunity nor be forced to become Malayanized. Positive government efforts to promote business training for Malays and to afford them

137

favored treatment in selected occupational areas and rural development projects were designed for long-run rather than immediate results.

The situation was even more disparate in British Borneo (the annexation of which will be considered below), where Chinese residents outnumbered the 10 percent Muslim Malay fraction of the population by more than two to one.[1] Residents of Borneo also resented the presumption of the mainland Malays that they alone were qualified to rule. Thus the overriding spirit of nationalism that characterized most other emerging states of post-war Southeast Asia was in Borneo largely submerged by communal differences.

Just as it was quite impossible to contemplate eliminating Malaya's economically active Chinese population, neither was it feasible for the conservatively pragmatic Alliance party coalition to give serious consideration to nationalizing British-owned plantations, tin mines, banks, and trading facilities. British management was both progressive and cooperative, paying taxes willingly and taking the lead in replanting rubber trees, replacing mining machinery, and improving processing operations. Whatever government funds were available could be better used to encourage new industrial development than to purchase already-functioning enterprises. Malaya's leaders also decided for the time being to stay linked financially to the British pound for the additional reason of avoiding balance of payments problems.

Transition to Independence

The encouraging economic gains and the governmental adjustments that the Malayan Federation was able to achieve despite the embarrassment of the Emergency rebellion rested on a fragile political base. The helpful presence of the British colonial administration could not be expected to continue indefinitely; the interests and resources of the United Kingdom were simply no longer adequate to warrant maintaining the Singapore naval base and garrisoned forces for the defense of its Malaya, Singapore, and Borneo possessions. Within the changing East Asian political context, colonialism could not long survive, and the process of British withdrawal would inevitably bring to the surface a variety of tensions, both domestic and international.

The difficulties which the Alliance party compromise encountered in its initial endeavors to bridge existing differences produced a tendency to exploit independence as a unifying issue. The Alliance election manifesto of 1955 offered amnesty to surrendered terrorists, but skirted the questions of union with Singapore, citizenship rights, and differences of language and religion. A vote for Alliance candidates in 1955 was interpreted as a move toward independence. The party accordingly attracted 81 percent of the vote and emerged in complete control of the Assembly, with virtually all of the elected candidates and nine of the forty-six appointed members.[2]

In the Malayan political context of the middle fifties, colored as it was by the fact of Communist rebellion and the demonstrated consensus to end colonial rule, the victorious Alliance party leadership was effective politically. It experienced little difficulty in persuading the British authorities to shorten the normal pattern of gradual progress toward self-government, as contemplated in the 1948 Federation Constitution. The obvious dangers of attempting independence without nationhood had to be balanced against the impossibility of maintaining colonial control in the face of overt rebellion and the impressive victory of the essentially conservative Alliance party. The logic of events overshadowed counsels of moderation.

The two years that elapsed between the election of 1955 and the achievement of independence in 1957 were busy ones politically. British authorities moved first to persuade the Malay sultans to accept substantial revisions in the Federation Agreement of 1948 and to participate on equal terms with Alliance party representatives in the independence preparations. British authorities at Kuala Lumpur speeded up the process of replacing European officials with qualified Malays. The role of the indigenous chief minister was expanded to include finances and economic policy, and also internal security. The sultans retained their dignity as titular heads of the several states, but the chief minister, not the high commissioner, now appointed their advisers.[3]

The task of drafting the new constitution was entrusted to an expert Advisory Commonwealth Commission (representing the United Kingdom, India, Pakistan, and Australia), which convened from June to October 1956. On difficult matters of communal relations, the Commission deferred to the National Council of the Alliance party to formulate acceptable agreements. The resulting compromise settlement was more pro-Malay than pro-Chinese. The Commission initially opposed according special constitutional privileges to the Malays on a permanent basis, in favor of a fifteen-year limitation and subsequent legislative regulation of such matters, but the Malay-dominated National Council rejected the Commission's idea in the end.[4]

The principal Chinese gain under the new constitution was provision for single-nationality citizenship to be accorded to all who met the stipulated requirements, which included place of birth or length of residence, an elementary acquaintance with the Malay language, and taking the oath of allegiance. Residents of Penang and Malacca could retain a semblance of dual citizenship within the Commonwealth. Special privileges for indigenous Malays covered favored eligibility (four to one) for public employment, access to one-half of the public lands that became available for occupancy, and advantages with respect to obtaining vocational licenses and scholarships. Such constitutional privileges were enforceable by successive paramount ruling sultans and by the several state rulers, and they could be altered only by a two-thirds concurrence of the Assembly. Islam became the official religion, under similar constitutional guarantees. English would be permitted in governmental and legislative agencies for ten years as an alternative to official Malay, after which time language questions would be subject to legislative control. The ruling sultan would be selected by his peers for single five-year terms, and the associated Rulers' Conference could discuss matters of national policy. The sultans could also participate in making judicial appointments, in settling disputes over state boundaries, and in preserving privileges accorded by the constitution. The constitution, a thoroughly professional document, was ratified on August 15, 1957, and implemented on August 31.[5]

Guarantees to alien residents were heavily qualified. Non-Malays were accorded freedom from interference in their business activities and in the exercise of all personal liberties (speech, assembly, and association), except when it might be necessary to suspend such rights for reasons of public order and security. Fomenters of disorder could be detained without trial for a maximum of three months during emergency situations, to be officially designated by executive ordinance. Such rulings could be rescinded only by joint action of both houses of Parliament.[6]

The political and constitutional compromises fashioned by the Alliance party system could, it was hoped, buy valuable time by muting communal antagonisms until more adequate guarantees of ethnic equality could be worked out. Meanwhile, the party's prestige rested on its achievement of early independence, on the charismatic qualities of Premier Tengku Abdul Rahman, and on the inauguration of state-promoted programs for industrial and rural development. The predominantly rural Malay communities were more easily pacified under the Alliance arrangement than were the urban Chinese centers, where the articulation of economic and political grievances was clearer. For a variety of reasons, the Alliance system held together through the 1964 elections, although it provided no basic solutions.[7]

Economic Development after Independence

Economic gains of a more general dimension were realized following independence in 1957. On the recommendation of a visiting World Bank mission, a Central Bank for

Malaya was set up to supervise the operation of commercial banks with respect to required reserves and interest rates. When it opened in 1959, the new bank assumed the added function of encouraging saving habits in order to provide additional resources for government development activities. Colonial practice in Malaya had already conceded as legitimate the public ownership of such facilities as railways, electrical generating facilities, and rice mills.

The Alliance party government, although conservative, was not averse to the exercise of state economic initiative in areas where it appeared to be useful. Progress in rural development was realized mainly in the construction of roads, buildings, and public works, plus the clearing, planning, and settlement of newly opened lands. A formal program sponsored by the Federal Land Development Authority (FLDA), dating from 1959, was directed by Deputy Prime Minister Tun Abdul Razak. The FLDA functioned not so much as an operations agency, but rather to direct, coordinate, and expedite the realization of agreed-on policy objectives. Tun Abdul Razak personally inspected various projects that were under way, staged regular briefing sessions covering development activities, and pressed officials to coordinate their efforts and to keep themselves informed on what was going on. By such methods, red tape was cut and public investment expedited with a minimum of graft and delay. For five years the FLDA managed to relieve crowded areas by setting up annually some 10,000 ten-acre plots on a priority basis of need. Chinese contractors were employed to clear the sites, and roads, schools, and water services were provided.

Small-holder rubber estates, with subsistence garden plots adjacent, proved particularly attractive, as long as world market prices were reasonably sustained. Less effective for the poorer farmers were the government-aided cooperative credit agencies, which provided in time almost half of the seasonal requirements for paddy cultivation in western and northern Malaya.[8] A number of irrigation dams were constructed near the Thai border, coupled with emphasis on the use of better seed rice and fertilizers.

Despite such efforts, and the fact that three-fifths of the Malayan labor force was devoted to food production, the country grew only 65 percent of its rice needs as of 1966. Malaya's natural rubber exports eventually encountered serious competition with synthetic substitutes produced in leading industrial states, with the Russian and Chinese markets being the main exceptions. At the conclusion of a decade of rural development efforts, the movement tended to run aground, due in part to the carry-over of routine habits of colonial administrative inefficiency and partly to the sheer inertia of villager habits.[9] Malay peasants simply did not become thrifty and industrious farmers in so short a time. Even so, Abdul Razak's accomplishments in the agricultural area were obviously significant.[10]

A more dependable area of economic activity was mining. In tin output, an annual production rate of some fifty thousand tons was maintained, facilitated by the use of new dredging equipment. Output could be restricted whenever necessary to maintain economic price levels, but this kind of production could not continue indefinitely, because the tin ore deposits were limited. Iron ore production in eastern Malaya multiplied substantially after 1950 with the aid of Japanese capital outlays. Five new areas were opened, so that the annual output by 1965 was seven million tons, compared with the prewar production of only two million. But thereafter production fell off. Malaysia's limited ore potential simply could not keep pace with the voracious appetite of the Japanese steel mills, for which more ample sources were being found in India, Australia, and South America. As of 1966, Malaysia's total remaining iron ore reserves were estimated at only forty million tons. Efforts to use the ore within Malaysia were handicapped by the lack of adequate fuel. Rubber-tree charcoal was used for the production of some twenty thousand tons of steel in 1967.[11]

The traditional entrepôt servicing operations for ocean-going vessels continued at Singapore and Penang. Expansion was registered in the processing and grading of regional products and in the servicing and repair of ships themselves. But such traditional activities could not be expected to

143

absorb more than a small fraction of the annual increment in labor forces of the several port areas. These numbered eighty thousand in Singapore and three hundred forty thousand in Malaya. Industrial expansion was the principal alternative.

The mainland government assigned the task of promoting new industry to the Malayan Development Finance Company, which was set up in 1960. Tax incentives were accorded to new industries covering the first five years of operations, with extensions of such privileges for those enterprises that proved capable of producing for export markets. The results were less than had been hoped for. Outside capital hesitated to commit itself, while most of the local Chinese family firms became only moderately involved in producing footwear, tires, leather goods, and cement. As of 1966, the manufacturing output in Malaysia accounted for an estimated 9 percent of production and employed only 7 percent of the work force.[12]

The surface evidences of economic progress were nevertheless clearly present in Kuala Lumpur, with its modern airport, new roadways, skyscraper office buildings, and automobiles, and its several handsome new mosques. The gain in annual gross national product was 7.6 percent in 1964 and 8.5 percent in 1965. It represented, however, more building expansion and infrastructure than enhanced output of consumer and export items, and underneath it all was the perennial problem of the maldistribution of the realized gains. Balance-of-trade figures and tax revenues showed serious losses in 1966, due in part to the slump of rubber prices to a twelve-year low and in part to Britain's withdrawal of its $210 million defense contribution following the resolution of the Confrontation crisis.[13]

The Singapore counterpart of the Malayan agency was termed the Economic Development Board. In the absence of resources for the development of basic industry, the only immediately feasible course was to assemble and process local and imported ingredients. These included electrical facilities, chemicals, paint, tires, and cement. More long-term plans included the production of sugar, flour, paper, fertilizers, and aluminum. Some ninety "pioneer industry" firms were started with official encouragement between 1958 and 1962. Many of the new plant facilities were concentrated in the Jurong area near the western end of the island, where port access was afforded. The largest were devoted to oil-refining operations and ship servicing. But the difficulties were many. Even if large-scale industrial output became possible, neighboring markets could not possibly absorb the products. Chinese firms, here as in Kuala Lumpur, disliked the risks of heavy capital outlay and the cost of hiring professional management personnel. Industrial employment increments in both Singapore and Malaysia were impressive, even though, by the early 1960s, they had achieved not more than half of their planned objectives.[14]

Urban development per se constituted a separate goal. Much of the labor surplus could be employed profitably in the construction of much-needed middle-class housing in both Singapore and Kuala Lumpur. Imported construction steel was nevertheless very expensive, and its purchase became a limiting factor. At the end of the queue were the displaced components of the urban working class. The urban Malays in particular were cut off from the support of friends and relatives living in rural communities while they were being progressively alienated from the traditionally enforceable mores controlling their behavior patterns. Crime and juvenile delinquency defied family or police control, and the ability of the Social Welfare Department to care for the indigent was minimal. Malay squatters lived in shanty homes put together from boxes, planks, corrugated roofing, and flattened petrol tins. The urban Chinese were less seriously uprooted, but they also lived in badly crowded tenement areas.[15] The total picture was far from rosy, and it was destined to deteriorate when political tensions increased during the late 1960s.

The economic progress achieved in postwar Malaysia, although surpassed by no other Southeast Asian state, appeared less impressive when subjected to critical examination. The relatively high per-capita income figures of U.S.

$279 for Malaya proper and U.S. $430 for Singapore were badly distributed. Many workers earned much less than the average, and both states faced difficulty in finding jobs for the increasing number of young people who entered the labor market annually. Meanwhile, latent factors of tension, relating to job access, language usage, and political opportunities, came to the fore. Faced with the problem of competing with alien residents, many Malays looked forward to implementing the constitutional provision that the indigenous tongue could become the official language by 1967. Proponents of the move tended to ignore the obvious shortcomings of the language, particularly in vocabulary and literature covering legal and governmental matters and in terms of world communications. On the other side, non-Malays naturally objected to the imposition of arbitrary limitations on their access to government positions and to the prospect that their superiority in English communication would be discounted.

Malay Nationalism and Relations within the Alliance Party[16]

Despite the fact that the modulation from British colonial rule to Malayan independence was peacefully achieved and did not involve any major shift in governmental and social leadership, the change nevertheless carried important political implications. Under British rule the elite Malay establishment, headed by the titular sultans, had been assured of the preservation of personal and cultural prestige as guardians of customary social values, including the Islamic faith. The de facto emasculation of the political powers of the sultan was less disturbing because educated Malay civil servant personnel from the top social strata were substituted for the more or less autonomous and uncontrollable district officials of precolonial times. As the recognized symbols of governmental authority and national identity, the several sultans continued to be important individually, and their status remained secure.

Similarly, British rule had sheltered the Malay villages

146

from the disturbing impact of economic modernization—in the form of plantations, tin mines, seaports, and cities generally—which had impinged on the Chinese, and Indian residents. Villagers continued to enjoy ready access to land for agricultural purposes and to fishing opportunities. They also tended to focus their political loyalties on their own particular states and sultans rather than on the incipient Malay nation as a whole. Thus neither from the elite strata nor from the peasant elements of the indigenous society did there develop in prewar times any significant evidences of nationalist sentiment or political unrest.

In between the two disparate but essentially traditionalist strata of the Malay world, three potentially nationalist movements emerged prior to World War II. The least representative of the three was a highly articulate Islamic reform group centering in the coastal cities, Penang and Singapore. In several respects, this group was similar to the Santri religious partisans of coastal Java. They were concerned with purifying the faith and developing a more egalitarian Malay society, but they attracted no mass following—partly because they included descendants of Arabic and Muslim Indian ancestry, and partly because they demonstrated little sense of loyalty to Malay traditions in general and to the several mainland sultans in particular.

The second group was made up of politically dissident Malays, drawn from the limited number of foreign-educated Malay youth (some of them of humble origins and trained in the University of Cairo), who entertained strong anti-colonialist convictions. They developed fairly close relations with similarly motivated Left-wing Indonesian opponents of Dutch rule. As educated Malays, they were not unassociated with the indigenous intelligencia, but most of them entertained little respect for the elite entourage of the sultan courts or for civil service personnel, because both were closely aligned with British rule. Since the declared goal of these dissidents was to bring about the end of colonial rule, possibly in collaboration with their revolutionary counterparts in Indonesia, they were kept under close surveillance by the colonial police. For this and other reasons, they

147

were able to attract no mass following. Representatives of the anticolonialist group were destined to establish tentative Indonesian contacts during the course of the Confrontation controversy in the early sixties.

The third and more representative group of Malay nationalists was drawn directly from youthful members of the English-educated civil service elite class. They sensed the threat of possible Chinese domination, politically as well as economically. The various associations sponsored by this group were more ethnicist than nationalist in character and were accorded considerable freedom. At the outset, they shared with the traditionalist elements the acceptance of British colonial rule, but when, during the first decade after the war, they were faced with insistent Chinese demands for political equality in the context of possible British withdrawal, they became alarmed.

In the end it was this group of ethnic partisans, rather than the Islamic reformers or the outright anti-colonialists, that established a substantial measure of rapport with the Malay population as a whole.[17] They tended to distrust the compromising UMNO collaborators within the Alliance party. Much the same could be said of the articulate younger elements of the Chinese and Indian communities, who envisaged a threat to their future citizenship status once British withdrawal left them vulnerable to both economic and political discrimination from a Malay-dominated government.

During the course of the middle fifties, considerable friction developed between the several member factions of the far-from-homogeneous Alliance party. The differences centered on communal rights and party leadership. All of the Malay UMNO factions were generally opposed to alien Asian interests, but for somewhat different reasons. Some of the Malays were orthodox religionists, while others professed to see in the Chinese community a direct political threat, whether capitalist or Communist. Traditionalists generally favored bolstering the prestige of the sultans as an essential means of maintaining national identity, while the more progressive Malays wanted to modernize the state.

The civil service class had jobs at stake and a vested interest in maintaining racial harmony as a condition for achieving early independence. The Tengku Abdul Rahman, as prime minister and leader of the UMNO, exploited all of the traditional symbols of authority (political, social, and religious) in his endeavors to attract the allegiance of divergent elements. Although personally tolerant of aliens, he dared not grant any substantial concessions to the Chinese if he wished to expand the influence of the UMNO.

The wealthy, Westernized leadership of the Malayan Chinese Association (MCA) faction of the Alliance group had less close rapport with the basic organizations of the Chinese community (secret societies, guilds, and labor unions) than the UMNO had with the mass of the Malays. The prestigious founder, Tan Cheng-lock, was becoming physically frail, and rival younger leaders, less Anglicized, were vying for MCA control. Most of them tended to keep one foot in the MCA camp and the other in some basic organizational connection. Chinese factions included rival linguistic groups, Kuomintang partisans against the Communists, trade unions against employers, and advocates of differing methods of defending the political rights of the Chinese against Malay discrimination.

In 1958 the leadership of the MCA passed to Lim Chong-eu, who attempted to establish more effective centralized control. He also demanded that the Chinese element within the Alliance grouping should be permitted a stronger role in determining policies. Several recalcitrant members were suspended when all MCA leaders were required to qualify as citizens. A less-important contingent within the Alliance, the Malayan Indian Congress, also found its younger members critical of the bland passivity of the leadership. Some branches rebelled, and centralized control was maintained with difficulty. Within the Alliance National Council, tension developed between the various racial constituencies when the Council ruled that its own chairman and that of the executive committee must invariably be Malays.

A showdown occurred between the Tengku and Lim

149

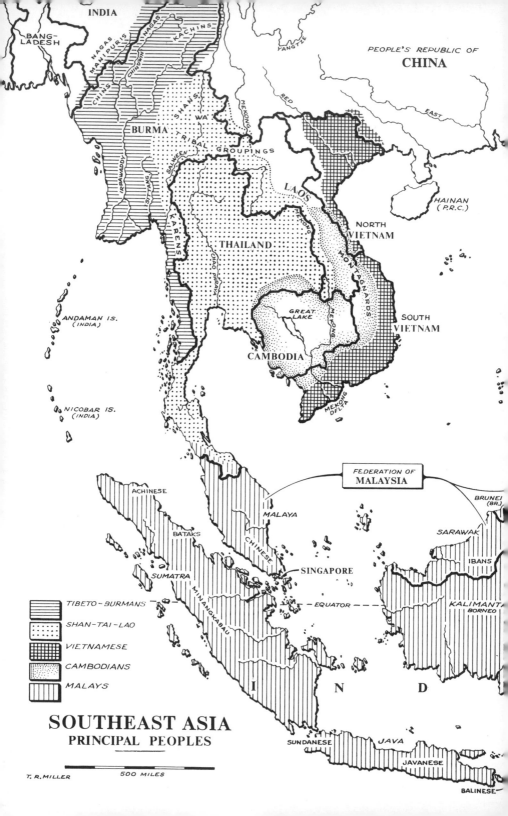

SOUTHEAST ASIA
PRINCIPAL PEOPLES

Legend:
- TIBETO–BURMANS
- SHAN–TAI–LAO
- VIETNAMESE
- CAMBODIANS
- MALAYS

T. R. MILLER   500 MILES

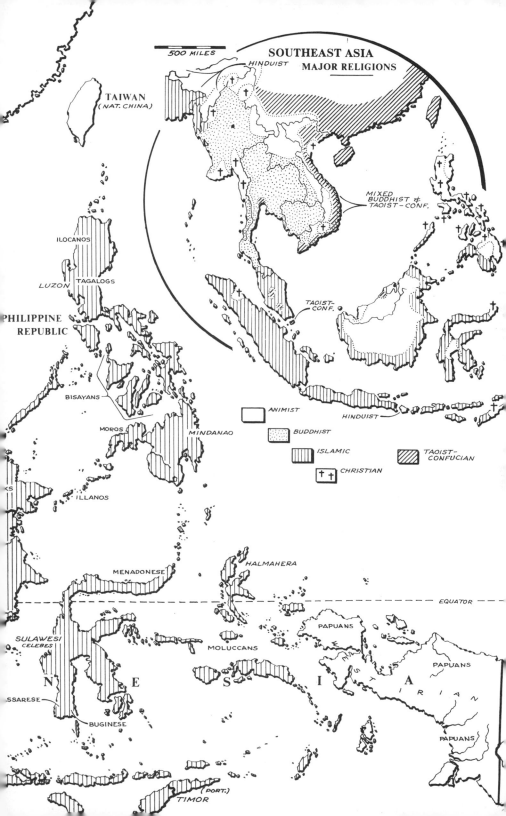

SOUTHEAST ASIA
MAJOR RELIGIONS

500 MILES

HINDUIST

TAIWAN
(NAT. CHINA)

MIXED
BUDDHIST &
TAOIST–CONF.

ILOCANOS

LUZON   TAGALOGS

PHILIPPINE
REPUBLIC

TAOIST–
CONF.

BISAYANS

MOROS   MINDANAO

ANIMIST

BUDDHIST

HINDUIST

ILLANOS   ISLAMIC   TAOIST–
                                              CONFUCIAN

                           ✝ ✝ CHRISTIAN

MENADONESE   HALMAHERA

EQUATOR

SULAWESI
CELEBES   PAPUANS

                      MOLUCCANS

N   E   S   I   A   PAPUANS

SSARESE

BUGINESE

(PORT.)
TIMOR   PAPUANS

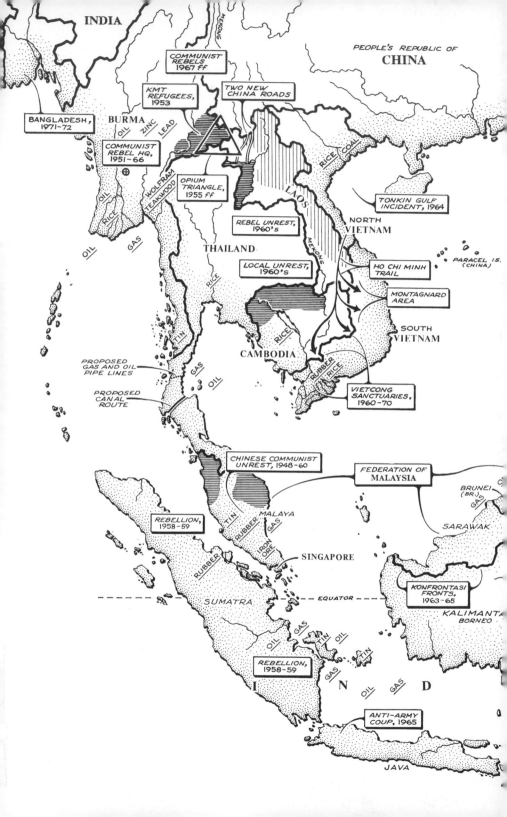

INDIA

PEOPLE'S REPUBLIC OF
CHINA

COMMUNIST
REBELS
1967 ff

KMT
REFUGEES,
1953

TWO NEW
CHINA ROADS

BANGLADESH,
1971–72

BURMA

OIL ZINC LEAD

COMMUNIST
REBEL HQ,
1951–66

RICE COAL

OPIUM
TRIANGLE,
1955 ff

WOLFRAM

TEAKWOOD

LAOS

TONKIN GULF
INCIDENT, 1964

OIL

RICE

REBEL UNREST,
1960's

MEKONG

NORTH
VIETNAM

OIL

GAS

THAILAND

RICE

LOCAL UNREST,
1960's

HO CHI MINH
TRAIL

PARACEL IS.
(CHINA)

MONTAGNARD
AREA

TIN

RICE

SOUTH
VIETNAM

PROPOSED
GAS AND OIL
PIPE LINES

CAMBODIA

RICE

GAS

OIL

RUBBER
RICE

VIETCONG
SANCTUARIES,
1960–70

PROPOSED
CANAL
ROUTE

CHINESE COMMUNIST
UNREST, 1948–60

FEDERATION OF
MALAYSIA

BRUNEI
(BR.)

GAS

REBELLION,
1958–59

TIN

RUBBER

MALAYA

RUBBER
GAS

SARAWAK

IRON
ORE

SINGAPORE

RUBBER

SUMATRA

EQUATOR

KONFRONTASI
FRONTS,
1963–65

KALIMANTAN
BORNEO

GAS

TIN

OIL

OIL

GAS

TIN

GAS

I

N

OIL

GAS

D

REBELLION,
1958–59

ANTI–ARMY
COUP, 1965

JAVA

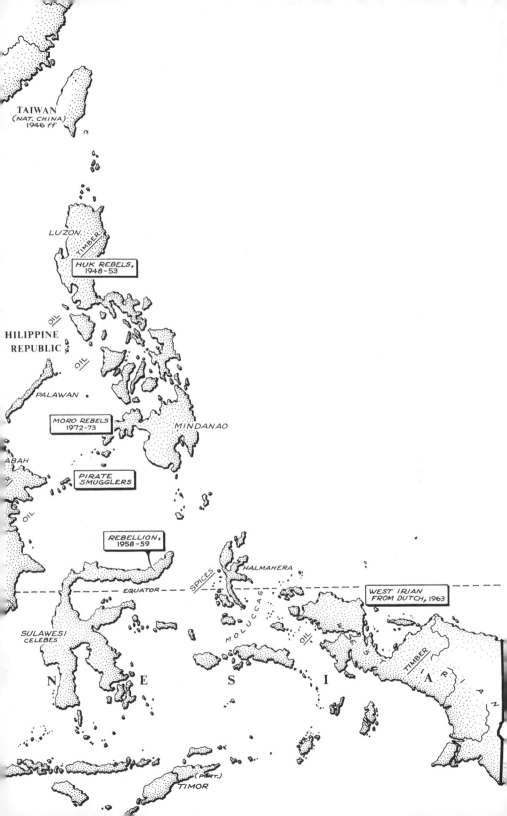

TAIWAN
(NAT. CHINA)
1946 ff

LUZON

TIMBER

HUK REBELS,
1948-53

OIL

HILIPPINE
REPUBLIC

OIL

PALAWAN

MORO REBELS
1972-73

MINDANAO

ABAH

PIRATE
SMUGGLERS

OIL

REBELLION,
1958-59

SPICES

HALMAHERA

EQUATOR

WEST IRIAN
FROM DUTCH, 1963

SULAWESI
CELEBES

MOLUCCAS

OIL

WEST IRIAN

TIMBER

N   E   S   I   A

(PORT.)
TIMOR

SOUTHEAST ASIA
1973

500 MILES

T. R. MILLER

SOUTHEAST ASIA
1939

500 MILES

COLONIES

moy
Swatow

TAIPEI
TAIWAN
(NAT.
CHINA)

INDIA
(BR.)

BURMA
(BR.)

NATIONALIST
CHINA

FORMOSA
(JAP.)

TONKIN

HAINAN
(FR. LEASE)

PARACEL IS.

SIAM

FRENCH
INDOCHINA

PHILIPPINE
ISLANDS
(U.S.)

LUXON

MANILA

**PHILIPPINE
REPUBLIC**

ANDAMAN
IS.
(BR.)

NICOBAR IS.
(BR.)

CAM-
BODIA

COCHIN-
CHINA

SPRATLY IS.
(BR.)

BR.
N. BORNEO

BRUNEI
(BR.)

SARAWAK
(BR.)

CELEBES

MALAY
STATES
(BR.)

SUMATRA

SINGAPORE
(BR.)

BORNEO

NETHERLANDS

EAST   INDIES

Iloilo
PANAY

PALAWN

JAVA

(D.

SULU
SEA

MINDANAO

Zamboanga

Davao

SABAH
(BR. N. BORNEO

CELEBES

SEA

PACIFIC

OCEAN

Menado

HALMAHERA

MOLUCCA

SEA

EQUATOR

SULAWESI
CELEBES

STRAIT OF MACASSAR

MOLUCCAS
SPICES

WEST

CERAM

N   E   S   Ambon   I   A   IAN

Macassar

BANDA

SEA

ARU
IS.

SUMBAWA

FLORES

(PORT.)

TIMOR
(INDON.)

ARAFURA   SEA

SUMBA

130° E

140° E

Chong-eu in July 1959 over preparations for the general elections of that year. Lim demanded in an open letter that the MCA be accorded 40 candidates (later 35) in the total of 104 instead of the promised 28, and that they be nominated by the MCA rather than by the Tengku. To block further pro-Malay constitutional amendments, 35 votes were needed. The Tengku called Lim's bluff and agreed to a compromise of only 32 Chinese candidates, all to be nominated by himself. Lim was denied a candidacy and subsequently resigned as leader of the MCA. The net result was to aggravate communal unrest within the MCA, but without providing any feasible alternatives for dissident elements. For educated Chinese, Alliance connections still provided the only means of access to government employ, available mainly in a number of technical areas where few Malays could qualify. The Alliance party won 74 of the 104 seats in the Assembly election of 1959.[18] During the ensuing two years, opposition to the Alliance in various camps continued to grow, but the dissidents failed to coalesce.

Singapore under Fading Colonial Rule

Self-government plans for Singapore after 1953 had moved directly from full colonial administration to an elected-majority Assembly of twenty-five in a total membership of thirty-two. The chief minister was the leader of the largest party in the Assembly, and he in turn selected the other five ministers. The first Singapore election, held in 1955, brought to power the stridently anticolonialist but otherwise conservative Labor Front party, which won ten seats in the Assembly. The Front was led by a lawyer of Jewish-Iraqui descent named David Marshall, who served as chief minister from 1955 to 1957. The principal opposition came from the Leftist-inclined Peoples Action party (PAP), led by the brilliant British-trained Lee Kuan Yew, with the backing of some trade unionists and several Marxists. Marshall's Front associate, Lim Yew Hock, took over as premier after Marshall made a bold but futile effort to establish political power over both troops and police, which remained under British control. Lim then moved to entrust security problems to a joint committee, including colonial officials and one Malayan member. He also attempted to prevent subversive elements from gaining membership in the Assembly.

The PAP reaction to Lim's increasingly conservative tendencies was at first ambivalent. Youthful Chinese members tried to influence the PAP to move in a Communist direction, but when the party won forty-three of the fifty-one seats in the 1959 Singapore elections, its representation fragmented quickly. One moderately Leftist faction founded the United Peoples party, which strongly opposed the prospective union with Malaya. In 1962 the Barisan Sosialis, a Marxist wing of the PAP, split off, leaving Lee Kuan Yew with a bare majority in the Assembly.[19]

What propelled Lee Kuan Yew and Tengku Abdul Rahman into the Malaysia union was the frightening prospect that the Singapore electorate might drift under complete Communist control. The loudly proclaimed denunciation of both colonialism and capitalism by Barisan Sosialis partisans appealed to frustrated youthful elements of Singapore's population. Both the Alliance and the PAP were castigated as enemies of the peoples' will, in spite of the fact that Lee himself advocated extensive welfare measures designed to reduce the existing inequities in both opportunities and wealth.

The possibility that Singapore would fall under Communist control developed significant international implications as well. With the British preparing to reduce their territorial holdings and security commitments in Southeast Asia, the Tengku had suggested in May 1961 the idea of an expanded Malaya Raya, in which the annexed 75 percent Chinese population of Singapore would be balanced by the North Borneo Malays. If something were not done, an independent, Communist-led Singapore might attract vigorous support from the strong PKI Leftists in Java and might also solicit the backing of the Sukarno government in pursuit of his favorite anticolonist Indonesia Raya scheme. If, alternatively, the partisan anti-Chinese Malays should

157

decide to support Sukarno's prospective Malay unity movement, the danger to Malaya itself could become serious.[20]

Singapore had much to gain economically as well as in terms of defence from union with Malaya. Union could conceivably afford the islanders wider employment, enhance production opportunities, and improve trading and investment outlets.[21] The move would end Singapore's colonial status on a positive note. Under the circumstances, Lee had no choice but to counter the anti-Malaysia agitation of his Communist opponents and to adopt a more conciliatory line with respect to the Alliance itself.

Meanwhile, Singapore and the Borneo states became a concern of world Communist policy. Resolutions passed at the World Federation of Democratic Youth Conference at Warsaw in August 1962 reflected the increased interest in Southeast Asia. Conference spokesmen accused British imperialists and their Malayan stooges of trying to block the efforts of anticolonialist peoples in the region. Radio Peking and Radio Moscow both encouraged Indonesian resistance to the proposed creation of Malaysia.[22] Communist agitators in Singapore also opposed the merger, in part, no doubt, because continued British control offered them a more convincing target for anti-imperialist propaganda, until the situation with Indonesia was made ripe for revolutionary objectives. In any case, it was significant that, in 1961, the PKI had been the first Indonesian group to advocate challenging the British move.

The original pattern for creating a broader Malaysian federation, as formulated in August 1961, would have permitted Singapore a considerable degree of autonomy. The local government would exercise control over labor and educational policies, and would have the use of 75 percent of its own revenue resources. To compensate for these privileges and for the concession of *jus soli* (place of birth) citizenship, the island's representation in the Federation House of Representatives was set at only fifteen seats, instead of the nineteen or more that the size of the population would have warranted. Sarawak, by comparison, got twentyfour seats, and Sabah sixteen. A vigorous advance was accomplished in August 1962, when a special referendum held in the island approved the merger proposal by a 71 percent majority. Another year of haggling over terms ensued before the union was consummated.[23]

The final terms of the compromise agreement left a number of economic and political provisions not fully clarified. Lee Kuan Yew, for example, agreed in the end to surrender 40 percent of the island's revenue collections to the central government, presumably in return for Malaya's agreement to set up a common-market arrangement. The latter was considered essential to Singapore's continued prosperity as an entrepôt and future industrial center. Kuala Lumpur later postponed implementing any customs agreement until some national program for industrial development had been worked out, a goal which was never realized. Few if any of the "pioneer certificates" for setting up tax-free industrial projects were ever granted to Singapore applicants following the merger. Another moot question was Singapore's tentative offer to lend 150 million Malay dollars, two-thirds of it to be tax free for five years, to aid the economic development of the associated Borneo states. This promise was coupled with the requirement that half of the needed outside labor would come from Singapore. The loan was never negotiated. A recurring political complaint related to the island state's inadequate representation in the Federal Parliament and the denial of the right of Singapore citizens, including Lee Kuan Yew himself, to aspire to election or appointment to federal or Malaysian state offices. The rules did not explicitly prohibit Singapore-based candidates from competing for Parliamentary seats in other sections of the federation, but the practice was not acceptable to Alliance leadership.[24] It proved to be one thing to sign the merger agreement and another to define and implement its terms.

Borneo Colonies and Malaysia

Another major problem connected with the creation of Malaysia concerned the incorporation of Britain's neighboring Borneo possessions within the federation. The move would provide the United Kingdom with a convenient opportunity to divest itself of colonial holdings that it could no longer defend and could not expect to retain indefinitely. From Kuala Lumpur's point of view, the absorption of Borneo peoples within the Federation would conceivably raise a barrier against China's southward expansion and also prevent the development of a Chinese population majority in the Federation, a real possibility after Singapore's population was added. Most Borneo peoples, including Chinese residents, disliked mainland Malays and preferred that the British protectorate be indefinitely continued. If that was not possible, however, the continued connection of Borneo with Singapore and Malaya was generally preferred to its incorporation into neighboring Indonesia or the Philippines. No one believed that the Borneo states were capable of proceeding alone, and it was recognized that some educated Chinese residents were obviously susceptible to Peking's propaganda.

The seeming similarities between the population of the North Borneo states and Malaya proper proved on examination to be superficial. The Malay-speaking people constituted only one of some twenty-eight identifiable language groupings in North Borneo, while less than 10 percent of the indigenous population followed the Islamic faith. Resident Chinese numbered 31 percent of Sarawak's population and 23 percent in North Borneo's Sabah. They were mainly traders, craftsmen, and small-scale rubber and tin producers. Literacy among the Chinese (50 percent) was almost three times that of the non-Chinese (17 percent). Four-fifths of the latter were engaged in agriculture (largely slash-and-burn) in what was otherwise a technologically sophisticated situation, featuring the innovation of outboard motors for river craft. The largest economic asset of Sabah was its virtually untouched timber resources. Sabah traders profited from smuggling operations with the lower islands of the Philippines. The tiny Brunei Sultanate, sandwiched in between Sarawak and Sabah, was rich in oil resources, but it constituted only a small fraction of the once-extensive domain of the ruling Brunei dynasty. Apart from oil, Brunei's economy was stagnant, and the paternalism of the wealthy sultan was debilitating. In 1946 the British government had taken over Sarawak and Sabah as colonial domains from the prewar "private" rulers, who were financially unable to sponsor essential developments. Many of the gains in education realized after the takeover benefited mainly the Chinese, who made up some 85 percent of the secondary school enrollment in Sarawak as of 1958.

By 1960 time was running out on Britain's costly long-run task of developing the Borneo territories politically and economically. Sarawak was still ruled by an appointed governor and a combined European-Malay civil service. Five of the executive council's ten men were selected indirectly by local municipal and district councils. The Legislative Council Negri was only half-elected, and indirectly so at that. Sabah was even more backward governmentally, with official members still dominating both executive and legislative councils down to 1961. The prospect of Malaysian merger had actually stimulated Sabah's first serious efforts at governmental modernization.[25]

Preparatory moves for the incorporation of the North Borneo territories into Malaysia were entrusted in 1961 to a commission headed by Lord Cobbold. The plan, as publicized in 1962, called for a twenty-four-member Sarawak representation in the central Parliament and sixteen from Sabah. Borneo authorities would retain autonomous control over citizenship and immigration policies and education and economic development funds, and would maintain preferred indigenous access to designated jobs. English was to be the principal language of instruction in government schools, and non-Muslim religions would not suffer official interference. The indigenous peoples would also enjoy a privileged position with respect to landholding. Local governors, sultans or otherwise, need not be Malays. The central Malaysian authorities would exercise predominant authority over finances, revenues, policing, and trade.

The newly emerging political parties in Borneo were communally based, but such ethnic groups were themselves

161

fragmented by economic and cultural differences. The Sarawak United Peoples party, for example, was both Chinese sponsored and Communist affiliated. It focused attention on labor rights, educational opportunities, and the abolition of restrictions of landholding and citizenship. The opposing Negara Sawarak party, as of 1960, was Malay oriented. These disparate groups were both associated in 1962 with Alliance party promoters from Kuala Lumpur, presumably because practical leaders appreciated the advantages of being on the winning side. Actually, the Alliance constituencies in both Sarawak and Sabah were many sided, including coastal Muslim and non-Muslim Malays, interior tribesmen, plus Chinese and Indians. Independent political groups were unable to compete effectively with the Alliance coalition organization.

The Status of Brunei

The Sultanate of Brunei was a special case. The British decision to turn over to the ruling Sultan the administration of the tiny oil-wealthy colony in 1958–59 caused more serious deterioration of government services than had been anticipated. The changes affected adversely the five-year National Development Program previously initiated under British direction. School construction and vocational training programs ran aground, as did road building, housing, market development, and health clinics. The money was available, for the sultan's government had meanwhile invested some $300 million abroad and continued to enjoy handsome profits from oil. What was lacking in Brunei was efficient governmental performance and the stimulation of popular economic incentives. The promised hospitals failed to materialize; newly opened lands were not readily accessible, and potential settlers often could not even find out how to apply for access. The occupants of new houses and recently opened lands, as well as the incumbents in new jobs, were more or less alienated socially and vocationally. High school graduates went jobless, and most of the overseas graduates found little demand for their services upon their return. The sultan's treasury could provide jet planes for his personal use, along with electricity, water services, radio programs, and sewing machines for some of the people, but all of it on a very limited scale.

The political modernization effort in Brunei started off with the promulgation of a constitution in 1959, which provided for the election of sixteen of the thirty-three-member Legislative Council. The sultan made no serious effort to develop an official party, but the economic stakes in the country were too high to be neglected by outsiders. Into this political vacuum entered the Ra'ayat party, led by an ambitious Arab-born native of Labuan, a promoter named A. M. Azahari, who developed supporting connections in both Indonesia and the Philippines.

In the absence of serious political competition, Azahari promised everything to indigenous malcontents. He denounced British colonialism, feudal privilege, Chinese capitalists, Malayan interference, and modernization generally. He advocated nationalism, socialization of oil properties, encouragement of Islam and pilgrimages to Mecca, and an end to vice. He also promised the restoration of the once-extensive powers of the Brunei sultan over neighboring Sarawak and Sabah. Azahari's Ra'ayat party won all sixteen of the elected seats in the local Legislative Council. Meanwhile, the disturbed sultan opted for union with Malaysia and asked for protection by British troops and police. An armed rebellion broke out in December 1962 at the instigation of Azahari, who was apparently intent on capturing the person of the sultan himself. It collapsed two weeks later with the arrival of a British commissioner and a few thousand Gurkha and Highlander troops. Azahari fled first to Manila and later to Indonesia, where he posed as prime minister in exile of Kalimantan Utara. The rescued sultan built new barracks for the Nepalese and Royal Brunei regiments and decided not to join Malaysia after all. He did not want to share his lucrative oil income, especially in view of the newly successful drillings of the Shell Oil Company. He also resented being denied equal political status with the sultans of Malaya proper.[26]

The abortive Brunei rebellion was significant beyond the narrow limits of its intrinsic importance. It demonstrated the variety of problems to be encountered during the process of liquidating colonial controls. The Indonesian government and Communist party (PKI) leadership supplied some training services and arms for the hard core rebel recruits for Azahari's "peoples revolution against colonialism". The locally-enlisted Brunei recruits had little understanding of the objectives of the subversionary effort, and most of them surrendered promptly when the British commissioner arrived. Azahari, posing as heir of the deceased sultan of Sulu, had also, as explained in chapter IV, cultivated tentative and unofficial connections in the Philippines, where Communist instigation was lacking but where politicians had acquired stock in his fictitious Kiram Corporation. Nicasio Osmeña, Azahari's principal legal backer, apparently hoped that his client could collect some ten million pounds sterling in liquidation of the alleged claims of the former sultan, who in the 1870s had signed the original rental agreement with the British Company of North Borneo. When the Philippines government later took over the negotiation, the Sabah annexation question emerged.[27]

Even if the sultan of Brunei had not changed his mind about joining Malaysia, the derailment of the Brunei experiment in constitutional government would have necessitated postponement. Indonesian officials did not make good their promise of armed help to the exiled Azahari, but the threat was sufficiently disturbing to both Sarawak and Sabah to ensure election victories in favor of Malaysian affiliation in both states. Within Brunei, the basic problems of modernization remained undefined, much less realized. Economic privation was not widespread, and the people paid no taxes. Political discontent, if present, found no avenue for expression. Despite the negative reaction to the Azahari fiasco in neighboring Borneo states, anti-Malayan sentiment persisted.[28]

Malaysia and the Origins of Confrontation

Against the background of the Brunei rebellion and the elections in adjacent states favoring union with Malaysia, the negotiations for Union were completed with little haggling. Lord Cobbold's Borneo Commission of Inquiry visited the region in 1961. The formulation of detailed arrangements by an Inter-Governmental Committee in 1962-63 was approved in a final round of negotiations held at London in June 1963. Meanwhile, Tengku Abdul Rahman and Lee Kuan Yew were struggling to conclude their own bilateral agreement. The contemporaneous action of the Maphilindo meeting in Manila accorded qualified approval of the Malaysian merger and seemed to afford opportunity for a settlement. The final remaining hurdle was the pro forma investigation by the United Nations team, which reached Borneo in late August to determine the wishes of the inhabitants themselves. Manila and Djakarta boycotted the investigation, ostensibly because the British organizers permitted only token representation (four observers each) of the two protesting governments. The visitors reported that hostile reactions against the Azahari escapade were still strong in both Sarawak and Sabah. They estimated that around one-third of the people approved the Malaysia scheme, while another third preferred it to accepting Indonesian or Philippines control. The final U.N. report was submitted on September 14. Legal arrangements for the merger were promptly completed two days later via the formal implementation of the prepared amendments to the Malay constitution.[29] Few of the authors anticipated the rough sailing which the newly launched craft would encounter.

The Commonwealth authors of the Malaysia merger were not fully aware of the political and psychological considerations involved in their decision as far as Sukarno and his government were concerned. Djakarta's protests of late 1962 and early 1963 had been discounted as face-saving rhetoric associated with the thoroughly discredited Azahari venture in Brunei. The strident character assumed by the anti-Malaysian challenge at the outset was also diluted somewhat by the July Maphilindo declaration. British sponsors anticipated that prompt action with respect to the matter could achieve a kind of fait accompli. Several weeks before the United Nations investigating team completed its report, London had scheduled publicly the actual date for implementing the merger.

What rankled most with Djakarta was Britain's brusque

165

initiative, disregarding Indonesia's basic concern that careful and considered attention be given to the wishes of the people directly involved. The Azahari election victory of 1962 probably raised Sukarno's hopes. National pride and personal face thus became important considerations both domestically and internationally. Sukarno's concurrent overt alignment with the so-called New Emergent Forces of Afro-Asia was associated with his commitment to make Indonesia the revolutionary arbiter of political developments in his part of the world. He denounced Abdul Rahman as partner to the neocolonialist conspiracy and therefore bereft of revolutionary credentials. The sheer effrontery of a Malaysian government allegedly representing only reactionary sultans and Chinese millionaires was unworthy of Sukarno's respect.[30]

As the third member of the Maphilindo group, the Philippines government also opposed Malaysia's creation. Manila was inclined to support Djakarta's challenge, but not to the point of encouraging armed confrontation and incurring possible outside intervention. President Macapagal revived the Azahari-Osmeña claim of 1962, arguing that the 1878 lease contract between the Sulu sultan and the British company would have to be liquidated before Britain's summary transfer of Sabah could become legally valid. Filipinos believed that they had a valid legal complaint. In addition, the timber and commercial resources of various regions of Sabah adjacent to the Philippines were potentially attractive as was the probability of further oil discoveries along Borneo's east and west coasts adjacent to Sabah.[31]

It was not surprising that the emergence of possible international conflict, with some measure of Communist instigation attending the otherwise orderly liquidation of British colonial holdings in Borneo, became a matter of concern to the United States as well. On numerous occasions, American officials had attempted to generate increased regional cooperation, such as the formation of the Association of Asian States in 1961 and the Maphilindo conference itself in 1963. In January 1964, President Johnson sent Robert Kennedy on a mediatory mission to Tokyo, Kuala Lumpur, and Bangkok. Kennedy talked with Sukarno in person at Tokyo and obtained his qualified agreement to seek a settlement over Malaysia by direct consultations. At Kuala Lumpur, Kennedy persuaded the Tengku to participate in three-cornered negotiations to be held at Bangkok under Thai auspices, provided that assurances were given concerning the territorial integrity and independence of Malaysia. Under further prodding from Kennedy, Sukarno agreed to a cease-fire for all regular Indonesian forces involved in the Confrontation, but he made no commitment to restrain the activities of irregular guerrilla forces operating along Malaysia's borders. The later crucial conversations at Bangkok ran aground on Sukarno's insistence that armed operations must continue until a political settlement acceptable to Indonesia was found. In a separate bilateral conference held at Phnom Penh, Abdul Rahman and Macapagal reached near agreement over the Sabah issue, only to have Manila in the end refuse to break with Djakarta. Hopes for a cease-fire evaporated in March 1964[32].

The same basic disagreement defeated efforts to find a solution at a later Tokyo meeting, sponsored by Japan, Pakistan, Thailand, and the Philippines. In the fall of 1964, Malaysia's complaint of aggression was taken before the Security Council of the United Nations. The vote of nine to two in Malaysia's favor was negated by the Soviet veto. Regional and world opinion thus failed to halt the controversy. When the United Nations later proceeded to elect Malaysia to the seat in the Security Council vacated by Czechoslovakia, in accordance with a compromise decision reached in 1963, Indonesia withdrew from the organization in angry protest.[33]

The Course of Confrontation

Confrontation started officially with Djakarta's flat rejection of the September 14 report of the United Nations committee. Indonesia's effort was essentially propagandist and subversive in character, rather than military. Sukarno boasted repeatedly that he would destroy the new state, but his government's overt moves were confined to desultory raids of "volunteers" across the southernmost borders of Sarawak, plus periodic commando raids along the shores of Malaya proper. Communist guerrilla elements from Indonesian Kalimantan also made contacts with dissident Sarawak Chinese. Indonesia leaders preferred not to precipitate international repercussions by staging a determined attack. Hostilities were contained by Malaysia's intensified police activities in Sarawak, and by the introduction of fifty thousand Gurkha and British land forces. Seventy warships undertook surveillance of Malaysian coasts.[34]

For Malaysia, the Confrontation threat was domestic as well as international. If the attack had been relentlessly pushed regardless of risk or cost, Indonesia's population of one hundred million could have swamped the eight-million, communally divided population of Malaysia. Britain's available military and naval resources were limited. The situation took a particularly serious turn in July and later in September 1964, when communal riots developed in Singapore. The principal antagonists were the pro-Indonesian Raya Malay group, possibly subsidized by Djakarta, and the equally radical pro-Communist Chinese.[35] The peace that was arranged was precarious at best.

Indonesia's propaganda appeal was essentially pan-Malay and anti-Chinese, but it varied according to the source. Communist PKI agitators wanted to unite all Malays in a rejection of colonial domination and Chinese capitalism. The Indonesian army, on the other hand, hoped to establish a bulwark against threatened Chinese Communist control over the strategic southern shores of the South China Sea. An Indonesia Raya was the only common objective. Sukarno himself exploited both approaches to justify his essential concern to enhance national prestige and his personal role as a revolutionary leader.[36]

The Malayan reaction was also mixed. A merger with Chinese-dominated Singapore and largely non-Muslim Borneo peoples carried limited attraction in terms of national identity on both sides of the South China Sea. Some of the highly partisan anti-Chinese Malays responded sympathetically to Sukarno's appeal for an Indonesia Raya. On the Borneo side, few indigenous Malays and Dyaks and none of the Chinese entertained any patriotic affinity for mainland Malaya. It was the actual Confrontation threat itself that eventually solidified majority Malay opinion and enabled the Alliance government party to win an overwhelming election victory in 1964. The party obtained 123 seats against a total opposition of 36. In 1965, anti-Sukarno rallies sponsored by the government began to attract positive popular support. Malaysian nationalism still had a long way to go.[37]

In contrast to Indonesia's tentative effort to promote revolution within Malaysia, the Philippines claim to North Borneo was based in part on political considerations relating to the Muslim population of the southern islands. Also involved was the aforementioned desire to extort a British monetary settlement of the residual claims advanced by the alleged descendants of the Sultan of Sulu of the 1870s. Meanwhile, the very stridency of Sukarno's aggressive challenge called for the Philippines to try to keep pace. The apparent dislike of both the Indonesians and the mainland Malays by North Borneo peoples might possibly find eventual expression in Manila's favor. In any case, it was difficult to withdraw in the face of Britain's contemptuous rejection of the Philippines claim.[37]

How Malaysia Fared, 1963-66

Sabah. Because the threat of Confrontation was less serious in Sabah than elsewhere, northernmost Borneo registered uninterrupted economic gains following its inclusion in Malaysia. For the first several years, most of the upper-level administrative posts continued to be occupied by experienced British officials and by transferred personnel from Malaya proper. As of 1964, only five of twenty such posts were locally filled. Administratively Sabah thus continued to operate very much under colonial patterns. British Commonwealth funds were used to complete the rebuilding of the west coast city of Jesselton, where two-thirds of the population of twenty-two thousand were Chinese. Another town reborn under similar auspices was Sandakan on the eastern coast. Construction of a road connecting the two cities was planned in an effort to open up valuable new lands for rubber estates, agriculture, and timber extraction. Less effectively administered was the copra-smuggling port of Tawau (70 percent Chinese), located further down the eastern coast near the Indonesian border. From Tawau, consumer goods were smuggled into Indonesia (partly by sea-going Buginese) and cigarettes into the Philippines. High-powered motor boats were employed to outrun the competing Moro pirates and the Filipino police.[39]

Moderate progress was made in terms of economics and trade. The easily accessible eastern coast of Sabah fronted on the Philippines, and northward toward Taiwan and Japan. The output potential was mainly in timber, palm oil, and minerals. With the aid of Filipino laborers, Chinese lumbermen expanded hardwood and other forest products by 75 percent from 1964 to 1967. Murut tribesmen who were moved from Sabah's mountainous hinterland to arable sections along the eastern coast (some fifty thousand families all told) adjusted badly, so that food production continued to lag some 40 percent behind local needs. The serious shortage of labor, especially in the skilled category, was not likely to be filled by unwelcome mainland Malays. Sabah's major untapped mineral resources, oil, copper, chrome, and bauxite related not at all to the commerce of the remotely accessible Malaysia ports facing on the Bay of Bengal.[40]

Sarawak. Sarawak experienced an even more serious trained labor shortage than Sabah, particularly in areas of port services and transportation, but it progressed more rapidly politically and governmentally than did its northern neighbor. When faced by the immediate threat of Indonesian Confrontation, opposition to Malaysia faded. The leadership of the Ibans and coastal Dyaks became firmly committed to affiliation with the Federation, although economic union with Singapore would have been preferred, along with British security guarantees. Even the far-from-homogeneous anti-Alliance Sarawak United Peoples party (mainly Chinese) adopted the role of the loyal opposition, despite the fact that it was Communist infiltrated. Alliance party propaganda was directed toward the Ibans and Dyaks rather than toward the Chinese. The latter were divided by language groupings, vocational specialties, differing ideological commitments, and wide variations of wealth and poverty. Most of the Sarawak ministries continued to be operated by experienced Malayan officials, but local political leadership was gradually taking over. The three indigenous elements of the Alliance grouping competed among themselves in the Sarawak election appeals, preferring to limit their cooperation to the postelection division of the spoils of victory. Observable trends suggested the prospect of increasing resistance to Alliance control, but in any case, the Sarawak body politic was giving evidence of signs of life.[41]

Singapore

The ensuing two-year political association between Malaya and Singapore was marred by an increasing measure of acrimony and distrust. Both sides were to blame. The UMNO section of the Alliance party, from the very outset, intervened in Singapore politics in support of Malay minority rights, while Lee Kuan Yew attacked with increasing vigor the pretensions of the Malayan Chinese Association (MCA) to represent the Chinese residents of all Malaysia, and its presumed role as custodian of patronage and jobs for the total Chinese community. Lee's particular Chinese antagonist was the president of the MCA, who also served as minister of finance in the Tengku's Alliance government. Subsequently, Lee also denounced the UMNO leadership within the Alliance as a privileged Malayan elite bent on exploiting the special constitutional rights of the community but unconcerned for the well-being of the Malay population generally.[42]

Premier Lee's clever argumentative approach scored high in debating points, but it lacked any realistic appreciation of what was politically wise or feasible. Whereas the Tengku tried to curb acrimonious political disputation, Lee

171

insisted that free debate was the essence of democracy. He called for a Malaysian Malaysia, operating along noncommunal lines and concerned for the interests of the mass of the population, regardless of ethnic affiliation, rather than the wealthy and elite elements alone. He challenged the Malays' claim for special privileges based on indigenous status by contending that the ancestors of most of them had actually migrated to the peninsula in early modern times, just as the Chinese had done in the nineteenth century. The Malay reaction was understandably angry.

Lee's first unsuccessful venture into Malaysian politics came in the elections of April 1964. The PAP elected only one candidate. The opposing MCA campaign was well financed and able to take advantage of the overpowering Alliance party issue of opposition to the Indonesian Confrontation. When racial rioting based essentially on Malay resentment of Chinese rule in Singapore broke out in August 1964, both Lee and the Tengku pretended that Indonesia instigation was to blame. The truce initiated by the two leaders shortly thereafter in an effort to curb racial antagonism lasted little more than a month before it was destroyed by increasing UMNO political intrusion into Singapore politics. Lee's strident advocacy of Malaysian Malaysia, although ostensibly noncommunal carried infuriating implications to all Malays that Chinese elements aspired to dominate the political and governmental spheres as well as the economic. Lee's primary objective was for his PAP to replace the MCA as the Chinese partner in the Alliance. The Tengku dared not risk such a gamble.[43]

Political and communal relations deteriorated steadily during 1965. Recriminations within the Federal Parliament reached the point of no return in May 1965, when the PAP spokesman proposed an amendment to the proposed reply to an address from the throne, suggesting that the Alliance coalition no longer represented any identifiable major constituency. This action precipitated a torrent of verbal abuse that ended any hope of accommodation between Kuala Lumpur and Singapore as long as Lee continued as premier. UMNO partisans advocated the arrest of the Singapore pre-

172

mier himself, but the Federation police limited repressive action to the expulsion of several allegedly subversive journalists. The Malaysian Solidarity Convention, which was convened shortly thereafter by the PAP, included several Chinese representatives from two Leftist groups in Malaya proper and two from Sarawak as well.[44]

The Solidarity approach, although theoretically concerned to bridge over ethnic differences, actually challenged Malay communalism and therefore fanned partisan hostility. Lee's vigorous advocacy of a democratic socialist basis for political alignments, emphasizing class differences rather than ethnic balancing, stimulated sharp ideological as well as personal antagonism to him within the Alliance camp.[45]

The Separation of Singapore

Under the developing circumstances, Premier Tengku Abdul Rahman decided in early August 1965 that Malaysia's political association with Singapore had to end. The forbidding alternatives were, on the one hand, to suppress the political activities of Singapore's PAP or those of the ultra nationalist Malay spokesmen, on the other, as a means of avoiding communal strife. The urgent consideration that had prompted the union with Singapore in 1962-63—namely, the definite threat of a Communist takeover in the entrepôt government—had largely faded by 1965. Malaysia now had less to fear politically from an independent Singapore than from the meddlesome interference of Lee Kuan Yew and his PAP followers. The Tengku rebuffed partisan demands that he arrest Lee, but became convinced that separation was the only way to avoid imminent bloodshed. The decision was announced on August 9, following Rahman's return from a prolonged period of hospitalization in London and after several days of communication with the Singapore authorities. Lee gave pained and reluctant consent, issuing a face-saving declaration of independence on the same day. Neither the British nor the Borneo representatives were consulted, aside from being informed of the impending action only a day or two before August 9.[46]

173

The PAP-Alliance rift ran so deep politically that it prevented giving serious attention to continued economic cooperation, which both sides had agreed at the time of separation was urgently important. Notable exceptions were the continued joint operation of the Malaysian Airways and the cooperative taxation of companies doing business in both states. Malaysia needed Singapore as a trade outlet because Port Swettenham and Penang were unable to handle essential commercial and banking services. Singapore's potential industrial development, on the other hand, depended in large measure on continued access to Malayan markets, raw material resources, and labor and water supplies. Neither party could make good the income derived from British defense installations, which were due to be closed down in the early 1970s, nor could they command the tax revenues needed for their separate defenses.[47]

Malaysia's communal problem continued to be serious because the difficulties to which Lee had called attention defied his own solutions and were destined to persist. The Tengku's rivals within his own UMNO, not to mention the partisan Islamic factions, were prepared to resort to riotous violence, as had been done at Singapore in 1964, to counter any political presumption on the part of the Chinese.[48] The years following the separation witnessed, therefore, the virtual repudiation of the promises of cooperation contained in the 1965 agreement covering both defense matters and economic relations. Communal emotion precluded rational discussion of even the elemental necessities. Reciprocal restrictions on passage of personnel across the Johore causeway, which were imposed periodically, actually halted daily ingress and egress.[49]

Fortunately for both Malaysian protagonists, the easing of Indonesia's Confrontation pressure started less than two months after their separation. The occasion was the October 1, 1965, coup of dissident military elements against the Indonesian High Army Command, staged with the support if not the instigation of the PKI leadership. With Sukarno eventually pushed aside, the successor Djakarta regime moved to recognize Singapore's independence in a desperately needed step to improve Indonesia's economic plight. By April 1966 Foreign Minister Malik had arranged to meet the Tengku at neutral Bangkok for peace negotiations. Premier Lee was not consulted.[50]

The negotiations involved concessions from both sides. The Tengku agreed to Djakarta's face-saving demand that the peoples of Sarawak be afforded an early opportunity to reconsider in a free election their 1963 decision to join Malaysia. He demanded, in return, that Indonesia's previous resumption of diplomatic and trade relations with Singapore should not involve any political or other form of collaboration that would be inimical to the security of mainland states of the Federation. The final peace agreement was signed on August 11, 1966. The Borneo states went along reluctantly; Sarawak regretted the exclusion of Singapore, where its foreign trade connections inevitably centered; and Sabah's leadership talked about reexamining the basic terms of federation. On the occasion of local elections in 1967, rival elements of the Sabah Alliance combination fell apart, amid quarreling over personal rivalries and states-rights claims. Brunei staged its separate Legislative Council elections and continued to remain politically aloof from Malaysia. The country weathered the storm, but basic problems still awaited solution.[51]

Malaysia after 1966: Leadership and Tone

The key person in the government of Malaysia after 1963 was Premier Tengku Abdul Rahman, who owed more to his native intelligence, to his English education in law, and to his reputation as a realistic pragmatist than he did to his minor princely rank. He was the cosmopolitan fourth son of the sixth wife of the sultan of Kedah. His mother was of Siamese-Burmese descent. His first wife was Chinese, as were two of his adopted children. Prior to World War II, he had attained the rank of district officer in the Kedah civil service, and as such he played a responsible role during the course of the Japanese occupation. His political performance as leader of the United Malay Nationalist Organization (UMNO) after 1951 and as negotiator of independence in 1957 was ably done. He had the additional advantage of being acquainted with both East and West in connection with the modernization program. He lacked oratorical skill and an imposing personal presence, but nevertheless maintained a close rapport with his people. The Tengku had a convivial personality; he was an enthusiastic golfer, socially relaxed, culturally interested, and religiously devout. He probably lost little sleep over his governing problems.[52]

Tun Abdul Razak, the deputy premier, was, by comparison, a commoner born in backward Pahang Province. He was less impressive personally than the Tengku but more popular among the Malay people. As minister of defense and minister of rural development, he had demonstrated substantial administrative capacity. No opposition leaders were able to match the influence exerted by these two UMNO personalities, even though critics accused their followers of being power hungry, capitalist minded, feudalistic, and communal in outlook.[53]

A surge of Malayan self-confidence developed in Kuala Lumpur following exclusion and virtual isolation of troublemaking Singapore and the collapse of Indonesia's Confrontation. Lee Kuan Yew had been put in his place; the enemy Sukarno was eliminated politically. Realization of the Maphilindo ideal awaited only the settlement of the Philippines dispute over Sabah. President Johnson's visit to Malaya in October 1967, accompanied by World Bank experts, added to the sense of pride and self-esteem. Rural development within the *kompongs* was making substantial progress, with several major barriers cleared away.

Political Problems after 1965

Following the exclusion of Singapore from Malaysia, a fairly close counterpart of Lee Kuan Yew's Political Action party appeared in Malaya proper under the name of the Democratic Action party. It was led by Devon Mair, a clever Indian politician of Kerala extraction who was reportedly a one-time Communist. The DAP advocated moderately Leftist but noncommunal policies akin to those of the PAP, including a neutralist foreign policy, neither anti-Communist nor anti-China. Malays generally resented the aggressive stance of the DAP, accusing its Chinese and Indian leaders of cultural arrogance and contempt for the asserted primacy of the Malayan language, politics, and religion.

Partisan Malay sentiment meanwhile accorded increasing support for the Pan-Malay Islamic party (PMIP), which enjoyed its principal following in the western provinces. Majority opinion in Malaya refused to follow the Tengku in his rational defense of the use of English in law courts, in the university, and in the commercial realm generally.[54] Nationalist spokesmen tended to accuse persisting British influence of perpetuating sympathetic concern for the rights of alien elements of the population who had been accorded entry in colonial times. Feelings of frustration affected youthful intellectuals of various ethnic backgrounds. Because the number of new jobs did not keep pace with the school-leaving group (aged fifteen to twenty-four), both youthful Malays and Chinese were critical of the Alliance party compromise between MCA capitalists and UMNO conservatives. Both groups were charged with being concerned mainly about creating and serving the interests of a small number of Malay entrepreneurs. Frustrated individuals either tended to abandon politics entirely or simply to proceed down the dead-end road toward racial conflict.

The expansion of educational opportunities profited little the poorer Chinese and Indian youth or the sons of Malay peasant-fishermen. Vernacular schools in the non-Malay languages could qualify for state subsidies only if they followed the syllabus prescribed by the government requiring the Malay language as a compulsory subject. At the secondary level, both Malay and English languages were required. At the University lelvel, English survived during the sixties, partly because the essential books were in English and the language was a prerequisite for overseas training. As of 1967, Chinese and Indian students earned

177

78 percent of the University degrees and made up from 90 to 95 percent of those studying overseas. Criticism centered on the dominant role which aliens played at the University of Malaya, as well as in the professional and technical aspects of government employment. In 1967 the government began to review exit permits for study abroad, with a view to encouraging greater Malay participation.[55]

Alliance party rule continued after 1965 more by reason of the absence of any unified opposition than because of meritorious performance. Less than 10 percent of party campaign revenues came from actual party members; the rest came from well-to-do Chinese and Indian sources and from assessments levied on the salaries of elected candidates.[56]

Parliament maintained the rules of decorum derived from polite British standards, but the government gave scant attention to opposition views, which admittedly were often fragmented and inarticulate. Reform proposals designed to relieve particular hardships and injustices usually started a chain reaction of claims and counterclaims, with debates colored by emotional overtones.[57] Expressions of sharp dissent made outside of Parliament were regarded as provocative of disorder and were therefore subject to police suppression. The by-elections of 1965 reflected defections from Alliance support by reason of communal sensitivity on both sides, plus increasingly virulent criticism of the misconduct of party officials.[58]

Serious trouble developed in late 1967. Devaluation of the Malayan currency in November triggered rioting by Chinese Labor party personnel in Penang, and the disorder spread quickly to adjacent areas of the mainland. An essential cause was the continuing Chinese distrust of the government's policies, which perpetuated their handicaps as second-class citizens. The Penang police stood firm; twenty-four non-Malay Labor party leaders were arrested and held prisoner without trial. But the government refused to employ the same degree of severity against excessive expressions of Malay nationalism by the Pan-Malay Islamic party, which were exhibited widely in the northeastern states of the Federation.

Communist agitators and secret society leaders were only peripherally responsible for the unrest. Public resentment was reflected in the refusal of cinema audiences in Penang to respond to the playing of the Malaysian national anthem. Particularly disturbing was the ease with which seemingly peaceful situations could erupt into violence. When trouble developed in Kedah and Selangor provinces over poor wages for rubber plantation workers, PMIP partisans attacked the Tengku for not insisting on the immediate implementation of the exclusive use of Malay as the national language. Few arrests were made, however. An informed observer commented: "Malaysia's future now hangs on whether the Alliance will have sufficient courage to hunt down the racialists with the same single-mindedness that it displayed in defeating the communists in the jungle." Moderates derived a measure of encouragement from the announcement by the sixty-four-year-old Tengku that he would postpone his planned retirement until after the 1969 elections.[59] But time was running out.

In terms of foreign policy, Malaysia's stance was heavily conditioned by the same factors of communal tension. The presence of an economically influential and politically dissident Chinese community incapable of being assimilated made relations with mainland China particularly sensitive. Fanatical Malay nationalism might drive resident Chinese into a second Communist-oriented rebellion. If a general war should ensue involving China, Malaysia would be far more vulnerable militarily than it had been in 1942. The Tengku flatly affirmed that Malaysia would simply surrender if faced with the threat of Great Power invasion. Except for frontier security relations, China would have more reason economically and ethnically to become involved in a future Communist-oriented rebellion in Malaya than it had demonstrated during the Vietnam civil war.

Despite the fact that Malaysia's historic, ideological, and political connections lay with the West, Kuala Lumpur's leadership by 1967 began to follow a more neutral course. With Commonwealth ties fading by reason of Britain's announced military withdrawal from Southeast Asia in the

179

early 1970s, and with America becoming disillusioned over the South Vietnam war, political adjustments seemed advisable.[60] In 1966 the USSR had agreed to purchase increasing amounts of Malayan rubber, and offered in exchange needed machinery and other industrial goods. China also provided an expanding market for quantities of surplus rubber. In May 1967 Kuala Lumpur further strengthened its diplomatic ties with Eastern Europe by establishing diplomatic relations with Yugoslavia and Rumania and with other Russian satellite states. Establishment of diplomatic relations with mainland China or with Taiwan was out of the question because of the domestic implications involved, but there was no inclination to discourage expanding trade with China.[61]

Independent Singapore

The traumatic experience of Singapore's exclusion from Malaysia at a time when British ties were fading and Indonesia's Confrontation was still threatening, bred initial discouragement and confusion. The fact that the people of Singapore enjoyed the highest living standard in all of Southeast Asia, constituted a psychological liability in view of the sharp juxtaposition of wealth and poverty. Confusion was evidenced when Left-wing labor unions struck because of the government's alleged "impolitic demands," at a time when sheer economic survival demanded the attraction of outside capital for industrial development. Union picketing and student demonstrations could be viewed by interested parties as heartening evidences of mass awakening, but for what tangible ends? One-half of the island's population was under twenty-one years of age. Nationalist enthusiasts who had been accustomed to attacking the British military installations as relics of colonialism began worrying about the loss of forty thousand jobs and the annual $85 million imperiled by Britain's impending withdrawal from military bases. Singapore's wage scale, relatively high by Asian standards, made difficult the competition with Hong Kong production, especially when large markets were not available nearby.

180

Old and new were confusedly mingled. The Chinese were adept at business, but also at secret societies and gangsterism. The Malays still valued leisure, and despondent Indian residents felt somewhat orphaned and downtrodden. The Raffles Hotel and the waterfront clubs persisted· in staging afternoon teas, holding cricket matches between the showers, and wearing jackets and ties for evening dinner. By contrast, the magnificent monument to World War II was dedicated to Chinese victims of the Japanese occupation.

That Singapore survived at all was a tribute not only to intelligent leadership and effective government management, but also to the capacity of the ordinary Chinese to make his way economically. The Chinese mastered useful educational skills, and usually espoused feasible political objectives in preference to idealized revolutionary goals.[62] Singapore's government moved to provide tax exemption for new industries as a means of providing jobs for the unemployed (13 percent as of 1965) and for the eight thousand annual youthful additions to the labor force. Budgetary innovations in 1966 called for no tax increases and provided liberal investment incentives. These included five tax-free years and limited tax liability for ten years thereafter for producers of items saleable overseas.[63]

When the needed increment in jobs failed to materialize in 1966, Premier Lee Kuan Yew inaugurated a vast program of high-rise apartment construction directed by a Housing Board Authority. The additions through 1967 amounted to some eighty-four thousand family units, and the continuing completion rate ran around twelve thousand flats per year. Each complex included a shopping center, school facilities, clinic, and telephones. Education with free tuition was made available to virtually all children of the island. A uniform school syllabus was followed, but language selection was made optional. Provision of health and hospital services reduced mortality rates, accompanied by family planning efforts and legalized abortions. Some of the youthful unemployed were absorbed into various forms of compulsory national service.[64]

Political opposition could offer few alternatives to compete with Lee's highly pragmatic efforts geared to economic survival. The Barisan Socialist party, for example, simply boycotted the 1964 Malaysian elections. Singapore representatives who attended the Havana Conference for Afro-Asian Solidarity thereafter garnered no useful ideas.[65] In mid-1967 the Socialists finally abandoned completely their thirteen-seat representation in the Parliament. The street demonstrations calculated to bring down Lee's Peoples Action party government encountered police suppression and repressive legislation. Parliamentary opposition collapsed. Meanwhile, Premier Lee retained Singapore's own membership in the Afro-Asian Organization, while continuing to back the presence of the United States in South Vietnam. He also advocated the promotion of diplomatic and trading relations with Eastern European countries, and the admission of Red China to the United Nations. He thus left the opposition little ground for maneuvering.[66] Even his failure to reach agreement on a common Malaysian-Singapore currency in July 1966 left the two monetary systems interchangeable on equal terms for the time being.

The question of the economic viability of Singapore could not be answered in the affirmative because of the continuing and cumulative problems to be faced. The 1965 unemployment figures of seventy thousand had increased to ninety thousand by 1968 in spite of the enormous expenditure in housing construction. Only seven thousand new jobs had been created annually, while ten to twelve thousand were needed. Production gains were registered in export items and in food; in fact, the output of eggs, chickens, ducks, and pigs so far outran the market that the government was forced to purchase some surpluses and put them into cold storage consignment in order to ease the glut. Forty-seven new factories were reported to be under construction in response to the tax reduction program, although manufactured items for export were still not in large supply.

A particularly encouraging economic development in 1967 was the growth of Japanese commercial and investment activity in Singapore. In that year, Japan's trade grew by 24 percent to surpass Britain as Singapore's largest non-

182

contiguous trading partner. Capital investment was mainly on a partnership basis, usually 51 percent Japanese. The planned drydock installation would accommodate ships of two hundred thousand tons, and a new fleet of small coastal craft would serve to complement ocean freighter services. The cost of such facilities was defrayed in part from Japanese reparations payments. Other Japanese investments in fixed assets and machinery promoted the production of steel plates and piping, nails, cables, batteries, tires, chemicals, plywood, veneers, and sugar. By the end of 1967, Japanese exports to Singapore exceeded imports from the island by three and a half times. The emerging version of the wartime Greater East Asia Coprosperity Sphere was capped by Japan's offers of access to staff-training programs in business management and technology.[67]

In spite of the fact that Britain's huge naval and air bases, which had provided more than one-fifth of Singapore's GNP, were scheduled to be abandoned in 1971, the United Kingdom continued to be economically important in Singapore. Large British trading companies and banks maintained headquarters at the city, where they still controlled much of Malaysia's overseas commercial operations. New British investments in fiberglass and petroleum were important. Prime Minister Lee Kuan Yew continued to attend the Commonwealth meetings at London, where his role clearly reflected an understanding concern that useful traditional relationships deserved to survive, even in the face of such difficult and devisive problems as that presented by Southern Rhodesia.[68] At a Ministerial Defense Conference at Kuala Lumpur in June 1968, Britain, Australia, and New Zealand all insisted that Singapore and Malaysia must endeavor to cooperate in defense matters if they expected Commonwealth assistance. If such cooperative efforts were forthcoming, Britain proposed to transfer its defense installations in both countries cost free. London also offered Singapore $120 million in economic aid in addition to the gift of the naval base and the three royal airports. It was also suggested that the naval ship-building facilities might be converted to civilian use by 1971. London subsequently promised to

183

install an experimental military airlift service east of Suez to contribute psychological, if not substantive, support in emergency situations.[69]

America's interest in the future status of Singapore's military facilities was also in evidence. Starting in 1968, the United States Navy began to investigate the possibility of formal arrangements for using former British naval and air force facilities on a contract basis, once they were turned over to Singapore. Such access would relieve pressure on American use of Okinawan and Philippines base facilities in the far Pacific. The Singapore government also enlisted the services of an American consulting firm to explore possibilities of developing an industrial complex for engineering and aerospace activities on the island.[70]

By the end of 1968, the statistical evidence of Singapore's economic progress was impressive. Foreign trade was up 11 percent over 1967, and cargo handling up 14 percent. Apart from the growing trade with Japan, much of the increment derived from dollar trade with Saigon and with China. Industrial production was up 30 percent from its previously low base. The new industrial center at Jurong involved an estimated hundred factories, plus a harbor, railway lines, shipyard, oil refinery, and steel-processing machinery. Much of the needed $225 million of capital allegedly came from Hong Kong, but American interests were represented by Allis Chalmers, International Minerals, Peoria Caterpillar works, Esso, and Mobil Oil. The Bank of America in early 1968 proposed making Singapore the headquarters of an Asian Currency Unit exchange program as a counterpart to the Euro-dollar system, in an effort to facilitate commercial transactions. The success of the Asian Currency Unit scheme would depend on the degree of cooperation extended by participating national currencies and the steady growth of trade volume.[71]

Nor did the Singapore authorities neglect the possibilities of increasing trade with the Communist bloc countries. Its trade with mainland China, for example, increased from $91 million in 1966 to $156 million in 1968. China purchased rubber and tin and sold a variety of its own manufactured products. Transactions were handled at Singapore via letters of credit issued by the Bank of China branch at Singapore. Local business interest in this growing China trade was significant enough to oblige the Singapore government to postpone on one occasion implementation of its threat to close the Bank of China for nonpayment of a fine imposed for operating without adequate reserves. Next to Hong Kong, Singapore was emerging as China's best source of foreign exchange.[72]

In conjunction with the arrival of the first Soviet ambassador to Singapore in January 1969, Russian warships cruising in the Indian Ocean were permitted to call at Singapore to use local bunkering services. Russian trawlers operating in the future from Black Sea bases were to be serviced at Singapore under contract. Soviet purchases of tin and rubber also suggested the prospect that Russian manufactures might find a future market outlet in the Singapore entrepôt. At the Chinese University of Nanyang, now government subsidized, ten Russian students were enrolled to study Mandarin Chinese, and Russian language facilities were provided for the training of local Chinese.[73] A visiting Russian delegation inspected the Nanyang language facilities in August 1968, following the conference of historians at Kuala Lumpur.

Racial Strife in Malaysia

The explosion of racial violence that followed the general elections of May 10, 1969, derived from tensions long present, but aggravated during the course of the hectic five-week election campaign. The basic factors of political and economic competition were strengthened by ethnic and cultural differences of long standing. Malays resented the alleged cultural arrogance of the Chinese, their superior economic status, and their educational aptitude. The Chinese on their side demanded political equality as the only available means of defending their economic future. The election contest was the occasion, rather than the cause, of the orgy of violence that began on May 13.

185

Recent changes in educational policy had contributed to communal friction. The Lower School Certificate examination, which had been used down to 1966 as a means of determining eligibility to enter middle school, had given a distinct advantage to English-educated Chinese and Indian candidates. Because proficiency in Malay was irrelevant to the examination, the test was accordingly discontinued in response to Malay demands. What was needed, constructively and from a detached point of view, was to make English instruction more accessible to Malay students to help them compete more effectively in the higher sectors of the economy and the government. Abolition of the LSC examination was actually part of the communal drive to establish Malay as the primary medium of instruction throughout the school system, including the University as well. Chinese opponents of the UMNO policy employed the language issue as a political weapon. They demanded the establishment of a Chinese language university on the pattern of the private Nanyang University of Singapore, which had been set up in 1956, quite oblivious to the fact that Nanyang had since been taken over by the Singapore government.[74] Frustrated Chinese youth generally became increasingly cynical toward the well-to-do MCA compromisers within the Alliance government, who allegedly put money interests above equality of political rights.

Events during the eighteen months previous to the election of May, 1969, demonstrated repeatedly that racial tensions were near the breaking point. The rioting in Penang in November 1967 had been generated in part by the devaluation of the Malayan dollar in response to London's action. Expressions of hostility were instigated by secret society agitators, with peripheral Communist agents trying their best to exploit the situation. PMIP partisans in nearby Kedah responded in kind to the Chinese riots.[75] A year later, in November 1968, the Alliance party government invoked the Internal Security Act, which dated from the Emergency crisis of the fifties, in order to curb Leftist political critics in Johore, Selangor (Kuala Lumpur), and Penang Island. Some 110 arrests were made for alleged violations of the Act. This episode contributed substantially to the emergence of the new Gerakan party, which was led by a variety of intellectuals, including Lim Chong-eu of Penang, the two Alatas brothers in Johore, and the respected Dr. Tan Chee Khoon of Kuala Lumpur. Gerakan leaders denounced the official revival of the "Communist bogey" issue as a weapon designed to punish political opponents and to divert attention from the exposure of governmental scandal and corruption.[76] The principal difference between the Gerakan party and other opponents of the MCA was the noncommunal emphasis of the Gerakans and their attack on the misuse of the Internal Security Act for political ends.

Observers of the Malaysian political scene three months before the election concluded that the well-financed Alliance party was in little danger of losing control, even though it advocated no positive issues. The party was in a strong position in Sabah, stood to lose a few seats in Malaya proper, and was in some trouble in Sarawak. In that state, the Alliance coalition had fragmented, with the complete defection of the Sarawak Nationalist party (SNAP), the partial defection of the Iban-centered Peseka party, and the appearance of the urban Chinese Leftist-oriented Sarawak United People's party, which directly challenged the debilitated Alliance grouping. But a political deal was still possible. At the time there seemed to be little prospect that the opposition parties of Western Malaysia, though growing stronger individually, could pool their efforts to end Alliance domination of the Assembly. The widest opposition appeal was enjoyed by the alien-sponsored Democratic Action party of Western Malaya, essentially anti-Alliance, but theoretically anticommunal and anti-Communist as well.[77]

As the election approached, it became apparent that the MCA was mounting no effective rejoinder to the severe criticism levied against it by Gerakan and DAP spokesmen. The Leftist Labor party of Penang, although officially boycotting the election, sympathized with the opposition. The UMNO countered the challenge by declaring that it could cooperate with no Chinese groups except the MCA, which

187

meant that Chinese who wanted to participate in the government would have to support the Alliance candidates. Those states that wished to have access to development funds from the center were also told that they would do well to back the Alliance election campaign. Any overt UMNO collaboration with the DAP, difficult in any case, would have opened the gates to devastating attacks from the partisan PMIP, while any contrary effort to organize an exclusively Malay government would damage race relations beyond repair. Time began to run out on the compromising Alliance arrangement.[78]

The West Malaysian elections, held on Saturday, May 10, produced an unanticipated polarization of sentiment at the expense of the middle-of-the-road Alliance party, especially so in the urban constituencies. Few observers had expected the party to retain its overwhelming eighty-nine-member Parliamentary majority of 1964, but not to the extent of losing twenty-three seats, mostly Chinese. Only 13 of the thirty-three MCA Alliance candidates were elected. Victory in Penang went to the Gerakan Peoples party, while the PMIP scored heavily in Kelantan, thus providing most of its twelve-member representation. Heavy inroads on Alliance majorities were made by the DAP in Perak and Selangor (Kuala Lumpur), reducing Alliance victories to narrow margins in both total votes and elected candidates. Two-thirds of the urban votes went to the Gerakan or DAP, who together won twenty-one seats, five of which came from constituencies previously represented by minor party incumbents; eight from the Alliance; and eight from older socialist groups that did not contest the election.

In a conventionally operated Parliamentary system, the 63 percent majority in Western Malaysia that the Alliance party maintained (66 of 104) would have provided a fairly comfortable governing majority, especially since the opposition was sharply fragmented. But control of constitutional alterations called for a two-thirds majority (or 70). By comparison, the DAP had 13 seats, the PMIP 12, and the Gerakan party 8. What was lacking at the center was the ability or the willingness of the UMNO leadership to heed the criticisms registered at the polls and to adjust its personnel and policies in order to reduce the growing dissatisfaction. The Tengku's reaction was very one sided. He blamed the MCA for permitting the victory of opposition candidates, who allegedly had won only by resorting to intimidation and blackmail. He later attributed the ensuing disorders to the instigation of Communists who were trying to overthrow the government. The long-term causes of political unrest were thus ignored.

As soon as urban election returns became available on Sunday, communal tensions began to mount, even though open rioting was some two days away. Particularly disturbing was the outcome in the Selangor state (Kuala Lumpur) elections, where the Alliance gained only fourteen of twenty-eight seats and could therefore anticipate difficulty in assuming control. The fear later proved groundless because four Gerakan members decided to remain neutral.[79]

The safeguards of the parliamentary system began to disintegrate on Monday, when Prime Minister Abdul Rahman declared that despite the rejection of the MCA by Chinese voters, no other Chinese-oriented party leadership would be allowed to participate in the government. He charged that the Chinese political opposition was in league with Communist agents for the promotion of common revolutionary objectives.[80] On Tuesday night, May 13, rioting began. It raged out of control for the better part of four days. Chinese shops and residences were burned and looted, and the mobs left more than 150 dead and uncounted victims maimed. Police plans to curb the prospective rioting proved to be too limited, too late, and badly directed. Unrestrained mayhem took over in an orgy of violence.[81]

Responsibility for arousing the wrath of the Malays was attributable in large measure to the activities of several Chinese student cliques within Kuala Lumpur. Clad in white shirts and tight trousers, and some of them carrying Mao's Little Red Books, the agitators invaded several Malay-occupied sections of Kuala Lumpur by car to vent their enthusiasm over the alleged Chinese election victory. The UMNO reaction was to recruit from peripheral neighborhoods angry Malay compatriots, acting presumably in self-defense, to stage a counterdemonstration parade to start on Monday evening. Clashes with the young Chinese agitators started approximately an hour before the scheduled time for the parade and defied all efforts at police control. What was lacking at this critical juncture was a serious effort on the part of UMNO leadership to reach some accomodation with respected representatives of the opposition Chinese. One such person was Dr. Tan Chee Khoon of the Kuala Lumpur branch of the Gerakan party, whose offer to cooperate to restore constitutional government was rejected.[82]

At the end of the four days of rioting, the UMNO leadership moved to establish arbitrary control. It forbade all political discussion and imposed a twenty-four hour curfew covering all West-coast communities. Tun Razak was designated to head the Emergency National Operations Council (NOC), which included a representative from both the MCA and MIC groups in the Alliance. Two MAC members and one Indian also agreed to join the new cabinet on a nonportfolio basis, although the body's authority for the time being was nil. Premier Tengku Abdul Rahman accepted the chairmanship of the new National Goodwill Committee, assigned the task of assisting pacification.[83]

Continuing tension produced a revival of communal rioting on June 28. Malay critics of the Alliance compromise arrangement first attacked the UMNO *in toto*, but later concentrated on the Tengku alone, demanding his resignation. Newspapers were obliged to suspend publication for an indefinite period.[84] Some slight improvement was in evidence by early July, after the Tengku's Goodwill Committee began to tour the several states in turn. The NOC also initiated job-training programs for the unemployed and set incentive awards for the encouragement of capital investment. Ostensibly, the training program was fashioned to serve the needs of the total community. Few Chinese and Indians accepted the government's program at face value, and many of the Malays also questioned Tun Razak's credibility. But the need for peace was urgent, and the situation quieted down. Razak's official explanation for the causes of the rioting still blamed Chinese accomplices of Communist agitators, but he also admitted some measure of Malay responsibility.[85] The effective government action was to forbid all public discussion of the basic problem of communal friction. The political price for avoiding another eruption of violence was high, but the net result was less forbidding than the alternative arbitrary imposition of military control, such as occurred elsewhere in Southeast Asia. Nearly two years elapsed before the postponed elections in Sabah and Sarawak were held and a semblance of parliamentary government was restored at Kuala Lumpur. The postriot story of Malaysia and Singapore will be described briefly in the concluding chapter.

1. J. M. Gullick, *Malaya* (London, 1963), pp. 164-73.

2. Robert O. Tilman, *Bureaucratic Transition in Malaya* (London, 1964), pp. 64-65.

3. R. S. Milne, *Government and Politics in Malaya* (Boston, 1967), pp. 124, 130-33, 237-47.

4. *Ibid.*, pp. 36-38; Gullick, *op. cit.*, p. 124. The Malayan political reform pattern was accelerated by eliminating the stage of appointive members of the Council and the period during which the Council's control over the selection of Cabinet members was confined to Ministries of minor importance only.

5. See Milne, *op. cit.*, pp. 38-42. The Emergency rebellion persisted legally until 1960. Similar emergency status was involved briefly in Singapore (1964), in Sarawak (1965), and in all Malaysia (1969).

6. Milne, *op. cit.*, pp. 87-95, 107-9.

7. *Ibid.*, pp. 43-7.

8. Gullick, *op. cit.*, pp. 187-96.

9. J. Norman Parmer, "Malaysia," in George M. Kahin, *Governments and Politics in Southeast Asia* (Ithaca, 1964), pp. 336-37.

10. See Gayl Ness, *Bureaucracy and Rural Development in Malaya* (Berkeley, 1967).

11. Gullick, *op. cit.*, 181-201; *FEER* January 6, 1966, pp. 644-46.

12. *FEER Yearbook for 1968*, pp. 239-39, 243-45.

13. *Ibid.*, pp. 234-36; *FEER*, December 9, 1965, pp. 464-65; *New York Times*, January 24, 1966.

14. Gullick, *op. cit.*, 181-86.

15. *Ibid.*, pp. 197-201.

16. See W. R. Roff, *The Origin of Malay Nationalism* (New Haven, 1967).

17. *Ibid.*, pp. 248-256.

18. Gordon P. Means "Malaysia—A New Federation in Southeast Asia" *Pacific Affairs* 36 (Summer, 1963), pp. 138-145.

19. Nancy McHenry Fletcher, *The Separation of Singapore from Malaysia* (Cornell Data Paper no. 73, 1969). pp. 12-22, 26-30.

20. Milne, *op. cit.*, pp. 49-60, 156-62.
21. Means, "Malaysia", *Pacific Affairs*, 36, pp. 146-150.
22. Milne, *op. cit.*, pp. 63-73.
23. Means, "Malaysia," *Pacific Affairs* 36, pp. 147-151.
24. W. A. Hanna, *The Formation of Malaysia* (New York, 1964), pp. 128-33.
25. *Ibid.*, pp. 133-38; Gordon Means, *Malaysian Politics* (New York, 1970), pp. 300-08.
26. *FEER*, September 19, 1968, pp. 556-82, article by Harvey Stockwin, "Venture Into Yesterday"; also Means, *op. cit.*, pp. 314-15.
27. Means, *op. cit.*, p. 315; *Pacific Affairs*, 36 (Spring, 1963), pp. 150-56.
28. Hanna *op. cit.*, pp. 139-51.
29. Means, *op. cit.*, pp. 315-16; Milne, *op. cit.*, pp. 64-8.
30. Hanna, *op. cit.*, pp. 1-3; Gunnar Myrdal, *Asian Drama: an Inquiry into the Poverty of Nations*, 3 vols. (New York, 1968). 1: pp. 218-20.
31. Parmer, *op, cit.*, p. 309; see also Means, *op. cit.*, p. 16.
32. Means, *op. cit.*, pp. 319-21.
33. Parmer, *op. cit.*, pp. 363-64; Hanna, *op. cit.*, pp. 1-3; Milne, *op. cit.*, pp. 190-97.
34. Anthony Short, "Confrontation in Sarawak," *FEER*, December 23, 1965, pp. 547-49.
35. Means. *op. cit.*, p. 343.
36. Hanna, *op. cit.*, pp. 7-14.
37. Means, *op. cit.*, pp. 335-45.
38. Myrdal, *op. cit.*, 1, pp. 217-18, note 1.
39. Milne, *op. cit.*, pp. 156-62; Hanna, *op. cit.*, pp. 52-54, 56-59.
40. Bob Reeco, "A Meaty Bone of Contention," *FEER*, November 28, 1968, pp. 486-89.
41. Robert O. Tilman, "The Sarawak Political Scene," *Pacific Affairs*, 37 (1964-65) pp. 412-26; see also *FEER Yearbook for 1968*, pp. 231-34.
42. Fletcher, *op. cit.*, pp. 35, 63-65, 72-75.
43. *Ibid.*, pp. 49-50, 62-65, 70. Malay resentment was aroused by the expropriation of residential areas intended for the erection of high-rise apartments for Chinese occupants. See also Means, *op. cit.*, pp. 335-43.
44. Fletcher, *op. cit.*, pp. 52-53, 60-65.
45. J. Norman Parmer, "Malaysia 1965," *Asian Survey* 6 (1966), 113-15; Milne, *op. cit.*, pp. 215-18.
46. Milne, pp. 217-18.
47. *FEER*, March 10, 1966, pp. 459-61; *ibid.*, March 24, 1966, pp. 554-55.
48. Milne, "Singapore's Exit from Malaysia," *Asian Survey* 6 (1966), pp. 174-84.
49. *FEER*, August 11, 1966, pp. 271-72.
50. *FEER*, June 2, 1966, pp. 431-34.
51. *New York Times*, April 17 and 20, 1966: *FEER*, March 18, 1966, pp. 519-21 and August 8, 1966, p. 299; *ibid.*, Annual Report for 1965-66.
52. Hanna, *op. cit.*, pp. 152-63.
53. Parmer, in Kahin, *Governments*, pp. 336-37.
54. Richard Allen, *Malaysia, Prospect and Retrospect* (New York, 1958), pp. 250-58; Means, *op. cit.*, pp. 353-56.
55. *FEER*. May 9, 1968, pp. 293-98.
56. Milne, "Political Finance in Southeast Asia," *Pacific Affairs* 41 (1968-69): 491-510. Even so, election expenses ran far below the level of costs prevalent in the Philippines.
57. Milne, *Government and Politics*, pp. 228-229.

58. Parmer, "Malaysia 1965," pp. 115-17.
59. *FEER*, December 7, 1967, pp. 425-27; *ibid.*, *1968 Yearbook*, pp. 233-34.
60. Tilman, *op. cit.*, pp. 64-66.
61. *FEER, 1968 Yearbook*, pp. 233-34.
62. Hanna, *op. cit.*, pp. 197-200, 205-6.
63. *New York Times*, January 20, 1967.
64. *FEER, 1968 Yearbook*, pp. 294-96.
65. *FEER*, February 3, 1966, "Singapore Politics."
66. *FEER, 1968 Yearbook*, pp. 291-94.
67. *FEER*, March 21, 1968, p. 547.
68. *New York Times*, September 8, 1966.
69. *FEER*, June 20, 1968, p. 602.
70. *New York Times*, July 6, 1969.
71. *Ibid.*, January 27, 1969.
72. *Ibid.*, May 26, 1969; *FEER*, May 29, 1969, p. 482.
73. *FEER*, January 23, 1969, p. 139.
74. Cynthia H. Enloe, "Issues and Integration in Malaya," *Pacific Affairs*, 41, (1968): 372-85.
75. *FEER*, January 18, 1968, pp. 106-111.
76. *Ibid.*, November 28, 1968, p. 467.
77. *Ibid.*, February 27, 1969, pp. 358-61; also March 27, 1969, p. 615.
78. *Ibid.*, April 17, 1969, pp. 122-3; *ibid.*, May 8, 1969, pp. 330, 333-34.
79. Felix Gagliano, *Communal Violence in Malaya 1969: the Political Aftermath* (Athens, Ohio, 1970), pp. 9-15.
80. Charles Mohr, "Malaysian Leader Orders Creation of Anti-Riot Force," *New York Times*, May 16, 1969, p. 3.
81. *FEER*, May 2 and June 5, 1969. pp. 435-38, 534.
82. *New York Times*, May 19, 1969; Gagliano, *op. cit.*, pp. 16-18.
83. *FEER*, May 22, 1969, pp. 435-38; *ibid.*, June 5, 1969, 534, 566-67; Gagliano, *op. cit.*, pp. 23-27.
84. *FEER*, May 29, 1969, pp. 479-81.
85. *New York Times*, May 18, 1969: Gagliano, *op. cit.*, pp. 23-37.

VII

INDEPENDENT BURMA, 1951–62: GOVERNMENTAL AND ECONOMIC PROBLEMS

Peculiarities of the Burma Situation

The problems faced by independent Burma differed in many respects from the situations in Thailand, the Philippines, and Malaysia. In contrast to Thailand, wartime Burma had suffered a larger measure of social and political demoralization, coupled with the wholesale destruction and dislocation of economic resources. Tens of thousands of former cultivators were surviving by minimal subsistence agriculture or were joining the many refugees in Rangoon and other protected urban centers. Most of Burma's prewar foreign workers, mainly Indians, had departed the country; Burma's new strata of youthful nationalist elite had displaced the prewar political leadership; and the steel frame of the colonial civil service had completely disappeared. Burma's precolonial symbols of governmental authority (the Royal Court, supreme *Hlutdaw* Council, provincial *Myowun* Governors, and township *myothugyi* headmen) were all lost beyond recall. The governing agencies were therefore dependent on the dubious popular acceptance of borrowed parliamentary institutions patterned on those of London. The dyarchy system, which had functioned from 1922 to 1936, had never been popular, and the tentative application of quasi-

194

responsible Cabinet rule prior to World War II had been very short-lived. Thailand faced no such problems in adjusting to post-war economic dislocation and an essentially alien governmental system.

As compared to the status of the independent Philippines, Burma's decision to leave the Commonwealth had denied to her the receipt of British assistance offered to restore productive facilities lost during the war. The United States supplied such aid to the Philippines down to 1959 under terms that, admittedly, somewhat limited the recipient's economic independence. Burma's experience of three years of revolutionary strife (1948 to 1951) also aggravated the country's economic problems. Premier Nu's government lacked access to adequate capital resources, functional patterns of trade relations with the outside world, and adequate defense facilities, all of which Manila enjoyed as a result of American assistance.

Burma differed from Malaysia in that indigenous hostility to Asian aliens was afforded unimpeded expression, with Indians providing the main target. Anti-foreigner sentiments were associated with anticolonialism and anticapitalism and thus tended to reinforce the government's affirmation of state control over economic matters. Although Burma's prewar experience with parliamentary institutions had been far more extensive than the degree of self-government enjoyed by colonial Malaya, the system as revived in Rangoon in 1951 had to function in a more complicated milieu. The ruling Burmans had to make adjustments not only with foreign residents, but also with alienated Karens, Shans, Kachins, Chins, and to some extent Mons and Arakanese. No convenient compromise was available on the Malaysian Alliance party model between varying elements of Burma's plural society. From the very outset, Burma's AFPFL nationalist leadership itself was far from complete agreement on political priorities, and the League itself began to disintegrate in 1957.

Like Malaya, Burma cherished the British tradition of civilian authority over the military. But when faced with the serious threat of civil strife in 1958, Burma's AFPFL felt obliged to submit to temporary control by an emergency army caretaker regime, which continued for the better part of a year and a half. The country was destined to revert to complete military dictatorship in early 1962.

The essential peculiarities of Burma's postwar situation can be characterized under several headings. Informed Burmese recognized the contribution that British technical and economic assistance could make in such areas as mining, oil, and timber, but they drew back from the risks involved. Acceptance of such aid could well mean the re-establishment of control and ownership of these essential operations by a number of powerful prewar colonial firms that had consistently opposed nationalist aspirations. Secondly, it was also apparent that any attempted accommodation to prewar legalities with respect to residence rights and property claims carried the awesome threat that hundreds of thousands of unwanted refugee Indians, including the wealthy Chettyar community moneylenders, would have to be permitted to return. The Chettyars held legal titles and mortgage claims to millions of acres of paddy land in Lower Burma. The fashioners of Burma's new constitution proposed to cancel such claims once and for all by a sweeping constitutional affirmation that the title to all real estate property lay with the state.

A third peculiarity of Burma's postwar policy involved the conviction entertained by progressive Socialist leaders that the mere rehabilitation of the prewar economy—which involved mainly the production of raw materials and food for export—would not suffice. These leaders were convinced by previous experience that Burma must make a substantial effort to achieve diversified industrial development. The painful shortages of manufactured goods experienced during the Japanese occupation had re-enforced the memory of privations endured during the depression of the early thirties. On both occasions, Burma's population had been victimized by adverse world-trade conditions that were entirely beyond their control. Burmans must learn to produce their essential needs. If alien entrepreneurs were to be denied control of such newly planned industry, economic development under state sponsorship and direction seemed to be the only feasible answer.

A fourth aspect of Burma's situation was the political and international implications of the experience of the forties: nationalist leaders were agreed that the country must never again become a theater of strife between contending world powers under conditions over which the victimized people could exercise no control. An ancient Burmese proverb affirmed that when elephants fight, the grass gets trampled. Burma's noninvolvement in the newly emerging Cold War called for persistent efforts to avoid alignment with the several contending forces, and in particular reaching a boundary accord with neighboring Communist China, with whom Burma shared a thousand-mile border. Peking must be given no excuse or provocation that might lead to future intervention or direct attack on Burma. Such a neutralist policy did not imply any cessation of government efforts to suppress the Communist rebel factions (some of whom found encouragement from China) or tolerance of outside intervention from any source.

Finally, Premier Nu and other culturally traditional Burmans were greatly concerned about curbing the social and religious demoralization that prevailed throughout the country. Such considerations could not easily be reconciled with the Socialist objective of achieving a nonexploitive utopian society. The basic premises behind Buddhism and Marxism were highly disparate. Buddhism counselled the "conquest of desire" in the context of a physical world that was considered to be both illusory and impermanent. Marxism by contrast posited a materialistic interpretation of history, based on Hegelian dialectic of continuing controversy involving control over the means of production of material goods.

These varying points of view did not clash head on because they operated in entirely different planes. Traditionalists emphasized the compelling need to revive the ethical and social values of Buddhism as a preliminary condition to pacification and social rehabilitation. Idealistic advocates of state socialism argued that their essential goal was to

197

end exploitation of Burman workers by capitalist employers, most of whom would be aliens, and thus make larger incomes available for Burman Buddhists to use in support of the monks and monastic establishments. In actuality, both goals proved very difficult to achieve. A large fraction of the Buddhist monkhood (*Sangha*) resisted the attempted imposition of disciplinary regulations and otherwise demonstrated a hopeless obscurantism. At the other pole of the dichotomy, an overburdened and ineffective governmental administrative system (whether operating under democratic or dictatorial direction) faltered distressingly in an effort to achieve a viable, socialized state.

The Principal Barriers to Planned Economic Development

The deterrents to hoped for industrial development were formidable. Essential fuel and ore requirements were simply not available in Burma, and long-staple cotton was lacking. Also absent were risk capital, business initiative, and a disciplined factory labor supply. Even where productive conditions were favorable domestically, comparable manufactured imports from abroad were usually found to be of better quality and cheaper. Added to such material difficulties was the innate conservatism of the predominantly peasant Burmese society. Villagers were reluctant to sacrifice the security of traditional social and cultural values for the possible gains of regimented economic endeavor, especially if monetary incentives were not explicitly provided. Social ties centered in family loyalties rather than around broader economic affiliations. The only enthusiastic advocates of state-sponsored economic development, therefore, were younger, literate Burmans who had acquired a superficial acquaintance with Marxist goals and were correspondingly impatient with religious traditionalism and petrified social custom.[1] Life habits and climate were more important barriers to thrift and dedicated industry than was Buddhism per se. Villagers simply preferred the more leisurely tempo of rural living, with its close family and community ties and its religiously saturated atmosphere, the latter more animist than Buddhist. But the problems of achieving economic accommodation to a more secularized industrial order were essentially social rather than religious.[2]

The case for government sponsorship and direction of economic development could be argued pro and con, but with little conclusive outcome. Private initiative could help meet short-term consumer needs, but alien elements would dominate the private sector if permitted full freedom. The basic goals of increased per-capita production and more equitable distribution of income were presumably less likely to clash under planned development than under a policy of laissez faire, but would the increase actually take place? Any successful channeling of forced savings to finance state-sponsored enterprises depended also on the capacity to absorb the friction generated by such efforts within the existing institutional structure. Available business and administrative experience could not be utilized as long as economic ends were persistently accorded second rank to political goals and ethnic prejudices. The general concentration of power in the hands of a largely self-appointed elite, such as Burma's AFPFL leadership, simply did not contribute to technical competence. Once they were committed to state operation of the economy, the Burmans found that the flexibility in administrative procedures needed to correct emerging problems was generally lacking. Those Burmans capable of mastering the essentials of engineering and business management usually suffered political interference, which added to their loss of cultural rapport with their own people.[3]

The cultural gap that developed between the traditionalist social milieu and the modernizing minority leadership carried especially deep-rooted negative implications in Burma. Implementation of drastic economic change called for popular recognition that governmental authority was legitimate and authentic and dedicated to desirable goals. Institutional structures must be strong enough to bridge personal rivalries and to contain such conflicts as could not be resolved. Imposition of arbitrary power could establish a semblance of order along traditionalist lines, but it could not inspire the confidence needed to elicit cooperation in creative change. A properly functioning civil society would have to be willing to accept the decisions of its rulers as authoritative and contributing to generally accepted goals. Where policies ran sharply counter to social inertia, the burden of proof had to rest with the advocates of substantive change. It is within the context of such complicating factors that the story of Burma's faltering efforts at democratic government and economic development under Premier Nu must be examined.

Burma's 1947 Constitution

Burma's new constitution vested executive authority, not in a popularly elected president, as in the Philippines, but in a prime minister responsible to a Chamber of Deputies, which was elected for a maximum term of four years. The Chamber could be dissolved and new elections called if the cabinet failed at any time to command majority support on a major legislative issue. The titular president was a figurehead selected on a rotating pattern by joint action of the two houses of Parliament; first a Shan, then a Burman, then a Karen, and so on. The president would exercise limited residual authority during interim periods between successive cabinets and serve as a watch dog against violation of constitutional provisions.

In contrast to the Philippines Senate, Burma's upper house, the Chamber of Nationalities, represented the several component states of the Union, which were quite disparate and ethnically delineated. Apart from the two-fifths representation of majority Burman elements, membership in the upper Chamber was allocated roughly in proportion to population. The Shan and Karen contingents each approximated one-fifth of the total, roughly equal to the combined Kachin, Chin, and Kaya (Karenni) representation.

The administrative structure of colonial Burma had been only partially Burmanized, so that few indigenous officials were capable of replacing the largely alien India and Burma civil service personnel. Premier Nu's cabinet was selected on the basis of political rather than administrative criteria, while few of the newly elevated Burmese officials below cabinet level had enjoyed previous experience in decision making. In terms of personnel, the government was severely handicapped.

The constitution as originally drafted under Thakin Aung San's direction was secular in character. It prohibited both clerical participation in political affairs and designation of Buddhism as the state religion. Equal citizenship rights were accorded only to indigenous residents within the Union. All citizens were guaranteed equality before the law; equal economic and educational opportunity; freedom of religion, speech, assembly, and political organization; plus the right of all adults to vote and to hold office. The judiciary was explicitly charged with protecting constitutional provisions and individual rights, free from exccutive or legislative interference.

State representation in the Chamber of Nationalities was copied in some respects from the Soviet pattern of minority participation. The several ethnic groupings elected to the lower Chamber were also designated to constitute their respective State Councils, which were accorded limited autonomy within the federal framework. Sessions staged by such councils must be presided over by governors or ministers appointed by the prime minister and removable by him. State Council legislation was subject to suspensive veto by the president of the Union and review by the Supreme Court on constitutional grounds. The separate state budgets were largely centrally controlled, since additional revenues beyond local tax collections could be allocated only by central authority. The constitution also provided that, after the first full decade of independence, the Shan and Kayah states, but not the other three, might opt for secession from the Union.[4]

Government under the AFPFL

Throughout the first decade of the independence period,

which witnessed two general elections, the Thakin-led Anti-Fascist People's Freedom League (AFPFL) dominated the Burman political scene. Cohesion within the League derived for the most part from the long-time personal association of its leadership in the nationalist struggle. The majority group had socialist leanings, although priorities varied and not all leaders were affiliated with the Socialist party. Rival leaders within the AFPFL generated personal support by sponsoring mass organizations composed of workers, peasants, or young people. Some politicians cultivated particular ethnic followings.

As the successor to Aung San and as the victorious leader over the multiple rebellions of 1948–50, Premier Nu became the perennial president of the League. His leadership was based on charismatic qualities, buttressed by his acknowledged concern for national welfare and honesty in government. Unfortunately, Nu was woefully deficient as an administrator, and also proved incapable of disciplining either his political entourage or his student following.

AFPFL victory in the first two general elections was a foregone conclusion. The initial voting was spread over a number of months in 1951 and 1952, as successive districts were cleared of rebel elements. The League won 147 of the 239 contested seats, with most of the remainder going to independent or to minority ethnic group candidates. The responsibility of the Parliament to the electorate was actually minimal, because the candidates were usually nonresidents nominated by the party, which also financed their campaigns. The outcome of the 1956 elections was almost identical, except that a Leftist National Unity Front opposition coalition emerged with a block of 48 seats.

Despite apparent party unity and the lack of outside challenges, by 1956 the AFPFL had begun to disintegrate. The government's performance in the areas of economic development and political pacification left much to be desired, and traditional friendships were giving way to tension and rivalry. Burma's political story after 1956 will be considered later.

The Context of Burma's Economic Problems[5]

The economic problems facing postwar Burma were difficult to solve. Enormous stretches of paddy land had reverted to semijungle; a large fraction of the cattle and buffalo population had died from rinderpest epidemics and other causes. The human death rate and incidence of illness had reached record proportions. All of the major British industries of prewar days were rendered inoperative by reason of scorched-earth measures performed by retreating armies. Virtually all river steamers had been destroyed, as had railway bridges, trackage, and rolling stock.

The departure of the Indians and their only fragmentary return after 1945 left no one to take the place of the Anglo-Indian railroad operators, the Chittagonian sailors who had manned the river steamers, and the Chettyar distributors of credits to the peasant cultivators. After the war, there were no more Indian freight handlers at the Rangoon docks and railway yards, and no more outcaste garbage collectors. Indian cloth merchants, civil servants, and professional people were also sorely missed.

Except for the dispossession of Chettyar holdings, Burma's leaders were not agreed as to what kind of tenure system or land redistribution policy would be desirable or feasible. The Land Nationalization Act of 1948, which abolished landlord holdings in excess of fifty acres, applied mainly to Lower Burma. In the north, traditional practice permitted borrowers to defray up to a three-year limit the accrued interest charges by granting lenders gratis access to land encumbered with debt. During wartime, cultivators in upper Burma had been able to take advantage of diversified cultivation opportunities in time of scarcity to pay off accumulated obligations in ever-cheaper currency. Land turnover was therefore minimal in the north, where village elders' jurisdiction continued to merit respect.[6]

Burma's youthful postwar nationalist leadership lacked both administrative and business training. Many were cata-

203

pulted into political and governmental roles that were far beyond their capacities. Members of the prewar Burma civil service who carried over into the independence period had previously been little more than routine operators who had little or no responsibility for making decisions. After 1951 they were subject to periodic intimidation by assertive local politicians connected with the ruling AFPFL. The secular-minded, pro-Marxist Thakins (Nu was a notable exception) lacked rapport with the Buddhist villagers, who had little appreciation of the government's grandiose schemes for economic development. The cultivators wanted credits to enable them to plant next year's paddy crop and a chance to sell their surplus rice for a good price.

Nu's government lacked authority as well as administrative capacity. It had barely survived the multiple rebellions of 1948–50. The symbols of traditional monarchial rule —a royal court and palace precincts, the white umbrella of divine monarchy, and the Sacred Sword—were all lacking. The deceased Thakin Aung San, rather than Nu, had been the hero of the independence struggle. Premier Nu's basic preoccupation from 1953 to 1956 was the revival of Buddhism. His convening of the Sixth Great Buddhist Council was coupled with construction of a costly cave assembly hall and an adjacent Peace Pagoda, where a tooth of Buddha, a gift from China, was enshrined. These acts had no relevance to economic development; Nu was trying to exploit traditional sanctions to bolster the dubious authority of his government as an agency of social integration, but there were many loose ends.

It was true, as critical American economic consultants affirmed during the 1950s, that traditional British-type colonial administration was ill suited to administer an ambitious program of state-directed economic development. But that was too much to expect. Colonial rulers had been effective economically: they had developed detailed land-settlement records; kept tax registers up to date; operated public works and health services; and maintained a disciplined hierarchy of officials extending down to village headmen, plus an effective police and court system. Such a program called for revival rather than denigration.

The emphasis on state sponsorship of industrial development was related in part to meeting consumer needs and in part to curbing the private industry sector, which alien Indians, Chinese, and possibly British would inevitably dominate. State sponsorship was conceived as a utopian ideal, and apologists insisted that socialization was completely compatible with democratic freedom and with traditional Buddhist values. A truly socialist society would end employer exploitation, provide popular health and education services, and promote general welfare and happiness. For the time being, however, the knowledgeable and motivated socialist leadership within the AFPFL government would have to make all the necessary decisions. The government did approve selected joint-venture projects operating on a basis of 60 percent state ownership, covering mainly oil and mining activities, but such efforts were intended to be short lived.

Expert Advice and Planning, 1951–53

The American-financed fashioners of Burma's economic development plans following the end of the rebellion were actually selected by Rangoon and responsible only to the Burman government. The costs for the initial two-year contract were borne by Washington's Technical Cooperation Administration. The group was headed by the engineering firm of Knappen, Tippetts, and Abbot, which was assisted by the Pierce Management Mining Engineers, with Robert R. Nathan Associates acting as economic consultants. Although no one questioned their technical competence, these advisory groups were unfamiliar with Burma's problems generally and with the motivating factors that conditioned the Burmese response to their proposals.

In early 1952, Knappen, Tippetts, and Abbot (KTA) submitted a preliminary report that set the tone of the entire operation. Sensing that various members of Premier Nu's Cabinet felt distrust and suspicion of American advice, the authors affirmed their sympathy for Burmese aspirations and urged the government and the people of Burma to undertake a bold and ambitious effort. In view of the fact that

205

the estimated 1951 per-capita productive output was only 60 percent as high as that of 1938, the proposed goal was to achieve by 1959 a 4 percent increase over the prewar per-capita standard. Anything less was characterized as not sufficiently attractive and challenging to generate maximum response. They affirmed that the requisite material resources were available and that the proposed achievement was definitely within the bounds of possibility.

The grounds for such optimism were argued in labored fashion. Investment needs for such a program over an eight-year period would total $1575 million. These funds could be mobilized if: (a) order was fully restored by 1954; (b) overseas rice sales of better than two million tons annually could continue at a minimum price of £ 50 per ton (the 1953 price was £ 60); (c) administrative agencies could be properly reorganized and motivated to meet new responsibilities. These were formidable conditions. Although it was assumed that the public sector would probably constitute two-thirds of the development program, the report suggested that private enterprise should also be encouraged, especially where efficiency of management was particularly important. Agriculture output must double, transportation improve, and selected new industries be established.[7] Presumably as an aspect of their deliberate shock treatment, the authors of the preliminary report denounced the routine colonial administration as being debilitating and "ill adapted to the requirements of a major economic effort."[8]

The official Burman reaction to the preliminary report was one of cautious approval. The secretary of the Ministry of National Planning, at an initial conference held at Nu's residence in March, 1952, argued that the people of Burma must rise to the challenge, even though he admitted that the investment proposals "may appear impractical and idealistic if judged in the light of the actual rate of investment and capital formation in the past."[9] With proper effort and new thinking, he said, he believed that the requisite administrative adjustments could be achieved and hindering bureaucratic inhibitions eliminated. The four proposed autonomous development corporations (for industry, minerals, agriculture,

206

and transportation) would, of course, have to be run on business principles.

Burma's Pyidawtha Program

Five months later at the widely attended *Pyidawtha* (Happy Land) Conference staged at Rangoon in August 1952, the official hesitancy had vanished. Premier Nu and other spokesmen enthusiastically acclaimed the projected socialist welfare state. Class exploitation would cease; the people's material needs would be met; and crime, disease, ignorance, and retrogression would be ended. An outmoded governmental system that had allegedly been designed to maintain foreign rule must be discarded so that bold decisions could be made, free from restricting departmental procedures. Risks would have to be taken, because indecision would itself entail excessive loss and wastage.[10]

The objectives espoused at the *Pyidawtha* Conference far exceeded the scope of the preliminary KTA report. They constituted a virtual inventory of Premier Nu's utopian aspirations, with little attention to implementation. Three million acres of paddy land (old and new) would be brought under production, and detailed attention would be paid to specialized aspects of peasant needs. A preparatory administrative structure for redistributing some nine million acres would also be set up, and provision would be made to expand housing, electricity, health, and lending services to such areas. Terms of tenure, purchase prices, and compensation payable to previous owners were not mentioned. *Pyidawtha* transportation plans stressed expanded river and air facilities, plus the restoration of prewar railway services (coupled with a plaintive plea for everyone to stop cheating). Urban housing plans were somewhat better formulated, but again with no estimates of magnitude or costs. Health needs were expertly outlined with WHO assistance, and education needs were similarly prepared with expert UNESCO help. Nu's favorite *Pyidawtha* project involved the allocation to each township unit of a sum amounting to $10,500 to spend as it pleased on locally selected material improvements. Local councils elected within the districts at various administrative levels would help administer the grants, with central government officials serving as executive agents. The tone of the *Pyidawtha* Conference was peasant oriented, exhortive, and promotional. It tried to generate popular understanding and acceptance of selected aspects of the proposed welfare state. Curiously omitted from the Conference agenda were references to the favorite promotional schemes of the socialists, including manufacturing and mining projects, electrical power installations, and water control systems. Forestry was also omitted.[11]

Premier Nu's romanticized version of the welfare state was actually more closely akin to his effort to promote religious revival than to any realistic program of planned economic development. The differences were deliberately drawn. Nu declared that Burmans could learn more from the Lord Buddha than from Karl Marx; his socialist associates in the cabinet, however, deplored the premier's lavish expenditures of effort and money on the construction of the artificial cave and the Peace Pagoda for the Sixth Great Buddhist Council. The thirty-million-*kyat* expenditure could obviously have been used productively elsewhere. Even in its essentially cultural sphere of increased piety or in creative scholarship, literature, and the arts, the two-year Buddhist Council extravaganza looked falteringly backward rather than forward.[12]

The comprehensive report of the KTA advisory group, submitted a year later in August, 1953, did nothing to dampen the excessive optimism of the *Pyidawtha* sponsors. It surmised that the entire cost of the development program could probably be financed from profits on rice exports alone, without having to resort to foreign borrowing as originally contemplated. The anticipated sale of some 2.3 million tons of grain per annum, even at somewhat reduced prices, would provide ample funds to finance the full development program.[13] As a further gesture of encouragement, the authors pointed out that the 7 percent of annual production sent abroad in colonial times as dividends to shareholders would henceforth remain in Burma as profits of state-owned corporations.

208

In its fairly obvious effort to maintain rapport with the government, the second KTA report avoided challenging excessive socialist predilections. The authors did cite the advantages to be realized from increased private sector participation in both housing construction and industrial operations, where market competition was needed to provide a spur to efficiency. They also underscored the importance of efficient management everywhere, calling for early restoration of law and order in the face of a discouraging outlook, and for reorganizing government operations. But on the whole, the authors found no reason to doubt that Burma should move forward with confidence in the execution of an ambitious development program.[14]

Implementation of Burma's Development Program

The government's proposal for state-sponsored industrialization included some sixty-five areas in all. Many of them were highly unrealistic because the essential conditions could never be met. Efficient management was not enlisted; order was not restored; incentives for peasant endeavors were not provided. Burma's total exports at the end of the 1950s were approximately only half of those of 1937.[15]

The unwisdom of espousing overambitious economic goals became evident in the preparation of the official budget for 1954-55, immediately following the formal acceptance of the KTA report. The proposed capital expenditure assignments were actually 50 percent higher than the liberal KTA recommendations (10.7 million *kyats* compared to 6.95 million), and continued to be one-third higher after being reduced in the final draft. The director of Nathan Associates later commented on the situation as follows: "Having worked for . . . two years to persuade the Government to adopt an ambitious and aggressive approach, the economic consultants were now obliged to try to persuade it not to go too fast. This first battle was lost."[16] So were most of the later ones.

At some point between the renewal of the Nathan Associates' contract at Burma's initiative and expense in August 1953, and the group's abrupt dismissal in late 1958, the question of the political and economic justification of their ineffective role became relevant. The average cost to the government per year for each one of the score of American consultants under hire was estimated at $45,000,[17] more than ten times the salary of a Burma cabinet member. In 1955 Rangoon tried to get the United States to buy enough of the country's surplus rice to cover the cost of continuing technical aid (some ten thousand tons), but Washington was not interested in sponsoring the project. A World Bank investigator reported at the time that the development program was being badly managed, that it was overambitious in its industrial objectives, and that it neglected adequately to promote agriculture, timber, and mining.[18]

The consultants' optimism of 1953 was brutally deflated by the collapse of the world rice market, starting in 1954–55. The standard price per ton dropped from a high of £60 to £44 in 1955, £36 in 1956, and £32 in 1959. Burma's unsold rice carry-over from the 1954 crop was 1.5 million tons, to which was added 1.8 millions more from the following year's output. The failure of the inefficient State Agricultural Marketing Board to collect and market the rice in some realistic fashion, coupled with the unavailability of storage facilities, resulted in the spoilage of extensive grain stocks. Under the circumstances, the government had no reason whatever to provide incentives for increased production. Collapsed prices and marketing failure thus largely demolished the unilateral financial basis on which the program's industrial expansion had been predicated.

Despite this serious setback, the American consultants continued publicly to exhort the government to move forward. In 1956 they privately considered advising against attempting anything more than minimal additions to investments in state industry, unless and until administrative standards were improved and order was restored countrywide. But in 1956, as previously, they repressed their misgivings and declared in somewhat equivocal fashion that pursuit of the second four-year program, as projected, was desirable if any real gains were to be achieved, and that the revised schedule was feasible if the necessary reforms were made.[19]

210

The consultants suggested more conservatively that the government encourage private investment in those economic spheres not reserved for the state, and that additional taxes be voted to counter increasing revenue deficits. Other proposals concerned the advantages of offering incentive increments in prices paid to peasants for improved quality paddy and for superior qualities of milled rice. For the time being it was to no avail. The net result of such tactics was to confuse whatever moderating influence may have been developing within high government circles.

The official apologist for the Nathan consultants, writing later in 1962, conceded that it would probably have been better if the first comprehensive report had been accompanied by an alternative and more modest proposal to be followed if the basic essentials for accomplishing the larger scheme could not be achieved.[20] The prevailing psychological climate was hostile to the salutary influence that visiting World Bank and other disinterested expert commentators subsequently tried to exert.

Premier Nu and Buddhist Revival

Premier Nu was easily the most popular political leader available within the ranks of the Thakin elite. His triumph over the multiple rebellions of 1948–50 had been a substantial government achievement. He was thoroughly Burman, a sincere Buddhist, an exemplar of traditional folklore wisdom, and free from venality.[21] He possessed both native intelligence and personal charm; his eloquence as an orator contributed much to his political influence. Nu obviously believed in democracy and also favored political and religious freedom.[22]

Premier Nu's personal limitations were nevertheless obvious. His political views were parochial, and his interest in religious values was cluttered by much traditional lore. His labored efforts to reconcile Buddhism with both communism and democracy, for example, reflected both wishful thinking and mental confusion. He was acutely aware

211

of social problems, but generally incapable of solving them; when he made right decisions, he often faltered badly in their execution. He became, after 1952, increasingly sensitive to criticism, often equating dissent with disloyalty. His wounded ego was involved in his eventual break with his long-time Thakin friends. In addition to his failure to coordinate efforts needed to realize domestic objectives, he made a number of dubious decisions in foreign aid categories, sometimes without consulting the ministers directly concerned.[23]

Nu's emphasis on Buddhist revival as a top government priority reflected his genuine social concern. Few Burmans could disagree with his affirmation that the teachings of the Lord Buddha could accomplish far more to heal Burma's distraught society than could the revolutionary counsels of Karl Marx. He insisted that reform would have to start with the restoration of discipline within the ranks of the Buddhist monastic community. All monks must eschew political activity, and disorderly members must be purged from the *Sangha*. Pseudomonk residents at many pagoda centers were known to be guilty of flagrant misconduct. They ignored the scriptural (*Vinaya*) rules of piety; they were also involved in alcoholism, robbery, and sex offenses.

Nu assigned the reforming task to his Ministry of Religion. It set up a hierarchy of ecclesiastical courts to enforce discipline and to adjudicate factional disputes. The direction of the more positive religious revival was assigned in 1950 to the Buddha Sasana Council, a lay organization headed by prestigious Buddhist judges of the High Court. The Council proceeded along traditional lines. It collected sacred relics from both Ceylon and India and later obtained the alleged Buddha tooth from China. It encouraged pagoda restoration, pilgrimages to famous shrines, and planting shoots of the *Bo* tree under which the Buddha found enlightenment. Government employees were encouraged to engage in meditation routines. The traditional *Dhamma* (fundamental law) examinations were revived under the Parliament's Pali University Act.

Government efforts to enforce the new disciplinary regulations quickly ran aground. In 1952 Premier Nu persuaded an assembly of eminent *Sayadaw* (royal teacher) abbots to approve his religious program, but to little effect. The newly established ecclesiastical courts proved powerless to enforce the basic initial requirement that all wearers of the yellow robe must register their identity. The government's accompanying assertion that regular law courts had jurisdiction over all criminal offenders, lay and clerical, was challenged by mass *pongyi* (monk) action. Premier Nu lacked the fortitude to assert his power. A subsequent alternative plan to set up a representative assembly within the *Sangha* was abandoned.

The decision to convene the Sixth Historic Council of Theravada Buddhism was made on the recommendation of the Sasana Council. A cave-type convocation hall large enough to seat ten thousand was constructed at considerable cost near Rangoon, adjacent to the new Peace Pagoda, where the Buddha tooth from China was enshrined. The Council convened in May 1954, with Theravada Buddhist leaders present from Ceylon, Thailand, Cambodia, and Laos. Some thirty countries were subsequently represented at sessions of the World Fellowship of Buddhists held at the cave. The conclusion of the two-year Council in 1956 was timed to coincide with the twenty-five hundredth anniversary of the Buddha's death. The labored recitation of some two thousand pages of the *Pali Tripitaka* scriptures dramatized the common devotion of the participants, but it accomplished little visible improvement in the conduct of Burma's *Sangha*. The program also became involved in the nationalist objective to establish Burma's role as the leader of world Buddhism. Mundane economic considerations fared badly in competition with such religious preoccupations.

Negative Factors in Government Performance

The difficulties encountered in making democratic government effective in Burma ran more deeply than the personalities and policies of premier and cabinet. Political factors, bureaucratic deficiencies, and even educational

213

policy influenced the situation. The politically dominant AFPFL personnel had achieved *pon* (glory) from their leadership in the national independence struggle, but they did not command full popular respect for their authority as rulers. Premier Nu was popular partly because he tended to be accomodating rather than demanding. He was an idealist rather than a pragmatist, a talker rather than a doer. The revolutionary activities in which he and his Thakin comrades had been involved during the forties had been unrelated to administrative problems and to the operation of democratic institutions. Nu's preachment of the values of democracy was popularly discounted because of the prevalence of corruption and official bungling. Even within the circle of Burma's Thakin elite, basic policy differences tended in time to assume the character of personal aggression.

Top government leaders could, of course, always find excuses for their failures by citing popular intransigence and lack of cooperation, bureaucratic stodginess, the activities of rebel elements, the survival of colonial traditions, or foreign intervention. The obvious need was for concentration on less ambitious objectives that could be realized.[24] Administrative officials, vulnerable to castigation by superiors when things went wrong, often had to perform locally under conditions of political interference and even threats of violence. Lacking, among other things, was popular acknowledgment of the authority of the government. The unconcealed contempt exhibited by politicians for careerist civil servants was balanced by bureaucratic resentment of interference from such mischievous political amateurs.

An inevitable result of the politician-bureaucrat controversy was that administrative agencies tended to avoid taking responsibility. Officials ritualized routine procedures that had been carried over from prewar colonial times and transferred all decision making, even down to trivial details, to overburdened authorities operating at higher levels.[25] They could also on occasion avoid the execution of difficult policies by reference to astrology and numerology.

214

An auspicious occasion and time must be selected for taking any specific action. It could be regarded as highly unfortunate, for example, that some dubiously qualified astrologer had mistakenly picked 4:20 AM on January 4, 1948, as the propitious time to inaugurate Burma's independence. Monastic influence, prompted by either traditional commitments or ignorance, could frequently block the execution of worthy policies. Under such circumstances, why should officials run the risk of provoking the ire of multiple critics and incurring the stigma of personal misconduct by any exercise of administrative vigor—especially when magical forces of astrology and *Karma* would presumably determine the outcome in any case?

Government activity thus became an exercise in official finesse, devoid of immediate social goals. The primary objective was to avoid trouble and to exploit cleverly one's opportunities for aggrandisement. Under the circumstances, a revision of the four-year plan, a change of ideological commitment, or a shift of cabinet personnel could realize only marginal improvement in faltering governmental endeavor. Villagers, on their part, discounted Rangoon's grandiose plans and promises, usually supported only trusted local leaders, and stayed aloof from officials and politicians, except where tangible needs (bunds, wells, pumps, roads) were clearly involved.[26]

Educational policies adopted during the middle 1950s contributed to political and governmental problems by offending minority groups and by diluting standards of instruction. Educated minority elite groups suffered from official abandonment of the use of English as a permissory language in government, courts of law, and schools. The required use of Burmese as the basis of all school instruction above the third standard in accredited schools effectively tended to handicap minority candidates in both university matriculation and government employ. Shans, Karens, and Kachins had previously been able to qualify with English as their second language.

Because the teaching of literary Burmese had long been neglected, school standards in the language were extremely

215

low. This situation was aggravated by lax disciplinary controls. The pass records in matriculation exams for students in government schools declined from a low 19 percent in 1952 to a pathetic 6 percent in 1957. Thereafter the minimal level of required performance was progressively lowered. The Burmese language lacked the precise vocabulary needed in law, government, and technical subjects taught in the schools. English instruction was still being used in university lectures in the mid-fifties, but classroom standards were less demanding than those of the thirties. Overburdened teachers were expected to prepare translations of English textbooks into Burmese for the use of badly prepared university students.

While standards were falling and the English-language door to learning was being gradually closed, the campus community was disrupted by a recurrence of political strife. The frustration generated by the overextended educational program lent general student support to the revolutionary protest organized by the so-called Leftist Progressive Student Force. Premier Nu and other Thakin cabinet members were reminded of their own similar record of student participation in politics after 1936 whenever additional disciplinary regulations were proposed.[27]

Burma's Eastern European Orientation

Various considerations influenced the Burma government to initiate a closer accomodation with the major Communist powers. Relations with China were a major concern. In the spring of 1953, Rangoon abruptly cancelled existing American-sponsored aid programs, including a road construction project leading northward into Upper Burma, a move which Peking could interpret as potentially hostile. The immediate cause of the break was Washington's failure to prevent American arms from reaching Kuomintang refugees in Burma's eastern Shan states, the arms presumably coming via Taiwan and Thailand. Washington's official ignorance of the arms delivery program added to Burmese distrust. U.S. refusal to continue financing the Nathan economic consultant team or to accept surplus rice in payment followed in 1955.[28] India also refused to purchase Burmese rice in 1955–56 on what Rangoon considered to be reasonable terms. Popular exasperation was fanned by rising costs of imported consumer goods, due to insufficient supply and to the declining value of the *kyat*.

Because the capitalist world, already regarded as suspect by ranking cabinet members, would not assist Burma in its time of need, the government undertook to find alternative outlets for the glut of unsold rice caused by the collapse of world prices in 1955. The Ministry of Trade Development ventured hopelessly beyond its depth in negotiating a series of barter deals with Eastern Europe.[29] The occasion was the Khrushchev-Bulganin visit to Rangoon in early 1956. The Russian visitors agreed at the time to accept on a barter basis one hundred and fifty thousand tons of Burma rice, which they promptly shipped to their desperately hungry North Vietnamese allies. Khrushchev also agreed to provide Burma at some future date with a technical institute, a modern hotel, and a sports stadium. Burmese purchasing agents, sent to Europe to find acceptable commodities available for early shipment in return for the barter credits, found that prices were high and choices limited. They ended up by ordering a surfeit of some one hundred thousand tons of cement, mainly from the USSR. Its arrival in Rangoon in May 1956, on the eve of the monsoon rains, clogged both port facilities and warehouses so that part of the cement suffered heavy spoilage in the rains. Meanwhile, negotiations for a U.S. loan of $25 million, plus a smaller sum to cover possible future sale of agricultural surpluses, dragged on for some eighteen months and were not concluded until March 1957.[30] A good rice crop in 1956 and Rangoon's eventual acceptance of more realistic prices permitted the disposal of two million tons of grain in 1957. Only one-seventh of the total sales of 1957 was made on a barter basis, compared to one-fourth in the previous year. Burma was learning the hard way.

A Tentative Transitional Move

Following the conclusion of the formal sessions of the Buddhist World Council and the holding of the general elections in May 1956, Premier Nu announced abruptly that he would take leave of the government for an indefinite period and retire to a monastery retreat; he left in June for what proved to be a nine-month absence. U Ba Swe was designated to act as interim premier, with the minister of industries, U Kyaw Nyein, second in line. Nu characterized his action as a kind of personal expiation for his party's dishonest performance in the May elections. His declared objective was to reform and purify the party organization, for which he continued to serve as president. His self-denying move commanded a degree of popular respect, although it was impossible to assess its results in terms of party reform.

In several respects, Nu's departure had a salutary effect. Reverting to a kind of interim defensive posture, the government began to deal more realistically with foreign trade problems, as indicated above, and also made serious efforts to establish priorities and to improve administrative performance. The revised second half of the eight-year development plan more than doubled the capital investment assigned to such production areas as agriculture, irrigation, mining, and forestry, and a visit by World Bank officials was scheduled for mid-1957. Farmers were provided incentives to expand productive efforts and to purchase needed chemical fertilizers. The land nationalization program, however, was still not clarified in terms of cultivator rights and rules of tenure, and the uncertain prospect of enforced collectivization discouraged peasant initiative. Nevertheless, a period of common-sense improvisation appeared to be in prospect, and for the good. Unfortunately, personal and ideological differences arose again following Nu's return to the premiership in March 1957.

Premier Nu's actions in 1957 reflected a considerable degree of mental and emotional confusion, which went far to unravel the fabric of the emerging revised program. He suspected that his Socialist party rival, U Kyaw Nyein, was endeavoring to push him aside politically. There ensued a bitter struggle for AFPFL party control, which came to an eventual head in early 1958. Meanwhile, ignoring the advice of cabinet colleagues, Nu requested the Soviet Union and Eastern Europe to provide agricultural and industrial advisers. The scheduled World Bank mission was accordingly cancelled. Khrushchev agreed to implement his previous promises of a technical institute, a modern hotel, and a sports arena. Adding to the growing confusion, the premier proposed in June 1957 that the entire development program be arbitrarily scrapped until law and order could be completely restored and other requisite preparations completed.

Nu also set up a Bureau of Special Investigation to function under his personal control. The Bureau was designed to expose and punish officials found guilty of nepotism, corruption, and inefficiency at all levels of the administration —an appallingly formidable task—but its net result was to instill overcaution among officials and virtual paralysis in decision making. After three months of chaotic confusion, Nu finally got around to making the kind of judicious policy reappraisal he should have made in June: he approved the vigorous pursuance of the revised four-year development program, with additional emphasis to be placed on joint-venture projects involving experienced British firms and the private sector generally, coupled with increased tax revenues and improved management standards.

But political feuding continued. On the occasion of the annual AFPFL Congress in January 1958, Nu as party president undertook to dictate the choice of secretary and also to challenge the role played by affiliated mass organization groups as constituent elements of the League. The latter move was primarily an attack on AFPFL-sponsored youth and peasant organizations, but it was also aimed particularly at U Ba Swe's labor union constituency and U Kyaw Nyein's Socialist party group. Nu's opponents countered by charging that he was using his personal control of the Bureau of Special Investigation to harass bona fide efforts to push forward in the economic field. Nu managed

219

to get his own party secretary installed, an action accompanied by vague promises of compromise. A permanent break within the ranks of the League was precipitated in late spring of 1958,[31] to be described shortly. Meanwhile, U Kyaw Nyein's pet prestige project, a steel mill for Burma (*sans* coal or iron ore), proved to be a hopeless fiasco, and Nu's British-built pharmaceutical plant produced millions of unusable yeast tablets. The entire program of economic development calls for examination at this juncture.

An Assessment of Economic Performance to 1959

The tangible accomplishments of the Industrial Development Corporation, directed by U Kyaw Nyein, were limited in both quality and extent. The best-conceived projects included a cotton-spinning and weaving factory, several sugar mills, and brick- and tile-making facilities. The cotton cloth factory ran into difficulties because its spinning operations called for a longer staple cotton than Burma could supply. In addition, the ball bearings in the machinery (supplied by China) proved faulty, and labor problems were encountered. Production at several badly located sugar mills was interrupted by flooding during the rains, and management was plagued by pricing problems and political graft. Sugar output by 1960 was only 58 percent of capacity. It took the Development Corporation until 1956 to get a brick factory into production, and then only with the assistance of a team of United Nations expediters from Germany. Roofing-tile facilities were longer delayed, even though the product was desperately needed to curb the disastrous fires that periodically swept crowded urban areas. The government-operated jute mill found itself obliged to import substantial amounts of fibre from East Pakistan, with the result that the cost of its high-quality bags ran exorbitantly high. An effort to exploit inferior coal resources found near Kalewa in the Chindwin Valley was abruptly discontinued in 1958 because the undertaking was found to be completely uneconomic. An electrical installation in Karenni, plus the pharmaceutical plant and steel mill, completed the list of industrial accomplishments. Many of the projects proposed initially were never launched at all.

Administrative incompetence in the public economic sector reached to the very top. The Economic and Social Board, headed by Premier Nu himself and including Kyaw Nyein and Ba Swe, neglected to delegate authority or even to establish a strong secretariat. The Board devoted far too much of its limited time to trivial problems, neglecting a broad review of programs and progress and failing to check whether decisions once made were ever implemented.[32] Specific projects were denied autonomy in determining prices, wages, and labor management policies. The delivery of raw materials for the manufacture of matches at Mandalay, for example, was held up by police who suspected illicit trade. The several joint-venture efforts initiated in the mid-fifties did not enjoy the unqualified support of the central Board and were denied operating autonomy. River transportation was assigned to Chittagonian crews, but other transportation and communications projects, as well as irrigation developments, progressed little beyond the initial stages.[33]

The economic gains that were realized in Burma during the late fifties owed relatively little to the government's planning program. For example, the private production of logs other than teak far surpassed the production of the government's teak monopoly. The joint project of the Burma Oil Company revived petroleum output by 1959 to 68 percent of prewar levels only to run aground because the general outlook was too discouraging to warrant investment of new effort and capital. With domestic prices for cooking oil rising, Upper Burma's output of groundnut and sessamum seed attained—without state aid—a 50 percent increment over 1938 levels. Paddy production in Lower Burma also expanded, after the pacification of 1958–59, to some 93 percent of prewar volume,[34] improving even more during the ensuing three years when price incentives for superior grain were offered to cultivators.

During this period, however, the traditional pattern of village life changed very little. Peasants still elected to

221

rest after the strenuous plowing and planting routines of the wet season, until the December–January harvest forced them into the fields again. They attended the November lenten holiday celebrations, which included pagoda worship, *pwe* dramatic performances, cock fights, and racing contests. It mattered little that interim employment was available in adjacent areas during slack agricultural seasons. Surplus earnings, if any, were seldom devoted to land improvement, but rather put into clothing and jewelry purchases and religious activities.

American observers in Upper Burma villages reported that government-sponsored propaganda for greater industry elicited little popular response. One village headman, who was genuinely concerned about maintaining good relations with district officials, sent an unemployed young client to a nearby town to attend a series of government-sponsored welfare lectures. On his return the young man did not bother to tell the village elders anything at all about the meetings. In another community, land redistribution moves by government agencies provoked a bitter factional fight. Even where public projects attracted local interest (tube wells, crop expansion, and tractor use), limitations on credit and unavailability of land inhibited any positive response. One enterprising milk distributor found that his suppliers watered their milk, his laborers were undependable, and his teashop customers failed to pay their bills on time. Another entrepreneur acquired loud-speaker facilities to rent to communities only to learn with dismay that his principal helper had pawned the equipment, batteries, and records and then decamped with the proceeds.[35] There was, essentially, no meaningful effort to assess the basic interests and needs of the peasants or to enlist the positive cooperation of recognized village leaders. Rural welfare needs obviously had little relevance to the political feuding that developed at Rangoon in 1958.

The Breakup of the AFPFL, 1958[36]

The political rift in government leadership in early 1958 was the most serious crisis since the rebellions a decade earlier. Premier Nu's handling of the situation reflected his reluctance to test the Parliamentary system when his League support ebbed away Instead of dissolving the Chambers and calling a special election to resolve the contest for control, he undertook to preserve his majority by soliciting the support of minority groups and opposition elements in the Chamber, including the Marxist-oriented National Unity Front (NUF), which demanded that Nu accept a plan for rebel pacification. Nu also enlisted the votes of two-thirds of the deputies from the Shan and Kaya states and the six conservative Arakanese members, four of whom were invited into the cabinet. Nu's June Parliamentary victory of 127 to 119 was nevertheless so narrow that he promised to call general elections in October following the end of the rainy season.

Premier Nu and his revamped cabinet undertook meanwhile to initiate a number of reform measures. An Indemnity Act was promulgated to encourage the surrender under liberal terms of all rebels still at large. Some minor successes were realized, but at the cost of antagonizing anti-Communist army officers, who were concerned that groups associated with the NUF would gain entrance into the government. As a second move, Nu staged a series of sixteen functional seminars at which various assembled groups were asked to suggest changes in areas of governmental activity. The seminar findings were significantly forthright. They reflected widespread resentment of AFPFL political interference with governmental administration, education, trade, and industry. Conservative spokesmen suggested that the monarchy be restored, that Buddhism be made the state religion, and that all government industrial ventures be turned over to private management. However valuable some of the ideas may have been, the plethora of uncoordinated proposals disrupted governmental cohesion and effectiveness during this critical period.

Political crisis developed in mid-September. The principal legal issue was Premier Nu's August decision to promulgate the annual budget by executive decree in order to avoid calling a new Parliamentary session, where his inability to command majority support would be exposed. Meanwhile routine government operations ground to a halt. Violence broke out between rival labor groups on the Rangoon docks, railway units struck, and pro-Communist elements began to talk about the need for a "people's struggle." The alternative to impending chaos and civil war seemed to be to call in General Ne Win's army to take control for a six-month emergency period, as provided by the constitution, until new elections could be staged in an orderly manner. Agreement was finally reached on such a move in late September, and the military caretaker regime accordingly took over from Nu's cabinet a month later. Burma's experiment in democratic government had clearly run aground, even though the constitution was still legally intact.

General Ne Win's Caretaker Regime, 1958–60

Despite the political damage inflicted by the army's takeover on October 28, 1958, the results were far from totally negative. The mere prospect of a more resolute government produced immediate improvements in the deteriorating situation. The danger of civil war quickly subsided, as did the fighting between dock workers and the protests of railway unions. With political pressures relieved, the several minority councils within the Parliament were permitted to elect their own presiding officers. Frustrated NUF Communist elements attempted to foment worker and student strikes as a step toward inaugurating a "people's struggle," but these efforts were successfully thwarted. The undertaking was abetted by Soviet embassy personnel, who charged on September 26, in the middle of the domestic crisis, that United States imperialist agents, acting in collusion with the Ba Swe-Kyaw Nyein faction, were conspiring to bring Burma into SEATO. Two constituent elements of the NUF, the Peoples Comrade party and the Burma Workers and Peasants party, persisted in their disruptive efforts for several weeks. By October 28, the Parliamentary leadership of the NUF agreed to assume the more conventional role of responsible Parliamentary opposition.

224

Not all of the pacification was easily achieved. During the course of several ensuing months, the army authorities arrested more than one hundred Leftist student agitators on subversive charges. Several score AFPFL partisans were detained on grounds of their abuse of authority, the culprits being drawn mainly from mass peasant and worker organizations and from trade unions. The regular jails eventually became so full that a penal colony had to be set up on an off-shore island. As disorders declined in the countryside, the trains began to run on schedule and even at night, with ticketless riding brought to an end. Tons of long-uncollected garbage were removed from Rangoon's streets, and hundreds of ownerless dogs were poisoned. During the course of the first year, an estimated one-eighth of the capital's population was removed from downtown squatter huts to three newly prepared urban sites on the city's outskirts. Although admittedly salutary, these actions were not universally popular.

More significant governmentally was General Ne Win's selection of an able, nonpolitical cabinet, responsible only to him, which included senior judges, academics, bank officials, and experienced bureaucrats. A distinguished Burman economist, teaching at Oxford, U Hla Myint, was appointed rector of Rangoon University. Intermediate administrative levels were staffed increasingly by army officers, who were assigned the direction of a variety of governmental boards and councils. These included the budget agency, transportation services, direction of housing construction, rural development, labor administration, mining, and oil extraction. An expanded Defense Services Institute, headed by Colonel Aung Gyi, undertook to train servicemen to perform a proliferating array of economic functions, such as banking, construction work, fishing, hotel operation, restaurants, department stores, and the distribution and servicing of automobiles and electrical appliances. Additional supplies of fish brought into the market by governmental agencies brought meat prices down, as did permission for the slaughter of cattle previously forbidden by Nu.[37]

One of the most dramatic moves by General Ne Win was his cancellation in December 1958 of the seven-year tenure of the Nathan Associates advisory team. It was permitted three months to wind up its affairs. He also dismissed most of the Russian advisers on land and rural development. Both actions were attributable in part to economy needs and in part to a general dislike of foreigners.

The Nathan group was blamed, with less than full justice, for the ineffectiveness of the Nu government's economic development program. The Nathan Associates chief actually left behind with the Rangoon authorities seventeen detailed memoranda of recommendations dealing with as many areas of the economy. A number of these proposals concerning the agricultural sector were subsequently utilized to good effect. They included permission for private domestic trade in rice, premium prices for quality rice for sale overseas, improvement of milling practices, more strict collection of taxes and loans, and a greater degree of autonomy in the operation of all public enterprises. Another recommendation was that a revised, British-type Land Survey Department begin a seven-year effort to rescue the land-holding records from their near-hopeless state of confusion. Less acceptable was the Nathan Associates' recommendation to expand the private sector by offering depreciation allowances for prospective foreign investors, three-year tax exemptions, waiver of taxes on reinvested profits, and duty-free entry of industrial production imports.[38]

The policy pursued by the caretaker government during the initially allotted six months was largely opportunist, involving few if any changes in long-range objectives. Major attention was devoted to the disciplining of so-called economic insurgents who were allegedly out to sabotage existing government regulations. The government denied further assistance to Burman peasants who defaulted on their loans and excluded from all business activity those who were found serving as heads of fictitious trading firms in order to provide cover for aliens who were doing business illegally. Chinese and Indian traders who were

226

suspected of violating commercial regulations had their business records and safety deposit boxes examined and were summarily deported if found guilty The Defense Services Institute became increasingly involved in both domestic commerce and foreign trade.[39] Under such circumstances, the government received minimal response from potential overseas investors to the tariff exemptions it offered and to its long-term guarantees against nationalization. The outlook was too uncertain for foreign capitalists to take the risks.

As the months passed, the army ceased to regard itself as merely an interim authority, but became a distinct political entity with an increasing stake in its continuing exercise of power. The army was predominantly Burman, drawing its newly enlisted personnel from village youth, who were more amenable than were the urban University students to discipline and indoctrination. Thus constituted, the armed services were strongly nationalistic and therefore unsympathetic to the autonomy aspirations of minority ethnic groups. The military opposed not only Communist rebels but student protesters as well, plus mass organization protagonists and religious partisans. It found an increasing number of things to do. In early February 1959, General Ne Win declared flatly that he could not possibly complete the necessary preparations for the general elections scheduled for April, and demanded more time. At first U Nu tried to hold the army leader to his pledge, but when faced by the threat of Ne Win's resignation and the prospect that U Ba Swe's "Stable" faction of the AFPFL would command a majority in the old Chamber of Deputies, Nu finally consented to the extension of military rule for another full year. A constitutional amendment extending the time period was accordingly approved, and the elections were rescheduled for early 1960.

The accomplishments of one and one-third years of army rule were limited for the most part to policing operations, pacification of the countryside, and encouragement of agricultural production. Local security activity included organizing many so-called solidarity associations at the

227

village level. Such volunteer groups were asked to assume a variety of responsibilities, from fire fighting and reporting an official corruption, to providing the army with anti-insurgency intelligence. Units of the solidarity agencies survived the caretaker period to constitute a residual base for the future activities of the army political faction.[40] Price incentives offered to peasants for delivery of superior quality rice had the effect of raising annual rice production to approximately the prewar level. This made possible the exportation in 1959–60 of some 1.7 to 1.8 million tons annually. Other economic gains, however, were minimal. Teakwood and oil production remained far below prewar levels.

The caretaker regime assumed a strongly nationalist and patriotic stance. Minority claims got short shrift. Ne Win cancelled the hereditary status of twenty-nine Shan Sawbwa princes. Most of them were permitted as individuals to continue to act as constitutional rulers of their respective states, but to do so they were forced to renounce their right to permanent tenure. By implication, the caretaker authorities also repudiated whatever remained of their ten-year constitutional option of secession. A tentative proposal for an autonomous Mon state in Tenasserim was rebuffed, and Arakanese discontent was mollified by the construction of a much-needed port jetty at Akyab. Burmese nationalist sentiment found expression when China invaded Tibet in 1959, as well as when personnel of the Soviet embassy became involved in local politics. As a kind of rejoinder, Ne Win revived negotiations with the United States for additional aid covering improvements in water and road transportation and for educational ends.[41] The government maintained its generally neutralist stance, however. Ne Win disavowed any intention to align with SEATO, but without specifically attacking the Treaty Organization itself. He also resumed efforts to settle the China border problem, and actually concluded the boundary treaty in early 1960.[42]

As election time approached in the autumn of 1959, public support of army rule waned rapidly. Arbitrary authority was widely resented, and Ne Win's government was clearly beyond its depth politically and economically. For these and other reasons the general was apparently not unhappy to find a way out of a difficult situation without any serious loss of face and with some credit to himself for honoring his promise to stage free elections. Some of his following who had tasted the fruits of power and distrusted politicians were less ready to surrender control. Although many military leaders entertained the hope that Ba Swe's less permissive Stable AFPFL would win out over Nu, the army stayed politically neutral. Actually the armed services surrendered none of their physical strength and maintained the exemption of its officer corps from civilian control. The publication of the caretaker regime's official apologia, entitled *Is Trust Vindicated?* (1960), provided political and psychological support for possible subsequent reversion to army rule. Colonel Aung Gyi's Defense Services Institute continued to train personnel for a variety of civilian roles, especially in such areas as transportation, trade, and deep-sea fishing.

Premier Nu's Return to Power, 1960–62

In a skilfully waged election campaign, U Nu's new Union party made the most of its political opportunities. It capitalized on popular resentment of army coercion, maintaining that representative government alone would give heed to the popular will and end the abuses of power. Nu repudiated the support of the Leftist National Unity Front, which he had courted in mid-1958, and promised sympathetic consideration of the wishes of all minority factions. At the same time, he acceded to the demands of traditionalist Burman politicians that Buddhism be made the official religion of the Union. His Buddhist cause gained windfall support when an albino calf elephant (a favorable religious omen) was transported to the Rangoon zoo in September 1959. The largest crowd in Rangoon's history welcomed the arrival. Ba Swe's and Kyaw Nyein's Socialist party propaganda, by comparison, aroused so little popular appeal, that they also began visiting pagoda shrines. At election time, Nu put his own portrait on the Union party's yellow ballot boxes (the color of the *pongyi* robe). He won an overwhelming preliminary victory in the December local elections, and then duplicated his feat in the general elections of February 1960. The voting took place in orderly fashion, and the electorate's decision was conclusive.[43] Ba Swe and Kyaw Nyein both failed to win seats in the new Parliament.

Premier Nu's political triumph was a victory for democracy and social traditionalism over army domination and socialist planning. But the aura of popularity reflected in the large Union party majority was deceptive. Nu headed a loose federation of highly disparate groups, including fanatical Buddhist partisans who were not amenable to his control, a number of liberal proponents of democratic principles of government, plus a variety of minority factions, each intent on achieving its own objectives. The largest single organized group, Thakin Tin's All Burma Peasants Organization (ABPO), was virtually a party unto itself. When Nu resigned the Union party presidency in March 1961 in favor of Thakin Tin, dissention began to spread. In January 1962 Nu lost control of the executive committee of the party, when Tin managed to corner all of the committee seats for his disciplined ABPO peasant faction. Nu's actual power as political leader thus eroded away in time.

The long-pondered State Religion Bill was finally approved in August 1961. Serious trouble developed a month later when the related constitutional amendment designed to ensure religious freedom for non-Buddhists came up for approval. On the appointed day, the authorities arranged a predawn session of the Parliament in order to avoid the embarrassment of facing picketing monks at the entrance of the building. Once the trickery was discovered, an angry *pongyi*-led mob attacked and damaged several Muslim mosques in Rangoon. Instead of acting vigorously to curb the religious fanatics, Premier Nu made a series of bland appeals to maintain national unity and cooperation.[44] The rioting eventually subsided, but it left a residue of distrust not only among Muslims, Hindus, and Christians, but also within the ranks of non-Burman Buddhists as well.

The task of dealing with minority autonomy demands was far more complex than the religious freedom question had been and was consequently even slower coming to a head. In late 1960 a Mujahid insurrection developed along the Chittagong borders of Arakan, reminiscent of the disorders of the immediate postwar period. The initial concessions to demands for autonomy included two proposed constitutional amendments that granted separate jurisdictional authority to the inhabitants of Arakan and to the Mons of Tenasserim. Both were scheduled for implementation in August 1962, presumably as part of a larger package. The Shan problem was particularly sensitive because of General Ne Win's cancellation of the hereditary rights of the Sawbwa princes. Nu had enlisted Shan election support by agreeing to reconsider both the role of the princes and the original constitutional permission for the Shan State to alter its status within the Burma Union after ten years time. Representatives of the approximately thirty units of the State administration were invited to assemble at Rangoon on March 1, 1962, for a conference on the subject. They included the respected Sao Shwe Thaike, the first president of the Burma Union. It was this move that precipitated the army coup of March 2.

The army leadership professed to see in Nu's policies the dire prospect of the disintegration of the Union. Members of the group had been waiting in the wings for two years for some such plausible excuse to intervene.[45] Ne Win's coup was abrupt and thoroughgoing. He arbitrarily declared the constitution abolished, together with the Parliament and the higher court system, affirming that democracy had proved to be unsuitable for Burma. No one was able to challenge his decision, and the principal personnel of the government, including Premier Nu and all of the assembled Shan chiefs, were taken into custody. Burma's postwar experiment with democracy had come to an end, with consequences that will be described in a subsequent chapter.

231

Both politically and administratively, the second Nu government had pretty well run aground. Nu's basic intentions were worthy, but he failed to coordinate his goals and to implement approved policy decisions. Although unable to keep his variegated followers in line politically, he tried to use both democratic means and the force of his own personality to bridge the huge gaps that separated the traditionalists from the minority modernist socialist elements, trying at the same time to conciliate the distrustful ethnic minority factions. His objectives were utopian rather than realistically conceived. He tried to wear too many hats: orthodox Buddhist, champion of religious freedom and minority rights, convinced proponent of democracy, and the enemy of greedy, exploitive and alien-dominated capitalism. He also suffered from the characteristic indiscipline of many of his countrymen, restive under restraint and too impatient to concentrate on detail. In this sense, the democracy which Nu espoused was backward looking and opposed to modernization,[46] while tolerating a surfeit of freedom.

The character and results of Premier Nu's final two years of rule were nevertheless recalled later by countrymen with some measure of nostalgia. His lackadaisical administration had witnessed the expansion of Burma's rice production to the postwar peak, with expanding overseas sales permitting the purchase of valued consumer goods. Nu had also held out some promise of democratic adjustment of tensions and a larger measure of freedom, which might possibly have been realized had the army not intervened.

1. Hla Myint, *The Economics of Developing Countries* (London, 1967), pp. 167-71; Lucian Pye, *Politics, Personality, and Nation Building: Burma's Search for Identity* (New Haven, 1962), pp. 48-65.

2. E. Sarkisyanz, *Buddhist Backgrounds of the Burmese Revolution* (The Hague, 1965).

3. Clifford Geertz, ed., *Old Societies and New States* (Glencoe, Ill., 1964), pp. 1-9, 21-26, 195-99; Manning Nash, *The Golden Road to Modernity* (New York, 1965), pp. 164-65, 291-311.

4. Louis Walinsky, *Economic Development of Burma, 1951-60* (New York, 1962), pp. 252-64.

5. This section is based on John F. Cady, *A History of Modern Burma* (Ithaca, 1958).

6. Nash, *op. cit.* pp. 16, 24-33, 52-57, 73-79.

7. Walinsky, *op. cit.*, pp. 80-91. See page 2 of the KTA report for quotation.

8. *Ibid.*, p. 108.

9. *Ibid.*, p. 96.

10. *Ibid.*, pp. 96-98.

11. *Ibid.*, pp. 99-109.

12. Hugh Tinker, *The Union of Burma* (London, 1959), pp. 165-83.

13. Walinsky, *op. cit.*, p. 119.

14. *Ibid.*, pp. 111-25.

15. Hla Myint, *The Economies of the Developing Countries* (London, 1965).

16. *Ibid.*, pp. 156-62.

17. From a privately circulated typescript by Robert Nathan, "Nathan Trip to Rangoon", February, 1959.

18. Walinsky, *op. cit.*, pp. 185, 218-20.

19. *Ibid.*, pp. 218-20.

20. *Ibid.*, pp. 371-81.

21. Josef Silverstein, "Burma", in Kahin, ed., *Governments and Politics*, pp. 113-19.

22. Nu's eloquent utterance on the occasion of independence illustrates his spirit: "We lost out independence without losing our self-respect; we clung to our culture and to our traditions, and these we now hold to cherish and develop in accordance with the genius of our people. We part without rancor and in friendship with the Great British nation which held us in fee." Quoted in Maung Maung Pye, *Burma in the Crucible Rangoon*, (1951), p. 211.

23. See Richard Butwell, *U Nu of Burma* (Stanford, 1963), chapters 7-9.

24. The best presentation of this point of view is in Pye's *Politics, Personality and Nation Building*, pp. 3-8, 124-27, 151-74, 244-66.

25. *Ibid.*, pp. 3-8, 136-44.

26. *Ibid.*, pp. 178-95, 199-207, 287-301.

27. Personal observations on the Rangoon University campus in 1955-56.

28. William C. Johnstone, *Burma's Foreign Policy: a Study in Neutralism* (Cambridge, 1963), pp. 118-34.

29. Walinsky, *op. cit.*, pp. 162-67, 176-84, 195-97.

30. *Ibid.*, pp. 190-97, 209-10. The loan by the America Export-Import Bank was repayable in twenty years at 4 percent in Burmese *kyats* and at three percent in U.S. dollars. Farm surplus grants were valued at $17.3 million.

31. *Ibid.*, pp. 185-90, 217-36.

32. *Ibid.*, pp. 475-76.

33. *Ibid.*, pp. 137-49.

34. *Ibid.*, pp. 298-317, 336-51.

35. Nash, *op. cit.*, pp. 218-31, 237-45.

36. This portion of the text is also based on Cady, *op. cit.*

37. *Ibid.*

38. From Robert Nathan typescript, *op. cit.*

39. Lucian W. Pye, "The Army in Burmese Politics," in John J. Johnson, *The Role of the Military in Undeveloped Countries* (Princeton, 1962), pp. 231-49.

40. *Christian Science Monitor*, June 27, 1960.

41. Cady, *op. cit.*, "Supplement," pp. 79-83.

42. Johnson, *op. cit.*, pp. 68-76, 101, 238.

43. Cady, *op. cit.*, "Supplement," pp. 32-34.
44. Johnson, *op. cit.*, pp. 148-57.
45. Butwell, *op. cit.*, chapter 18.
46. Richard Butwell, "The Four Failures of U Nu's Second Premiership," *Asian Survey*, 2 (March, 1962); 3-11.

VIII

INDONESIA'S VENTURE IN DEMOCRATIC GOVERNMENT, 1949-57

The Post-Independence Setting for Indonesia

The similarites between independent Indonesia and Burma were superficial compared to their major differences. Both governments were led by political personalities drawn from an entirely new postwar elite strata, who were concerned to eliminate foreign political and economic control but were handicapped by the pluralistic nature of their respective societies. But Indonesia was several times larger than Burma both geographically and populationwise and had never, prior to the imposition of colonial Dutch rule, functioned as a national political entity. Srivijaya and Malacca, prior to 1200 and during the 1400s, had controlled little beyond areas adjacent to the Straits leading to the South China Sea, while Majapahit Java (1293 to 1520) had controlled only minor portions of Sumatra and Borneo. Unlike Burma's two decades of experience with representative government prior to World War II, Indonesians had simply witnessed the authority and prestige of their traditional ruler system erode progressively under colonial rule, with little to take its place. Remnants of the Sultanate system survived in the outer Islands, while the Buginese, Macassarese, and the Moluccan islander traders had retained their sense of regional and economic identity.

Although the great majority of Indonesians espoused the Muslim faith, they were far from homogeneous in culture. The Achenese in northern Sumatra entertained a fanatical commitment to Islam that long antedated the conversion of the rest of the archipelago and that carried a Sufi mystical quality all its own. Javanese Muslims were themselves divided between the orthodox Nahdatul Ulama faction, the politically fanatical Darul Islam strong in western portions of the island, the conversion-motivated *santri* traders of the northern port cities, and the modernized Muhammadijah reform sect with cultural roots in distant Cairo. By contrast, the interior population of central and eastern Java, although nominally Muslim, continued loyal to their indigenous pre-Islamic *adat* traditions,[1] while the *priyayi* ruling-class who had collaborated with the Dutch still clung to their fading Hindu-related caste pretentions.[2] Bali island, to the east of Java, remained culturally Hindu, entertaining little or no affiliation with Islam but a fairly close cultural identity with the peoples of eastern Java. The Amboinese islanders, Menadonese at the extreme northeastern corner of Sulawesi, and the Bataks of upper Sumatra were largely Christianized.

With minor exceptions, all indigenous Indonesians joined hands to be rid of Dutch colonial control, but they did not emerge from the independence struggle an integrated nation. They were less xenophobic than the Burmans, partly because they were more cosmopolitan in their outside contacts, and partly because Dutch colonial policy had not permitted the diversion of agricultural land to foreigners as had been the case with Burma's Chettyar moneylenders. Distinct portions of Indonesia were so disparate politically and socially, in fact, that observers agreed that the state could probably be held together only by the exercise of strong centralized control.

The leader of the unification effort for a decade and a half was Bung Sukarno. He capitalized on his personal

236

charisma to dramatize the nationalist cause. He differed sharply from Nu in both personal character and political tactics. As an ardent Buddhist and a man of democratic convictions, Burma's Nu undertook to reconcile divergent political groups within his country. Sukarno, on the other hand, had little respect for party politicians, tried to divert popular attention from basic social and economic problems, and eventually assumed arbitrary control of the government in alliance with the army. He later used the Indonesian Communist party as a makeweight against his Islamic political enemies and enlisted nationalist support by involvement in foreign policy ventures. Sukarno was prepared to appropriate Dutch property and other foreign investments for nationalist ends, but not from any dedication to socialist goals.

Except for the topmost level, Indonesia's postwar leadership was neither well trained nor experienced. The few European-trained Democratic Socialists were highly intelligent and well motivated, but they lacked rapport with the indigenous population. The total educated group was very small. In 1940, for example, fewer than 250 persons graduated from Westernized High Schools, while college graduates numbered only 37.[3] The Dutch-educated intelligentsia could be characterized as culturally adrift and spiritually lonely. In the religious fanaticism and anti-colonialism of the postwar period, all allegations of Dutch origin were automatically discredited. The Cairo-trained Muhammadijah modernists were only slightly less alien. The wealthy among them built schools and mosques, promoted sports and scouting activities, and delivered thoughtful sermons and lectures. But the modernist reformers could not really compete with Nahdatul Ulama champions of Koranic orthodoxy or with the proselytizing *santri* trader group.[4] The Darul Islam fanatics of Western Java were capable of launching a traditional "holy war" against heretics and backsliders.[5] It is within this confusing context of cultural objectives that one must judge Sukarno's platitudinous *Pantja Sila* principles of democracy, social justice, faith in God, nationalism, and humanity, with no effort made for precise definition or implementation. By contrast, the principal social foundations on which Javanese villagers relied were neither Western nor Islamic. A primary concern was to maintain community harmony and peace, to be achieved in part by the periodic observance of ceremonial meals, termed *slametans*. These were staged on an ad-hoc basis by the several households as circumstances required, usually around sundown, after the day's work. Attendance by all those invited was practically compulsory, and constituted an earnest display of good intentions to promote community harmony. The numerous spirit inhabitants of the village, some helpful and others mischievous, were also presumed to be present, and their cooperation was enlisted in similar fashion. The brief eating ceremony closed with the chanting of an Arabic prayer from the Koran, but the ritual itself was older than Islam.

The *slametan* has been interpreted as depicting the triumph of social harmony and civilization over the crude violence of primitivism. Just as the amoral spirits of nature retreated before civilized Javan conquest of the jungle, so could selfish individual concerns become amenable to positive social control rather than to confusion and disorder. Javan cultural values called for "mutual adjustment of independent wills," for emotional restraint, and for regulation of behavior. Civilized society must fit things together (*tjotjok*), including marriages, manners, clothes, food and medicines, frustrations, and even personal grief. Within this traditional cultural context, many Javanese villagers found dogmatic Islamic monotheism aggressively strident. Occurrences of party strife within the experimental postwar democratic system were regarded as similarly crude, if not uncivilized.[6] Any endeavors to realize sociopolitical accomodation for the nation as a whole in the *tjotjok* fashion would clearly run into difficulties. It was partly on this basis that Communist party organizers familiar with the Javan scene were later able to enlist a substantial Javanese peasant following by stressing the communal aspects of Marxist social objectives.

Independent Indonesia's Economic Problems

The economic losses suffered by Indonesia during the course of the Japanese occupation stemmed more from deteriorating facilities and the disintegration of the social fabric than from physical destruction per se; in fact, more overt destruction was suffered during the postwar Dutch police actions than during the Japanese occupation. But wartime deprivation was dire. From 1942 to 1946, all interisland trade ground to a halt. Destitute urban Javanese returned to their native villages, and the already crowded arable land had to accomodate a population some 15 percent larger than the prewar total. In the outer Islands, plantations unable to market their output were occupied by subsistence squatters, or were used for grazing areas. Deforestation increased, as did soil erosion, road deterioration, and the silting up of rivers and harbors.[7]

The war experience also aggravated the disintegration of traditional patterns of social cohesion, a process that had started during the thirties. The groups that suffered most grievously were the Javanese white-collar *priyayi* official class and the Chinese traders and moneylenders. Both were exposed not only to Japanese discrimination, but also to Indonesian national resentment for having allegedly been allied with the colonial Dutch. By contrast, the Japanese tended to encourage partisan Muslim organizations, along with nationalist-oriented worker and youth groups. The youthful nationalists who came to the fore politically made up in enthusiasm and daring what they lacked in experience. Many of them gravitated into the army, which became in time one of the few disciplined organizations within the islands. Unfortunately, the colonialist economic and administrative structure disintegrated before any effective alternative could be created.[8]

A major problem was to find a substitute for the Dutch and Chinese business communities of colonial times. Indonesian traders tended to be more peddlers than entrepreneurs. The goods they handled passed through many hands, earning minimal profits, before any bona fide consumer-purchaser was found. Peddling was essentially a contest of wits, deception, and patience, which could contribute little to enlarging the volume of production and trade. Many clever Chinese traders managed to survive in the postwar nationalist climate by taking on Javanese license-holders as partners. The Dutch held on for the better part of a decade as operators of large commercial houses, oil operations, plantations, and tin mines. The Chinese were somewhat less vulnerable than Europeans, but as in Malaysia, they were unassimilable non-Muslims and were denied full rights as citizens. Some Outer Island groups, such as the Sumatran Minangkabau and Bataks and the Macassar and Buginese traders, demonstrated a degree of economic initiative, but their experience and capacities were limited.[9]

The usual employment tactic of educated Javanese was to join the expanding government bureaucracy, which under independence attained several times its prewar dimensions. The public service operated as a kind of outdoor relief for the educated classes. Many of the new officials literally had nothing to do. Whatever recovery was achieved in Indonesia down to 1953 was largely the accomplishment of returned Dutch technicians and businessmen, who enjoyed a substantial assist from the trade boom that accompanied the Korean War. The Dutch sold off all their accumulated supplies and made substantial advances in restoring production. Most of the revival was accomplished in the Outer Islands, where nationalist sentiment was less strong and where the oil wells, mines, and plantations were located. Export sales were expedited by official devaluation of the *rupiah* in 1950, a move that also facilitated the retirement of old debts.[10] By 1953 the gross output level equalled that of 1938, but the economy as a whole was demonstrating no resilience.[11]

Production levels ran aground after 1953 for various reasons. For one thing, the export boom attributable to the Korean War tapered off and was followed by a period of doldrums. Difficulties encountered in renewal of Dutch plantation leases discouraged expenditures on rubber replanting, and the general atmosphere of political uncertainty forbade additional capital investments. Squatters were difficult to expel from the plantation areas, and the new Indonesian foremen were less efficient than their Chinese predecessors had been.

Economic conditions for the common people, especially in overcrowded Java, improved only marginally. The island could not feed its people, and the needed imports were difficult to come by. The early fifties witnessed a threefold increase in the price of rice and a one-third rise in the overall cost of living in Java. The decline in the world price of rice after 1954 helped but little, since it was accompanied by a fall in total Indonesian exports in both volume and unit value. The growing adverse balance of payments was accompanied by budgetary deficits.[12] The faltering efforts of the Indonesian government to cope with such problems will be examined after describing relevant aspects of the new government itself.

Centralized Control in the New State

The Republic of the United States of Indonesia, which the Dutch surrendered control of in 1949, was a federation that included the central nucleus of Java and fifteen minor states in the Outer Islands, most of which were of Dutch creation. The federated arrangement was logically designed to take account of local interests and traditions, including divergent linguistic and cultural peculiarities. From the beginning, however, Indonesian leaders began to suspect that the Dutch intended to exploit the federal principle for their political and economic advantage. The issue was brought into impressive focus in early 1950, when an abortive rebellion was launched by a motley assortment of demobilized colonial troops, led by a Dutchman named Westerling. Indonesia's abrupt response was to set up a unitary state system in July 1950, under which autonomous privileges might be accorded by the central authority but could not be claimed as local rights. At this juncture, parochial loyalties were subordinated to the generally entertained conviction that central control was essential if national political and economic goals were to be achieved.[13]

The conflicting demands for central direction and local

241

autonomy proved difficult to reconcile. Few informed observers denied that some measure of local participation was necessary and desirable, even between the several parts of Java. The proper functioning of popular sovereignty (democracy) required that deference be paid to public opinion. But the precise definition by the unitary government of the character and extent of such autonomous rights involved inescapable contradictions. The strong traditional preference (among Javanese in particular) to legislate by consensus, so as to ensure that policy differences would not harden into hostility, gave rise to endless delays. Attempted adjustments invariably ran aground in prolonged and inconclusive debates that majority vote could not properly resolve.

The problem of achieving consensus was particularly difficult with respect to economic differences. Once the threat of Dutch manipulation had disappeared, both political and military leaders in the Outer Islands objected to the fact that the central government profited from the export of non-Javanese tin, copra, rubber, and oil but neglected local needs for roads, schools, and other facilities. They also complained that Javanese candidates were selected for most of the prestigious civil-service posts, to the exclusion of capable non-Javanese. Even when central revenue resources were made available to meet urgent local needs, the bureaucracy frequently bungled the projects, and Javanese civil servants attracted most of the blame.[14]

The problem of action by consensus was complicated by the pattern of representation set forth in the Constitution, which followed the Dutch practice of proportional representation in the selection of Parliamentary delegates from multiple-candidate districts. The result was a proliferation of party organizations. Prior to the first general election of 1955, the Provisional Assembly, whose membership was nominated roughly in proportion to the assumed political strength of the numerous party groups, functioned as an advisory parliament. Although the successive cabinets were supposed to be responsible to the parliamentary membership, no clear majorities emerged. For this reason, President Sukarno was usually able to influence the composition of successive cabinets by selecting the formateur, who was periodically assigned the task of assembling the new ministers. The President also influenced the role of army leadership and nominated the foreign service elite, and was empowered by the Constitution to enact emergency legislation.

From the outset, President Sukarno took advantage of his stragetic role as the theoretical representative of the people as a whole to pose as the guiding genius of the Indonesian revolution. He developed a strong dislike for party politicians, especially if they were non-Javanese, and preferred to work with the functional representatives of occupational groups, the army, and manageable cultural units. Although extremely popular in Eastern Java and everywhere regarded as an authentic national hero, Sukarno did not command universal acclaim. His dislike for the strong Masjumi party, largely *santri* and Outer-Island oriented, was only in part because of his secularist opposition to the establishment of an Islamic state. He related much better to the more conservative Nahdatul Ulama faction (which defected from the Masjumi in 1952) because it was Eastern Javanese and therefore more sympathetic to his political objectives. Sukarno's own Nationalist party (PNI) was 86 percent Javanese supported and the PKI Communists, with whom he later collaborated, were almost 90 percent Javanese.[15] As president, Sukarno exploited all possible ambiguities in the still tentative constitutional situation at the expense of the Sumatran vice-president, Hatta, and the first Masjumi prime minister, Natsir, who became, in time, his bitterest rival.[16]

A survey of the Indonesian political scene as it emerged in the crisis of late 1952 reveals its many complications and numerous divergencies. The two most articulate parties in demanding early elections were Sjahrir's Socialists (PSI) and the Masjumi Council of Muslim Associations. The PSI emphasized economic reform policies and democratic socialism. It enjoyed some support from one influential army faction, led by Colonel Simatupang, an officer

243

with Christian antecedents who was posted at Djarkarta; otherwise it commanded little physical backing or popular support. The Masjumi party became almost entirely a Sumatran affair following the defection of the Javanese Nahdatul Ulama from the Council in 1952. The Masjumi was also backed by a powerful North Sumatran military contingent, led by Colonel Simbolon. Muslim politicians generally insisted that Islam alone could offer a lasting solution for the country's problems and that religion must become the focus of both political and social aspirations. The Masjumi in particular espoused an amorphous kind of Islamic brotherhood and the cause of federalist autonomy.[17]

The major army faction at Djakarta, led by Colonel Nasution, was flatly opposed to parliamentary rule whether by the provisional representative body or by an elected successor. Nasution advocated outright authoritarian control by President Sukarno, backed by army sanctions. A third army faction at the capital included the younger officers and was led by Lieutenant Colonel Lubis, head of the army intelligence bureau. He was jealously hostile to both Simatupang and Nasution. As an opportunist, Lubis was inclined for the time being to support President Sukarno's efforts to bridge the developing political rifts and to keep extremists under control. The one thing that all three army factions had in common was opposition to the Communists.

Vice-President Hatta was associated in 1952 with Premier Wilopo, with the prestigious Sultan Hamengku Buwono as minister of defense, and with the able Sumitro as minister of finance, all of whom were progressive nationalists. They were bent on curbing the size and political pretensions of the army factions, through action by the Provisional Parliament. The Wilopo cabinet also included PNI Nationalists and Masjumi members, but it was generally Western oriented and European trained. Sukarno's PNI followers were primarily Javanese nationalists, representatives of the traditional governing classes and landholders of Central and Eastern Java. They were ultrapatriotic, interested in patronage considerations and in bureaucratic privilege. They included many government workers whose meager salaries had to be supplemented by moonlighting.[18] Sukarno was a Javanese hero, and his PNI organization was the strongest political organization in the island.

In the early fifties, the revived Communist party (PKI) was also becoming a predominantly Javanese organization, with a carefully modulated political approach. By supporting Sukarno's opposition to the Masjumi religionists, mainly Sumatrans, the PKI, by 1952, had earned his tacit permission to recruit its own mass following. The party's phenomenal recovery from its near demise following the Madiun rebellion of 1948 was due to the dedicated efforts of its youthful leader, D. N. Aidit, who was prepared to exploit nationalist fervor as well as existing social and political tensions present within Javanese society. Communist propaganda appealed to plantation and trade union workers and to youth and women groups, all of whom might otherwise have aligned with the more principled PSI Socialists. The opportunist PKI propagandists also established rapport with nominally-Muslim East Javan villagers in defending their cooperative *adat* traditions against the *santri* partisans, being careful not to attack Sukarno and his particular constituency support. The popular following recruited by the Communists within Java, by 1955, was some five times the estimated party membership itself.[19]

A political crisis developed in Djakarta on October 17, 1952, when Nasution's army faction challenged the Parliament. The army tried to bluff a coup by directing some three hundred partisans to attack the Parliament building and then converge on the president's palace. The group demanded the abolition of the Provisional Parliament. Colonels Nasution and Sematupang then demanded and obtained a direct confrontation with Vice-President Hatta and Premier Wilopo in the palace itself, with Sukarno acting as a kind of presiding mediator. Tensions ran high, but Sukarno's emotional appeal for unity won the day. The government survived, but barely so. Nasution resigned his command on December 5, an action balanced by the departure of Defense Minister Hamengku Buwono on January 1, 1953. A principal consequence was the acceleration of

245

preparations for the long-deferred elections. The electoral law was approved on April 1, 1953, and balloting preparations got under way.[20] The crisis of 1952 did not directly concern the PKI, which continued its opportunist tactics of supporting Sukarno and the new Ali Sastroamidjojo government of 1953.

Sukarno's political tactics were also opportunist. He took advantage of his well-nigh invulnerable status as president and national hero to stand aloof while awaiting a conclusive demonstration of party disagreements and democratic futility. All the while he continued to tolerate Communist propaganda, although it was calculated to undermine constitutional authority and was financed increasingly by blackmail contributions extorted from resident Chinese, with the cooperation of the Chinese embassy and consular staffs. He permitted Nasution to return from army retirement in 1955, with the enhanced rank of major general and the title of army chief of staff. He strengthened his own PNI organization and encouraged the anti-Masjumi tactics of the orthodox Nahdatul Ulama Muslims in Java. Otherwise he was content to see the colorless Ali Sastroamidjojo government flounder during the course of the ensuing two years over political divergencies and increasing corruption, problems that he as president did nothing to try to solve. The Ali cabinet finally fell apart in August 1955, just prior to the scheduled elections, giving place to the even weaker government of Premier Harahap of the Masjumi faction. The last two years of the Provisional Parliament's performance were undistinguished. Parliament did little to improve administrative efficiency, to curb corruption, or to come to grips with the problem of Outer Island autonomy. It also failed to limit the legal prerogatives of the office of president or the political activity of the army.[21]

Economic Recovery and Early Development Plans

A primary deterrent to economic development throughout Indonesia was the fact that customary attitudes and values were, for the most part, irrelevant to industrial regimentation. Industrialization required coordinate efficiency, monetary savings for investment purposes, careful record keeping, and an awareness of the value of time, all of which were largely alien to the values the people cherished, including their taste for artistic expression and entertainment. Javanese generally were reluctant to leave their crowded island home and face a strange milieu—even if, as was customary, the entire family went along. Furthermore, the mutual help tradition (*gotong rojong*) of the Javanese rural community was imperilled in urban settings, and particularly if associated with long-term government-sponsored projects.

One informed Indonesian spokesman summarized the problem as follows:

> Ability to work hard and struggle for a better standard of living over a long period of time inevitably depends on the subordination of external values of economic life to deeper . . . cultural values. . . . It is no use providing good seeds and teaching good methods of cultivation . . . unless the villager's values of life are changed. . . . By far the greater part of the confusion, the failures, and the corruption which . . . plague economic enterprise in Indonesia can be essentially reduced to the immaturity of the new culture which is developing.[22]

From the superficial point of view of the foreign economic observer, the development potential for Indonesia was encouraging. The land and resources of the Outer Islands in particular could be developed by utilizing surplus Javanese labor, especially in the production of oil, tin, bauxite, and rubber. Sugar, coconut, and tobacco held limited promise, and the production of food could be expected to do little more than keep pace with local demands. Population mobility needed to be improved and educational opportunities expanded. The government had also to provide guarantees for the security of continuing business operations, for effective direction of the nonprivate economic sector, and for at-

247

tracting outside capital resources. Indigenous business experience would presumably develop in time, along with adequate savings accumulation.[23]

In Indonesia as in Burma, theory and reality diverged sharply. Efforts throughout the 1950s to subsidize migration from crowded Java to the Outer Islands accomplished the transfer of only 220,000 persons, whereas the annual increment of employable heads of families in the same island was nearly 300,000. Even if the annual rate of migration during the 1960s had been multiplied ten times and combined with a decline in fertility, Java's sixty-two million people (as of 1960) would reach some eighty-one million by 1975. Desperately needed, therefore, was a combination of vigorous and continuing improvement of agricultural techniques and employment opportunities outside the agrarian sector.

A competent technical assistance team, sponsored by the United Nations and headed by Benjamin Higgins of the Massachusetts Institute of Technology, undertook in the early 1950s to advise the Indonesian government on economic and financial matters. The team's formal report, presented in 1952, was both enlightening and realistic. It pointed out that extensive public investment in Outer Island resources would aid Indonesia's balance of payments problem but would contribute little to the employment of surplus Javanese labor. Basic needs included the expansion of all forms of transportation facilities within and between the islands, plus community development projects in housing, education, and cottage industries, all designed to employ local labor. Large industrial efforts, such as the Assahan Valley Power Development project in Sumatra, could make possible the production of fertilizers, aluminum, paper, and glassware. At the same time, agricultural improvements should be undertaken to achieve self-sufficiency in food production, and there should be a proliferation of indigenous small-scale factories for producing a variety of consumer needs. If sustained growth was to be achieved, a major effort was required, utilizing domestic savings and earned foreign exchange to supply a major portion of capital needs.[24] The authors also insisted that, if production was to keep pace with population, careful planning was necessary that would take into account local values and social dynamics. The report established dependable norms; it was up to Djakarta to work out the details.

Before the Indonesian government could undertake to implement the suggested development program, it encountered budgetary deficits and rising prices. Since military and policing costs constituted a heavy drain on the revenues, the responsible Wilopo government of 1952 proposed to retire some sixty thousand members of the army and thirty thousand police.[25] The move was much resented by those affected and helped precipitate Nasution's previously mentioned demonstration of protest on the part of the army, which challenged the leadership of the civilian parties in the government. President Sukarno backed Wilopo in rebuffing the half-hearted coup, even though he shared the army's dislike of civilian party activities. The civilian democratic Wilopo cabinet, an assembly of top administrative talent, was forced to resign in mid-1953 under pressure of highly emotional nationalism and petty politicking. Wilopo's successor, Premier Sastroamidjojo, was much less forthright and exercised diminishing authority, weakened by the negative attitude of both the president and the army. His government fell in August 1955 over its abortive effort to remove squatters from plantation areas in Sumatra.

Economic affairs in Java did not improve. In 1954 inflationary pressures forced the Bank of Indonesia to suspend its legal reserve requirements. A brief flicker of hope appeared in early 1955, when the value of the *rupiah* was temporarily stabilized and the psychologically significant Bandung Conference was staged. But the parliamentary elections held in September of the same year witnessed the virtual elimination from Parliament of the Democratic Socialists, who were the principal supporters of rational economic development plans.

The events of 1953–55 also marked the eclipse of Vice-President Hatta's steadying influence and the advent of ultranationalism and religious partisanship. Hatta's policies (cooperation with the Dutch, law and order, and economic needs) had become too unexciting to satisfy Java's revolutionary youth or the army leadership. Both groups felt constricted by his emphasis on reform and economic discipline. Parliamentary factions in general staged a less than inspiring performance. The need for some authoritative symbolism and the potency of a nationalistic mystique constituted for many an attractive alternative to confused political feuding, to a proposed Islamized state, or to possible Communist regimentation. President Sukarno's commitment to nationalist incitement and continuing revolutionary instigation was destined in time to find strange bedfellows, with the army leadership aligned on the one side of him and the revolutionary PKI on the other. All three agreed in opposing democracy and political parties. From the standpoint of implementing economic development plans, this emerging coalition became part of the problem, contributing nothing to a possible solution.[26]

The Elections of 1955

The Indonesian election campaign of 1955 was conducted with vigor and enthusiasm, for expectations were high. Electioneering was encouraged; both candidates and the press were free to discuss issues and to criticize the government. Attention was nevertheless diverted from important domestic issues by Sukarno's widely heralded Bandung Conference, which was held in the spring of 1955, featuring the participation of Asian and African states to the exclusion of the West. Nationalism became the dominant issue in the election, focusing on Sukarno personally and on the vindication of what was assumed to be Indonesia's enhanced place in the world. Patriotic aspirations provided a kind of tent under which a score of minor party groupings, centering around personalities and regional issues, could find a semblance of cohesion. The diversion was particularly attractive to corrupt Outer Island officials engaged in lucrative smuggling activities. Religion was clearly the second

250

most potent factor in the election. The cause was championed at the village level by *desa* headmen and religious teachers. The defection of the orthodox Nahdatul Ulama weakened the Masjumi appeal in Eastern and Central Java and defeated any possible attainment of a convincing Masjumi parliamentary plurality.

Elections results were inconclusive. The two principal protagonists, Sukarno's Nationalist PNI and the Masjumi party, gained precisely the same number of seats in the new Parliament, fifty-seven each. The PNI seats came largely from Java and those of the Masjumi from Sumatra. The strength of orthodox Islam in Java was reflected in the forty-five victories registered by the Nahdatul Ulama candidates, rivals of the Masjumi. The renovated Communist party emerged with a surprising thirty-nine seats. These four parties commanded 90 percent of the votes and 77 percent of the seats. The remaining fifty-nine seats were shared by no fewer than twenty-four parties; most of them reflected little more than their several ideological and regional peculiarities. The principal casualty, as previously indicated, was the highly articulate Socialist Party, which proved unable to compete for popular support and virtually dropped out of the political picture as a party organization.

The Communist campaign was conducted with vigor and imagination. The party polled 4.6 million votes in Central and Eastern Java, some 850,000 in Djarkarta and Western Java, and around 525,000 in Sumatra. It was an amazingly well-financed campaign, with an estimated 200 million *rupiahs* expended for hired buses, entertainments, and the distribution of posters, soft drinks, kites, and straw hats. The tone, pitched to appeal to workers and peasants, was ultranationalistic and ostensibly pro-Sukarno, anti-Masjumi, and anti-PSI. The party collected most of its funds by assessing local Chinese residents under pressure, supposedly with the cooperation of personnel connected with the Chinese embassy and with an assist from the Bank of China. The latter controlled remittances sent to relatives in China. That the PKI political effort was no flash in

251

the pan was demonstrated by the results of provincial elections held in Java in 1957, when the Communist candidates took over several seats held by Sukarno supporters.[27]

It is not surprising that the three other major parties were genuinely alarmed by the Communist political performance, even though the extent of the outside support was not immediately apparent. All three were determined not to permit Communist party participation in the new government, even though Sukarno urged that such action be taken to dilute the Masjumi influence. The Harahap government gave way in March 1956 to a coalition cabinet led by PNI's Sastroamidjojo, Masjumi's Natsir, and the Nahdatul Ulama. The disparate factions found it difficult to cooperate on any positive legislative program, notwithstanding their common hostility to the Communist movement. Sharp disagreement developed when Natsir demanded that corruption be curbed. By the end of 1956, a number of rebellious colonels began to challenge the authority of the central government, especially in Sumatra.[28]

Although the election contest was fairly conducted, it was largely irrelevant to basic economic problems. Issues that were given no explicit consideration included the difficulties of Outer Island autonomy and trade, the antidemocratic influence of the army and the president, and what to do about relieving popular discontent, which was being so effectively exploited by the PKI. The psychological urge for consensus persisted, even though cabinet members within the same party disagreed over what to do and the bureaucracy was mired down in petty controversy. The military heroes of the nationalist struggle felt cheated of the rewards they believed were due them. A perceptive Socialist spokesman commented that, "The future role . . . of the parliamentary system . . . will depend on the ability of the parties to rebuild themselves gradually into effective instruments of political power, able to cope with the concrete issues of the nation."[29]

252

The Demise of Parliamentary Democracy

Governmental and political developments following the elections of 1955 were far from encouraging. The essentially anti-Communist coalition cabinet headed by Premier Ali Sastroamidjojo and the Masjumi's Natsir was poorly integrated. It failed to act vigorously against official corruption as Natsir, presumably for political considerations, demanded. From their position outside the government, the Communist leadership was able to make political capital by citing the government's ineffective performance and by insisting that most political party activities were financed through official corruption, including allocations appropriated from foreign aid funds. By the time the cabinet had formulated a revised economic development program in late 1956, the program was already inadequate to meet ever-growing needs. The plans included no provision for enlisting managerial or business talent, for accelerating migration from Java to underdeveloped areas of the Outer Islands, for the better regional allocation of resources, or for the assignment of adequate funds for industry and education. The long delay in reaching any basic decisions had permitted the initial enthusiasm of the independence dynamic to spend itself. To the increasing evidence of partisan rivalry (whether regional, party, military vs. civilian, or simply venal), Sukarno added the emotionally charged demand that Dutch Irian (West New Guinea) be annexed, while problems of economic development were being pushed aside.

In 1956, despite the urgency of unsolved domestic problems, President Sukarno embarked on a world tour, which included visits to the United States, the Soviet Union, and Communist China. He was particularly impressed by the flattering attention accorded him in Moscow and Peking and by his exposure in both capitals to the alleged advantages of planned economic development on the Communist model. Lacking confidence in Western democratic procedures, Sukarno became fired with a sense of revolutionary mission

253

to lead his people out of their wilderness of political frustration and economic confusion.

The factional rifts that developed within the Indonesian body politic during the latter half of 1956 were both deep and complex. Basic popular grievances related to inflationary price increases, widespread corruption, and faulty allocation of limited financial resources. Such problems were compounded by personal antagonisms between civilian and army leaders, rivalries within the ranks of the army itself, and Outer Island dissatisfaction with the allocation of export earnings. Two abortive coups were staged by army malcontents in August and November 1956, directed respectively at corrupt cabinet personnel and at Major General Nasution, army chief of staff. Increasing political pressure was put on Natsir by Sumatran elements of the Masjumi party to withdraw from the Ali cabinet, a demand he countered with increasing difficulty. Army commanders assigned to various areas of Sumatra, denied adequate funds to pay and to support their troops, stepped up the illegal bartering of such exportable items as copra and rubber in order to realize additional local income.[30] Many of the saleable items were appropriated from former Dutch plantations that were still occupied partly by squatters.

The difficulties of the government were further aggravated by the actions of President Sukarno who, in October and November, declared that Western democracy was unsuitable for Indonesia and must be abandoned. The pursuit of nationalist revolutionary objectives must be revived, including the exclusion of the Dutch from Irian and the assertion of the leadership of Indonesia within the East Indies area. He argued that the party system must be buried and that a new democratic system be devised capable of protecting weaker groups from exploitation by allegedly predatory party factions. The Communists in particular gave enthusiastic support to President Sukarno's proposals.

In a dubious attempt to challenge the president's anti-democratic orientation and, presumably, to bridge the growing rift between Djakarta and the provincial authorities,

Vice-President Hatta, himself a Sumatran, resigned his ,elected post in December. He then openly attacked Sukarno's advocacy of continuing revolutionary activity as destructive of national unity and completely unproductive. He insisted that revolution could not properly be regarded as an end in itself, that it was at most a preliminary to constructive efforts to reach new adjustments and useful compromise decisions. Revolutionary tactics, he argued, would inevitably play into the hands of Communist partisans associated with the cause of proletarian revolution directed from abroad, but his rational protest was completely unavailing. Hatta's abdication of his legitimate role in the government left Sukarno without any highly placed antagonist within the state structure who was capable of contesting his political manipulations; it also set the stage for a series of Outer Island rebellions.

Three Sumatran military coups occurred at two-day intervals, starting on December 20. The first move was by Lieutenant Colonel Achmad Hussein, who assumed control over the provisional government of West Sumatran Padang, by setting up a ruling council composed of military personnel and civilians. Two days later, Colonel Simbolon, who had collaborated with Nasution in 1952, took a similar action at Medan in Northern Sumatra. He was followed by Lieutenant Colonel Barlian at Palembang in the south of the island. All three dissident officers asserted their loyalty to the Republic, urged that Hatta resume his vice-presidential role, and affirmed their opposition to Sukarno's authoritarian (and presumed Javan) rule. Chief of State Nasution managed to achieve an early accomodation with Simbolon, who was reassigned elsewhere, but Hussein and Barlian continued to defy Djakarta's authority for several months. It was the inability of the Ali cabinet to reassert control over rebellious regional factions that brought about its disintegration. Natsir's Masjumi group withdrew in January 1957.

The first formal exposition of Sukarno's rationale for the "Guided Democracy" system came in a speech of February 21, 1957. He proposed to set up a cabinet of mutual cooperation (*gotong-rojong*) that would include representatives of all the major parties, coupled with an advisory national council, in which basic functional groups would participate. The council would include leaders of important economic, social, and religious groups, plus such governmental categories as the civil service, army, and police. This advisory body would presumably represent the dynamic forces of the society, and would operate under Sukarno's personal chairmanship. Meanwhile, the cabinet would represent all varieties of political opinion, not excepting the Communists, and would exercise plenary authority. Sukarno also argued that Indonesia must henceforth follow an independent foreign policy in order to enhance national ends through accelerated revolutionary activity.[31]

PKI spokesmen hailed the speech as a commitment to resume the aborted revolutionary endeavor that had begun in 1945. On the day after the speech, Communist-organized mass demonstrations developed in Djakarta and elsewhere in ostensible support of Sukarno's revolutionary program. They continued for more than two weeks, with youth squads defacing public buildings, churches, embassies, and hotels with PKI slogans in a crescendo of unrest. The agitators were eventually curbed by army intervention on March 11, but not before the Ali Cabinet had been completely discredited. The cabinet resigned on March 13, and Guided Democracy had begun.

Meanwhile, in early March 1957, a new epidemic of regional revolts began. In the Greater East, one Lieutenant Colonel Ventji Sumual declared parts of Sulawesi (Celebes), the Moluccas, and the Lesser Sunda Islands separated from Djakarta's control. As in the previous December revolts, the new movement was pro-Hatta and was roundly condemned as such by the Communists as well as by Sukarno. A long-simmering Kalimantan rebellion also flared up, and dissidents again raised their heads in southern Sumatra. Following Nasution's suggestion, Sukarno declared a state of siege and imposed central army control over all disaffected regions.[32] One effect was to legalize the *de facto* authority of virtually all local army commanders. The net result was to strengthen the power of General Nasution throughout the Republic.

Sukarno's new orientation was vigorously challenged by former Vice-President Hatta, but with little effect. National unity and independence, he declared, could not possibly be enhanced by government collaboration with a Communist party organization associated with the cause of worldwide revolution, directed from the outside. Hatta denounced Sukarno's proposed council as both unconstitutional and redundant, suggesting that governmental stability would be better achieved if Sukarno took over personal responsibility for operating a presidential cabinet as long as martial law prevailed. During the interim, Hatta argued, Sukarno should undertake to consult with all party leaders and other knowledgeable experts concerning policy decisions. Hatta's ideas died aborning, partly because Sukarno had no desire to accept the onerous task of directing government operations personally. Other opponents of Sukarno's proposals felt that Hatta would have been more effective if his declared opposition could have been launched from within the government itself. That democracy could have been saved at this late date is impossible to affirm, but with Hatta gone the cause lacked any strategically placed champion who could challenge the drift toward totalitarian control.

The precise circumstances attending the drift toward Guided Democracy will be considered in chapter IX. It is relevant here to summarize the reasons for the expiration of representative democracy in 1957. In Indonesia, it had never been a hardy animal. Seven years was a short time for the body politic to adjust to a strange environment where popular expectations were highly inflated, and the political experience and responsibility of party leaders were minimal. Furthermore, Sukarno's role was a negative one. Unlike Premier Nu of Burma, the Indonesian president was never sympathetic to the democratic experiment. On occasion he had done much to thwart the efforts of responsible leaders like Hatta, Natsir, Sumitro, and Wilopo, who were struggling to cope with formidable administrative and economic problems.

257

Apologists for Sukarno have argued that his ritualistic nationalism took control only after constitutional means had failed to produce solutions. The nationalists were more concerned with the crucial task of regional integration than were the problem-oriented administrators. It can be questioned in rejoinder, whether artificially-stimulated national unity, emanting largely from Java alone, was of much use in dispelling the essential causes of the tensions that were reflected in the confused political spectrum. The cultural dichotomy between populous and highly civilized Java, with its long tradition of empire and social maturity, and the economically endowed Outer Islands, with their more flexible atmosphere, could not have been bridged easily under any circumstances. The potential for governmental and economic leadership lay largely within the non-Javanese segment, which Sukarno persistently opposed. The unifying influence of his personality and charisma would have been far more effective if it had been used in support of those who sought solutions for regional and economic problems.[33]

A somewhat more basic analysis, one that is divorced from personalities and governmental fumbling, relates to the rootlessness of the postindependence government of Indonesia in terms of cultural authentication. Javanese political traditions, including the colonial period, generally provided little basis for a nonauthoritarian government responsible to the will of the people. Rulers were traditionally regarded as responsible to some kind of cosmic moral order to which the people also owed respect and allegiance. There simply was no viable traditional concept of the validity of individual rights that governments were obliged to respect. The best government was one that ruled by consensus, but in paternalistic fashion. Such practices as debating controversial issues in public, holding formal votes in Parliament, and involving a score or more of competing parties in general elections were novel and exciting to most Indonesians, but they usually served mainly to advertise differences of opinion and to aggravate political tensions.

The pragmatic test of democracy in Indonesia added

258

little to its theoretical credentials. In the absence of a supporting clientèle, political corruption became the primary source of party income. Elected officials in the Parliament or local councils could become just as venal as were the members of the appointed bureaucracy. Dutch colonial rule, while maintaining much of traditional authority at the village level, had destroyed the historic symbols of governmental authority at the center. Contrary to Burma and the Philippines, Indonesia had been afforded by the Dutch no meaningful acquaintance with democratic theory or procedures. Others have pointed out that a constitution providing for single-member parliamentary constituencies instead of proportional representation and affording adequate provision for the encouragement of local initiative in economic development would have been helpful. But any future Indonesian government that was not militarily imposed must face the inescapable task of legitimizing its authority by means of constructive performance.[34]

A comment by a member of a United Nations Advisory team, as of 1957, is particularly relevant:

> [Indonesia's leaders] seek more "businessmindedness" on the part of their people but are opposed by their own desires to hold on to . . . mutual aid and familistic concepts. They would like to be a blend of traditional village life and the modern world of trade and commerce and advanced technology. . . . The wish to increase efficiency in government and business conflicts with the desire to retain . . . paternalism. . . . No clear political . . . decision as to the proper role of foreign enterprise has yet been made. . . . [They are also] ambivalent about the role in their society of . . . modern competitive . . . individual enterprise.[35]

What was lacking, in other words, was a clear delineation of the kind of society they really wanted to build. The task was far from easy.

---

1. Clifford Geertz, *The Religion of Java* (Glencoe, Ill., 1960), pp. 227-49, 255-77, 288, 349-63.

2. Selosoemardjan, *Social Change in Jogjakarta* (Ithaca, 1968), pp. 362-74; S. Takir Alisjabana, *Indonesia: Social and Cultural Revolution* (New York, 1966), pp. 3-12.

3. Selosoemardjan, *op. cit.*, pp. 372-84; James Legge, *Indonesia* (Englewood Cliffs, N. J., 1964), 120-27.

4. Geertz, *op. cit.*, pp. 121-42, 148-76.

5. George M. Kahin, *Nationalism and Revolution in Indonesia* (Ithaca, 1952), pp. 326-32.

6. Geertz, *op. cit.*, pp. 12-29, 112-18.

7. Goege C. Allen and Audrey B. Donnithorne, *Western Enterprise in Indonesia and Malaya* (London, 1957), pp. 74-77.

8. Clifford Geertz, *Peddlers and Princes: Social Change and Modernization in Two Indonesian Towns* (Chicago, 1963), pp. 7-17.

9. Benjamin Higgins and Jean Higgins, *Indonesia, Crisis of the Millstones* (Princeton, 1963), chap. 3 and 4.

10. W. F. Wertheim, *Indonesian Society in Transition* (The Hague, 1959), pp. 120-31.

11. Douglas S. Paauw, "Economic Progress in Southeast Asia," *Journal of Asian Studies*, 23 (November, 1963): 69-92.

12. Benjamin Higgins, *Indonesia's Economic Stabilization and Development* (New York, 1957), pp. 1-2.

13. L. G. M. Jaquet, "The Indonesian Federal Problem Reconsidered," *Pacific Affairs*, 25 (1952): 170-75; George Kahin, "Indonesia" in *Major Governments of Asia* (Ithaca, 1963), pp. 594-95.

14. Gerald Maryanov, *Decentralization of Indonesia as a Political Problem* (Ithaca, 1958), pp. 13-16, 32-33, 39-45, 61-62.

15. Rupert Emerson, *Representative Government in Southeast Asia* (Cambridge, 1955), p. 240; Kahin, "Indonesia" in *Major Governments*, pp. 626-35.

16. Kahin, *Major Governments*, pp. 569-72, 598-606.

17. Arnold C. Brackman, *Indonesian Communism* (New York, 1963), pp. 178-86.

18. C. A. O. Van Niewenhuijze, *Aspects of Islam in Post-Colonial Indonesia* (The Hague, 1958), pp. 52-66.

19. Ruth McVey, "Communism and the Transition to Guided Democracy" in A. Doak Barnett, ed., *Communist Strategies in Asia, a Comparative Analysis of Governments and Parties* (New York, 1963), pp. 148-62.

20. Brackman, *op. cit.*, pp. 180-82.

21. Guy Pauker, "Indonesia," in John J. Johnson, ed., *The Role of the Military in Underdeveloped Countries* (Princeton, 1962), pp. 207-9; also B. and J. Higgins, *op. cit.*, pp. 78-85. The Wilopo Cabinet included Sultan Hamengku Buwono, Sumitro, Djuanda, and Sjafruddin. It had been preceded by three cabinets headed in turn by Hatta, Natsir, and Sukiman, the latter two representing the Masjumi party. Premier Sastroamidjojo followed Wilopo in August, 1953 (PNI and Nahdatul Ulama), with Harahap's cabinet from August, 1955 to March 1956, and again by Sastroamidjojo to March 1957.

22. Alisjabana, *op. cit.*, pp. 116-25; Kahin, *Major Governments*, p. 622.

23. B. and J. Higgins, *op. cit.*, chap. 3.

24. B. Higgins, *Indonesia's Economic Stabilization*, pp. 71-77 and chap. 4.

25. *Ibid.*, pp. 23-24, 109-10.

26. B. and J. Higgins, *op. cit.*, pp. 85-93. Leading members of the Wilopo cabinet were all Dutch trained.

27. Herbert Feith, "Toward Elections in Indonesia," *Pacific Affairs*, 27 (1954): pp. 263-69; See also Kahin, "Indonesia" in *Major Governments*, p. 616 and Brachman, *op. cit.*, pp. 217-21.

28. Herbert Feith "The Dynamics of Guided Democracy," in Ruth T. McVey, ed., *Indonesia* (New Haven, 1963), pp. 312-14.

29. Soedjatmoko, "The Role of Political Parties In Indonesia," in Philip W. Thayer, ed., *Nationalism and Progress in Free Asia* (Baltimore, 1956), pp. 130-39. See also McVey, *Indonesia* pp. 313-18, and Wertheim, *op. cit.*, pp. 342-46.

30. Kahin, "Indonesia" in *Major Governments*, pp. 621-26.

31. *Ibid.*

32. Herbert Feith, *The Decline of Constitutional Democracy in Indonesia* (Ithaca 1962), pp. 544-48; Legge, *Authority and Regional Autonomy in Indonesia* (Ithaca, 1957), pp. 33-37.

33. For alternative points of view on this central issue, see L. H. Palmier, *Indonesia and the Dutch* (New York, 1962), pp. 180-94, and H. Feith, *Decline of Constitutional Democracy*, pp. 600-08.

34. Kahin, "Indonesia" in *Major Governments*, pp. 628-38.

35. Selosoemardjan, *op. cit.*, pp. 362-74.

IX

FROM INDONESIA'S
GUIDED DEMOCRACY TO
MILITARY DICTATORSHIP

The Inauguration of Guided Democracy

The abandonment of Indonesia's experiment with constitutional democracy within a scant eighteen months after the first general election was depressing on several counts. It was the first of several governmental fiascos in post-colonial Southeast Asia that involved the near collapse of endeavors at economic development as well. Sukarno's alternative brand of Guided Democracy also triggered an orgy of chauvinistic nationalism that seriously damaged relations with Malaysia and, by 1965, threatened a political debacle domestically. The dismal situation was complicated by problems of overpopulation and by marginal involvement in the Cold War.

Sukarno's initial effort, made in March and April, 1957, to form a ruling cabinet centering around his PNI nationalist party, but including representatives of the three other major political organizations, was quickly abandoned. The Masjumi and Nahdatul Ulama Muslim parties flatly refused to be associated with the Communists. Acting as formateur himself, Sukarno then undertook to designate his own cabinet. He persuaded the unaffiliated and colorless Djuanda Kartawidjaja to act as Premier of a cabinet built around his own PNI group and the cooperating Nahdatul Ulama, leaving out the Masjumi and the Communists. Hatta on this occasion refused Djuanda's offer of a ministerial post. A month later, Sukarno selected an advisory council of forty-three members representing "functional" non-political groups in an ostensible effort to establish a basis for achieving a broad consensus. The unity achieved, however, was one of idea-starved sycophants. Only the co-operating army leadership maintained governmental authority outside the capital in those situations where regional friction flamed into periodic violence.

Widespread resistance to this Sukarno-army domination developed in late 1957 and early 1958 but was not coordinated. On November 30, 1957, a group of fanatical young Muslim followers of Lieutenant Colonel Zulkifli Lubis attempted to assassinate Sukarno in a grenade attack. Lubis and fellow dissidents fled to Central Sumatra.[1] Many Masjumi leaders also fled Djakarta following their harrassment by government-protected youth gangs. In January a group of Sumatran Masjumi rebels issued an ultimatum demanding the resignation of the Djuanda government. When the ultimatum expired on February 15, the group proclaimed the Revolutionary Government of the Republic of Indonesia, headed by Sjafruddin Prawiranegara, which enjoyed strong backing from several local military commanders. Another group of rebels in northern Sulawesi immediately announced their own support of the Sumatran movement.

Another factor contributing to the confusion at this juncture was the government's seizure of Dutch properties throughout the islands—partly to divert attention from political grievances and partly to mollify Sumatran dissidents. All Dutch plantations, mines, oil properties, factories, and trading facilities were seized. Previous confiscations had been limited to railways, airlines, and the Bank of Indonesia and had been mostly in Java. The action was more a gesture of nationalist assertion than a move toward socialization. Most of the seized properties were turned over to loyal local officials, both civilian and military, who permitted the people to exploit newfound opportunities.

The expropriation of comparable non-Dutch Western capital holdings came two years later, all of it carrying only vague promises of eventual compensation.

Some clandestine American military aid got through to the several rebel movements. It was presumably given on the assumption that the dissidents were not promoting territorial disunity but challenging Communist infiltration at Djakarta, as Hatta had done at the time of his resignation. When the limited nature of the rebel movements became evident, American assistance was hurriedly disavowed. The Sumatran revolts collapsed by May, and the north Sulawesi effort faltered in July, 1958.

The collapse of the rebellions of 1958 produced serious political consequences. For the time being the leaders of the Masjumi party were discredited, as were virtually all of the ablest pro-Western leaders who opposed Sukarno's Guided Democracy and his continuing tolerance of the PKI.[2] The abortive rebellions gave Sukarno an opportunity to denounce his political opponents as tools of the American imperialists and to appeal for military aid from Eastern Europe for his Irian campaign. Javanese PKI leadership seized the occasion to denounce the Sumatran colonels in the name of the displaced workers who had temporarily occupied the Dutch plantation properties.[3]

The complete implementation of the Guided Democracy system came in early 1959, legally bringing an end to any pretense of parliamentary democracy. When the rump of the 1955 Assembly, acting as a Constituent Assembly, refused the proposal of Sukarno and Nasution to reactivate the draft Constitution of 1945, which provided for a strong executive officer, all political activities were abruptly banned. On July 5, 1959, Sukarno published a presidential decree activating the 1945 Constitution; three days later he announced the formation of a new cabinet, which he proposed to head personally in his dual role as president and prime minister. He required that all new cabinet ministers give up their previous party affiliations, but still saw to it that all major party groups except the Masjumi

264

and the Socialists were represented in the new cabinet and in the major planning and advisory groups.

In August of 1959 Sukarno spelled out more explicitly the goals of Guided Democracy. He focused attention on three basic points: providing food and clothing for the people; restoring internal security; and continuing the struggle against imperialism, which involved gaining control over West Irian from the Dutch.[4] A further move, in September, reorganized the several regional governments to bring them under more strict control of the central authority, thereby negating somewhat the increasing Communist influence within the elected regional assemblies of Java. Sukarno's concept of Guided Democracy had enjoyed from the outset the active support of Nasution and the army command, which favored an authoritarian government. Army influence gained in 1958–59, following the collapse of the several rebellions and in the face of increasing PKI strength in regional elections. Many Indonesian civilians began to think that Guided Democracy might indeed be some improvement.[5] The last remnants of parliamentary democracy disappeared in 1960 when Sukarno completed the dissolution of the elected parliament.

Sukarno's Guided Democracy experiment can most charitably be judged as a sincere but misguided effort to bridge the cleavages existing within the Indonesian body politic. As presidential leader, he made the most of his personal charisma to divert attention from divisive issues by deliberately fanning nationalist and revolutionary emotions. An excerpt from his *Manifesto Politik* (*Manipol*) will illustrate:

> I am obsessed with the romanticism of revolution. . . . A state which does not grow in a revolutionary way will not only be crushed by its own people, but also will be swept away by the typhoon of universal revolution . . . leading to the formation of a new world free of colonialism, free of exploitation . . . free from oppression. . . . Guided Democracy means swiftly increasing state ownership and control . . . [and] rejection of Western values. . . . The old

house with its creaky boards and hinges is not merely [to be] renovated, but razed.

To this declaration of revolutionary purpose should be added Sukarno's dedication to the five principles of *Pantja Sila*, namely faith in God, nationalism, humanitarianism, popular sovereignty, and social justice, which could function as a bag of verbal magic capable of providing sanctions for almost any assumed point of view.[6]

It is not difficult to recognize that liberal Western government institutions were ill adapted to the requirements and capacities of emerging Asian states, since uninhibited expression of divergent points of view could threaten to destroy the state. It is also arguable that controlled discussion under purposeful leadership was needed to enlist popular acceptance of governmental authority. Superficially viewed, Guided Democracy appeared to embody some of the accepted traditions of Javanese civilization, facilitating general discussion of common problems in an effort to achieve consensus and harmonious cooperation. But nationalism and revolution propagated for their own sakes provided no basis for positive and constructive solutions of urgent problems.[7]

The three-sided pattern of control that emerged under Guided Democracy was a strange amalgam of arbitrary government, army power, and Communist propaganda. The government, as directed by Sukarno on a nonparty basis, took full advantage of the leader's personal charisma and his ill-defined role as president. His prestige as a political hero above partisan strife and as an articulate spokesman of national aspirations was widely acknowledged. He had no rivals as an orator and as a manipulator of the symbols and rituals of nationhood. But Sukarno needed something more substantial than oratory and personal prestige to maintain his role as leader. A cooperating army command provided him the physical resources needed to cope with Outer Island rebellions or with the political impasse that party intransigence might pose. He also needed the assistance of the PKI to help dramatize the cause of anticolonial nationalism and revolutionary fervor.[8] Neither the army nor the Communist propagandists could push the other aside as long as Sukarno stood in the middle, performing his balancing act. The charade lasted until October 1, 1965.

The Army and the PKI in Guided Democracy

Within the troika of Guided Democracy, the political influence of the army was never fully commensurate with its physical powers. Army leaders exploited their status as the heroic instruments of the freedom struggle and the embodiment of national ideals. They claimed the right and duty to share actively with political groups the responsibility for promoting the welfare of the nation.[9] Even so, the army leaders were usually not capable of effective political intervention. They were far from agreement in their own purposes and concerns, since military interests tended to be parochial and personal, rather than national or international in character. General Nasution and associates at the center backed Java's authority, while commanders in the Outer Islands developed a competitive stake in local trading and sources of revenue and in the supervision of nationalized foreign enterprises. The armed services possessed neither the interest nor the capacity to promote economic reforms and nationwide development.[10]

The legal authority of the army stemmed from Sukarno's declaration of martial law in April 1957, but it persisted long after the emergency period had passed. Wherever rebellion flared or was incipiently present, army commanders displaced top civilian officials. Naked military dictatorship was seldom imposed, for the bureaucracy was a needed ally. Army prestige required some legal justification for any overt defiance of civilian rule. Military leaders were prominently represented in both the cabinet and in Sukarno's Advisory Council. They also assumed the self-appointed role of custodians of patriotism, staging Heroes' Days, patriotic rituals at gravesides, and sponsoring the Veteran's Legion, and the National Front for the Liberation of Irian. They also promoted the participation of youth and worker corps in training programs for the people's defense, covering crisis indoctrination and recent military history.[11]

The Communist party also developed an impressive promotional routine. Under the leadership of Party Secretary Aidit, the advocacy of doctrinaire Marxism and direct peoples action was muted in favor of support for Sukarno's goals and of clever exploitation of traditional value symbols and institutions. Communist slogans found their way into ceremonial presentations at village festivals and popular dramatic performances. Home visits were made to discuss popular grievances, not on a class-warfare basis, but with the ostensible idea of arriving at some kind of consensus, *adat* fashion. At the outset, special attention was paid to the development of the Central Labor Organization (SOBSI), to promote the struggle against capitalism and to recruit voter strength.[12]

The handicaps the party faced were nevertheless formidable. The army was hostile, as were the several Islamic parties, the bureaucracy, and the fading *priyayi* elite. Radical-minded Socialist intellectuals were expelled. Virtually all other political camps, including the army, were also recruiting their own mass organization support. Communist propagandists had to prove that such rival efforts were not genuinely concerned about the needs of nonprivileged workers and peasants. The PKI sponsored a Peoples Cultural Association, interested in welfare projects, educational programs, and expression in the creative arts, which proved effective. By 1957 the party had captured council control in a dozen regencies in local Javan elections, gains that outstripped the performance of any rival political group at the time.

Taking advantage of the fact that the party was denied any substantive participation in the central government, PKI spokesmen fanned popular criticism of official shortcomings. They also denounced sterile religious partisanship, elite disregard of villager grievances, and evidences of economic decline. Party membership surpassed two million by 1958, and supporting mass organizations grew even more rapidly. Sensing the possibility of accession to power by electoral procedures, PKI spokesmen began to extol the holding of elections, along with freedom of speech, press, and assembly, but not to the point of breaking with Sukarno. He, meanwhile, was trying to domesticate the PKI and to utilize it to promote his own "functional" youth, worker, peasant, and veteran National Front groups.[13]

The PKI realized little success with the SOBSI labor unions and gradually abandoned their promotion. The labor approach was handicapped by the fact that the popular demand for jobs themselves was greater than were the needs for minor wage and hour adjustments. Labor unions served generally as addenda to political organizations; their members were better at staging demonstrations than at serving as union officials. In the Outer Islands, military authorities suppressed any initiatives by plantation workers to take over former Dutch properties. Eventually Guided Democracy flatly outlawed strikes in all vital economic categories, so that SOBSI units lost their morale, membership, revenues, and political importance.[14] Much more effective was the party's distribution of pro-Peking literature within its membership and in selected Chinese communities, where pride in China's enhanced political stature attracted widespread admiration.[15]

Among the Javanese villagers, Communist agitators advocated land reform, salaries for headmen, improved wages for workers, lower interest rates, reduced landlord claims on the crops, and cooperative aid projects. They also exploited traditional tensions with the Muslim *santri* critics of surviving *adat* practices. They criticized the government effectively for failing to carry out its own reform legislation of 1960. Under such stimulation, the party grew steadily, attaining an estimated four and a half million members by 1963.[16] Such gains were not reflected in any comparable growth of party influence in the central government, however. The first PKI cabinet role began in March 1962, when two nonportfolio posts were assigned to Aidit and to his lieutenant, Lukman. The PKI leaders were more free thereafter to communicate with their Outer Island cadres, but they realized little other advantage. Aidit argued in vain that more direct Communist party participation in public affairs could help arrest social and economic deterioration, which threatened, if unchecked, to turn popular despair into anger and violence.[17] The response from the army leadership in particular was a flat negative.[18]

Controversy between the army and the PKI was never far below the surface. A crisis developed in 1959–60, when the principal Communist newspaper was banned temporarily because it denounced the alleged dishonesty of army members of the cabinet. Regional army commanders in Sumatra, Borneo, and Sulawesi, acting independently at the time, actually outlawed the party within their respective jurisdictions for denouncing army profiteering in the use of expropriated Dutch properties. The party managed to recover a measure of freedom in Java only because Sukarno intervened personally as its sponsor and protector. The sixth National Party Congress convened in 1959, despite army objections, only after obtaining direct permission from the president. Sukarno appeared in person to address one party session. When all political party activities were finally banned in 1960, Aidit gave pro forma acceptance to the ruling, but he continued to blame governmental deficiencies on the bureaucracy and the army. The "bureaucratic capitalists" were abusing governmental authority for personal profit, displaying contempt for social objectives, and exhibiting neither the inclination nor the ability to solve economic development problems, Aidit claimed, but because his words were denied wide circulation, such criticisms were ineffective. The more radical pro-China faction within the party began subjecting Aidit's policy of calculated moderation to increasing criticism.[19] Direct action tactics were nevertheless out of the question as long as the armed services front stood firm.

Differences between Sukarno and the high army command were largely submerged in the surfeit of nationalist agitation, to be discussed below. Despite the army's dislike of Sukarno's tolerance of the Communist activity, General Nasution and his principal associates felt confident that they could contain any direct PKI thrust for power. Friction erupted within the cabinet on occasion. In 1959 the army drove Sukarno's attorney general from office when he tried to press corruption charges against the headquarters command. Sukarno later kicked Nasution upstairs to be chief of staff of the combined services in order to place his own nominee in the top army post. He also transferred three regional commanders who were too blatantly anti-Communist.[20] Sukarno's delicate balancing act could not continue indefinitely.

The Widespread Abuse of Government Power

The Guided Democracy regime tended to aggravate the abuse of government power. Sukarno was in part to blame, since he made no determined effort to curb corruption and displayed virtually no interest in solving economic problems. At its best, army leadership provided an element of stability, holding the nation together while buying time to gain experience and governing competence. At its worst and in the absence of responsible civilian control, it degenerated into a rivalry-ridden parasite preying on the state.[21] Proponents of Guided Democracy, trying to find a scapegoat for the sorry state of affairs, usually attributed the system's failure to the inherited evils of colonial rule and the continuing machinations of capitalist imperialism.[22]

Under the new system, bureaucratic decay was infectious and progressive. Army personnel occupied approximately one-third of the cabinet posts, and high officers issued directives to regional commanders relating to civilian responsibilities whenever it suited their interests to do so.[23] The continued tenure of the civil servants depended in large measure on their conformity to army policy, and they were left free to supplement their inadequate salaries by taking on extra jobs or levying exactions on clients. The continuing escalation of consumer prices, which multiplied seven times from 1951 to 1961 and even more rapidly thereafter, left them no alternative. Con-

271

formity to a public image of avowed loyalty to the "revolutionary struggle" took precedence over official honesty and effective administration. In the charged atmosphere, even such tangible objectives as steel mills, power installations, and the transportation infrastructure took on the character of semisacred public monuments.

Elaborate bureaucratic regulations set some parameters for payoffs, police bribes, and falsification of accounts, but they did little to promote administrative efficiency. Licensed businesses had to cultivate helpful political connections, since both police and judges were subject to executive interference. Peasants (in Java particularly) had to sell their surpluses to government agencies at fixed prices and were subjected to unpaid labor exactions in the off season. The tendency was to cheat wherever possible. The rigors of the system were softened only by avoiding strict enforcement of regulations and by practicing corruption in moderation. Indonesia developed no concentration camps, and no confessions were exacted by torture, since the game was still played by some accepted rules.[24]

The Dimensions of Economic Decline

Indonesia's economic decline reflected a number of tendencies toward stagnation dating from the prewar depression. Increased population pressure in Java after the war and the failure of Javanese to migrate to the Outer Islands in large numbers aggravated the evils of shared poverty. Many products of the colonial period, such as sugar and coffee, were no longer economically profitable in terms of the world market, and yet the arbitrarily low price for badly needed rice provided no incentive for peasants to abandon their traditional crop routines. Rice imports multiplied by five times from 1955 to 1958, absorbing one-fifth of the foreign currencies acquired from Outer Island exports. Trade between Java and the Outer Islands declined, primarily because the Islands sold almost 80 percent of their surpluses abroad, and very little to Java. This situation improved economic conditions in selected Outer Island regions but also afforded opportunities for profitable smuggling on the part of local armed services personnel. Because the central government lacked control over foreign trade, it could not find the foreign exchange needed for essential imports. The coordination of export production and import needs was also hindered by declining output from the newly nationalized foreign investment properties.

The moderately encouraging 2.5 percent annual gains in real per capita income realized during the Korean War boom were completely dissipated by 1957. Consumer prices rose some 20 to 40 percent in 1958 and reached an increase of 50 to 100 percent by 1961. The mounting political crisis over West Irian afforded opportunity for Sukarno to complete the expropriation of Dutch enterprises, to be followed by the seizure of British, American, Swiss, Danish, Belgian, and French properties, with only vague commitments regarding compensation. During the course of the West Irian crisis from 1957 to 1961, an estimated sixty thousand Dutch personnel departed Indonesia, incurring some two billion dollars in property losses. During the same period, most government-sponsored cooperatives collapsed, as part of the general decline of production and trade.[26] In the face of increasing inflation, the pay of civil servants had to be supplemented by rice allocations and subsidized housing accomodations.

Meanwhile, the Five Year Development Plan, which competent foreign economists had helped formulate in 1956, fell completely apart. A new Eight Year plan, implemented with little conviction in 1961, was grandiose in the extreme. It included some 335 designated projects and the expenditure of 240 million unavailable *rupiahs*. The Planning Council itself was politically oriented, and unable amid the plethora of slogans and symbols to coordinate the responsibilities of the agencies concerned.[27]

In the early sixties, the game of soliciting aid and loans from outside governments to make good trade imbalances largely played out. Down to 1961, Indonesia had received from the United States some $380 million in economic credits and surplus agriculture products, plus grants-in-aid

273

amounting to an additional $146 million. Other grants were obtained in 1962. Japanese reparations payments came to $400 million, and the Soviet Union advanced credits totaling $833 million, most of it in military hardware, during the course of the West Irian crisis. Preliminary requirements for price stabilization were examined during the post-Irian lull in early 1963, but the undertaking was sabotaged by the Malaysian Confrontation extravaganza, starting in late 1963.[28]

Despite all of the ominous signs, Indonesia's economic decline and price inflation did not precipitate an immediate political crisis for a variety of reasons. Selected areas of the Outer Islands, like Medan in northern Sumatra, were relatively unaffected. Most Javanese villagers could still survive by subsistence agriculture and barter trade, in situations that violence could do nothing to improve in any case. Civil servants received special allowances and took on additional jobs. Miserably paid Javanese laborers who were reduced to semistarvation were helpless. Governmental deficiencies and inadequate employment, like such natural disasters as flood, drought, earthquakes, and volcanos, might properly be conceived as portents of the approaching end of an era, but they seemed at the time to be beyond political control and must therefore be endured.[29]

Foreign Policy and the Irian Crisis

Starting in 1958, the Djakarta government assumed the self-appointed role of revolutionary leadership in regional affairs and active participation on the world scene as well.[30] Indonesia's stance with respect to the Cold War was slanted toward the so-called New Emerging Forces of Asia, Africa, and Latin America, which were declared to be in confrontation with the surviving remnants of the Old Established Forces of Capitalist Imperialism. During his visit to the USSR early in 1959, Sukarno was encouraged to adopt the new orientation. Moscow apparently saw in the emerging Indonesian role an opportunity to challenge the presumption of Western primacy in Southeast Asia and also to acquire an ally against the threat of possible Chinese dominance once the West was excluded.

This new Indonesian foreign policy found overt expression in the decade-old quarrel with the Dutch over the requested cession of Western New Guinea (Irian). In the Dutch agreement of 1949, The Hague had conceded to Djakarta the sovereignty over Indonesia proper but insisted that West Irian was an entirely separate issue. Later negotiations on the Irian problem produced negative results. Dutch pride and vested interests (missionary as well as business) were involved, coupled with a sense of commitment to the welfare of the primitive Papuan inhabitants. The Papuans differed ethnically and culturally from Indonesians in general, and most of the area had never been a part of the Islands empire prior to Dutch arrival. Except for some meager timber and oil resources, West Irian was of no value commercially, and its climate, topography, and forest cover presented formidable impediments to development.

The quarrel defied solution. Dutch spokesmen argued that the disposition of West Irian had no connection with Indonesian independence and that Djakarta lacked both the capital and skills required to develop the region. This position was generally supported by Australian authorities, who were entrusted with administering the eastern half of the island. Indonesian spokesmen, on the other hand, insisted that continued Dutch occupancy was both illegal and politically intolerable and that the integrity of the emerging Indonesian nation depended on the eradication of this final relic of Dutch colonial control. A joint Dutch-Indonesian commission, visiting the area in 1950, had produced two bulky reports presenting diametrically opposite views as to the alleged wishes of the inhabitants.[31] The discussions thereafter ran firmly aground.

The bilateral quarrel over West Irian took on international significance following three abortive efforts, from 1954 to 1957 on the part of the Indonesian authorities to obtain United Nations approval of resolutions calling upon the Dutch authorities to resume negotiations on the issue. Representatives of the Communist governments and most of the Afro-Asian states in the General Assembly supported the Indonesian resolutions, but the necessary two-thirds majority was lacking. The sympathy of Western governments for the Dutch position was strong, and even those who abstained from voting, as did the United States, were accused of contributing to the failure of the Indonesian effort.

The Irian question took on serious economic implications during the rebellion crisis situation of 1957–58. Anger over Dutch intransigence found expression in the previously mentioned seizure of Dutch properties, including shipping companies, hotels, banks, factories, trading firms, and plantations. West Irian was as much excuse as cause. Formalization of the nationalization procedures followed within the year, which also witnessed the departure of most of the Dutch nationals involved.[32] The ensuing regional rebellions occupied center stage for the time being, coupled with Sukarno's suppression of political party organizations. But the West Irian problem did not go away.

Indonesia's trend toward international alignment with the Communist bloc began in 1957. The United States and Britain were then accused of having supported Dutch colonialism prior to 1949 and of exercising a kind of regional paramountcy in derogation of Indonesia's leadership aspirations. The widespread dispersion of American land, air, and naval bases throughout the Western Pacific area was objectionable to Djakarta, as was the British presence in Singapore, Malaya, and Northern Borneo. But the United States still provided valuable economic aid, and as long as Indonesia's strained relations with China persisted over the rights and status of the Chinese residents within Indonesia, the American and British presence was not entirely unwelcome.

Djakarta's relations with the two Chinas continued to be tense from 1957 to 1960. Indonesian hostility was at first directed at residents who supported Nationalist China, mainly because Chiang's America-allied regime was suspected of assisting the Outer Island rebels. But both the Djakarta government and the army eventually began harassing all resident Chinese regardless of their supposed

276

loyalties, banning all organizations, rural trade activities, and schools. When in 1957 Peking protested such mistreatment of Chinese, a series of highly contentious negotiations ensued. The resulting Dual Nationality Treaty, which was finally ratified in 1960, obliged all Chinese residents seeking Indonesian citizenship to renounce Chinese nationality and thus forego Peking's protection.[33]

Indonesian foreign policy began a major shift in 1960. Because Sukarno was determined to wrest West Irian from the Dutch, the position that other nations took on this issue determined the state of their relations with Djakarta. The repeated refusal of the United States to abandon its allegedly neutral policy and to sell arms to Indonesia finally pushed Sukarno and the army into closer relations with the USSR. When the Dutch dispatched an aircraft carrier to West Irian waters in mid-1960, Sukarno severed diplomatic relations with The Hague, and the armed forces prepared for war. At this juncture the visiting General Nasution was warmly welcomed by Moscow and promised massive military aid to be covered by a Soviet loan of half a billion dollars.

Also implemented in 1960 was an earlier agreement for Soviet economic aid, which included the same type of technical institute previously offered to Burma and Cambodia. It was to be located at Ambon, capital of the South Moluccas territory. A group of potential Indonesian instructors was sent to Odessa for training, with the instructional program including shipbuilding, merchant marine maintenance, and administration. The project was related to Indonesia's ambition to control the eastern seas adjacent to West Irian.[34] Delivery of additional purchases of Soviet arms came in early 1962. Moscow thus bid high to gain Indonesia as a military ally in Southeast Asia, presumably in order to embarrass the West, but also to be in a position to challenge China's competing efforts to acquire political influence in the East Indies.[35]

The threat of a major Cold War confrontation that developed in 1961-62 over near-worthless West Irian territory carried ominous overtones. Indonesia adopted military registration and started drilling recruits, with the government releasing press reports of "victories" won. In March, 1962, some one thousand Indonesian volunteers reportedly invaded West Irian via both ships and parachute. Pressure mounted on a world-wide scale to persuade the Dutch to negotiate. When contrary resolutions submitted by the two sides to the United Nations General Assembly sessions of 1961 both failed adoption, a face-saving mediatory effort was launched by Acting Secretary U Thant, in which America's Ellsworth Bunker played a leading role. Agreement was finally reached in August, 1962. West Irian was assigned temporarily (from October, 1962 to May 1963) to United Nations administration before being turned over to Indonesia. Some time before the end of the decade, the Papuans would be afforded opportunity to decide, with United Nations cooperation, whether Indonesian control should be continued or ended.[36]

Domestic Implications of the Irian Crisis

For Indonesia, the domestic and economic implications of the West Irian crisis were almost as significant as was the international impact. The army exploited growing national fervor to sponsor a broadly inclusive National Front agency (labor, peasants, veterans, youth), under the direction of local commanders. The primary role of the Front was to expand the influence and power of the army and to counter the PKI's mass indoctrination efforts among similar functional groups. Sukarno became sufficiently perturbed by the army's initiative to launch a tentative Front organization of his own. His tactic thereafter was to support the PKI indoctrination program; this support included a personal appearance before one Communist party assembly and continuing exhortations to promote revolution. Indicative of his rising popularity was Sukarno's acquisition in 1962 of the title of president for life and his additional designation as grand leader of the revolution.[37]

The exorbitant costs of the Irian military adventure helped throw Indonesian finances into complete disarray.

For the several years involved, the military absorbed an estimated 75 percent of the annual budget allocations, plus incurring a huge debt of $800,000,000 for Soviet-supplied military equipment and supplies. This orgy of spending wrecked all plans for economic development. Monetary inflation multiplied. The rupiah prices of standard consumer items in 1962 averaged almost fifteen times those of 1953.[38]

The Indonesian Communists, like the army and Sukarno, also tried to turn the West Irian crisis to political account. The exhibition of overt cooperation between Indonesian nationalists and the Soviet government in an atmosphere of patriotic frenzy helped to dampen any effective expression of anti-Communist sentiments by opposition party groups. But the balance could not be maintained indefinitely. The Soviet Union after 1960 was heavily compromised in favor of the Djakarta government because of its arms deals and extension of lavish credits. Moscow was clearly more interested in countering Western influence and possible Chinese competition in Southeast Asia than in improving the lot of the Javanese worker or peasant. If Guided Democracy was ever to be replaced in time by a Maoist National People's Democracy, the PKI must be prepared at the appropriate moment to abandon its subservience to Sukarno and to the army, in line with Peking's policy of challenging alleged Soviet revisionism and compromises with bourgeois mentality. Such was the position adopted by Lukman's growing pro-Peking faction within the PKI, in opposition to the less adventurous policy of Party Secretary Aidit.[39]

Evidences of the PKI's growing alignment with Peking policy emerged as early as 1960. Partly as a means of soliciting party funds from vulnerable Chinese businessmen, the Indonesian Communists took up the defense of the rights of the resident Chinese community of Java against the abuses imposed by the government. Late in 1960 the PKI aligned with the traditional pro-Albanian and anti-Titoist policies of Peking. Aidit still argued that Communist parties worldwide, including the PKI, should be permitted opportunity to work out their own domestic policies free of external alignment or dictation. But the growing rift between the Russian and Chinese versions of the Communist world role could not be ignored. China's example and leadership were more closely attuned to Asian problems than were those of the Soviet Union. Maoists suggested that the much-maligned Old Established Forces might well in the end include the power-balancing and revisionist Soviet Union as well as the capitalist West. China's viewpoint supplied a psychological antidote to popular apathy, to the banality of Sukarno's patriotic extravaganzas, and to the army's abuse of power.[40]

Confrontation of Malaysia

The golden opportunity that the eventual West Irian settlement of 1962 afforded Sukarno to shift attention to crucially important economic problems was lost, although some attention was given to reform measures in late 1962. Customs levies were raised on luxury imports; plans were made to cut the military budget, to lift martial law, and even to assign soldiers to serve in work brigades. Consultations covering more basic economic recovery measures continued far into 1963. As late as May a tentative effort was made to implement monetary stabilization plans recommended by the International Monetary Fund. The reform program eventually ran firmly aground. It was unpopular with the profiteering bureaucracy and with the army, and as an expression of world capitalism it was anathema to the PKI. The army objected particularly to the proposed reallocation of available revenues.[41] Under the circumstances Sukarno opted for the anti-Malaysia Confrontation policy as a means of avoiding for the time being needed but painful economic adjustments and because it provided a political diversion to counter the threatened clash between his army and PKI allies.

The first overt expression of opposition to Malaya's proposed accession of Singapore and North Borneo territories had been made in late 1961 by the PKI. It declared that

280

the proposed union was designed to perpetuate British control over oil, tin, and rubber resources in the area and was also intended to suppress patriotic nationalist aspirations of the peoples involved. Following the settlement of the Irian crisis in August 1962, Sukarno gambled in December by according support to the previously-mentioned abortive Azahari revolt in Brunei. In early 1963, in the wake of the Brunei fiasco, Sukarno initiated his "Crush Malaysia" agitation.[42]

For the PKI, the Confrontation project provided three attractions. It could dramatize the pretended nationalist stance of the Communist party while providing a morale-serving outlet in Borneo for revolutionary energies that were denied overt expression in Java. Guerrilla operations against North Borneo might also give the party an opportunity to develop a people's militia of volunteer revolutionaries who would constitute the nucleus for an eventual PKI army. (Such a proposal for Java had been vetoed repeatedly by the army command.) But even if these two primary objectives should fail, the party reasoned, the Confrontation challenge would promote Indonesia's continuing alienation from the West and its closer alignment with the Communist bloc. The moderate wing of the party, led by Secretary Aidit, opposed involvement in any full-scale war over Malaysia as "adventurous army-sponsored nonsense." He was prepared nevertheless to challenge the creation of Malaysia through guerrilla operations and to capitalize on the opportunity provided to nationalize all British-owned properties in Indonesia proper, just as Dutch holdings had been expropriated previously.[43]

Although army leadership could not afford to permit Sukarno and the PKI to monopolize the nationalist cause, the military's rather hesitant decision to challenge British Malayan policy was based on reasons otherwise sharply at variance with those advanced by the Communists. Defense of national interests and prestige would obviously support the army's claims to budgeted funds that it might otherwise be denied. The army would also insist that Indonesia be fully consulted in major decisions relating to the settlement of all regional affairs, which the British were not prepared to do. Conservative army spokesmen argued that Malaya's proposed annexation of Singapore and the Borneo states, which were under Chinese economic control, might add to the threat of Peking's eventual domination of the strategically important shores of the South China Sea. The army thus tried to capitalize on Malayan anti-Chinese sentiment as a means of promoting Pan Indonesian sentiments in Western Malaya. The army harbored few illusions that Borneans would welcome Javanese control or that an overt military challenge of Malaysia was feasible. The air force was inclined to be somewhat more adventurous.

Sukarno's own stand on the Malaysia Confrontation struggle was derived mainly from considerations of political opportunism and personal prestige. Although it was apparent that Indonesia expected to inherit some Bornean possessions once the British departed, Djakata insisted that no ambitions for territorial aggrandizement were involved. But saving face was a perennial consideration. Sukarno posed as a plebian nationalist opponent of the Old Established Forçes of the region, represented by the aristocratic Tengku Abdul Rahman and by Britain, who were ignoring Indonesia's wishes and allegedly moving to encircle it in time-honored imperialistic fashion. Sukarno also charged that Malaysia was the creation of colonialist promoters who had previously rendered aid to Sumatran rebels in opposition to the nationalist cause. His own heroic stance would therefore help keep alive the spirit of revolutionary nationalism and also enhance his personal standing within the emergent Afro-Asian world.

Although a number of ulterior considerations were obviously involved, Britain's refusal to pay due respect to Djakarta's concern over the launching of Malaysia became an important reason for the Confrontation. At first, activities were confined to Borneo, where Indonesian guerrilla forces attempted to infiltrate Sarawak and Sabah. Indonesian trade with the Singapore entrepôt was legally banned, but clandestine delivery of marketable goods to Singapore by both official and unofficial Indonesian agencies undercut the anticipated negative economic impact of the embargo. Meanwhile, Commonwealth forces sent to Sarawak and Sabah rendered the guerrilla operations generally ineffective. Manila refrained from making any overt move against Sabah, but it was prepared to assert its tentative claim to the shores of the Sulu Sea in case the Indonesian Confrontation proved successful.

The resulting tensions were brought under a measure of temporary control through outside conciliation. In January 1964, President Johnson sent Robert Kennedy to Southeast Asia, where he managed to set up a temporary cease-fire arrangement. Conferences were staged at Bangkok in February and March, with Thai officials offering to act as a kind of referee for the Maphilindo representatives. No meaningful agreement was reached, but some time was gained. The several heads of state met later at Tokyo, on June 20, in an abortive effort to arrange for troop evacuation from affected Borneo territories. In August and September 1964, almost a full year after the initial break, a number of Indonesian volunteer units staged overt attacks on coastal areas of Malaya proper. Although the situation carried ominous implications, the operations fell far short of an all-out effort to crush Malaysia. Indonesia's position was not enhanced by its later withdrawal from the United Nations in protest. During most of 1965, continuing Indonesian attacks assumed the guise of political vendetta rather than actual warfare.[44]

Indonesian army leaders began in time to suspect the ulterior motives of the more aggressively inclined Communist PKI. They therefore refused to permit the creation of a Communist-infiltrated militia and also criticized the air force's accompanying bombing raids as both futile and hazardous. The army committed few if any of its first-line troops to Borneo and suffered fewer captured personnel than did either the air force or the navy. Following the exclusion of Singapore from Malaysia in August 1965, fears that Malaysia might fall under Chinese control noticeably lessened.[45] Meanwhile, Sukarno's Guided Democracy experiment was running out of material resources. Although concern to end Confrontation via some graceful exit was clearly present in Djakarta from early 1965, the PKI and its air-force allies continued to endeavor to make political capital from Confrontation policies.[46] Productive efforts toward pacification did not become possible until months after the abortive anti-army coup in September.

The September 30, 1965, Coup and its Political Aftermath

Exaggerated reports of Sukarno's declining health that circulated during the summer of 1965 helped precipitate the inevitable showdown between the Army High Command and the Communist leadership. Each side suspected the other of plotting a coup, thus putting a premium on prior action to forestall the other party. During the course of the Malaysian Confrontation the PKI had sided with dissident elements in the armed forces, particularly those who were sympathetic to Confrontation and the planned creation of a people's militia. Leaders of one army division based in Central Java were included among the dissidents, as were elements of the palace guard battalion commanded by Lieutenant Colonel Untung.

It is unclear what part the PKI leadership played in launching the 1965 coup attempt. Fragmentary evidence indicates that they did not participate in its inception. Nevertheless, the party leadership, represented by Aidit, became actively implicated in the coup activities of October 1 and afterwards. Whether PKI participation was direct and official remains to be satisfactorily answered. Although the Communist party membership generally was not involved in the coup at all, as individuals they were completely exposed to reprisals since they lacked weapons and trained military units capable of defending themselves against army reprisals.

The break came on the night of September 30, when the plotters attempted to assassinate seven top-level army chiefs in their homes. Elements of several army and airforce units, plus trained youth groups who were affiliated

284

with the PKI, backed the effort.[47] Six of the intended victims were killed, several of them after being transferred to Halim Air Force Base and turned over to youth group leaders. General Nasution escaped from the rear of his house, suffering serious ankle injuries. General Suharto, the man who was subsequently to crush the coup, was not included among the intended victims, possibly because of his friendship with Untung or because of his reputation of political neutrality. The rebel officers appeared to be a mixed group ideologically, but they had all participated in the ultranationalist appeals of Sukarno and the PKI under Confrontation, while the more conservative higher command had at times indicated some reservations. In similar fashion, the vulnerable *abangan* peasantry of Java and adjacent islands had responded positively to PKI agitation for economic and social revolution, without themselves becoming overt Marxists.[48]

It appeared for a brief time as if the coup might succeed. On the allegation that the action had been planned to forestall a similar move by the army, Sukarno himself was influenced to take refuge at Halim Air Force Base, the rebel headquarters. A previously prepared list of forty-five proposed members of a new Revolutionary Council was there presented to Sukarno for approval. The list included several pro-Sukarno generals and a number of non-Communist civilians, many of whom had not been consulted, as well as Communist leaders; the mélange made little political sense. In the end Sukarno refused to accept the proposed Council, but he did not react negatively to the coup itself, apparently hesitating to commit himself until the outcome was obvious. During the early hours of October 1 General Suharto sorted out the unreliable units and commanders from the forces at his disposal. Through a combination of persuasion and intimidation all suspected regular army personnel either came over to Suharto's side or withdrew to Halim Air Force Base. At midnight when Suharto's forces began moving on Halim, the coup leaders and most of their troops fled to Central Java.[49]

Whether or not they were justified in doing so, the

surviving Army High Command accused PKI leaders and unidentified Chinese Communist agents of participation in the assassination plot. The Communists in rejoinder argued that they were in no way involved, pointing out that no preparations had been made to stage supporting mass demonstrations or to defend the party membership in case of failure. They insisted that they were actually acting in cooperation with Sukarno, who responded by trying to excuse them from blame. It was nevertheless obvious that the party had been prepared to capitalize politically on the elimination of political enemies within the Army High Command in the continuing contest for political control. In any case, the gruesome episode of October 1 provided the army with a plausible excuse to implement previously prepared plans for a thoroughgoing anti-Communist purge. The effort enlisted widespread support from partisan Muslim elements whom Sukarno had long excluded from power, from conservative student groups, and for a time from the *peranakan* (Indonesian-born) Chinese.

Retaliatory anti-Communist measures began toward the end of October. A specially selected paratrooper unit (RKPAD) introduced both training facilities and weaponry into Communist-infested regions of Central and Eastern Java to assist the Muslim population in liquidating the "enemies of Allah." The bodies of the murdered generals were exhumed in an effort to intensify the emotional response. Once aroused, the mobs made little distinction between the pro-PKI Chinese and the non-Communist Chinese. As the break with Peking widened, anti-Chinese prejudice added to the bitterness of religious and political strife. PKI leadership everywhere was marked for liquidation. Secretary Aidit sought escape by withdrawing into the mountains of Eastern Java, but paratroopers pursued and killed him on November 22, 1965.[50] In February 1966 the Communist party and all of its affiliates were officially banned.

The army-instigated suppression eventually took on the character of a holy war, its frenzied mood arising from the release of long-sustained tensions and frustrations.

Estimates of the number of victims ran as high as half a million. The party leadership in Java was completely eliminated, although the seedbed for revolution still survived in regions where peasant and worker grievances were compounded by hatred and vengeance. Overt rebel resistance continued in Kalimantan far into 1967, whereas underground opposition in Java persisted into the following year. Thousands of suspects were jailed. As late as 1968, well over one hundred thousand prisoners still awaited sorting out to determine which ones should be obliged to stand trial.[54] The army-instigated anti-Communist campaign in Central and Eastern Java took care not to attack the numerous pro-Sukarno loyalists. Many of his countrymen continued to regard him as the national hero and accepted with reluctance the New Order foreign policy that gradually emerged under General Suharto, repudiating the Confrontation stance and turning to the non-Communist West for economic assistance.[52]

Modulation to Full Army Control

The generally favorable popular reaction to the suppression of the coup and the liquidation of the Communist party included no immediate demand for an end to Confrontation. Powerful nationalist emotions already generated over the "Crush Malaysia" issue could not be released abruptly, and no party group was willing to accept responsibility for advocating an abrupt change of policy. Sukarno continued to command wide popularity in many parts of Java, and he had more at stake than anyone else in maintaining the militant stance. But the operational aspects of Confrontation steadily declined in the context of army-Communist feuding. With the passage of time, the nationalist furor gradually subsided, and a face-saving formula was found for the eventual reassignment of Sukarno's power. General Suharto, as top army commander, avoided challenging Sukarno directly, partly to maintain his personal advantage over his former superior officer, General Nasution, and partly to refrain from precipitating a possible rebellion by

287

supporters of Sukarno in Central and Eastern Java.[53]

Sukarno's principal—but abortive—attempt to recover personal control, made in early 1966, appealed to nationalist issues and to personal prestige. He endeavored to fan the embers of the Malaysian Confrontation fire and to block attempts to halt the operation. He tried to disband the anti-Sukarno youth group[54] and, in late February 1966, formally removed General Nasution from his previous post of minister of defense. On February 24 he designated a new one-hundred-member cabinet, including some with Communist affiliations. This move was the signal for violent student rioting, both pro and con.[55] Sukarno successfully cowed a group of assembled politicians into approving his newly proposed cabinet and condemning opposition student agitation, but the army intervened some two weeks later. During the course of a cabinet meeting, troops surrounded the Presidential Palace, bent on arresting the Leftist leader Subandrio. Sukarno and Subandrio fled to the Summer Palace at Bogor by helicopter, but to no avail. Confronted there by army representatives who had pursued him, Sukarno was obliged to sign over his presidential powers to General Suharto and to abandon his cabinet-forming pretensions.

On the following day, March 18, Suharto arrested fifteen Leftist members of the proposed cabinet, including Subandrio, and outlawed the PKI. He then revised the cabinet membership, retaining several of Sukarno's choices. But the new faces portended significant changes. They included Adam Malik, formerly leader of the Nationalist-Leftist Murba party, who became the new foreign minister. Sultan Hamengku Buwono of Jogjakarta took over the multiple roles of deputy prime minister and minister of financial, economic, and development affairs.[56] At the meeting of the Provisional Consultative People's Congress in June 1966, 120 of its members were arbitrarily excluded for suspected PKI affiliations. The rump Congress then proceeded to elect General Nasution as the new legislative chairman. It also revoked Sukarno's title of president for life and formally approved Suharto's assumption of executive authority.

In July General Suharto announced the formation of a completely new cabinet, which excluded most of the Sukarno supporters. Although Sukarno retained for a time his titular post of prime minister, Suharto assumed firm control of the functioning cabinet, filling himself the position of minister of defense and security. In August, with Suharto himself as chairman of the presidium, the long series of trials began for those implicated in the September coup attempt. The trial of Subandrio in particular added fuel to the increasing hostility to Sukarno. Even so, the final political emasculation of Sukarno was delayed until the March 1967 session of the Provisional Assembly, when he was banned from further political activity during the course of the contemplated election campaign. Suharto was formally designated acting president.

The End of Confrontation

Beginning in May 1966 Adam Malik took the lead in seeking a reconciliation with Malaysia. A series of meetings were first held at Bangkok, with a Filipino representative present along with the Kuala Lumpur spokesman. Malik was convinced that Indonesia must seek the broadest possible re-establishment of its international relations, and Sultan Hamengku Buwono supported him by insisting that economic stabilization be regarded as the overriding consideration of domestic concern. The slogan of *Ampera* (the message of the peoples' suffering) replaced *Nekolim* (anticolonialism and anti-imperialism) as the key word of public rhetoric.[57] *Ampera* spokesmen argued that only the PKI and China wanted Indonesia and Malaysia to go to war. Suharto's conciliatory military mission visited Kuala Lumpur in May, and by June direct negotiations with Tun Razak were concluded at Bangkok resulting in a halt of Confrontation activities. The "Crush Malaysia" policy was dead, but back in Indonesia protests by Sukarno and ultranationalists delayed the signing of a formal treaty until August. In the formal agreement most of Indonesia's previous demands, such as removal of British bases, were disregarded, although as a face-saving gesture full diplo-

289

matic ties were not to be established until after referendums were held in Sabah and Sarawak to determine if the Borneo people wished to remain in the Federation.[58]

The arguments for abandoning Confrontation were compelling. The groups that had been most directly associated with it—Sukarno's personal following, the PKI and the air force, the imprisoned Subandrio, Nahdatul Ulama, and to some degree Nasution and the PNI—were all discredited politically. The undertaking had an unquestionably deleterious effect on the near-desperate economic state of the country, and its complete repudiation was a condition for receipt of any Western assistance in recovery. Sponsors of the venture had incurred high risks for achieving dubious goals. The peoples of North Borneo could not stand alone, and they had demonstrated no interest in joining either Indonesia or the Philippines. Abandoning *Konfrontasi* and rejoining the United Nations in September 1966 paved the way for Malik to solicit needed financial assistance from Western sources. By the time diplomatic representatives were finally exchanged in August 1967, the Kuala Lumpur Malays welcomed their brothers from the islands into the new Association of Southeast Asian Nations (ASEAN), dedicated to a policy of Asian solutions for Asian problems.[59] Thus faces were saved all around.

Sympathetic observers of the events of the year following the coup were impressed by the skill and patience demonstrated by General Suharto in his carefully deferential but essentially firm downgrading of President Sukarno. Apart from the relentless purging of the Communist elements by the military party, about which serious reservations can be entertained, Suharto's gradual displacement of Indonesia's acknowledged national hero successfully forestalled the potential political convulsions that could have torn Java apart. The freedom afforded to the charismatic leader to continue to have his way for a time without suffering arbitrary suppression demonstrated the characteristic Javanese concern to develop consensus support of new policies and goals, while avoiding direct challenge.

From the abandonment of Confrontation, the Suharto

regime moved in time toward the restoration of confiscated foreign properties and the encouragement of new capital investment. Nor did Suharto repudiate—as did his contemporaries, the army leaders in Burma, Thailand, and South Vietnam—the prospect of early restoration of a semblance of democratic rule. Elections were scheduled for mid-1971. Emotional and pyschological tensions continued to be present, but Suharto recognized that they could not possibly be relieved by the exchange of abuse or by making scapegoats of opponents.[60] Reservations could still be entertained as to whether the exercise of arbitrary authority by army agencies, with its attending temptations to abuse power, could cope with the staggering economic and social problems left over from Sukarno's orgy of nationalism and revolution.[61]

The Task of Economic Recovery

The problem of economic recovery was extremely critical. Civilian associates whom Suharto had brought into the cabinet took a sober and realistic view. Several of them had participated in earlier governments: Adam Malik was a former Marxist associate of Tan Malaka, now turned pragmatist; the Dutch-educated Hamengku Buwono was admired as a princely nationalist, honest and intelligent.[62] They were later joined by the able economist Dr. Sumitro as minister of trade in the June 1969 cabinet. He had served in a similar capacity in several governments of the fifties, but had suffered a ten-year exile following participation in the abortive Sumatran rebellion of 1958. Continuing administrative problems were still complicated by widespread corruption and abuse of power. Popular hostility to foreigners, especially resident Chinese, was complicated by the dead weight of popular prejudice and fanatical religious partisanship. Suharto's new government was nevertheless an important step forward in the transition from cabinets composed of competing interest groups to a body of able technicians responsible directly to the president.[63]

Initial efforts to curb mounting price inflation, under-taken amid the veritable buyer's stampede of late 1965, were palliative at best. The most forthright move was a decree issued in December requiring holders of old *rupiahs* to exchange them for new, at the rate of one thousand for one, while making a ten percent "contribution to the revolution." Government officials and the army received additional increments in salaries and allowances in the form of rice and housing aids.[64] Chinese hoarders at the time were trying desperately to exchange their *rupiahs* for U.S. dollars at rates of thirty or forty thousand to one. The new money somewhat relieved the government's printing costs, but the volume of currency in circulation recovered quickly from the 10 percent reduction.[65] Living costs almost tripled between January and March 1966, and interest rates rose as high as 15 to 20 percent per month.

Sultan Hamengku Buwono promulgated a new pattern of trade control in April. The new regulations, subsequently revised, were aimed at expanding exports and encouraging development-oriented imports and domestic industry gen-erally. He accorded import priorities to food, raw materi-als, and spare machinery parts in an attempt to relieve high food costs and the virtual paralysis of industry. Buwono and Malik also sought relief from international debt obliga-tions plus new aid grants to facilitate recovery from bank-ruptcy.[66]

The seriousness of Indonesia's economic plight at the end of 1966 continued to be most discouraging. The govern-ment owed some $2.5 billion (including interest) to foreign creditors and was asking to borrow more. Factories were producing at 40 percent of capacity, while locomotives and freight cars were traveling an average of only 12.5 miles per day. Transportation problems included some 2,000 miles of unrepaired roads, approximately 50 percent of all motor vehicles out of commission, and a Djakarta harbor badly in need of dredging. The inflationary panic quieted down during the course of the year, but the price level in Decem-ber 1966, was still some seven times that of December 1965.

Only in a long-term perspective could encouraging signs

be found. A small portion of increased export revenues was being allocated for investment purposes. Prospective foreign investors responded only after being accorded a five-year tax holiday, the right to repatriate their earnings, and guarantees against expatriation. Credits up to $180 million for needed food, raw materials, and engine parts were received from the United States, the Netherlands, and West Germany, plus new planes and an aircraft assembly plant. The rice output slowly expanded. Hamengku Buwono halted several grandiose construction projects characteristic of the Sukarno regime, and promising state-operated enterprises were permitted a larger measure of autonomy. The nightmare of hopelessness gradually gave way to a new spirit of pragmatic endeavor.[67]

One factor that greatly hampered the revival of economic activity was the continuing persecution of the resident Chinese population. In April 1967 President Suharto undertook for the first time to discourage officially continuing expressions of racism and the mistreatment of Indonesia's approximately three million Chinese. Adam Malik also emphasized the need to cool emotions and to observe the norms of humanity and justice, pointing out that racial tension would seriously damage Indonesia's attractiveness to foreign capital investors. Even so, mobs repeatedly attacked the Peking embassy and consular quarters, with violence spilling over into the Chinese quarter. No one tried to conceal the ugly reality of Indonesian racial prejudice and the victimization of alien residents. Further naturalization of Chinese residents was ruled out, and those already nationalized were pressured to adopt Indonesian names.

It was simply not popularly feasible for the average politician to follow Suharto's and Malik's appeals for racial tolerance. Nor could one expect police and army officers who themselves had been extorting protection money from Chinese shopkeepers in order to supplement their meager pay to display enthusiasm for protecting the rights of aliens in general. An impoverished nation and a poorly paid bureaucracy were in no mood to resist the temptation to

293

wring money from the relatively prosperous Chinese. And yet without Chinese participation, domestic commerce and business activity would continue to stagnate.[68]

Evidences of Improvement

The economic situation in Indonesia showed definite but inconclusive signs of improvement by 1969. The price spiral was reduced to a 120 percent increment in 1967, to a manageable 85 percent in 1968, and finally to negligible dimensions in early 1969. Meanwhile, annual budgets were brought into a semblance of balance, and $2.7 billion of domestic debts were rescheduled for payment over an eight-year period. Previously nationalized oil installations and plantation estates, mainly in Sumatra, were restored to owner management, and controls over export activities were relaxed. Some $400 million of credits were advanced by the United States, Japan, and other lenders (31 percent of it from the U.S.), and subsidies were reduced for those state industries that were being inefficiently managed. Substantial investment gains were realized in off-shore oil prospecting and in mining exploration. Bauxite ores were found in the Riau Islands off Singapore, additional tin deposits near Bangka Island, and promising if currently inaccessible iron ore, copper, and nickel resources in West Irian and Sulawesi. Indigenous business initiative was still limited, and exports continued to lag behind target levels, due in part to poor domestic transportation facilities, smuggling activities, and falling world prices in tin and rubber.[69]

Other aspects of the economic recovery problem were more deeply seated. In crowded Java and Bali, the population was outrunning the food supply, with rice production gains of only 1.6 percent annually compared to a 2.4 percent gain in population. Two decades of independence had produced no real agricultural progress, except in favored areas outside of Java. Funds were not available for land clearance and for improved water accessibility to serve the Javanese who wished to migrate to the less densely populated Outer Islands. Many Javanese were reluctant to move in any case, and few Outer Islanders welcomed their arrival. In point of fact, Djakarta alone probably attracted non-Javanese immigrants in excess of the number of Javanese who sought new homes in the rest of Indonesia. Both industrial employment and population shifts demanded alteration of long accepted social structure and values, and many peasants hesitated to surrender the final security of resort to subsistance agriculture.[70] Even such long-established industries as sugar and textile production found it increasingly difficult to compete in quality and price with products available overseas under conditions of tight money, obsolete machinery, and heavy taxes. Cultivators who had grown sugar cane for generations resisted shifting to rice production. Newspapers added to social tension by publishing emotional outbursts attacking Chinese grafters and corrupt bureaucrats and army officers, who reportedly were waxing rich and powerful.[71]

The welcome halting of the demoralizing price spiral in early 1969 was not without its immediate handicaps. It was accompanied by a virtual cessation of new domestic investment and by contracting consumer demand. No longer was there need, as had previously been the case, to buy frantically before prices went up further. The new five-year economic development plan promulgated in 1969 aroused more skepticism than enthusiasm. The lack of efficient, honest, and skilled administration was obvious during the first quarter of 1969, when only an estimated 20 percent of the funds expended were actually put to positive use. In the private sector, the absence of organizational and managerial talent contributed to popular inertia and lassitude. The rusty wagon would not start easily. The public economic domain was snarled in red tape with army personnel unwilling to surrender the economic perquisites of power. Some slight improvement was noted in the recovery of confidence on the part of Chinese businessmen, but they were understandably hesitant to risk putting their savings into trade and productive enterprise until the rules were more clearly defined. Meanwhile, the foreign debt rose to some three billion dollars.[72]

The conditions of economic recovery were easier to

specify than to realize. More effective operation of government agencies in all areas was sorely needed, but with some flexibility. Central authority must exercise better control over distant provincial officials but must also grant autonomy to responsible directors of government projects. Economic needs must take precedence over political considerations, and yet it was obvious that increasing foreign investment could again arouse strong nationalist opposition. Political factions long excluded from power were not likely to accord the same wholehearted support to competent economic leadership that General Suharto himself was giving. If development programs were expected to enlist wide acceptance privately or officially in both Java and the Outer Islands, they would have to take the entire national interest into account in convincing fashion. Profit incentives had to be provided for potential investors at all levels of the society, including the three million Chinese residents. A more genuine awareness was needed of the character and magnitude of the problems to be faced.[73]

The Trend toward Army Rule

Despite the fact that General Suharto did not aspire to become an Indonesian dictator and was concerned to enlist the aid of the best civilian brains in the demanding task of economic recovery, it was difficult under the circumstances to find a feasible alternative to army rule. Former Vice-President Mohammed Hatta made an abortive effort to sponsor a new reformist Muslim party to serve as a vehicle for adherents of the still-banned Masjumi and Socialist (PSI) parties. Suharto refused to approve Hatta's plans because of the obvious influence of the 1958 rebels within the organization. Hatta was eventually given a nominal role as advisor to the president in 1970. The final legitimization and consolidation of rule by Suharto and the army occurred in March 1968, just one year after Suharto became acting president. At the fifth session of the Council, Suharto was appointed president until March 1973, at which time a newly elected or appointed group would convene and select the next president.

Elections for approximately two-thirds of the new Assembly membership (the remainder were appointed) were scheduled for July 1971. General Nasution's previous demands for new elections to be held in 1967 and then in 1968 had run aground, partly because of the difficulty of reaching agreement on the new electoral law between the army and the political parties. The army wanted the right to nominate one-third of the Council and Parliament, as well as to utilize single-unit constituencies instead of proportional representation (thus almost eliminating the minor parties). This controversy was solved by a compromise in 1969, but the delay resulted in a postponement of the elections until 1971 and a corresponding extension of army rule.[74]

The continuance of army rule actually implied the lack of any feasible alternative rather than wide popular support. Many army personnel regarded the uniform as a license to steal from or otherwise abuse their fellow countrymen They collected minor contributions, including cigarettes, from travellers at road blocks. They rented out rifles for ten dollars a day. Soldiers interfered with trade by commandeering cars and food and by continued smuggling of copra and rubber from Medan and south Sumutran ports. Suharto's reduction of the army budget in 1967 by one-third made more difficult his faltering efforts to curb such irregular exactions. The central government made little attempt to reduce the excessive measure of autonomy exercised by regional army commanders, who often acted in the role of governors, because Suharto simply could not dispense with their support. Central authority decreased in almost direct ratio with the distance from Djakarta.[75]

The alternatives to army authority were narrowly limited. Too many Indonesians remembered the political confusion of the middle fifties to have much faith in the revival of the democratic process. The satisfaction of urgent economic needs could better be left, presumably, to non-political experts such as Malik, Buwono, and Sumitro. The secular nationalists were badly splintered, while religion was too potent an issue to be ignored, but too divisive to be governmentally useful. Proponents of Islam resented the post-war doubling of the Christian population (to a total of ten million),

297

partly because many of the converts were Chinese. Orthodox partisans continued to denounce the animistic customs of rural Java and insisted that all schools stress Islamic studies, whether or not they were relevant to defined social and economic ends. Aspiring politicians outside the ruling coterie, such as Generȧl Nasution, solicited backing from both the Nahdatul Ulama and Masjumi adherents, while former Premier Natsir and others sounded like U Nu of Burma when they declared that only a revival of Islam could dissipate Indonesia's moral bankruptcy and restore faith in spiritual values. A fraction of the reforming Muhammadijah group and some former Masjumi party members affiliated with the Partai Muslimin Indonesia (PMI), but Suharto refused to permit important ex-Masjumi figures, such as Roem or Natsir, to lead the party. The government got a member of the Suharto regime, Mintaredja, installed as PMI chairman.[77]

Some older groups did re-emerge. A revived Sarekat Islam opposed secularization, whether liberal or Marxist, and denounced the democratic system as part of an American capitalistic plot. Another conflict in the already schism-ridden society appeared in the form of the "generation of '66" composed politically of active and impatient youth groups who had helped topple Sukarno. They complained that the political influence which they had earned was being denied them by a dominant military elite that was reluctant to move forcefully to relieve society's ills. Indonesia's aspirations for consensus were far from realized.[78]

Widespread realization that an early return to political party activity was both dubious and risky was balanced off by tangible evidence that imposed stability by the military also carried a heavy price, both immediate and long-term. The new electoral law for the 1971 elections retained proportional representation but allowed the government to appoint 22 percent of the lower house and one-third of the upper. In addition, former PKI members and suspects, along with the otherwise generously represented army, were prohibited from participating in the elections.[79] The outcome will be examined in the concluding chapter.

298

In late 1969 Suharto strengthened his hold on the military establishment by a complete reorganization. Naval and the air-force operational units, as well the army, were placed under the control of the president as chief of the armed forces and of his deputy chief, General Panggabean. This new organization provided for the first time a semblance of centralized control of all the Indonesian armed forces. Meanwhile, army personnel also exercised extensive control within the government bureaucracy. They occupied six cabinet posts, virtually all of the provincial governorships, plus the eighteen military districts which were being ruled in war-lord fashion. Sergeants and corporals functioned as mini-kings in many villages. As of early 1970, army officers also operated the state oil company, the airlines, much of the overseas trade, and many of the Outer Islands plantations. Retired army personnel were regularly kept on the government payroll in other capacities. Many Indonesians who appreciated the dangers of political confusion and possible economic collapse were convinced that risks had to be accepted in order to escape the abuses of authoritarian rule. But the moot question of whether constitutional government under civilian control could be achieved for Indonesia was not likely to be decided by a single election attempt.[80]

1. Arnold C. Brackman, *Indonesian Communism, a History* (New York, 1963), p. 242; also Daniel S. Lev, *The Transition to Guided Democracy: Indonesian Politics, 1957-1959* (Ithaca, 1966), pp. 33-37.

2. Leslie Palmier, *Indonesia* (London, 1965). pp. 193-94; Lev, *op. cit.*, pp. 133-47; Herbert Feith, "The Dynamics of Guided Democracy" in Ruth McVey, ed., *Indonesia* (New Haven, 1963), pp. 322-25.

3. J. D. Legge, *Authority and Regional Autonomy in Indonesia* (Ithaca, 1957), pp. 202-5; George M. Kahin, "Indonesia" in Kahin, ed., *Major Governments of Asia* (Ithaca, 1963), pp. 646-49.

4. Feith, in McVey, *op. cit.*, pp. 358-66; Lev, *op. cit.*, pp. 269-89; Bernhard Dahm, *History of Indonesia in the Twentieth Century* (New York, 1971), pp. 189-96.

5. Feith, in McVey, *op. cit.*, p. 359; Howard Palfrey Jones, *Indonesia: The Possible Dream* (New York, 1971), pp. 236-44.

6. S. Takdir Alisjabana, *Indonesia: Social and Cultural Revolution* (New York, 1966), pp. 128-36.

7. Feith, in McVey, *op. cit.*, pp. 325-27.

8. Kahin, *op. cit.*, pp. 636-43.

9. Soedjatmoko, "The Role of Political Parties in Indonesia", in Philip W. Thayer, ed., *Nationalism and Progress in Free Asia* (Baltimore, 1956), pp. 139-40.

10. Feith, in McVey, *op. cit.*, pp. 325-30.
11. *Ibid.*, pp. 331-36.
12. Donald Hindley, *The Communist Party of Indonesia, 1951-1963* (Berkeley, 1964), pp. 119-22; Justus M. Van der Kroef, *The Communist Party in Indonesia* (Vancouver, 1965), pp. 44-125.
13. Hindley, *op. cit.*, pp. 282-86.
14. Evert Hawkins, "Labor in Transition," in McVey, *op. cit.*, pp. 248-71.
15. Donald Earl Wilmott, *The Chinese in Semarang* (Ithaca, 1960), pp. 32-35.
16. Van der Kroef, *op. cit.*, pp. 227-30; Ruth T. McVey, "Communism and Guided Democracy," in Doak Barnett, ed., *Communist Strategies in Asia* (New York, 1963), pp. 159-60, 174-77.
17. McVey, in Barnett, *op. cit.*, pp. 167-77.
18. Hindley, "Political Power and the October 1965 Coup in Indonesia," in *Journal of Asian Studies* 26 (February, 1967): 237-40.
19. Feith, in McVey, *op. cit.*, pp. 336-42.
20. Kahin, op. cit., pp. 655-58.
21. Guy Pauker, "Indonesia," in John J. Johnson, ed., *The Role of the Military in Underdeveloped Countries* (Princeton, 1962), pp. 221-24.
22. Willard A. Hanna, "Nationalist Revolution and Revolutionary Nationalism," in K. H. Silvert, ed., *Expectant Peoples, Nationalism and Development* (Stanford, 1963), 134-37.
23. Feith, in McVey, *op. cit.*, pp. 378-83: Kahin, *op. cit.*, pp. 658-65.
24. Feith, in McVey, *op. cit.*, pp. 360-402.
25. Douglas Paauw. "From Colonialism to Guided Democracy," in McVey, *op. cit.*, pp. 155-75.
26. Benjamin and Jean Higgins, *Indonesia: the Crisis of the Millstones* (Princeton, 1963), pp. 94-100.
27. Paauw, *op. cit.*, pp. 182-206.
28. *Ibid.*, pp. 214-61; Kahin, *op. cit.*, pp. 674-87; Feith "Indonesia," in Kahin *Governments and Politics of Southeast Asia* (Ithaca, 1964), p. 267.
29. Feith, in McVey, *op. cit.*, pp. 400-09.
30. Feith, in Kahin, *op. cit.*, p. 365.
31. L. Maetzemaekers, "The West New Guinea Problem," *Pacific Affairs*, 24 (1951): 131-42.
32. Feith, in Kahin, *op. cit.*, pp. 203, 206, 210.
33. Leslie Palmier, *Indonesia* (London, 1965), pp. 195-96; Kahin, *Major Governments*, pp. 679-87.
34. Bureau of Educational Affairs, "Soviet and Eastern European Educational Projects in Less Developed Countries of Africa and Asia" (Washington, 1966), p. 20.
35. Feith in Kahin, *op. cit.*, pp. 265-268; Palmier, *op. cit.*, p. 196.
36. Feith, in Kahin, *op. cit.*, pp. 268-70; Palmier, *op. cit.*, p. 196.
37. Alisjabana, *op. cit.*, pp. 158-60.
38. *Ibid.*, pp. 155-58: Kahin, *Major Governments*, pp. 670-87: B. and J. Higgins, *op. cit.*, pp. 94-100.
39. McVey, in Barnett, *op. cit.*, pp. 180-89.
40. *Ibid.*, pp. 182-89
41. Feith, in Kahin, *op. cit.*, pp. 269-70.
42. John O. Sutter, "Two Faces of Konfrantasi: Crush Malaysia and the Gestapo," *Asian Survey*, 6 (October, 1966): 523-27. For a discussion of the Brunei revolt, see chapter VII.

43. Franklin B. Weinstein, *Indonesia Abandons Confrontation. An Inquiry into the Functions of Indonesian Foreign Policy* (Ithaca, 1969), pp. 4-5.

44. Daniel S. Lev, "Indonesia, 1965: The Year of Confrontation," *Asian Survey*, 6 (February, 1966): 103-110.

45. *Ibid*," ," pp. 5-9

46. *Ibid.*, pp. 3-4, 10-11; See also Donald Hindley, "Indonesia's Confrontation with Malaysia: A search for Motives," *Asian Survey* 4 (1964): 904-13.

47. For a review of the best Dutch articles of the episode, see B. B. Hering in *Pacific Affairs*, 41 (1968-69): 611-13. Also Basuki Gunswan, *Kudeta Staatsgreep in Kjakarta* (Meppel, 1968).

48. Jean Contenay, "Smoking Volcano," *FEER* (January 11, 1968), pp. 70-71.

49. D. S. Lev, "Indonesia, 1965," pp. 104-5; John Hughes, *Indonesian Upheaval* (New York, 1967).

50. Jean Contenay, "Heritage of Blood," *FEER*, December 14, 1967, pp. 509-16; *ibid.*, November 23, 1967, pp. 357-61.

51. Donald Hindley, "Political Power and the October 1965 coup in Indonesia," *JAS*, 27 (1969): 237-49.

52. Jean Conteay, "Another Blood Bath?" *FEER*, November 23, 1967, pp. 367-71; see also *FEER*, November 2, 1967, pp. 224-25 and *ibid.*, August 24, 1968, p. 349.

53. Weinstein, *op. cit.*, pp. 13-20.

54. *Ibid.*, pp. 21-28.

55. *FEER*, March 18, 1966, pp. 503-4, 507-8.

56. Robert Shaplen, *Time Out of Hand* (New York, 1969), pp. 136-43.

57. Weinstein, *op. cit.*, pp. 31-36.

58. *Ibid.*, pp. 38-62, 70-84.

59. *Ibid.*, pp. 85-88.

60. Adam Malik, "Promise in Indonesia," *Foreign Affairs* 46 (January, 1968), pp. 292-303.

61. *FEER*, August 18, 1966, p. 295.

62. *FEER*, September 28, 1967, pp. 556-62.

63. Guy J. Pauker, "Indonesia, the Age of Reason," *Asian Survey* 7 (1968): 133-39; *FEER*, June 20, 1968, p. 591.

64. *FEER*, December 9 and 30, 1965, pp. 451, 581-83: *Bulletin of Indonesian Economic Studies*, no 4 (June, 1966), pp. 2-3.

65. *New York Times*, January 24 and February 24, 1966.

66. *FEER*, April 28 and June 16, 1966, pp. 216-18, 519-22; *Bulletin of Indonesian Economic Studies*, no. 7 (June, 1967): 18-25.

67. *FEER*, April 13, 1967, pp. 61-63: *New York Times*, January 20, 1967.

68. Charles Mohr, "Indonesia Moves to Contain Anti-Chinese Riots," *New York Times*, April 29, 1967, p. 6.

69. *FEER, 1968 Yearbook*, pp. 197-204; *FEER*, November 23 and 30, 1967, pp. 344 and 394; *New York Times*, January 19, 1968.

70. See Guy Pauker, "Political Consequences of Rural Development Programs in Indonesia," *Pacific Affairs* 41 (1968): 386-402.

71. *FEER, 1968 Yearbook*, pp. 201-4.

72. O. G. Roeder, "The Sleeping Beauty Awakes," *FEER*, March 10, 1969, pp. 403-05; *New York Times*, July 8, 1969.

73. Douglas Paauw, "From Colonialism to Guided Democracy," in McVey, *op. cit.*, 243-48.

74. *FEER*, April 13, 1967, pp. 61-63; *New York Times*, April 20, 1967.

75. *New York Times*, May 7, 1967.

76. Guy J. Pauker, "Indonesia, the Age of Reason," *Asian Survey* 7, (February, 1968); 139-46.

77. *FEER*, January 25, 1969, pp. 156-59: *ibid.*, May 23, 1968, pp. 388-89; *ibid.*, December 28, 1967, pp. 570-71.

78. Husein Rafe, "Insja'llah—God Willing," *FEER*, April 4, 1968, pp. 26-29; *FEER*, November 28 and December 12, 1968, pp. 388-89, 600.

79. *Bangkok World*, February 14, 1968.

80. *New York Times*, February 7, 1969; O. G. Roeder, "Reprieve for Politics," *FEER*, March 20, 1969, p. 521.

X

THE TWO VIETNAMS

The Roots of Political Fragmentation

The political and cultural fragmentation that has characterized postwar Vietnam stemmed in some measure from divergent historical traditions and the frequently demonstrated North-South rivalry. Tonkin had experienced 1,000 years of Chinese rule plus another 550 years of independence before lower Annam was brought under Vietnamese control. The Mekong delta was taken away from Cambodia only in modern times. Throughout the middle sixty years of the 1600s, the Trinh dynasty of the North had attacked Nguyen rule in the South, and the dynastic and sectional feuding was revived in the latter decades of the 1700s. Vietnamese peoples everywhere were jealously proud of their cultural and historical identity, but political rivalry, whether active or latent, prevailed between the Sinicized North, the court-oriented region of Hué in central Annam, and the less homogeneous South, with its variant peoples and dialects. Northerners as a rule were more aggressively inclined and better disciplined. Immigrant Chinese, for example, found economic opportunity available only in Cochin-China, not in the North.

However variously the significance of such historical factors may be assessed, seventy years of French colonial rule clearly magnified older differences. The indigenous elite of Cochin-China by 1941 were trained in French or in

303

the Latinized *Quoc Ngu* script, which closed the door to the Confucianist classics still cherished by mandarin families in the North. Saigon was a French city, and neighboring Cholon was inhabited by overseas Chinese, who dominated trade in the delta area. In an arc extending above the two cities were located the French-owned rubber, tobacco, and tea plantations, while indigenous landlords shared ownership of the newly developed ricelands of the Mekong delta. French officials ran the government, and the traditional family-oriented village communal units were replaced by tenant farmers.

Although the practice of traditional rites for ancestral spirits had eroded somewhat in immigrant communities, they were still widely pervasive. The six hundred thousand Cambodian Buddhists still residing in the delta followed their own patterns of spirit propitiation. In Cochin-China, direct French rule had destroyed the mandarin tradition. The façade of emperor rule at Hué, including the Chinese-style authentication of Heaven's Mandate, survived down to 1945, although it was wearing thin. In August of that year Emperor Bao Dai abdicated and assigned the care of the remains of his royal ancestors to the emerging nationalist-Communist regime of Ho Chi Minh. Calendrical ceremonies soliciting the assistance of the spirits of the royal clan as guarantors of good government and national welfare were abandoned, however, and governmental authority in mandarin-oriented Annam and Tonkin was thus deprived of its moral and religious sanctions. Ancestral remains continued to be revered by the vast majority of the Vietnamese population, but divergence from ancient tradition was distinctly evident in the South.

French-ruled Cochin-China spawned a variety of social and religious innovations both before the war and after. Cao Dai, a Westernized version of traditional animism born in 1919, was a syncretic amalgam of ideas and practices partly Asian and partly Western in origin. Cao Dai incorporated prominent features of Chinese Confucianism and Taoism, Buddhism, Christianity, and Islam, down to traditional spirit routines. The basic symbol was the all-seeing

eye of God, surrounded by solar rays; this image was enshrined in an elaborate temple located about fifty miles
west of Saigon. Taoist-type mediums communicated directly
with Cao Dai, the central Spirit for which the cult was
named. Worship routines were designed to contribute to
spiritual understanding, peace of mind, and dedication to
social responsibilities. The evangelistic fervor of the cult
attracted several hundred thousand adherents during the
1920s, and by 1947 it claimed several million followers.

Following World War I, both forms of Buddhism, Maha-
yana and Theravada, staged significant revivals in Central
Annam and Cochin-China. Buddhism was strong in both Hué
and Saigon, although divided by factionalism. In 1938 a
reformist Buddhist sect called Hoa Hao was developed in
the Mekong delta by an anti-French monk. After enjoying
protection by the Japanese during the course of the occupation, the Hoa Hao leadership in 1945 joined the Cao Dai and
the Trotskyite Communists of Saigon in opposing both the
restoration of French control and the leadership pretensions
of the Vietminh from the North. The more orthodox Maha-
yana Buddhists of Saigon and Hué were both strongly
opposed to French rule and to Catholic Christian influence
as sponsored by Ngo Dinh Diem. The widely scattered
Catholic minority of some one to two million people—not
all of whom were pro-French—developed distinct political
as well as religious affiliations.[1] However much nationalist
aspirations may have provided the overriding issue in postwar Vietnamese politics, factional and religious divisions
within the South constituted formidable barriers to permanent
unification.

The Democratic Republic of Vietnam (DRV), 1954

The Vietminh victory over France at Dienbienphu in May
1954 and the resulting settlement worked out at Geneva in
July contributed substantial advantages to the Communist-
led nationalist coalition at Hanoi. Since representatives of the
Vietminh and France were the only signatories of the Gene-

va settlement, to the complete exclusion of the Bao Dai regime and its newly installed premier, Ngo Dinh Diem, the Ho Chi Minh government alone gained full diplomatic standing. It also enjoyed unchallenged authority over the North and political prestige throughout the entire Vietnamese-inhabited domain. As the residual sovereign in the South, France was pledged to cooperate in arranging elections to be held in 1956 to determine what form the contemplated unification would take. British and Russian cosponsors of the Geneva Conference were presumably also committed to holding elections, and the unilateral American statement promised not to oppose the unification effort if a free choice were guaranteed. The two-year interim provided by the settlement would afford time for Hanoi to develop a more effective governmental and economic system in the North; it would also postpone for a time the difficult task of devising and installing an administrative structure for the less-homogeneous and politically factionalized southern half of the country.

The principal political problem faced by Hanoi derived from the elimination of the unifying anticolonialist issue, which had facilitated the capture of the nationalist movement by the Communist Lao Dong (Workers) party within the Vietminh coalition. The government's imposition of rigid disciplinary controls was unavoidable if ordered recovery was to be achieved from the orgy of anarchy and near-famine occasioned by three years of Japanese occupation and nearly eight years of anticolonial strife. The aura of heroic leadership centering around Ho Chi Minh and General Vo Nguyen Giap would dissipate in time.

Following the revival of the Lao Dong party in 1951 (it had ostensibly been dissolved in 1948), Communist-type control was introduced into all areas directly administered by the Vietminh. Village assemblies of from ten to twenty-five members, locally elected, were assigned various routine administrative responsibilities. They could make policy proposals and recommendations subject to review by political and administrative committees at the higher provincial and regional levels, following the familiar "democratic centralist" pattern fashioned in the Soviet Union. If occasion demanded, upper-level committees could call on the support of General Giap's military forces, which maintained closer rapport with the country people than did most of the official Lao Dong spokesmen. All decisions covering property rights, taxes, budgets, and public works had to have upper-level approval; minor decisions by lower level councils could stand only if they were not vetoed from above.

The problem of extending this type of governmental balancing apparatus to an alien countryside was formidable. The surfeit of committee selections, meetings, and discussion of details was completely alien to the discarded mandarinate system. Government functioned in three interrelated categories. The army exercised substantial political influence but was itself infiltrated by political commissars and party cells. The civilian bureaucracy had to integrate with the plethora of village, district, and provincial councils, topped by the National Assembly and the cabinet. Meanwhile, the Communist party structure was busy establishing functional cells at all levels of the government hierarchy, as well as in schools, hospitals, factories, religious groups, women's and youth organizations, and among the montagnards. At the top level of the National Party Congress and the Presidium, the leadership of government and party overlapped.

At the outset, trained party organizers were too few in number and too concentrated geographically to encompass all elements of the population. Locally recruited propagandists usually reflected rural values and aims, which were not concerned with socialist objectives.[2] This integrative task could not be accomplished without the application of coercive measures and the accompanying risk of abuse of power. The "land to the tillers" reform decree of December, 1953, had attracted little support from the peasantry, mainly because the country was on the verge of famine and because there simply was no surplus land to distribute, except in areas later abandoned by Catholic refugees fleeing to the south. Rice, sugar, and cloth rations were very meager, and their distribution was liable to administrative abuse.[3]

Ho Chi Minh's superior organizing ability and his stature

307

as national hero contributed to the aura of patriotism generated by the Vietminh during the anti-colonialist struggle. The propaganda tactics pursued by General Giap and other leaders stressed the enlistment of local support, including that of the montagnards, plus the harassment of all pro-French elements. Manpower had to be pitted effectively against superior armament. The success of Vietminh operations, down to 1954, had depended in large measure on the dramatization and exploitation of grievances attributable to the colonial presence. General Giap's pragmatic approach exhorted the people "to fight the kind of war which you are best prepared to fight [and] do more when you are able."[4]

French withdrawal from the north in 1954 altered the political context. The Geneva agreement's partition at the seventeenth parallel (explicitly designated to serve military purposes only) benefited the other participating parties more than it did the Vietminh. For the French, the agreement provided an opportunity for an orderly exit from an impossible situation. For the Peking Chinese, it afforded a breathing period needed to ease the economic drain occasioned by the Korean War and to initiate economic recovery measures. The Soviets profited in Europe by partially isolating the United States and by facilitating an arrangement with the French covering future defense cooperation against Germany. Moscow also forestalled a distant and profitless military involvement in Vietnam without overtly sabotaging its Communist protégé. The British gained stature as the prestigious, honest broker who promoted accomodation and peace. For the United States, whose anti-Communist bluff had been called and whose efforts to create an effective security system for Southeast Asia were left far from realized, the two years' leeway afforded by the Geneva agreement could also be used to establish the Diem regime, delaying the promised elections as long as possible. The Manila Pact for SEATO was negotiated, and there was time to make a less hectic assessment of essential American interests in Southeast Asia.

The North Vietnamese authorities could ill afford after 1954 to double their immediate problem of government organization by taking on the South as well. Marxist patterns proved difficult to establish even in areas already under their unchallenged control. But food-deficient Tonkin desperately needed commercial relations with the Mekong delta region if a viable economy was to be developed. Vietminh spokesmen charged that the North had been sold out at Geneva, "denied the fruits of victory that they felt were honestly and morally theirs."[5] This difficulty became more clearly apparent when, in early 1956, the French defaulted in their commitment to help arrange for the promised elections by withdrawing their military forces three months prior to the July deadline. In view of the urgent internal problems faced by Hanoi's DRV authorities and the lack of resources for military protest, an armed rejoinder was impossible. Not one of Hanoi's friends was willing to reopen the Vietnamese conflict in view of the French withdrawal and the increasingly firm commitment of the United States to support Ngo Dinh Diem's successor government.

North Vietnam suffered a serious blow to its morale and to early economic recovery efforts as a result of the abrupt withdrawal southward of more than eight hundred thousand refugees within the ninety-day grace period permitted by the Geneva settlement. The Catholic three-quarters of the refugees were actively encouraged to make the move by the resident hierarchy of bishops and priests, who since 1951 had condemned Hanoi's pro-Communist orientation. God had allegedly moved south. Even the parishioners of the ten Vietnamese bishops who had identified with the nationalist cause were attracted by the Catholic-led government at Saigon and by guarantees of American and French assistance. In Tonkin, Catholic distrust of Ho Chi Minh had attained almost fanatical levels by early 1954, probably surpassing in intensity any opposition to him to be found in the south. But many people's fears subsided somewhat following nationalist celebrations of the Vietminh victory at Dienbienphu,[6] so that in the end almost half of the resident Catholic population remained in the North. Hanoi gained one-half million acres of vacated rice lands to be redistributed and also lost many implacable enemies as a result of the exodus. Ho's popularity as a national hero was unassailable. Washington's considered estimate as of early 1954 was that he would win a four-to-one victory in any direct nationwide voting contest with Emperor Bao Dai.

The second largest fragment of the southbound refugees consisted of families of officials and of the French colonial army. They no doubt had ample reason to anticipate rough treatment from the Vietminh authorities for both political and ideological reasons. Such evacuees, along with elite Catholic refugees, were destined to play a prominent role at Saigon through the 1960s. Their migration was really one aspect of the program of military detachment provided for in the Geneva settlement. The contrary movement of anti-French Vietnamese going northward, drawn mainly from the population of the Annam littoral, numbered only an estimated one hundred fifty thousand. Some five to ten thousand active Vietminh partisans stayed behind. Hanoi discouraged northward migration because North Vietnam lacked the financial resources needed for resettlement of the immigrants and partly because Ho and Giap recognized some advantages to be derived from the continued activities of Vietminh adherents remaining in the South.[7] Their initial assignment was political rather than military, preparing for the elections to be held in 1956. Overt struggle against Diem's repressive measures was delayed until the last quarter of 1957.[8]

North Vietnam from 1954 to 1960

The relative priority that Hanoi authorities gave to domestic matters, both economic and political, from 1954 to 1960, can be understood only in the context of prevailing circumstances, urgent needs, and the availability of proferred aid. The debilitating anti-French struggle had been fought largely in the Tonkin area, which had therefore experienced near-total destruction of railways and industrial installations, plus a general dislocation of agricultural activities. If a viable state was to be achieved in overcrowded North Vietnam, it could presumably be accomplished only by con-

310

centrating on the development of Tonkin's industrial potential. This would involve syphoning off surplus agricultural population to construct and man the newly planned industries. The task was far from easy. An entirely new course had to be plotted and implemented by an administration that was very inexperienced and not universally accepted. Furthermore, communist-type regimentation ran counter to family solidarity, reverence for ancestral remains, the norms of the mandarinate administrative tradition, and the intimate association of peasants with their land.

It was not until the autumn of 1955 that a National Planning Board and a Central Statistical Office were finally set up at Hanoi, with Russian and Chinese experts present to assist in their operation. (North Vietnam's trade had meanwhile switched to Communist-bloc nations.) The first three-year plan allocated 38 percent of available development funds to industrial construction, 23 percent to transportation and commerce, 20 percent to agriculture and irrigation, and the remaining 19 percent to education and social needs. The emphasis on industrial modernization was accompanied by several politically motivated moves that were related marginally to the execution of the plan. These involved liquidation of noncooperating landlord and moneylender elements by People's Courts, a tactic designed both to please and to impress the peasantry. But because the forced-draft program of collectivizing of the land offered virtually no positive incentives to the cultivators, the program met with considerably less than full cooperation.[9]

Serious difficulties developed in 1955–56. Typhoon and flood damage played havoc with the 1955 rice crop, raising the food deficit for the ensuing year from the normal two hundred thousand to nearly five hundred thousand tons. The resulting famine prompted Chairman Khrushchev, on the occasion of his Burma visit in early 1956, to purchase some one hundred fifty thousand tons of Burma rice on a barter basis to be shipped directly to hungry Hanoi. At the same time, the repeated effort made by the DRV to solicit cooperation on the part of the Saigon authorities in restoring normal communications and commercial relations prepara-

311

tory for reunification was futile. Diem denounced Hanoi's requests as designed for infiltration and propaganda purposes.

A serious peasant rebellion developed in North Vietnam in 1956. An immediate cause was the severe pressure exerted by Truong Chinh, the China-oriented Communist party's first secretary, in favor of rapid agricultural collectivization and for the forced transfer of workers to employment in construction and industry. Popular tension eventually forced Ho Chi Minh himself to take over the party secretaryship from Truong in October, 1956, and to replace the government's deputy minister of agriculture. Meanwhile the growing disaffection within the intellectual community of North Vietnam (doctors, writers, journalists, artists, lawyers, and engineers) came to a boil in the Vietnamese version of the "Hundred Flower" episode in China. Again, Truong Chinh was the principal target. For a period of three months, from September to December 1956, a torrent of criticism emerged. The inevitable repression imposed in early 1957 subjected more than three hundred critical intellectuals to gruelling indoctrination sessions in a correctional program that persisted throughout the year. Uncooperative persons within the group were sentenced to hard labor. Persistent efforts were made thereafter to mobilize all educational, cultural, and scientific leadership in support of the government's objectives.[10]

A policy crisis developed at Hanoi during the concluding months of 1957 following a September visit by Marshal Voroshilov, president of the Supreme Soviet of the USSR. The Russian visitor criticized Hanoi's lack of progress, and Ho Chi Minh, clearly on the defensive, departed in October for a two-month visit to Moscow in an attempt to mend relations. Following Ho's return in December, the pendulum swung back sharply in favor of the Soviet's peaceful coexistence and industrial development policies, with help coming from Eastern European countries. Soviet grants and credits for the ensuing three-year period exceeded aid coming from China by some 60 percent, in support of a policy of political and economic consolidation within North Vietnam. A Soviet technical and scientific assistance agreement was signed in March 1959. At the same time, Ho was careful not to offend Peking, which he visited in August 1959 on the tenth anniversary of the Maoist triumph. His task of placating both sides of the Communist world was destined to become increasingly difficult.[11]

Hanoi's second three-year plan, launched in 1958, placed emphasis on cooperative agricultural enterprises and industries related thereto. Former owners of nationalized firms covering many sectors of industry were asked to become managers of joint stock company operations. By 1960 state agencies were reportedly running some 80 percent of North Vietnam's transportation facilities and 90 percent of its industries. More than 80 percent of the arable land was collectivized by 1960, and state cooperatives performed many services previously provided by small businesses.

North Vietnam in 1960

By concentrating during the 1950s on economic objectives, Hanoi's industrial development program accomplished substantial gains. Production of coal, cement, lumber, and electrical energy expanded, and textile, plywood, paper, and sugar factories were put into operation. Railways leading northward to the China border were improved. A steel mill with an annual capacity of two hundred thousand tons was in operation by 1960, as was a small but useful bicycle plant. By 1961, Soviet contributions to North Vietnam's development program surpassed the previously larger Chinese effort.[12] Nevertheless, the economic outlook for Hanoi in 1960 was still far from promising. Clothing and housing were scarce except for favored party leaders, and severe food rationing was in operation as a result of harvest failure. Peasants were apparently learning how to utilize the blackmarket in disposing of withheld rice and meat products; their truculent mood was reinforced by widespread resentment over their loss of freedom as cultivators. Despite the difficulties encountered in economic development, North

313

Vietnam's new five-year plan drafted by Russian advisors and projected in 1960 included a Soviet commitment to train five hundred student technicians from Vietnam. So little was the Soviet Union interested in the early union of the two Vietnams that it had proposed in 1957, the membership of both in the United Nations.[13]

Changes were in the offing, due in part to growing divergence between Chinese and Soviet world policies. Instead of continuing to pursue an economic development objective, Hanoi's political and military partisans began to advocate, with substantial encouragement from Peking, increasing involvement in the efforts of South Vietnam Vietminh to undermine the American-supported but highly unpopular regime of Ngo Dinh Diem in Saigon. Ho Chi Minh's associate, Le Duan, himself a Southerner, returned from an extended two-year tour in the South in late 1957 to advocate stronger support of the tactics of anti-Diem partisans. If and when Diem should fall, pro-Communist elements in the south must be in a position to assert themselves. Hanoi's reaction was slow; not until the end of 1958 did it decide to take a more belligerent role. Formal party approval came in May, 1959, and full implementation of the militant policy came in September 1960.[14]

The first formal constitution for North Vietnam, which was promulgated on January 1, 1960, was a characteristically Communist document. Extensive power resided in the person of the president, who was to be chosen by each newly elected National Assembly every four years and assisted by the Executive Presidium. The president was the ceremonial chief of state, the promulgator of laws, and the nominator of the premier and the cabinet, over which he presided on occasion. The National Assembly, first elected on May 8, 1960, would meet twice yearly and was empowered to amend the constitution by a two-thirds vote. Previously selected delegates to represent the party in South Vietnam were carried over as nominal members of the new Assembly. The Standing Committee of the Assembly, functioning between its formal sessions, could scrutinize the activities of both the Council of Ministers and the supreme judicial agencies.

314

Ho Chi Minh was elected president, and his long-time Communist associates occupied key government and party positions, which overlapped at the top levels. The Politbureau inner council of the Communist Lao Dong party supervised important state functions, including propaganda activities. At the lower levels of government, People's Councils (Soviets) elected by adult suffrage were made responsible for ensuring the execution of laws and decisions initated from above, including policing operations and the use of government funds. The Councils exercised little or no discretionary power.[15] Whatever else the character of the constitution of 1960 may have indicated, it appears fairly obvious that it was not designed as an instrument capable of easy extension or acceptance in South Vietnam. Communist partisans by no means dominated the resistance to Ngo Dinh Diem, and political disunity was multiplied in a bewildering variety of sectional and sectarian interests.

Despite the reluctance of senior leaders at Hanoi, including Ho and Giap, to become actively involved militarily in South Vietnam at the cost of shelving the new Russian-sponsored five-year plan, it was nevertheless becoming increasingly apparent in the famine-prone North that economic development, so assiduously pursued since 1955, could not get very far without access to the potential of surplus food and exportable plantation products available only in Cochin-China. Younger pro-Chinese elements within the Communist Party took the initiative in September, 1960, to elevate Le Duan, the southerner, to the office of first secretary of the party. At the same time, the pro-Peking ideologist, Truong Chinh, who had been demoted from the secretaryship in 1956, rose again to the third-ranking position within the party hierarchy.[16] The decision called for support in more overt fashion of the activities of militant South Vietnam Leftist cadres attacking the Ngo Dinh Diem regime, beyond the previously dispatched 4,500 Vietminh organizers and propaganda agents of southern origin, who had returned to a familiar environment of relatives and friends.[17]

Hanoi was presumably less interested in hastening Diem's downfall per se, which appeared to be inevitable in any case, than it was in maneuvering Communist party promoters within the resistance effort into a position to profit from that event as a step toward accelerated unification. Thus, the same issue which had occasioned the rift between Ho and Admiral d'Argenlieu in May 1946 again came to the fore. By contrast, the major opponents of Diem in the South, including elements of the emerging National Liberation Front, formally organized in December, 1960, were much less concerned with early unification than with ridding their country of an oppressive American-supported government.

The Limits of Washington's Early Commitment

The American decision to sponsor and to finance Ngo Dinh Diem as the premier of Emperor Bao Dai's Associated State of Vietnam was from the outset a dubious political gamble. Diem did not have a personal following, and his previous administrative experience was limited to a mere three months of service to the new Bao Dai Emperor in 1933. On the positive side, he came from an influential mandarin family with high Catholic affiliations in northern Annam. He was adjudged a man of integrity, a moderately anti-French nationalist, and an ardent anti-Communist. He had declined previous offers to serve in Bao Dai's cabinet, once during the Japanese occupation and again in May 1949, when he was asked to be premier immediately after the emperor had returned to Hué on France's invitation. Ho Chi Minh had even offered Diem a cabinet appointment in March 1946. Diem heatedly rebuffed Ho's offer on the ground that the Viet Minh leader had murdered his mandarin brother, Ngo Dinh Khoi.

Diem's contact with Americans, at first unofficial, dated from August 1950. By the spring of 1953, when he was a resident at the Maryknoll Fathers Catholic mission in New Jersey, Washington was seriously interested in ascertaining his political views. It was with active American support that Diem, on June 18, 1954, finally accepted the emperor's renewed invitation to become premier. He took over as titular head of government on July 7, but was permitted no role in the ensuing Geneva Conference.[18] How far the United States would back him in his difficult assignment was unclear at the time.

United States hesitancy to become involved militarily in the affairs of Indochina at the time of Diem's accession is a matter of record. In view of the Korean ordeal, American army leaders, especially Generals Ridgeway and Gavin, were determined to avoid becoming involved in another Asian ground war where they could not tell friend from foe. Policy statements prepared by the Joint Chiefs of Staff as far back as 1952 nevertheless reflect Washington's serious concern lest the Chinese military action exhibited in Korea be subsequently transferred to Southeast Asia. Such a move, the Joint Chiefs affirmed, could bring all of Southern Asia under Communist control and possibly even influence Japan to come to terms with China. A memorandum of 1952 suggested that the United States should therefore be prepared to cooperate with the French and the British in assisting the peoples of Southeast Asia in economic development and in countering threatened Chinese aggression. The principal condition was that colonial authorities should agree to grant political freedom to their peoples and, at the same time, keep their own forces in place during the emergency, as was happening in Malaya. As a means of halting Chinese aggression, the Joint Chiefs as of May 1954 were prepared to contemplate the use of atomic weapons together with air and naval operations along the China coast, but opposed embarking on a ground war in Indochina.[19]

French requests in early 1954 for American assistance in the Dienbienphu affair called for additional planes and some four hundred trained mechanics to service them. Although the Joint Chiefs agreed to consider granting one-half of the French request, President Eisenhower intervened. He insisted that any such belligerent move would require Congressional action, and declared that the United States in any case would not so act without full British cooperation and continuing French participation. Eisenhower said, "The United States cannot and will not be put in a

317

position of salvaging British Commonwealth interests in Malaya, Australia, and New Zealand. . . . [and would] go to Congress to intervene with combat troops only if France stayed in the fight." With respect to Indochina, he continued, France would be expected to internationalize the conflict by permitting the United States to participate in the planning, while simultaneously granting to the associated Indochina states some real measure of freedom. He flatly refused to "bale out colonial France."[20]

At the end of May 1954, the Joint Chiefs rejected any substantial military involvement in Indochina. The May 26 statement ran as follows:

> With reference to the Far East as a whole, Indochina is devoid of decisive military factors, and the allocation of more than token forces in Indochina would be a serious diversion of limited U.S. capabilities. . . . Committing to the Indochina conflict naval forces in excess of the Carrier Task Force [requested by the French for Dienbienphu] . . . or basing substantive air forces in Indochina would involve maldeployment of forces and reduce readiness to meet probable Chinese Communist reaction elsewhere in the Far East.

American countermeasures to any overt Chinese invasion of Indochina would more properly include the blockade and bombardment of China's coastal cities, the seizure of Hainan Island, plus the possible use of Nationalist Chinese, Thai, and Filipino ground troops.[21]

American policy during the course of the Geneva Conference continued to oppose any ceasefire or French withdrawal requiring the attendant abandonment of Vietnam to Communist rule, as Secretary Dulles repeatedly affirmed.[22] But Washington's concern did not at the time contemplate any unilateral commitment to underwrite the newly installed Diem government or any overt repudiation of the Geneva settlement. On July 7, the date of Diem's arrival in Hué, Dulles cabled Bedell Smith at Paris as follows:

> Since it is undoubtedly true that elections might eventually mean unification of Vietnam under Ho Chi Minh, . . . they should . . . be held as long after ceasefire agreement as possible and in conditions free from intimidation. . . . No date

should be set now, and . . . no condition be accepted by [the] French which would . . . prevent effective international supervision.[23]

Ambassador Smith's reply on July 18 reported that American press contacts with Chinese spokesmen indicated that Peking very much desired United States acceptance of the settlement, particularly the requirements that Indochina be neutralized and that all foreign military bases be barred from Southeast Asia. Smith concluded that the United States "as a member of the conference" had no moral reason to avoid the obligation of accepting the settlement.[24]

The Early Years of the Diem Regime.

Diem's immediate task as premier was to create an alternative governmental structure to take the place of the decaying French colonial administration. The prospects were most discouraging. Governmental authority was disintegrating; saboteurs were active in Saigon; the army was hostile to the new regime; Diem did not even possess a palace guard.[25] Experienced anti-French nationalist officials were few—especially so in the former Cochin-China colony, which had been governed by French civil servants. It was only with American encouragement and funds that Diem acquired the support of some three thousand Cao Dai troops and enlisted the assistance of a Filipino friend of Colonel Edward Lansdale to recruit and train a palace guard. As head of CIA's Saigon Military Mission, Colonel Lansdale also assisted in the propaganda field. He prepared and circulated leaflets to discourage Vietminh deportees from going northward and to encourage the registration of refugees arriving from the North.[26] When friction between Diem and General Nguyen Van Hinh reached the breaking point in October 1954, two of Hinh's key subordinates were invited by Lansdale to visit the Philippines, where they were detained beyond the October 26 deadline for a projected anti-Diem coup. The crisis passed with Hinh's departure for France a month later, but the morale situation at Saigon continued to be dismal. Few persons thought that the Diem government could possibly survive the elections promised for 1956. One Francophile group of Vietnamese was barely dissuaded from migrating to the island of Madagascar.[27]

A disproportionately large percentage of the new official-dom recruited by the Diem regime, including appointees to regional and district posts, came from the Hué area of central Annam and from the Catholic refugee population from North Vietnam. A majority of the top personnel were French speaking, and an estimated 40 percent of the original nonelected Assembly members were former civil servants. The North Vietnamèse dialect was not easily understood in the South, and many refugees shared the prejudices of Diem's personal entourage, who viewed most Southerners with unconcealed contempt. Southerners occupied only half of the cabinet posts at Saigon; they filled only a third of the higher civil service ranks. Officials were fairly familiar with routine administrative procedures, but they retained the *fonctionnaire* habit of avoiding responsibility for making decisions.[28] Diem's successful resettlement of the Northern refugees, accomplished with generous American financial assistance, added many useful supporters of the new regime, but the procedure contributed negatively to his own acceptance by the general population of South Vietnam. The aggressive role of the Ngo Dinh family, with brother Nhu dominating Saigon, brother Can in lower Annam, and Bishop Ngo Dinh Thuc at Hué, was particularly resented by elite elements, including those who had been allied with the French. These dissidents included top army leadership and spokesmen for the sect organizations.

Diem managed to deal with his enemies one at a time. The first of a series of crises arose in October 1954, with the Francophile General Nguyen Van Hinh. President Eisenhower tilted the balance in Diem's favor by channeling essential American aid only to Diem's government. General Hinh finally elected to depart for France on November 29.[29]

A second and more serious crisis developed in March 1955, when Diem moved to withdraw from the Cao Dai and

320

Hoa Hao sects the financial subsidies long provided them by the French. Both sects ruled over semiautonomous delta provinces and operated their own private armies. Diem refused to compromise, and matters reached an impasse. It was again a moot question for a time whether the abrasively stubborn Ngo Dinh leadership could survive. Bao Dai and the French wanted Diem replaced by someone more conciliatory and acceptable to Hué. A proposal to oust the family clique was formally transmitted to Saigon from France, where the emperor was temporarily in residence. The idea received at the time a considerable measure of support from General Lawton Collins, then serving as American ambassador at Saigon. Diem had already demonstrated his complete lack of respect for democratic methods of accommodation, his distrust of all advice coming from outside the family circle, and his presumptuous sense of family rectitude and divinely sanctioned authority. The opportunity that was here afforded to displace him gracefully by conceding to the Emperor's wishes was destined not to recur.

The regime was saved by Diem's stubbornness and by the audacious action taken by the so-called Revolutionary Committee headed by his brother Nhu. Its members invaded the palace and threatened the life of Bao Dai's army emissary, who had been sent to summon Diem to report to the emperor at Cannes. Meanwhile, the two hostile religious sects failed to coordinate their resistance efforts, so that both succumbed in April to the combination of financial and military pressure, coupled with the strategic use of bribes. In May when the same threatened Bao Dai military emissary undertook to utilize aid proffered him by the Binh Xuyen police force—a semi-bandit organization with its own 2500-man army that operated lucrative rackets in Saigon and Cholon—, elements of the regular army under General Duong Van Minh came to Diem's support. Under Nhu's direction, the troops crushed the Binh Xuyen and laid waste the section of Cholon that it had previously controlled. Thereafter, Nhu included the emperor himself in his purging list.

Because Diem refused to seek accomodation with either of the still dissident religious sects, ten of the eleven subgroups of the Cao Dai and virtually all of the Hoa Hao following began cooperating secretly with the underground opposition to his government. Nevertheless, a successful series of operations against such formidable enemies—all ostensibly in the interest of anticommunism, according to Nhu—confirmed Diem's self-confidence and also Washington's faith in his appointed destiny. Nhu himself took over many of the lucrative vice operations of the Binh Xuyen. In October 1955 a specially arranged plebiscite forced a choice between Diem and Bao Dai and resulted in a 98.2 percent victory for the former.[30]

The final victory of the emerging Ngo Dinh family dynasty came in the spring of 1956. Impressed by the kind of anti-Communist, anticolonialist miracle unfolding at Saigon, United States authorities lent support to Nhu's proposal to end the French presence prior to the scheduled departure date in July. In March 1956 Diem flatly rejected Hanoi's renewed proposals to arrange for the election promised at Geneva. The French military withdrawal came that April. Despite the continuing hostility of the religious sects and other opposition elements, the Diem government actually generated a measure of popularity during 1956, mainly because the ousting of Bao Dai and the French was generally approved. Few Southerners, aside from the hard-core Vietminh partisans, favored the immediate holding of nationwide elections. The North itself was facing at the time its own rebellious peasant and intellectuals' convulsions, as has been previously indicated.

From the official Saigon point of view, there was no reason for Diem to accept the gamble involved in holding the elections promised for 1956 in the Geneva settlement, especially since American influence had displaced that of France. Plebiscites and elections, after all, were useful political expedients only if they demonstrated ostensible support for the ruling authority, the actual sanction for whose power resided elsewhere.[31] The moralistic viewpoint of Secretary Dulles was psychologically akin to that of Diem, even though his supporting considerations differed. For the Puritan Dulles, Godless Communism was evil incarnate, and any neutralist stance in the context of the world confrontation struggle between good and evil, freedom and slavery, was adjudged immoral. The enthusiastic American Catholic support for the Diem regime by Cardinal Spellman and Jesuit institutions in particular added a further dimension to the Secretary's Manichean dichotomy.

The Diem Regime Takes Form

The drafting of South Vietnam's Republican Constitution which was completed in March and promulgated in October 1956, was the handiwork of Diem's cabinet. It was reviewed by his own carefully selected National Assembly, in which his brother Ngo Dinh Nhu and Madame Nhu were prominent members. The cabinet was made responsible to the president, who was to be elected for terms of five years. The president was accorded the power to initiate laws for Assembly approval and to legislate by decree on occasion. A three-fourths vote of the Assembly was required to override a presidential veto. The president also controlled the judiciary, made budgetary allocations, and managed foreign policy, including the making of war and peace. The elected single-chamber Assembly of 123 members was forbidden to debate important proposals in which the president indicated a direct interest. Cabinet officers could not be members of the proposed Assembly.

Political activities under the new regime were similarly under executive control. Diem's official National Revolutionary Movement (NRM) party, centering in the Assembly membership, was assisted by the National Revolutionary Civil Servants League, whose job was to electioneer and get out the vote for the NRM. No other party was legally authorized to function. Nonofficial candidates could run for office, but only as independents without party organization support. Particular groups that in 1955 had supported Diem's campaign against the Binh Xuyen and also his anti-French policies were incorporated bodily into the NRM.[32]

323

Nhu's so-called Personalist Labor party functioned mainly as a secret espionage system to gather incriminating evidence on opposition elements and to solicit political favors and graft. It also functioned politically in the extreme south as an alternative to the NRM. Constitutional provisions for freedom of the press and of association were empty guarantees. The president could censor the press, refuse to concede meeting privileges, and imprison political opponents, including Assemblymen, on allegations of Communist affiliations. Non-Communist opponents of Diem had to abandon political activity or turn subversive.

In the end a wide assortment of lawyers, teachers, students, businessmen, religious leaders, and army generals aligned secretly with various opposition movements.[33] By a law of May 6, 1959, Diem ruled that capital offenses to be tried by military tribunals should include the airing of complaints about prices, distortions of economic difficulties, provocation of disturbances, and sabotage of government policy generally, along with overt subversionary efforts and crimes against the state and property. Under Nhu's leadership, the government's allegedly anti-Communist policy attained after 1959 a crescendo of near frenzy.[34]

The repressive system was rationalized in various ways. Diem's assumption of "Heaven's Mandate" as the savior of Vietnam was presumably authenticated by his near-miraculous triumph over his many enemies in 1954–56. The regime also appropriated ideological support from the doctrine and philosophy of personalism, acclaimed enthusiastically by Ngo Dinh Nhu. It was based on an adaptation of existentialism as propounded by the French philosopher Mounier, but was given in Saigon a strongly antiliberal and arrogantly puritanical interpretation.[35] In theory personalism was intended to promote the free development of intellectual, moral, and spiritual capacities and to encourage dedication to civic duty and disciplined living. Nhu's emphasis was on "discipline." He discounted the validity of various American reform proposals and the offering of incentives to enlist popular support as misplaced idealism at best and as unwarranted interference in South Vietnam's internal affairs at worst. Meanwhile, sycophants within Diem's entourage systematically kept unpleasant facts from coming to his exalted attention. By 1959 Diem was becoming extremely sensitive to any expressions of organized opposition, even to the point of juggling military commands to the detriment of rebel suppression in order to curb the influence of army critics.[36]

At the administrative levels of government, Diem replaced with his own appointees the governors of all thirty-nine provinces and stripped the subordinate territorial units of virtually all autonomous authority, budgetary or otherwise. Some 233 district chiefs, all centrally appointed, functioned mainly as agents to transmit orders down to a total of around 16,000 village and hamlet units.

Appointed officials at the village level replaced the traditionally elected councils for handling basic functions, such as tax collections, police duties, and the distribution of government propaganda. Within the smaller hamlet units, family groupings at two levels (twenty-five-member units and five-member units) completed the highly centralized system of governmental controls.[37] It was an open question which of the two Vietnam regimes, North or South, was the least democratic.

One of Diem's first moves in the area of economic reform, taken in August 1956, was to exclude all alien residents (predominantly Chinese) from participating in eleven designated business and professional categories. These included moneylending, rice milling, and transportation services, plus the distribution of such commodities as meat, coal, wood, silk, and scrap iron. The Chinese population centered at Saigon's sister city of Cholon, where some three hundred thousand aliens resided. The arbitrary anti-Chinese regulations did nothing to improve economic conditions, since no other group was available to take up the slack in most of the designated areas. The law was widely circumvented by assigning titular ownership to indigenous wives or their children. (Only locally born persons could be classified as citizens.) Diem also attempted to break up existing Chinese Associations based on common language or provincial origin, which had long functioned to govern, care for, and discipline the several communities.

Diem's announced purpose was to force the Chinese to

choose between assimilation or expulsion from Vietnam before Red China was in a position to champion the rights of overseas Chinese throughout Southeast Asia.[38] Taiwan did not assist the local Chinese.

Due in large measure to the receipt of generous aid from the United States,[39] the Saigon regime was not in as dire an economic plight after 1954 as was its counterpart to the north. Even so, the economic problems faced by Diem were formidable. Saigon's traditional dominance as the primary port of French Indochina lapsed with the loss of Cambodian and Laotian trade. Some eighty-five thousand local jobs were cancelled when the French Expeditionary Corps departed in 1956. Except for plantations and urban properties, French investments were widely liquidated. Rice and rubber exports continued, but little else. Primary needs included the repair of irrigation and transportation facilities and the urgent revival of full plantation production. The resettlement and relief of displaced peasants and refugees from the North was completed, thanks to American aid. Some 150 new sites in the central highlands, capable of accomodating more than 200,000 persons, were made available by 1957. Inflationary pressure and commodity shortages were eased by the importation of American consumer goods, which the authorities sold for overvalued *piasters* to local merchants. Such payments, along with assessed customs dues went into "counterpart funds" for the use of the government.[40]

From 1957 to 1960, the emphasis in American aid shifted from relief needs to economic development. Roads, bridges, railways, and canals were repaired. School enrollment multiplied three times from 1955 to 1958, with the facilities at the three universities at Saigon, Dalat, and Hué expanded to accomodate some twelve thousand students. New industrial installations included factories for producing paper, glass, chemicals, textiles, and sugar. French capital developed coal mines near Danang, and a hydroelectric installation was built with the help of Japanese reparations. The early gains realized in agricultural output slowed by 1959 because of growing unrest and disorder in the countryside. Between 1960 and 1962, South Vietnam's exports declined by 50 percent, with United States aid funds having to take up the slack. Meanwhile, an increasing proportion of American aid was diverted to military assistance.[41]

The Land Reform Effort

One of the most disappointing aspects of Ngo Dinh Diem's reform efforts related to changes in land ownership and use. The need was urgent if restive peasant cultivators of Cochin-China were to be persuaded to accept the Diem regime. Some 2.5 percent of the population owned around half of the arable land, whereas 70 percent of the title owners claimed a mere 12.5 percent of the total. Much of the previously cultivated land had been abandoned by absentee landlords, and the delta irrigation and drainage facilities were in dire need of repair. Unless some tangible incentive could be offered to cultivators to stimulate recovery efforts, peasant villagers would prefer to side with the Vietminh propagandists, who supported free cultivator access to all abandoned landlord holdings. Political considerations weighed heavily against the land reform implementation. The concurrent efforts of the Diem police to eliminate all Vietminh supporters were strongly backed by the landlords, who contributed both prestige and revenues to the Saigon regime. In a situation where a bold program of reform was required to counter growing peasant unrest dating from the prewar period, Diem's program was both too cautious and too tardily implemented to meet the need.

Land reform moves had actually begun in early 1955, when two legislative reform measures were initiated to reduce tenancy rentals to 25 percent of yields and to guarantee three- to five-year occupancy rights. Diem's comprehensive Land Distribution Ordinance came in October 1956. The new law required that larger landholders surrender ownership of rice lands above the 100-hectare limit (247 acres) that each was permitted to retain; they would receive from the government payment at an agreed price for such surrendered lands in the form of 3 percent bonds redeemable in twelve years. Occupying tenants were accorded prior purchase rights, and they could acquire full title from the government by payment of the redemption price, interest free, over a six-year period. The total amount of rice land available for redistribution under the terms of the ordinance, including a substantial area acquired from the French government, was approximately 685,000 hectares. Enormous areas of plantation holdings were not affected, along with other nonrice cultivation. Church land holdings of some 150,000 hectares were also unaffected by the law.

Diem's land-reform proposal was essentially a compromise effort designed to retain the support of the landlords, while offering what purported to be an opportunity for cultivator ownership. Even if the reform had been fully and promptly carried out, it would have left the vast majority of the tenant farmers, not to mention those tenants who continued working on the plantations and the reserved 100-hectare plots, without any realistic prospect of keeping up with their six-year payment schedules. Actually, long delays ensued. Preliminary land surveys had to be completed and procedural problems resolved relating to price determination. The 3 percent bonds could be worth little if inflation should continue during the twelve-year period. Then came the problem of the actual administration of the approved transfers. Final acceptance of the program took another full year. In situations where neither landlord nor tenant could establish clear claims, strategically-placed government officials, including members of the Ngo Dinh family, were able to acquire valuable property. The first issuance of temporary titles to cultivator-tenants came in 1960; two years later, the entire program foundered.

Various difficulties were encountered. Owners objected that original price estimates were too low, and they succeeded in dominating the Special Agrarian Court set up in November 1957 to adjudicate disputed land claims. Cultivators, on the other hand, objected to being asked to pay the purchase price, especially when officials began trying to collect back rentals and taxes covering the long period of irregular occupancy. If annual payment obligations were to be kept at manageable size, the redemption period would have to be

328

longer than six years. Many potential recipients of land deemed it unsafe to accept government-distributed titles, in the face of Vietminh reprisal threats against anyone who collaborated with the landlord class and the officials. When the redistribution program was abandoned in 1962, only 110,000 hectares had been transfered to temporary and insecure cultivator control. The Saigon government had meanwhile come to regard any expressions of peasant opposition to the alleged land reform program as politically motivated and essentially subversive.[42] In 1962, land reform efforts modulated to the so-called strategic hamlet program, in which security concerns took priority over cultivator interests.

Opposition to Diem in South Vietnam

A principal factor contributing to the growing unpopularity of the Saigon regime down to 1960 was the power-hungry parochial outlook of its leadership. In the absence of any dependable following in the southern part of South Vietnam (except for the resettled Catholic refugees), Diem reserved most decisions, including trivial administrative details, to himself and his family. Nhu and his imperious wife shared the palace precincts and functioned as virtual autocrats in the South. Can, another brother and a thoroughly un-Western mandarin traditionalist, dominated even more effectively the central Annam area, without holding any official government post. Both Nhu and Can were interested in bribery and graft as well as power. Catholic Bishop Thuc of Hué, the third brother, exercised wide influence politically in upper Annam, exhibiting an arrogance and crusading fanaticism that offended even his local Catholic constituency.[43] Bishop Thuc fired the liberal rector of the University of Hué and otherwise rode roughshod over Buddhist sensitivities in the Hué area.[44]

Early evidence of such nepotism had prompted the previously mentioned efforts by responsible Vietnamese and French residents in April 1955 to remove Diem and his family from power. From officials of his immediate entourage, Diem demanded complete subservience, rejecting any independence of mind. Beyond the family circle, Diem favored northerners generally and Catholic refugees in particular in his appointments to high administrative posts. Many of the new refugee villages were ruled by their Catholic priests. Catholic laymen assigned to government posts in the provinces usually had difficulty establishing rapport with the local people and eventually provided vulnerable targets for the Vietminh opposition, with its People's Courts.[45]

Frustration took a devastating political toll after 1957. Many qualified and responsible ex-officials departed for France. Others defected to the North or joined the Leftist resistance. Unable to countenance or to make accomodation with any expression of organized dissent, Diem elected to counter his opponents head on, as he had previously done with the sects, with Bao Dai, and with the French. Political participation was countenanced only if it operated within the tradition of respect for mandarin authority. Alienation of protesting groups became cumulative. Diem's uncompromising stance was sustained by a kind of nostalgia for things Annamese and by a conservative mentality that disdained efforts to attract popular support through ameliorative reform and social welfare efforts. Thus Ngo Dinh Nhu preferred to encourage villager self-help and self-discipline while holding out little or no incentive for peasant cooperation, even when the United States offered to pay for the incentives.[46] From 1954 to 1957 the Diem police imprisoned or liquidated an estimated fifty to one hundred thousand opponents. They were mainly Vietminh veterans, but included also military leaders, students, and professional men, as well as peasants and montagnards. The brutality, thievery, and general abuse of power exhibited by the army and the civil guard encouraged the population as a whole to respond positively to the propaganda of the trained South Vietnam veterans of the Vietminh who returned to their homes from the North.[47]

An orderly challenge to Diem's authority was attempted by a group of South Vietnamese elite assembled at the

Caravelle Hotel in Saigon in April 1960. The eighteen prestigious political leaders included representatives of the Cao Dai and Hoa Hao sects and a dissident Catholic group. Ten of the eighteen had been cabinet ministers in previous governments. Calling themselves the "Bloc for Liberty and Progress," they drafted and released to the foreign press a document of grievances and reform demands criticizing Diem's practice of nepotism and calling for constitutional revision in the direction of a freely elected assembly and responsibility for the cabinet, plus the encouragement of foreign and domestic enterprises. Members of the Caravelle group were promptly arrested and consigned to jail without advancing any formal charges or affording them any chance for a hearing.[48]

In mid-September 1960 the American ambassador, Ellbridge Durbrow, reported by cable to Washington that a coup against Diem could be anticipated for two reasons: the first was the steadily rising hostility to Diem reflected at all levels of the population, and the second was the conviction of non-Leftist critics that the rapidly expanding influence of the Vietcong (Communists) in the countryside carried the threat that the Communists would profit substantially from Diem's growing unpopularity.

Ambassador Durbrow's recommendations were far-reaching. The United States should press for important changes at Saigon in both leadership and policy; Nhu and Police Chief Tran Kin Tuyen could be removed by giving them ambassadorial assignments; the dependable Vice-President Tho should become the new minister of the interior; Nhu's secret Can Lao party should be disbanded; favoritism in the assignment of military ranks and posts must stop; and responsible leaders from nonofficial party groups should be selected for ministerial posts. Furthermore, Durbrow recommended, high officials should be required to publicize their property and financial resources, and the National Assembly should be permitted not only legislative initiative but also the right to investigate abuses of political authority. The widening gap between the news media and the government must be closed. Peasants must be granted not only a better price for their paddy, but also some compensation for forced *corvée* labor and aid for dislocated agroville communities in line with the assistance previously accorded to refugees from North Vietnam. The ambassador solicited consideration and comment on what he realized was a large order.[49]

In November 1960 came the surprise attack on the Presidential Palace by three paratrooper battalions led by dissident younger officers. They gained control of the palace temporarily and offered to let Diem continue in the role of figurehead president if he would get rid of family advisers and consent to constitutional changes and a reform government. Diem played along for time, pretending to accede to the demands until loyal troops arrived to put down the coup. It was shortly after this debacle that the respected Phan Quang Dan, a Harvard-trained physician, was arrested for alleged involvement in the uprising, a highly dubious accusation. He had previously criticized the Caravelle reform demands as not going far enough. Phan was consigned to prison on Poulo Condore Island, where he was tortured in a futile effort to exact a confession. He regained his freedom only after Diem's fall. It was in such a political context that the Hanoi-supported National Liberation Front (NLF) organization emerged in late 1960 as leader in the struggle to oust the American-supported regime at Saigon.

*South Vietnamese Resistance to Diem
and its Relations with Hanoi*

During the years of the anti-French struggle, the Dai Viet rebels had been active in central Annam, but elsewhere in the South the fighting had been on a small scale. Following the Geneva settlement, many of the anti-French militants previously resident in coastal Annam elected to move northward, while most of those resident in southern Cochin-China decided to remain. Thus it developed in many areas of the extreme South that Vietminh partisans managed from the outset to assume full control locally, assigning landlord properties to cultivators and collecting taxes to support their own governmental operations. Everywhere in South Vietnam, Vietminh propaganda stressed land redistribution, reduction of rents, and opposition to usury and official corruption.[50]

Diem's efforts to repress surviving elements of the Vietminh in Annam encountered little effective resistance at first. During the initial two years, the principal focus of nationalist hostility was the presence of the French and puppet Bao Dai, sentiments shared by Diem himself. Many of the opponents of French influence, including the southern sect groups, the Buddhists, and even some of the Catholic refugee elements were also opposed to immediate unification with the North. Diem's suppression of Vietminh leadership began as early as November 1954, when he arrested the membership of a southern group called the Committee for the Defense of Peace and the Geneva Agreements. The victims included Nguyen Huu Tho, the lawyer son of a plantation manager, who had previously suffered imprisonment in 1950 for stirring up student unrest. Tho was destined in 1962 to become the first elected head of the National Liberation Front.[51] While the French were being pressed to leave, Diem issued a special police ordinance in January 1956 authorizing the imprisonment of all presumed Vietminh adherents. Those who managed to escape the police net had virtually no choice thereafter but to band together in self-defense.[52]

Because the government's land reform program was long deferred and not very attractive in any case, villager resentment in particular mounted cumulatively against Saigon-appointed officials, tax collectors, and landlords. Politica persecuted anti-Diem adherents, therefore, found prote and recruited allies throughout the countryside. 1958, the resistance effort in the villages be d, with the convening of Peoples pecific purpose of eliminating resident a executions numbered around two hundred victims in 1958 and perhaps double that number in 1959. Diem countered the Peoples Courts by setting up in 1959 his own military courts empowered to suppress all dissent.[53] At the same time, veterans' groups in the south, presumably acting under the direction of agents from Hanoi, stepped up their enlistment of guerrilla fighters. The Resistance Veterans Declaration, issued in March 1960, solicited support from all dissident groups. The declaration proposed replacing Diem by a coalition government, and demanded the withdrawal of the American influence and presence, plus the implementation of the Geneva agreement looking toward the eventual unification of all Vietnam. Particularly significant at this juncture was the Veterans' complaint that Hanoi was not affording substantial support for their more militant stance.[54]

Just as French intransigence had made possible the Communists' capture of the nationalist movement prior to 1954, the continuing United States support of the repressive Diem regime strengthened the influence of more radical elements within the southern resistance movement. The emerging anti-Diem movement centered around a number of disparate nuclei. Many of the southerners affiliated with the Vietminh were themselves not Communist oriented. They included representatives of the religious sects, urban politicians, doctors, lawyers, teachers, and architects, as well as the villagers and the montagnards. With relatively little support from the north in arms or fighting men,[55] guerrilla terrorist bands composed mainly of southern volunteers found shelter among the generally sympathetic population and exercised quasi-control over an estimated 75 to 80 percent of the countryside by the end of 1959. The Diem government acted as if the regime would lose irreparable face if it responded positively to the most legitimate of the peasant or urban dissident demands. Anti-Diem sentiment rose as Saigon's official and army morale declined. It was under such circumstances that the Hanoi authorities decided with some reluctance to undertake a more militant role.[56]

Hanoi's effort to take over the direction of growing insurgency in the South presumably dated from May 1959. The Third Congress of the Lao Dong Communist party, held at Hanoi from September 5 to 19, 1960, sanctioned for the first time the proposed militant program of South Vietnam's Self-Defense United Front. On December 20, at a meeting held in the south, the National Liberation Front was formally launched. The event was publicized by the Hanoi government in late January 1961. The First Congress of the NLF itself was not staged until in February 1962, when Nguyen Huu Tho, who had escaped from jail in 1961, was elected its first president. A professional journalist became secretary-general of the Front. Included among its five vice-presidents were a doctor, an architect, a Buddhist monk, and a montagnard tribal leader. The Central Committee membership included a Catholic, a Cao Dai leader, and a Buddhist monk. These facts supply little support for the official Washington view that the NLF was an agency created and directed by Hanoi as part of its deliberate program of "aggression from the North."[57]

A more judicious assessment of the situation was made by Douglas Pike, a member of the State Department's USIS staff in Saigon during the crucial years of the early 1960s. Pike concluded that North and South Vietminh groups differed significantly from the outset on questions of tactics, priorities, and timing. Hanoi advocated the early political unification of Vietnam as promised at Geneva, but it refused down to 1960 to press the issue at the cost of interrupting economic development activities under way in the North.[58] The threatened Vietminh partisans in the south, who were of necessity enemies of the Diem regime, wanted Hanoi to move more rapidly beyond the merely organizational and political support that had characterized its role down to 1960. The southern contingent paid lip service to Communist goals, but unification was for them a deferred objective to be realized only after the wishes and interests of the South Vietnamese people were taken fully into account. Hanoi undertook a measure of direction over the existing Vietminh anti-Diem struggle as early as 1959 by sending in advisers, but it provided no substantial numbers of arms or troops prior to late 1963, after Diem's assassination. Pike concluded that whereas the National Liberation Front, after 1960, did not function as a purely South Vietnamese movement, it could not accurately be described "simply as a hammer in the hand of the long arm of the

335

DRV."[59] Scholarly French and American studies have emphasized the point that the widespread violence that engulfed the South Vietnam countryside by 1959 was essentially locally instigated and had no essential relevance to any planned conquest from the north.

The progression of the Leftist resistance effort can be delineated by reference to three successive declarations made in 1960. The appeal of the Resistance Veterans publicized in March 1960 solicited support from widely disparate malcontents, as indicated above. The concluding proposal of the Veterans Declaration was that the victors over Diem should consult realistically with the Hanoi DRV authorities to restore relations between North and South and to arrange for holding joint elections. By comparison, the formal resolution adopted by Hanoi's Lao Dong party congress in September 1960 in support of the armed struggle of the South put primary emphasis on defeating the United States as the enemy of unification.[60] The formal Ten Point program affirmed by the newly formed National Liberation Front in December 1960, also denounced U.S. imperialism, but advocated the "gradual unification of the country by peaceful means, on the principle of negotiations and discussions between the two zones." The Ten Points also called for an independent economic program for the South, the creation of a national army, protection of the legitimate rights of foreign residents, a foreign policy of peace and neutrality, opposition to any aggressive war, and safeguarding the peace of Southeast Asia.[61] These latter considerations were not dictated by Hanoi.

Efforts to find a more widely accepted basis for opposition to Diem continued into 1962. On the occasion of the convening of the NLF's First Congress in January, a group composed of some one hundred southern-chosen delegates, the Hanoi government made a significant counter move by announcing the formation of the Communist Peoples Revolutionary party of South Vietnam. The party's platform called for the replacement of the Diem regime by "a Democratic coalition" dedicated to a program of economic restoration, land and rent reforms, the exclusion of U.S. advisers, and the normalization of north-south relations as a step toward unification. Hanoi's sponsorship in 1962 of this more definitely Communist-oriented organization reflected its concern to counter the apparent bourgeois tendencies within the NLF.[62] The evidence indicates that both within and outside the NLF, various anti-Diem groups were unwilling to let Hanoi's propagandists gain exclusive advantage from the prospective downfall of the Saigon regime.

America's Expanding Advisory Role, 1961–64

The new Kennedy administration, which came to power in Washington in January 1961, faced a difficult decision with regard to Diem. Qualified expressions of official State Department satisfaction over Diem's survival of the November coup also suggested that his authority could be substantially enhanced by implementing already approved reform measures and by taking strong disciplinary action against official corruption. As usual, Diem was unresponsive to Washington's polite suggestions. Official advisers to the American administration, including Frederick Nolting, the new ambassador at Saigon, stressed the lack of any satisfactory alternative to Diem and also questioned America's moral right to discard a government that it had sponsored and supported for six years and that was now completely dependent on continued aid. Catholic partisans in America, led by Cardinal Spellman, a long-time friend of the Kennedy family, were also strongly in favor of Diem.[63]

The distressing dilemma of whether or not to support an unpopular dictatorship as part of the world struggle against Communism was, of course, far from novel. Informed non-official observers in South Vietnam, as of early 1961, supported Durbrow's negative views of late 1960. They were highly dubious of the wisdom of supporting the Diem regime in a situation where the essential problem was political and where continued American support could easily prove to be self-defeating. Virtually the entire American newspaper corps in South Vietnam was convinced that, granted the mood of the Diem regime and its growing unpopularity among all

337

elements of the population, Washington must find, before it was too late, an alternative government able to resolve the increasing disaffection in the cities and counter the influence of the Communist agents in the countryside. Guerrilla operations based on hostility to a government that was unsympathetic to popular demands could not be countered by direct military suppression. America's anti-Communist crusade was in danger of being engulfed in a political morass.[64]

American critics also stressed Diem's shabby treatment of Phan Quang Dan. As the sole opposition member elected to the National Assembly in 1959, Dan had been denied his seat by Diem's police on the spurious charge of currying votes by offering free clinical service. Dr. Dan's critical comment to Dennis Warner on America's policy cut deeply:

> The only message the Americans bring is anti-Communism. They criticize the Communists for the very things they countenance here. The North Vietnamese regime at least has the advantage of being true to itself. It does attempt to work for the poor masses. Here it is just the reverse. . . . The Americans intervene when they want to. Why don't they intervene when moral issues are at stake?[65]

Washington's options were circumscribed by the authoritarian stand of the Ngo Dinh regime and by the downright hostility exhibited by Nhu, who actually blamed the attempted coup of November on American instigation. The tense situation created by the November crisis provided no appropriate context for Washington to make reform recommendations, unless it was prepared to insist on their implementation.

President Kennedy's policy problem was complicated by other international considerations that commanded his attention in early 1961, including the Bay of Pigs fiasco in Cuba, the West Berlin crisis, and the attempt to neutralize Laos. His Laos policy aroused the anger of Marshal Sarit of Thailand, and to assuage Bangkok's fears, the United States concluded a bilateral treaty of defense with Thailand. Diem promptly asked for similar assurances. The defensive stance which Washington was obliged to assume elsewhere in the world seemed to underscore the need for a firm position in South Vietnam, regardless of the peculiarities of the situation in Saigon. American intelligence estimates agreed that Saigon's efforts at pacification would be futile unless a more vigorous military initiative was pursued along with administrative reforms as well. Operational agencies argued in rejoinder that additional advisory personnel could help Diem improve governmental operations and that intensification of covert activities might alter the discouraging situation. By May 1, 1961, Washington decided to withdraw from Laos if possible but to defend Thailand and South Vietnam from the assumed menace of Communist domination.[66] A new treaty of Amity and Economic Relations had been negotiated with Saigon in April.

The expanded American advisory program was more psychological than military, partly because Diem flatly rejected any proposal to introduce alien troops. The "Program of Action for South Vietnam," prepared in Washington and dated May 8, assigned to ambassador Nolting at Saigon the difficult tasks of strengthening popular loyalty to the "free government of South Vietnam" and of improving Diem's reputation in allied and neutral countries. The detailed operational plans as revealed in the *Pentagon Papers* dealt mainly with efforts at espionage and psychological warfare to be conducted by the Military Assistance Advisory Group headed by Colonel Lansdale and by associated CIA agencies. They included American penetration of the governmental, military, and political agencies of South Vietnam in order to obtain data covering possible anti-Diem coups and also to identify individuals with "potentiality of providing leadership in the event of the disappearance of Diem." An accompanying Joint Chiefs of Staff Memo of May 10 suggested that Diem be encouraged to request that the United States fulfil its SEATO obligation with respect to the defense of Laos.[67]

The concurrent Washington decision to increase economic aid to the Diem government raised no objections from Saigon, but it contributed nonetheless to long-term problems. The already heavy annual American aid contribution ($13.70 per capita as of 1960, second only to that given to sparsely populated Laos)[68] was substantially augmented. The increased volume of consumer goods imports, designed to generate counterpart funds for government use, stimulated the inflationary spiral. In the face of decline in export earnings, the South Vietnamese economy was unable to absorb the surfeit of consumer imports. Declining revenues forced the government to resort to deficit financing, with living costs rising as the value of the piaster declined.[69]

The Domino Theory in Application

The contradictory considerations which Washington was attempting to reconcile were illustrated by the equivocal report that Vice-President Lyndon Johnson submitted on May 23, at the conclusion of his special mission to Southeast Asia. The report accepted the domino theory of cumulative threat with no qualifications and also reflected the contradictory views he encountered at Saigon:

> The battle against Communism must be joined in Southeast Asia with strength and determination to achieve success there . . . or the United States inevitably must surrender the Pacific and take up our defense on our own shores. . . . There is no alternative to United States leadership in Southeast Asia. . . . [Otherwise] the vast Pacific becomes a Red Sea.

The report then proceeded to expound an opposing point of view. Johnson argued that the presence of American combat troops in South Vietnam was neither required nor desirable in view of the strength of anti-colonial sentiment in the country and because any overt attack by the Communists at the moment was highly improbable. He added that:

> The greatest danger Southeast Asia offers . . . is not the momentary threat of Communism itself, [but] rather . . . hunger, ignorance, poverty, and disease. We must . . . keep these enemies the point of our attack.

The Vice-President also conceded that Diem was remote from his people and surrounded by persons less admirable than he; even so, Johnson argued, the United States must decide whether to support him or to let Vietnam fall. Thai-

land's Sarit, he added, was "more staunchly pro-Western
than many of his people. . . . If Sarit is to stand firm against
neutralism, he must have—soon—concrete evidence . . .
of United States military and economic support." The United
States must, therefore, rise to the Southeast Asian challenge
and not throw in the towel, even though present action might
lead to major commitments in the future.[70] The Vice-
President's confused memorandum gave ominous warnings
of things to come, when he himself would take over policy
determination.

The principal thrust of United States opposition to the
pro-Communist Vietcong and Pathet Lao rebels in 1961 and
1962 took the form of covert guerrilla operations by rangers,
paratroopers, marines, and airplane pilots. Colonel Lansdale's program in South Vietnam was only one of several in
progress. Some nine thousand Meo tribesmen in Laos were
recruited and trained by the American Military Assistance
Advisory Group at Vientiane. Thai ranger volunteers numbering around six hundred were used for aerial intelligence
and supply operations in Laos. Filipino anti-Huk guerrillas,
recruited by Colonel Lansdale in Manila, were included
in the ranks of the Filipino Construction Company provided
for work in South Vietnam. By and large, the operations
branch of the CIA constituted the principal agency of the
United States countermeasures in 1961.[71]

A shift toward more active military involvement was
recommended in the report submitted by General Maxwell
Taylor following his own visit to South Vietnam in October
1961. Taylor broached the need to persuade Diem to solicit
outright American or other military assistance as a means
of salvaging the deteriorating situation. He doubted that
Diem's government alone, with its mistaken tactics and its
faltering administration, could ever succeed in frustrating
the increasingly effective efforts of the Communists to
win over the South Vietnam population. Additional American
"advisers" might promote needed flood control and coastal
surveillance; they could also defend the areas where they
were stationed and generally improve governmental performance, thus liberating Saigon's forces for more offensive

341

action. But Taylor was convinced that the rescue of South Vietnam would also require some U.S. troop commitment, including helicopters and air support up to the level of from eight to ten thousand men, whether Diem realized the need or not. Such a move, he argued, would improve morale in the South, exert a sobering effect on the enemy, and discourage escalation of aggression. Diem must be persuaded to ask for assistance, and the immediate flood relief problem would provide a convenient cover. He concluded: "NVN (North Vietnam) is extremely vulnerable to conventional bombing. . . . There is no case of fearing a mass onslaught of Communist manpower into SVN and its neigh‑boring states."[72]

General Taylor's escalation proposal encountered sharp criticism. The State Department's Bureau of Intelligence Research stressed the heavy risks involved in undertaking overt armed intervention: They pointed out that the Diem regime did not command the confidence of its own high civilian and military officials and that Diem stubbornly refused to delegate authority, to the point of provoking administrative paralysis. It would be patently unwise to commit the United States to the support of such a feeble regime. American forces would become involved in a losing struggle, facing an impossible task "in the midst of an apathetic or hostile population." Far from being intimidated, Hanoi would match the American troop escalations, while bombing threats against the north would elicit a strong supporting response from both Moscow and Peking. Although Secretary Rusk supported the view that reforms within the Saigon regime were necessary, he sided with the Defense Department's spokesmen and with Walter Rostow of the White House staff that Diem should be influenced to ask for outside military assistance.

The formal Rusk-McNamara Memorandum of November 11 covering the problem ran, in part, as follows:

> The loss of South Vietnam to Communism would . . . make pointless any further discussion about the importance of Southeast Asia to the free world. We would face the near certainty that the remainder of Southeast Asia and Indonesia

would move to a complete accomodation with Communism. . . . The loss . . . would not only destroy SEATO, but would undermine the credibility of American commitment everywhere.

The memorandum further specified that the contents of Diem's contemplated letter requesting American military aid should include references to Hanoi's violations of the Geneva Agreement, to South Vietnam's immediate need for flood relief assistance, and to the absence of aggressive intent on the part of the United States. Diem should also emphasize his own alleged efforts to improve his government's organization and performance. President Kennedy's reply to Diem, not surprisingly, would be affirmative, indicating that America's previous compliance with the Geneva neutralization of South Vietnam would be resumed once DRV violations ceased. Ambassador Nolting was assigned the additional task of insisting that in return for American aid, Diem should expand the political base of his government, cooperate more effectively with his subordinate officials, and permit United States participation in decisions covering economic and military matters.[73] Kennedy's final decision to bolster South Vietnam's military strength short of sending combat troops was announced on November 16, 1961.[74] This publicized action undercut completely the ambassador's demand for reforms, which only elicited Diem's angry refusal to comply.

Reform Endeavors Run Aground at Saigon

State Department recommendations advanced at Saigon in early November 1961 included the decentralization of control over administrative and military operations throughout South Vietnam, better coordination of intelligence agencies, and greater freedom of public expression. Nolting's proposals encountered bitter incriminations from the Palace at Saigon, coupled with planted newspaper stories suggesting the possible need for South Vietnam to reconsider its relations with America. Comparable tactics were being employed by General Sarit in Bangkok and by Prince Sihanouk

343

in Phnom Penh. The net result was a defensive and apologetic effort on Washington's part to dispel this distrust of American motives and to reaffirm commitments to increased military and budgetary aid.

For better or for worse, the United States government was committed by late 1961 to defeat the threat of Communist control of South Vietnam by strengthening rather than altering the Diem government, under the disquieting assumption that any attempted governmental change would probably lead to chaos. When the Presidential Palace at Saigon was bombed in February 1962, the two pilots involved concentrated their attack on the wing housing the Ngo Dinh Nhus. President Kennedy responded by enunciating his "greatest possible backing" of Diem as a gesture to discourage local sympathy for the attackers. The one captured pilot was forced by the police, under torture, to assert that America had been party to the bombing plot.[75]

Washington's repeated affirmations of its commitment to Diem's government had the unfortunate result of stifling all reform proposals advanced by the non-Communist opposition. The successive elections had been a mockery of the democratic process. Candidates for the Assembly and for the presidency were screened by the Diem-dominated Assembly, and opposition voters were openly intimidated. In the presidential election of 1961, Diem won Saigon by a seven to four majority, while in the less-articulate countryside, his majority was 91.5 percent. One of his few sharp critics was the former defense minister, Dr. Phan Huy Quat. His Committee for National Union convened an ad hoc assembly at Saigon in June, 1961, which attracted some one thousand representative spokesmen covering the entire spectrum of anti-Diem and anti-Communist sentiment. They demanded a genuine democracy, administrative reform, decentralized control, and eventual national unification. This first mild protest was tolerated, but a subsequent challenge from the same group was not. In March 1962 Dr. Quat publicly challenged Ambassador Nolting's unqualified support of the Diem regime. He demanded the release of the vast number of political prisoners, legalization of the non-

344

Communist opposition, and the holding of genuinely free elections for a new National Assembly. Thereafter, all pronouncements by Quat's committee were prohibited. Dr. Quat was arrested and eventually brought to trial in 1963, only to be acquitted in the end for lack of incriminating evidence. The concept of tolerating a legalized opposition and permitting it a political hearing was alien to Diem's mandarinate ideas of political authority.[76]

Saigon's anti-Vietcong program changed form in 1962, from the earlier American-sponsored agroville pattern of rural development, calculated to give villagers some evidence of the government's concern for their welfare, to the strategic hamlet system. Whereas the agroville approach had stressed development of such facilities as electricity, schools, and clinics, the new program was primarily political, intended to inhibit Vietcong contact and infiltration. The objective was to separate the guerrillas from access to essential aid from villagers, in the form of food, taxes, shelter, and recruits, and thus drive dissidents into the open. In the many situations where such contacts could not be prevented, the peasants were forcibly removed to new hamlet centers that were capable of adequate surveillance. Abandoned village sites and those presumed to be under Vietcong control were completely destroyed. At the same time, government military forces were increased by some two-thirds and provided with American helicopters and other forms of transportation. The local Civil Guards and the Self-Defense Corps in loyal villages were provided with arms.[77]

American support of the strategic hamlet system was based on a dubiously valid analogy with Malaya's successful anti-Emergency tactics. Whereas the anti-Communist British forces in Malaya had encountered no difficulty from rural Malays in the transfer of alien Chinese squatters to points beyond the reach of Communist Chinese guerrillas, the situation was otherwise in South Vietnam. Peasant resentment was almost universal over the uprooting of an indigenous population who treasured their family ties and adjacent ancestral graves.[78] Ngo Dinh Nhu's policy of forceable transfer also provided no genuine security from guerrillas apart from that which the inhabitants themselves could provide. In most situations, Saigon officials and the police avoided exposing themselves by staying overnight in vulnerable hamlets.

American evaluation of the strategic hamlet program varied from Secretary McNamara's wishful conclusion that it might permit an early phasing out of American troop commitments, to more realistic assessments by other observers. Secretary Forrestal commented in February 1962 that many innocent and easily persuaded villagers were among the alleged twenty thousand Vietcong casualties reported for 1961. He argued that the sacrifices demanded of peasants in the new hamlet system outweighed any benefits that they could realize and that villagers everywhere resented Diem's dictatorial rule. Similarly the State Department's Roger Hilsman, in his report of November 1962, found no grounds for optimism. He found that the influence of the Vietcong was growing stronger in urban as well as rural areas and that pacification was years away. Hilsman also reported that coup plots were rife among elitist elements, but that their success would tend to reverse whatever momentum the government's counterinsurgency efforts may have achieved. He saw no hope of restoring Saigon's authority as long as counterinsurgency efforts were associated with the widespread use of air power and artillery attacks on suspected peasant communities. To be successful, the strategic hamlet program must be integrated with systematic efforts at pacification, not with preventive military deterrence.[79]

During the course of 1962, approximately one-fourth of the sixteen thousand hamlets scheduled to be included in the program were established. They were located mainly in the coastal plains of central Annam. Few were attempted in the Mekong delta area, where rebel partisans were particularly influential. American ameliorative efforts to afford direct assistance to pacification ran aground on restrictions imposed by the government.[80] Nhu's philosophy of personalism stressed duty and discipline, countenancing no

346

coddling of villagers. During the same year of 1962, some ten thousand additional American troops were sent to Vietnam as non-combat advisers. They suffered casualties of thirty-four killed and eighty-five wounded.[81]

Rejoinder from the National Liberation Front

Although the general military capacity of the South Vietnamese government improved noticeably in 1962, such gains were far from conclusive. The regular forces of the Communist side also improved their training, arms, and leadership. They managed to make good their manpower losses by recruiting locally some five thousand men to their army of now twenty thousand. Government forces outnumbered the guerrillas by eight to one, but the discipline and morale of the latter were superior. By avoiding direct armed confrontation and concentrating effort on enlisting popular support, the Vietcong managed to reoccupy most of the areas that had been overrun by government forces. They took over many of the strategic hamlets secretly by working from the inside. The personnel of the guerrillas continued to be largely southern in origin, although an increasing number of trained Vietminh organizers, also mostly southerners, were sent down from the North. Vietcong weapons were still mainly of French and American manufacture. The vulnerable aspects of Saigon's political front at the close of 1962 were summarized by Professor Scigliano as follows:

> Needed reforms were not instituted, criticism was still strongly controlled, outside advice strongly resented, and American motives highly suspected. The Vietnamese leadership seemed to be more than ever isolated from its own people, and public morale . . . was at a low. . . . The political situation worsened.[82]

In contrast to the harsh strategic hamlet system, which alienated many of the villagers, the National Liberation Front's policy was designed to reach maximum accomodation with them. The NLF guaranteed poor tenant cultivators low rental costs or assigned them lands from former

347

French plantations or abandoned landlord holdings. The average small holder was not forced to share his limited acreage with his poor tenant neighbor, and sympathetic well-to-do farmers who cultivated plots of their own and accepted reduced rental returns on the remainder were not attacked. Taxes assessed in kind went to support the NLF.[83] Cultivators were not given title deeds to transferred lands, ostensibly so that they would not suffer if government forces regained control, but partly because Communist policy probably did not contemplate private ownership on a permanent basis. Taken as a whole, the NLF land policy enlisted willing and widespread support from the peasants, who, while they had little affinity for Communism or North Vietnam rule, were disillusioned with Saigon's land reform program. Many professed to see in the American-supported Diem government a successor to French puppet rule. The Saigon regime was characterized as the friend of the landlord class rather than the cultivators, as well as being dominated by arrogant northerners and a limited Catholic clientèle.[84]

The four-point NLF manifesto issued in July 1962 was specifically designed to elicit support in the south. It proposed the emergence of a national coalition government that would enable South Vietnamese to settle their own affairs. Along with neighboring Cambodia and Laos, South Vietnam should constitute a neutral region, with all three nations retaining full sovereignty. In the ultimate task of promoting the interests of the Fatherland (a term frequently used by Hanoi), Vietnamese must deal with Vietnamese in reaching a common agreement. Reunification must be realized "step by step on a voluntary basis with consideration given to the characteristics of each zone, with equality, and without annexation of one zone by the other." The manifesto policy's effect on Vietcong morale was reflected in a decline of the monthly defections for the guerrilla forces, which dropped from an average of 600 during the spring months of the same year to a mere 350 during the summer.[85]

The Downfall of Diem in 1963

The overthrow of the Diem regime was the work not of the NLF, but of dissident army officers and leaders of the Buddhist community. Army disaffection stemmed largely from feuding that had begun in 1955 and from Diem's denial of formal military command to anyone who demonstrated any independence of mind or will. Commanders assigned in and around Saigon were all pro-regime. Advancement in rank was made dependent on uncritical and abject loyalty. Diem's policy also set rival generals against each other. This device saved him in 1960, but was destined to fail in 1963. Army leaders did not trust each other and were not sure what the American reaction would be to attempted coups. The abortive effort of November 1960 had been the work of junior officers; the palace bombing of February 1962 was a limited effort of Air Force pilots bent on destroying the Ngo Dinh Nhus. The army's final move in November 1963 was accomplished by several senior-rank army officers, with the collusion of a previously loyal commander of Diem's own palace guard. Political-military rivalry reached crisis proportions within Saigon long before there was any prospect of defeating the Vietcong forces in the countryside.[86]

Growing Buddhist opposition to Diem was attributable mainly to resentment over the favoritism shown to Catholic immigrants from the north and to the president's demonstrated lack of respect and trust for the majority Buddhist community. As in the case of the alienated Cao Dai and Hoa Hao sects, religion provided a rallying point for an otherwise widely divided opposition. American policy for a time tried to exploit Buddhism as a popular faith capable of opposing Communism, but the effort ran aground in the face of Diem's intransigence.

Serious trouble developed at Hue on May 8, 1963, when government troops opened fire on a Buddhist demonstration protesting the banning of public ceremonies in honor of the faith. (A similar Catholic celebration had been permitted several weeks earlier.) Nine persons were killed, a deed for which both Diem and Archbishop Thuc, his brother, were locally considered responsible. The government refused to acknowledge any blame, charging that Communists had sponsored the Buddhist protest. The self-immolation of eight monks and writers between June and October constituted for the enraged Buddhists a dignified and purifying protest against Diem insensitivity to a suffering populace and to life itself. These human sacrifices cast indelible shame on the government, which Madame Nhu intensified by her contemptuous references to "monk barbecue shows."

A confrontation developed between American embassy personnel and President Diem on June 12, when Deputy Ambassador William C. Truehart, substituting for vacationing Frederick Nolting, insisted that the Buddhist rift must be healed if the United States was to continue its association with the Saigon government. Diem gave a grudging pledge to that effect on June 16, but nothing of significance came of it. Meanwhile, Nolting himself was called to Washington in early July for consultations, only to learn that he was being replaced as ambassador in late August by Henry Cabot Lodge. Upon his return to Saigon, Nolting was obliged to deal with a July 7 police attack on members of the American press who were observing at the time a Buddhist protest procession in Saigon. As a long-time Diem supporter, Nolting was obliged to point out, in protest, that the United States stood for freedom of religion and for an open society where the press could report news events without hindrance. For the first time, however, he omitted his customary references to Diem's "dedicated and courageous leadership." President Kennedy's concurrent renewal of America's pledge to counter Communist aggression was irrelevant and did nothing to dispel Diem's growing hostility.[87] On July 11 Ngo Dinh Nhu faced down protesting senior army officers, who dared not move boldly because all troops in Saigon and vicinity were commanded by officers loyal to Nhu.[88]

Directly prior to his departure from Saigon Ambassador Nolting persuaded Diem to announce publicly that he would conciliate Buddhist discontent. The statement was issued on August 15. But these efforts went for naught, for on

350

August 21, the very day before the arrival of the new ambassador, Nhu's own CIA-trained special forces attacked pagodas throughout the entire country, jailing some 1,400 monks. During the operation, telephone lines leading to the American Embassy were severed. On the following morning the government radio attributed the action to army units, not to the special forces.[89] Nhu also started the rumor that he was initiating peace negotiations with Hanoi via French and Catholic intermediaries.[90] American relations with Ngo Dinh Nhu had reached the point of no return, but how could he be removed without toppling the entire Ngo Dinh Diem regime?

The best alternative, from the American point of view, was to retain Diem as titular president, while eliminating the influence of his brothers and enlisting the services of prominent opposition leaders in a new cabinet. No one acquainted with Diem believed that he would ever accept any such arrangement. If the overthrow of the regime was unavoidable, many felt it should be performed by ranking army leaders who had a stake in the continued prosecution of the pacification program, rather than by a less responsible group. But potential coup leaders themselves required assurance that American officials, both civilian and military, would not sabotage their hazardous endeavor and would continue to cooperate actively with the emerging successor regime. Ambassador Lodge approved CIA contacts with the conspirators and received authorization from Washington to support any promising coup attempt. He nevertheless refused to give official assurances as requested and reserved the option of disowning the entire operation if it should fail.[91]

Under the circumstances the anti-Diem rising did not come off, as anticipated, in late August. Rivals within the Saigon military leadership were mutually distrustful. Most of them entertained particular loyalties to Buddhist, Catholic, or other religious groups. Some were known to be aligned with Nhu, others with the CIA and a few were even suspected of Vietcong connections.

The months of September and October were characterized

by uncertainty and confusion of counsel. The authorized contacts of CIA personnel with the plotting generals continued in desultory fashion, much to the displeasure of the local American military command, especially General Harkins. Harkins wanted to base American relations with Diem entirely on the issue of the continued prosecution of the war, and he accordingly ordered military personnel under his command to avoid contact with dissident leaders. He distrusted the sponsors of the coup and questioned their ability to assume leadership of the government once Diem was removed. High army officials at Washington tended to agree with Harkins, reasoning that since the coup was apparently off, Americans had better try to get on with the war.[92]

A contrary view came from the newly arrived Ambassador Lodge, who was supported by intelligence services within Washington. Lodge was convinced that the Diem regime would have to go if the prosecution of the war was ever to be vigorously resumed. State Department specialists insisted that Diem had lost control in Saigon, and that brother Nhu, if left in power, would not only abandon the war but have the United States forces out of the country within six months. Robert Kennedy proposed with refreshing candor that if Diem was the cause of threatened failure, he would have to go, and that if it became clear that the war could not be won, the United States should completely withdraw.[93] Meanwhile, General Duong Van Minh and his principal associate, General Tran Van Don, insisted that prompt action against Diem was necessary to prevent a strengthening of pro-Vietcong sentiment because of rising popular resentment. They declared that the salvaging of army morale was a critical issue.[94]

In the end, American policy was determined by the logic of events rather than by argumentation. Ambassador Lodge exerted pressure for some kind of a conciliatory response from Diem by suspending minor aspects of the economic assistance program, but without success. Lodge asked Diem why at least some of the imprisoned Buddhists and students could not be released, so that the schools could be reopened. Down to the very eve of the coup, official Washington suggested that further postponement might permit more careful examination of future contingencies.[95] Lodge pointed out meanwhile that to turn over coup information to Diem would "make traitors of us all" and also ensure the destruction of army leadership essential for the future prosecution of the war. The final Washington authorization dated October 30, 1963, stated: "Once a coup under responsible leadership has begun, it is in the interest of the U.S. government that it should succeed."[96] Lodge delayed his scheduled departure for Washington in anticipation of developments. In the end, Vice-President Nguyen Ngoc Tho himself moved to support the coup.

A pivotal figure in the overthrow of Ngo Dinh Diem was the youthful Major General Ton That Dinh, military governor of Saigon and commander of Corps III. Although appointed by Nhu, Dinh had become disillusioned with the regime and was influenced by General Tran Van Don to detach himself from Nhu. The plan of the latter was to lay a trap for the conspiring Generals by having Dinh start a false coup a day before the designated time, in order to tempt the dissidents into the open where they could be crushed. Although not fully trusting the information transmitted by Dinh, the coup leaders advanced their own plans by twenty-four hours (to the afternoon of November 1). Concluding erroneously that the move was connected with Dinh's counterplot, Nhu initially ordered his supporters to withhold defensive action, only to find the palace infested, and rebel control extending over police headquarters, the radio station, and the airport. When Nhu tried to call General Dinh by phone, he was not available. Ambassador Lodge's tentative offer of safe evacuation to the Ngo Dinh brothers had been refused on the previous day.[97]

Diem and Nhu escaped via an underground passage to an overnight refuge in Cholon. In a final act of pride and bravado, they attended mass the following morning at a Jesuit church in Cholon, making no attempt at further concealment. A weapons carrier picked them up, and the officer in charge, under circumstances that can only be conjectured, shot both brothers while en route to the Joint

General Staff headquarters.[98] Madame Nhu had meanwhile departed for the United States where she was extravagantly feted by Fordham and Georgetown Universities and other Catholic institutions. The Christian version of Heaven's Mandate died very hard. President Kennedy's tragic assassination three weeks later in Dallas left Washington's monumental miscalculation of Vietnam to be handled by his successor in office, President Lyndon Johnson.

Successors to Ngo Dinh Diem

A French observer has characterized the Saigon political scene following Diem's death in clarifying detail.[99] Although few local residents mourned Diem's passing (even Catholic spokesmen admitted his deficiencies), there existed virtually nothing in the way of organized administration to take his place. Several leaders of the army junta responsible for the coup including Chief of State Duong Van Minh, would have preferred to take time to set up a functioning democracy rather than to run a military dictatorship. But they proved incapable of directing policy in the emergency. Army counsels were divided, but most of the officers believed, with some reason, that the time was not right to encourage full popular political participation. Personal rivalries emerged. The Buddhist majority had no positive program to offer. The Cao Dai and Hoa Hao sects had long played the opportunist's role. Even the released political exiles, such as Dr. Phan Quang Dan, volunteered no specific suggestions apart from holding new elections.

The people at first were in no mood for serious matters in any case. The tension was relaxed; the Saigon press was free; night life revived, relieved of the prudery of Madame Nhu; university students elected a council, previously outlawed. Positive direction was nevertheless lacking. Vice-President Nguyen Ngoc Tho, the best carryover from the Diem era, took over the presidency of the Ministerial Council, but he lacked influence with the army and with non-Catholic civilians. Tho invited none of the courageous civilian leaders who had previously defied Diem to participate in the new government. Under-secretaries within the various ministries moved upward, but they usually exercised as little authority as Tho did himself. The top posts in the end were occupied by army selectees, chosen allegedly on the basis of their anticommunism, discipline, and devotion to duty. For the time being, political activity was confined within the framework of an overriding concern for national survival militarily, to the neglect of other pressing problems.

The interests of many important elements of the body politic, including the peasantry, were in no way represented by the army junta that assumed control after Diem's fall. The participants, for the most part, were French-trained military officers, highly individualist in temperament, strongly anti-Communist, and mainly Cochin-China born. None of them had previously been entrusted with high command or administrative responsibilities. The coup leader, General Duong Van Minh, was robust, direct, and personally popular, but he was indecisive. He lacked the ability to take essential governmental or military actions in the face of interference by army associates who were preoccupied with political affairs. Secretary McNamara's investigative report dated December 21, 1963, suggested as a serious possibility that the next several months could witness the collapse of effective anti-Communist resistance. Most of the Diem-appointed provincial officers had been dismissed, creating an administrative vacuum. The strategic hamlet program was disintegrating, and new province chiefs were receiving no direction from Saigon. McNamara added that Lodge and Harkins were not cooperating, and that the entire Country Team needed better personnel. The Vietcong continued to expand their control in areas south and west of Saigon. Infiltration from the North, he added significantly, did not constitute a major problem as yet, but the tentative alignment of Hoa Hao and Cao Dai sect leaders with the government promised little more than a neutralist position on their part.[100]

Ambitious younger army officers who were standing in the wings included Ky, an air force officer of northern antecedents;

355

Khanh, an ambitious opportunist, allegedly pro-American; and Thieu, a pro-Catholic moderate. Neither the original junta nor any of the seven successor regimes that appeared during the ensuing nineteen months made any substantial effort to revive the land reform program (not to be resumed until 1971),[101] or to undertake administrative improvements or economic development efforts. Big Minh lost out to Khanh in January, 1964 amid a welter of factionalism that persisted throughout the year. Low Army morale was reflected in the increasing rate of desertions, which averaged six thousand a month during 1964 and rose thereafter to eight thousand a month. Civilian attitudes were colored by war weariness, defeatism, and a spreading sense of terror. Only a massive escalation of American aid and military power prevented a threatened collapse.[102]

By mid-1965, the United States was committed to support virtually any regime at Saigon, whatever its credentials, that was prepared to fight the alleged threat of Communism. As Gunnar Myrdal later commented: "The very weakness of the Saigon government increased the United States dependence on it."[103] The several post-Diem governments and the Americanization of the war will be covered in a subsequent chapter.

Post-Diem Communist Relations

Vietcong activities within the South Vietnam countryside had intensified during the final three years of the declining Diem regime, and its downfall in late 1963 afforded an even greater opportunity. In 1964 occurred also the first southward intrusion of organized contingents of the regular North Vietnam army, prepared to take full advantage of the confused situation. The propaganda line of both the Liberation Front and Hanoi authorities changed substantially. By mid-1964, spokesmen for the NLF held out no prospect for negotiation with "American lackeys" in control at Saigon. They proposed setting up a neutralist coalition regime, with eight ministers drawn from the Paris emigré group, six Communist party representatives, and four from the Saigon

356

opposition group. The DRV spokesmen from Hanoi were not in complete agreement with the NLF. As of November 1964, they proposed the convening of a "Fatherland Front" conference to formulate policy and to assume control over relations with supporting Communist nations. A principal difficulty was that Soviet-Chinese rivalry operated to aggravate differences between the DRV and the NLF.[104]

The international problem was relatively new for South Vietnam. The NLF established contact with Peking in mid-1963, but did not post any permanent delegation at the Chinese capital until September 1964. Some of the NLF leaders welcomed China's encouragement of any settlement that would oust American forces from South Vietnam, whether it meant unification or not. Hanoi, on the other hand, although committed to the defeat of the Saigon junta and supporting Americans regarded any pacification short of unification with the south as a virtual defeat of its primary objective. Peking could presumably use a South Vietnamese satellite ally to balance the increasingly pro-Soviet regime in the north as a means of promoting the cause of China's leadership of Asian communism. The NLF provided China with a convenient weapon with which to belabor not only Soviet revisionism, but also the entire role of the United States in Southeast Asia. Peking presumably did not like the NLF advocacy of neutralism, but it did welcome the Vietcong cheers raised over China's dramatic nuclear weapons demonstration in October 1964. In its relations with the Soviets, the NLF found some common ground in Moscow's support of the proposal to neutralize South Vietnam. The Russians were fully committed to protect their North Vietnam protégé from destruction, but Moscow's leaders would like to avoid, here as in Laos, a costly military confrontation with the United States, which could only serve to enhance China's long-run influence in the area.[105]

American diplomacy, if emancipated from the fixed assumption of a monolithic World Communist conspiracy, might have exploited such differences to advantage, but that effort had to wait until the advent of Henry Kissinger. Douglas Pike's comment, relating to 1965, is relevant: "Unlike China, the Soviet Union had a great deal to lose and nothing to gain in a continuation of hostilities in South Vietnam." A Burma fearful of China and bent on pursuing the "Burmese Way to Socialism" on an Eastern European pattern could serve as an alternative Southeast Asian base for Soviet influence quite as satisfactorily as would the more vulnerable Vietnam.[106] As of early 1965, Hanoi propaganda continued to stress the need for unification and the cooperation of all Vietnamese in solving their problems. The NLF, on the other hand, was talking about the need to neutralize South Vietnam and to settle its problems without outside interference. Unfortunately, the American initiation of extensive covert attacks on North Vietnam during 1964 and the overt bombing offensive that began in February 1965 tended to erase the potential NLF-Hanoi divergence of interests with respect to unification and also the sharp differences between Chinese and Soviet policies covering the situation. One of the few issues on which the Communist world could agree was the defense of North Vietnam from American aggression.

1. Kenneth P. Landon, *Southeast Asia, Crossroads of Religion* (Chicago, 1947), pp. 192–200.

2. Bernard B. Fall. "Local Administration Under the Viet Minh," *Pacific Affairs* 27 (March 1954): 50–57.

3. See Gunnar Myrdal, *Asian Drama: An Inquiry into the Poverty of Nations*, 3 vols. (New York, 1968), I: 170–73, 228.

4. Douglas Pike, *Viet Cong. The Organization and Techniques of the National Liberation Front of South Vietnam* (Cambridge, 1966), pp. 41–46.

5. *Ibid.*, pp. 33–38, 52–53.

6. Jean Lacouture, *Vietnam Between Two Truces* (London, 1966), pp. 102–108; Bernard Fall, *Le Viet Minh. La Republique Democratique du Vietnam, 1945–1960* (Paris, 1960), pp. 336–40.

7. Myrdal, *op. cit.*, pp. 399–400.

8. Neil Sheehan et al., *The Pentagon Papers, New York Times*, (New York, 1971), pp. 72–75.

9. William Kaye, "The Economy of North Vietnam," in P. J. Honey, ed., *North Vietnam Today* (New York, 1962), pp. 105–115.

10. Philippe Devillers, "The Struggle for Unification of Vietnam," in Honey, *op. cit.*, pp. 29–34; also Nhu Phong, "Intellectuals, Writers, Artists," *ibid.*, pp. 70–77.

11. See also P. J. Honey, *Communism in North Vietnam, its Role in the Sino-Soviet Dispute* (Cambridge, 1963), pp. 43–74.

12. Informed estimates by Kaye indicate $450 million given by China in the early years and $365 million by the USSR.

13. See the introductory chapter by Honey (pages 1-24), by Kaye (pages 112-115), and by Devillers (pages 24-34) in Honey, *North Vietnam Today*. See also Lacouture, *op. cit.*, pp. 35-38.

14. *Pentagon Papers*, pp. 75-77.

15. Nguyen Ngog Bich, "Vietnam—An Independent Viewpoint," in Honey, *op. cit.*, pp. 128-34.

16. See Fox Butterfield's account in *Pentagon Papers*, pp. 70-77.

17. *Ibid.*, pp. 61-114.

18. Robert Scigliano, *South Vietnam Under Independence* (East Lansing, 1963), pp. 12-13, 194-96.

19. *Pentagon Papers*, pp. 27-35.

20. *Ibid.*, pp. 35-38.

21. *Ibid.*, pp. 44-46.

22. *Ibid.*, pp. 46-47.

23. *Ibid.*, p. 47.

24. *Ibid.*, pp 48-49.

25. Edward Lansdale, in *ibid.*, pp 53-66.

26. *Ibid.* One of Lansdale's leaflets deliberately misrepresented Vietminh policy respecting property and money holdings, reduced currency value by half, and tripled refugee registration. Another discouraged persons about to migrate northward by ship by suggesting precautions against the danger of bombing or submarine attacks.

27. *Ibid.*, pp. 60-61.

28. *Ibid.*, pp. 47-50.

29. Brian Crozier, "The Democratic Regime in Southern Vietnam," *Far Eastern Survey* 24 (April 1955): 49-55.

30. *Ibid.*, pp. 12-13, 212; Dennis Warner, *The Last Confucian*, (New York, 1963), pp. 101-6.

31. *Ibid.*

32. Scigliano, *op. cit.*, pp. 78-82.

33. *Ibid.*, pp. 26-34, 75-78, 88-90. Saigon's ambassador to Washington in 1965, Vu Van Thai, related how, as an anti-Diem nationalist, he was approached in Saigon by Communist agents in a futile effort to enlist his political cooperation, only to have the same agents denounce him to Nhu's agency as a subversive who had been in touch with the Communists.

34. Lacouture, *op. cit.*, pp. 20-31.

35. *Ibid.*

36. Myrdal, *op. cit.*, 1: 403-5.

37. Scigliano, *op. cit.*, pp. 30-34.

38. Bernard B. Fall, "Vietnam's China Problem," *Far Eastern Survey* 27 (May 1958): 65-72; Lacouture, *op. cit.*, pp. 30-31.

39. From 1955 to 1960, the United States treasury met an estimated 62 percent of the regularly budgeted expenses of the Saigon government, amounting to some $1.4 million. It contributed a smaller, but increasing, amount for economic, technical, and military assistance. The totals were approximately twice the volume of aid contributed to Hanoi by Communist sources. See Lennox Mills, *Southeast Asia* (Minneapolis, 1964), pp. 275-321.

40. Scigliano, *op. cit.*, pp. 101-110.

41. *Ibid.*

42. *FEER*, (May 16, 1968), pp. 350-51.

43. A fourth brother, Ngo Dinh Luyen, was posted as ambassador to London. The father of Madame Nhu, who later turned against the regime, was ambassador to Washington.

44. Lacouture, *op. cit.*, pp. 108–111. In mid-1963 Bishop Thuc was summoned to Rome in a move to forestall a Catholic rebellion against his authority at Hué.
45. Scigliano, *op. cit.*, pp. 47–68.
46. Pike, *op. cit.*, pp. 57–73.
47. *Pentagon Papers*, pp. 71–72.
48. Pike, *op. cit.*, pp, 53–55.
49. *Pentagon Papers*, pp. 118–19.
50. Pike, *op. cit.*, pp. 46–49.
51. *Ibid.*, pp. 53–55.
52. *Ibid.*
53. *Pentagon Papers*, pp. 75–78.
54. *Ibid.*, pp. 70–78.
55. George McTurnan Kahin and John W. Lewis, *The United States and Vietnam* (New York, 1967), 111–120.
56. Devillers, *op. cit.*, in Honey, pp. 36–46.
57. *Aggression from the North; the Record of North Vietnam's Campaign to Conquer South Vietnam*, Department of State Publication 7893 (Washington, 1965).
58. Pike, *op. cit.*, p. 310
59. *Ibid.*, pp. 310-26.
60. See Lacouture, *op. cit.*; also Devillers in Honey, *op. cit.*, and Kahin and Lewis, *op. cit.*
61. See Kahin and Lewis, *op. cit.*, appendix 6, pp. 388-95.
62. Pike, *op. cit.*, pp. 136–45.
63. Scigliano, *op. cit.*, pp. 84–85.
64. See a dispatch from Saigon from Seville R. Davis, "How Long Can the President Wait?" *New York Times*, early 1961.
65. Warner, *op. cit.*, pp. 112–13.
66. *Pentagon Papers*, pp. 108–14.
67. *Ibid.*, pp. 118–26.
68. Milton C. Taylor, "South Vietnam: Lavish Aid, Limited Progress," *Pacific Affairs* 34 (1961): 242–46.
69. Robert Scigliano, "Vietnam: A Country at War," *Asian Survey* 3 (January 1963): 48-54.
70. *Pentagon Papers*, pp. 127–30.
71. *Ibid.*, pp. 130–38.
72. *Ibid.*, pp. 141–47.
73. *Ibid.*, pp. 150–53.
74. Marcus J. Raskin and Bernard B. Fall, *The Vietnam Reader* (New York, 1965), pp. 384–86.
75. *Ibid.*
76. Lacouture, *op. cit.*, pp. 51–60.
77. Scigliano, in *Asian Survey*, *op. cit.*
78. Milton Osbourne, *Strategic Hamlets in South Vietnam*, Cornell Southeast Asia Project, data paper 55 (Ithaca, 1965).
79. *Pentagon Papers*, pp. 112-14; *New York Times*, July 1, 1971, pp. 6-8.
80. *Pentagon Papers*, pp. 117-30. George Kahin, *Governments and Politics in Southeast Asia* (Ithaca, 1964), pp. 445-48.
81. Mills, *op. cit.*, pp. 93-94.
82. Scigliano, in *Asian Survey*, *op. cit.*
83. Pike, *op. cit.*, pp. 276–79.
84. *FEER*, May 16, 1968, pp. 350–51.
85. Pike, *op. cit.*, pp. 350–58, 364.

86. Kahin, *op. cit.*, pp. 435–36; *New York Times*, July 21, 1963.

87. *Pentagon Papers*, pp. 197–201; see also dispatch by Hedrick Smith, *New York Times*, July 21, 1963, and Lacouture, *op. cit.*, pp. 71–80.

88. *Pentagon Papers*, p. 165.

89. *Ibid.*, pp. 165–66, 194–201.

90. Lacouture, *op. cit.*, pp. 82–85.

91. *Pentagon Papers*, pp. 170–72.

92. *Ibid.*, pp. 201 213.

93. *Ibid.*, pp. 203–5, 211–12.

94. *Ibid.*, pp. 217–19.

95. *Ibid.*, pp. 216–19

96. *Ibid.*, pp. 230–31.

97. *Ibid.*, p. 232.

98. Warner, *op. cit.* pp. 10-13.

99. Lacouture, *op. cit.*, pp. 93–101.

100. Kahin, *op. cit.*, p. 442.

101. Post-Diem governments moved to facilitate peasant purchase of land by providing permanent titles and by doubling the period (twelve years instead of six) during which payment for land could be made. But not until after the election of 1967 was provision made to staff the Land Reform Administration. By that time, the opportunity to purchase had largely disappeared. See *FEER* May 16, 1968, pp. 350-52. The law was revived in 1970 and reimplemented in 1971, but French and other landlord claimants began reasserting their titles in 1973. See *New York Times*, January 14, 1974, pp. 1, 10.

102. Wesley Fishel, "Vietnam, the Broadening War," *Asian Survey* 6 (January, 1966): 49-55.

103. Myrdal, *op. cit.*, 1: 405-08.

104. Pike, *op. cit.*, pp. 102, 162-65, 319-20, 358-62.

105. *Ibid.*, pp. 339-42, 367-70.

106. *Ibid.*, pp. 367-370.

XI

POSTWAR CAMBODIA
AND LAOS

The Postwar Freedom Movements

The postwar political problems arising within the former French protectorates, Cambodia and Laos, were by no means identical. The Cambodians were largely homogeneous ethnically and culturally, being the inheritors of a classical civilization of impressive dimensions and occupying the heartland of their once-extensive empire. The only large minority groups consisted of some 420,000 Vietnamese and a much smaller number of Chinese immigrants, both of whom had entered Cambodia during the period of French rule. By contrast, a substantial fraction of the smaller population of Laos did not speak Lao-Tai at all and did not even share the Buddhist faith of the Mekong Valley Lao.[1]

French Laos had been divided into a number of distinct administrative districts. Champassak was in the south; the governmental center of Vientiane was in the central part of the valley; the royal capital at Luang Prabang was further up stream; the interior state of Xieng Khouang, centering on the Plain of Jars, lay north of Vientiane. The vast mountain domain lying behind Champassak and adjacent to Annam contained a great variety of unassimilated *Moi* (slave) tribesmen, ethnically akin to the early Khmer and Indonesian inhabitants. The northern mountains contained a medley of *Kha* (savage) tribesmen, plus tribal Thai, and the more recently arrived Yao-Man and Meo montagnards extending southward from the Tonkin-China border areas. The Meo in particular had moved southward into Laos in late modern times.[7] Whereas Cambodia was held together by long-established cultural and kingship traditions, the peoples of Laos could hardly qualify as a nation at all.

French colonial rule had been acceptable in both countries largely because it was culturally tolerant and politically less onerous than the alternative prospects of Siamese or Vietnamese suzerainty. The Japanese conquest, here as elsewhere, had discredited French prestige, and by 1945 the invaders had encouraged the appearance of anti-colonial movements in both countries. The Khmer Issarak (freedom) movement was headed by a prewar newspaper editor, Son Ngoc Thanh, who had spent a portion of the war period in Japan and whose nationalist following included youthful Cambodians of middle-class background who were both anti-French and anti-royalist. The Khmer Issarak lost its leader when the returning French arrested Son in late 1945 and exiled him to France.[3] The rebels were also cut off from Thai assistance following Bangkok's enforced surrender of Battambang and Siemreap in 1946 and the displacement of the anti-French Luang Pridi Free Thai government in 1947. The Issarak rebel headquarters had to be shifted eastward to the Cochin-China border, where the movement barely managed to survive in cooperation with the Vietminh. The actual freedom struggle in Cambodia became a contest between King Norodom Sihanouk and the French, with youthful nationalist supporters standing impatiently off stage.

The Lao Issara (Free Lao) faction of the immediate postwar period was largely a princely clique, opposed to the pro-French Prince Boun Oum of Champassak and to the equally Francophile court at Luang Prabang. The dissident princes were determined to exploit the anticipated demise of French colonialism to enhance their personal status and power. On the approach of the returning French in 1946, the Lao Issara partisans fled to Bangkok. Most of them returned to Laos in 1949 in response to a vaguely defined French offer of qualified self-rule. Several of the returnees gained posts in the Vientiane government almost immediately, and by 1953 a majority of the Vientiane cabinet were former members of the Lao Issara. Boun Oum had made an earlier accomodation with the French in 1946, along with his younger protégé, Phoumi Nosavan, and the two became leaders of the conservative faction within the Laos government.[4] Two brothers among the dissident Lao princes—the former military viceroy, Phetsarath, and the French-trained engineer, Souphanouvong—both refused to accept the French accomodation. Phetsarath was denied pardon by the jealous king and was forced to live in exile until 1957. He died in 1959. His younger brother, married to a Vietnamese, aligned himself with the Vietminh nationalists in the anti-French struggle. He was seriously wounded on one occasion. In 1953 Souphanouvong helped organize the Pathet Lao (Lao country) rebels, who were centered along the Laos-Tonkin border.

The political spectrum within Laos was almost entirely elitist, but widely divergent otherwise. It included, from Right to Left, the following factional leaders: (1) the colorless pro-French King Sisavang Vong; (2) the aggressively power-hungry Boun Oum of Champassak; (3) the wealthy Sananikone faction of Vientiane; (4) the anti-Communist nationalist Prince Katay D. Sasorith; (5) his neutralist half-brother Prince Souvanna Phouma, who was willing to seek accomodation with the Hanoi-allied nationalists; (6) his half-brother Prince Souphanouvong, a Francophobe allied with Hanoi; and (7) the Pathet Lao rebels, composed mainly of Meo tribesmen, allied with the Vietminh. Most of the political rivals in this confused situation appear to have been more concerned with personal status and goals than with national ends.

The French authorities treated the incipient freedom movements with just enough deference to avoid provoking open revolts within the two countries. Paris' major initial concession, made in mid-1946, was to authorize in both protectorates the election of an Advisory Constituent Assembly. The two constitutions, which were drafted and approved within the ensuing year, were similar but not identical. Both documents designated the respective kings as sovereign rulers within the bounds of the French Union (which meant continued French control of finances, foreign relations, and domestic administration). Both kings had authority to prorogue the authorized elected Assemblies whenever the occasion demanded and to postpone or modify specific legislative enactments. Whereas the Cambodian constitution accorded wide suffrage rights and a measure of parliamentary majority control over the cabinet, the Laos document restricted suffrage rights severely and provided that only one-third of the cabinet would be held responsible to a majority of the Assembly. The Upper Chamber Councils in both countries were appointed or indirectly chosen and designed to be both pro-royalist and pro-French. Paris took minimal chances.

The Assembly elections, which were held in late 1947, produced differing results. In Laos Boun Oum's dominant royalist faction encountered little opposition. Boun Oum took over the permanent presidency of the Upper Council, which exercised most of the power awaiting the formation of a cabinet. It was mid-1949 before the Lao Issara exiles were persuaded to return from Bangkok. At that time Prince Katay D. Sasorith was asked to become the first premier. In Cambodia, the election of 1947 afforded opportunity for the nationalist followers of the exiled Son Ngoc Thanh to organize as the Democratic party and to conduct a vigorous campaign. In the face of poorly-co-ordinated opposition, the party won a two-thirds victory, sufficient to dominate the newly elected Assembly. King Norodom Sihanouk satisfied the Assembly leadership initially by appointing several of them to cabinet positions and to other prestigious posts, while he himself assumed leadership in demanding more meaningful concessions

365

from Paris. In the face of accumulated frustrations, the Assembly eventually became so restive that the king felt obliged to prorogue the body in September 1949.[5] For two years thereafter, Sihanouk carried on the government with the aid of the Council alone.

Following a similar Democratic party victory in the second Assembly elections held in September 1951, the membership demanded and received royal permission for the return of Son Ngoc Thanh from France. The returned exile went into hiding in early 1952, paving the way for the king himself to take over the premiership in June, with Assembly approval of his exercise of full emergency powers. Shortly thereafter, the Assembly was prorogued for a second time, and the constitutional structure was abandoned indefinitely.[6] The king-premier nevertheless continued his relentless if abortive efforts to obtain from France some more meaningful definition of "independence within the French Union." He journeyed in person to Paris in January 1953 and the following June took up temporary exile in Bangkok to continue his protests.

French intransigence gave way in August 1953, when Paris finally accorded to Cambodia control over the army, the police, and the judiciary.[7] When Sihanouk eventually returned to Phnom Penh in November 1953, he was hailed as a national hero.[8] The Democratic party resistance largely disintegrated, and the princely opposition faction (Sisowath) was completely emasculated.[9] Accompanying concessions made to Vientiane gave the Lao Issara faction a majority of the cabinet posts in October 1953. Laos was accorded full but theoretical independence within the still-undefined French Union,[10] to be implemented as soon as the exigencies of the military struggle with the Vietminh would permit.[11] Vientiane's formal acceptance of membership in the French Union contributed to France's fatal 1954 military gamble at Dienbienphu near the Tonkin-Laos border.[12] The final liquidation of colonial rule in the two countries was accomplished at the Geneva Conference in mid-1954.

366

Laos and Cambodia under the Geneva Agreement

Although the Geneva Declaration of 1954 outlined the future of Cambodia and Laos in almost identical terms, significant differences can be noted in their post-Geneva roles. Suspension of hostilities in both countries was made subject to inspection by the International Control and Supervisory Commission, which included representatives from India (as chairman), Canada, and Poland. Both states were forbidden to join any military alliance or to request foreign aid in war materials, in the operation of military bases, or from instructional and fighting personnel. These conditions were sufficiently restrictive to prevent either state from accepting membership in the forthcoming SEATO, but they proved otherwise unenforceable.

With reference to Laos, the Geneva agreement was qualified by the explicit acknowledgement of existing military arrangements already worked out with France.[13] Laos could retain the services of a 1,500-man French training mission for the projected 25,000-man Royal Army, plus French operation of two bomber bases and the continued presence on Laotian soil of some 3,500 French troops for most of the remainder of the decade. A smaller French military teaching mission assigned to Cambodia until 1963 lacked comparable importance. The United States supplied much of the war material for both groups. Whereas members of the International Commission found little to do in Cambodia, especially after the collapse of Son Ngoc Thanh's futile rebellion in late 1954, they encountered enormous difficulties in Laos because of inadequate travel facilities and lack of freedom of contact. Not the least of the problems was the Polish representative's ill-concealed partisanship in favor of the Pathet Lao.

The situation in Laos moved in a vicious circle that prevented any effective resolution of the temporary de facto partition. In the eyes of the Francophobe Prince

Souphanouvong, the continuing French presence plus increasing financial support accorded to Vientiane by the United States compromised the independent status of the Laotian government. The Pathet Lao military units refused therefore to amalgamate with the Royal Army, and supporting Vietminh forces operating in the northern provinces bordering Tonkin declined to withdraw. The refusal of the pro-Communist faction to honor the terms of the Geneva Declaration provided the Vientiane authorities with an excuse to permit the continued presence of foreign military advisers. Their ostensible justification was that the country was still threatened by the Communists. The pro-American faction headed by Prince Katay Sasorith, who served as premier through much of 1955, denied to the Pathet Lao any participation in the elections of that year.

An alternative point of view was taken by Prince Souvanna Phouma, who tended to regard the Pathet Lao as dissident nationalists rather than hostile Communists, and favored efforts to reach an accomodation with them.[14] In this endeavor, Souvanna enjoyed some French support in favor of promoting national unity. Shortly after Souvanna himself took over the premiership in 1956, he visited both Hanoi and Peking in the company of Katay in an effort to reconcile some of the difficulties. The lavish reception which was accorded the two Lao princes in Peking, where protestations of friendship were balanced off by exhibitions of military might, followed the traditional pattern of vassal tributary missions. The result was an improvement in the climate of Vientiane and Pathet Lao negotiations and the formation of a tentative National Union Government.

The National Union Government proved to be a fragile affair. Prince Souphanouvong was designated minister of finance and planning and one of his associates was made minister of religion. The Pathet Lao was permitted to function as a political party, and supplementary elections were projected for 1957 to permit selection of Assembly representatives from their area of control. In Vientiane,

Souvanna Phouma defended his conciliatory approach with difficulty in the face of sharp opposition from Prince Katay and Boun Oum, who were backed by Thai representatives and by spokesmen for the United States. Premier Souvanna resigned for a time in favor of the insistent Katay, who flatly denounced the Pathet Lao as agents of the Viet-minh and demanded full restoration of the two occupied frontier provinces, Sam Neua and Phong Saly. After two months of political confusion, Souvanna returned to power in late 1956 and resumed his efforts at conciliation.[15]

The talks eventually ran aground over policy differences and efforts to accomplish something more than a token integration of the Pathet Lao military units into the Royal Army. Economic Minister Souphanouvong's ambi-tiously conceived development plans for agriculture, indus-try, and the social services were totally unrealistic and were coupled with demands that Vientiane accept economic aid from China to match that being accorded by the United States. Efforts to heal the breach failed in part because Communist propagandists exploited effectively the deep-seated distrust that the Meo and Yao-Man peoples of the mountainous Tonkin border area felt toward the Mekong Valley Lao elite at Luang Prabang and Vientiane. A Rightist government under Premier Sananikone took over at Vientiane in June 1958.

Souvanna Phouma while premier had contracted addi-tional agreements with France covering monetary, reve-nue, and economic matters, plus continuance of the privileged legal status of resident Frenchmen. It was not until the end of the decade that French political influ-ence and military aid tapered off. French economic and technical assistance persisted far into the 1960s.[16] The attempted American displacement of French influence at Vientiane will be considered in a subsequent context.

In contrast to the contradictory role played by the titular authorities of Laos in defining and implementing the Geneva Agreement, Cambodia's King Norodom Sihanouk assumed a commanding and forthright stance. Appearing in person at Geneva in 1954, he refused to accord any

369

recognition whatever to the pro-Vietminh forces of the Khmer Issarak still operating in border areas. He extracted from Peking's Chou En-lai explicit recognition of the exclusive legitimacy of the Phnom Penh regime. As a corollary to his promise not to permit Cambodia to become a foreign military base, he demanded and obtained Chou's approval of the complete withdrawal of all Vietminh forces as well. The insistent Cambodian spokesman asserted his unqualified right, as a sovereign prince, to act in defense of Cambodia in any fashion consonant with the terms of the United Nations Charter, even to the point of arranging for foreign military bases. The wearied Soviet spokesman, Molotov, finally gave consent. Vietminh forces were accordingly withdrawn unconditionally from Cambodia in mid-October 1954.[17] Cambodia thus affirmed within the theoretical limits of its security needs the right to rearm and to contract alliances. It remained for Norodom Sihanouk in 1955 to reconcile domestic political differences under a revamped constitutional structure.

The only substantive political requirement stipulated for Cambodia and Laos under the Geneva Declaration was that both countries should implement their existing constitutions by holding elections in 1955. All citizens were to be permitted to vote, and both governments were to abstain from reprisals, whether individual or collective, against previously hostile elements of the population.[18]

Sihanouk as Political Leader

King Sihanouk managed the transition to independence with considerable political skill. As a first move in preparation for a return to constitutional rule, he staged in February 1955 a French-style plebiscite, which approved by almost unanimous vote his management of affairs. In March he stepped down as king in favor of his father, Prince Sumarit, and took up a new role as political boss. In preparation for new Assembly elections scheduled for September 1955, Prince Sihanouk organized the Peo-

370

ple's Socialist Community, or Sangkum party. He undertook to attract the support of all loyal subjects by advocating a socialized egalitarian democracy theoretically capable of meeting the needs and aspirations of the population as a whole. He also made a sustained effort to enlist the support of younger politicians. With election opponents of his own carefully selected Sangkum candidates tabbed as virtual traitors, the king's party won a convincing 83 percent victory at the polls.

In an effort to direct the policy of the formless Sangkum majority in the Assembly, Sihanouk convened at Phnom Penh a series of semiannual People's Congress forums, over which he presided personally. At these sessions cabinet ministers and their subordinates were required to respond to particular questions and complaints; policy disagreements between ministers and elected assemblymen were aired. Questions of overriding importance could be submitted later to popular plebiscite decision. In such an atmosphere of relatively free discussion, the opposition Democratic party became increasingly ineffective. In successive elections of 1958 and 1962, the official Sangkum party encountered no effective challenge.[19]

Prince Sihanouk's apparent political success was somewhat less impressive when examined closely. He was vulnerable to criticism from several sides. Conservative leaders in the government objected to his cultivated intimacy with China. He visited Peking in 1956 and sent his son to China for secondary schooling. The norms of the traditional tributary relationship with the Middle Kingdom were in evidence. Opponents of his Sinophile policy staged an abortive protest effort in 1959. When a serious cabinet crisis developed in early 1960, Sihanouk staged another plebiscite extravaganza that elevated him to the perennial rank of chief of state. By this time, youthful Sangkum incumbents were becoming unhappy in their powerless official roles and were resenting the favored status of the Royal Khmer Socialist Youth Group, which Sihanouk had helped sponsor in 1957. Elements of the Communist-

371

oriented Pracheachon (People's Group) party in 1962 accused the king of leading Cambodia into membership in the United States-sponsored SEATO alliance. Sihanouk responded by arresting spokesmen of the party and charging them with treasonable connections with an outside power; at the same time he denounced SEATO in forthright terms. He persisted in his earlier practice of including Leftist youth leaders in his slate of official party candidates and of subsequently assigning them posts in government.

The successful political finagling of Cambodia's chief of state may have tarnished the shining symbol of divine kingship, but the immediate effect was not serious. Sihanouk enjoyed the aura of authentic descent from both branches of Cambodia's ruling dynasty, the Norodoms and the Sisowaths. He retained at Phnom Penh the custody of the symbols of divine royalty: the several crowns, the sacred sword, the white umbrella canopy, and the bejeweled silken cap.[21] The charismatic Sukarno of Indonesia and Nu of Burma could not in any way equal Sihanouk's combination of kingly stance and ability as a master politician, nor could they match his political resilience. Sihanouk's game would play out in time, for some of his political assets were subject to erosion.

Sihanouk's performance as political actor was in many respects masterful. He scheduled weekly receptions for persons seeking redress of grievances, following the tradition of the rulers of thirteenth-century Sukhotai. He endeavored systematically to revive national pride in the achievements of the Khmer builders of Angkor Wat, the Bayon, and neighboring classical monuments. From Cambodia's Buddhist tradition, he undertook to generate sanctions for the promotion of such moral practices as self-denial, mutual aid, personal honesty, and concern for human need over personal privilege. His rapport with the conservative peasantry and the Buddhist monks helped keep radical intellectual and political ferment under effective control, albeit at the expense of retarding economic and social adjustments.

Sihanouk became his government's foremost public relations officer. He sponsored activities especially designed to enlist the interest and cooperation of the younger Western-educated elite. He staged movie spectacles with himself as star actor, demonstrated his substantial gifts as a musician, and became Cambodia's leading orator. He elevated popular participation in a reformed program of public education to the level of a patriotic duty. He dramatized the traditional annual plowing ritual, replete in royal regalia and sandwiched in between flag-bearing children and a cheering column of peasants. The parade proceeded around a modern stadium track, with a modern tractor plow bringing up the rear. On one occasion, he celebrated the opening of a public medical dispensary by appearing in brightly colored Manila shirt and trousers and handing out flowers to the girls while mingling with the enthusiastic crowd.[22] This kind of showmanship was effective for a time, but it eventually reached a point of diminishing returns.

Two important minority groups in Cambodia constituted bothersome but manageable problems. The three to four hundred thousand Vietnamese residents worked mainly as plantation laborers, craftsmen, and merchants. As a group, they were generally distrusted by the Khmer majority as overaggressive intruders and as possible sympathizers with rebel elements led by Son Ngo Thanh and his Vietminh backers. The second minority group were the Chinese, numbering some three hundred thousand and mainly Fukien and Cantonese speaking. They dominated Cambodia's retail trade, along with rice brokerage, moneylending, and coastal fishing. Characteristically apolitical, industrious, and business minded, Chinese youth made acceptable sons-in-law for some of Cambodia's elite, but the Chinese were otherwise unassimilated. In 1958 Sihanouk cancelled the privileged status previously enjoyed by the five designated congregations of Cambodia's Chinese under French rule, but he avoided any overt harassment. He eventually permitted Chinese schools to use Communist-oriented text-books, and most of the local Chinese language newspapers fell under the political influence of agents of Peking.

373

Since Sihanouk was convinced that the greatest threat to Cambodian independence was the possibility of future Thai and Vietnamese control, he was prepared to seek a long-term defensive accommodation with China.[23]

Faltering Efforts at Economic Development in Cambodia

For Sihanouk, the objectives of economic development as well as ideological commitment were subordinated to considerations of national security and survival. Some improvements were realized in educational facilities. Improved teacher training facilities were expanded, and a new technical institute was set up. A two-year development plan was formulated in 1956, but its dimensions were severely limited. Competence in the French language continued to be a symbol of cultural status, rather than an avenue to training in science and technology that might contribute to economic development. Cambodians usually found it easier to obtain second-hand technical information from Bangkok journals, even though the Thai themselves employed imprecise Sanskrit-derived terms in such discussions.[24] Even where objectives were clearly delineated, Cambodia was able to provide from indigenous sources neither the capital nor management needs. An overvigorous development effort, in any case, would inevitably play into the hands of alien entrepreneurs, with little profit to the Cambodians themselves. Since relatively few Cambodians were hungry, agricultural expansion did not appear to be a particularly urgent need. The government's preliminary announcement that private foreign investment would be welcome on the basis of 60 percent indigenous participation attracted few inquiries.[25]

Phnom Penh's two-year plan of 1956–58 produced a plethora of ineffective government agencies and some improvement of transportation facilities. Behind the building activity and other evidences of material improvement at Phnom Penh, the traditional social and economic order continued little changed. Annual per-capita income continued to be approximately $120, and the balance of

374

external trade was increasingly adverse. Elite families sent their sons to France for a Western education, a principal asset in finding government employment. Official moves in the direction of the nationalization of foreign trade pinched the resident Chinese, but Cambodians generally seemed little concerned with improving their own economic prospects.[26]

During the immediate postindependence years, economic advances within Cambodia were related mainly to foreign aid projects. The most important improvements included the new airport at Phnom Penh, with its connecting highway into the city, plus the new seaport of Sihanoukville on the south coast, all gifts of France. The United States undertook the difficult task of constructing a highway from the new port city across the mountains to the capital. Other gains included school facilities, light industry in the form of cotton mills, sugar refineries, timber mills, an auto assembly plant, and a juice bottling works. A plywood factory promised by China never got into effective operation, while the dams and irrigation works planned for southwest of Phnom Penh were never completed. Highway and railway traffic increased a moderate 8 to 10 percent during the two-year plan.

When state control of credits and foreign trade was expanded at the end of the decade, economic activity tapered off. Permits required for private enterprise undertakings were denied except for basic commodity needs. The enhanced importation of industrial equipment starting in 1961 produced a near cessation of consumer imports. Increased trade deficits were aggravated by an almost 20 percent drop in export earnings (mainly rubber). The purchase of building steel, cement, machinery, and electrical equipment overseas also declined in time. Meanwhile, the country's basic resources in agricultural potential, forest products, and minerals (iron, copper, manganese, and gold) were little touched.[27] Despite the enormous tourist attraction of Cambodia's Angkor monuments, the tide of visitors lagged because of inadequate plane services and hotel accommodations.

In 1963 Sihanouk showed his impatience with American and French assistance by shifting to a pro-China orientation following a visit to Peking early in the year. An element of political blackmail may have been involved. The action was taken ostensibly because Washington refused requests to curb radio attacks on Sihanouk that were allegedly emanating from Khmer Issarak spokesmen in Thailand.[28] The pro-China move was not popular: it provoked one schoolboy riot and an abortive political revolt led by the younger members of the cabinet itself. Sihanouk nevertheless persisted by inviting Liu Shao-chi to visit Phnom Penh in May 1963. Later that year Cambodia joined Albania in cosponsoring China's bid to enter the United Nations. From Yugoslavia Sihanouk obtained the promised installation of three hydroelectric plants. To discourage students from studying in France, he cancelled the acceptance of scholarships provided by the Union of Khmer Students in France. In November 1963 Sihanouk requested the termination of all United States economic and military assistance, which had previously averaged around $40 million per year. The pro-China stance was destined to continue for several years, presumably for other than economic reasons.

The Problem of National Identity in Laos

The presumption that landlocked Laos could best achieve nationhood and progressive modernization through contacts with neighboring Thailand was somewhat less true than appearances indicated. On the positive side were ethnic identities, trade connections, similarities of language, social institutions, and religion. Even the sharp political differences that had developed during the period of Siamese control in the mid-nineteenth century and during the fifty years of French rule were not insurmountable. By comparison, the brief contacts with Communist China and the North Vietnamese that the peoples of Laos made after 1949 were both culturally alien and politically embarrassing. The non-Buddhist tribal elements in Laos

376

already distrusted the Mekong Valley elite but found even less in common traditionally with the Vietnamese or the Chinese.[29] Pathet Lao propaganda, for example, persistently utilized the idea of loyalty to the Laotian kingship as a cohesive political factor in soliciting the cooperation of other tribal groups within the country.[30]

The problem of achieving nationhood for Laos was nevertheless both complicated and formidable. The Lao population of over one million who resided along the left bank of the Mekong River constituted a frontier projection of the eight to ten million Lao peoples living in northern Thailand. Proceeding up the several left bank tributaries of the Mekong into the mountainous hinterland, the population shaded off into four or five identifiable groups of so-called *Tai* tribesmen. At one extreme were the partly assimilated Black *Tai*, who had adopted Buddhism and an Indian-type script and who recognized princes and priests as classes differentiated from the mass of commoners. By contrast, the Red *Tai* had developed no system of writing and were committed to an unadulterated animist religion. The eventual acculturation of all tribal *Tai* by their Laotian neighbors was generally assumed, but even with improved means of communication with the outside world, the process would take a long time. Mountaineers generally preferred not to be disturbed in their traditional life patterns.

Residing in more remote regions adjacent to the *Tai* tribesmen, but alien ethnically and linguistically, were many varieties of semi-indigenous inhabitants. The valley Lao referred to them by the perjorative name of *Kha* (savages), as previously indicated. Such groups had been left behind during the course of major population migrations, and were for the most part passive and unaggressive peoples. Acculturated Khmer elements resident on both sides of the lower Mekong Valley above the Cambodian border, called *Khmu* by the Siamese, accepted Buddhism and identified with kinsmen living in both Thailand and Cambodia. The *Khmu* disliked both the Lao-Thai and the Vietnamese.

The presence of many of the Meo and Yao-Man peoples in northern Laos probably dated from mid-nineteenth-century disturbances in South China. They differed from the older resident *Tai* and *Kha* tribesmen, and were more closely akin to peoples found in much larger numbers in northwestern Tonkin and across the China border. As newly arrived intruders, the Meo in particular penetrated mountaintop areas unoccupied by the older inhabitants. The frontal or southern edge of the Meo advance proceeded as far as Xieng Khouang (Plain of Jars) and penetrated at some points into the northernmost reaches of Thailand. They were largely subsistence farmers, who produced opium as a cash crop. The Yao-Man immigrants were considerably less mobile and aggressive than the Meo.

The Meo tribesmen were destined to play a significant role in the postwar history of Laos, for they became active on both sides of the armed controversy. One Meo leader named Faydang helped Souphanouvong organize the Pathet Lao, while two others, Touby Lyfong and General Van Pao, found service with the Lao governor of Xieng Khouang and at Vientiane. This dispersion of affiliation reflected an obvious lack of political cohesion among the widely scattered Meo tribesmen. In neighboring Tonkin, their cooperation was actively enlisted by the Vietminh. Peking was also apparently interested in eliciting Meo support along the Laos-China border by devoting considerable energy and resources to constructing roads into the Phong Saly province and southward toward the Mekong River above Luang Prabang. Because both the Laos government and the Thai authorities failed in efforts to conciliate the tribal frontier inhabitants, the latter tended to develop stronger political ties with their more solicitous Communist Tonkinese neighbors. After the Laos Conference of 1962, to be described below, the United States sponsored economic aid and refugee programs to help the Laos government maintain a measure of control over the more vigorous tribesmen.[31] The situation could not be explained in terms of Vietnamese aggression or the Cold War dichotomy. Most Lao peoples had their own interests in mind.[32]

378

Political Developments in Laos to 1959

Political developments at Vientiane following Souvanna Phouma's abortive effort in 1956–57 to integrate divergent political elements were concerned mainly with the relationships of members of the 200 elite family factions. They dominated the royal court, the cabinet ministries, the civil service leadership, and the army command. They intruded somewhat into the apolitical Chinese business community of Vientiane in areas of real estate and transportation.

Under the new Laos constitution of 1955, the person of the king was legally sacred, and his extensive authority was buttressed by religious sanctions. He selected the prime minister, declared wars and negotiated treaties, and functioned as protector of the Buddhist state religion. The nine-member cabinet was theoretically responsible to an assembly elected at five-year intervals, convening annually in May. The older royal council of twelve elder statesmen, under Boun Oum's chairmanship, was legally designated as the National Assembly. The pattern of democratic procedures vaguely outlined in the constitution was largely irrelevant to the strident competition for power and wealth within the ranks of the French-educated elite. The political incumbents regarded their privileged position as an inherent right and, in practice, were not held legally accountable for abuse of power.

With the probable exception of Boun Oum and Phoumi Nosavan, who maintained close connections with Bangkok, Laotian leaders of all political persuasions were not enthusiastic about cultivating close relations with Thailand. The neutralist Premier Souvanna Phouma flatly refused, in 1955 and later, to accept repeated Bangkok proposals that the Pathet Lao threat against the Laos government be brought to the attention of SEATO. Peking allegedly threatened intervention if SEATO was called in.[33] Nor did Vientiane welcome the alternative concept of organizing a "Buddhist bloc" as an alternative regional defense agency. Thai intervention was not welcome, since any augmentation of Bangkok's political or military presence might conceivably threaten the survival of the precarious state. The memory of Marshal Pibun's wartime irredentist claims to Laos territories in Samaboury and the Champassak district west of the lower Mekong was still fresh.[34]

The revived coalition government formed at Vientiane in November 1957, following prolonged negotiations between the neutralist Souvanna Phouma and his pro-Communist half-brother, Souphanouvong, survived less than a year. The central government's concurrent recovery of the two Pathet Lao border provinces, Phong Saly and Sam Neua, was largely fictional, but the pretended reunion did provide a reason for the International Control Commission to adjourn its activities. In the supplementary elections held in May 1958, the Patriotic Laotian Front party (Pathet Lao) and Souvanna Phouma's allied Peace Party won thirteen of the twenty-one contested seats. Election appeals by Pathet Lao candidates denouncing official corruption and calling for peace were so disturbingly effective that the previously quarreling conservative factions were obliged to close their ranks in order to maintain a coalition majority within the full Assembly.[35]

Against the prevailing tradition of government for the benefit of the elite classes, the opposition delegates solicited support from peasants, monks, and nonstatus intellectuals by promising a reformed government free of corruption. Political relations became strained. All elected provincial delegates were housed in plain army barracks while attending the Vientiane Assembly sessions. Opposition assemblymen tried to enlist support within the expanding ranks of the army and police and from minor administrative and technical personnel, many of whom had been recruited from peasant stock. Prominent among the malcontents was the half-*Kha* Colonel Kong Lê, who had fought with the French against the Vietminh and was destined to play a prominent role in the 1960–61 crisis. He owed his enhanced position mainly to his army connections and to marital ties.[36]

The gap between the elected delegates and their several

380

constituencies was frequently as great as that between the newcomers and the traditionally privileged class. The services of governmental agencies were at best available only in areas near urban centers, and even these areas lacked sewer drainage, dependable piped water, hospital care, and fire protection. Despite their dislike of greedy politicians, the Valley Lao as well as many tribesmen made poor revolutionaries because they shared a traditionally cynical and apathetic attitude toward government as a source of welfare services.

American financial and military assistance, designed to buttress the royalist regime as a barrier to communism, may have helped to demoralize rather than strengthen the recipients. American funds covered the salaries and wages of teachers, policemen, soldiers, and civil servants, but the Lao elite also profited enormously. Illicit access to American jeeps, army clothing, and blankets became part of the normal perquisites of power and office. American consumer goods sent in from 1955 to 1957 to absorb the flow of dollar credits provided the principal opportunity for graft. Their value was credited to the government account in *kip* at the legal rate of thirty-five to the dollar, while the items were actually sold in the Laos market or in Thailand for three to four times the legal price. No profiteer in such lucrative operations was ever brought to account. Because Lao consumer capacity proved unable to absorb the volume of such gratis imports, more than 70 percent of the American contributions were later transmitted in the form of import-license dollars, which were also regularly manipulated at alternate official and blackmarket rates to the profit of those in authority.

When an American congressional investigation discovered that an estimated 60 percent of the goods and import licenses never served their intended purposes, drastic measures were devised in a futile effort to remedy the situation.[37] In June 1958, with the dual purpose of ending the misappropriation of aid funds and of challenging the presumed pro-Communist drift of Souvanna Phouma's coalition government, Washington suspended temporarily all monthly aid payments, amounting to several times the regular tax revenue collections. Before the new exchange rate of eighty *kip* to the dollar could be stabilized, Souvanna Phouma's government collapsed amid an orgy of personal and factional bickering.[38]

The emerging cabinet headed by the influential Phoui Sananikone, leader of the so-called Rally of Laotian People, was stridently anti-Communist. But the new government also proved to be even more financially irresponsible than the previous regime had been. Despite Phoui's acknowledged experience and ability, he was widely distrusted. He dismissed from the cabinet all neutralist and pro-Communist members. Newcomers to the cabinet included several members of the American-sponsored Committee for the Defense of the National Interest (CDNI), which was explicitly pro-Western in outlook and ostensibly dedicated to the eradication of corruption and communism. General Phoumi Nosavan, protégé of Prince Boun Oum and a member of the CDNI, became the new minister of defense, while other CDNI leaders were assigned to the ministry of foreign affairs.

Phoui Sananikone's eighteen-month association with the CDNI faction was at most a marriage of convenience. In foreign affairs, the regime tried to play an independent political role, cultivating close relationships with both Ngo Dinh Diem and Norodom Sihanouk. Phoui rebuffed suggestions that the International Control Commission be asked to return and also rejected Secretary-General Hammarskjöld's proposed visit on behalf of the United Nations in March 1959.[39]

The CDNI Experiment

The CDNI membership was recruited from younger educated elements of the marginal elite strata whom the genuine elite regarded as presumptuous upstarts. Committee spokesmen talked much about justice, honesty, improved administration, and reform of the law courts.

They also criticized the alleged growing indiscipline of the monks, including gambling and alcoholism. They participated in the Junior Chamber of Commerce and sponsored Boy and Girl Scout organizations. The CDNI also praised the Philippines Operation Brotherhood, an American-financed medical mission sent to Laos. For a time the CDNI even enjoyed the patronage of Crown Prince Savang Vatthana, who addressed one of its meetings in person and whose protocol officer functioned as a regular member of the committee. The committee's considerable funds came from sources other than business and graft, and it enjoyed strong army support via General Phoumi Nosavan. American sponsorship, although not advertized, was widely assumed.

The CDNI experiment was too theoretical and detached to be politically effective. The committee established only superficial contact with the Lao villagers and the Buddhist clergy and made no effort to counter disaffection among the hill tribes. Village chiefs were expected to journey to the main roads for interviews, since committee members traveled only by car. Rhetoric about governmental improvement did little to generate social reform or to eliminate entrenched privilege. Committee members themselves coveted houses, cars, and night-club entertainment. By contrast, the Pathet Lao organizers emphasized their personal sacrifices and dedication to the welfare of the hill tribesmen, even though they, too, were economically ineffective.

The CDNI participated in the final phases of the Sananikone government in 1958–59 and continued their role in the successor Boun Oum-Phoumi Nosavan regime, which took over in December 1959. The new government won a landslide victory in the elections of April 1960 by assessing high fees on prospective candidates and by manipulating polling booths. Little or nothing remained of the committee's reforming pretenses.[40] The CDNI joined in demanding dissolution of the National Assembly itself and in calling for the trial of Souphanouvong for treason.

Meanwhile, the political crisis occasioned by the displacement of the coalition government in mid-1958 had led to a revival of guerrilla warfare. The renewed threat afforded occasion for the new leadership to raise their aid requests from America to cover military preparations as well as civil government and police costs. By October 1958 the United States resumed aid payments that it had suspended the previous June, until they covered more than 90 percent of total government costs. Corruption was revived on a wider scale than ever. Phoui Sananikone subsequently refused to join a proposed anti-Communist crusade advocated by Marshal Sarit of Thailand and President Ngo Dinh Diem of South Vietnam,[41] which seems to have been an initial objective. The United States' first venture at political manipulation in Laos was less than an impressive performance.

Economic Development Problems in Laos

Concomitant American efforts to stimulate production and trade in Laos ran completely aground. Financial aid to cover costs of expanding army and police forces prior to 1958 had boosted business activity, but the profits went largely to alien entrepreneurs. Because of official ineptitude and thievery, government planning never got beyond the working-paper level. Total tax revenues covered less than half the costs of routine nonmilitary services, and some 70 percent of the tax total was derived from customs duties levied on imports of capital and consumer goods provided from American sources. Local income taxes, starting with a miniscule 1.5 percent levy, were payable by only a very small portion of the population. Police and army groups paid no taxes at all.

The normal incentives designed to stimulate economic activity were largely inoperative in Laos. Most of the people preferred the meager security of subsistence farming, with its assured base and its traditional calendrical rites, to the uncertainties of a money economy and wage employment. Wage earners, from 1958 to 1962, made up only 12 percent of the population, while the nonproductive refugee group increased to around 10 percent. Some 65 percent of the rapidly expanding urban population of Vientiane and four-fifths of the inhabitants of other cities were still engaged at least marginally in agriculture. Even so, the same cities had to import grain from Thailand because of impaired transportation on the Laos side of the river.[42] Meanwhile, inflationary pressures raised consumer prices in *kip* some four-fold from 1958 to 1962, while prices paid for peasant-produced surpluses only doubled. Illness incurred by displaced refugees took a heavy toll.[43]

American aid helped initiate a number of agricultural programs covering rice, poultry, stock raising, and forestry, but results were disappointingly meager. Approximately one-quarter of American aid funds went for road construction, education, health, and public administration. The other three-quarters were devoted to enlisting and equipping the thirty-thousand-man Royal Laotian Army. Recruits were easy to find because the pay was generous by Laos standards, but the undisciplined Royal Army proved unable to cope with the smaller but more determined Pathet Lao forces.[44] Laos represented the acme of the underdevelopment problem: a fragmented political structure, an inadequate administrative system, lack of trained and experienced manpower, fiscal irresponsibility, incapacity to generate savings from local production, plus sadly deficient infrastructure facilities in areas of health, roads, communications, housing, and electrical power.

Efforts at economic and political development were also hampered at times by rivalry between French and American advisers. The French group, which numbered only eight hundred in 1950, increased by four or five times during the ensuing decade. They communicated more readily with the Lao elite and were far more familiar with the total scene than were the newly arrived Americans, whose presence the Europeans resented. French officers continued to train the fledgling Royal Army, while its essential equipment, supplies, and pay came from American sources. After the French military training units eventually withdrew in 1959, the former colonial power continued to provide several thousand advisers and essential facilities for secondary education, public works, and legal and fiscal areas of government. The United States provided an expanding embassy staff and an extensive AID mission, including a Program Evaluation Organization charged with supervising the distribution of military assistance. An American teacher training school was constructed and staffed near Vientiane, and additional training activities for teachers were conducted in Thailand, the Philippines, and the United States. Some four hundred new village schools were built with American funds.[45]

American-French rivalry developed on a number of fronts. The French resisted American pressure that English be made the second language of the schools. They also opposed the view that Laos should develop closer commercial and cultural relations with kindred anti-Communist Thailand, for whom French colonials entertained no love. Whereas the United States Information Service prepared reading materials in the Lao-Thai language covering cultural aspects of the Laotian past, the French counterpart agency stressed the cultural significance of the European experience. Few of the French-educated Lao favored identity with the Thai. As late as 1967 the American AID mission at Vientiane held up school construction projects until the use of English instead of French for instructional purposes was officially confirmed.[46]

While French and American aid dispensers were competing for priority status in Vientiane, the local rulers found relatively little to say in their own behalf. Since the hill folk of the interior were not regarded as politically important and lacked reception facilities in any case, the government's radio propaganda was addressed almost exclusively to the Buddhist Lao in the Mekong Valley. The principal themes were loyalty to the divine ruler at Luang Prabang and support of the Communist-threatened Buddhist faith. Hanoi and Pathet Lao spokesmen, particularly Prince Souphanouvong, countered by stressing the need to protect the revered Laotian king from the domination of "exploiter imperialists" and their corrupt Vientiane lackeys. They also feigned support for the orthodox Buddhist hierarchy against betrayal by the Gallicized secularism of the heterodox Lao elite.[47] The Hanoi Vietminh also solicited positive support from neighboring hill tribesmen by promoting road construction, home industries, and the trained indoctrination of selected tribal leaders. Hill peoples were moved from crowded lowland areas into less densely populated regions of Sam Neua and Phong Saly, where Pathet Lao Meo control centered.[48] The montagnards of interior Tonkin and adjacent Laos felt that they had a friend in the Vietminh, who trained their leaders, aided them economically, and provided them with military assistance.

Vietnamese propaganda in Laos apparently attracted little positive support from the tribal *Tai* and *Kha* peoples. It did succeed in neutralizing any potential antagonistic response from the Buddhist Lao peasantry. The latter saw little reason why they should risk death by fighting either in defense of the self-centered Vientiane regime or to maintain control over remote regions in the country's interior. The American-financed and French-trained Royal Lao Army, as will be indicated shortly, failed repeatedly to stand up to Pathet Lao-Vietminh attacks. The subsequent American-recruited "Clandestine Army," like the Pathet Lao forces, was drawn largely from Meo tribesmen, whose leaders were accorded officer training in the United States.[49] Otherwise the population of Laos exhibited little revolutionary enthusiasm or patriotic devotion.[50]

The apolitical Buddhist tradition was not an effective anti-Communist ploy. Veneration of the monks and the *wat* shrines persisted, along with popular regard for traditional Thai music, art, and dancing.[51] Leading Buddhist champions, such as Nhouy Abhay, decried the growing indiscipline, ignorance, and impiety among both clergy and laity in Laos, and the clergy complained of governmental interference. But as an ally of the Vientiane government in its supposed struggle with communism, the attempted exploitation of Buddhism was notoriously ineffective. The real cultural conflict was between traditional social values and the seductive attractions of Western movies, motorcycles and cars, radios, air conditioners, and modern dancing troops. Children of poor families attended monastic schools, mainly because modern education was not available to them. Younger monks were usually anxious to learn English in order to qualify for remunerative jobs in government service or the army, with little regard for the Pali Scriptures or the *Vinaya* discipline of Buddhism. Such problems of religious decay and cultural confusion had little relevance to popular susceptibility to Communist propaganda or to promotion of national resistance to America's Cold War enemies.[52]

Political Developments in Laos, 1959–62

The dominance of Premier Sananikone's Rally of the Laotian People came to an end in late December 1959 in a bloodless army coup staged by Phoumi Nosavan's CDNI faction. Sananikone provided the occasion when he tried to remove several CDNI cabinet members in favor of his personal cronies. The coup leaders denounced prevailing corruption, but then cancelled their reforming credentials by staging controlled elections in April 1960. Phoumi's army group took no chances. Districts were gerrymandered; polling booths were controlled; and candidates had to produce receipts for tax payments for five years, make substantial election deposits, and submit to education tests. Thirty-four CDNI candidates were elected, compared to half that number from the Rally party, plus six Independents.[53]

The new short-term cabinet was headed by the colorless Prince Somsanith, while Phoumi took over the crucial post of defense minister and the self-appointed role of leader of the Social Democratic (CDNI) party. Opposition developed. Prince Souphanouvong and nine other leading Pathet Lao politicians who had been imprisoned without trial since July 1959 managed with some local cooperation to escape from jail. They proceeded northward where they resumed political activity and guerrilla resistance. The Somsanith government was itself overthrown on August 9, 1960. Captain Kong Lê's paratrooper force simply took over at Vientiane while all the princes were absent at Luang Prabang attending cremation ceremonies for the deceased King Sisavang Vong. Kong Lê acted at the instigation of disgruntled politicians, but the action was widely interpreted as a sincere protest against the government's abuse of power, alleged American interference in Laotian affairs, and the persistence of civil war.[54] Pathet Lao influence was also clearly in evidence. Souvanna Phouma returned to Vientiane to negotiate a compromise settlement with Captain Kong Lê, who had ventured far beyond his depth politically. Boun Oum refused to accept the settlement.

A counterrevolution quickly got under way. Phoumi Nosavan, the principal loser in August, proceeded from Luang Prabang directly to Bangkok to confer with Marshal Sarit and thence to his home base at Savannakhet in southern Laos. He there began preparing for a military move against Vientiane, still held by Kong Lê's well-armed paratroopers. Backed initially by the compromise agreement and later approval by a majority of the Assembly, Souvanna Phouma meanwhile obtained royal confirmation of his premier's role as Somsanith's successor. In an effort to avoid a recurrence of civil strife, Souvanna also accepted the new king's suggestion that he confer with Phoumi Nosavan at Luang Prabang to try to work out some agreement. The price Souvanna Phouma had to pay for attempted reconciliation was high. On August 31 Phoumi was named deputy prime minister and minister of the interior, in charge of police. This concession alienated Kong Lê and the Pathet Lao moderates, and it also failed to influence Phoumi to abandon his own military preparations at Savannakhet and to return peacefully to Vientiane. Phoumi was assisted in his military plans by Bangkok's Sarit and eventually by American support as well.

More promising was Souvanna's balancing attempt to conciliate the Pathet Lao, which controlled two northern provinces and had made unwelcome a succession of royalist officials sent to Xieng Khouang since mid-1959. As soon as Pathet Lao leaders learned that Phoumi had decided not to be associated with the new regime, they responded positively to Souvanna, while taking advantage of the opportunity to extend the areas of their control. Preliminary contacts began in late September, and negotiations with Souvanna were actually initiated formally at Vientiane on October 11, 1960.

The United States reaction to these developments was equivocal. The American ambassador at Vientiane, Winthrop Brown, believed that Washington should go along with Souvanna's apparently sincere effort to achieve reconciliation, but he was overruled by the Pentagon and the CIA. In late September, Air American planes joined those of Marshal Sarit in delivering supplies for Phoumi's growing army at Savannakhet, while similar military supplies were being denied Kong Lê's forces. Thailand subsequently imposed a food blockade on Vientiane. Washington then sent to Vientiane a special emissary who suspended cash-grant aid and demanded that Souvanna reopen negotiations with Phoumi. As a condition for the resumption of cash-grant payments, Souvanna himself finally agreed on October 17 to approve the sending of American military aid to Savannakhet, but only on condition that such arms should be used against the Pathet Lao and not against Kong Lê. The pledge given by the American negotiator on this occasion proved unenforceable.

The situation took on a more ominous aspect when, during the course of the application of American financial pressure, the Soviet ambassador, Abromov, offered to meet the urgent fuel needs of Kong Lê's Vientiane forces. The arrangement was later expanded to include military hardware as well. Air-lifted Soviet supplies sent via Hanoi began to arrive at Vientiane early in December. Plagued by military desertions elsewhere, the forces available to the Souvanna government proved unable to stem the attack launched from Savannakhet. The embittered premier fled by plane to Cambodia on December 9. The capital fell to Phoumi on December 16 after a determined struggle that saw Soviet artillery manned by Vietnamese gunners contributing to the defense.[55]

The vacillating role which the Eisenhower administration had played in Laos ended in January 1961 under discouraging circumstances. The Soviet government was openly allied with the Pathet Lao; the conciliatory Souvanna Phouma was in exile; Kong Lê's nationalist paratroopers were fighting on the side of the Pathet Lao, while trying to maintain some kind of a separate identity of command. The American aid program and the CIA agency were allied with the most reactionary and corrupt faction in Laos, acting in collaboration with the avaricious Marshal Sarit of Thailand, all in an ostensible effort to save the country from Communism. Once having recovered Vientiane, Phoumi failed to press operations against his enemies into the interior. Morale problems were involved. In early 1962, when a small Vietminh-Pathet Lao force entered the vicinity of the royal capital of Luang Prabang, the defending Royal Army fled. As a contribution to fading morale, an American force of nearly two thousand marines was introduced into adjacent territories of Thailand in March, 1962.[56]

Presumably because too little was at stake in backward Laos to warrant an armed confrontation between Soviet and American power, a compromise was arranged later in 1962. Both major parties agreed to "neutralize" the country under the restored rule of Souvanna Phouma, who had been previously twice rejected by the Americans. The resulting policy approximated the one that had been proposed by informed French observers in 1955.

A Critique of American Policy in Laos

American military policy in Laos down to 1962 assumed that any participation in the Vientiane government by Pathet Lao representatives would constitute an important victory for the World Communist conspiracy. Washington and Bangkok envisaged the possibility that Laos would be occupied by China-supported North Vietnamese forces, which would then be in a position to threaten all of Southeast Asia. Washington's desertion of the coalition arrangement in 1958 in favor of the anti-Communist Rightist faction miscarried politically and afforded Hanoi a plausible argument that American intervention in Laos constituted a revival of colonialism.

American policy also misjudged what was feasible and desirable in terms of economic development activity in Laos. Efforts based on Marshall Plan European concepts made little sense. Massive American monetary contributions, which attained in 1962 a per-capita level of $192, far exceeded the capacity of the economy to absorb them. The few well-placed Laotians who had access to imported luxury goods and import-license dollars profited enormously, while the economy as a whole realized few advantages. Spiraling prices and the falling value of the *kip* moved imported items well beyond the reach of the population as a whole. Electrical appliances such as radios and air conditioners, along with outboard motors, automobiles, and construction machinery had little relevance to popular needs. Even where rural development programs and educational facilities were constructively fashioned, the necessary cultural adjustments failed to keep pace, and tangible implementation faltered.[57]

An American Congressional report of 1959, entitled "United States Aid Operations in Laos," was both frank and informative. It concluded that the American-sponsored Royal Laotian army (30,000 troops) was twice the size required, and that attendant expenditures had led to widespread corruption. Carelessly drawn contracts for engineering services, road construction, and ferry barges had been violated beyond any possibility of correction by the operations mission or by auditing control. Laos' International Cooperation Administration rationalized such admitted maladministration on the grounds that, without American aid contributions, the country would have fallen to the Communists.[58] Actually, flagrant official corruption in Vientiane gave credence to Hanoi's anti-American propaganda, despite widespread Laotian aversion to Vietnamese or Communist control.

Clearly, Laos did not fit into the dichotomy of the Cold War. Marxism had limited relevance in a land where the prevailing atmosphere was one of veneration for the environs of the royal palace, with its caparisoned elephants, golden palanquins, and royal attire; with its royal white umbrella and the golden betel nut service of the court. Also alien to the modern world were the reverence due to Buddhist temple precincts, the annual plowing ritual, and the pageantry of the New Year celebrations. The new symbols of elitist status, such as dust-producing automobiles, were offensive and to many suggested wealth unearned and unsanctified, and subservience to the banality of American largess.[59] Nor did SEATO seem to fit. It actually revived the profound distrust, shared historically by the Laos people, of Thailand's presumptuous role.[60] Laotians had appreciated French protection from Bangkok after 1893 and were aware that France as a member of SEATO was currently hostile to what Paris regarded as the blundering American presence in Laos.[61]

Meanwhile, Marshal Sarit at Bangkok and his Right-wing allies at Vientiane did everything they could to encourage international involvement in Laotian security problems. In 1959 Premier Sananikone and Sarit collaborated in drafting a blueprint for defense, based on a formal appeal to the United Nations and an extension of American military involvement. At the same time, Vientiane also tried to reach agreement with the Diem regime at Saigon for military cooperation against the shared Communist threat. Abortive efforts to enlist SEATO's protection were repeated in 1960, at the instigation of Boun Oum and Phoumi Nosavan in response to Sarit's urging. When the move failed, the angered Thai dictator suggested that he might have to seek direct accomodation with Peking and Moscow, the kind of blackmail tactic previously used by Sihanouk. American military guarantees followed.[62]

American policy failed to delineate precisely what the aid program to Laos was intended to accomplish. The United States reacted in piecemeal fashion to unanticipated crisis situations, which the Vientiane conservative elite exploited to their personal advantage. What was needed was a long-term effort for government improvement, for the selection of responsible leadership, and for the enhancement of social values shared by the Laotian people. What the American presence in Vientiane actually fostered was an envied "Little America" mentality, featuring improved housing, radios and air-conditioning units, a post exchange commissary, and English language training for school children, servants, and chauffeurs.[63]

The Neutralization of Laos, 1962

Reacting to the deepening Laos crisis following his inauguration in January 1961 and plagued by the Bay of Pigs fiasco in Cuba, President Kennedy decided to abandon the futile CIA policy of supporting the anti-Communist but irresponsibly corrupt government of Boun Oum and Phoumi Nosavan, and to encourage instead the elevation of a new coalition government again headed by the Prince Souvanna Phouma.[64] The task was not easy, nor was success assured. In pursuit of this objective, Washington solicited Soviet pressure at Hanoi to moderate Vietnamese aggressiveness in Laos in return for American abandonment of a policy of military confrontation. A neutralist coalition would give Laos an opportunity for pacification and a chance to survive as an independent, non-Communist state, albeit a highly vulnerable one. The alternative commitment of American forces to remote Laos would involve serious complications, including the awesome threat of precipitating strife among the world powers. In March 1961 Kennedy proposed to recall the International Control Commission and to invite Souvanna Phouma to return to Vientiane as premier.[65]

Moscow had equally cogent reasons to seek a settlement in Laos. It would afford opportunity, with minimal loss of prestige, to end the costly Soviet airlift to Vientiane and remove Laos as a danger zone of possible military confrontation. Warfare in Laos would invite overt Chinese invasion of both that country and Tonkin, a contingency that Moscow and Hanoi alike wanted very much to avoid.[66] In other words, the issues at stake in Laos were not commensurate with the risks entailed.[67]

394

Preparatory negotiations for a Laos settlement involved the participation of fourteen states and required more than a year to complete. The initial move, made at Geneva in May 1961, called for reciprocal pledges not to use Laotian territory as a base for intervening in adjacent countries. A second milestone was reached at a Rangoon meeting in September 1961, when it was agreed that half of the new coalition cabinet should be selected from Souvanna Phouma's neutralist followers and the other half be divided equally between the Boun Oum-Phoumi Nosavan faction and Leftist adherents of Souphanouvong. The Rightist faction, understandably opposed to any diminution of its power, demanded continued control of both the defense and interior ministries as well as the authority to approve four of Souvanna Phouma's selectees.[68] Souphanouvong agreed to enter the newly planned cabinet as one of the deputy prime ministers (the other was Phoumi) and as minister of economic planning, but he would give no prior commitment to integrate his Pathet Lao troops with the Royal Army. The Pathet Lao forces, by 1962, actually controlled approximately half of the territory of Laos, not counting the Vietminh-controlled border supply routes leading into South Vietnam.

In order to force eventual compliance by the Boum Oum faction, the United States government moved in February 1962 to withhold its monthly contribution of some three million dollars to cover routine government expenses. An indignant Marshal Sarit at Bangkok thereupon volunteered to make good a portion of the sum denied to Phoumi and Boun Oum. The situation was deadlocked for a time. Phoumi publicized a fictitious propaganda story that ten thousand Chinese troops had invaded the Nam Tha province above Luang Prabang. The Thai government was eventually mollified by the presence of a token American marine force of some 1,800 along the Thai-Lao border and by the negotiation of a bilateral American agreement pledging unqualified defense assistance in case Thailand were attacked. Phoumi's cause collapsed completely in May 1962, after the Royal Army contingent assigned to defend Luang Prabang had fled in a panic across the Thai border as previously indicated. Souvanna Phouma was persuaded to return from Europe to set up a new coalition cabinet at Vientiane. Boun Oum resigned as premier in June.[69] The deadlock was formally broken by the Soviet-American arranged conference at Geneva between Boun Oum, Souvanna Phouma, and Souphanouvong.[70] The sullen Phoumi remained on at Vientiane, encouraged in his continuing but futile resistance by his Thai relative and mentor, Marshal Sarit.

The new coalition government was officially installed on June 23, 1962. It was a syncretic amalgam, far from unified. The balance between the two antagonistic deputy prime ministers Souphanouvong and Phoumi, was weighted in the direction of the latter, who also served as finance minister. Since the Treasury was able to limit the funds available to Souphanouvong's ministry of economic development, a complete paralysis developed in economic policy. Many of the foreign advisor technicians began to depart in August, including some eight hundred American military aids.[71]

Phoumi, meanwhile, had developed a number of private interests. Taking advantage of his position as finance minister, he managed a lucrative chain of gambling casinos, controlled liquor and perfume imports, and had a monopoly on the smuggling of gold flown out of Europe for distribution via the Bank of Laos. His performance amounted to official thievery. These abuses reached such a point in late 1962 that United States agencies again refused to underwrite the cost of routine government expenses unless Phoumi ceased his indiscriminate use of printing-press money. The value of real wages had been reduced by half, and the *kip* was devalued to around 240 to the dollar. Phoumi was finally stripped of his last remaining military command and expelled from Laos in 1965, after having become involved in two abortive coups. He took up exile residence in South Thailand.[72]

The international ratification of the Laos neutralization agreement was accomplished at Geneva on July 12, 1962. Thirteen nations participated, including the governments of neighboring Burma, Cambodia, Thailand, North and South Vietnam, plus China and India. The Western signatories included Britain,. France, the Soviet Union, Poland, Canada, and the United States. All of the parties affirmed their willingness to respect the sovereignty, territorial integrity, and neutrality of the Kingdom of Laos and pledged nonintervention in its affairs. Military entry by outsiders was forbidden, as was the use of Lao territory as a base for armed operations. No political conditions were to be attached to future contributions of economic aid.

The effective enforcement of such restrictions was clearly beyond the capabilities of the revived International Control Commission (made up of Canada, Poland, and India with India as chairman), but the pattern set up was nonetheless significant. The action ostensibly eliminated Laos for the time being as a focal point of world conflict. Violations of the agreement occurred, but because they could not be openly acknowledged, they tended to be apologetic and limited in character. Before any substantial progress could be made to implement plans for a unified Laotian army, events in Saigon overtook the endeavor, and it was destined never to be realized. Pathet Lao participation in the coalition government came to a de facto end in 1963, although the four abandoned cabinet posts continued to be held open for their de jure incumbents. The Pathet Lao was allowed to maintain a legation headquarters at Vientiane.

Despite the resumption of aggressive action on the part of Leftist rebel forces around the Plain of Jars and also in southern Laos, where Boun Oum continued to act as inspector-general of the armed forces, the end of the first year of the new regime found Souvanna Phouma commanding an increasing measure of political support, especially from civil servants and military officers.[73] Moscow was able to influence Souphanouvong but failed to maintain any continuing restraint on Hanoi's aggressive tendencies, possibly because of China's exertion of powerful counterpressure. After Ngo Dinh Diem's overthrow at Saigon in late 1963, North Vietnam developed an overriding interest in the overthrow of successor Saigon governments.[74] The results of the neutralization effort thus fell far below the optimum expectations of Washington, but only the most violently anti-Communist partisans would argue that the compromise endeavor was a mistaken move.[75]

Sihanouk's Foreign Policy, 1958–63

As previously indicated, Prince Sihanouk's foreign policy was based on his basic concern to preserve the independence and territorial integrity of Cambodia. He resisted threatened intrusions by Vietnamese and Thai neighbors and tried to maintain some kind of diplomatic balance between contending forces in the Cold War. In 1958 he opened diplomatic relations with North Vietnam and accepted an offer from the Soviet Union to set up an advanced technological school.[76] With respect to events in Laos, Sihanouk advocated in 1959 that the country be neutralized under international guarantees. He specifically approved the Kong Lê coup in August 1960 and advanced a plea that both Cambodia and Laos be neutralized. When Souvanna Phouma was obliged to flee Vientiane in December 1960, he set up a temporary government-in-exile at Phnom Penh.[77] Sihanouk's advocacy of a compromise settlement in Laos continued undiminished into 1962.

Meanwhile, the prince became increasingly concerned over boundary problems nearer home. Eighty years of French colonial rule had served to extend the boundaries of the Cochin-China colony at Cambodia's expense, and French economic development in Cambodia (plantations and trade) had encouraged the infiltration of more than four hundred thousand Vietnamese settlers. Neither these settlers nor the approximately six hundred thousand persons of Khmer ancestry who continued to reside in the Mekong delta portion of Cochin-China were easily assimilated. Cambodia's leaders could have entertained little or no hope of ever recovering its pre-nineteenth-century

398

control of the lower delta. But amid the growing disorders encountered after 1959 by the Diem regime at Saigon, Phnom Penh raised repeated complaints about the ill treatment of Khmer residents in Cochin-China and periodic violation of Cambodia's borders by South Vietnamese forces. By 1962 Diem began to register countercomplaints that Vietcong rebel units were finding sanctuary in border regions of Cambodia. Another territorial dispute developed in the late 1950s over ownership of several small off-shore islands in the Gulf of Siam.[78] Relations between Sihanouk and Diem continued to be sharply abrasive.

Cambodia's border friction with Thailand centered mainly on the Thai occupation in 1954, following the French withdrawal, of the ancient border temple site of Preah Vihear (Phra Viharn in Thai). The land in dispute was not substantively important, but future claims and saving face became heavily involved. Presumably Thailand's irredentist aspirations, which had been asserted overtly during the war, were not dead. The outcome of the Preah Vihear controversy could therefore prejudice the future bargaining position of the losing party.

For four years the dispute was conducted on the level of discussion of the legalities of the case. Virtually all of the maps used by both the French and the Thai down to the 1940s showed the site lying within Cambodia's borders, and Bangkok had actually handed it back to the French in 1947. Thai protagonists, however, referred to relevant documents connected with the 1907 treaty of cession, which stipulated that the revised boundary through the area's Dangreb mountains region should follow the watershed, which would shift the temple to the Thai side of the border.

The controversy reached an acrimonious phase in 1958, following Sihanouk's flirtations with Peking. Emotion replaced legal argument. Thailand's Premier Thanom Kittikachorn charged that Sihanouk was deliberately enlisting Chinese intervention, that Cambodia's quarter-million Chinese residents would presumably align themselves with the Communist side (carrying ominous implications for Bangkok's Chinese), and that Cambodia would become henceforth an avenue for Communist infiltration into Thailand. Thanom's allegations reflected Bangkok's growing impatience with Cambodia and were also calculated to enlist the positive support of the Americans, who were involved at the very time (1958) in substituting the anti-Communist Sananikone government in Laos for Souvanna Phouma's coalition regime. Reciprocal recriminations multiplied, and diplomatic relations were broken off in November 1958. Under United Nations and American mediation, the border negotiations were resumed in 1959–60, resulting in an eventual agreement to assign adjudication of the dispute to the International Court of Justice at The Hague. Meanwhile, the level of invective of press and radio denunciations reached a new high.

The nine-to-three judgment of the International Court in 1962 in favor of Cambodia's claim came precisely at the time of the formation of the new neutralist Souvanna coalition cabinet in Vientiane. The double setback for Bangkok fanned the exasperation of Marshal Sarit and Foreign Minister Thanat Khoman. Sarit threatened to defy the court ruling, and Thanat wondered aloud why Washington had conspired to humiliate its ally in favor of a pro-Communist nation, citing Dean Acheson's role as counsel for Cambodia and Philip Jessup's membership on the court itself. Bangkok's eventual reluctant acceptance of the court decision contained a reservation to the effect that Thailand would utilize in the future any legal process available to challenge the decision. Cambodian forces took possession of the Preah Vihear site in January 1963, amid denunciations from Phnom Penh of the Thai government's contempt for its international obligations. Sihanouk thereafter made the formal and unconditional recognition of Cambodia's existing frontiers an essential preliminary to diplomatic relations.[79]

Sihanouk's Pro-Communist Orientation

Sihanouk's abrupt pro-Communist diplomatic orientation was apparently based on the conviction that it would be advisable to hedge against the possibility of a Communist victory in South Vietnam. Assuming that the American presence would effectively restrain Saigon and Bangkok, as in the Preah Vihear controversy, then the cultivation of cordial relations with the USSR and Communist China might serve similarly as a moderating influence on Hanoi. America was expected to curb hostile propaganda emanating from Bangkok and Saigon, and was asked to offer explicit guarantees of Cambodia's current boundaries. Sihanouk frankly conceded, under questioning, that his new pro-Communist tactics might eventually land Cambodia in the Communist camp, but even so, he argued, the state would survive, and that was his major concern. If Communist agitation should later develop into a serious domestic threat, Phnom Penh could always return to a pro-Western alignment. Sihanouk trusted none of his immediate neighbors, except possibly Souvanna Phouma.

The contrary American assumption that the major threat to Cambodia's security was Communist inspired was unacceptable at Phnom Penh. When Ambassador Kenneth Young proposed in 1962 from Bangkok that the United States help Cambodia defend her borders, violated by the Vietminh, by providing helicopters and amphibious personnel carriers, Sihanouk denounced the proposal as deliberately calculated to embroil his country in the Vietnam war.[80] A year later, he threatened that unless the Western powers assembled a conference to neutralize Cambodia, as had been done for Laos in 1961–62, he would invite Chinese forces to defend his borders. Although China, the Soviet Union, and North Vietnam approved the conference idea, President Kennedy countered by suggesting that all concerned countries simply submit "official letters of guarantee." When Ambassador Young repeated his offer to bolster Cambodia's military defenses, a strongly negative reaction developed in Bangkok. General Praphat Charusatien, the new deputy prime minister, threatened to cancel all of Thailand's commitments with reference to the Cold War if Cambodia were so armed.[81]

Following Ngo Dinh Diem's death in November 1963,

401

Prince Sihanouk expelled a dozen American military advisers, while keeping on their French counterparts. American efforts to repair the breach ran aground in 1964, mainly because of the worsening situation in South Vietnam and the continuing intransigence of Bangkok. Arguments that the Vietminh were the only ones violating Cambodia's soil and that the stipulated conditions for holding the proposed conference were unacceptable were to no avail.[82] America's investment of much diplomatic effort and some $350 million in aid to Cambodia since 1954 produced few results.

Sihanouk's unequivocal alignment with China occurred during an eight-day visit to Peking in October 1964. As part of the departure ceremonies at the Peking airport, in the company of Chou En-lai and Liu Shao-chi, the prince expressed regret that he was not born a proletarian and proclaimed China as Cambodia's number one friend and brother in arms. He added: "The solidarity between us is unbreakable; United States imperialism can never separate Cambodia and China." Phnom Penh's complete severance of diplomatic relations with Washington followed in May 1965.[83]

Meanwhile, Sihanouk was making maximum use of the opportunity afforded by his anti-United States stance to obtain economic and technical aid from Communist-bloc countries. China contributed two cotton mills, a plywood factory, a glass plant, and a market for some of Cambodia's exports. The Soviet bloc provided minor irrigation dams and a tire factory, plus a tractor assembly plant from Czechoslovakia and a thermal plant from Yugoslavia.[84] Russia also completed the long-promised Khmer-Soviet Friendship Institute of Technology, for which a Cambodian staff had been in training in Eastern Europe since 1961. The Institute included five faculties, each geared to admit fifty students per year, in architecture and engineering, textile technology, mining, electrical engineering, and agricultural hydraulics. It was staffed at first by twenty-five Soviet professors who lectured with the aid of French interpreters. The

Chinese and Russian ships that began docking at the port of Sihanoukville in growing numbers were suspected by Americans of landing arms for the use of the Vietcong in the Mekong delta, but such allegations were difficult to prove.

As of 1967, the only Western power that remained active in Cambodia's aid program was France. She supplied some three hundred teachers, plus technical aid for building bridges, air strips, port facilities, railway equipment, and an oil refinery. France contined to be the largest supplier of imports and was second to Singapore as a market for Cambodian rubber.[85]

Cambodia's Domestic Problems

Sihanouk's internal security measures in 1966–68 oscillated between armed repression and offers to take malcontent leaders into the government. He nationalized basic trade and credit services in order to keep Chinese entrepreneurs under restraint. When he discovered that political disaffection prevailed within the China Friendship Association, he threatened to recall the Cambodian ambassador from Peking. Meanwhile, he refused to participate in any of the Southeast Asia regional organizations, with the exception of sending observers to the successive sessions of the Mekong Valley Development Committee. Down to 1969 he also avoided connections with the World Bank, the International Monetary Fund, and the Asian Development Bank established at Manila.[86]

In reply to the initial charges made by Saigon that military supplies destined for the Vietcong were being imported via Sihanoukville, the Phnom Penh authorities in 1966 invited the International Control Commission to examine some 250 cargo manifests dating from 1964–65, in which no such incriminating items were found listed. Sihanouk flatly denied charges that armed Communists were making chronic use of Cambodian border sanctuaries, while complaining bitterly on occasion over alleged anti-Communist violations of the eastern boundary. He finally made re-

403

luctant exceptions for the latter in situations involving hot pursuit of enemy troops.[87] Peace of a sort was maintained both internally and externally, but in the face of increasing domestic and international tensions. Cabinet changes in 1967 were made without any reference to the wishes of the National Assembly or to the ruling Sangkum party.

By early 1968 Sihanouk faced a rising chorus of protest from conservative elements within the Sangkum leadership, primarily in the army. Sihanouk's Leftist orientation and the country's deepening economic stagnation and decline were challenged. The variety of accumulated industrial installations acquired mainly from Communist sources made good propaganda copy for the regime, but their operation was uncoordinated and badly administered. The surface appearance of economic progress lacked substance. The aura of modernity in Phnom Penh, with its heavy traffic, tourist shops, French-provided airport, and absence of beggars, belied the continued backward character of the largely subsistence rural economy. Industrial and trade difficulties were aggravated in 1966 by a poor rice crop and in 1967 by declining jute and cotton production. A slight gain in rubber production did little to offset such losses. Consumer import goods were in short supply and highly priced.

The prince-premier tried for a time to counter dissent by proposing private economic development, only to find that little capital and enterprise were available. The tourist trade was limited to a small fraction of its potential because of the lack of hotel accomodations.[88] Late in 1968 Sihanouk endeavored to improve relations with China and the Vietminh by declaring that Cambodians could espouse Communism if they liked, provided only that the country's independence be preserved, along with personal freedom of choice. He entered no objection to the wearing of Mao badges by Peking embassy personnel, but he demanded that China halt the flood of Red Books and badges being sent to Cambodia. He also indicated his support of both the Vietminh and Vietcong as Vietnam nationalists, but not as Communists.[89] Such maneuvering may have served temporary objectives, but by 1968 Sihanouk's equivocal tactics were reaching the point of diminishing returns. Signs of a change in the temper of Phnom Penh became evident in early 1969. In February President Nixon indicated his willingness to recognize Cambodia's boundaries in return for restored diplomatic relations, suggesting that other contemplated proposals would be conditioned on Cambodia's favorable response. Faced with the prospect of an eventual cessation of war in South Vietnam, Sihanouk undertook to prepare a place for himself at the peace table. He let it be known that following the restoration of peace, he would not oppose the continued presence of United States military forces in Southeast Asia, even in Thailand. Bangkok's spokesmen were not favorably impressed. At the same time, Phnom Penh established contact for the first time with the International Monetary Fund and the Asian Development Bank. By April 1969, a new orientation seemed definitely in prospect, although few observers expected that Sihanouk himself might have to go.[90]

Meanwhile, other important issues were raised. Washington submitted evidence to Phnom Penh in early 1969 describing the cargoes of fourteen ships that had docked at Sihanoukville from November 1966 to January 1969. These ships—eleven Chinese and three Russian—had discharged some 14,350 tons of military ordinance, far more than Cambodia could possibly use. Most of these supplies had been handled ashore by a designated trucking firm associated with army officers of the Cambodian general staff, including a member of the princely Sisowath family. The destinations were eleven indicated supply bases across the South Vietnamese border. The Washington documents also disclosed, according to reliable press coverage, that the transport operations were financed in Hong Kong dollars transmitted through the Chinese and North Vietnamese embassies.[91] Sihanouk reacted in March by roundly denouncing the presence of Vietminh and Vietcong regiments within Cambodia. Simultaneously he started negotiations at Phnom Penh with Pan American Airways for permission to use Cambodian airports in

405

return for American financing of deluxe hotel facilities at both Siem Reap and the capital.

Despite this promising start, diplomatic rapprochement was not achieved easily. When President Nixon indicated on April 16 that the United States would definitely "recognize and respect the sovereignty, independence, neutrality, and territorial integrity of the Kingdom of Cambodia within its present frontiers," Sihanouk suggested that Thailand and South Vietnam should be asked to do likewise. At the same time, he assured China that Cambodia had rejected in advance any attempted imposition of political conditions in connection with future American aid and that contemplated restoration of relations with the United States did not indicate resumption of friendly relations. He nevertheless called attention to the admitted presence of some thirty thousand North Vietnamese forces inside the Cambodian border nearest to Saigon, complete with staff headquarters, hospitals, supply depots, and rest areas.[92] One month later the pendulum swung in the other direction. Sihanouk denounced President Nixon's pledge as worthless because the phrase, "within its present boundaries," was allegedly less specific than "Cambodia's present frontiers." Finally, on June 11, 1969, an agreement was reached that permitted Washington to re-establish relations at the legation level.[93] Both Communist-power embassies outranked, in terms of protocol, the restored American diplomatic establishment.

Sihanouk's opportunist game was obviously playing out in the context of the continuing war. His efforts to divert growing dissent by reference to Cambodia's glorious past persisted. Angkor Wat demonstrated not only the country's cultural genius, but also Khmer competence in engineering. Sihanouk praised the Buddhist ethic of community concern and self-help as the forerunner of the "socialist revolution" of the modern day. But showmanship was no substitute for disciplined economic goals, government performance, and the cultivation of friendly relations with immediate neighbors. The war had lasted too long. Only peace would permit the realization of the economic development plans prepared by the Mekong Development Committee. The successful mobilization of technical and capital resources required for such multiple hydraulic installations would cost only a small fraction of the material losses incurred by continued warfare. Cambodia needed, in particular, a relatively simple water-level control facility at the top of the Tonle Sap connection leading from the Great Lake, which would raise the permanent level of the lake by several feet. The problems blocking the implementation of such plans were regional and international, with Cambodia as much victim as cause.

Sihanouk's *denouement* came in 1970, after a full year of mounting criticism from military and political opponents. The circumstances will be covered in a later chapter.

Political Fragmentation within Neutralized Laos

The civil strife that erupted in interior Laos in late 1962 and more seriously after March 1963 was highly confused. Pathet Lao opposition to Kong Lê's forces was initiated by hard-core Communist elements, even while Souphanouvong was still cooperating within the Vientiane government in compliance with the moderate Soviet line. When the Leftist prince subsequently defected from the coalition, he found himself less able to exercise control of the rebel organization than previously. The first aggressive action of the Vietminh forces under Hanoi's direction was designed to seize the strategic border areas and to control mountain paths leading southward. The action was in obvious violation of the Geneva Agreement, which prohibited the entry of foreign troops into Laos, but Hanoi had no other way to circumvent by land the barrier of the demilitarized zone (DMZ). The Vietminh also appropriated late-arriving Soviet military supplies originally intended for Kong Lê's forces near the Plain of Jars.

The American rejoinders to Hanoi's aggressive actions were also in technical violation of the neutralization

407

agreement, although somewhat less flagrantly so. Air American transport planes, run by the CIA but operating technically under private contract with Vientiane, undertook to supply the essential needs of Kong Lê's hard-pressed paratroopers. One early difficulty was that American ammunition did not fit the Russian rifles. The paratroopers nevertheless managed to withdraw and to survive as a unit. American agencies also organized and supplied by air their own "White Star" Meo guerrilla forces, who operated in hill areas adjacent to and behind Pathet Lao lines. Small arms and matching ammunition were included in bags of rice air-dropped at designated points. Such supply activities were supplemented by raids performed by some two score propeller-driven bombers bearing Laotian Air Force markings, manned by Air American pilots with the assistance of trained Thai personnel. On the ground, the regions traversed by the Ho Chi Minh Trail were infiltrated by CIA-recruited montagnard units from South Laos (Operation Hard Nose), with little success. Teams of infiltrators from South Vietnam were also introduced in Laos by various means after 1963.[94]

The Russians presumably feared driving Hanoi into the arms of China, and so brought no effective pressure to halt admitted North Vietnamese violations of Laotian neutrality. Moscow thus went along with violations by both sides, on the assumption that America would continue to support Souvanna Phouma and that North Vietnam would not provoke any final showdown with the legal Laos government. Meanwhile, Prince Souphanouvong continued to cultivate the support of minority tribesmen and anti-government Lao nationalists. He kept his own government apparatus intact and tended to regard the Vietminh alliance as only a temporary necessity. He continued to be strongly opposed to American intervention and to the conservative lowland Lao elite. Just as the Royalist Lao entertained reservations regarding Bangkok's support, so Pathet Lao leadership was distrustful of eventual Vietnamese domination.

Conservative elements within the Vientiane government,

became seriously fragmented after 1963. At least three factions could be identified. Deputy Prime Minister Phoumi Nosavan controlled only a portion of the armed police and was becoming increasingly unpopular. His youthful security officer, General Siho Lamphoutacou, joined hands in May 1964 with the top commander of the guard troops, General Kouprasith Abhay, in an effort to displace Souvanna Phouma. But they acted without consulting Phoumi, who refused to go along. Siho's hurried coup had actually pre-empted another move planned by Bangkok authorities allied with the Sananikone faction. Siho's abortive move aggravated existing friction within the armed forces of Laos, and served to undermine further Phoumi's fading power.[95] In February 1965 open fighting broke out in Vientiane between forces still loyal to Phoumi and a contingent of regular troops under the command of General Abhay. Although several cabinet ministers sided with Phoumi, Abhay's troops kept control of the airport and eventually forced Phoumi to seek refuge in South Thailand, as mentioned previously.[96]

In 1966 open conflict developed between a group of disgruntled air force pilots and the army. Eleven veteran pilots, led by the recently demoted General Thao Mah, bombed the headquarters of General Abhay and then defected to Thailand. Bangkok refused Abhay's request for surrender of the defectors, who were characterized under a Thai court ruling not as criminals but as political refugees. Mah's record as a combat pilot with many missions to his credit was in some respects far more reputable than that of the corrupt Abhay.[97]

Premier Souvanna Phouma's middle-of-the-road faction attracted increasing popularity, but it lacked organized political and military support. He received some army backing from Kong Lê, but Lê was showing signs of a mental breakdown from the continued strain, and his own troops forced him into exile in early 1966.[98] In the general confusion, the tenacious Souvanna Phouma virtually won out by default, with the support of Americans and the toleration of the Russians. He was no longer a mere figurehead; nor was he, as he had been previously adjudged by Washington, simply a weakling compromiser with the Communists. He emerged as virtually the only remaining political hope.

America's own ambiguous conduct in supporting the Meo-recruited "White Star" guerrilla and the "Clandestine Army" prevented Washington from entering any strong public protest against the more flagrant Vietminh violations of the Laotian frontiers. A kind of stand-off situation developed, involving the connivance of both the United States and the USSR.[99] Following the Tonkin Bay episode of August 1964, planes from American aircraft carriers began conducting reconnaissance and fighter-cover operations over areas of northern Laos. By 1966 American planes also flew from new bases developed in northeastern Thailand.[100] Pacification in Laos was not possible; the limit was an effort to balance increasing tensions. One casualty was the older pattern of living in a peaceful past before Laos became a focal point in the Cold War controversy.

Economic Debacle in Laos

The neutralist Vientiane authorities would not lack offers of economic assistance, once pacification should be attained. Generally speaking, French aid fitted best, although it fell far short of the total volume of the American contribution. The reputation of France as the best source for cultural and educational borrowings long persisted among the Lao elite. France provided teaching staffs for schools of medicine, law, and administration, and for vocational and secondary training in general. Additional French plans included a school of agriculture, river dam construction, cotton mills, tin mining, oil exploration, and the tapping of the enormous iron ore reserves discovered in Xieng Khouang province.[101]

American aid, both civilian and military, was so massive that it tended at times to be more disruptive than helpful. As of late 1967 American personnel assigned officially to Laos numbered some six hundred civilians and two hundred nonuniformed army men. Both the government and the economy faltered over assimilating the volume of aid. The diversion of peasant manpower to army duty, plus the general disruption of agricultural activities, put an end to the normal rice surplus output. Revenue collections covered only a small fraction of routine costs of administration.[102] A foreign exchange operation, worked out by the International Monetary Fund, Britain, Japan, and France, assisted the United States in meeting budgeted expenditures amounting to some $33 million a year. The volume of other American economic and educational aid rose from $54 million in 1956 to almost $69 million in 1968. A relatively small proportion of this assistance was capital equipment. American military expenditures on the new seventy-five-thousand-man Laotian army, both regular and clandestine, were estimated at several times the amount of the economic assistance. Such efforts blunted the Pathet Lao advance, but Lao troops were still no match for the better disciplined Vietnamese.

The government's financial situation became increasingly difficult. Imports amounted to twenty times the value of annual exports (mainly opium and forest products), while tax revenues brought in considerably less than 10 percent of total expenditures. Foreign trade earnings were not even sufficient to pay for needed bicycle imports. Revenues were derived mainly from import duties, from opium sales, and from an 8.5 percent tax on gold shipments arriving from Europe for distribution at blackmarket rates in Saigon and among the Bangkok Chinese. Transit gold shipments reached some fifty kilos in 1966–67, but thereafter suffered drastic curtailment as a result of the European monetary crisis of mid-1968.[103]

The economic gulf separating the artificial affluence enjoyed by the privileged Lao elite and the average villager living in a subsistence barter economy could not be bridged. New schools, roads, and wells served the general good, but the widespread graft that permeated government circles was demoralizing.[104] The Filipino volunteer medical aid team, called Operation Brotherhood profited similarly from American largess, both in high salaries paid participants in Laos and in the $30,000 in overhead management fees collected by Manila organizers. Actually the team failed to identify with the medical needs of Lao peoples generally. Many American-provided import items calculated to absorb the abundant dollar exchange found

411

no bona fide purchasers in Laos and were accordingly sold in Thailand for two and a half times their cost in Laos.[105]

Economic prospects within the two-thirds of the countryside not under Vientiane's control were far more gloomy than in the capital area. The Pathet Lao faction also lacked vigorous leadership and positive goals. It was even more dependent on Hanoi for directions and funds than was the Vientiane regime on United States aid, and Meo morale suffered from increasing Hanoi interference.[106] The Pathet Lao headquarters at Sam Neua near the Tonkin border was described by a visitor in 1968 as a morass of overlapping bomb craters. American saturation bombing had engendered bitter resentment against the American puppets at Vientiane, who presumably authorized or consented to the unremitting bombardment. Because of the deepening barriers thus developed, national unification could not be assumed in the foreseeable future. Rebel resistance could continue indefinitely.[107] Tribesmen who opposed the Pathet Lao received food and arms assistance via Air America drops, but they were only moderately better off. The inadequate care which Vientiane authorities had given the sixty thousand refugees from combat areas since 1960 tended to arouse more apathy than loyalty.

In contrast to the regions under Laotian control, whether Vientiane or Pathet Lao, the military camps maintained by the Vietnamese in hill country bordering Tonkin were described by visitors as being well disciplined and well defended. The North Vietnamese were in a position to dominate their several spheres of control, but they were still distinctly alien.[108] If the country survived as a political entity, it would be because Laotians generally, including Souphanouvong, would not willingly acquiesce in Vietnamese control, and because more of the Mekong Valley elite began to exhibit some genuine concern for the welfare of tribal groups in the hinterland.

Aspects of the Pacification Problem

The fiction of princely cooperation within Laos was maintained. Souvanna Phouma reserved four ministries in the official cabinet for the Pathet Lao faction. Souphanouvong was himself in theory still deputy premier and minister of economic planning, and the two brother princes continued to communicate periodically, either directly or through the Pathet Lao headquarters at Vientiane. Actual power within the government was shared by Souvanna Phouma and leaders of the powerful Sananikone faction, with which General Kouprasith Abhay was allied by marriage. Following the elections for the Assembly in 1967, Souvanna brought into the cabinet several able younger members of the conservative Boun Oum faction. The aging Souvanna continued to be the key to any reconciliation, however.

The political situation in Laos continued to defy rational evaluation along Cold War lines. Vientiane continued vigorously to denounce the Vietminh intervention, but Souvanna still maintained friendly relations with both Moscow and Peking.[109] The resident Soviet representative favored maintaining the assumed neutrality of Laos and winked at the massive character of the American aid program, including Air America operations among the hill tribes.[110] The Chinese, on their side, continued to employ several thousand laborers on the new roadways leading from the Mekong Valley border eastward into the Pathet Lao country. For Souvanna Phouma, the neutralization of Laos continued to be a political and geographical imperative.[111] He was much less disturbed than were the American and Thai observers when in 1968 Pathet Lao attacks threatened several provincial capitals in southern Laos. He alleged that Souphanouvong was interested in increasing his theoretical representation in the cabinet from four ministries to six, but argued that the rebel tribesmen were incapable of undertaking to organize any rival government. Communist ideology appeared to play a very insignificant role in the confused situation.[112]

A temporary opening for renewed negotiations was afforded by the American cessation of the bombing of North Vietnam and the start of the Paris peace talks in November 1968. Prince Souphanouvong took the initiative in suggesting the new effort. Souvanna Phouma replied by inviting the Pathet Lao representatives to assume the four cabinet posts reserved for them and to agree to integrate their armed forces with the Royal Army. The Vientiane National Assembly also opened the door for negotiations with Hanoi

413

as well.[113] Moscow favored the move, in part, as a means of reducing China's influence in contiguous Laos territory while there was still time, preferably as part of the Paris peace negotiations. Chinese propaganda, on the other hand, continued to denounce Souvanna Phouma as a traitorous collaborator with the American imperialist aggressors. Hanoi followed the more moderate Russian line, acknowledging that Souvanna Phouma could be a helpful factor in a possible settlement in Laos. In February 1969, the Soviet ambassador to Laos, Minine, visited both the Pathet Lao headquarters and Hanoi in support of the negotiation proposal.[114]

Formal negotiations began in May 1969 with the arrival at Vientiane of both the long-absent Hanoi ambassador, Le Van Hein, and Mikhail S. Kapitsa, the director of the Southeast Asia section of the Soviet Foreign Ministry. Le Van Hein met with both Souvanna at Vientiane and with the king at Luang Prabang. The premier repeated his offer to permit full participation of Pathet Lao representatives in the Vientiane government, but he refused to seek a halt in the American bombing raids in all parts of Laos as long as an estimated forty to fifty thousand Vietminh troops occupied Laotian territory. Le Van Hein's presumed counter offer was that Vietnamese forces would agree to stay out of the Mekong Valley proper, but would occupy border regions of Laos as long as the war with Saigon continued. The Soviet spokesman professed continuing concern to safeguard the neutrality of Laos as defined in 1962, while permitting the local population to resolve their own political differences. Contrary to the alarm expressed by the Bangkok press over the alleged deterioration of the situation in Laos,[115] it seemed likely that any final pacification of Laos must await the termination of the war in South Vietnam.

1. For background discussion, see John F. Cady, *Southeast Asia: Its Historical Development* (New York, 1964), pp. 550-57.

2. *Ibid.*, pp. 419-29.

3. *Ibid.*, pp. 550-51.

4. John F. Cady, *Thailand, Burma, Laos, and Cambodia* (Englewood Cliffs, N.J., 1966), pp. 21-28.

5. Roger Smith, "Cambodia," in George M. Kahin, ed., *Governments and Politics in Southeast Asia* (Ithaca, 1964), pp. 608-613.

6. Virginia Thompson and Richard Adloff, "Cambodia Moves Toward Independence," *Far Eastern Survey* 22 (August, 1953): 108-111.

7. Michael Leifer, "Cambodia and Her Neighbors," *Pacific Affairs*, 34 (1961-62): 361-64.

8. Smith, *op. cit.*, pp. 613-15.

9. Sisouk Na Champassak, *Storm Over Laos* (New York, 1961), pp. 18-20.

10. Donald Lancaster, *The Emancipation of French Indochina* (New York, 1961), p. 51.

11. Roger Smith, *op. cit.*, pp. 533-34.

12. Frank Le Bar and Adrienne Suddard, *Laos* (New Haven, 1959), p. 144.

13. Marcus G. Raskin and Bernard Fall, *The Vietnam Reader* (New York, 1965), pp. 96-99.

14. Sisouk Na Champassak, *op. cit.*, pp. 25-37.

15. *Ibid.*, pp. 40-58.

16. Le Bar and Suddard, *op. cit.*, pp. 145-48.

17. Smith, *op. cit.*, pp. 615-618.

18. Raskin and Fall, *op. cit.*, pp. 96-99.

19. David J. Steinberg, *Cambodia* (New Haven, 1959), pp. 18-21; Smith *op. cit.*, pp. 619-25.

20. Michael Leifer, "The Cambodian Opposition," *Asian Survey* 2 (April, 1962): 11-16; Leifer, "The Cambodian Elections," *Asian Survey*, 3 (September, 1962): 20-24.

21. Oden Meeker, *The Little World of Laos* (New York, 1959), pp. 153-54.

22. *FEER*, June 6, 1963, p. 529.

23. Steinberg, *op. cit.*, pp. 28-30, 40-45: Smith, *op. cit.*, pp. 636-37; Meeker, *op. cit.*, pp. 165-69. Other minority groups such as the Cham-Malays, the Lao-Thai, and tribal peoples were not serious problems.

24. Steinberg, *op. cit.*, pp. 57-58.

25. Smith, *op. cit.*, pp. 653-62.

26. Francis Renoir, "Between Two Friends," *FEER*, December 31, 1964, pp. 675-76.

27. *New York Times*, April 5, 1963, and January 19, 1968.

28. Renoir, *op. cit.*, p. 676: Leifer, "Cambodia: the Politics of Accomodation," *Asian Survey* 4 (January, 1964): 674-79.

29. Joel Halpern, *The Lao Elite* (New Haven, 1958), pp. 37-39.

30. Joel Halpern, *Tribal Peoples of Laos* (New Haven, 1958), p. 27.

31. *Ibid.*, pp. 6-29.

32. Arthur J. Dommen, *Conflict in Laos: the Politics of Neutralization* (New York, 1964). See review by Joel Halpern in *Journal of Asian Studies* 24 (August 1965): 703-04.

33. R. Gavin Boyd, "Communist China and SEATO," in George Modelski, ed., *SEATO* (Vancouver, 1962), p. 177.

34. Le Bar and Suddard, *op. cit.*, pp. 148-50.

35. Smith, *op. cit.*, pp. 544-46.

36. Halpern, *Lao Elite*, pp. 39-40; Halpern, "Observation on the Social Structure of the Lao Elite," *Asian Survey*, 1 (July 1961): 25-32.

37. Halpern, *Lao Elite*, pp. 39-40; 86th Congress, 1st session, House Report No. 546, "United States Aid Operations in Laos," (1959), pp. 11-14.

38. Bangkok opposed Souvanna's government because he refused Thailand's urging to seek assistance from SEATO on the ground that the Pathet Lao movement threatened the security of Laos.

39. Sisouk Na Champassak, *op. cit.*, pp. 61-68. The author was a member of the CDNI.

40. Joel Halpern, *Government, Politics, and Social Structure in Laos* (New Haven, 1964), pp. 4, 9-14, 34, 87.
41. Smith, *op. cit.*, pp. 545-51.
42. Joel Halpern, *The Economy and Society of Laos* (New Haven, 1964), pp. 129-134.
43. Le Bar and Suddard, *op. cit.*, pp. 157-61.
44. Meeker, *op. cit.*, pp. 92-99.
45. Le Bar and Suddard, *op. cit.*, pp. 86-87. UNESCO and the Colombo powers also contributed educational aid.
46. Halpern, *Government, Politics*, pp. 20-28.
47. Halpern, *Economy and Society*, pp. 12, 31, 73-76.
48. *Ibid.*, pp. 82-83, 162-65.
49. *Ibid.*, pp. 6-8, 20, 25, 36-37.
50. *Ibid.*, pp. 14-19, 40-41, 80.
51. *Ibid.*, pp. 84-85.
52. Halpern, *Government, Politics*, pp. 49-60; Halpern, "American Policy in Laos," *Michigan alumnus quarterly review* 67 (1967): 213-219.
53. Sisouk Na Champassak, *op. cit.*, pp. 128-38. Political classifications vary.
54. *Ibid.*, pp. 154-63. The instigator of the coup was Quinim Pholsina, who later became minister of information.
55. See Dommen, *op. cit.*, pp. 147-70.
56. Smith, *op. cit.*, pp. 551-56.
57. Barbara Halpern and Joel Halpern, "Laos and America—a Retrospective View," *The South Atlantic Quarterly* 63 (1964): 175-87.
58. 84th Congress, 1st session, House Report no. 546, "United States Aid Operations in Laos," (1959), pp. 3-6; see also B. and J. Halpern, *op. cit.*, pp. 175-87.
59. B. and J. Halpern, *op. cit.*, pp. 177-83.
60. George Modelski, "The Asian States' Participation in SEATO," in Modelski, ed., *SEATO*, p. 47.
61. Leicester C. Webb, "Australia and SEATO," in Modelski, *op. cit.*, p. 75.
62. Modelski, "The Asian States' Participation in SEATO," in Modelski, *op. cit.*, pp. 148-53, 183.
63. See B. and J. Halpern, *op. cit.*, pp. 177-87.
64. Halpern, *The Lao Elite*, pp. 85-89.
65. Saville R. Davis, "A Fresh Wind in Laos," *New York Times*, February 15, 1963.
66. Gavin Boyd, "Communist China in SEATO," in Modelski, *op. cit.*, pp. 177-80
67. Seymour Topping, "Gain for Khrushchev," *New York Times*, June 14, 1962.
68. Smith, *op. cit.*, pp. 556-60.
69. *New York Times*, August 24, 1962 and April 5, 1963; see also Dommen, *op. cit.*, chap. 10.
70. Roger M. Smith, *Cambodia's Foreign Policy* (Ithaca, 1965), p. 182.
71. 88th Congress, 1st session, Senate Document no. 12, "Study Mission to Southeast Asia" (March, 1963).
72. *New York Times*, February 4, 1965.
73. Smith, in Kahin, *op. cit.*, pp. 560-63
74. Stuart Simonds, "Laos: A Renewal of Crisis," *Asian Survey* 4 (January, 1964): 680-84.
75. For a negative view, see Frank Trager, "Never Negotiate Freedom," *Asian Survey* 1 (January 1962): 3-11.

76. Smith, in Kahin, *op. cit.*, 662-67; Seth S. King, "Sihanouk—Prince Under Pressure," *New York Times Magazine*, September 13, 1964.
77. Smith, *Cambodian Foreign Policy*, p. 178.
78. *Ibid.*, pp. 153-62, 166-70.
79. *Ibid.*, pp. 140-52.
80. *New York Times*, September 2 and 14, 1963.
81. *Ibid.*, November 29 and December 1, 1963.
82. Smith, *Cambodia's Foreign Policy*, pp. 203-5.
83. Seymour Topping, "Cambodia Hails Link with Peking," *New York Times*, October 7, 1964.
84. *FEER, 1968 Yearbook*. pp. 129-33.
85. Policy and Coordinating Staff, Bureau of Educational and Cultural Affairs, "Soviet and Eastern European Projects in Less Developed Countries of Africa and Asia" (Washington, 1966).
86. *FEER, 1968 Yearbook*, pp. 129-33.
87. *Ibid.*, p. 35; *FEER*, April 28, 1966, pp. 35, 183-84.
88. Roger Smith, "Cambodia Between Scylla and Charybdis," *Asian Survey* 8 (January 1968): 72-79.
89. *FEER*, November 28, 1968, pp. 479-83.
90. *FEER*, February 20, 1969, p. 304; *New York Times*, April 9, 1969.
91. *New York Times*, April 6-8, 1969; see also C. L. Sultzberger, "Foreign Affairs: the Sanctuary," *ibid.*, April 20, 1969. Similar evidence was reported in 1968.
92. *New York Times*, April 13 and 16, 1969.
93. *Ibid.*, May 20, June 12, 1969
94. Dommen, *op. cit.*, chap. 13: *Pentagon Papers*, New York Times (New York, 1971), p. 239.
95. *New York Times*, May 3, 1964
96. *Ibid.*, February 4, 1965.
97. *Ibid.*, October 25, 1966.
98. *Ibid.*, March 4, 1966.
99. See Dommen, *op. cit.*, chap. 13. Defense Secretary Melvin Laird, in 1969, admitted to periodic American troop invasions across the Laos boundary to rescue stranded airmen, but not to American sponsorship of Laotian forces operations.
100. *FEER*, January 13, 1966.
101. J. Halpern, "Laos, Future Prospects and their Limitations," *Asian Survey* 6 (1966): 59-64; *FEER*, July 28, 1966, p. 139.
102. Halpern, "Laos, Future Prospects," *Asian Survey*, 6, pp. 63-64; Seymour Topping, "Changes in Vientiane," *New York Times*, December 21, 1963.
103. *FEER*, August 25, 1966, pp. 365-67; *ibid.*, October 17, 1968.
104. *New York Times*, January 20, 1967; Anthony Short, "The Differential Economy," *FEER*, December 24, 1968 and January 23, 1969, pp. 161 and 614-16.
105. T. D. Allman, "The Dollar Props in Laos," *New York Times*, February 10, 1969.
106. Paul F. Langer, "Laos: Search for Peace in the Midst of War," *Asian Survey* 7 (January 1968): 80-85.
107. Jacques Decournay, "Where is America?" *FEER*, August 15, 1968, pp. 318-20.
108. Guy Hannoteaux, "The Savage Peace," *FEER*, November 21, 1968. pp. 405-7. Air America food deliveries to the "White Star" anti-Pathet Lao guerrillas amounted annually to an estimated 900 tons.

417

109. Langer, *op. cit.*
110. *FEER, 1968 Yearbook.* pp. 225-26.
111. *New York Times,* September 21, 1966.
112. *FEER,* March 28, 1968, pp. 597-600.
113. *FEER,* November 28, 1968, p. 468; *New York Times,* February 22, 1969.
114. *FEER,* February 27, 1969, pp. 340-42.
115. *New York Times,* May 5, 11, 15, 18, 1969.

XII

MILITARY RULE
IN THAILAND,
1957–69

The Army Coups of 1957–59

The triumph of Marshal Sarit Thanarat over his erstwhile political associates, Pibun and Phao, in the autumn coup of 1957 came not from any positive action on the part of the victor, but largely by default. Sarit took advantage of popular revulsion against the sterile opportunism of Pibun and the orgy of fraud perpetrated by Phao to push both of them into exile. Following the disgracefully rigged elections of February 1957, Sarit and the army permitted student and press criticism to continue long enough to deny the winners of the election any semblance of popular backing. Sarit's own newspaper, *Thanakit*, joined the chorus against the corrupt government and even echoed the Leftist demand that Pibun abandon his pro-American stance. The criticism was led by the so-called Economist party, made up of former supporters of Pridi's policies and of the Bandung Conference, defenders of the now-suppressed Hyde Park orators, and several labor union factions. To have the army supporting the anticorruption cause was indeed too good to last very long.

Sarit installed as interim premier the able civilian administrator Pote Sarasin, one-time head of SEATO.

The customary ritual election for confirmation of the new regime was staged in December 1957, after which General Thanom Kittikachorn was elevated to the premiership with some semblance of legality. The participation in the December election of only 13 percent of the eligible voters reflected the political apathy that prevailed once the "rascals" had been ousted. Sarit's "Independent candidates" dominated the new Assembly, and Sarit himself departed for Walter Reed Hospital in Washington, D.C., for prolonged emergency treatment of a chronic liver ailment.[1]

When Sarit returned to Bangkok in June, he found that Premier Thanom was losing control of the situation. Party criticism was mounting; the press was demanding reform; labor-union and student protests were denouncing the political opportunism and venality of members of the new Assembly. In October 1958, Sarit pushed the faltering Thanom aside, took over the premiership, and substituted an appointed Revolutionary Council for the elected Assembly. Exactly one year later, on his return from a trip to England for medical treatment, Sarit set up an unabashed military dictatorship. Apart from promulgating a tailor-made Interim Constitution, based on the de facto situation, he made no pretense of legality. Sarit simply affirmed that his move was necessary to rescue the country from the Communist threat that was allegedly being transmitted via Laos and Cambodia and finding expression through local political factionalism.

The new regime was ostensibly dedicated to public welfare and freedom, to human rights, nation, religion, and monarchy, but Sarit's first moves included arresting uncooperative assemblymen, along with intellectuals and student critics; closing down a dozen newspapers; and forbidding all protest meetings. When the dictator's liver ailment flared again, the United States government sent Walter Reed physicians out to Bangkok rather than run the risk of the political crisis that Sarit's third absence might precipitate. By 1959–60, Marshal Sarit had apparently qualified as an effective champion against the menace of communism in Southeast Asia.[2]

Sarit's control was convincingly unassailable. His Revolutionary Council, expanded to 240 members, drew more than half of its personnel from the armed services. The rest were selected from among conservative politicians, businessmen, professional people, academicians, and intellectuals. A safe three-fourths majority was needed for making any constitutional changes. Sarit himself commanded the army, navy, and air force and served as director general of police and as chairman of the National Economic Development Council. As premier, under the terms of the Interim Constitution, he also exercised control over the judiciary. He assumed power to suppress any activity that he deemed inimical to law and order or dangerous to the security of the state or the throne. All cabinet ministers and administrators of state enterprises were responsible to him.[3] Having enjoyed since 1952 the lucrative post of chairman of the national lottery, along with other economic perquisites of power to be described below, by 1959 Sarit was already a person of ample private means. The pattern of virtual martial rule that he established continued for more than a full decade, long surviving Sarit's own death in 1963.

The Roots of Political Apathy

The peasantry and the urban masses of Thailand had learned since the 1930s to regard political activity as generally a matter of rivalry among elite factions and therefore peripheral to their own essential interests. The electorate could entertain no realistic expectation of exercizing political control in the name of the people and in the promotion of their interests. Even if overt political activity had been legal and feasible for workers and villagers, the required organizational structures were lacking and the issues were not clearly defined. The government did not let situations arise that could provide a common grievance for large segments of the population. In any case, appeals on the part of the ruling clique for voluntary popular support were far less effective than

421

was the use of the police, the civil service, and the press to promote the government's ends directly. The people generally appreciated the government's periodic willingness to provide irrigation controls, electrical power, improved roads, and expanded educational facilities. But few voters entertained any illusions that the customary abuses of governmental authority could be corrected through any kind of election performance.[4]

Politics in Thailand, in other words, was a game played by the ruling clique for essentially personal interests. Elected assemblymen easily forgot their campaign promises and even their party affiliations. Personal mobility facilitated jockeying for advantage, and party leadership posts usually went begging.[5] Because the parties represented no articulate constituency, the disciplined military faction could exert physical control and also exploit the sanctions of bureaucratic authority. Army ministers in particular had access to graft from a variety of sources including military assistance contributions from abroad.[6]

The absence of any effective political alternative to authoritarian rule was, in a sense, a by-product of the country's avoidance of colonial control. In contrast to the other Southeast Asian states, where the struggle for national independence spawned a new revolutionary, nontraditionalist elite, Thailand witnessed the emergence of no such group. Luang Pridi's coterie of Free Thai followers was Bangkok's closest approximation to the pattern, and it had been thoroughly discredited by accusations of regicide and communism. In the Thai tradition, the Royal Court itself had initiated governmental reforms. The Westernized "promoters" of 1932 had espoused the same ends, but always within the traditional bureaucratic framework. Siam's avoidance of colonial rule had preserved legal and administrative continuity. The idea of the king as the symbol of sovereignty persisted, as did social and religious customs. Furthermore, Thailand escaped the devastation of World War II, and cultivator ownership of land was generally maintained. How long such traditional political habits could withstand mounting pressures associated with social and economic change was a moot question. In other Southeast Asian countries, democratic experiments had tended to outpace attendant social changes.[7]

No political initiative whatever could be anticipated from the Buddhist monastic order (*Sangkla*) in Thailand. The government's department of religious affairs exercised a tight rein over the monastic community; the Supreme Patriarch was a venerable figure who enjoyed little power. Rules prohibiting political activity on the part of the monks were strictly enforced, offenders being promptly disrobed. There was no prospect of duplicating in Thailand the political role played by Buddhist monks in Burma, or South Vietnam. The monasteries absorbed the time and energies of some two hundred and fifty thousand men, many of them neophytes, and required substantial funds for the support of the community. Some monasteries owned land and had other capital funds available for economic purposes, but the *Sangkla* itself exercised almost as little initiative economically as it did politically.

The Functioning of the Military Dictatorship

Marshal Sarit's economic policy was paternalistic and in many respects constructive. It promoted public improvements in fields of transportation, health, electricity, and water facilities. It encouraged private investment in many areas, following suggestions made by World Bank advisers. It also sponsored public enterprises through the National Economic Development Board, of which Sarit himself was head. The government extended compulsory public education from four to seven years, expanded the scope of vocational training, and established a new university at Chiengmai. Urban improvements included better streets and traffic control, sanitation facilities, housing regulations, and the elimination of street hawkers and beggars.

On the negative side was the government's denial of civil liberties and legal protection against the abuse of authority. Arrests were made on suspicion, and executions

423

were conducted, on occasion, without trials. Year-end Chinese arsonists, bent presumably on collecting insurance on their own property, were shot out of hand on unproved allegations that they were Communists. Labor unions were banned on similar grounds, and opposition newspaper offices were smashed by destructive gangs, while the police were busy elsewhere.[8]

Below the upper levels of administrative and military police initiative, the traditional bureaucratic system continued to function routinely. Civil service membership, under regulations that were essentially hierarchical rather than political in their application, provided security and status. Below the upper-secretary levels of the several ministries, civil service standards extended downward through a maze of services to the population in general. Alien businessmen, shopkeepers and craftsmen occupied a kind of political limbo between officialdom and the people. State-run business enterprises, operating outside the regular bureaucracy, provided sources of monetary gain for highly placed management personnel, but seldom did any profit from them reach the treasury. At all levels of the bureaucracy, it was customary to supplement wages by collection of such fees and gratuities as opportunity afforded.[9]

Entry into the civil service was conditional on passing qualifying examinations administered by various service ministries. University faculties functioned primarily as civil service institutes. A candidate's place on the register was determined by his grades on the examinations, qualified by his familiarity with applicable rules, evidence of formal education and language competence, and absence of any political or criminal disabilities. Promotion within the civil service was attained by direct selection, as were opportunities for overseas educational training.

The system discouraged administrative innovation. New procedures could sometimes be introduced on the initiative of foreign advisers, acting in cooperation with Thai associates, but only if upper-level political support was assured. Such changes proved feasible in the technical areas of fiscal administration, medical training, engineering, mining, and agricultural experimentation. Otherwise, the bureaucratic system generally provided its own built-in sanctions for conformity, with status regarded as more important than creativity. The lower ranks of the civil service had to pay deferential respect to superiors, regardless of their ineptitude or dishonesty. The traditional status system could itself sanction essential changes without incurring accusations of social disruption, but critical businessmen and political agitators, on the other hand, could be stigmatized as being in contempt of royally sanctioned authority and thus unworthy of public respect.[10]

Marshal Sarit and his military successors made wider use of the symbols of kingship than their predecessors had done. Pibun had regarded the king as a kind of personal rival who must be kept in the background and permitted only limited public exposure. Sarit, on the other hand, utilized the sacrosanct status and popularity of the royal family to enlist the allegiance of the people and to encourage their acceptance of governmental authority. This deliberate cultivation of loyalty to the monarchy involved occasional risks of royal initiative. In the course of an address at Thammasat University in 1967, the king ventured to deplore the prevalence of corruption throughout the government. In 1968, he criticized the long delay in implementing the new constitution. Subsequently, to the annoyance of the military leadership, he deprecated the indiscriminate bombing of hilltop villages of Meo tribesmen in the north.

Ordinarily, the opportunity for royalty to exercise political initiative, except as solicited by the government, was virtually nil. Thus, in June, 1968, the king did not suggest any changes in the membership of the new Senate, selected by the army leadership, or in the similarly chosen cabinet of 1969. As exploited by the military rulers, monarchical prestige was becoming a slowly wasting asset in the late 1960s. It was nevertheless manifestly obvious that changing political and economic conditions could in time generate sufficient protest in student, business, and intellectual circles to make them capable of finding support from the essentially liberal sentiments of reforming westernized royalty.[11] This actually occurred in November, 1973, when Generals Thanom Kittikachorn and Praphat Charusatien were driven from power.

An Era of Economic Accomplishment

What Sarit's military dictatorship sacrificed in terms of political freedom was redeemed in some measure by his inauguration of an era of remarkable economic expansion. Much of the growth was the fruition of beginnings made during the Pibun-Phao period, including the establishment of a modern statistics and budgeting system, the National Economic Development Committee, and the Investment Board. A team from Indiana University set up a useful training program in business administration. Pibun had also invited an expert mission from the International Monetary Fund to examine trade and marketing practices and another from the World Bank to criticize the operation of the manifold government enterprises, including railway and harbor operations and development loan services. The resulting studies were pragmatic rather than ideological in tone. They furnished a basis for effective implementation of the ideas of a number of Thai economists who had studied abroad and who were given a full hearing by the premier-dictator.[12]

A key document was the International Bank report, completed in 1959.[13] The report focused attention on the gross mishandling of the scores of government enterprises, their lack of defined objectives, their patchwork budgeting, and their complacent inefficiency. It argued that government responsibility should be concerned primarily with transportation, irrigation, and social improvement. The basic economic need identified in the report was the creation of a climate for private investment, both domestic and foreign, and curtailment of competitive public participation in industry. Agricultural production should also be

426

expanded and diversified by government initiative, and credits should be provided for small-scale business ventures.[14] Such expert outside advice provided a basis for Thailand's Six-Year Plan, which emerged at the end of the fifties under Sarit's leadership. Just as the origins of the plan preceded Sarit's advent to power, the full effects of the resulting program became apparent only after his death in 1963.[15]

The differences between the economic policies of Pibun and Sarit were less in substance than in implementation. Pibun's primary concern, until 1957, was negative; he would end alien domination of Thailand's business economy by substituting a plethora of governmental enterprises, some of them monopolistic in character. In the course of time, a total of some 140 officially sponsored projects were developed, covering a great variety of regulative and manufacturing operations. This effort to emancipate the country from alien economic control also afforded opportunity for personal profit for those placed in control.[16]

Sarit changed the emphasis to promote incentives for privately operated business enterprise, provided it was willing to solicit official association and protection. Private enterprise could afford to employ competent administrative talent, at salaries several times those of the civil service scale, minus the customary expectation of tenure and tax privileges, school fees, and housing allowances. Firms that agreed to initiate selected capital-intensive industries (such as truck assembly and the manufacture of tires, chemicals, metals, and electrical equipment) could apply for exemption from business taxes and customs dues on essential capital imports. Import rebates available for new industries in less strategic categories ranged from one-third to one-half of the normal customs rates. A similar kind of encouragement for small-scale enterprise was accorded by making credit services available from government-operated provincial and agricultural banks. The number of small-industry applicants rose in time to some thirty thousand.

Sarit himself, as chairman, transformed the restructured National Economic Development Board into a separate Ministry of National Development by absorbing a variety of relevant agencies from other government departments. Partly because of the continuing vested interests of the political and governmental elite in the scores of governmental enterprises originated by the preceding regime, Sarit abolished very few existing operations, contrary to the World Bank's recommendations. The essential change was in the encouragement he gave private investors to expand production and services.[17]

The economic gains realized by Thailand under Sarit's Six-Year-Plan (an annual GNP increment of 6 percent by 1963 and 8 percent by 1966-68) can be attributed to a number of factors. Basic was the increasing encouragement of the Chinese business community, centering in Bangkok, to participate in expanding enterprise. The results were hesitant down to 1963, but more vigorous thereafter.[18] Social assimilation of the economically elite Chinese community proved increasingly feasible. Both government and business developed a stake in correcting unproductive practices and in maintaining rapport with worldwide contacts and services. Opportunities for business training overseas, especially for sons of army generals, improved the levels of Thai technical competence to a point surpassing that found within the local Chinese community.

Expert foreign assistance, including private foundation help, contributed substantially to agricultural improvements and crop differentiation. Advances were made in maize, kenaf, jute, kapok, tapioca, sugar cane, and poultry, all made more easily marketable by improvements in interior road transportation. Supplementary employment opportunities were afforded by a number of construction projects, including transportation services and small-scale industry. It was the private sector of the economy that forged ahead. By 1964 some 86 percent of the GNP came from nongovernment enterprise, stimulated by a total of some $400 million total investment from overseas.[19]

Unfortunately the encouraging statistics on gross output per year took little or no account of the growing disparity of wealth within the country. The Thai elite—including the princely holders of vast areas of urban real estate, rental properties, and hotels—profited enormously from the construction boom in Bangkok. At the same time, the government showed virtually no concern for providing more satisfactory living accomodations for the newly arriving migrants from the countryside who crowded into urban slum areas, frequently as semisquatters. Because labor unions were outlawed, the wages of workmen and servants continued to be miserably low. Food prices and bus fares were kept down by limiting rice exports and by transportation subsidies.

The Prevalence of Official Corruption

The perennial problem of official corruption in Thailand stemmed mainly from the woefully inadequate salaries provided for civil servants, even at the upper levels. A 1957–58 survey, covering a random sampling, revealed that the top officials of the civil service received only $70 a month, and others as little as $35.50. As late as 1968, the dean of a university faculty was paid around $150 per month under the civil service; public school teachers received as little as $27. Even when cost-of-living allowances and wages from multiple jobs were added, the income of public servants was grossly inadequate in terms of rising costs. No substantial salary-scale increments had been provided since 1952. Understandably, the search for ways to augment income became a fundamental preoccupation of civil servants at all levels. The demand was particularly compelling at the upper levels because rising standards of living created expectation of status material goods, such as houses, clothing, cars, and golf club memberships.

It was a general practice of the police to take advantage of wealthy persons who found themselves in vulnerable situations and without political protection. Because the Chinese business community was generally denied access

429

to political power in its own right, individual firms or groups could be pressed to contribute financially to police protectors and official patrons as a condition for continuing in business. No laws protected alien business interests from official harassment, and noncooperative Chinese could be framed, arrested, and deported.

Starting in the late 1950s, Bangkok's military political elite, led by Marshal Sarit, elected to join up with those whom they had failed to defeat. Sometimes competent Chinese businessmen were enlisted in the government's own economic program by assigning them to well-paid managerial posts involving appropriate kickbacks. The allocation of economic permits, quotas, and licenses could be manipulated in return for contributions paid to the distributing official. A further step, initiated before 1957 and becoming widespread in the sixties, was to encourage Chinese firms to solicit official favors by appointing leading political figures to their boards of directors and allocating to them blocks of stock in the enterprise. The range of official participation extended from importers to hotel owners and even massage parlor operators.

Virtually all of the "promoter" groups, except Pibun's own clique, became heavily involved in the directorship game. By 1958 Generals Phao and Sarit and their associates had developed some 175 identifiable business connections; Phao alone was involved in 26 firms. (Generals Thanom Kittikachorn and Praphat Charusatien were secondary members of the Sarit group.) Chinese business firms could generate profits for all concerned, especially if they enjoyed access to government contracts and other favors. While scandals connected with overt mismanagement of government corporations were less easily concealed, official graft through directorships was not subject to close public scrutiny. Phao exercised control over the opium trade suppression until 1957, while Sarit ran the national lottery and Praphat the Bangkok pork-trade monopoly. The government's tobacco monopoly was particularly profitable, as was the production of potable spirits and playing cards.[20] Income available from the surge of American aid and visiting military

430

personnel in the mid-sixties, plus the growing tourist trade, added substantially to the prosperity of Thai business and real estate operators.

The extent of the abuse of political power for private profit was dramatized by the enormous fortune—some $140 million dollars—that Sarit left behind on his death at fifty-five, from accumulated lung, kidney, liver, and heart complications, in December 1963. The fortune came to light when several of the heirs contested the will, which had been drawn up in 1959. The total assets of the estate were frozen, pending examination of the sources of the fortune to determine how much had been stolen from government agencies. The bulk of the estate was willed to Sarit's second wife, who had acted as a kind of general manager, but twenty minor wives claimed titles to their several homes, and two sons contested their allegedly niggardly allotments of $50,000 each. The state treasury eventually recovered $25 million, much of which had been stolen from the National Lottery Bureau by simply not declaring winners with regularity. It was eventually disclosed that Sarit had shares in some thirty enterprises, including a match factory, a brewery, a theater, an insurance company, a bank holding a monopoly of gold imports, and several construction firms doing extensive business in government contracts. The will was finally validated, with appropriate deductions, in early 1969.[21]

Despite the damaging disclosures of General Sarit's financial irregularities, his name was the object of little criticism, public or private. It was remembered instead that he had established order, initiated an economic boom, and shown everyone who was boss. Sarit had simply been more successful in his financial dealings than others had been who were engaged on a smaller scale in similar operations. Few in high positions wanted a thoroughgoing investigation of official corruption. The standard justification of Sarit's authoritarian but allegedly benevolent government was stated by Foreign Minister Thanat Khoman, who also held the rank of colonel in the army. Western political institutions and practices, he affirmed, simply did not suit Thailand. Sarit had stabilized authority

431

through the elimination of divergent and divisive political elements intent on promoting their selfish interests.[22]

Sarit, SEATO, and Laos

General Sarit endeavored, quite understandably, to adapt the SEATO Manila Pact to Thailand's purposes. The signatories had agreed to consult on common defense measures if the security of a member state was threatened, but they conditioned any overt response to requirements stipulated in the constitutions of the several consulting states. Both Pibun and Sarit tried to transform SEATO into a defense alliance that would serve to counter alleged Communist threats from states peripheral to Thailand. When British and French representatives in particular proved unwilling to employ SEATO resources to resolve the factional rivalry developing in Laos during the middle fifties, Bangkok's insistence that SEATO intervene in favor of the Boun Oum-Phoumi Nosavan faction ran aground. The International Control Commission itself refused to judge the Pathet Lao movement in violation of the Geneva Convention of 1954. Bangkok thereupon became involved in an effort to enlist United States support of the Thai point of view.[23]

Several tactics were tried. The most effective was to interpret any move to recognize the de jure position of the Pathet Lao faction, in a pro-China gesture on the part of Cambodia's Norodom Sihanouk, or any evidence of Vietminh intrusion into areas bordering North Vietnam, as a Communist-engineered threat to Thailand and to all of Southeast Asia. The continued presence in Thailand, dating from the 1940s, of some forty thousand Vietnamese refugees from French rule was also interpreted as a potential threat from Hanoi. If and when such representations fell short of enlisting the desired American action, the Bangkok leadership repeatedly suggested that they themselves might move in a pro-China or pro-Soviet direction. This kind of blackmail was tried by Pibun in 1955, by Sarit in 1956, 1960, and 1962, and by Sarit's

432

successors on later occasions.[24] For these and other reasons, relations between Bangkok and Washington were strained from time to time, despite the general pattern of agreement. The death of Secretary of State John Foster Dulles in 1957 added to the strain. Within Thailand, the idea of fashioning a policy independent of United States influence was a perennially popular nationalist theme, even if it was not always seriously entertained.

When Marshal Sarit's group took control from the Pibun-Phao faction in the fall of 1957, Souvanna Phouma had just returned to power in Vientiane and was trying to include the leaders of the Pathet Lao faction in a coalition government that was designed to unify the country. The merger was legally confirmed in the May 1958 elections, which saw nine of the Lao Patriotic Front (Pathet Lao) candidates enter the Assembly, while Prince Souphanouvong and an associate joined the cabinet.[25] This move was anathema to Sarit. Upon his return from Walter Reed Hospital in the summer of 1958, he gave full support to the efforts of the American-sponsored Lao Committee for the Defense of the National Interest (CDNI) to drive Souvanna from power. Sarit's protégé and cousin, General Phoumi Nosavan, entered the new Sananikone cabinet as defense minister, as indicated in chapter XI. The Pathet Lao rebels thereupon reasserted their autonomy in the border provinces of Phong Saly and Sam Neua, and efforts at unification ran aground.

For approximately a year thereafter, until September 1959, Marshal Sarit maintained a strongly belligerent attitude. He proposed to dispatch Thai occupation troops under the SEATO umbrella. Failing to obtain SEATO cooperation in such an effort, Sarit's next move was to help Phoumi Nosavan push Phoui Sananikone aside in December 1959, in favor of CDNI and army rule. The usual confirmatory election was staged in April 1960, under the control of the Laotian army, which saw to it that all Pathet Lao representation was eliminated from the Assembly. This arrangement was disrupted in August 1960, when Captain Kong Lê's paratrooper battalion seized Vientiane and Souvanna Phouma resumed efforts to set up a coalition government.[26]

The ensuing Laos crisis has already been described, but not in the context of Thai politics. Marshal Sarit interpreted America's temporary acquiescence in the return of Souvanna Phouma to power as an intolerable sell-out to the Communists. During the ensuing months, he blockaded the shipment of supplies to Vientiane, again threatened direct Thai military intervention if SEATO did not act, and publicized the fact that he had initiated discussions with the Soviet ambassador concerning cultural exchanges and trade expansion. Thailand, he insisted, had no desire to intervene in Laos but must nevertheless act to defend its vital interests by preventing the alleged Communist takeover. Foreign Minister Thanat Khoman accused the United States of unconcern over Thailand's security needs. The SEATO sessions held at Bangkok in November 1960 witnessed a determined Thai effort to abolish the unanimity rule. Bangkok insisted that if the Communists continued further to consolidate their power, the Thai response would be military force.[27]

When the Thai-supported Rightist army of Boun Oum and Phoumi Nosavan attacked Vientiane in December 1960, Kong Lê's outnumbered forces, partly Soviet supplied, put up a far more vigorous resistance than had been anticipated. The Boun Oum attack stimulated widespread anti-Thai sentiment within Laos and threatened to precipitate a general war.[28] The eventual neutralization of Laos, accomplished by negotiations at Geneva extending through 1961 and into 1962, also caused a near rift in Thai-United States relations.[29] In February 1962, Bangkok dispatched thirteen units of the Thai army to the northern border province to the west of Luang Prabang, presumably to counter a threatened Pathet Lao invasion from the Nam Ta valley of Laos, which failed to materialize.

Bangkok-Washington tensions were finally eased in March 1962 by the negotiation of a bilateral agreement that committed the United States, outside of the SEATO context, to aid Thailand's defense in case of attack. Bangkok, in return, agreed to accept Souvanna Phouma's control over both the defense and interior ministries. The problem then shifted to Vientiane, where Boun Oum at first refused to comply with Bangkok's agreement. The temporary withdrawal of American economic aid from Vientiane, starting in March 1962, forced Boun Oum to surrender power, after which the desperate Phoumi Nosavan, with some encouragement from Bangkok, tried to scuttle the entire coalition arrangement. 1800 American marines were sent to the Udorn base in northeast Thailand as indicated in chapter IX, and Vice-President Johnson visited Bangkok in May to convey additional assurances. The Rightist cause collapsed in June, 1962, when the Royalist Laotian forces near Luang Prabang fled into Thailand, and Phoumi Nosavan finally surrendered control over the defense and interior ministries.[30]

The Bangkok representative was not even present at Geneva during the final month of the Laos negotiations, and the July 9 Declaration of Neutrality was signed only by the Thai ambassador to Bonn. When the United States began withdrawing the marines from Udorn shortly thereafter, Bangkok's reaction was acid. An officially inspired *Bangkok Post* article of June 24 declared that in the absence of security guarantees, Thailand "may be forced into accomodating itself to the conditions surrounding it, in the hope that the Communists, who are coming closer and closer, will live and let live."[31] The words might have been those of Sihanouk. Sarit's complete identification with the pro-Thai anti-Communist clique of Boun Oum and Phoumi Nosavan thus compounded American difficulties in the Laos affair.[32]

Thailand's Other Borders

Marshal Sarit's personal relations with Prince Sihanouk of Cambodia were far more acrimonious than those with Souvanna Phouma of Laos. Lacking in Thai-Cambodian relations were the close ties between the Buddhist hierarchies and the language similarity and ethnic kinship that prevailed among the lowland Lao on both sides of the Mekong. Sihanouk's periodic advocacy of a neutralist Laos was roundly denounced by Sarit as arrogant treachery, "a pig challenging a lion to a fight." Thai anger was further aroused over the assignment of the Preah Vihear (Phra Viharn) border temple to Cambodia by decision of the International Court of Justice in June 1962. General Praphat reflected widespread official sentiment in Bangkok when he advocated outright defiance of the decision. Dean Acheson's role as legal counsel for Phnom Penh in this case and Philip Jessup's membership on the court, plus the previously authorized delivery of American small arms to Cambodia, suggested treachery on the part of Washington. Marshal Sarit finally accepted the court's judgment under pressure from the outside, but he did not renounce Thailand's claims. He made no secret of his contemptuous opinion of Sihanouk as a vulgar, juvenile, and psychopathic upstart. In 1963 Thanat Khoman commented that "Sihanouk was kissing the crocodile [China] in the hope that he will be the last to be eaten." At the end of the same year, the Cambodian leader responded to news of the death of Sarit by staging a nationwide celebration. There was no love lost on either side.[33]

Thailand's border relations with Malaysia were also of some concern to Bangkok. Rivalry related to the predominance of Muslim Malays in the four border provinces of South Thailand and in Bangkok's historic exercise of nominal Siamese suzerainty over several of the adjacent Malay states down to the 1909 treaty with Britain. A strong cohesive factor was present, however, in the common concern of Thailand and Malaysia to suppress Communist terrorists (largely Chinese) operating along the frontier. Joint information centers regarding such activities were established at Songkla and at Kuala Lumpur. Thai border police acted primarily to protect officials posted in the border provinces. For the most part, they did not seek trouble by acting aggressively, nor did they make any serious effort to stop the extensive smuggling of rice

across the Malaysia border, which profited all concerned
—including the Thai railway officials and the police.
For the time being, the Communist menace took precedence over irredentist considerations on both sides.[34]

Thailand showed little concern over actual or potential
violations of the Burma border. Officials exercised some
oversight of Karen dissidents occupying the lower Salween
River Valley and over Burmese rebels operating near the
Three Pagoda Pass exit leading from Moulmein. Border
relations treaties were everywhere correctly maintained.
Thailand refrained particularly from making any overt
gesture toward kindred Shan State dissidents on the Burma
side beyond the Chiengrai frontier on the north.

Post-Sarit Thailand

The succession to Sarit was shared mainly by Marshal
Thanom Kittikachorn and General Praphat Charusatien.
Thanom became the prime minister, and Praphat the
supreme commander of the army and air force, plus
minister of defense and of interior. Second in line were
Pote Sarasin, as minister of economic development and
Thanat Khoman as foreign minister. Premier Thanom
acted as a kind of political front man, concerned ostensibly
with examining the irregularities of the Sarit estate,
curbing official corruption, continuing the development of
the economy and of education facilities, and, eventually,
preparing a new constitution. General Praphat was a
determined and reactionary politician who commanded
deference because he controlled the means of forcible
coercion, which constituted the essential sanction behind
the government. He was particularly disdainful of proposals
to return to constitutional government.

On the basis of Thanom's faltering performance as
fill-in premier for Sarit in 1958, many observers
viewed him as unequal to his task, yet the post-Sarit team
held together throughout the remainder of the decade.
Differences and rivalries developed from time to time
within the government elite, but all members had a stake

in maintaining a common front against continuing but uncoordinated criticism. As long as the economy continued to expand, the critics could either be ignored or be silenced under martial law as Communist subversives.[35] Bangkok's military authorities were also able after 1965 to take full advantage of the increased American military assistance available because of the worsening war in Vietnam. Such aid helped make the army and the air force, both under Praphat, unassailably strong politically, besides affording additional opportunities for private gain for the government elite in general. The Thai Navy, with its liberal traditions, was far outdistanced.

Well-publicized efforts to curb corruption reflected the government's concern to quiet the rising chorus of adverse comment, both domestic and foreign. Pote Sarasin, for example, ruled against the acceptance by high military officers of lucrative roles in the management of government corporations already operating at a loss. One general and his wife were convicted of extortion, and an air vice-marshal was arrested for gambling and embezzling the funds of the royal household. Public criticism was far from satisfied with such occasional measures, but little else could be done, for Praphat commanded not only most of the military and police power but as minister of interior he also controlled the vast majority of the civil service. The only prospect for governmental change—apart from student protest and the unlikely development of serious unemployment, which could crystalize the grievances of an articulate middle class—was the possibility of a rift within the military itself, led perhaps by jealous younger officers in the time-honored coup pattern.

Stopped from demanding long-overdue improvement of their status and wages, the mass of the apolitical civil service tended to accept in a kind of conspiracy of silence the prevailing abuses of power.[36] The 8 percent rise in living costs from 1964 to 1967 was not matched by any comparable increment in civil service pay or wages for labor. The most vulnerable non-official group, aside from the Chinese business community, were the journalists. They lived by their wits and were subject to threats of censorship and police repression. Some were in the pay of politicians; others jockeyed for government favors; few were secure enough to risk criticising the government.[37] Even so, matters in 1967-68 were improved over the situation in Sarit's time. Publication of particular newspapers was suspended from time to time, but no longer did thugs break in during the night to wreck the papers' presses with the police nowhere around.

Aspects of Thailand's Economic Development

The substantial gains in economic output realized by Thailand during the first half of the sixties were further increased during the second half of the decade. Under the Industrial Promotion Act of 1965, more than three hundred foreign firms applied for the proferred tax and customs privileges covering new ventures. The applicants were mainly Japanese and Taiwanese companies, with U.S. firms running third. The resulting industries covered a wide spectrum of products, from textiles to electronics, rubber tires, fertilizer, and cement, as well as tin smelters and oil refineries. Meanwhile foreign trade increased substantially in volume, with the deficit trade balance arising from the surfeit of imports being covered by foreign currencies earned in the tourist trade. State enterprise also expanded moderately, mainly in the improvement of transportation, education, and health services and the building of dams and power plants. By 1967 Thailand's accretions in foreign investment amounted to some $300 million, and the country's total financial reserves approximated $1 billion.

Thai capital, as opposed to foreign, tended to concentrate on the construction of houses, hotels, and entertainment facilities in urban areas where quick profits could be realized from transient foreign residents. The number of tourists reached almost four hundred thousand in 1967, an increase of 85 percent over 1964. Five entire hotels and parts of several others were leased by the U.S.

military to accommodate visiting army personnel.[38] The volume of commercial bank loans increased by 60 percent from 1962 to 1965, and the demand thereafter exceeded the available funds. Interest rates ranged upward from 15 percent per annum.

Many Thai army leaders and other officials made substantial investments in entertainment facilities— restaurants, bars, massage parlors, and brothels—to serve visiting Americans from Vietnam and other bases. The general commanding the air forces set up his own highly profitable tourist agency assigned to handle visiting servicemen who arrived by air. Private operators of entertainment premises usually found it advisable to solicit political protection by assigning to appropriate police officials a small block of stock plus memberships on their boards of directors. Bangkok authorities evinced no enthusiasm for repeated offers from the American embassy, in response to public complaints, to declare such entertainment areas off-limits to visiting service personnel.

Expansion of agricultural output fell far behind attainments in industry and construction. Paddy farmers got too little for their rice to enable them to purchase fertilizers and modern equipment. Government services available to the farmers were meager. Rice trade controls limited the exportable surplus in order to keep the domestic price stable and required exporters to pay a heavy tax premium to cover a substantial portion of the difference between the low domestic prices and those prevailing overseas.[39] At the same time, the rising value of arable land in the central plain made difficult the transition from tenancy to cultivator ownership. The government proposed to assist tenants who wished to purchase land by paying off vacating landlords in government bonds, Land Bank shares, or stock in other state enterprises, but the idea encountered strong resistance. The problem of cultivator ownership was growing because of population increase, and it would become critical if too long

440

neglected.[40] Peasants in the south were somewhat better off than those in the north, presumably because of clandestine marketing opportunities in Malaya.

Increasing American activity within Thailand (in terms of technical assistance, construction of ports and airfields and related communication facilities, and the eventual presence of some fifty thousand air force personnel) constituted an asset economically, but was something of a liability socially and politically. American construction projects, such as the Sattahip port facilities, six airfields, and connecting roads, employed a large number of Thai workers at $45 per month, which was better than the standard wage, and involved the importation of several hundred million dollars worth of construction equipment and fuel. By 1967 the United States had spent some $960 million in such aid projects, not counting the lavish spending of military and other visitors.

Problems arose on both sides. Americans complained of lack of official cooperation, governmental corruption and inefficiency, and wholesale thefts of supplies and fuel from U.S. bases.[41] Families residing in Bangkok found rental prices for houses so high that owners could recover the entire cost of new construction within four or five years. Customs regulations on consumer goods for the *ferang* (foreigner) population were both irksome and punitive. The Thai population generally resented the high income and living standards enjoyed by foreign residents. Many complained, with reason, that social and ethical standards among the young were eroding away under massive American impact, of which the R & R visitors constituted only a part. Some American residents showed lack of respect for Thai culture, government, and royalty. Bangkok's elite particularly resented the readiness of free-spending American servicemen to treat their female companions as dates rather than as prostitutes. Those Thais who were able to tap the flow of American largess were allegedly being demoralized in the process, while those who were not able to share in it were both angry

441

and frustrated.[42] Few observant *ferang* residents of Thailand questioned the conclusion that the massive culture confrontation centering at Bangkok was good for neither side.

Thailand's new Five-Year Development Plan, prepared in 1966 with the aid of a team of World Bank experts, was only partly implemented. The plan called for further diversification of production, additional attention to transportation and irrigation improvements, coupled with a conservative monetary policy. The government's agricultural program was assisted by Rockefeller Foundation help and by a United Nations-sponsored program to diversify production. An annual output growth of from 8 to 10 percent was contemplated. The government proposed to concentrate greater effort, in the form of artesian wells, water control dams, and electrical power installations, in the impoverished northeast. Some deficiencies cited by the World Bank report were ignored: the inequitable distribution of newly created wealth, the meager return permitted to peasant producers, and the tardy development of the country's potential mineral wealth and other natural resources.[43]

The most inefficient aspect of the Thai economy continued to be the government-operated enterprises. Even when technically qualified persons were put in charge, they seldom dared discipline the protégés of political leaders who were assigned to their employ; nor could managers obtain funds to cover deficits without paying deference to the same politicians. If an able engineer's performance appeared to discredit any of his bungling associates who had high connections, he was likely to be arbitrarily isolated from the operation because his presence had become embarrassing.[44] Another problem was that in various phases of economic activity potential or aspiring Thai entrepreneurs faced impossible competition with the Chinese on the one side and the government enterprises on the other.

The most promising developments included the discovery of tin ore and gas in the Gulf of Siam. Substantial offshore deposits were thought to be capable of raising Thai tin production to a level of two-thirds that of Malaysia.[45] In 1968, the Thai government signed contracts with a number of large oil companies for explorations along the coast and offshore on both sides of the isthmus. Tentative plans were prepared for the construction of an isthmian canal or pipe line.

American Military Aid to Thailand

Before 1959, American military aid to Thailand was principally in the form of improved communications and transport facilities. Some $30 million were spent developing a telecommunications system linking all the important cities of Thailand, Laos, and South Vietnam. An additional $150 million were similarly spent after 1959 to include contacts with Manila. A modern highway was completed northeastward to Korat (later to be extended to the Laos border), and railway connections were completed to the Nongkai terminus on the Laos border opposite Vientiane. The formal military assistance agreement concluded in October 1960 permitted United States planes access to more than a dozen civilian airports in Thailand and to three military fields. Substantial contributions of military hardware began in 1961 with the transfer of twenty troop-carrying but unarmed helicopters, later to be used at Udorn during the brief period of American marine occupancy.[46] Other helicopters were added in time and permitted after 1967 to carry arms. American military aid amounted to an estimated $42 million in 1966 and $80 million in 1967.

The rationale on which such assistance was solicited by the Thai related in part to the Laos situation, previously described, and in part to the increasing evidence of disaffection in the Korat plateau region in the northeast. Bangkok tended to exaggerate the Korat danger for obvious reasons. Unrest in the area stemmed from corrupt administration, chronic poverty, poor soil, bad roads, and inadequate water supply. Because of its poverty and relative isolation, the Korat region had long provided the least attractive governmental posts in the entire country and drew, correspondingly, the least able and responsible officials. One disgruntled political faction was led by Phayom Chulanout, a former member of Parliament, but the widespread discontent was largely uncoordinated. Some footloose young people were invited to North Vietnam, where they were trained in subversive guerrilla tactics. Korat discontent did provide both Peking and Hanoi a target for hostile radio propaganda, although few of the villagers had radios. It took the crisis in Laos during 1961-62 to force Bangkok authorities to start implementing its long-prepared plans for improving Korat area roads and water resources, and health and education facilities. Improvement was very slow.

At no time, however, did it appear likely that a situation could develop in the Korat area similar to that in South Vietnam. For a time in 1967, rebel bands allegedly perpetrated one official assassination per day,[47] but the insurgents had little room to hide and no easy access to food and military supplies. The excitement of guerrilla activity wore off in the face of physical hardship and inadequate incentive. Violent sabotage against governmental authority usually alienated more people than it enlisted. A reporter described the rebel groups as frogs trying to find water rather than as fish swimming in a sea of peasants.[48] For all Thai citizens, Bangkok was the seat of government, where the king lived and where authority centered. Occasionally officials assigned to the northeastern provinces realized tangible improvements, but the American-provided anti-insurgency units from South Vietnam contributed little to the solution.[49]

The many Lao-Thai northeasterners who came to Bangkok to find excitement and employment were more characteristic than were the scattered jungle guerrillas. The migrants were culturally alien to a degree, spoke a Lao dialect, preferred a diet of glutinous rice and Lao-type music, and were usually more strictly Buddhist than were the urban Thai. Many found employment driving *samlors* (three-wheeled motor taxis) or in construction projects, where the work was hard and the wages poor. Their serious

444

objectives were to save money and return with enhanced prestige to the more congenial Korat environment, where they could buy land and buffalos and live in the accustomed peasant fashion. Far from being budding Communist revolutionaries, they were highly competitive individualists. Many found temporary living quarters in the Buddhist temple quarters of the capital; others lived miserably in slum or squatter settlements. They were discreetly respectful of the Bangkok police. The authorities threatened on one occasion to implement existing regulations banning *samlors* from the crowded Bangkok streets, only to relent at the last moment after a host of *samlor* operators lined up as much-publicized donors to the blood banks of the Bangkok hospitals.[50]

Northeasterners had their continuing differences with the central valley Thai, but better administration and economic improvements, rather than military suppression and anti-Communist propaganda, were the answers to the unrest. Marxism generally had little appeal to the Thai people, partly because it was notoriously alien and probably Chinese, but also because it was largely irrelevant to social and political problems. Within the loosely structured traditional social order, where change was still taking place, the Thai population, including the neglected northeasterners, still enjoyed some opportunity for mobility.[51]

Education and Intellectual Currents in Thailand

The negative effects of Thailand's long-persistent cultural continuity were particularly in evidence in the area of education and intellectual development. Public education progressed during the fifties and sixties in terms of the numbers served, but not in the quality of the performance. Education absorbed almost as much of the central budget as did the army, and the two were not unconnected. General Praphat as minister of interior exercised control over all of the elementary school teachers, who, though not under the Department of Education, made

445

up the largest single unit of the civil service. Starting pay at the elementary teachers' level in 1968 was 540 *bahts* per month ($27), and increments averaged annually 40 *bahts* a month or two dollars. Despite some helpful monetary and advisory assistance from UNICEF sources, the standards of elementary instruction continued to be dismally low. Discontent developed over Praphat's failure to make good his repeated promises for improvement of teachers' wages, but the malcontents had no means of pressing their demands.

Education at the upper levels, including the universities, was far more closely linked to civil service standards than to any meaningful intellectual orientation with the outside world. A high school diploma was needed to qualify for a low-level, class-four appointment, while a university degree was required to merit class-three status. Qualifications for both categories were limited to the memorization of requisite factual information and familiarity with governmental procedures. Because overseas scholarships were allocated mainly for more scientific and professional training, scholarly study in such fields as philosophy, religion, and history—subjects that were assumed to have little bearing on practical governmental affairs—was neglected. Because no civil service examinations were based on historical knowledge, the subject attracted few male students and not the brightest group of the girls. Hence, few recipients of advanced degrees were prepared to view their cultural heritage in a detached or critical fashion. Educational concentration on civil service requirements encouraged conservatism and caution even among those who otherwise might have reason to question the status quo.[52]

Political favoritism played an important role in appointments to higher levels of the civil service and selection for overseas study, which became the stepping stone to the higher ranks. It was the sons of generals who now qualified for overseas scholarships, just as the princes had done prior to 1932. An important American oil company contract of 1968, for example, required that $100,000

446

be set aside annually for educational training in the States covering disciplines relevant to the oil industry. Company officials were dismayed to find that only 10 percent of the list of Chulalongkorn University candidates nominated for such scholarships possessed the academic competence and ability to do the work. But no official would take the risk of altering the list, partly because General Praphat himself was rector of the university. On other occasions, university administrators were known to have altered students' grades in order to give advantage to favored individuals.[53] Acquiring of university degrees and passing civil service examinations called for memorizing formal lecture notes; the same was true for technological training. For this and other reasons, creative scholarship in the humanities and the sciences tended to be neglected. The rules of the game called for following the Chulalongkorn University motto of "seniority, order, and tradition." Meanwhile democracy survived only as a verbalized ideal, while historical study called for repetition of accepted details, duly mythologized and romanticized.[54]

What little genuine intellectual activity was going on within professional circles—law, clergy, journalism, and academia—was generally lacking in profundity, originality, and critical stimulation. The intelligentsia valued books as status symbols rather than for reading purposes. University students accumulated lecture notes, and the lecturers themselves seldom visited the libraries. Peace Corps observers reported that high school teachers with college degrees usually read nothing at all. The limited circulation of books cancelled out any economic incentive to write and to publish. Original editions of books of recognized value rarely exceeded two to four thousand copies.

Barriers to freedom of discussion were culturally as well as politically imposed. Heretical and critical ideas were taboo, and reinterpretations almost invariably fell within the accepted framework of custom. The prevailing norms for literary excellence were clarity, persuasiveness, and entertainment, but always in support of traditional value systems. Advantageous association with persons of influ-

447

ence took precedence over detached scholarship. The most widely distributed book in Thai translation (some twenty-seven thousand copies) was Carnegie's *How To Win Friends and Influence People.*[55]

On balance, the stultifying influence of conservative tradition in Thailand far outweighed the influence of emerging critical comment. The most articulate innovators found it advisable to conform outwardly, once they got married, found a job, and acquired a stake in the established order. Only a few incorrigible rebels dared to challenge the prevailing climate of opinion. Generally speaking, the Thai feared the Chinese and communism, looked contemptuously at their regional neighbors, and resented Western criticism of things Thai. National pride and the romanticization of tradition produced few radicals. Even so, the direct impact of the outside world on Thailand (Bangkok in particular) and the demands for social and governmental change inherent in the economic advance of the new, educated elite were to have an increasing rather than a diminishing effect.

Thai-American Relations

Although the American military presence in Thailand was welcomed in the crisis situation of 1964–66—even to the point that contingency arrangements were made for the use of U.S. ground troops to defend the Laos border—it became irritating when prolonged to 1968–69. For one thing, Bangkok became increasingly sensitive to hostile allegations emanating from Peking and Hanoi, and echoed in Phnom Penh, that Thailand was becoming an American colony. The receipt of American weapons and extensive construction and aid programs, all of which carried financial perquisites, continued as before to be welcome. But when the buildup of American air force personnel attained thirty-five thousand by 1966 and more than forty-thousand by 1968, without exerting any decisive effect on the outcome of the war in Vietnam and Laos, the American presence reached the point of diminishing political returns for Bangkok.

The assignment of the actual number of American troops was kept secret through 1966, and for many months thereafter no public acknowledgement was forthcoming that a major portion of bomber operations against the pro-Communist forces in Laos and Vietnam originated from protected bases in Thailand. Large B-52 bombers used the 3.5 kilometer runways of U Takeo airfield near the new port of Sattahip on the Gulf of Thailand. American jet bombers flew from Takli base in central Thailand, and fighter bombers from the Korat field. Lighter aircraft, including reconnaisance planes and helicopters, used three other American-built fields near the Laos border. Don Muong airport near Bangkok served as a distributing center for U.S. aircraft, both military and transport. By 1969 the total American investment in military facilities in Thailand amounted to an estimated $1.5 billion.[56] A nervous Bangkok officialdom affirmed repeatedly that the Americans were there only on invitation.

Even more distasteful to Bangkok were the occasional American proddings toward administrative reform and the somewhat ironic offers of American expertise, gained in South Vietnam, against rising guerrilla insurgency in Northeast Thailand. Such expert help was accepted in 1966, but reportedly only when accompanied by grants of some $40 million dollars for police support and $60 million for army units assigned to the pacification tasks.[57] In the absence of any real improvement in official performance, the American funds that poured into Thailand provided mainly additional opportunities for favoritism and corruption.

The Hanoi-trained guerrilla agitators recruited from the Thai-Lao population of the Korat were usually local boys whose formal education had not gone beyond four grades. Their prospects were otherwise bleak, and Hanoi agents offered them not only further education and moderate compensation, but participation in what promised to be an exciting enterprise. The Thai security forces sent in to put down such subversives often aggravated local unrest by mistreating those villagers who were not rebellious. The presence of thousands of American troops at the four Korat plateau airfields, whatever their contribution to Thailand's security, served to aggravate official graft and to provide a target for Hanoi's anti-imperialist propaganda. Marxism as such had little or no appeal to the Korat plateau population, who continued to function within their traditional social and ideological framework.[58]

Apart from strengthening the political and military domination of Thailand by Bangkok's army dictatorship, America's role in the country had little relevance to the alleged threat of Communist domination. Neither North Vietnam nor China had any compelling reason to violate Thailand's Mekong River boundary or to seek political control. The country's total rice export potential of less than 1.5 million tons per year would satisfy less than 1 percent of the food needs of China's 750 million people. Hanoi, of course, wanted to disrupt guerrilla fashion the operation of hostile air bases in Thailand, but the Vietminh armies seldom approached the Mekong boundary. The American presence thus related to no immediate threat of invasion, and the corrupting influence of the dollar inflow contributed nothing to ease popular resentment over rising prices and depressed income throughout most of the countryside. Government reform efforts whether constitutional or administrative continued to languish.[59]

As of 1967, Thailand's leadership was prepared to see the profitable American war against the Communists continue indefinitely so long as the fighting took place elsewhere than on Thai soil. They were unhappy, therefore, when President Johnson halted the bombing of targets in the Tonkin sector of North Vietnam in the spring of 1968, following the Tet offensive, under circumstances to be described later. Then came the hesitant Washington reaction to the Pueblo seizure off the Korean coast, the eventual cessation of all North Vietnam bombing, the initiation of the peace talks at Paris, and the beginnings of American troop withdrawals from South Vietnam in 1969. Such developments suggested to Thai the ominous conjecture that the American intervention was either unable or unwilling to establish its authority throughout the region and that an inconclusive peace for either South Vietnam or Laos would leave Thailand vulnerable as the principal Southeast Asian collaborator with the United States. For domestic reasons as well as international, Thai spokesmen in 1968-69 began to characterize the American military presence in their country as both objectionable and unnecessary. In the summer of 1969, President Nixon and Foreign Minister Thanat Khoman were reported to be agreed that it would be unwise to use American troops in Thailand for putting down domestic rebellion. The contingency plans of 1964-65 for possible use of American ground forces against an overt invasion via Laos were no longer applicable. Thanat expressed confidence that Thailand could contain internal threats without American help, and suggested that China was too heavily involved domestically and along its Soviet frontier to play any major role for the time being in Southeast Asia. He concluded that once the war in Vietnam was ended, American forces would be expected to withdraw from Thailand, save for possible agreement as to their continued use of Port Sattahip and the adjacent Takeo airbase.[60]

Thailand's Relations in Regional Context

Foreign policy declarations by Thai government spokesmen had long been related to domestic politics as well as to international bargaining. Thus the Sinophobe Marshal Pibun had paid temporary deference in 1955 to Chou Enlai's Bandung Conference idea of peaceful coexistence. General Sarit, when angling for Pibun's overthrow in 1957, registered a desire for closer trade relations with Peking as an appeal for local Chinese support, a position which he repudiated in 1958.[61] General Praphat, in 1963, had suggested greater flexibility with respect to the Cold War dichotomy, but again only temporarily. Thanat Khoman made the same kind of calculated ploy in 1969 in proposing secretly the opening of diplomatic and commercial conversations with Moscow, Hanoi, Peking, and Pyonyang, only to run afoul of Praphat. The American reporter who disclosed the information about Thanat's proposals was summarily expelled from Bangkok as a troublemaker.[62] General Praphat reacted by directing his trade spokesman to interview the resident Taiwan ambassador, denouncing Thanat's trade proposals. Thanat was later driven from power in the military coup of 1971. It must be assumed that knowledgeable foreigners discounted periodic Thai maneuvers. Even so, the basic trend in 1968-69 was clearly a cooling off of American-Thailand relations.

In pursuit of the more immediate goal of regional cooperation within Southeast Asia, Thanat Khoman demonstrated a more consistently positive record. With the exception of the short-lived Maphilindo Association of 1963, from which Thailand was omitted, Bangkok was in the vanguard of all such efforts. The headquarters of SEATO was established at the Thai capital, with Pote Sarasin acting for a number of years as the organization's secretary general. Despite its limited Southeast Asian membership (only Thailand and the Philippines) and the virtual defection of France and Pakistan, Thanat made repeated but vain efforts in the Sarit tradition to prod SEATO into accepting some measure of responsibility for halting the rebellion in neighboring Laos. Denied any meaningful security role, SEATO eventually concentrated on developing a regional program for the improvement of health and education, including the proposed establishment of a Graduate College of Engineering at Chulalongkorn University. Such activities served to conceal both SEATO's ineffectiveness as a security shield and its essential function as a clearinghouse for anti-Communist intelligence.[63] From first to last, SEATO was more façade than substance.

The Association of Southeast Asia (ASA), which included Thailand, Malaysia, and the Philippines, was founded at Bangkok in July 1961. Its purpose was to promote regional cooperation in the social, cultural, and economic fields;

more specifically, the stated objectives included the possible promotion of a regional common market, a co-ordinated industrial development program, and economic specialization.[64] Such goals proved completely unfeasible, so that the organization's actual accomplishments—beyond exhortation to friendship and cooperation—were virtually nil.

Thailand was also one of four Southeast Asian members of the Asian and Pacific Council (ASPAC), which was initiated at Seoul, South Korea, in June 1966. The Council also included Malaysia, South Vietnam, the Philippines, Taiwan, South Korea, Japan, Australia, and New Zealand. Despite the obvious anti-Communist orientation of the Council members as a whole, their interests and concerns varied widely. At the second annual session of ASPAC, held at Bangkok in July 1967, Thai spokesmen took the lead in efforts to solicit Council cooperation in stemming the tide of "Communist aggression" that allegedly continued to pour fuel on smoldering discontent and to put lethal weapons in the hands of subversives. Japan's foreign minister explained that his only concern in the Council was to establish a forum to promote a candid exchange of views covering common political, economic, and social problems in a relaxed atmosphere. The Malaysian spokesmen responded by warning against establishment of overlapping agencies. The cautious Australian representative advocated that the Council function only to clarify problems of common interest.[65]

The final ASPAC communiqué in 1967 opposed further nuclear testing, expressed sympathy for the plight of South Vietnam, but was otherwise not anti anything or anybody. A Laos observer who was present expressed gratification that his views were taken into account in the final communiqué, but the precise points were unclear. In the end ASPAC pushed political and security matters aside. It set up in Taiwan a Center for Cultural and Social Exchange, a registry of technical experts, and a center for food and fertilizer technology, plus a kind of economic brain trust in Bangkok.[66]

453

A subsequent effort to obtain a more general integration of Southeast Asian countries was made at Bangkok later in 1967, with the launching of the Association of Southeast Asian Nations (ASEAN), which superseded ASA and broadened its membership to include Indonesia and Singapore. As in all previous instances of attempted regional integration, Thanat Khoman maintained that the group should also be willing to accept security responsibilities, but he argued to no effect. On this occasion, such action was not at all feasible because two members, the Philippines and Malaysia, were quarreling over the disposition of Sabah in North Borneo. President Marcos of the Philippines managed to echo Thanat's hope that ASEAN could become something more than a cultural and economic clearinghouse by concerning itself with the coordination of regional defense efforts and with the ordering of diplomatic alignments for security purposes. Eventually ASEAN, like its predecessors, placed priority on promoting regional economic development, although within a world context and with diminishing concern for the strict avoidance of power-block affiliations. How strongly the United States government may have encouraged such efforts at regional cooperation was never clarified.

The difficulty of achieving regional agreement, even on a fairly simple issue, was illustrated at Bangkok in the spring of 1969, when a UNFAO meeting tried in vain to formulate regulatory measures covering the rice trade, in particular the disposition of surplus miracle rice grown in the Philippines and Thailand. Japan and Australia raised sharp objections to providing any special privileges, and even the two countries involved developed divergent views.[67] Regional coordination, however desirable, was destined to remain a perennial problem.

Adoption of Thailand's New Constitution

One of the major concerns espoused by Prime Minister Thanom Kittikachorn following Sarit's death was to press for an early drafting of a new constitution, partly to brighten

Thailand's image in the West. The work of the drafting committee was accordingly accelerated, and the document was accordingly placed before the appointed reviewing Assembly in November, 1964.[68] Some press comment was elicited at the time, but more than three and a half years passed before the document was formally approved and proclaimed in June 1968. The plan called for an elected House, an appointed Senate, and a cabinet that was ostensibly royally appointed but actually responsible to the military leadership dominant in the government. Adoption was postponed in 1965, 1966, and 1967 allegedly because of critical events in Laos and South Vietnam. The government was clearly reluctant to encourage any political activity or free discussion during what was considered an emergency situation.[69] General Praphat, the proposed constitution's most determined opponent, expressed concern in 1966 over what would happen in some future election if the Communists should endeavor to take over the country by buying the necessary votes.[70]

The discussion of the document was highly inconclusive. Pote Sarasin led the pro-election group within the government, although he admittedly saw no alternative to military rule. Bangkok's leading journalist, Kukrit Promoj (the brother of Seni, a descendant of Rama II, and a member of the drafting committee), took a cynical view of the prospects for the development of any real democracy under the proposed document. He pointed out that, apart from the army, organized articulate political parties did not actually exist. Critics entertained ideals without ideology, attacked grievances without a chance to enlist popular backing, and lacked financial support to champion their unformulated remedial programs. Seni Promoj, whose political connections went back to the Free Thai movement and the Democratic party, was prepared to challenge army rule in the Bangkok-Thonburi elections. But he also was under no illusions that an elected Assembly under the proposed constitution could alter materially the character of the government.[71]

Repeated postponements occurred. Although revision of

the constitution was completed before the end of 1966, the proposed submission of the document to the appointed Constituent Assembly on January 1, 1967, was put off. The next selected date—December 5, 1967, the king's own birthday—was also passed over. Meanwhile, in October 1967 Praphat took over full command of intensified anti-insurgency efforts, alleging that pro-Communist agents from Hanoi had actually infiltrated the government and were the source of delays in ratifying the constitution.[72] The document finally had to be approved at three separate readings by the ad hoc Assembly and then transcribed on palm leaf books prior to submission to the king. Finally, the Royal Household Bureau had to designate an auspicious time for its presentation.[73]

Articulate elements of the urban population became increasingly impatient over the delays. *Siam Rath*, Kukrit's paper, denounced the government's allegations that the imminence of the Communist threat would probably prevent the holding of elections, which were required within 240 days after the promulgation of the constitution. The Communists, argued the editor, exercised no effective control anywhere in Thailand.[74] The *Daily News* of March 1 alleged that the government itself, not the Communists, threatened to deny the voters their rights. Other papers called for new faces in politics representing the younger generation and ridiculed the pretense that no auspicious day could be found to present the document to the king before September 1968.[75] The king himself finally joined the protestors, claiming that he saw no reason to delay longer the promulgation of the constitution and adding that numerous propitious days could be found.

In the preliminary elections for district and provincial councils, held in December 1967 and January 1968, candidates were forbidden to hold meetings or to discuss political issues, national or international. The elected bodies so chosen were supposed to function only as administrative agencies and were intended primarily to identify local leaders for the convenience of Bangkok. These arrangements drew acid comments. Seni Promoj asked why elections

MILITARY RULE IN THAILAND

should be held at all if party leaders and elected assemblymen and councilors were forbidden to consider political grievances and to propose appropriate remedial measures.

Two incidents at the northern provincial capital of Chiangmai illustrated the difficulties of achieving governmental decentralization. Bangkok took an assembled group of provincial assemblymen to task for daring to exclude from one of their regular sessions the noncooperating representative of the central government in order to be able to discuss freely among themselves the selection of a complaints committee. Also disapproved by Bangkok was the distribution of mimeographed lists of nominees for the offices of speaker and deputy speaker of the assembly. Such illegal political actions, Bangkok charged, could generate divisions between officials and the people and thus invite chaos.[76] The government also objected to a meeting of mayors and their under-secretaries at Chiengmai, functioning as members of the League of Municipalities. The objective of the sponsors was to inform themselves on governmental policy and to exchange views on how to improve municipal government. The reporting editor, for example demanded that General Praphat's Ministry of Interior, which controlled municipal government policy, revise its approach and remedy the numerous problems raised.[77] Time seemed to be running out for dictatorial rule from Bangkok.

The Constitution Itself

The primary concern of the authors of Thailand's new constitution, as finally promulgated by the king on June 8, 1968, was apparently three-fold. The document was designed, first, to present to the outside world an attractive image of the "democratic" character of Thailand's government; second, it would support the continuing exercise of authority by the military within the aura of

457

traditional royal sovereignty and prestige; and third, it endeavored to afford to political groups and their elected assemblymen some minimal opportunity to influence policy.

The basic statements of the rights and liberties of the Thai nation (Articles 24 to 44) covered all the time-honored guarantees of freedom: equal protection under the law, freedom of religion, presumption of innocence until proved guilty, exemption from arbitrary imprisonment, and the inviolability of one's dwelling and property under law. The exercise of freedom of speech, press, and assembly were nevertheless expressly limited by legal restrictions designed to maintain public order and good morals. In any case, these freedoms were all subject to suspension under emergency conditions. Voters must be Thai nationals and at least twenty years of age; the mentally infirm and persons held under court or prison detention were excluded. The Buddhist clergy were explicitly denied political participation. Members of the Parliament were free to act in the chamber as individuals, but not under mandate to any organized group or party. Acting constitutionally as members of Parliament, they would be exempt from arrest, detention, or other legal liability. The democratic façade was skillfully contrived for external observers.

The emphasis on royal authority was intended primarily for domestic consumption. Thailand was declared to be a democracy, with the king exercising the functions of sovereignty, which derived inherently from the Thai nation. Army rule was nowhere mentioned. The king was above the law and provided the essential sanction for governmental authority. His appointive Privy Council functioned apart from the cabinet, the elected Parliament, or political parties, following the traditional Thai pattern. The king was also designated as head of the armed forces and was empowered to declare war and to proclaim martial law. He could dismiss government officials below the under-secretary level, dissolve Parliament, and authorize new elections. Subject to the countersignature of the army-selected president of the Parliament, the king appointed the Senate and the Council of Ministers.

The wording suggested a reversion to pre-1932 standards, but in actuality the king could act only on the advice of his ministers, who themselves functioned apart from any effective parliamentary control in accordance with the policies determined by the Council as a whole. The king changed not a single name of the lists of senators and ministers submitted by army leaders for his approval in July 1968. The emphasis upon royal authority and patronage as defined in the constitution could become politically significant in some future contest for control within the military itself, but hardly otherwise.

The elected membership of the House of Representatives outnumbered the senators by the ratio of four to three, but the legislative powers of the House were limited. All money bills must carry the prior endorsement by the president of the Council of Ministers, and the budget of the previous year remained in force until a new set of appropriations was approved. The military elite selected and controlled the membership of the Senate and promoted the candidacy of official party nominees for the House, who would invariably constitute the largest and best disciplined single party unit in the lower chamber. Proposed constitutional amendments must be approved by a two-thirds vote of the combined House and Senate, and even then might be remanded for a plebiscite by joint decision of the president of the Parliament and the king.[78]

Despite its limitations, the very promulgation of the new constitution opened the door for public discussion of a number of political issues that had previously been taboo. Several newspapers pressed Prime Minister Thanom to explain his selection of members of the army-dominated Senate. Why, for example, had he omitted the name of the former president of the Constituent Assembly and one time premier, Thawee Bunyaket, who had on several occasions tried to accelerate the approval of the constitution? Thanom's halting reply was that he did not want to infringe on Thawee's resolution not to be involved again in politics. The sixty-one senators on active army duty had been chosen, he said, because they had played important roles in maintaining national security. The additional thirty service personnel, he continued, were actually retired and now functioning in civilian capacities. Eight of the twenty-nine designated civilians had served on the committee to frame the constitution. The remainder were knowledgeable persons who had previously been national assemblymen or were outstanding in their several professions.[79]

A more potent issue raised by the press in the summer of 1968 concerned the declining prestige of the civil service and the official abuse of power.[80] A series of anonymous articles in the *Bangkok World*, entitled "Civil Service Performance and Morale,"[81] pointed out that growing dissatisfaction among civil servants of classes two and three had produced some nine thousand resignations between 1962 and 1967. The main problems in the Civil Service were overstaffing,, underpay, compulsory moonlighting, and widespread dishonesty. Modest salary increments introduced in 1967 had not kept pace with rising living costs, not to mention the larger earnings currently available in private sectors of the economy. Single-step annual increments amounted to only $7.50 per month, and less than 10 percent of the employees at any given grade could merit double promotions. Top positions were coveted allegedly because of the bribes and commissions available to the incumbents, and economic expansion was hindered by official demands in the form of gratuities, gifts, and shares of stock. Only the rich and those with advantageous political connections could obtain selection for overseas study.

The indictment concluded as follows:

> The Thai Civil Service no longer represents honor and efficiency. . . . Many dedicated officials have resigned . . . because . . . their colleagues rely on the Service for a dishonest living . . . , (often) their superiors. . . . [Needed was the emergence of] a new code of morality, where civic and national responsibility, . . . personal integrity and self-respect . . . , and promotion by ability are the components.

460

The remedial measures proposed included a general reduction of staff, removal of the universities from civil service control, the exercise of greater care in appointments and tenure decisions, systematic purging of the unfit, leading to complete overhaul of the entire structure.[82] Such candor suggested the degree to which the mere appearance of the new constitution had changed the political climate. It also explains why the constitution was destined for early repudiation.

Thailand and Vietnam Peace Negotiations

Bangkok's lack of enthusiasm for the Paris peace talks reflected its dismay over the kind of settlement likely to emerge and concern over America's diminishing role in Southeast Asia. Officially Bangkok hoped that the Paris negotiations would run aground, that the bombing of North Vietnam would be resumed, and that Americans would decide to stay on in the region until Thailand's Communist enemies were completely destroyed.[83]

A leading Thai-language paper, *Siam Rath* argued editorially in early 1968 that America's earlier failure to eradicate Communist aggression in Korea and Laos had contributed to the stalemate in South Vietnam. The United States should therefore take advantage of the Pueblo seizure to revive the war in Korea. A negotiated peace in Vietnam might entail worse consequences than would result from overt Communist subversion, for it would probably see American forces pull back into Thailand itself.[84] Thanat Khoman argued that no successor coalition governments in either Vientiane or Saigon could be expected to survive the withdrawal of American financial support, on which both had become abjectly dependent, so that an eventual Communist takeover in both countries had to be assumed.[85]

Thailand's actual leverage with respect to influencing the terms of a possible peace settlement was very limited. Some six thousand ground troops had been sent in 1967 for a year's service in South Vietnam, and they had been replaced by twice that number in 1968. The troops had on the whole given a good account of themselves, although they were used mainly in noncombat roles, with the result that their casualties were minimal. If and when the peace negotiations reached the stage of considering tangible details, Bangkok as a participant hoped to be permitted to share in formulating the terms of any final settlement.[86] The limitations on Thai influence arose from the fact that the entire expenses· of the services performed by the two Thai contingents had been defrayed by the United States, at a cost some three times that required for the services of comparable American units. Bangkok was also compensated by gifts of American aircraft and other armament not connected at all with the service in Vietnam.[87] In early 1969 these gifts had reached the magnitude of surface-to-air missiles. Thailand's participation in the Vietnam War had cost Bangkok very little.

The only really articulate critic of the Bangkok government's policy was the conservative Seni Promoj. Speaking as head of the Democratic party, he pointed out that Thailand's panicked acceptance in 1964–65 of American offers to prepare and utilize Thai airfields for belligerent purposes had opened the country to possible retaliatory raids from both the Pathet Lao and the Vietminh. A better policy, he argued, would be to try to come to terms with the victims of American bombing attacks. When President Nixon visited Bangkok in mid-1969, he paid deference to the sensitivities of the Thai government by not asking to confer with critic Seni Promoj, as he had done with opposition leaders in the Philippines.[88] Thanat's own insistence that American forces must be prepared to withdraw from Thailand at the end of hostilities in Vietnam was related to the problem of finding a basis for settlement with Hanoi.[89]

The incipient Meo rebellion in the northern Thai provinces adjacent to the cis-Mekong Samaboury area in Laos was only peripherally associated with the Pathet Lao problem. Most of Thailand's Meo and Yao tribesmen were

462

fairly recent immigrants from the north and had experienced little direct contact with Thai government authorities. Distrusting lowland interference, the tribesmen resented in particular Bangkok's efforts to resettle several thousand of them in valley areas that were more easily capable of surveillance, and they had accordingly returned to their cooler hilltop retreats. Small insurgent bands, recruited from them presumably by rebel instigation, took vengeance locally on hated police and welfare officials with whom they were in disagreement.

Stigmatizing such insurgency as a Communist-instigated plot to set up an autonomous state, General Praphat's forces attacked "rebel" Meo villages by air strafing, using napalm. The result was to alienate previously non-hostile tribal elements.[90] American and other protestations of the excessive severity of such policies found welcome support from King Bhumiphon himself, who commented to University students that few Meo even knew what communism was about, and that the problem of tribal relations was less simple than some military leaders assumed.[91]

Parties, Issues, and Elections

A number of weeks passed following the official promulgation of the new constitution before legislation was enacted to permit the legal organization of political parties. The officially-sponsored United Thai Peoples Party (UTPP) was fashioned on authoritarian lines in the late summer of 1968. Prime Minister Thanom Kittikachorn, stressing national unity, social advancement, prosperity, and security, initiated the party's formation, while Air Force General Dawee Chulasapya acted as its Secretary-General. The party's nucleus included a number of nonmilitary personnel, some of them former members of the National Assembly, plus an amalgam of social workers, business, and professional leaders. The basis for their selection was challenged, because the political records of some members was dubious, while other selectees were entirely new to politics. Furthermore, the size of the party

463

bureaucracy was insufficient to satisfy the expectations of all politically ambitious candidates, especially those residents in provinces distant from Bangkok.[92]

Some of the malcontents organized the rival Free Peoples League, which enlisted the backing of General Praphat as chief patron. Announcing itself as strongly anti-communist, the League's membership included more than one hundred provincial leaders who had previously been members of Parliament and who aspired to regain such status. For a number of months it appeared likely that a political rift might develop within official ranks. In late September, Thanom, Dawee and other UTPP leaders were invited to attend a League rally at the official military residence of General Praphat. Before some four hundred guests, Thanom affirmed his political solidarity with Praphat both in the government and by reason of family ties and exhorted members of the League to strive for unity and national development. In rejoinder, League spokesmen demanded substantial changes in the UTPP character that would permit their participation in party affairs.[93] The UTPP leadership staged its own joint session on November 22, 1968, at which League spokesmen charged ominously that both the structure and the policies of the official party were borrowed from communist patterns. This unseemly feuding prompted press comment to the effect that the reading public was wearied of such sterile controversy, while substantial grievances and major policy issues were being ignored.[94] It was not until the very last weeks of the campaign that General Praphat finally indicated his full support of the official list of candidates. Many of the pro-Praphat malcontents who could not get on the party ticket ran as independents.

The only effectively organized nonofficial party was the conservative Democrat party, or *Prachathipat*, a group formerly led by the deceased Khuang Aphaiwong and now by Seni Promoj. The party centered at Bangkok and included in its ranks prominent navy personnel as well as royalists and professional men. Seni and his followers were at work long before formation of the party was legally authorized. The Democrats participated in the municipal elections of the capital area held in July 1968 and won approval of nearly all of their candidates for councilmen. Their activity was later extended outward from the capital as far as limited financial and personnel resources would permit. But like other opposition groups, they were denied official sanction to hold meetings or to establish branch headquarters in provincial areas. Whereas Democrat party rallies in Bangkok attracted enthusiastic crowds, those of the UTPP were ill organized and marred by heckling. The Democrat party eventually nominated 192 candidates, only 27 less than the full slate of the UTPP. Seni and associates were under no illusions that the new constitution was adequate or that prevailing electoral procedures afforded any real prospect of defeating the official party. They were nevertheless determined that protest sentiment should achieve some kind of articulate expression.

Considerably to the Left of the conservative Democrat party but far short ideologically of the hardly visible China-sponsored Thai Patriotic Front were a number of minor party groups. The most articulate among them were the Peoples party, or *Prachachon*; the Economic Front group centering in the Northeast; and the Bangkok-centered Labor Front. Such opponents of the government were all denounced officially for allegedly giving aid and comfort to communist subversives. On April 8, 1968 the moderately critical newspaper *Kiattisak* had argued editorially as follows:

> The Communists' objective is to win the minds of local residents by looking for shortcomings of local officials . . . in order to destroy the confidence of the people. . . . If the people dislike the authorities, they will surely become tools of the Communists. . . . Local officials must demonstrate proper behavior and must mix with the local residents. . . . It is the duty of the government to see that such a policy is effectively carried out.[95]

The total number of candidates registered by early January for the 219 seats numbered well over 1,000.

465

Most of them were independents, since the nonofficial parties were afforded little opportunity to organize themselves on a countrywide basis.[96] The campaign conducted by the government was pitched in low key. Only in the final week were vigorous efforts made by means of television and rallies to answer insistent charges of corruption and mismanagement. A number of Democrat party rallies in Bangkok aroused enthusiasm, but the rural Thai as a whole were apathetic, convinced that no important changes could be realized by voting. Scattered Communist efforts to disrupt procedures aroused virtually no support in response. The election was conducted on February 10 on a nationwide scale and with minimal disorder.

The result of the election was something less than an overwhelming victory for the government party, which elected only 75 of its 219 candidates. The Democrats won all 21 of the Bangkok and Thonburi seats and 36 others outside the capital area. Independent candidates won 72 victories, while 5 minor parties collected the remaining 15. How many of the independents would back Praphat rather than the prime minister would depend, no doubt, on what kind of tangible incentives each was able to offer them. If all the dissidents should join with the opposition Democrats, they could outvote the UTPP membership. The greatest demonstration of independent strength was in the northeastern region, where Leftist parties had been expected to make a more impressive showing. Few observers believed that the new constitutional structure could withstand any serious controversy within the ruling military hierarchy. General Dawee Chulasapya himself referred to the constitution casually as "only a draft, . . . a temporary document."[97] In actuality, the constitution lasted less than three years.

Cabinet changes made following the election were all in the direction of strengthening the authority of the army. A stanch former supporter of Sarit and the army, Buchana Attakorn, was called home from the Washington embassy, to which he had been politically exiled in 1967, and made

Minister of Economic Affairs. In May 1969 he openly challenged Thanat Khoman's previously-mentioned gestures in the direction of developing trade relations with Red China.[98] Air Marshall Dawee Chulasapya was put in charge of the ministry of communications as an additional assignment, and the previous incumbent was transferred to the ministry of industry. These moves were presumably designed to strengthen army control over economic affairs. The director-general of police, Prasert Ruchiwarong, a rival of Praphat and a supporter of Thanom, took on additional duties as minister of health. Another close military follower of Thanom was assigned a roving ministership attached to the office of the prime minister. Thus were trusted and tried military colleagues enlisted to bolster the army's authoritarian cabinet, paying no deference to democratic norms or to the admission of greater civilian participation.[99]

1. David A. Wilson, *Politics in Thailand* (Ithaca, 1962), pp. 33-34.
2. Frank A. Darling, *Thailand and the United States* (Washington, 1965), pp. 114-17, 181-89.
3. *Ibid.*, pp. 190-96; David A. Wilson, "Thailand: A New Leader," *Asian Survey* 4 (1964): 711-15.
4. Wilson, *Politics.* pp. 33-34.
5. Fred W. Riggs, *Thailand: Modernization of a Bureaucratic Policy* (Honolulu, 1966), pp. 167-77.
6. Wilson, *Politics*, pp. 33-34.
7. Donald Hindley, "Thailand: The Politics of Passivity," *Pacific Affairs* 41 (1968): 358-64.
8. William J. Siffin, *The Thai Bureaucracy: Institutional Change and Development* (Honolulu, 1966), pp. 151-59; Darling *op. cit.*, pp. 190-96.
9. Siffin, *op. cit.*, pp. 151-59.
10. *Ibid.*, pp. 160-90, 224-53.
11. *Ibid.*, pp. 250-53; T. H. Silcock, *Thailand: Social and Economic Studies in Development* (Canberra, 1967), pp. 98-100.
12. Silcock, *op. cit.*, pp. 17-25.
13. *A Public Development Program for Thailand* (Baltimore, 1959).
14. See Elizer B. Ayal, "Some Crucial Issues in Thailand's Economic Development," *Pacific Affairs* 34 (1961): 157-64.
15. Silcock, *op. cit.*, pp. 21-25.
16. *Ibid.*, pp. 261-63.
17. *Ibid.*, pp. 264-80.
18. Ayal, *op. cit.*, *Pacific Affairs* 34: 160.
19. Silcock, *op. cit.*, pp. 283-307.

20. Riggs, *op. cit.*, 247-71, 305-10.
21. *New York Times*, July 10, 1964, and April 6, 1969.
22. See Darling, *op. cit.*, pp. 196-97.
23. Donald E. Nuechterlein, *Thailand and the Struggle for Southeast Asia* (Ithaca, 1965), pp. 140-46.
24. David A. Wilson, "Bangkok's Dim View to the East," *Asian Survey* 1 (1961): 13-17; *New York Times*, May 3, 1964.
25. Nuechterlein, *op. cit.*, pp. 140-46.
26. *Ibid.*, pp. 146-57.
27. *Ibid.*, pp. 157-84.
28. *Ibid.*, pp. 174-78.
29. *Ibid.*, pp. 182-94.
30. *Ibid.*, pp. 221-43.
31. *Ibid.*, pp. 245-49.
32. *Ibid.*, pp. 210-220.
33. *Ibid.*, pp. 221-22, 258; *FEER*, May 30, 1963, pp. 458-59; Wilson, "A New Leader," p. 715.
34. *FEER*, September 26, 1968, p. 612. Peking's radio propaganda from late 1955 tried to unite the Thailand Patriotic Front with border communists.
35. Wilson, "A New Leader," pp. 711-715.
36. Hindley, "Thailand," pp. 355-58.
37. David A. Wilson, "China, Thailand, and the Spirit of Bandung," *China Quarterly* 2 (1967): 108-110.
38. *FEER*, May 16, 1968, p. 360.
39. *New York Times*, January 19, 1968.
40. See Takeshi Motooka, in *Japan's Future in Southeast Asia* (Kyoto, 1966), pp. 15-27.
41. *FEER*, March 6, 1969, pp. 417-18.
42. *FEER, 1968 Yearbook*, pp. 336-39, 345.
43. *FEER*, March 18, 1966, p. 500.
44. Riggs, *op. cit.*, pp. 339-40.
45. *FEER*, June 2, 1966, p. 452.
46. George Modelski, "The Asian States' Participation in SEATO," in Modelski, ed., *SEATO* (Vancouver, 1962), pp. 96-103.
47. Frank C. Darling, "Thailand: Stability and Escalation," *Asian Survey* (February 1968): 120-26.
48. *FEER*, December 2, 1967, pp. 539-47.
49. J. L. S. Girling, "Northeast Thailand: Tomorrow's Vietnam?" *Foreign Affairs* 46 (January 1968): 388-97.
50. Hindley, "Thailand," pp. 365-70; Robert Textor, *From Peasant to Pedicab Driver*, Yale Southeast Asia Studies (New Haven, 1961), pp. 12-20, 24-44.
51. David A. Wilson, "Thailand and Marxism," in Frank Trager, ed., *Marxism in Southeast Asia* (Stanford, 1959), pp. 100-101.
52. *Ibid.*, pp. 65-68.
53. Based on first-hand observation of author.
54. Unpublished study by Ray Downs, "Changing Thai University Student Attitudes," Bangkok, 1968.
55. Unpublished study by Herbert P. Philipps, "Observations on Siamese Intellectual Life," Berkeley, 1967.
56. *FEER*, April 18, 1968, pp. 173-75.
57. *New York Times*, January 24, 1966.
58. "Symposium on Northwest Thailand," *Asian Survey* 6 (July 1966): 349-80.
59. Darling, "America and Thailand," *Asian Survey* 7 (April 1967), 213-25.

60. *New York Times*, August 11, 13, 1969
61. Wilson, "China, Thailand", pp. 96-107.
62. The expelled correspondent, Stanley Karnow, wrote for the *FEER*. Thanat denounced him as "an outcast from a Polish ghetto." *FEER*, June 27, 1969, p. 608.
63. Modelski, *op. cit.*, pp. 104-7.
64. Darling, *Thailand*, pp. 167-78, 196-205.
65. *Bangkok World*, July 6, 1967.
66. *FEER*, June 26, 1967, p. 652.
67. *Ibid.*, May 1, 1969, pp. 286-88.
68. *Ibid.*, November 12, 1964, pp. 341-42. Reported by Gopinath Pillai.
69. Nuechterlein, "Thailand: Years of Danger and Hope," *Asian Survey* 6 (1966): 119-22.
70. *New York Times*, December 18, 1966.
71. *Bangkok World*, August 22, 1968.
72. *FEER, 1968 Yearbook*, pp. 335-37.
73. *Siam Rath*, April 15-16, 1968.
74. *Ibid.*, February 28, 1968.
75. *Lak Muang*, March 8, 1968, and *Prachathipatai*, April 9, 1968.
76. Editorial in *Phoen Din Thai*, March 20, 1968.
77. *Kon Muang*, March 20, 1968.
78. For full text of constitution see *Bangkok World*, section II, of May 5, 1968.
79. *Bangkok World*. July 18, 1968.
80. *Ibid.*, taken from a *Chao Thai* editorial.
81. *Ibid.*, August 7, 12, 29, 1968.
82. *Ibid.*, August 29, 1968. Contributed by Likit Hongladaron.
83. *FEER*, June 12, 1969, pp. 611-13.
84. *Siam Rath*, February 28, 1968.
85. *FEER*, September 12, 1968, pp. 506-7.
86. *Ibid.*, February 20, 1969, pp. 314-15.
87. *Ibid.*, December 28, 1967, pp. 583-87; May 8, 1969, p. 316; June 2, 1969, pp. 606-7. The latter two items contain information relating to Stanley Kornow's expulsion from Thailand.
88. *Ibid.*, September 12, 1968, pp. 506-7; *New York Times*, July 28, 1969.
89. See *New York Times*, June 1, 1969, for information concerning the ASPAC meeting in Japan.
90. *FEER*, April 25, 1968, pp. 218-20.
91. John Stirling, "Meo Revolt Smolders in Hills of Thailand," *New York Times*, April 14, 1969.
92. *FEER*, January 16, 1969, p. 82.
93. *Bangkok World*, October 1, 1968.
94. *Ibid.*, November 23, 1968.
95. *Siam Times*, April 14, 1968.
96. *FEER*, January 16, 1969, pp. 8, 82.
97. *Ibid.*, February 13 and 27, 1969, pp. 261 and 350.
98. *Ibid.*, May 15, 1969, p. 368.
99. *Ibid.*, pp. 368-69.

XIII

BURMA UNDER MILITARY
SOCIALIST RULE

The army's seizure of power in
Burma on March 2, 1962, was politically rather than ideologically moti-
vated. The effective military rule that Thailand's Marshal
Sarit had demonstrated since 1958 probably contributed
some psychological stimulation, but the principal causal
factors were domestic. The major political consideration
prompting the authors of the coup was nationalist concern
to preserve the political and territorial integrity of the
country, which seemed in danger of falling apart under
Nu's democratic government. If public doubts were entertained about the competence of the army to govern, the
generally responsible character of the sixteen-month
caretaker regime could be cited, along with the obvious
fact that Nu's own cabinet and administration were hardly
models of statesmenlike foresight and efficiency.

The Army's Seizure of Power

The army's abrupt intervention on March 2 was both
sweeping and thoroughgoing. Premier Nu and most of his
cabinet were arrested and detained indefinitely without
trial, along with all of the representatives of the Shan
States who had assembled at Rangoon on his invitation.
Among the fifty-two persons arrested were Chief Justice

Myint Thein, Thakin Tin head of the All Burma Peasants Organization (ABPO), and the former president of the Union, the Karen Mahn Win Maung. Declaring flatly that parliamentary democracy had proved to be unsuitable for Burma, General Ne Win swept aside the existing governmental structure—including the constitution itself, the representative assemblies, and the top-level court system —and substituted military rule. In mid-April the American representatives of the Ford and Asia Foundations were obliged to leave Burma. Fulbright Foundation activities were also suspended, along with the British and the American-sponsored English language training programs.[1]

The army coup encountered no effective protest, and the reaction of the general public was one of reluctant acquiescence. Physical resistance was impossible in any case, and the muted complaints of civilian political spokesmen lacked both fervor and popular backing. Burman opposition to the possible disintegration of the Union was widely shared, and Ne Win's previous record as head of the caretaker regime had earned him respect as a nationalist champion. The emerging authoritarian government was secularist rather than religiously committed, and socialist oriented in a vaguely utopian fashion.[2] Optimists hoped that a second limited exhibition of disciplined control might serve to bridge political and social rifts and restore Burma's lost sense of national cohesion and purpose.

The official blueprint and rationale for the new military regime was set forth in a publication entitled the *Burmese Way to Socialism*. The document was issued on April 30, 1962, and it reflected evidence of hasty improvisation. Its proposals were so utopian and theoretical in tone that their ultimate political and economic implications were far from clear. The document affirmed that exploitive capitalism must give way to social justice in an effort to meet the people's essential needs for food, housing, clothing, and jobs. Self-discipline must displace selfish profit seeking, easy living, and parasitism, so that the country's available human and material

471

resources could be developed in balanced fashion in the interest of the well-being of the nation as a whole. The state itself, or group cooperatives functioning under governmental control, would henceforth direct productive efforts. Favored treatment of employers would give way to rewards to laborers, based on the value of effort expended in terms of production. The new system would not exclude middle-class participation, but it would rest essentially on a peasant and worker foundation. The armed forces would act to defend the new order. Bogus acts of charity and piety would be disallowed (a slap at Nu), and a comprehensive bond of patriotic concern would be generated to encompass all indigenous ethnic groups regardless of origin, religion, or language differences.[3]

The contemplated anticapitalist program would be sponsored by a monolithic political organization called the Burma Socialist Program party. Executive leadership would be lodged for the time being in a self-appointed Revolutionary Council. The "Burmese way" would avoid slavish copying of foreign patterns and would pay no deference to the democratic principle of permitting opponents to criticize either objectives or methods. Governmental objectives were tied in with earlier plans to curb the role of the Chinese and Indian business communities, which were to be replaced by centralized state control of the economy.

At the outset, Ne Win tried with little success to recruit Council members from a variety of political constituencies and to enlist the individual cooperation of experienced administrative personnel in promoting his idealized socialist goals. A few of the second-level Leftist leaders within the AFPFL and some of the ABPO peasant group leaders agreed to assist the Revolutionary Council, but membership in the Council from the beginning was predominantly military. The cultural orientation of the ruling group was rural rather than urban, authoritarian rather than modernist. Precedence was accorded to the goals of order and unity. Party discipline was imposed on township and village officials and on the police as well, until the eventual organization of peasants and workers councils

472

should prove feasible. Displacing the older governmental structure and also the capitalist business community were army-sponsored and directed economic and governing agencies, operating under direction from the center but enjoying substantial internal autonomy.

It can be assumed that Ne Win himself was not the principal author of the *Burmese Way to Socialism*, for he was not an economist nor a doctrinaire Marxist. But once the socialist goals were affirmed, the authoritarian trend developed increasing momentum within the army leadership. The intelligent pro-Western Colonel Maung Maung had been ousted from his army connections prior to the coup of March 2, and the democratic socialist Brigadier Aung Gyi, who opposed the stampede toward nationalization of the economy, was excluded from the Revolutionary Council in early 1963.[4] The relentless drift toward Communist-patterned regimentation, with the army rather than a party hierarchy acting in support, was due less to initial design than to attendant circumstances and events.

The only political grouping that responded enthusiastically to Ne Win's appeal for collaboration was the National Unity Front (NUF) and its associated Marxist theoreticians. Burma's educated elite, including high-level officials active in previous governments, flatly rejected the imposition of army dictatorship, however much some of them may have sympathized with espoused socialist goals. In the end, the higher levels of the judiciary and administration, faculty and students, the press and the business community, and eventually the Buddhist monks all refused to support the Burma Socialist Program party. Minority groups also distrusted Burman army domination, and Ne Win's own revived National Solidarity Association cadres enlisted fewer recruits than they had done in 1959. It was in the absence of any serious political competitors that NUF volunteers (especially U Ba Nyein) and the Communist-oriented army leadership, supported by avaricious officers hungry for the perquisites of power, gained ascendency within the Revolutionary

473

Council.[5] Because freedom of criticism was denied, popular discontent remained inarticulate, even among lower echelons of the Council hierarchy itself. The proposed organization of peasants and workers councils failed of realization.

Since the Burmese Socialist Program party was essentially a projection of governmental and military authority, it developed no popular base of political power. The Revolutionary Council eventually decreed, in October 1963, that party promoters were authorized to draw on the government treasury to cover both their political expenses and their personal and family needs. The accompanying explanation was that party workers who were dedicated to promoting the well-being of the working class as a whole should not have to worry about providing their own food, clothing, and shelter.[6] The new regime was, of course, not unique in substituting slogans for the implementation of policy objectives. But it was singularly unable to enlist popular cooperation, to improve governmental efficiency, or to achieve espoused goals.

The harshness of the discipline imposed by the Revolutionary Council government extended far beyond that demonstrated by army rule under the earlier caretaker regime. New policies were surprisingly puritanical in character, forbidding such bourgeois vices as horse racing, public gambling, beauty contests, and Western dancing. Golf and football survived, along with the traditional all-night *pwe* dramatic performances. The emphasis in education shifted away from social studies, humanities, and religion and onto science and technology, which presumably would contribute more directly to social and economic progress. Under the new emphasis, national accomplishment would be measured not by traditional Buddhist norms, but by evidence of intelligence and industry. Religion and education must both function to serve socialist objectives as defined by the Revolutionary Council.

A demonstration of General Ne Win's dictatorial mood occurred on the University of Rangoon campus shortly

474

after the opening of the new school year in June 1962. The customary student protest against the so-called 3-F ruling (which required dismissal of students who failed examinations three consecutive times) developed into a riot on July 6. When the police proved unable to curb the disorder with the use of hoses and tear gas, they requested army support. A local magistrate refused the request of the assigned military unit to authorize the use of firearms, but General Ne Win gave such permission on his own authority. Several score students were killed, and the army pursued the remainder into the dormitories. Army vehicles hauled the dead bodies away. When angered students on the following day placarded the university student union building with insults directed against Ne Win and his recently estranged wife, the general authorized the building's total demolition. Thus disappeared the symbol and reality of student freedom. The university was closed for a month. When trouble again developed in 1963 at the opening of the second term in November, the university was closed down for an entire year. The government meanwhile reorganized both curriculum and regulations, following patterns approved by the Revolutionary Council.[7]

Problems of Authority and Control

The initial political problem to which Ne Win addressed himself was the curbing of multiple rebellions. The National Liberation Alliance, which had been formed by Karens, Kachins, and Shans in 1960, had been temporarily appeased by Premier Nu's promises of greater autonomy. Following the coup of March 2 all minority elements saw their fears of Burman domination confirmed. Ne Win's early hope to enlist non-Burman support via government contributions to their educational and economic development needs was not fulfilled. The reaction of Shan leadership was particularly bitter, for the safety of their representatives who had assembled at Rangoon on Nu's invitation had been betrayed. Shan hostility

475

intensified following the early death in November 1962 of the imprisoned Sao Shwe Thaike, the first president of the Union of Burma.[8]

The Kachin rebellion that developed in northern Burma was in many respects the most difficult to curb. Christian Kachin leaders had protested Premier Nu's move to make Buddhism the state religion, and ethnic hostility buttressed religious differences. Since government forces managed to control only the communication facilities along the major routes of travel, the rebel Kachin opposition had plenty of room to hide. The most vigorous contingent of the Kachin Independence Army, under the command of the charismatic Naw Seng, operated along the China-Burma border to the east of Myitkyina. Some of the Kachin rebels profited by supplying the rebellious Naga tribesmen along the Indian border with military supplies sent across from China. Other Kachin rebels established contacts with the outside world via northern Thailand.[9]

Karen dissidents of the Irrawaddy delta, the lower Sittang and Salween Valleys, and intervening watersheds, although distrustful as always of Burman rule, were not capable of mounting any unified effort to challenge the new military dictatorship. Border areas contiguous to Thailand extending northward from upper Tenasserim passed beyond the control of Rangoon. In comparison with the widespread opposition of minority peoples, the chronic rebellion of the White Flag Communists centering around the northern reaches of the Pegu Yoma Mountains (between the upper Sittang Valley and the Irrawaddy) was relatively easy to contain. The drift of government policy toward an increasingly Communist economic orientation might conceivably provide a basis for their conciliation.

Efforts at Pacification

After some inconclusive military gains at the expense of rebel bands during the first fifteen months of the military regime, Ne Win adopted a more positive approach.

476

In June 1943 he set up the first of a series of conferences designed to pacify dissident elements. Leaders of the various rebellious groups met government spokesmen at Rangoon under assurances of safe conduct. Some Burman Communist spokesmen were flown to Rangoon from near the China border. Despite the fact that the rebels were promised full amnesty and an opportunity to participate in the new revolutionary order, the conciliatory efforts accomplished disappointingly little; in fact, they actually encouraged the revival of demands for regional and ethnic autonomy, denial of which had been the occasion of the coup originally. The White Flag Communists in particular wanted recognition of their full administrative control of occupied areas, including preservation of their land reforms.[10]

The only tangible success realized in Ne Win's pacification efforts was the signing of a truce in March 1964 with the more conservative faction of the Christian Karens, led by Saw Hunter Thamwe. This group was no longer willing to follow the pattern of Mahn Ba Zan's younger faction in collaborating with the White Flag Communists and hoped that the paper concessions obtained with the truce might provide a basis for eventual peace. Ne Win agreed to assemble at some opportune time a convention of representatives of Burma's indigenous races to draft new constitutional provisions covering their future role in the Union. He agreed to re-examine the boundaries of the existing Kawthoolai Karen state, with a view to its possible inclusion of the Karen-inhabited areas of Tenasserim and the Irrawaddy delta. In all such areas the government's local security and administrative committees would henceforth include Karen representatives. A joint committee of government appointees and representative Karens was established to supervise the terms of the truce. Rangoon hoped that the pattern thus formulated would prove acceptable to Kachin and Shan dissidents as well, but such proved not to be the case.[11]

Meanwhile, the Revolutionary Council made persistent efforts to exclude all Indians and Pakistanis from Burma.

The victims included many business and professional men who had long made Burma their home. Beginning in November 1962 Indian residents were required to pay an annual foreign registration fee of approximately $10 (U.S.) on pain of deportation. Applications for citizenship cost $50, plus the customary bribes and gratuities. Attempts to obtain court review of alleged inequities were usually futile; thus from 1962 to 1967 an estimated 177,000 Indians and Pakistanis left Burma. Precautions were taken to prevent departees from taking along their accumulated savings, including X-raying their stomachs at the airport.[12]

After August 1963 the Ne Win dictatorship abandoned efforts to reach accommodation with civilian critics as well as with rebel groups. Among those arrested at the time were socialist-democratic leaders such as U Ba Swe and U Kyaw Nyein, plus the former chief justice and Buddhist lay leader, U Chan Tun, and the editor of the *Nation* newspaper, U Law Yone. Determination of policy devolved thereafter on such doctrinaire Marxists as Brigadier Tin Pe, who had served without distinction as minister of mines under the caretaker regime, and U Ba Nyein, a disciple of econometrics and a committed advocate of Mao Tse-tung's brand of patriotic communism.

Drift toward a Communist Economic System

During the first year of Revolutionary Council rule, Brigadier Aung Gyi was given leeway to proceed with the task of nationalizing the economy on a moderate, pragmatic basis. He undertook to develop a mixture of private and public investment by promoting joint-venture enterprises. He also extended the policy of incentive price differentials to encourage the delivery of high-grade rice suitable for export by the Agricultural Marketing Board. Private traders could dispose of low-grade rice as they wished. The 1962 growing season witnessed a substantial increment of rice acreage (some 84,000 acres) and production of a surplus for export of 1.8 million tons. In early 1963 a majority of the seventeen-member Council vetoed the incentive program, forcing Aung Gyi's retirement from the government that March.[13]

The new nationalization policy sponsored by Ba Nyein rejected all incentive appeals as part of a thoroughgoing effort to eliminate the private bourgeois sector from both commerce and industry. He ignored pragmatic considerations and stressed the need for greater popular dedication to the welfare of the total worker-peasant population. Through the public media and through the staging of annual seminars, he undertook a program of exhortation and indoctrination in support of government policy. As soon as genuine popular cooperation was achieved, he proposed to set up two councils (soviets), one for peasants and one for workers, which would share in the direction of policy. Pending such time, he promised to curb all "class enemies," including indigenous and alien entrepreneurs, while encouraging the people's industry, honesty, and social dedication. His efforts aroused little affirmative response. The intelligentsia were thoroughly alienated by army rule, and military suppression was popularly resented.[14] Leaders of the official Socialist Program Party (*Lanzin*) obviously did not trust the membership very far. Of the 185,000 candidates for membership, some 54,000 were connected with the army and 15,000 were peasant leaders; full membership numbered only 9,000, including the required affiliation of all upper-echelon officials. The Revolutionary Council executive cadre included approximately a score of persons. The talk of representative councils of peasants and workers was therefore highly theoretical.[15]

The nationalization policy was pursued relentlessly from 1963 through 1965. The state first took over, with minimal compensation, all private banks and trading companies, including the surviving remnants of the large British colonial corporations and the two score joint-project enterprises. Foreign banks were forced to liquidate their assets, including two banks previously operated by Communist China as a means of influencing the local Chinese business community. The government agencies that took over responsibility for filling the services gap were for the most part inexperienced and lacking discipline. The Council decreed a standard work week extending from Monday through Saturday noon. Efforts to collectivize agricultural holdings were limited at this point to setting up model cooperative villages on the Israeli pattern. In 1963 government credit agencies undertook the difficult task of financing the planting and harvesting of the yearly rice crop. Private trade in rice for export purposes ended in July 1963, with no premium prices permitted thereafter.

The immediate results of the nationalization program in terms of lowered output and unemployment were most discouraging. In the industrial and mining sectors and in transportation activities, approximately a thousand private firms closed down in 1963, leaving an estimated two million workers without jobs.[16] The greatest government shortages were in management personnel and technical skills. Required fuel and raw materials were lacking in many instances, and adequate spare parts for machinery and transport were simply not available. The State Agricultural Marketing Board was particularly inefficient in matters of business. When rice exports began a progressive decline, the volume of imports was cut proportionately, so that industrial equipment, raw materials, and consumer goods became increasingly inadequate.[17] At the same time, conservative fiscal policies left about 10 percent of the available foreign credit exchange unused, resulting in an actual increment in foreign currency reserves in 1964. Because private investment opportunities were virtually nil and purchasable goods in short supply, savings deposits also increased, and internal debt, both public and private, declined.[18] The collapse in private trading was reflected in the 70 percent decline in newspaper advertising in late 1963. In 1964 the government began the practice of exercising control through People's Stores of the sale of such essential commodities as salt, cloth, cooking oil, soap, and electrical supplies. Quantities proved inadequate, and distribution facilities were woefully deficient. The continuing

480

forced departure of Pakistani and Indian merchants aggravated deficiencies in basic trading operations.[19]

In May 1964 the Revolutionary Council initiated an effort to bring wealthy hoarders and other "class enemies" under more effective control. It ruled that all existing currency notes above the 50 *kyat* level (around $10) were no longer legal tender and must be exchanged for newly printed substitute currency. Because holders of large amounts of currency were permitted to obtain immediately only a portion of the exchanged currency due them, many acquiesced only partially. Those who dragged their feet or who were caught trying to evade the decree suffered severe penalties. The move was accompanied by an extensive propaganda barrage on the part of Ba Nyein to publicize to the *ludu* (masses) the beneficial objectives of the government's program and to solicit increasing popular cooperation.[20]

Meanwhile, General Ne Win moved to restrict sharply the entry of alien visitors and reporters, explaining that he did not want to have foreigners looking on while "housecleaning" was in progress. Ordinary visas were limited to twenty-four hours, and the recipients were usually prevented from venturing outside Rangoon. Foreign journalists who had been critical of the regime were denied re-entry. The mobility of resident foreign diplomats was also curbed. They had to request permission from the Foreign Office for travel outside Rangoon, submitting a full statement of their intended itinerary. Burmese officials and all party members were also obliged to obtain approval from the top before issuing or accepting social invitations involving foreigners, and afterwards the Burmese had to report in full what was said and done during the course of their conversations with aliens. Wiretapping was widely practiced as a means of espionage.

The suppression of all public criticism of government policy, starting in 1964, included even statements by high army officers occupying such posts as minister of information and minister of trade development. The effect was corrosive on morale. Some army personnel no doubt

481

worked diligently at their often-boring tasks, trying to curb corruption and to keep rebel movements divided and at bay, but such efforts were usually not long sustained. The university student population continued under heavy surveillance by the police. The despoiled and frustrated middle-class Burmans were denied any opportunity for articulate or organized protest. Quiet expressions of cynicism with respect to declared government objectives were widely prevalent, but virtually no one was prepared to risk rebellion. General Ne Win was the boss and would brook no dissent. His customary petulant mood was aggravated by a chronic nervous affliction. On one notorious occasion, he chanced to meet a critic of his regime on the Maymyo golf course and actually struck him down with a golf club.[21]

Decline in Industry and Agriculture

The decline of Burma's industrial activity continued unrelentingly. Small private industry gradually died, partly as a result of government harassment, and partly because owners could no longer procure raw materials or machinery repairs. The public sector monopolized the credits available for both operations and maintenance. Ex-employers known to have funds were obliged to keep their discharged workers on their pay rolls. Regional state banking institutions acted as treasury units for their several districts. Particular banks were assigned functionally to serve the needs of agriculture, industry, foreign trade, or private accounts. The Union Bank supplied the government with needed cash by buying its bonds. Tax revenues and the receipts from the retail People's Stores were all put into the same till.

The decline of industrial output was widespread. Tin ore output in the lower peninsula, which had amounted to some 6,000 tons in 1939 and 1,624 tons in 1951, officially fell to zero in 1965. The stores, tools, and explosives required for mining were simply unobtainable, and what little ore was extracted was delivered to dealers who sold it across the Thai border for higher prices. The once profitable teakwood industry virtually collapsed from lack of coordination. Total domestic output declined by an estimated 3 percent in 1965–66, and the volume of imports dropped a dismal 43 percent during the same year, far below the level of essential needs. One of the few progressive moves was made by the official directors of the People's Oil Company, successor to the old Burma Oil Company, who enlisted the help of Rumanian and Japanese drilling technicians in successful exploration along the lower Arakan coast and offshore.[22] Rumanian drilling teams in the older Chauk oil area discovered additional gas, and Japanese-financed American efforts did the same off the Tenasserim-Martaban coast.

The continuing decline of agricultural production affected far more people than did the difficulties with industry, and was therefore more important politically. The inefficiency of the government's agricultural credit program and its associated policy of monopoly control of the rice trade were major contributing factors. Cultivators were afforded little incentive to produce efficiently, since the government-provided crop loans, which were advanced by installments during the course of the growing season, were not carefully supervised and were often used for other purposes. Many cultivators elected to follow the less costly and unproductive routine of broadcast planting a portion of their rice lands, instead of the more laborious transplanting procedures essential for a normal crop. Under the circumstances, no amount of official exhortation could counter the careless tactics of the cultivators. Only 43 percent of the crop loans advanced by the government for 1964–65 were ever repaid, partly because substantial portions of the crops were not worth harvesting. The generous advance of agriculture credits also contributed to inflation because the huge volume of money thus put into circulation could not be absorbed by the limited amount of consumer goods available from legal sources of supply.[23]

There was little incentive for the average cultivator to

dispose of his surplus rice to the government at the low official price of 350 *kyats* ($70) per one hundred baskets, and thereby risk attack by insurgents. One alternative was to sell most of his surplus to the rebels and black marketeers for 480 *kyats* per one hundred baskets, thus sacrificing his cloth and salt rations from the People's Stores. The usual tactic was to deliver to the government only enough rice to obtain essential rationed items, and to use the remainder for barter. The net result was to deprive the government of rice for export, which in previous years had provided some 70 percent of the foreign exchange used to pay for needed imports. Rice exports dropped from a high of 1.8 million tons in 1963 to 1.3 million in 1965, 1.1 million in 1966, 600,000 in 1967, and a mere 300,000 tons in 1968. Flood damage accounted for part of the decline in 1966–67, along with Karen insurgency in the delta. But the negative peasant reaction to government policy was the major contributing factor.[24]

Unwilling to alter official policies and unable to coerce the vast peasant population, the authorities continued their ineffective propaganda approach. Peasant seminars were staged annually in the dry season. In 1966, the seminar met at Rangoon, and two thousand selected representatives attended. Official spokesmen extolled the government's services in providing cultivator credits, making available four thousand tractors at seventy-eight stations along with fertilizers and pesticides, plus arranging favored access for peasants to rationed supplies. Seminar participants were also reminded that landlords and moneylenders no longer claimed a major share of the cultivators' incomes and that family plots had been enlarged. But a greater measure of discipline would have to be maintained in the future, the government warned. Crop loans would have to be repaid; paddy lands must no longer be transferred to fruit and maize production; water control systems must be maintained; and some use must be made of tractor services.[25]

Peasant spokesmen invariably responded by airing their own grievances. They complained that the rental cost of tractors was prohibitive and that the deep Russian plows cut through the soil pan, so that the water drained away. The low price cultivators got for their rice and the cost of delivery to remote collecting depots contrasted sharply with the high price of cloth, cooking oil, and salt. All complained that civilian officials and army personnel treated them arrogantly.[26]

An appropriate opportunity for the Revolutionary Council to undertake a serious review of the faltering economic control system came in the late months of 1967. A serious consumer rice shortage developed in a number of urban areas, precipitating rice riots in some twenty towns. The government was obliged to relax its controls over a number of consumer items in short supply and to permit purchasers legally to obtain essential food items from nongovernment sources. But as soon as the new crop appeared in early 1968, the restrictions were reimposed. All accumulated stocks of rice were ordered surrendered to the official Trading Corporation under threat of confiscation. The net result was negative. Hoarding of rice became the general practice, despite periodic visits of police from house to house, and the system of distributing consumer goods via the People's Stores began to falter badly.[27]

Distribution Problems: The People's Stores

The exercise of state control over virtually all aspects of the retail distribution of consumer goods through so-called People's Stores dated from 1965. The results were discouraging. The scarcity of goods in the stores themselves, due in large measure to poor distribution from the center, spawned a thriving black market. During the first half of 1966, when exports slumped 15 percent below the 1965 rate, the government responded by cutting back imports by almost 50 percent, thus adding to shortages of consumer goods and to the slowdown of investment and production.[28] Only in situations of dire scarcity were private traders permitted temporarily to handle staple

485

items at prices above those legally payable at the stores and considerably below the black-market rate.

At the local level, the operators of the People's stores had little or no incentive to do an efficient and conscientious job. To augment their inadequate 82 *kyat* ($17) monthly wages, most of them began to deal surreptitiously with black-market operators. Nationwide distribution was notoriously bad, so that all travelers departing from Rangoon by whatever means included in their luggage such items as soap, cloth, and salt. Electrical appliances, when available, were sold only to purchasers who deposited the burned-out items that were to be replaced. Cotton cloth was in such perennial demand that the buyer at the head of the queue had to take the item that happened to be on the top of the pile at the time.

Life in Ne Win's Burma reflected a mixture of the old and the very new. Light festivals at the end of the Lenten season still flourished, as did the all-night *pwe* performances. Both actors and audiences demonstrated their traditional lively sense of humor: The *pwe* comedian, in reply to the clown's persistent questioning, explained that the bandits featured in the dramatic performance had recently found jobs in the People's Stores.[29] Soccer was the most popular afternoon sport, and in the absence of festivals and *pwes*, the cinemas provided the only form of nightly entertainment. Otherwise, Rangoon was virtually a dead city at night. A novel aspect of daily life was queuing up at the People's Stores, but many householders found it easier to patronize the black market. "Professional buyers," otherwise unemployed, realized a quick profit on whatever the stores had to sell by disposing of goods to private dealers. Goods in limited supply were sometimes distributed by lot to successful ticket holders. Cinema managers employed Chinese and Indian youths to peddle the best tickets in the streets at premium prices. Scalpers occasionally cornered the tickets to popular football matches. The press commented quite openly: "It is glaring as daylight that our parasites get their stuff through links and connections with the respective branches of government." Ne Win admitted publicly that Burma's economic situation was a "deplorable mess."[30]

The government nevertheless took no effective measures to improve conditions. Official spokesmen addressing the assembled annual workers and peasants seminars castigated the people for refusing to cooperate and implied that the prevailing difficulties were evidence of the fact that stronger discipline was needed. A few orthodox ideas got across, especially after Ne Win's visit to Washington in September 1966. Burmese officials renewed tentative contacts with the World Bank and the International Monetary Fund, but aside from restoration of the modest U.S. aid program in small-arms assistance, no results were forthcoming. Permission for students to study in the United States continued to be denied, and most of them persisted in going to Eastern Europe.[31] Students ceased going to China after the break of June 1967.

In late 1967 Ne Win began to permit publication in the press of occasional critical comments with reference to prevailing difficulties. In November 1967, for example, an officer in the Ministry of National Planning was permitted to challenge the budget previously submitted by the Revolutionary Council. The critic maintained that the report failed completely to recognize the seriousness of the economic crisis the country faced. He argued that Burma's agriculture could not survive unless incentives for increased production were restored. He advocated free domestic trade in grain, relaxation of governmental controls over many consumer items, and complete decontrol of such essential items as salt, *ngapi* (fish paste), and prawns. Funds available for investment should be loaned at interest wherever they could be productive, and the many faltering public enterprises must be reorganized. The budget-balancing practice of curtailing the importation of essential equipment and raw materials for production was denounced as sheer folly. The critic concluded by urging that a high-level conference should be assembled without delay to consider the need for basic policy reforms.[32]

Another such critical column, attacking the prevailing

security regulations, appeared in the *Working People's Daily* in early 1968. The author was Thakin Ba Thoung, who was famous as the composer of Burma's national anthem. He challenged the prevailing security system as "unnecessary, uncalled-for, and amateurish," especially so in areas of local police surveillance. What Burma needed most was not the release of political prisoners, as Ne Win had recently conceded, but rather permission for ordinary citizens to earn a livelihood through the relaxation of trade restrictions. Why should the socialist ideal be equated with the denial of personal freedom through gratuitous police interference, including threats to cancel ration cards unless security regulations were meticulously observed? Another basic problem was official corruption and highhandedness. An accompanying letter to the editor denounced in even more severe terms official "power intoxication, . . . haughtiness, and conceit" as the principal obstacles in realizing cherished goals.[33] The bland editorial rejoinder pointed out that Burma was still better off than many other countries of the world. Its people had adequate food, shelter, and clothing, and were not in physical jeopardy.[34]

Educational and Social Adjustments

A new educational reorganization plan was introduced in November 1964, following the year-long shutdown of the university. The revised program divided the university into several autonomous institutes, with the major emphasis placed on science and technology. Student political activities were strictly forbidden, and matriculants were assigned to appropriate curriculum programs with minimal freedom of choice. The social sciences focused on Marxist interpretations within a very narrow context. The political science syllabus emphasized the *Burmese Way to Socialism*, the constitution of the Socialist Program party, and a tract entitled *Correlation of Man and His Environment*.[35] English-language instruction and the humanities were generally downgraded, with courses in

488

Western literature entirely eliminated. History retained a bit more of its integrity as a discipline, with emphasis at the honors level placed on modern Burmese history. Premedical instruction at the upper levels was conducted by Polish and Czech lecturers. The separate, Soviet-built Rangoon Technical Institute was run by competent Russian instructors, who lectured to the students in faltering English.

Attendance at the various university centers increased substantially, from 20,600 students in 1964–65 to more than 33,000 in 1967–68, but academic standards deteriorated alarmingly. Entrance requirements were lowered, but even so only 12 percent of the candidates for university entrance in any particular year qualified as matriculants.[36] Preparatory school standards, already low in the fifties, declined further following Ne Win's nationalization of mission high schools in 1962 and his complete exclusion of all missionary personnel in late 1965. But education still afforded virtually the only available avenue for the enhancement of social status.

Meanwhile, the educational program became increasingly divorced from traditional social values. An American observer intimately acquainted with several Upper Burma communities commented:

> The problems that surround the individual as he pushes past the village, town, and family to gain a University degree are strong evidence that . . . the price of progress has been social tragedy.[37]

Thus the Marxist doctrine of class struggle fitted very badly into the Burmese social context. The Burmese tradition, in any case, encouraged no expectation that the government would be genuinely concerned about the welfare of the ordinary citizen.[38] Most persons refused to credit U Ba Nyein's pretensions of such concern; attempts to implement his Communist formula, colored by exhortations borrowed from Mao Tse-tung, were irrelevant to the actual situation. The commercial

489

fiasco of the People's Stores and the fact of officially promoted economic paralysis made no sense. An Eastern European diplomat was reported to have commented: "It would not be so embarrassing if the government did not call it socialism."

Religion under the Revolutionary Council

General Ne Win inherited from Premier Nu the difficult task of dealing with monastic partisanship. Prohibiting overt religious demonstrations settled nothing of importance. No endeavor was made to improve positive adherence to the code of monastic discipline found in the Buddhist scriptures or to encourage their study, as Nu had undertaken to do with disappointing results.[39] The essential task of registering all genuinely ordained monks, so that spurious wearers of the yellow robe could be readily identified, failed utterly.

General Ne Win's religious policies differed drastically from those of Premier Nu in terms of objectives and methods of realizing them. When *pongyi* political demonstrators in Mandalay protested his abandonment of Buddhism as the official state religion, Ne Win ordered troops to fire on the procession, and several monks were killed. Such overt demonstrations ceased, but the general experienced no more success than Nu in his two efforts to register the *Sangha* membership in 1962 and 1964. Marxist partisans within the Revolutionary Council favored challenging the validity of the Buddhist tradition itself for failure to contribute to the realization of socialist goals.

Burmese religion, although in a sad state of decline, continued to function at a variety of social levels. Primitive aspects of religion related to planting and harvest rites, to Buddhist lenten and new year's celebrations, and to reverence for sacred objects and taboos. *Nat* spirits, associated with natural objects such as mountains, river, lakes, village sites, and family homes, continued to be propitiated in routine fashion. Food for

the omnipresent *spirits* was provided at festival occasions associated with Buddhist calendrical celebrations. Thus the basic tradition of canonical Buddhism
functioned in Burma in close juxtaposition with more
primitive rites and at levels impervious to modernist
influences, including Marxist propaganda. Life-cycle
ceremonies, such as the *shinbyu* initiation of youth
into the monastic community for a minimal period, and
the ear-boring ceremony for girls, persisted with little
change. Buddhism still provided a potent symbol of
Burma's national identity. Ethnic and social traditions
ran far deeper than the surface evidences of rivalry and
contention between competing economic and political
ideologies.[40]

Both the liberal, Western approach to political and
social problems and the contrary viewpoint of Marxist
secularism were culturally alien to Burmans. Ne Win's
special brand of Burmese socialism had degenerated into
little more than an agency of popular oppression. In
the hierarchy of Burmese Buddhist values, industry,
thrift, and the accumulation of wealth were not worthy
social objectives unless associated with particular acts
of Buddhist merit, such as construction of pagodas or
contributions to the needs of monks. The doctrine of
Karma, the law of deeds, provided a more effective
sanction to ethical conduct than could any kind of disciplined dedication to governmental objectives, however
rationalized. Pious monks continued to command respect
as the custodians of religious truth and as exemplars
of morality.

A resurgence of Buddhist devotion began in 1968. It
developed in part as a foil to government policy, but
also as an angry popular reaction to alleged Communist
plundering of a number of religious shrines in Lower
Burma. Popular participation in Buddhist festivals increased, and Ne Win himself visited the Buddha Gaya
shrine on one of his trips to India, bringing back a
sapling allegedly derived from the Bodhi tree that had
sheltered Gautama.[41] In prospect was a definite swing

of the cultural pendulum in the direction of traditional values that were rooted deep in Burmese experience but unrelated to dire economic needs.

Domestic Opposition to the Ne Win Regime

Popular hostility to continuing army rule was widespread but uncoordinated. Opposition elements were splintered along ethnic lines and also as a result of varying reactions to Communist efforts to exploit the general dissatisfaction. A secretive National Liberation Council (NLC) had been organized as early as 1963, under the leadership of Bo Let Ya, Bo Kya Doe, and Dr. Ba Maw's son-in-law, Bo Yan Naing. Kya Doe managed to assemble a small National Liberation Army near the Thai border in May 1965. It was later driven across the border in the area of the Three Pagodas Pass, protected in its retreat by a local Karen force led by one Bo Mya's group in Tenasserim, and the dissident Karens. NLC maintained thereafter a kind of jungle headquarters from which to conduct desultory raids across the Burma line; meanwhile, however, the Council failed to reach cooperative agreements with Shan and Kachin rebels.[42]

The Karen dissidents split four ways. A conservative Christian faction, led by Saw Hunter, came to terms with the government in 1966 under terms previously described. A more radical younger faction collaborated to some degree with the White Flag Communists operating from hill areas that bordered the middle Sittang Valley. Bo Mya's group in Tenasserim and the dissident Karens in the delta operated as semibandits, raiding local People's Stores to obtain supplies for needy villagers, in return for concealment and food.

Upper Burma dissidents were split in comparable fashion. An anti-Communist Shan Unity Preparatory Committee offered in the spring of 1969 to enter into a cease-fire arrangement preparing for peace negotiations with the army regime. Some fifteen hundred Shan rebels reportedly surrendered their guns, but acceptable peace terms were not forthcoming, and the dissident elements revived their Communist alignment. The once-aggressive Kuomintang refugees in the Kengtung State ceased military activity so long as their opium operations were unmolested. Along the middle reaches of Burma's China border, Peking-supported Burman Communists invaded the northern Shan States in 1967 as far as Kutkai, where they were repulsed by government forces. Two Kachin rebel groups, one led by Naw Seng and the other by Zaw Tu, maintained relations with the Chinese border authorities but had none with the Burman Communists.[43]

In 1967–68 the Burman Communist movement itself split into rival factions over the question of relations with Communist China. Contributing to the China policy feud was the official diplomatic break with Peking in 1967 (to be described below), which was precipitated by aggressive activities by Red Guard demonstrators in the Rangoon schools. In the early months of 1968 government forces managed to overrun the long-occupied Pegu Yoma Communist headquarters, which reduced the twenty-year-old rebellion to mere nuisance proportions. Meanwhile, the pro-Chinese Burman Communist faction, led by the venerable Thakin Than Tun, challenged his long-time anti-China associates, U Ba Tin (Goshal) and Yebaw Htay. The embittered feud ended finally in the assassination of Than Tun on September 24, 1968.[44]

Meanwhile, General Ne Win made concerted efforts to develop better rapport with his own people. During the first ten months of 1967, he released some 750 political prisoners and removed 34 consumer items from the controlled list. The government's housing construction program was expanded in 1967, and improved health and security benefits were provided for urban workers. During his periodic trips through the countryside, Ne Win began listening to popular complaints concerning the price of consumer goods, nutritional problems, factory unemployment, trade restrictions, and

493

lack of incentives for rice production. The immediate psychological response was encouraging, but few tangible improvements were forthcoming.[45]

Foreign Relations of the Revolutionary Government

There was little difference of opinion at Rangoon on the necessity of avoiding involvement in another World War and maintaining friendly relations with China. From 1956 to 1960 both Nu and Ne Win made persistent efforts to work out a settlement of the 1,360-mile China border. Mao Tse-tung's negotiators were generally cooperative, and an agreement was finally reached by the retiring caretaker regime in early 1960, followed by extensive surveying operations by a Burmese army unit.

The formal border agreement was signed by Premier Nu in Peking in October 1960. In terms suggesting a possible revival of the traditional vassal-suzerain relationship, China stipulated that Burma must not permit its territory to be used by a third party for aggressive purposes against China. While affirming its right of self-defense, Burma pledged that possible international resistance to Chinese moves along the borders of India, Laos, or Thailand would not be based on Burma's soil. On January 4, 1961, the anniversary of Burma's independence, an exchange of ratifications between Burma and China was completed at Rangoon covering a supplementary Treaty of Friendship and Mutual nonaggression.[46]

After 1962, under the Ne Win regime, Burma's policy toward China became even more carefully neutralist than before. The Marxist aspects of the *Burmese Way to Socialism* provided an ideological basis for rapprochement that had previously been lacking. Government personnel exchanged frequent visits. China responded by extending to Burma a loan of $84 million in return for Rangoon's agreement to provide rice to China on a barter basis. The loan was intended for the construction of irrigation works and factories to be installed by Chinese technicians. Only a small fraction of the loan was actually used.[47]

Meanwhile, the Revolutionary Council government maintained only minimal relations with the United States. American embassy and consular personnel were permitted little or no contact with government officials or with civilians in general. A prior American agreement signed with Nu in 1961 to provide military equipment for the army at discount prices to the total value of some $42 million, was honored by Washington. Shipments of small arms continued, though unpublicized, for the six ensuing years. Another agreement, under which the United States undertook to pay approximately half the cost of constructing an improved trunk road running from Rangoon to Mandalay (some $30 million), was cancelled for reasons which can only be surmised.[48]

By contrast, Ne Win's relations with the USSR improved progressively after 1962. Russian technicians were invited to complete several of the projects promised by Chairman Khrushchev in 1956, including a luxury hotel, a sports stadium, and the Rangoon Technical Institute. Other items were cancelled. Moscow's growing friendship with Burma involved the implied repudiation by Moscow of the Burma Communist party in favor of balance of power considerations. The Soviet government wanted among other things to maintain via Burma an assured entry into Southeast Asia as a balance against the prospect of growing Chinese influence there.

The increasing number of Burmese economic contacts with Eastern Europe was matched by the West only in the case of Canada. Canadian assistance had been solicited during the rule of the caretaker regime in financing and constructing new roadways and bridges to connect Rangoon with two satellite cities built to accommodate the removed squatter population. Canadian wheat shipments provided counterpart funds to help meet local costs, to purchase construction materials, and to hire engineers. As a gesture of good will, Brigadier Tin Pe of the Revolutionary Council accepted an invitation to attend the Montreal Trade Fair in 1966, and the Rangoon authorities permitted an increasing number of Burmese students to go to Canada.

But generally speaking, the overriding concern of the Ne Win government to maintain internationally a neutralist stance discouraged solicitation and acceptance of any substantial amounts of foreign aid. The rationale for such a policy was that Burma must learn how to develop its own economic resources, and that the temporary economic difficulties must be endured as part of the price of avoiding involvements in dangerous situations developing elsewhere in Southeast Asia.[49] Particularly ominous to Rangoon was expanding American intervention in Vietnam, coupled with Bangkok's consent for American planes to use newly constructed airfields in Thailand for bombing raids on Laos and North Vietnam. Burmese authorities insisted that their strictly neutralist stance implied no enmity toward any of the several contestants, provided they agreed to omit Burma from their plans. Rangoon's refusal in 1966 to utilize a three-million-dollar, interest-free loan offered by Communist China and to deny the entry of Chinese experts to implement the contemplated projects prompted a protest visit from Chou En-lai.[50]

In an apparent move to balance off his repeated visits to Peking and Moscow, General Ne Win journeyed to Washington in September 1966. The visit was decidedly low key. Ne Win requested that no formal reception be staged and refused to enter into economic or political talks in a serious way. At a dinner reception President Johnson acknowledged Burma's effort to pursue an independent foreign policy and affirmed America's desire to help the peoples of Southeast Asia live and prosper free of the threat of outside interference or aggression. Johnson looked forward to the day when the energies and resources currently expended in conflict could become part of a great cooperative effort to improve living conditions for all the peoples of Southeast Asia. Ne Win responded by hoping that his visit might contribute to better understanding, but he refused contact with the press and enjoyed playing his specially arranged golf game with an old acquaintance, Gene Sarazen.[51] The visit probably rendered Ne Win somewhat less suspicious and hostile to American activities in Southeast Asia, but its total effect was obviously meager.

A Break with China, 1967

Peking was far more insistent on obtaining Burma's cooperation internationally than Washington had been. In the spring of 1966 China's Liu Shao-chi and Foreign Minister Chen Yi made a formal visit to Rangoon in a futile effort to persuade Ne Win to abandon his proposed Washington visit and to denounce the American presence in South Vietnam. Liu's failure in this endeavor may have contributed to his subsequent discrediting in China. By early 1967 the Rangoon press began complaining that propaganda efforts associated with China's developing Cultural Revolution were impinging on the Chinese residents of Burma. The approximately three hundred Chinese technical experts present within Burma at the time were accordingly restricted in their movements. But Burma was courting no trouble. As late as May 1967 Burma's police surrendered to Chinese custody a number of Kuomintang agitators captured along the frontier.[52]

Peking's motives in precipitating the rift of June 1967 were far from clear. Efforts to influence Burma's Chinese community to identify themselves with the aims of the Cultural Revolution may have been designed to balance off the losses in prestige sustained during the previous year in Indonesia, but the connection is unclear. The move may also have been designed to strengthen the pro-China Than Tun faction of the Burma Communist party in its feud with Goshal and Yebaw Htay. A third suggestion is that Peking was angry with Ne Win and wished to embarrass him as a renegade Marxist. After the break occurred, the Peking radio began denouncing the Revolutionary Council as "fascist, racist, and reactionary" and exhorting the Burmese people to rebel, seize power, and strike Ne Win to the ground. It also praised the cause of the White Flag Communist "liberators."[53]

Trouble started in the Chinese-language schools of Rangoon in late June 1967 with the distribution of Maoist badges provided by the embassy. When efforts to coerce resident Chinese students to conform to the Maoist propaganda line were challenged, partisan elements barricaded school buildings against the police and abused both teachers and news photographers. Those who manned the barricades were sent food by the Chinese Embassy. Violence subsequently spread to the Chinese business district, where, in the absence of police restraint, Burman mobs sacked many of the stores. When a Chinese Embassy guard fired into the ranks of a protesting group, the premises were overrun and one member of the Embassy staff was killed. Police action eventually halted the violence, but not until a Chinese mob similarly threatened the Burmese Embassy in Peking.[54] The extent of the furor and violence obviously exceeded the wishes and intentions of both governments. Meanwhile, Ne Win's popularity within Burma gained significantly.

The Burmese press reflected the government's anger. It charged that Chinese Embassy authorities had acted contemptuously. It recalled that Ne Win had four times visited Peking and that he had cooperated loyally in restraining the border refugees. Peking's radio had been gratuitously insulting, leaving little room for reconciliation. The government arrested two hundred Peking sympathizers and closed down the pro-China Burmese-language newspaper. Ne Win also expelled around five hundred Chinese technicians, plus the local correspondent of the *China Daily Mail*, and then recalled Burma's ambassador to Peking. A seven-man economic mission from the Soviet Union was invited to visit Burma in August and September of 1967. Burma also resumed the purchase of small arms from America, after a selected defense team visited a Tokyo military exhibit to indicate what they wanted. American pilot instructors arrived to train crews to operate several new F-86 fighter aircraft. Whatever expectations Peking may have entertained of strengthening the Than Tun Communist faction ended with his assassination in September 1968. Burma did not qualify as an Asian Czechoslovakia, and Ne Win emerged as a national champion.[55]

The principal gain from the Sino-Burma quarrel went to the Soviet Union and its Eastern European allies. But Burma also developed improved relations with West Germany and Japan, neither of which could be charged with harboring anti-Chinese or pro-Russian designs. In connection with Chancellor Kiesinger's visit in November 1967, West Germany offered to purchase Burma's rubber and tin and agreed to supply in return needed industrial machinery in the amount of $20 million. Burma's newspaper coverage, meanwhile, was extended to include items furnished by sources in North Korea, both the Vietnams, and Prague.[56] In somewhat equivocal fashion, the Burmese government announced that it would not oppose a victory for the Vietcong in South Vietnam if it were clear that Chinese influence and control were not enhanced thereby.[57]

Friction within Rangoon's Revolutionary Council developed in late 1968, apparently from General Ne Win's disillusionment over the feasibility of the ideas set forth in the *Burmese Way to Socialism*. His boldest move was made in November, 1968, when he invited thirty-three of his one-time AFPFL associates, led by past Premier Nu, to propose solutions for the problem of national disunity. Their recommendations of May 1969, will be considered later. Brigadier Tin Pe and Economic Advisor Ba Nyein countered Ne Win's move at the time by expanding the government's nationalization program to include most of private enterprise that had survived previous actions. The *Guardian* newspaper questioned the wisdom of such gratuitous nationalization in view of the dismal outcome of previous efforts.[58]

Eventually relations with China began to improve. In

connection with his visit to West Pakistan in early 1969, Ne Win conferred with Chinese spokesmen over terms of a possible reconciliation. His price at the time was that China cease supporting the faltering Burmese Communist rebellion. No immediate settlement of differences was realized, but tensions relaxed and Burma's neutralist stance persisted. The Chinese Embassy at Rangoon ceased efforts at pro-Maoist agitation in the schools and eased its previous pressure to influence Chinese youths to go to China for advanced educational training.[59]

Relations with India and Thailand

One item of border friction with India concerned the illicit trade conducted from China across northern Burma to rebel leaders active in India's Naga hills. Burma's Kachin tribesmen acted as intermediaries in transmitting not only small arms but also valuable items such as watches, cameras, radios, and cutlery, all saleable in India, as a means of financing both the Kachin and the Naga-Mizo rebellions. As a means of getting their savings out of Burma, Indian merchants there paid for Chinese goods in *kyats* and accepted in return IOU statements payable in Indian currency. This troublesome situation became the subject of negotiation between Rangoon and India's Premier Indira Gandhi during the course of her visit to Burma in March 1969. Ne Win then agreed to make a concerted effort to halt such smuggling operations as part of the implementation of boundary treaties previously negotiated with both India and Pakistan in 1967.[60]

Another point of difference with India involved the continuing exodus of long-time Indian residents of Burma under punitive measures imposed by the Revolutionary Council, which denied them any legal opportunity of earning a livelihood by trading. Mrs. Gandhi and Ne Win agreed that some sixty thousand Burma-born Indian residents of Lower Burma would be made eligible to obtain full citizenship rights. Ne Win's concession in this instance was grudgingly given, as was evident in accompanying official press comment. The *Working People's Daily* declared that Burma's friendly treatment of foreign residents was conditional on their positive identification with activities designed to promote national welfare, including political noninterference and nonusurpation of economic power. Some four-fifths of Burma's Indian population were not included within the treaty terms and continued to be denied the opportunity for obtaining citizenship rights.[61]

Problems developing in Burma-Thailand border relations from the early 1950s were settled amicably. In 1952–53 Burma had objected to Bangkok's approval of the use of Thailand's airfields by American-manned planes, based on Taiwan, to supply arms to the Kuomintang forces in Burma's easternmost Shan States. Thailand later assisted the evacuation to Taiwan of some six thousand refugees, using the same airfield facilities. Meanwhile the Thai asked Burma to permit their use of the Salween River for teak-log shipments downstream to the Moulmein mills, without incurring prohibitive customs dues. Burma's counter request concerned the free marketing of minerals of Burma origin across the Thai borders. The volume of trade in both directions was slight. Such matters were eventually covered by the 1955 Treaty of Friendship, which also included travel regulations and extradition rights.

Relations were also improved by mutual gestures of good will. In connection with his visit to Thailand in 1956, Premier Nu contributed a substantial sum toward the erection of a new canopy to cover the giant statue of Buddha located on the ruined palace site at Ayuthia, which the Burmans had destroyed in 1767. Marshal Pibun made a friendly rejoinder by accompanying an elite Thai dancing troup to Burma as a contribution to cultural exchange. Golf teams also exchanged visits. Some minor troubles developed later at the southernmost point of Burma's Tenasserim coastal province, where Thai fishermen were accused of infringing on Burmese waters. Less easily negotiated were Rangoon's charges that Thai officials tolerated the presence along the interior Tenasserim frontier of refugees from Burma who were hostile to the Revolutionary Council. In the north, the Thai permitted the posting of a Burmese consul at Chiengmai as a somewhat ineffective means of checking clandestine shipments of arms to rebel elements still active in the Shan States. Relations remained formally friendly.

Prospects for Change in Burma's Policy

In May 1968 the government convened at Rangoon a Central People's Workers Council in a move that was widely proclaimed as a major step toward the realization of long-promised popular participation. The fourteen hundred delegates included workers by brain as well as brawn who had been selected more or less arbitrarily. The sessions became unusually acrimonious. Several delegates proposed that the annual seminars be discontinued unless the government was prepared to satisfy legitimate complaints. Others insisted that the principal obstacle to the exercise of workers' rights and privileges actually derived from official policies. For example, workers in the People's Stores could not live on their meager wages unless they resorted to stealing and black-market dealings. The government was doing nothing about the rising prices of food and the growing unemployment in factories and mills, both public and private, which were closing down for lack of machinery replacements and raw materials.[62]

The outcome of the sessions was, inevitably, negative. General Ne Win's concluding address criticized both the organizing committee and the assembled delegates. He insisted that any decision to transfer responsibility from the official Socialist Program party to the contemplated Workers and Peasants Councils must await satisfactory cooperation on the part of the latter. The following ex-

502

cerpt from Ba Nyein's concluding address, as reported in the official press, reflected the government's point of view:

Workers and peasants . . . can make or mar the Socialist Revolution. . . . All the means of production, transportation, and distribution have been nationalized. The workers today work for themselves and for the country, . . . not for the benefit of any employers. They must . . . show a greater sense of responsibility and discipline in their work . . . , not so much slackening on the job, so much malingering. . . . They are late in coming, early in leaving, slovenly in work. . . . The old antagonistic stance against administrators, managers, supervisors, and superintendents must be replaced by a spirit of cooperation, comraderie, and . . . venture for the common good.[63]

Although by 1968 the "Burmese way to socialism" had reached a dead end in efforts to achieve social justice and freedom from want, the prospect for constructive change was dubious. If General Ne Win were to pass abruptly from the scene, Brigadier Tin Pe, Colonel Than Sein, and Ba Nyein would be left in full control. One alternative prospect would be a struggle for power within the armed forces, which would benefit no one. The most hopeful possibility was that the doctrinaire Marxist leadership within the Council could be phased out, which would give Ne Win the opportunity to enlist a different kind of leadership for both policy determination and administration. Ne Win was still needed to control the army and to awe restive civilian elements, but he was not adjudged capable of revising policies without help from the outside. It would be difficult under any conceivable circumstances to deny the army leadership the perquisites of power it had so long enjoyed. But there was probably less corruption and peculation at high levels of Burmese government than among ruling groups elsewhere in Southeast Asia, partly because the opportunities for graft were more limited. Whatever happened, the army would still be around and could not be ignored.[64]

The Advisory Board Report

Against this background of persisting hope that some valuable experience might be realized from Burma's faltering effort at socialization, the deliberations of the Internal Unity Advisory Board in early 1969 took on significance. The body was commissioned on December 4, 1968, and continued its sessions until May. Its thirty-three members could hardly be objective, for they included a number of political and governmental leaders who had been detained in jail. A former Union president, the Karen Mahn Win Maung, was designated chairman. Cabinet members from previous regimes were ex-Premiers Nu and Ba Swe, plus Kyaw Nyein and Raschid. The Board was asked to propose political and constitutional changes calculated to solve the problem of national disunity.

The findings of the group, as submitted in May 1969, received full publicity in the press and some initial indication of qualified acceptance by General Ne Win. The majority report, attributed to U Nu and supported by eighteen of the 33 members, proposed the restoration of constitutional government. At the outset, Nu would resume the post of premier, and all available members of the 1962 Parliament would reassemble to legalize the selection of General Ne Win as the new president of the Burma Union. Nu would continue in office until the constitutional powers of both the legislative and judicial branches were re-established and the sovereign rights of the people guaranteed. He would then resign as premier, and President Ne Win would be empowered to select a new cabinet, presumably responsible to the legislature. Members of the Unity Advisory Board would continue to be available for counsel as a kind of elder statesman group. One of the first responsibilities of the new president would be to convene a national convention, representing all parties and nationality groups, to draft a new constitution. The report also suggested that an Arakan and a Mon state be added to the Burma Union membership.[65]

An eleven-member minority report of the Board also recommended important changes, but not in the direction

504

of restoring democracy. They proposed that a single-party Socialist system be created to include broadly functional representation of workers, peasants, political intelligentsia, and technicians. Democracy was rejected, but so was military rule. The minority reports recommended that state control be relaxed over minor activities in the economic field while continuing the regulation of large-scale industry. Foreign capital investment was flatly rejected. At intermediate levels of the economy, cooperative and joint state-private ventures would be encouraged, but no impediment should be placed in the way of small-scale private business. Kyaw Nyein and two other dissidents revived the argument for systematic socialistic planning, including the stipulation that the autonomous powers of the several constituent states of the Union be limited to noneconomic cultural matters.[66]

The merits of the several proposals tended to be lost in the ensuing welter of personal invective. Nu was the principal target of the government media. Even prior to the appearance of the report, both Burmese- and English-language papers denounced Nu for allegedly seeking to return to power by appealing to Buddhist partisanship and repeated bribe accusations dating from the Peace Pagoda period. What was lacking was a forum in which the proposed reforms could be examined with some measure of objectivity. In the end General Ne Win refused to break with his defiant army associates and rejected all of the proposed reforms.[67]

A basic weakness of the Board's report was its failure to pay adequate attention to the grievances of ethnic minority peoples, some of whom would trust the integrity of Nu, but few of whom would accept any cabinet selected by Ne Win. Their membership in the eventual Constituent Convention, as proposed by Nu, did not guarantee approval of their demands for effective control over mining, timber, and other forms of economic productivity within their several states. Both political and ethnic pacification were far removed in time.[68]

Nu's Challenge to Ne Win

For U Nu, the publication of the report was the culmination rather than the initiation of his challenge of army rule. A year earlier, in May 1968, Nu and his associates had attracted wide public attention in Rangoon by sponsoring efforts to collect relief funds for victims in the typhoon-devastated Arakan coastal area. The government objected, but it could hardly justify interference with such charitable activity. Later in the year Nu toured various major cities of Burma, including Moulmein and Mandalay, not as an aspiring politician but ostensibly as a lecturer on Buddhism. Everywhere he drew huge crowds. Operators of pony carts and buses cut fares to bring eager hearers to his lectures, for his presence was contagious. In the context of the dismal record of the Revolutionary Council, people tended to forget Nu's own faltering performance as premier and to regard his 1960-62 regime with a sense of nostalgia.

It was partly to remove his embarrassing presence that Ne Win consented, in June 1969, to Nu's request that he be permitted to journey to India to obtain medical attention and to visit Buddhist shrines. From India Nu proceeded to Thailand on the invitation of Marshal Thanom Kittikachorn to inspect the canopy at Ayuthia, which he had helped sponsor in 1956. It was in Bangkok that Nu made contact with dissident Burman revolutionaries, including kinsmen of the former Adhipati Ba Maw. He denounced the oppressive Revolutionary Council regime as flagrantly Fascist. It had disrupted the Burmese economy, provoked minority rebellion, and arbitrarily imprisoned political critics. The so-called nationalization program he castigated as open thievery of citizens' property for the personal profit of the army officers responsible.

From Bangkok Nu proceeded to London, where he met the militant rebel leader Bo Let Ya. While in London, Nu urged overseas Burmans to no longer sit idly by while their country was being ruined. Burmese patriots must unite to expel the usurpers, he urged, since the ruling military clique was impervious to persuasion. He received space in the British press, but no encouragement from the London government. Proceeding to New York in early September, Nu conferred with his long-time personal friend at the United Nations, U Thant, and addressed representatives of that body. He indicated via the New York press that his first objective was to broaden the existing "liberated area" located near the Thai border, so that a credible exile government might raise a standard to which all dissident groups could rally. The eventual popular rising he envisioned would include opposition elements within the Burmese government and the army.[69] But as had been the case in England, Nu's hope of attracting official support in the United States was disappointed, although he apparently did gain some private backing.

Although the odds against the early success of Nu's revolutionary initiative were obviously forbiddingly high, Ne Win's regime became increasingly unpopular and defensive. The abrupt retirement of Brigadier Tin Pe in November 1970 was one straw in the wind. Abler and more responsible leadership must be found, preferably by peaceful means. The task was becoming increasingly difficult because of the continuing exodus of former cabinet personnel. U Ba Swe made his way to Thailand in late 1972. The pickings were getting thin.

Whether democracy could again become effectively operative in Burma was a difficult question. It may be relevant in this connection to quote from a speech by Premier Nu himself delivered before the India Council of World Affairs in November 1960:

> The democratic system of government, although the most desirable, is at the same time the most difficult . . . to operate. . . . Democracy simply cannot be forced on a people, however enlightened the rulers may be. The basic principles of democracy have to be applied in such as way as to suit the local conditions, local beliefs, and local customs. This means a slow process of gradual growth and . . . education. . . .

507

Most of the countries of Asia have been independent
for just over a decade. This fact makes doubly unfair the
question 'Are Asians fit for democracy?' I suppose the
correct answer to this question is: 'Ask in a few hundred
years time, and I will tell you not only whether the
Asians but all other peoples of the world are fit for democracy.' . . .
Having come to power by democratic means, many of
our leaders have fallen prey.. . to . . . evils and have
thereby forfeited the confidence of their peoples. In a
long-established democracy, such a government would be
thrown out by the electorate at the next election if not
sooner. . . . These same corrupted leaders are . . .
often tempted to evade the democratic consequences of
their conduct by adopting unfair means to perpetuate
themselves in power. . . . In Burma, we have a saying:
'Only a gold cup is good enough to hold a lion's fat.'
Similarly, only good men can successfully operate a
democratic system of government.[70]

1. See Lucian Pye, "The Army in Burmese Politics," in John J. Johnson, *The Role of the Military in Underdeveloped Countries* (Princeton, 1963), pp. 153-57.

2. John H. Badgley, "Burma: the Nexus of Socialism and Two Political Traditions," *Asian Survey* 3 (February 1963): 89-91.

3. William C. Johnstone, *Burma's Foreign Policy* (Cambridge, 1963), Appendix IV, pp. 313-17.

4. Badgley, *op. cit.*, pp. 89-91: Josef Silverstein, "First Steps on the Burmese Way to Socialism," *Asian Survey* 4 (February 1964): 716-21.

5. Josef Silverstein, "Burma," in Kahin, ed., *Governments and Politics in Southeast Asia* (Ithaca, 1964), pp. 133-46: Fred M. Van der Mehden, "The Burmese Way to Socialism," *Asian Survey* 3 (March 1963): 129-35.

6. R. S. Milne, "Political Finances in Southeast Asia," *Pacific Affairs* 41 (1968-69): 499.

7. Eye-witness report, orally communicated, by Lucien Pye.

8. *New York Times*, November 22, 1962.

9. *Ibid.*, August 2, 10, and 13, 1963; George A. Theodorson, "Minority Peoples in the Union of Burma," *Journal of Southeast Asian History* 5 (March 1964): 6-14.

10. *New York Times*, August 2, 1963; Silverstein, "First Steps," pp. 716-21.

11. For the terms of the peace, see *New York Times*, April 13, 1964.

12. Silverstein, "Burma," in Kahin, *op. cit.*, p. 152.

13. Badgley, "Burma," pp. 91-95.

14. For a discussion of the China parallel, see Maurice Meisner, "Utopian Goals and Ascetic Values in Communist Chinese Ideology," *Journal of Asian Studies* 28 (November 1968): 101-10.

15. *Feer, 1968 Yearbook*, "Burma: Politics," pp. 121-122.

16. *FEER*, May 30, 1963, p. 494.

17. Silverstein, "First Steps," pp. 716-21.

18. *FEER,* April 1, 1968, pp. 134, 136.
19. *New York Times,* August 3, 1963, and January 13, 1964.
20. *Ibid.,* December 2, 1966.
21. John Ashdown, "Burma's Political Puzzle," *FEER,* September 17, 1964, pp. 516-19.
22. *FEER,* April 21, 1966, p. 167.
23. *New York Times,* December 1, 1966, and April 28, 1967.
24. *FEER,* November 28, 1968, p. 500.
25. *Ibid.,* May 26, 1966, pp. 417-19.
26. *Ibid.,* March 21, 1968, pp. 510-11.
27. *Ibid.,* March 14, 1968, p. 444.
28. *New York Times,* January 20, 1967.
29. *Ibid.,* December 2, 1966.
30. *Guardian,* May 30, 1968, by Soe Naing.
31. John H. Badgley, "Burma's China Crisis," *Asian Survey* 7 (November 1967): 753-61.
32. *FEER,* November 23, 1967, p. 352.
33. *Guardian,* May 31, 1968, a letter from U Mya Han.
34. *Ibid.,* editorial for May 30, 1968.
35. Badgley, "Burmese Intellectuals," *Asian Survey* 9 (August 1969): 611-13.
36. *FEER, 1968 Yearbook,* "Burma: Social Affairs," pp. 123-24.
37. Badgley, "Burmese Intellectuals," pp. 611-13.
38. See Htin Aung, *A History of Burma* (New York, 1967).
39. Fred van der Mehden, "Buddhism and Politics in Burma," *Antioch Review* 21 (1961): 166-75.
40. John Brohm. "Buddhism and Animism in a Buddhist Village," *Journal of Asian Studies* 22 (February 1963): 155-57.
41. *FEER,* December 12, 1968, p. 601.
42. *Ibid.,* September 7, 1967, pp. 453, 460-62.
43. Louis Kraar, "Thailand," in *Time Magazine World,* February, 1967.
44. Frank N. Trager, "Burma; 1968—A New Beginning," *Asian Survey* 9 (February 1969): 104-14; *FEER,* June 12, 1969, p. 603.
45. *FEER, 1968 Yearbook,* p. 122; also *FEER.* February 1, 1968, p. 185.
46. Daphne Whittam, "The Sino-Burmese Boundary Treaty," *Pacific Affairs* 34 (1961): 174-83.
47. Badgley, "Burma," pp. 89-95.
48. *Bangkok World,* May 22, 1968.
49. Johnstone, *op. cit.,* pp. 294-300.
50. *New York Times.* May 2, 1967.
51. *Ibid.,* September 8 and 9, 1966.
52. *FEER,* September 30, 1967, pp. 630-31.
53. Badgley, "Burma's China Crisis," pp. 753-61
54. *FEER,* September 30, 1967, pp. 630-31; *ibid.,* November 12, 1967, pp. 314-17.
55. Badgley, "Burma's China Crisis," pp. 753-61.
56. *FEER,* February 1, 1968. p. 185; *ibid.,* October 3, 1968, p. 65.
57. Badgley, "Burma's China Crisis," pp. 753-61.
58. *FEER,* January 9, 1969, pp. 40, 44, 92.
59. *Ibid.,* February 20, 1969, 311; and June 12, 1969, p. 603.
60. *Ibid.,* March 20, 1969, pp. 583-85; and April 7, 1969, p. 124.
61. *Ibid.,* May 22, 1969, p. 440.
62. *Ibid.,* May 22, 1969, pp. 387-88.

63. *Guardian*, May 26, 1968.
64. *FEER*, January 9, 1969, p. 92.
65. *Ibid.*, July 3, 1969, p. 8.
66. *Ibid.*
67. S. C. Banerji, "The Nu Burmese Way," *FEER*, June 22, 1969, pp. 697-98; *ibid.*, "Ideas Galore," *FEER*, July 3, 1969, p. 8.
68. *FEER*, January 6, 1969, pp. 105-6.
69. *New York Times*, August 12 and 31, and September 10, 1969.
70. U. Nu, "Asians and Democracy," *Burma Weekly Bulletin*, November 24, 1960, p. 287.

XIV

VIETNAM—1963
THROUGH 1967

Political Fragmentation and the Emergence of Khanh

The circumstances attending the overthrow of the Diem regime complicated the task of finding an effective substitute government capable of enlisting the allegiance of the peoples of South Vietnam. The Catholic refugees from North Vietnam, who numbered around six hundred thousand, were more free from dissention than were other political elements, but this group's morale was shattered following Diem's death. The other political factions that had joined in challenging the regime (three score in number) developed rifts immediately following the coup. The armed forces leadership itself was divided between the several services and commands and between the allegedly pro-French and anti-French factions, as well as by personal antagonisms.

Regional and religious rivalries aggravated the political problem. Three major factions emerged within the Buddhist community. The central Annamite leadership at Hué and Danang, whether Buddhist or Catholic, was jealous of Saigon's presumed domination. The Annamese elite, less Westernized than their counterparts in Cochin-China, were politically assertive and haughty by reason of their traditional associations with the royal court.[1]

The South Vietnamese generally resented the presumptuous role played by the more aggressive Northern Vietnamese refugees, especially in the government and the army. The principal faction of the Cao Dai sect, residing to the west of Saigon along the Cambodian border area, abandoned its previous cooperation with the anti-Diem National Liberation Front in an endeavor to obtain maximum guarantees for local autonomy. The Hoa Hao sect in the delta also resisted external control. The southernmost portion of Cochin-China, below the delta proper, was firmly under NLF control, while the six hundred thousand alien Khmers who lived in the delta and the equally numerous hill peoples to the north of Saigon acknowledged only limited allegiance to Saigon.

As far as indigenous governmental institutions were concerned, South Vietnam was virtually bankrupt. The Confucianist mandarin tradition, represented by the repudiated Emperor Bao Dai and by Diem himself, was thoroughly discredited. Diem's long-continued efforts to keep the opposition divided by resort to rigged plebiscites and managed elections had generated little popular enthusiasm for electoral processes.[2] Religious sect groupings functioned under hierarchical control, usually within defined geographical limits. Diem's centralization of bureaucratic control had been everywhere unpopular, especially where locally selected leaders had been displaced by Diem's appointees. For these and other reasons, any successor government at Saigon would experience difficulty in establishing administrative control, not to mention promoting economic improvements.

The actual repository of power in South Vietnam following Diem's death was a clique of some fifty military leaders, most of them ambitious younger men who had been trained by the French. Their varying political allegiances (Buddhist, Catholic, Cao Dai, Dai Viet, Hoa Hao) were usually lightly held, for ideological commitments were subordinate to personal associations and ambitions. The alternative civilian leadership was equally limited in number and conservative in inclination. Some of the civilian leaders were distinguished intellectuals and professionals who lacked any organized political support and were unable to agree among themselves. They downgraded the youthful military group as academic ne'er-do-wells who lacked both intellectual and political credentials. The military leaders, furthermore, tended to be either pro-French or pro-American and therefore lacked nationalist appeal. Duong Van Minh (Big Minh) was a popular exception, for he had defied the Japanese during the occupation and had suffered rough treatment. The previous administrative experience enjoyed by either the civilian or military elites was minimal.[3]

Although Washington was financing the Saigon regime almost totally and was therefore presumably able to exercise some measure of direction and control, the efforts that were exerted were halting and largely ineffectual. In general, American policy at the outset tried to encourage responsible civilian participation in government and preferred to deal with military figures who were not identified with the pro-French clique.[4] Despite his personal popularity, the easy-going General (Big) Minh proved disappointing as a government leader. He was teamed with Nguyen Ngoc Tho, the titular Premier, a Catholic who had been carried over from the Diem regime. Whereas Diem and Nhu had previously made all of the decisions, Minh, by comparison, was indecisive, unaggressive, and generally lacking in the ability to formulate and execute policy. The Council of Notables that Minh and Tho brought together to draft a new constitution spent much of its limited time in sterile debate. Minh failed to counter efforts of his army associates to block a possible transition to responsible civilian leadership. American efforts to promote the coalescence of the many disparate political factions into a limited number of identifiable party organizations also failed. Meanwhile, the government abandoned the strategic hamlet program as both futile and wasteful.[5]

By early 1964 the faltering Minh-Tho government faced mounting consumer complaints over rising prices, worker strikes, and local student demonstrations. One aggressive clique of military officers, led by the power-hungry

General Nguyen Khanh, centered in the Hué area. They criticized Minh's alleged neutralist tendencies and his supposed encouragement of a French-conceived peace negotiation effort—a rumor apparently calculated to elicit American acquiescence in the change of leadership. Minh mounted no serious resistance to Khanh's successful February coup; with American encouragement he kept himself politically available for some six months thereafter as nominal head of the Military Council.

Although General Khanh was a French-trained officer, he had acquired a semblance of nationalist credentials for having twice defected to the Viet Minh during the course of the anti-colonialist struggle. His political support was drawn from the generally pro-Buddhist Dai Viet nationalist faction of the Hué region. His principal associates in the coup were General Tran Thien Khiem, a cadet classmate at Dalat Academy, plus the disgruntled Dai Viet General Do Mau and the outspoken, pro-Buddhist Colonel Nguyen Chanh Thi. Khanh selected three civilian vice-premiers, one of them a returned Right-wing Catholic exile from Paris and another a prominent banker-economist. But Khanh's coup generated no positive popular response.[6]

American Policy Problems in Early 1964

The alarming deterioration of the authority and effectiveness of the Saigon government, a process that had started months before the anti-Diem coup, was clearly the central problem in South Vietnam during the early months of 1964. The Vietcong admittedly controlled at least half of the forty-three provinces up to an estimated 85 percent effectiveness and were influential in a number of others. Desertions within the South Vietnam army were alarmingly high; draft dodging was increasing; and governmental administration operations between Saigon and the villages were disintegrating.[7] American civilian advisers were more effective in recognizing shortcomings than in finding solutions, as will presently be indicated, for the problem was extremely complicated. It was almost equally baffling to attempt to improve military performance.

Since overt military operations against the North were rejected as being overly risky and not feasible at the moment, American attention was focused on a program of covert activities designed to harass and sabotage enemy transportation facilities and other installations wherever accessible. It was admitted that such activities would not have any decisive or immediate influence on governmental performance in the South or on Hanoi's policies, except to serve as a possible deterrent to increased intervention from the North. But they would, of course, constitute a first step in a military program that could be diversified and escalated in the future.[8]

General Maxwell Taylor, speaking for the Joint Chiefs of Staff in January 1964, declared that the stakes for victory over Communist insurgency in South Vietnam were compellingly high. Such "wars of national liberation" must not be allowed to succeed. An American defeat in this instance would allegedly affect adversely the political orientation of all of Southeast Asia, plus India, Taiwan, South Korea, and Japan, and could damage the American image in Latin America and Africa as well.[9] Taylor concluded that the United States must make the ranking service commander at Saigon responsible for the total U.S. program in Vietnam and take over from the Saigon authorities the actual direction of the war. The United States should organize and direct large-scale commando raids against North Vietnam, using South Vietnamese and some Chinese Nationalist volunteers to destroy military facilities on the ground and to mine port approaches along the sea coast. Planes operating under South Vietnamese cover would conduct reconaissance and paratrooper drops.[10]

Harassment operations against the North as developed during 1964 were conceived and implemented by agencies of the CIA. As part of the program, "Operations 34A" conducted raids along the North Vietnamese coast using

South Vietnamese-manned junks. Rumors and other forms of propaganda were employed in psychological warfare. Less successful was the despatch and support of ground raid operations within both Laos and North Vietnam; few survivors ever returned. Elsewhere within northern Laos, several score Air America planes and other craft purporting to belong to the Royal Laotian government began to bomb Pathet Lao and North Vietnam forces and facilities. As a means of intensifying the psychological impact, the bombing was designed to become progressively more intense as operations approached ever closer to the Tonkin border. Jet fighter escorts based in Thailand were added later, and by mid-1964, U.S. destroyer patrols were sent into the Gulf of Tonkin to gather intelligence and to provide psychological support for coastal raids conducted under Operations 34A. The plans assumed that direct bombing raids on Tonkin, if and when undertaken, should include among selected targets the industrial installations that Hanoi had worked so hard to develop during the 1950s.[11]

American Relations with Khanh

Although American advisers were annoyed that Minh and Tho were pushed aside before they had an adequate chance to prove themselves, they were pleased that General Khanh was responsive initially to U.S. advice, as Diem had never been. Khanh conceded that the South Vietnamese must win their own fight, which would require an improvement of morale and popular acceptance of the government. The United States finally decided to support the Khanh government and to seek to undermine Vietcong morale by discouraging North Vietnamese assistance, but to veto any future coup ventures.[12] For the first several months, Saigon propaganda featured General Khanh as the instrument of national survival and as a would-be reformer, American style. His declared objective was to serve his people's interests by improving agriculture and transportation, together with providing protection against rebel intruders. Through his weekly propaganda broadcasts, Khanh proposed to set up an elected assembly to replace the disbanded Council of Notables; to permit free peasant use of unpurchased land; to suspend land taxes; and to provide food, health services, and housing needs. The well-advertised program was more sound than substance, however, and its limited effect was quickly dissipated by Khanh's toughened execution of his new draft law.[13]

It did not take long to discover that Khanh's inexperienced and unpopular regime was no match for the National Liberation Front politically or militarily. In considering possible policy alternatives, Washington undertook to determine the actual extent of the infiltration and influence from the North. One report indicated that most of the estimated nineteen to thirty-four thousand Vietminh troops in the South were southern born. Ambassador Lodge's expressed concern over the shakiness of the Saigon regime was confirmed on May 4, when General Khanh asked privately for an early American declaration of war against Hanoi. He also indicated that a ten-thousand man special forces contingent was needed to carry out preliminary operations. Khanh agreed at the time to make no public announcement of his request, but it was evident that Saigon had virtually abandoned any hope that Southern forces could defeat the Vietcong. Khanh's propaganda campaign about governmental and social reform efforts was thereafter abandoned in favor of a straight military approach. Ambassador Lodge himself recommended the initiation of bombing raids on the North. To cope with the deteriorating military situation, General William C. Westmoreland replaced General Harkins as chief of the Military Assistance Command, while General Maxwell Taylor took over from Lodge as ambassador,[14] with Deputy Under-Secretary of State Alexis Johnson as his assistant.

In anticipation of the need for Congressional approval of the contemplated prosecution of warfare against North Vietnam, a draft resolution, dated May 25, was prepared in Washington for possible future use. It affirmed that

Communist North Vietnam and Communist China (the USSR was not mentioned) had promoted intervention in South Vietnam and Laos in violation of international agreements of 1954 and 1962, and that Washington was reponding to requests for aid from the two threatened governments. While the United States entertained no ambition to dominate Southeast Asia, it "regarded the preservation of the independence and integrity of South Vietnam and Laos as vital to its national interest and to world peace." The resolution continued:

> If the President determines the necessity thereof, the United States is prepared, on the request of the Government of South Vietnam or the Government of Laos, to use all measures, including the commitment of armed forces, to assist that government in defense of its independence and territorial integrity against aggression or subversion supported, controlled, or directed from any Communist country.[15]

Although President Johnson backed away for the time being from the full implications of plans for attacking North Vietnam, he did move in June to assign General Taylor to the top diplomatic role in Saigon, as previously indicated. The immediate crisis involved the tensions between rival generals in Saigon and the growing defection of previously supportive Dai Viet and Buddhist political factions. The president also had to take into account the uncertainties of American opinion in an election year. Part of the White House inquiry called for a CIA intelligence report on whether the rest of Southeast Asia would necessarily fall to the Communists if North Vietnam gained control of Laos and South Vietnam. The requested report ran in part as follows:

> With the possible exception of Cambodia, it is likely that no nation in the area would quickly succumb to Communism as a result of the fall of Laos and South Vietnam. . . . A continuation of the spread of Communism in the area would not be inexorable, and any spread which did occur would take time—time in which the total situation might change in any number of ways unfavorable to the Communist cause.

It was recognized that China's prestige as a Communist world leader would gain at the expense of the USSR if South Vietnam should fall, but the United States could deter further military aggression by China or North Vietnam by power exerted from Pacific island bases. Another CIA report also pointed out that "the real roots of Vietcong strength lay in South Vietnam." Despite this detached assessment, Washington decided officially that the United States must avoid suffering any humiliating defeat.[16]

Events of July Through September 1964

Developments in late July and early August relentlessly expanded America's role in the conflict with North Vietnam. Reacting resentfully against Washington's continuing pressure to launch an emergency build-up of anti-guerrilla forces, General Khanh, supported by Air Marshal Nguyen Cao Ky, broke his promise of silence by demanding an open declaration of war on North Vietnam. Khanh made his speech before a unification rally, while Ky later talked to reporters about secret contingency plans already formulated with Washington's approval. In the heated encounter which ensued between Ambassador Taylor and Khanh on July 23, the latter told of the actual capture of drafted North Vietnamese soldiers and demanded that legal recognition be given to the fact of Hanoi's belligerency. On the following day, Khanh called Taylor's bluff by asking whether he should resign his government post.[17]

The ambassador's report to Washington on July 25 reflected alarm. For the United States to react completely negatively to General Khanh's "March North" agitation would increase dissatisfaction with the U.S. role. Taylor proposed an alternative policy of permitting Saigon's participation in contingency military planning against the North. Such a course would serve to underscore the sobering realities behind Khanh's reckless sloganeering, while affording time to better stabilize the Saigon government.[18]

Associated with the American response program was the July 30 launching of two amphibious Operations 34A raids on off-shore islands northward in the Gulf of Tonkin. On August 2 the U.S. destroyer *Maddox* also moved into the gulf, ostensibly on an intelligence mission, where it clashed with several enemy gunboats charged with countering the hostile 34A units. Three PT boats were sunk by destroyer gunfire and by carrier planes that were conveniently available. The *Maddox* returned with a second destroyer on the following day, when two additional Operations 34A attacks were also executed. The separate moves were not associated tactically, but the psychological connection was obvious. A second gunboat attack on the destroyers occurred in the early morning of August 4, and the American response included carrier plane bombing raids along the North Vietnam coast.

Whether or not they were intended to do so, the destroyer incidents provided the occasion for proclaiming a case of unprovoked aggression by Hanoi and for obtaining Congressional approval for the draft resolution of the previous May, with minor changes in wording. The relevant sentences ran as follows:

> The Congress approves and supports the determination of the President . . . to take all necessary measures to repel any armed attack against the forces of the United States and to prevent further aggression. . . . The United States is prepared, as the President determines, to . . . use . . . armed force to assist any member or protocol state of the Southeast Asia Collective Defense Treaty requesting assistance in defense of its freedom.[19]

Despite the dubious assumptions behind the alleged provocation‚the way was cleared legally for the initiation of attacks on North Vietnam if and when the president should decide that the circumstances were propitious.

It was at this crucial juncture that U.N. Secretary-General U Thant, with the help of the Russians and the support of Adlai Stevenson, U.S. ambassador to the U.N., completed arrangements for initiating peace negotiations with Hanoi. Rangoon was to have been the place of venue

520

and January 1965 the meeting date. The proposed conference had been long in preparation. Washington nevertheless flatly rejected the proposition as "insincere"[20] and denounced a contemporaneous proposal for a cease-fire in Laos as likely to damage further the morale of Saigon. Instead, the president sent a warning message to Hanoi by the visiting Canadian member of the International Control Commission.[21] It was a fateful decision. Preparations for military escalation that had been secret now became less so. The only immediate change in tactics was to abandon the costly and ineffective airdrop of saboteurs into Laos and North Vietnam and to order U.S. destroyers to stay at least twenty miles off-shore. Admittedly, such tactical plans did not constitute a coherent program strong enough to influence Hanoi's policy.[22]

Ambassador Taylor's reports of mid-August were most discouraging. Although General Khanh's "March North" agitation had bolstered military morale somewhat, he still did not command the confidence and trust of the suspicious and jealous members of his own cabinet, who lacked a common loyalty and purpose. For the most part, the people of Saigon were both confused and apathetic. Outside the capital, the government controlled only one-third of the rural areas and fewer than half of the cities. Taylor gave Khanh only a fifty-fifty chance of lasting out the year. The Vietcong, by contrast, were better armed and better led than ever before and had no difficulty replacing their losses in men and equipment. The ambassador made no attempt to explain the difference.[23] He warned Washington in a later report that as long as the American base in South Vietnam was so insecure, it would be unwise to get involved militarily with North Vietnam and possibly China. The United States should make no crusading commitment against the North until Khanh's own forces pushed the enemy away from the doors of Saigon. The sending of U.S. reinforcements to Danang and Saigon would afford time to obtain some reading on Khanh's performance. Only in case of the threatened collapse of Khanh's government would it be advisable for the United States to initiate attacks on the

521

North independent of assurances as to Saigon's performance.[24]

Events in late August proved that the ambassador's forebodings were well grounded. On August 7, Khanh placed the country under martial law, convened the Military Revolutionary Council which approved a new dictatorial constitution on August 16, and assumed himself the post of Council President previously occupied by General Duong Van Minh. The elevation of Khanh to the role of semi-dictator was opposed initially by older conservative Generals of the Council, but their hostility was mollified temporarily by assurances and concessions. The real struggle developed between dissident Buddhist elements in Saigon and Central Annam, who resented the elevation of anti-Buddhist officers and the displacement of Duong Van Minh, leader of the anti-Diem coup of 1963, and the opposing Christian groups. The latter saw in Generals Khanh, Thieu, Khiem, and Thi some assurance of protection against the hostile Buddhist majority. Buddhist rioting began in Saigon on August 21, the anniversary of Ngo Dinh Nhu's raiding of the pagoda premises of the city in 1963. Trouble spread to Hué and Danang, and violence continued for nearly a week. In Saigon, the Buddhist militants were joined by student mobs denouncing military dictatorship and demanding freedom of the press, democratic elections, and civilian rule.

Chaos prevailed for several days. Catholic partisans invaded the city, acting either under official encouragement or full toleration by the police. They burned the student headquarters and cheered for General Khanh. Order was finally restored on August 26-27, after General Khanh, acting under American and Buddhist pressure, promised a new constitution and included both General Duong Van Minh and Tran Thien Khiem in an interim state Council. Khanh then withdrew to Dalat for an indefinite period to recover from the physical and mental exhaustion sustained during the crisis. Continuing American pressure with help from a moderate Buddhist faction, both concerned to avoid civil war, contributed to Khanh's return to Saigon on September 4 and his resumption of the role of Premier.

A final episode of political violence took place on September 13-14, when a group of reactionary Dai Viet and Catholic military officers staged an abortive coup at the Saigon airport, aimed primarily at the Young Turk supporters of Khanh. They came very near succeeding, being defeated in large measure by the efforts of Air Commodore Nguyen Cao Ky and Corps I General Nguyen Chanh Thi. From this episode forward, the Young Turk officer group constituted the effective locus of power in South Vietnam, capable of controlling Khanh himself, the façade of civilian officials, and the continuing hostile senior Generals faction. From the outset, General Nguyen Van Thieu was the ranking officer of the younger group.[25]

Washington's official reaction to the events of late August and early September was one of confused alarm. Spokesmen for the Joint Chiefs of Staff were convinced that only a vigorous military response against Hanoi could prevent the complete collapse of the U.S. presence in Southeast Asia and the assumed dire consequences.[26] One of Secretary McNamara's associate secretaries on the Pentagon staff commented more directly on the Saigon problem, as follows:

> "If . . . South Vietnam disintegrates or their behavior becomes abominable, [the U. S. would have to] disown South Vietnam, hopefully leaving the image of a patient who dies despite the extraordinary efforts of a good doctor. . . . During the next two months [prior to elections] because of the lack of 'rebuttal time' to justify particular actions, which may be distorted to the U. S. public, we must . . . give the impression that we are behaving with good purpose and restraint."[27]

The pessimism dissipated somewhat following Khanh's resumption of control with enlisted civilian support. The brothers Bundy, speaking respectively from the White House and the State Department at the time, believed that Khanh's government might survive for several months, although it would be too exhausted to think of staging attacks on the North, as had previously been advocated. For the time being, American emphasis should focus on improving official civilian morale by all possible means, including pay raises and spot improvement projects.[28]

The Last Months of 1964

The dismal weeks of the late summer and early fall in South Vietnam cast their shadow over the ensuing American presidential election. Between mid-August and late September, the Democratic candidate and incumbent, Lyndon Johnson, shifted his stance from his earlier flat rejection of Senator Barry Goldwater's demands for an American escalation of the war, including the bombing of North Vietnam, to a qualified admission that such measures might eventually have to be adopted. Some kind of commitment that attacks would be made against the North became essential to salvaging morale in the South. Some American proponents of the bombing attacks, including Walter Rostow, argued unconvincingly that the Hanoi leadership would probably sue for peace rather than see their hard-won industrial gains of the fifties destroyed by bombs. The only effective way to escalate the war seemed to be by bombing attacks. On the advice of the American ambassador in Moscow, attacks designed to close the port of Haiphong were vetoed in the interest of preserving world peace.

United States advisers, meanwhile, intensified their efforts to set up a civilian government as a substitute for faltering military rule. They supported the selection of a Cao Dai political leader, Phan Khac Suu, as chief of state, while elevating Saigon's mayor, Tran Van Huong, a former school teacher, as the new premier. The two were to be assisted by an appointive High National Council of nine civilian members. Khanh continued to serve with waning enthusiasm as army chief of staff; Khiem replaced ambassador Vu Van Thai at Washington; General Minh was discarded, later to find exile in Thailand.[29]

Unfortunately the Suu-Huong regime commanded little

authority. A gloomy Pentagon intelligence report contemplated the possibility of complete disintegration of governmental and military authority and the exit of American forces within six months. Ambassador Taylor's November report indicated that counterinsurgency efforts had run aground and that the northern provinces still threatened secession. Premier Huong's faltering efforts to keep the army out of politics held out little hope, and factionalism was rife at all levels of government. Taylor concluded: "War weariness and hopelessness pervade South Vietnam. . . . We are playing a losing game."[30]

At a high-level conference in Washington from November 27 to December 1, the emergency decision to carry the air war to the North was finalized—but not without misgivings. Available details indicate that President Johnson was particularly insistent that South Vietnam's leaders be required to stop their bickering if America was to continue its support. Ambassador Taylor's simple reply to Johnson was that "we must temper our insistence." He pointed out that General Khanh as army commander was intriguing against Premier Huong, and that a clique of younger officers within the Military Revolutionary Committee, headed by Nguyen Cao Ky, was acting independent of Khanh within the civilian High National Council. Taylor would solicit improved cooperation among the leadership in return for the promise of eventual bombing attacks. Information concerning the bombing decision was transmitted to several British Commonwealth allies. Premier Wilson of the United Kingdom refused approval and cooperation; Australia and New Zealand reacted less negatively, but with no enthusiasm.[31]

The only articulate, high-level protest to the decision was advanced by Under-Secretary of State George W. Ball at the November sessions. Fortified by the considered conclusions of various Washington intelligence agencies (the CIA, the State Department's Bureau of Intelligence Research, and the Pentagon's Defense Intelligence Agency), Ball challenged the assumption that the proposed bombing attacks would break the will of Hanoi to prosecute the war. Rostow's thesis, based on European analogies,[32] was declared unsound because North Vietnam was basically an agricultural country, economically decentralized into a myriad of self-sufficient village units. The disruption of newly created industrial facilities (largely nonmilitary) and of associated internal transportation agencies would therefore have no crucial effect on the daily lives of the vast majority of the population. Bombing would not deter Hanoi's war activities—much less those of the Vietcong, who would be fully supplied with guns and munitions by Communist allies.[33] William Bundy subsequently entered a mild protest that bombings would extract no concession from Hanoi and would also provide no hope for substantial improvement of the situation at Saigon.[34]

The contest for leadership in Saigon entered a more overt phase in December, 1964, when a number of younger military officers, led by Ky and Thi, exacted a pledge from Khanh to support their demand that President Suu force the retirement of two score senior army officers, including General Duong Van Minh. When the drastic proposal was negated by the civilian High National Council on December 17, the young turk military activists seized five of the nine members of the Council and proceeded on the following day to set up their own Armed Forces Council, chaired by Khanh, to assume authority over future decisions relating to the military establishment. When they were denounced angrily by Ambassador Taylor on December 20 for staging an illegal coup and tearing up the governmental charter designed to ensure civilian participation, the activists flatly refused to back down. Air Vice-Marshall Ky criticized the High National Council for blocking the necessary retirement of Minh and senior Delat Generals, who had failed their chance to rule. He implied that the five detained Council members lacked proper anti-Communist commitments. Thus both the civilian High Council and the conservative senior army group were driven from power, and the newly-formed Armed Forces Council held the upper hand. General Khanh directly challenged Ambassador Taylor's further interference on behalf of Washington.[35]

On January 11, 1965, Secretary Rusk accordingly cabled Taylor "to avoid actions which would further commit the United States to any particular form of political solution" to Saigon's turmoil; if another military regime emerged, Rusk continued, "we might well have to swallow our pride and work with it."[36] Meanwhile the bombing plans against North Vietnam were being perfected, and the date for initiating them was set for February 20.

Political Changes and Military Escalation

When Premier Huong in January 1965 undertook to counter rising opposition from the Buddhists and from the now anti-American Khanh, a double shift ensued: Khanh ousted the Huong Cabinet on January 27, only to face a series of Dai Viet-sponsored countercoups several weeks later. The conservative Colonel Pham Ngoc Thao made a second abortive move against the Young Turk group on February 20, an action that postponed the American bombing deadline scheduled for that date. On the following day Ky, Thi, and Thieu, acting as spokesmen for the victorious armed forces council, obliged the isolated Khanh to resign his post and flee the country. The Young Turk element preserved the appearance of civilian control for several months thereafter in the person of Premier Phan Huy Quat, a fellow northerner of Ky, with Suu continuing on as nominal chief of state. Basic policy divisions were not resolved, mainly because Quat's Buddhist supporters advocated peace negotiations, whereas the Armed Forces Council favored Washington's already determined policy of sending bombing raids against North Vietnam. The State Department's white paper *Aggression From the North* was issued on February 28, and air strikes above the seventeenth parallel began on the following day.[37] The fragile façade of civilian leadership lasted until June, 1965.

The differences that developed among the several agencies of the U.S. government over implementing the expanding military program in South Vietnam stemmed mainly from the varied contexts in which each agency functioned. The White House and upper-State Department agencies were concerned primarily with the Cold War, world opinion, national pride, and the domestic political impact. For armed forces leaders, careers and professional pride were at stake. The several intelligence agencies (CIA, State, and Defense) were more detached and objective because they bore no direct operational responsibilities; unfortunately, the validity of their informed judgments was not recognized at higher levels. In Vietnam the army faced the baffling task of defeating an enemy who was not easy to identify. Mounting combat difficulties influenced General Westmoreland and his staff to make insatiable demands for additional troops and facilities and to resent all politically imposed limitations on freedom of operations. Ground soldiers in time came to respect the resourceful tenacity of the Vietcong more than the often undisciplined performance of their own ARVN allies.

The difficult task of advising and directing a Saigon government desperately in need of improving its performance was left to American embassy personnel and recruited civilian agency officials. The very necessity of maintaining the feeble government made any effective American direction of its program impossible. Ambassador Taylor, for example, had to accomodate to the changes wrought by successive coups, which he was unable to control. He had to deal with General Westmoreland's purely military approach on the one hand, and with a hypersensitive government at Saigon on the other. When the dramatic landing of the marines at Danang on March 8 had far less psychological and political effect than had been anticipated, Westmoreland raised his original reinforcement request from eighteen thousand to some seventy thousand in the same month. As a nationalist, Premier Quat was far from happy over the entry of any sizeable alien forces, especially the invited Koreans, Australians, and New Zealanders. He also conditioned his approval of American reinforcements on an unqualified commitment to suppress the Vietcong rebellion. Ambassador Taylor's negotiations with Quat eventually ran firmly aground. Specific authorization for American troops to assume combat roles was eventually forthcoming at the end of June, when General Westmoreland called for combat reenforcements totalling some 200,000 troops, with no ceiling in sight.[39]

The essential American embarrassment developed from the failure of the bombing raids on the North to produce expected results. Designated targets were frequently missed, and the services-preferred pattern of a progressively advancing bombing threat in the direction of Hanoi-Haiphong and toward the China border was vetoed for political reasons by Washington. Far from intimidating the North Vietnamese, the raids perceptively hardened their determination to resist.[40] The bombings had no discernable effect on the Vietcong operations in the South and very little in dispelling defeatism at Saigon. A Pentagon analyst suggested at the time that some 70% of America's concern was to avoid a humiliating defeat, which could easily follow the collapse of the Quat government.[41] It was in the light of this dismal military prospect that Westmoreland's reenforcement requests mounted. President Johnson's confused response to increasingly hostile world opinion and to rising domestic criticism in early May was to order a five-day halt in the bombing. His apparent reason was not primarily to obtain a favorable response from Hanoi, but mainly to exploit the expected lack of response as a means of eliciting a positive reaction from world opinion.[42]

Governmental Change and Military Escalation

In late May Premier Quat got caught in the cross-fire feuding between the neutralist Buddhists and the belligerent, anti-Communist Catholic factions. With Quat's acquiescence, but contrary to the wishes of Ambassador Taylor, Quat's fellow Northerner General Nguyen Cao Ky took over as premier and as head of the Executive Council on

June 19. General Nguyen Van Thieu (a Catholic and friend of Khiem) headed the newly formed National Leadership Committee. As a conciliatory gesture to Hué partisans, General Thi was also admitted to the ten-man military junta. United States agencies abandoned for the time being the objective of civilian rule, in favor of a factionally balanced military junta. Ky established fairly good relations with Americans, but he was too much the alien Northerner, too flamboyant and too undignified to qualify as a respected ruler by traditional mandarinate standards.[43] The harried Taylor gave place to Henry Cabot Lodge, who returned to Saigon as ambassador in July.

A distinct shift of emphasis in South Vietnam was apparent following the accession of the military junta in June, 1965. Opposition to the repeated requests by Westmoreland for additional combat divisions melted away in both Saigon and Washington. By November the U.S. troop strength had risen to 175,000; Communist forces meanwhile increased to some 63,000, reportedly finding no difficulty in obtaining supplies or in replacing their losses. Westmoreland asked for 154,000 additional troops in November and in January raised his total needs to 459,000.[44]

Opposition to the seemingly endless military drain appeared in the State Department and among the civilian staff of the Pentagon. Under-Secretary George W. Ball's protest to President Johnson on July 1, 1965, again reflected intelligence agency findings. He pointed out that Western troops operating in a civil war situation, in jungle terrain, where the population refused cooperation, could not win a guerrilla war that the South Vietnamese themselves had been losing for some time. Ball argued that a compromise solution arranged with Hanoi would be far better than an indefinitely protracted war involving ever-increasing costs in money, manpower, and critical world opinion. Potential United States losses in terms of national humiliation, loss of credibility in commitments made elsewhere, and world influence generally had been grossly exaggerated. With Thailand's help, Ball said, the Mekong River line could be defended and a Chinese threat averted; Korea must not be pressed to provide more troops. NATO allies would welcome such evidence of American maturity; Moscow would be happy, and so, perhaps, would Charles de Gaulle. The criticism that would inevitably attend any compromise solution would have no permanent effect. Ball proposed specifically that U.S. forces be limited to a maximum of 72,000 men while search for a compromise peace was in progress. Saigon could be informed of the plans after substantial progress in negotiations had been made.[45] This reasoned State Department protest was echoed in a subsequent memo from Assistant Secretary of Defense John T. McNaughton, who saw in the developing stalemate the ingredients of "an enormous miscalculation." He suggested that U.S. reputation would not be seriously impaired by a compromise settlement, which did not rule out a coalition government, a free decision by the South to deal with the Vietcong and Hanoi, and a possible rejection of Saigon's ruling junta. The American commitment to the South had been fully honored already.[46]

Rationale for America's Belligerent Role

The official State Department apologia for massive American participation in the war was contained in the previously-mentioned White Paper No. 7839, *Aggression from the North*, which appeared in late February, 1965. Its essential argument ran as follows:

> Vietnam is not a spontaneous and local rebellion against the established government. . . . The hard core of the Communist forces attacking South Vietnam were trained in the north and ordered to the South by Hanoi. . . . For more than ten years, the people of South Vietnam . . . have fought back . . . these efforts to extend Communist power south across the 17th parallel. The United States has responded to the appeals of the Saigon government . . . in defense of . . . freedom.[47]

531

Secretary Rusk did not encourage any critical examination—even by the Department's own Bureau of Intelligence—of the factual accuracy of the basic premises of the White Paper. The precise nature of the revolutionary struggle in South Vietnam and the actual extent to which the security and vital interests of the United States and world freedom were involved went unexplained. Determined efforts on Washington's part to mobilize American patriotic sentiment in support of the war policy produced inconclusive results. Even within South Vietnam, escalated military activity had an adverse effect on the population's attitudes toward both the Saigon regime and the American presence. Within the United States, the policy of "more troops and more profits, draft the poor and reward the rich" (in the words of James Reston[48]) was destined in time to erode the artificially stimulated public support of the escalation policy.

Washington's official rationale for the new phase of the air war was made more explicit in President Johnson's *ex parte* Baltimore speech of April 7, 1965:

North Vietnam has attacked the independent nation of South Vietnam. Its object is total conquest. . . . It is a new face of an old enemy. Over this war—and all Asia—is . . . the deepening shadow of Communist China. The rulers of Hanoi are urged on by Peking. . . . The contest in Vietnam is part of a wider pattern of aggressive purposes. . . . Our objective is the independence of South Vietnam and its freedom from attack. . . . In recent months . . . . it became necessary for us to increase the confidence of the brave people of South Vietnam who have . . . borne this brutal battle for so many years with so many casualties. . . . We have no desire to devastate that which the people of North Vietnam have built with toil and sacrifice. We will use our power with restraint. . . . But we will use it. . . . We will always oppose the effort of one nation to conquer another nation. We will do this because our own security is at stake.[49]

The disaffection and civil war raging in South Vietnam were ignored.

American air operations, concentrated mainly in the South, increased rapidly during 1965. From around 1,000 sorties per month in January 1965, the number increased to 7,500 in July and reached 12,000 by October. The attacks were directed mainly against assumed centers of Communist concentration; these centers were often identified by little more than rumor, so that mistakes were inevitable. The most significant result was a sharp increase in the flight of villagers from the affected areas. Refugees totaled 400,000 by July and nearly 600,000 by September.[50]

Bombing forays above the seventeenth parallel, starting on March 1, 1965, concentrated on transportation and production facilities assumed to be manufacturing war materials. They forced the dispersal of North Vietnam's civilian population and industry to less exposed areas, but did little to hamper the war effort. The port of Haiphong, through which quantities of Soviet military supplies entered, was exempt from air attack on the assumption that the desired response from Hanoi could be obtained otherwise, and also out of respect for Moscow's unconcealed determination to prevent the Americans from destroying Ho Chi Minh's government. For similar reasons the principal irrigation control facilities serving the Tonkin delta were not systematically molested. Before the bombings began, Hanoi was known to be in possession of antiaircraft defenses provided by the Soviets, but the tolls the Vietnamese gunners levied on attacking U.S. aircraft, both land and naval based, were far heavier than had been anticipated.

Meanwhile, the rapid increment of American troop commitments proceeded apace. The number was 53,500 by mid-1965, and 277,000 by mid-1966, not including the large contingent of naval personnel or the nearly 50,000 (largely air force), who were sent into Thailand after 1965. The mobility of American forces was greatly increased by the massed use of helicopters. The allied forces were supplemented by the transfer to South Vietnam at American expense of some 48,000 South Korean combat troops, for which the Seoul government was handsomely compensated with several U.S. destroyers and full equipment for two additional South Korean divisions. A Filipino construction detachment was sent to South Vietnam and a smaller medical unit to Laos, for which Manila was similarly well rewarded. Australia and New Zealand contributed small but effective contingents. It is significant that no effort was made to enlist Formosan troops for service in Vietnam. No Chinese would have been welcome in the North or South. Shifting the major burden of combat duties to nonindigenous forces contributed nothing to the effectiveness of the conscripted South Vietnamese forces, however, whose morale continued to be low and who suffered heavy attrition from desertions.

Reasons for Differences in Performance

An important deficiency in American policy planning for South Vietnam was the absence of any realistic explanation of the superior performance of Vietcong guerrilla forces and supporting Vietminh units from the North, as compared with kindred troops from the South. The obvious fact of better leadership and better motivation left unanswered the basic question, Why? Excessive factionalism within the South was as much a consequence as a cause of the widespread unpopularity of successive governments unable to command trust and allegiance.

Anticolonialist nationalism was present everywhere in Vietnam, North and South. It contributed to the rejection of successive European-oriented leaders, from Bao Dai to Diem, to Khanh, to Ky. Both Diem and Quat strongly protested on nationalist grounds the introduction of alien combat troops, and the foreigners became increasingly unpopular as a result of the more aggressive "search and destroy" tactics that they inaugurated in late 1965. Civilian casualties were heavy and many mistakes were made. Enforced abandonment of homes and the vagaries of refugee survival could hardly be expected to generate

534

loyalty to Saigon and love for the Americans. The conduct of ARVN troops toward villagers was notoriously predatory, in contrast to the role of the Vietcong, who had to depend on the resident population for both recruits and food supplies.[51]

What gave the communist side its positive appeal in the South was Hanoi's effective exploitation of a long-developing revolutionary situation that had little to do with Marxist propaganda or even anticolonialist nationalism. The very elimination of French rule and of the discredited Diem regime brought to the surface inherent regional and parochial rifts that colonialism had papered over. Wide cultural gaps separated Christians from Buddhists, city dwellers from villagers, and the semi-Westernized, class-conscious elite from the mass of the population. From the educationally privileged group in the South were drawn the army officers, government officials, landlords, and professional classes. Vietcong and Vietminh agents, by contrast, enlisted the support of deprived elements of the populations of the delta, the coastal plains, and even the mountainous interior for ends the people themselves could appreciate. People's Courts eliminated Saigon officials, landlords, and usurers; trained cadres taught the youth to read and to acquire useful technical skills, as well as to fight. Promising young men were thus given opportunities for leadership in the NLF army and the new social structure that the old order had denied them. The positive result was to provide hope for a more adequate livelihood and a share in political power for those willing to accept responsibility within the National Liberation Front program. The Vietcong were quite capable of taking reprisal on those who refused to go along,[52] but they also provided positive reasons to cooperate.

The cumulative effects of armed destruction throughout much of the countryside and the mistreatment of local populations by ARVN, Korean, and American troops reinforced the almost universal distrust of an unresponsive Saigon government. The revolutionary appeal of the NLF became so popular in time that the United States itself initiated a so-called revolutionary development program of its own, only to encounter credibility difficulties. Within the context of popular demand for revolutionary change— political, social, and economic—the NLF advanced a reasonably effective claim to the allegiance and disciplined support of the people of South Vietnam, including many non-Communists. Even after the sheer military power generated by the United States checked the prospect of an early Vietcong triumph in late 1965, the Saigon government remained unable to command popular respect and allegiance, or the dedicated service of its own officials.[53] American grants and expenditures provided employment and government revenues, but they also encouraged widespread corruption. Few high officials at Hanoi, unlike those at Saigon, were accumulating savings in Swiss bank accounts. Washington's "aggression from the North" rationale was thus no valid explanation of the issues involved.

The Communist Side: Hanoi, China, and the USSR

North Vietnam's firm refusal to enter into peace negotiations under the threat of American air bombardment derived in part from Hanoi's remembrance of the failure to implement the Geneva Agreement of 1954 and partly from loyalty to nationalist aspirations long sustained. Although Communist regimentation in the North was in many circles unpopular, it was nevertheless dedicated to defined social and economic objectives, which was more than could be said of the Saigon government. Ho Chi Minh was the unanimously acknowledged symbol of the independence movement, a bona fide national hero. His birthday was regularly celebrated by non-Communists in the South as well as in the North. As a pragmatist and a realist, he saw in Communist principles and techniques a means of accomplishing nationalist goals. No one accused him of subordinating Vietnamese interests to those of China or the USSR. A French biographer affirmed that: "Of all men alive today, Ho is perhaps the one who has shown the . . . ability to wield power . . . rooted in national aspirations."[54]

The acknowledged superior coherence and discipline of the population of North Vietnam, both civilian and military, derived in large measure from cultural homogeneity and commitment to the nationalist cause. Under the revolutionary Hanoi government, leaders tended to emerge not by reason of social status or military power, as was the case in the South, but in large measure as a result of personal dedication and performance. The Vietminh party structure and bureaucracy included many persons of humble origins who would have been denied such opportunity under colonial rule or under the traditional Confucianist mandarin system. Vietcong leaders in the South were attempting in the late fifties to promote a similar social revolution at the village level, under difficult circumstances. Concern for national independence and opposition to the colonialist landlord group and the Gallicized military bureaucracy that dominated the Saigon government, characterized both the Vietminh and the Vietcong revolutionaries far more than did alleged subservience to any worldwide Communist conspiracy.[55]

And yet the two revolutionary groups differed. Following the overthrow of Diem, Hanoi's interests related to a broader international context than was reflected in the viewpoint of the emerging National Liberation Front in the South. The North was far more concerned with early realization of national unification and also less ready to accept a coalition government and a neutral stance with respect to the Cold War. And Hanoi's leaders differed among themselves, as well. President Ho Chi Minh, Prime Minister Pham Van Dong, and Defense Minister Vo Nguyen Giap recognized the necessity to avoid offending neighboring China, but they were also extremely wary of anything suggesting Vietnamese subservience to China, militarily or politically. Ho preferred to solicit major military support and diplomatic protection from his long-time friends in Moscow, who alone could provide needed antiaircraft weapons. The Soviet Union could also insist effectively that the port of Haiphong be kept open for the delivery of military supplies, and the continued receipt of Soviet assistance carried no threat of physical domination of the country. Ho's primary objectives, therefore, were to obtain the cessation of American intervention in the South; to eliminate completely the rule of the alleged U.S. puppet junta at Saigon; and to promote the early unification of Vietnam as promised at Geneva in 1954. Hanoi was also concerned that the South's Liberation Front not stray too far from orthodox Lao Dong Communist party guidelines.

The rival pro-China faction at Hanoi, led by General Nguyen Chi Thanh and Party Chief Truong Chinh, was more concerned than was Ho about maintaining Communist orthodoxy and waging the "anti-imperialist" war to the bitter end. Whereas Ho and the pro-Soviet group were willing to settle, presumably, for an interim period of autonomy for South Vietnam under the Geneva Agreement pattern of 1954, without insisting on domination by Communist elements within the emerging coalition, the more doctrinaire pro-China faction was prepared to wage a prolonged guerrilla struggle, conducted along ideological lines, against both Saigon and the American presence.[56] The differences suggested Moscow's greater concern to end the costly struggle in South Vietnam, which had no bearing on Soviet security per se.

Ho Chi Minh's essential personal role at Hanoi was to bridge factional rivalries and to maintain cooperative relations with both Communist powers, whose national interests had begun to diverge sharply, partly with respect to Vietnam, but primarily because of north Asian border claims and rivalry for world Communist leadership. Whatever opportunity Washington may have had to exploit to American advantage the differences developing between Peking and Moscow disappeared in 1965 with the initiation of bombing attacks on North Vietnam. The elimination of the American presence in South Vietnam and the preservation of Communist North Vietnam were virtually the only issues on which the rival Communist world powers could agree.

China's stake in the indefinite continuance of the war was conceivably much greater than was either Moscow's or Hanoi's. In 1965–66 Peking was prepared to leave to the Soviet Union the principal burden of supplying North Vietnam's military needs via the port of Haiphong, which Washington could presumably close only at the risk of incurring open conflict with the Soviet Union. Soviet use of China's railways was grudgingly conceded, and a Chinese labor force of some forty thousand helped keep overland transportation approaches to Hanoi under repair. Meanwhile, Peking gave primary attention to preparing the defenses of its long Siberian frontier, to developing a nuclear arsenal, and to the eventual internal struggle against alleged bourgeois deviations by Liu Shao-ch'i, whom Mao denounced as China's Khrushchev.[57] Peking's ultimate concerns may have included winning Hanoi away from its Soviet alignment (once Ho's presence was removed), thus reducing the potential rivalry of the Russians as well as the threat of the American presence in South East Asia. For the time being, however, China was not averse to permitting the two super powers of the West to expend their military resources indefinitely in an interminable Vietnam struggle. The divergent attitudes of Peking and Moscow were eventually reflected in the qualified Soviet support for efforts at peace negotiations, at first in 1964 and later in 1967–68, in contrast to China's strong opposition at the time to any such negotiations.[58]

American Efforts to Improve Governmental
Performance at Saigon

Renewed efforts by American agencies to strengthen the popular appeal of the Saigon government were largely ineffective. The so-called "revolutionary development" program of 1965-67 included revisions of the earlier agroville stockade defense efforts and the strategic hamlet system, both of which had been intended to bolster Saigon's influence by contributing needed assistance to the people and intensifying governmental surveillance.[59] Efforts to deny Vietcong access to populated areas where they might obtain supplies and recruits resulted in separating villagers from their means of livelihood and also from the vicinity of their ancestral tombs. Those who refused to cooperate with the revolutionary development program were suspected of being in league with the rebels and were therefore vulnerable to punitive military action. When the tactics of the Vietcong became increasingly aggressive and demanding, the villagers were caught helplessly in the middle.

The revolutionary development program, as initiated in June 1965, was promoted by integrated cadre units each numbering approximately sixty people. The functions of some two-thirds of the cadre members were related to military and intelligence duties. The other one-third predominantly American, was concerned primarily with civilian needs, such as improvement of administration, better medical and educational services, economic improvements, and census enumeration. Discipline within the respective cadre groups was strict, and the participants were well paid as an incentive to greater efficiency. The program in one sense was designed to compete with the efforts of the Vietcong to maintain *rapport* with the villagers. Particularly helpful were cadre efforts to assist peasants in completing their paddy harvests and in the sale of their surpluses. Such remedial efforts would have been more successful, however, had they been undertaken earlier. In the context of intensified military escalation of 1965-66, crops, fruit trees, and homes were frequently destroyed, and the promised compensations to peasants for such losses were often dissipated by local graft.

By 1966 the revolutionary development system began faltering badly. Surveillance replaced assistance. Increasing numbers of noncooperating peasants and sus-

540

pected Vietcong sympathizers were jailed and subjected to pressure to provide intelligence regarding the rebellion as a whole. The number of persons so detained by 1968 was estimated at around one hundred thousand. Proven Vietcong captives who refused to act as double agents were frequently "accidented." Meanwhile, the American Special Forces (Green Berets) were also recruiting mountain peoples under U.S. pay, while the CIA operated its own independent intelligence apparatus, euphemistically called the Provincial Economic Units (PEU).[60]

The pacification efforts were conspicuously ineffective in the Mekong delta region, where peasant opposition to landlord interests continued to be strong. A mere 2 percent of the Cochin-China population had previous owned some 45 percent of the arable land. "Revolutionary development" was therefore a meaningless phrase unless land redistribution reforms were effectively implemented, and the political elite at Saigon simply did not favor any such economic change.[61] Delta areas controlled by the Cao Dai and Hoa Hao communities were little influenced by the Vietcong, but the two sects also resisted Saigon's direct control. Increasing use of defoliants and napalm in Vietcong-infiltrated areas intensified the popular hatred of the American presence and distrust of the Saigon junta, which was dependent on American support.[62]

The Refugee Problem

The torrent of peasant refugees produced by pacification efforts constituted a new class of rootless urban mendicants. They added enormously to the relief problems of both Saigon and the American command. United States apologists claimed that such displaced persons had "voted with their feet" in favor of the Saigon authorities and against the National Liberation Front. But by 1967 the same spokesmen had begun to emphasize more realistically the political "value" of the creation of refugee groups as a means of depriving the Vietcong of essential rural support. But what value for whom? Such arguments

541

begged the essential problem of enlisting the positive allegiance of the South Vietnamese people. The ease with which such refugee camps could be infiltrated by Vietcong agents was to be dramatically demonstrated in the Tet offensive of early 1968.

By the end of 1968 the total number of displaced persons had reached an estimated five million, or around 30 percent of the total population. Most of the displacement was the result of Allied measures (bombings and artillery fire) rather than those of the Vietcong, who had a positive stake in keeping the villagers in place.[63] Some two million Vietnamese, by official count, occupied the designated refugee centers. A substantially larger group crowded into Saigon and other urban centers wherever any kind of livelihood could be scrounged. Uncounted numbers moved to live with relatives. The fraction of the refugee population that qualified for governmental relief, after negotiating the barriers of red tape, received for two months a daily stipend of eight *piasters* per person (some twenty cents) plus a daily diet of one pound of rice for six months. All refugees were virtually destitute on their arrival, having been unable to salvage such valuables as livestock or household possessions. The lack of basic needs of clothing, housing, land, and employment opportunities produced widespread apathy and bitterness, plus increasing resort to thievery, begging, and prostitution.[64]

The volume of American AID funds allocated for relief purposes increased substantially after 1965. Rice surpluses from many Mekong delta areas, normally marketed in population centers, were diverted and taxed by Vietcong agents, necessitating American importation of two hundred thousand tons of rice annually for urban consumption. United States contributions to regular government expenses, both civilian and military, were provided for the most part via counterpart funds derived from the government-controlled sale of commodity imports. Thievery, official graft, and black-market chicanery flourished, accompanied by heavy inflationary pressures in the form of price increases. When funds so generated were combined with the expendable pay of the growing numbers of American troops and employment income available at bases under construction, too many dollars were simply chasing too few consumer goods. Currency manipulation and black-market operations in stolen Post Exchange commodities and other looted supplies added to the economic demoralization.[65]

American-Vietnamese Relations

It was primarily the all-pervasive corruption that poisoned popular attitudes toward the officials of the Saigon government. Abuses of power tended to increase with the availability of additional American funds covering rental and service costs, plus the construction of roads, military facilities, health facilities, and schools. American standards of consumption were high, and the conduct of jealous Vietnamese officials reflected their concern to provide comparable standards for their own families by tapping the same dollar flow. Officials who signed large contracts regularly took a percentage rake-off; building contractors skimped on cement and sold the surplus on the black market; job applicants invariably had to resort to bribery. Observers conceded that virtually everybody was somewhat to blame (but some more than others), and that the resultant situation constituted the demoralizing problem that was South Vietnam.[66]

Cooperative relations between American military advisers and their Vietnamese counterparts became the exception rather than the rule. The wide psychological gap was aggravated by language difficulties, disparities in pay, and resentment over official American prodding. Vietnamese leaders did not welcome American "advice." Some countered with the suggestion that it was the Americans who needed advisers.[67] South Vietnamese soldiers avoided wherever possible the dangers and fatigue of strenuous campaigning in the jungle. Luncheon breaks sometimes lasted for two hours or more, and most of the troops returned "home" to relatively safe places in the evenings. Sagging morale was reflected in high desertion rates.[68]

Attendant American advisory officers, who were usually on one-year assignments and whose effectiveness was rated by their ability to get along with their Vietnamese counterparts, tended to mute their criticisms and to close their eyes to irregularities.[69] The more competent officers among the Vietnamese often ran afoul of their own area commanders, who had a vested interest in their authority and resented suggestions from below. The high command usually refused to dismiss incompetent officers, who in turn failed to check the predatory tendency of ARVN soldiery. Government officials enmeshed in a welter of corruption were ineffective in implementing any reform legislation.[70]

A particularly sensitive area of friction developed in connection with American efforts to enlist the support of the mountain tribesmen in the fight against the Vietcong. Neither the resident Mon-Khmer nor the other Malayo-Polynesian groups spoke Vietnamese, and both were traditionally regarded with contempt and aversion by the coastal lowlanders. The tribesmen on their side entertained no liking for the Vietnamese, including the Vietcong. Their grievances were many. Choice areas of their slash-and-burn holdings above Saigon had been appropriated by Ngo Dinh Diem for settlement of Catholic refugees after 1954, and subsequent rural pacification efforts had forced many of them to assemble as refugees at or near provincial centers. In the process, traditional montagnard society crumbled away in situations of estrangement and cultural confusion.

Vietnamese officials resented allegedly gratuitous American recruitment of montagnard youth into Special Forces units. The mountain people could not discard their darker skins, their cultural and language peculiarities, and their own ingrained prejudices. Contacts with the Vietnamese promoted neither understanding nor friendship. Younger montagnards, once in contact with wage employment, radios and loud speakers, guns and helicopters, and other aspects of a more modern life style, seldom wanted to return to hillside farming.[71] America's military escalation in tribal areas thus created a completely new dimension of the social adjustment problem.

American Efforts to Initiate Peace Negotiations,
January 1966

An American effort to initiate peace negotiations was formally launched in January 1966, supported by extensive publicity and full diplomatic orchestration, in an obvious effort to mobilize the support of world opinion. The offer allegedly included no prior conditions. Washington disclaimed any desire to establish military bases in South Vietnam or any permanent American presence in Southeast Asia and proposed a cease-fire, free elections, reunification of Vietnam if desired by both North and South, plus encouragement for the creation of a neutralized Southeast Asia. President Johnson pledged, in addition, an American contribution of one billion dollars for development of the Mekong Valley project, in which North Vietnam would be free to participate, once peace was restored. All bombings would halt as soon as there was any prospect of successful negotiations.[72]

That informed Soviet authorities were not entirely unsympathetic to the American peace proposals, was suggested by the arrival at Hanoi on January 7 of the Russian Foreign Office Secretary for Southeast Asia, A. N. Shelepin. During the course of his week's stay in Hanoi, Shelepin talked with President Ho Chi Minh and other ranking government and party officials about the terms of the American peace offer. Whether by inclination or (more probably) out of concern that Peking not be allowed to profit from his endeavors, Shelepin apparently exerted no overt pressure on North Vietnam to start negotiations, but he did obtain a list of Hanoi's counterrequirements. As reported in Hong Kong, these included unconditional cessation of American bombing attacks; early withdrawal of all American troops from the South; and recognition of the National Liberation Front as the sole representative of the South Vietnamese people. The indigenous population

545

must be left free to settle their own affairs without outside interference.[73] The two sides were obviously still far apart.

Whatever chances for accommodation of differences may have been possible in January 1966, were dissipated the following month by an acceleration of violence. In early February, a small-scale but highly effective Vietcong raid was made against the American helicopter base at Pleiku in the highlands of central Annam. The invaders succeeded in placing explosive charges not only on the airstrip but also against barrack walls. The raid was supplemented by mortar attacks from close range, using American-made 81-mm caliber weapons. Blame lay clearly with the negligent security units of the South Vietnamese army, and some measure of collusion was apparently involved in an operation that had entailed such extensive preparations. Washington authorities elected to regard the embarrassingly costly episode as a cynical reply on Hanoi's part to President Johnson's peace proposals. The immediate response of the American air force was a massive retaliatory air attack on North Vietnam, but how the bombing raid would improve the security of American air bases in the South was not explained. The major casualty was the peace offer itself.[74]

The Honolulu Conference and Its Sequel

Disappointed by Hanoi's negative response, and stung by the mounting criticism by Senator Fulbright's Foreign Relations Committee, in late February President Johnson hurriedly called a conference with Premier Nguyen Cao Ky at Honolulu. Preparation for the meeting was obviously minimal: Key White House and State Department participants were given a scant hour's notice to prepare for departure. Aside from President Johnson's concern to steal the press headlines from Senator Fulbright, he hoped to commit Premier Ky to undertake sweeping governmental, social, and land-reform efforts calculated to attract greater popular support for the Saigon regime. He promised to convene a later session to receive reports on what had actually been accomplished in specific areas. He would want not just phrases, but "coonskins on the wall." The conference ended with the tall Texan throwing his arm around the diminutive Premier as a gesture of encouragement.[75]

The ill-conceived Honolulu episode had two unfortunate results. It embarrassed Ky politically by stigmatizing him as an alleged American stooge, and it also encouraged the Saigon junta as a whole to presume on Washington's support in purging their ranks. The principal victim was General Nguyen Chanh Thi, the locally popular but increasingly insubordinate commander of the First Corps area centering at Danang in the north. General Thi had been one of the heroes of the abortive anti-Diem attack on the Presidential palace in November, 1960. He had returned from exile following Diem's death, and in January, 1964, assisted General Khanh's seizure of power. As an aggressive member of the ten-member National Security Committee, Thi had been a rival of General Ky for the post of premier in June, 1965, and personal enmity between the two persisted. As continuing commander of Corps I, Thi was endeavoring to consolidate his political position by soliciting local Buddhist support against the Saigon leadership.[76]

General Thi's insubordination developed in the context of a quarrel between the commander of the adjacent Second Corps area, General Vinh Loc, and Premier Ky at Saigon. Vinh Loc had objected strenuously to the American initiative to enlist volunteers from mountain folk residents of the central highlands for a "United Front . . . for Oppressed Races" to be used against the Vietcong. Following the Honolulu Conference, Secretary of State Dean Rusk brought pressure on Ky (ambassador Lodge refused the assignment) to transfer the troublesome General Vinh Loc to a less abrasive post in the Psychological Warfare Ministry. When Loc defied Saigon's orders, General Thi and the pro-Thieu Deputy Prime Minister General Nguyen Huu Co tried to exploit the situation in an effort to embarrass Premier Ky even

547

more. When Ky acted on March 10, with the approval of other Saigon members of the armed services National Leadership Committee, to deprive Thi of his First Corps command, trouble developed. The official announcement of Thi's resignation indicated that it had been tendered for reasons of health (sinus infection), and General Westmoreland, on the very next day, made Thi a face-saving offer of treatment for his illness at the Walter Reed Hospital in Washington.[77]

The Struggle Movement Crisis at Hué

Saigon's dismissal of the popular General Thi brought Hué's smouldering Buddhist discontent to white heat in the so-called "Struggle Movement" led by the Buddhist monk, Thich Tri Quang. The movement was conceived as a kind of third-force alternative to the American-advised "military bandit" government at Saigon and the equally objectionable National Liberation Front. It included non-Buddhist opponents of the war and other elements critical of the American presence, and some of its Buddhist leaders in particular attacked the Americans for growing evidences of social and moral degradation, extending from corrupt officials to bar girls and prostitutes. At the end of the initial five days of local anti-Saigon agitation, General Thi defied his ordered retirement and reoccupied his headquarters at Danang temporarily, announcing that the armed forces under his command would support popular demands for social justice and civilian rule. During the latter part of March, the focus of anti-government agitation shifted to Saigon, with students supporting both Buddhist and Catholic reform demands. Premier Ky abandoned his initially defiant stance to proclaim on March 25 several conciliatory promises to convene an officially selected Constitutional Convention plus subsequent approval of its work by popular referendum and the holding of elections later in 1966. Because these promises were accompanied by disciplinary threats against uncooperative officials and soldiers, massive popular protests erupted at Hué, where an estimated 20,000 demonstrators included uniformed soldier participation. Less massive protests occurred at Saigon, coastal Nhatrang, and interior Pleiku.

The government's first rejoinder was ineffective. Two battalions of marines were airlifted to the Danang air base on April 4-5, a move accompanied by General Thieu's allegations that the protests were instigated by Communist agents. Marshal Ky proceeded to Danang in person, but his negotiations were to no avail. The marines were not permitted to leave the base, and Ky himself later apologized for the false allegations of Communist involvement. He also promised the convening of an elected Assembly, disavowal of punitive disciplinary action against officials, and the immediate assembly on April 12-14 of a so-called National Political Congress to fashion a reforms agreement. Although boycotted by both Buddhist and Catholic organizations, the assembled Congress did obtain Army Directory approval of an early shift to civilian rule, elections to be staged within four months, encouragement of political party activity except for Communists and neutralists, coupled with freedom of the press, assurances of official amnesty, and appeals for an end to destructive demonstrations. The moderate Buddhist leadership generally accepted the proposals as satisfactory, so that popular demonstrations tended to subside. But Corps I area continued outside Saigon's control.

The final phase of the government's suppression of the Struggle Movement at Danang and Hué was initiated in the middle of May. On May 7 and 14, Marshal Ky repudiated many of the pledges given in April, by affirming his determination to remain in power throughout the ensuing twelve months and to resist the presence of either Communist or neutral elements in any elected Assembly. In a secret meeting on May 14, the military Directory at Saigon decided to recapture Danang by force. The gruesome process continued from May 15 to 23. The city's armed defenses collapsed, but both anti-Saigon and anti-American feeling ran high. Nine Buddhist immolations, seven of them nuns, occurred from May 29 to

June 4. Meanwhile, Buddhist resistance at neighboring Hué flared into rioting, but military defense was hopeless and resistance collapsed on June 19. The University was closed for an indefinite period, with many students who had participated in the demonstrations suffering imprisonment. Buddhist elements in Central Annam were permanently alienated from Saigon's authority. Desultory friction continued in the South throughout the summer of 1966, but the army junta was firmly in control.[78]

Washington's official reaction to the Struggle Movement episode was one of unmitigated gloom. Following one White House meeting, Assistant Secretary McNaughton foresaw the prospect of imminent economic collapse in South Vietnam, with no apparent progress realized in military or pacification activities. William Bundy envisaged for the United States a future of mounting costs, growing casualties, and increasing political embarrassments. Under-Secretary George Ball saw no attractive options except to cut activities to a minimum in preparation for inevitable disengagement. Actually, the only tangible shift in American policy at this juncture was to authorize the bombing of oil supply depots in Hanoi and Haiphong, a move which had long been advocated by the Joint Chiefs of Staff.[79]

During the Struggle Movement, the Saigon junta led by Premier Ky succeeded in ousting the troublesome General Thi as Corps I commander, but at the cost of the near collapse of the authority of the regime. The situation in 1966 differed from that of 1963 not in the intensity of popular protest against Saigon authorities (including Buddhist immolations), but rather in the fact that army mutiny was localized at Danang and Hué and that American authorities backed the challenged government, as they had not done for Diem in the fall of 1963. Saigon's promises of substantial political concessions in April and May of 1966, offered as means of halting street demonstrations, were presumably exacted as the price of immediate American support, but these promises were half repudiated during the final month of the struggle and were destined never to be carried through except in highly qualified form.[80]

The crisis also witnessed a continuing purging of the military command. During the three months period, General Thi was succeeded as a commander of I Corps by four Generals before Saigon finally found one who would cooperate fully with the eventual suppression of Buddhist resistance at Danang and Hué. All five were cashiered or exiled by a special military tribunal in early July.[81] In the end, Buddhist political resistance was left with virtually no representation within the ruling army group. Pro-Buddhist General Duong Van Minh retired for some four years (until 1970) to exile in Thailand, and General Tran Van Don transferred his efforts to the political arena. Don first challenged Ky's political leadership in 1967, and later, as an elected Senator in 1969, attacked the dominant role of President Thieu himself, but all to no avail. Meanwhile, the clerical leadership of the Buddhist opposition was fragmented by internal factional controversy and by the arrest of several of its leaders. Monk spokesmen tended to be more emotional than rational, and politically more negative than positive, but the cards were stacked against them in any case. Rivalry among top military leaders at Saigon remained as a perennial aspect of the political scene, but President Thieu after the 1967 elections saw to it that the command of troops in the immediate environs of Saigon were always amenable to his personal control. Buddhist political opposition eventually focused its hostility on the allegedly pro-Catholic President Nguyen Van Thieu and his allegedly corruptionist ally General Nguyen Huu Co.[82]

Columnist James Reston of the *New York Times* commented on the political scene in South Vietnam, not too inaccurately, as follows:

> The present Saigon government is a coalition of war lords. The propaganda of Honolulu has not prevailed over the

traditions of Saigon. There is no cohesive national spirit
. . . for the simple reason that there is no nation. It
is a tangle of competing individuals, regions, religions,
and sects. . . . Washington is relying on myths.[83]

The same columnist raised still more relevant questions
a month later:

> What justified more and more killing in Vietnam? . . .
> By [the President's] own definition, this struggle can-
> not succeed without a regime [at Saigon] that commands
> the respect of the South Vietnamese people. . . . The
> President's orders are sending more and more Americans
> into battle to replace the Vietnamese who are fighting
> among themselves. . . . [The proper alternative course]
> was to make clear to all the contending South Vietnamese
> leaders that the United States was going to limit its
> reinforcements, its military and economic aid, its casual-
> ties, and its military operations to a minimum until they
> had composed their differences. . . . The President's
> commitments in this war involve not only a handful of
> generals who seized power, but involve the Vietnamese
> people and the American people as well. . . . Our prom-
> ise was to help South Vietnam, not to destroy it.[84]

The demonstration of military feuding and regional
dissonance during the course of the imbroglio of March
and April, 1966, afforded an opportunity for Washington
to insist on basic governmental adjustments and to review
critical issues of both leadership and policy. Moderate
spokesman of the National Liberation Front could have
been accorded a hearing. In actuality, President Johnson's
unreserved commitment of support to Premier Ky accorded gratuitously at Honolulu and later at Hué ruled
out any such adjustment. In the end Ky emerged trium-
phant, although increasingly distrusted by his military
associates. Buddhist partisanship, Annamese regionalism,
and student opinion drifted further away from their already
limited allegiance to Saigon.

The Honolulu Conference was followed by another
characteristic public relations endeavor. At a hurriedly
convened White House press conference on April 22 (the
official stenographers arrived late), President Johnson

reacted sharply to a speech delivered by the recently returned ambassador to India, John Kenneth Galbraith, which was critical of Washington's Vietnam policy. Galbraith had pointed out that America's rigid pursuit of exclusively anti-Communist goals had often aligned the power of the United States with despots and military adventurers. He questioned whether South Vietnam was really important as a "bastion of freedom" or a "testing place for democracy." President Johnson cited in rejoinder Ambassador Lodge's rather equivocal assessment that the Honolulu Conference had initiated competition among South Vietnamese about who cared most for the underdog. He also cited Lodge's reservations about the wisdom of staging early elections under existing circumstances. Johnson concluded by affirming his assurance that America would prevent the North Vietnamese from swallowing up the people of the South by force and that a constitutional government would emerge in good time.[85]

Meanwhile, the monetary and inflationary crisis at Saigon reached the point of near economic collapse. The early months of 1966 had seen consumer prices increase at a rate of 10 percent per month. Within a two-week period in June, the black-market rate for *piasters* jumped from 140 to the dollar to a high of 250, compared to successively elevated official rates of 35 and 80 to the dollar. Rice imports from overseas to the Mekong delta region, where normally there was surplus rice, rose to an annual rate of 450,000 tons, which was more than twice the amount actually harvested in 1966. In Saigon, motor cars were priced at seven times their import valuation. In March 1966 the glut of ships trying to discharge cargo at the up-river Saigon port forced vessels to wait outside the river entry at Cape St. Jacques for a full three weeks, and several additional weeks often passed before they could reach the docks. Raising the official exchange rate to the level of 118 *piasters* to the dollar eventually produced a semblance of monetary order, but price levels continued to rise.[86]

553

The French Peace Initiative of September 1966

Another round of peace proposals was precipitated by President de Gaulle's visit to Phnom Penh in September 1966. In anticipation of the announced departure of de Gaulle, Secretary of State Dean Rusk had informed Foreign Minister Couve de Murville that Washington was prepared to abide by the Geneva agreements of 1954 and 1962, to neutralize both Laos and South Vietnam, and to join Hanoi in a phased withdrawal of both American and North Vietnamese troops under international supervision. While at the Cambodian capital, de Gaulle communicated with the Foreign office spokesman for Hanoi, Nguyen Thuong, and with the Liberation Front spokesman, Nguyen Van Hieu. In his publicized address delivered at Phnom Penh, the French president underscored the necessity for some advance commitment on the part of the United States. American forces should agree to withdraw over a suggested two-year period, during which time some "international arrangement" could be made to organize the peace. The world powers, he insisted, must agree to end all interference in the affairs of Vietnam.[87]

President Johnson's counteroffer to de Gaulle's suggestion was to schedule withdrawal of American troops from South Vietnam provided North Vietnam would halt its armed infiltration and recall its forces "present illegally" in the South. Hanoi found the term "illegally" objectionable and flatly refused to equate its own participation in the struggle for Vietnam's independence and unification with the allegedly aggressive presence of troops from half-way around the world. As a preliminary to peace negotiations, Hanoi insisted that American bombing of the North must cease and assurances of U.S. withdrawal be given.

At the opening sessions of the United Nations General Assembly in mid-September, the American spokesman adopted a somewhat more conciliatory stand. Ambassador Goldberg denied that America was prosecuting a "holy war against Communism." Washington sought no permanent military establishment in Southeast Asia, was not endeavoring to overthrow the Hanoi government, and did not wish to impose a military solution of the Vietnam problem. Reunification, of the country, he continued, could be determined later by the exercise of the free choice of the people, North and South.[88]

Goldberg's speech was followed by a moving address by France's Couve de Murville before the U.N. General Assembly, which ran in part as follows:

> As this merciless war continues, the question is no longer so much one of knowing why there is fighting and what the objectives are on each side. It is more and more one of knowing if the very survival of the Vietnamese people and its future as a nation are not at stake. . . . Confronted with this material and human tragedy, what is the meaning of ideologies, political calculations, power plays? If at the end of the combat, Vietnam were nothing more than ruins and sorrow, . . . what meaning can these . . . acts of intervention [have] whatever their source? . . . A somber fatalism hovers over this war, which . . . seems to prevent both adversaries from simultaneously stating their readiness to negotiate. . . . Is it imaginable . . . that such an overture [can] come from a side other than that of the great power . . . whose intervention has been one of the basic elements of that escalation and which alone is therefore in a position to make the new move?

The speech received little publicity, and public comment varied. Richard Nixon, in an address delivered in late September before the World Conference on Peace, emphasized the need for even-handed justice throughout South Vietnam if popular support of the government was to be achieved.[89] The implications were not clear. Overseas comment was skeptical of the president's declared desire to effect a peaceful settlement in Vietnam, since his proposals appeared to be tailored more specifically to meet the exigencies of domestic politics and general foreign policy considerations. It was also clear that powerful elements in the administration, including the Joint Chiefs of Staff, opposed any suggestion to withdraw

American forces or to abandon expensive installations. The president's proposal to permit the Vietnamese people, both North and South, to determine their political futures, combined with the neutralization of all Southeast Asia, was conditioned on premises that neither Hanoi nor Saigon would accept. It was difficult to determine where political and public-relations improvisations ended and considered policy commitments began.[90]

The Manila Conference of October 1966

Following the abortive French initiative, President Johnson decided to convene at Manila a top-level conference of representatives of the seven allied nations participating militarily in the Vietnam War. The meeting was designed ostensibly to bolster morale, but it was also intended to serve domestic political purposes with reference to the upcoming congressional elections in early November. Johnson's opening address to the Conference stressed the need to develop a closer partnership among Asian peoples to oppose Communist aggression, which presumably threatened the security of them all. The United States was prepared to help, but the Asian peoples themselves must take the lead in making needed improvements in domestic economic and social conditions. His encouraging report on the progress of the Vietnam War was supported by General Westmoreland's comment that the "kill ratio" had improved from two to one in the allies' favor in January 1966, to seven to one in September, with corresponding improvements in troop morale.

Premier Ky's response was skillfully presented and tailored to please; it covered all of the appropriate topics but took some liberties with the facts. He boasted that the Communists had been checked on every battlefield and that the revolutionary development (pacification) efforts were achieving concrete results. Civilians would be asked to take over more of the governing responsibilities at Saigon in the future, so that the military would be free to perform their more appropriate duties. Inflation remained to be curbed, and dictatorship must in time give way to constitutional government. Local elections were planned, along with land redistribution. Ky also insisted that the war on poverty, ignorance, and disease would continue to be waged relentlessly and that the inequities on which Communist propaganda thrived would be progressively eliminated. All of this was obviously designed for Washington's ears.

In the area of new proposals, Ky declared that Saigon wanted peace, but not at any price. He announced that, starting on November 1, individual insurgents would be offered an honorable way to renounce rebellion and to integrate with the national community. He ruled out direct negotiations with the Vietcong as a group and any offer of amnesty to hard-core rebels, who would all have to leave the country. He reported that the new Constituent Assembly, elected in May and already convened in September, would prepare for early elections to be staged behind the protective screen of South Vietnam's pacification forces. The constitution was expected to be completed within six months, and general elections were scheduled later in 1967. Meanwhile, the expanding activities of American combat forces would continue to challenge the main guerrilla bands and Vietminh regulars from the North, leaving Saigon's ARVN forces to support the pacification effort.[51]

The concluding communiqué of the seven-nation conference summarized the accomplishments of the sessions. The allies, as heretofore, were determined to resist aggression and to preserve the right of the South Vietnamese people to choose their own government through pending elections. They also agreed that the cornerstone of any national structure for South Vietnam must be the promotion of popular confidence in the honesty, efficiency, and justice of the government's efforts to "forge a social revolution of hope and progress." The projected program would endeavor to improve electrical supply, water resources, educational and health facilities, refugee training, agricultural credits and modernization, inflationary difficulties, and land reform. Some progress was made despite numerous difficulties, but initial expectations had little correspondence with the situation in many areas of the countryside.

The declared purpose of the Manila group—to pursue peace by discussion, negotiation, or reciprocal reduction of violence—needed much clarification. The enemies of the South Vietnamese people were described as seeking to "obtain by force and terror what they have been unable to accomplish by peaceful means." South Vietnamese spokesmen deplored the "partition brought about by the Geneva agreements in 1954" and insisted that they were trying to "resolve their own internal differences . . . through the democratic process." Saigon would ask its allies to withdraw their forces and evacuate military installations within six months after Northern "military and subversive forces are withdrawn,"[92] but no effort was made to define precisely those "military and subversive" elements whose complete withdrawal was made the condition of peace. Many areas of South Vietnam, particularly in the delta region, had been out from under Saigon's control since Diem's time, when few if any organized North Vietnamese forces were present. Did the term "Northern subversives" include the Southern-born Vietcong? The Manila Conference dealt superficially with a highly complicated problem.[93]

Differences within the Washington Administration, 1966–67

Serious questions about the military effort in Vietnam had meanwhile found expression in the Pentagon in mid-1966. A report of August 19, prepared by the Institute of Defense Analysis at Secretary McNamara's request, pretty thoroughly discredited the bombing operations in North Vietnam. The raids had obviously failed to impair Hanoi's ability or determination to support military activities in the South and had actually strengthened patriotic motivation to support the war. The North's essentially agricultural economy had survived the enforced dispersion of newly developed industrial plants, while available transport facilities and manpower recruitment had continued to move the essential military supplies, which the USSR and China still provided for Hanoi. Proponents of the air war had failed to take into account the remarkable tenacity and recuperative power of the North Vietnamese people. The report found no evidence that continued bombings at any level would end the war in the South and concluded that it would be less costly and more effective to construct a transportation barrier across the Laos panhandle.[94]

These findings and others were incorporated into specific proposals sent to the president by Secretary McNamara on October 14. He recommended that the costly and largely ineffective bombing operations be curtailed, that full recognition be given to the fact that victory was impossible without improved performance on the part of the Saigon government and army, and that the enemy be convinced that the United States really intended to withdraw once the North ceased its interference. Differences between Hanoi and the Vietcong should be exploited during negotiations by affording the latter a role as negotiator and in the proposed postwar government. Marshal Ky's government controlled only 25 percent of the population, while the Vietcong were recruiting heavily in the delta and showing no signs of flagging morale.[95]

The Joint Chiefs registered a sharp rejoinder to the Defense Secretary's memorandum, claiming it was inaccurate in its evaluations and destructive of morale in any case. They characterized the bombing operations as an American trump card that must not be discarded and recommended that political constraints relating to the bombing be minimized. Only the unconvincible, they argued, would doubt "the sincerity, the generosity, and the altruism of U.S. actions and objectives."[96] Thus did the rift emerge within the Pentagon.

Secretary McNamara subsequently criticized the excessive costs of the bombing operations, arguing that the interdiction of southbound traffic during the daytime could be accomplished by half of the current number of sorties. Air strikes outside South Vietnam had cost some $250 million for each of the twenty months since intensification began in March 1965, while they had inflicted total damages on enemy facilities and supplies of only $140 million. They had also cost the United States an average of one airman for every forty sorties, had killed some one thousand noncombatants per week, and had also alienated world opinion, while accomplishing little to deter the war effort. Further escalation of such operations would therefore be both futile and dangerous, McNamara believed. The United States, he argued, was not committed to expel those South Vietnamese presently in the Vietcong camp, to keep any particular government in power at Saigon, to ensure that an eventual popularly chosen government in the South was non-Communist, to keep North and South permanently divided, or to continue to put more effort into the contest than the corrupt, apathetic, and vulnerable government itself was doing.[97] It was at this juncture, in the spring of 1967, that the secretary ordered the systematic compilation of the documents that were later published as *The Pentagon Papers*, in order to determine where along the road American policy had gone astray.

The candid opinions of the military leadership were almost as gloomy as those of the Defense Department's intelligence agency. A reported conversation between President Johnson and Generals Wheeler and Westmoreland in April 1967 revealed that the generals supported their requests for 100,000 additional troops above the current number of 470,000 by insisting that the war had become a contest of attrition. If there were no troop increments, the outcome was touch and go; with the requested addition of two and one-third divisions, the struggle could go on for three more years; with an additional 100,000 reinforcements (up to a 570,000 total), it might be limited to two more years. General Wheeler admitted that the bombing operations were running out of worthwhile fixed targets, except for ports and other forbidden sites.[98] Meanwhile, the Joint Chiefs continued efforts to generate public and Congressional support for the faltering bombing program, which they had privately discounted. They also warned that public criticism of the rationale of the American presence in South Vietnam in alleged defense of the "free woild" could produce embarrassing consequences.[99]

Renewed Pacification Efforts, 1966-67

One principal thrust of American policy at the operational level during 1966 and 1967 concerned the expanded pacification program. Although the major concentration focused on security measures (census taking, identity cards, intelligence collection, and hearing of complaints) the operation was highly varied. In the area of land reform, for example, some 57,000 farmers, mainly squatters, were given titles to 273,000 acres of land during 1966. Unpaid taxes and rents were voided on all lands redeemed from NLF control. Some success was realized in organizing youth, women's groups, and cultivators into functioning units for self-help in agricultural, health, educational, and public works projects. Pacification teams now remained for a full year, and their efforts were supplemented by follow-up contacts. The initial results, measured quantitatively, fell far behind established performance quotas, reaching only 25 percent of the hamlet objective, but results as of late 1966 were modestly encouraging.[100]

Pacification efforts encountered increasing administrative difficulties in early 1967. Saigon forced the dismissal of several Corps I Vietnamese administrators on grounds that they were espousing third-force movements within Dai Viet and Buddhist circles. Others were found guilty of nepotism in the selection of personnel. Bureaucratic agencies, both military and civilian, began contesting access to available funds. The American Office of Civil Operations itself competed with related activities of the CIA and USIS, as well as with the semiautonomous Rural Development Committees.

The pacification program reached the point of near collapse in May, 1967, particularly in the area of Hué, where South Vietnamese forces failed to protect pacification teams assigned to cooperating hamlets. The ARVN forces preferred to withdraw at night to safe quarters, leaving villagers and team members exposed to retaliation by the Vietcong. The people thus betrayed were understandably bitter. It was alleged in Hué that Saigon's leadership encouraged such ARVN laxity as a means of punishing the local population for the rebellion of the previous year. Guerrilla elements penetrated both Hué and nearby Quang Tri almost at will. A *New York Times* investigator provided the following explanation of the near debacle:

> Failure of security is a symptom of . . . the overwhelming corruption that infests every phase of Vietnamese life. . . . There is simply no sense of unity, no feeling that winning the war must come first, no understanding that unless there is a contented peasantry, there is no room for the opulent society of the Government of Vietnam.[101]

In a desperate effort to salvage the faltering civil operations program, Ambassador Bunker acceded in early June 1967 to the army's request that the services command take over direction of the program from State Department personnel. A civilian presidential appointee, Robert Komer, was assigned to get the program back on the track under the overall command of General Creighton Abrams. Komer was a vigorous man with a reputation for efficiency, but he was new at the task and had to operate within the unresponsive milieu of army command headquarters, where his presence was resented. In the task of protecting the hamlet teams, matters actually got worse instead of better. The basic problems of friction between army and civilian pacification agencies were simply not amenable to military solution. Time was running out on the project.[102]

Part of the growing morale problem related to the fact that ARVN officers resented being pushed aside militarily. Army malcontents regarded their pacification role as suitable only for a militia, beneath the dignity of real soldiers. Particularly relevant were reported instances of overbearing attitudes toward ARVN forces displayed on occasion by Korean army forces. A more basic problem was the absence of any political consensus among South Vietnamese people in general on what values were being served by the continued prosecution of the war. Personal, family, class, and factional considerations were given priority, along with opportunities for monetary aggrandizement. The "Swiss-bank-account mentality" was contagious, extending downward from the top levels at Saigon. Provincial officials and ARVN leaders became rivals in the game and cooperated badly. When the active election campaign began in July 1967, political differences and local rivalries emerged to aggravate residual friction.[103] Even so, an essential objective of the pacification effort came to be the encouragement of popular participation in the elections.

The Elections of 1967

The selection of the Constituent Assembly occurred on September 11, 1966. The 530 candidates, grouped in 11 slates, were drawn largely from urban middle-class circles and army personnel. All were carefully screened to eliminate dissidents who were not committed to the anti-Communist struggle. The candidates were permitted, during the lifeless two-week campaigning period, to discuss no controversial issues whatever. Several organized campaign meetings in the capital area attracted only 200 listeners at most.[104] The 117 members who were finally selected represented, not surprisingly, groups that were friendly to the government. Twenty members were drawn from the army, and another 25 from Provin-

563

cial and Municipal Councils. Hoa Hao and Cao Dai representatives totalled another 17, with others coming from the Dai Viet Nationalists of central Annam and from a variety of resistance groups. Included among the 30 North Vietnamese members of the Assembly were many drawn from the Catholic refugee group. The Constituent Assembly convened in late September 1966, under the chairmanship of a former civilian premier, Phan Khac Suu, and settled down to six months of serious work preparing the draft constitution. The document was completed in March 1967.[105]

Meanwhile, in December, village and hamlet elections for Council committees and local chiefs were authorized by Premier Ky to be staged in the early spring of 1967. Such elections were limited to those communities presumed to be secure—an estimated 1,000 of the 2,500 villages and some 4,000 of 14,000 hamlets. All qualified eighteen-year-old residents could vote, barring those adjudged to be Vietcong adherents, leftists, neutralists, or other supporters of the Communist cause. The elected local committees, numbering six to twelve members, would serve as legislative agencies and also as electors of the village chiefs. Saigon empowered its appointed provincial chiefs (usually army officers) to dissolve any local council adjudged to be ineffective or vulnerable to control by a pro-Communist or neutralist majority. The vagueness of the law as designed by Premier Ky thus permitted sweeping government control of the local committees.[106]

South Vietnam's central constitution, as approved on April 1, 1967, was a very conservative document, reflecting the cautious views of its authors and the generally negative attitude of the ruling junta. Army henchmen in the Constituent Assembly controlled more than the one-third voting strength required for vetoing undesirable provisions. The American pattern of a strong, four-year presidency emerged, with the president granted power to select the prime minister and to reorganize the government without soliciting majority congressional approval.

The Armed Forces Council continued intact, although its previously exercised supremacy was limited by possible negative action of a majority of the elected Assembly. The Council could still "advise" the president regarding army reorganization and officer promotions, which were the areas where real power was vested. Constitutional provision for an "opposition party" within the elected bicameral Congress, operating by implication on the two-party pattern, actually tended to curtail free political expression within the body itself. Members were theoretically not to be held criminally liable for actions *in camera*, but offending spokesmen could be sharply censored. A vague Bill of Rights section held out hope that worker representatives at some future time might help determine wages and working conditions. It also proposed that farmers should be assisted in becoming property owners, but did not specify how. In the end, real power, including the presidency itself, was destined to remain within the disciplined army command.[107]

The considerable advantages enjoyed by the government party by reason of its control of the radio, travel facilities, and the press (three major newspapers were suppressed during the election campaign) were enhanced by the fact that the Generals within the Armed Forces Council closed their ranks behind a single slate of candidates. This was an action which rival civilian aspirants were unable to duplicate. Friction was caused in the army by allegations that Premier Nguyen Cao Ky had started his unofficial campaigning for the Presidency long before the permitted date, thus offending his army rivals. The Council accordingly acted at the insistence of Ambassador Bunker, who was concerned lest the developing factional rivalry within the army forces Council should erupt into open strife. In the ensuing emotion-laden three-day sessions in June, 1967, the army majority selected ranking Chief of State, General Nguyen Van Thieu as the Presidential candidate, naming Marshall Nguyen Cao Ky to the largely innocuous Vice-Presidential slot. Aside from his strong army support, Thieu enjoyed the active backing of a conservative Catholic group and the Hoa Hao sect faction.

Premier Ky accepted his political rejection grudgingly. He announced that "since in any democratic country, you have a right to disagree", he intended to resist militarily the actions of any elected civilians of which he disapproved, whether neutralist or Communist.[108]

In view of the fact that the faltering pacification program was itself dependent on the continuing protection afforded by the ARVN army forces, it was scarcely possible that any elected civilian candidate for the Presidency could have assumed political leadership in Saigon.[109] Assurance was lacking that the military would even permit the newly elected Congress to function as intended if actual control by the army command was threatened in any way. The elections, in other words, might redistribute in some more cooperative fashion the control exercised by the ruling elite, but they were unlikely to generate any sense of popular participation in government affairs or any public confidence in the effectiveness of aid coming from the Saigon authorities.[110]

The handicaps suffered by nongovernment candidates were both inherent and contrived. Most of them lacked functioning political party organizations, and few were known to the electorate even by name. All aspirants for office had to be highly circumspect in what they said, because the ruling junta continued to reserve the power to disqualify any candidate considered to be pro-neutralist, pro-Communist, or in favor of a compromise peace. Seven of the eighteen proposed tickets were actually disallowed. The Buddhist slate for the Senate was ruled out on a technicality, and the group was also forbidden to use its selected lotus symbol. The United Buddhist Church faction accordingly declared the election a sham. Buddhist critics denounced the exclusion from the election debates of such basic questions as peace and the neutralization of an independent South Vietnam. They also denounced the overwhelming American presence, with its alleged backing of the army candidate for the presidency. Saigon's former ambassador to Washington, Tran Van Dinh, declared flatly that the elections were meaningless "so long as the ultimate supervision . . . is in the hands of a foreign-powered military clique which has a vested interest in a particular outcome."[111] Generally speaking, the cautious ethnic minorities and the non-Buddhists tended to support the army ticket, along with the well-organized pro-Thieu Catholic party. (The latter elected no fewer than forty of the sixty Senate seats it contested.) The three most prestigious nonjunta military leaders—Minh, Thi, and Khanh—were all in exile and ex-Minister Au Truong Thanh was barred as a candidate because he advocated a negotiated peace. The leading civilian candidates for the presidency—Suu, Huong, and Quat—ran against each other, which served to fragment the antijunta sentiment.[112]

Public participation in the September 3 election was widespread, mainly because concerted official pressure was applied to get the people to vote. But the campaign aroused no popular interest, and many irregularities were reported. Voting booths in some areas ran out of ballots, and vote buying was common. The most serious abuse was the encouragement of double voting by army personnel, once as citizen and a second time as soldier. Army candidates ran particularly strong in the Second Corps area.[113] Some ballot boxes, improperly sealed, were stuffed en route to Saigon, according to passengers on the planes that delivered them. The cumulative evidence of a variety of irregularities, backed by Buddhist and student demonstrations, was later disallowed by the reviewing Constituent Assembly by the far-from-unanimous vote of fifty-eight to forty-three.[114]

Two surprising results emerged from the election. Although easily in the lead in the field of ten candidates, Thieu and Ky received only 37 percent of the votes. On the other hand, the best-known civilian candidates ran slightly behind the second-place winner, a relatively unknown lawyer named Truong Dinh Dzu, who had dared to advocate a coalition government following future peace talks with the Vietcong. For this aberration, Dzu was subsequently jailed for five years.

Although the holding of elections in war-torn South

Vietnam was itself a notable achievement from the American point of view, the performance was not impressive to most of the participants. The limited degree of freedom of expression permitted during the campaign tended to take the safe form of intensified criticism of the allegedly intrusive role of the United States in the internal affairs of South Vietnam. Opposition civilian parties, and particularly the Buddhists, flatly condemned U.S. interference.[115]

However much the elections may have served to legitimatize before American and world opinion the authority of the Saigon government, the traditional Vietnamese Confucianist idea of authority via Heaven's Mandate was far from met. President Thieu's government proved incapable of easing the burdens of the people and of promoting peace and harmony within the nation. In addition to being president and the supreme commander of the armed forces, Thieu also controlled the police and appointed both the premier and the cabinet. Vice-president Ky was reduced to the role of ex-officio chairman of three advisory councils: one covering cultural and educational affairs; a second, economic and social concerns; and the third, the ethnic minorities.[116] In competition with the powerful presidency and the army, the elected Congress lacked both cohesion and substantive power. Subsequent United States efforts to influence Thieu to broaden the civilian base of his political support invariably ran aground on military considerations. Meanwhile, the mass of the people, especially villagers, refugees, and Buddhist malcontents, wanted primarily to end the war.

The Situation as of Late 1967

Despite the elections and an apparent improvement in the allied military situation in late 1967, the political and economic scene in South Vietnam contained many elements of concern. Retail prices rose approximately 50 percent in 1967, and the export volume fell to the level of a meager $16 million, as compared with the very modest figure of $85 million realized in 1960. Nine-tenths of the foreign exchange available to the Saigon government came from direct dollar expenditures locally.[117] With America's total military expenditures on the war running over $2 billion a month, the surfeit of money in circulation could be absorbed only by America's subsidized shipment on government account of luxury consumer imports valued at several hundred million dollars per year for purchase by those who possessed the dollar currency. Without such ameliorative efforts, price inflation would have gotten completely out of hand. The government was thus kept reasonably solvent financially, but American contributions to cover local administrative and military costs and to control inflationary pressures served also to widen the gap between rich and poor, or often the corrupt on the one hand and victims of wartime violence on the other. Responsible elements of the population were becoming increasingly concerned over the decay of social and cultural values.[118] Distinguished Vietnamese exiles at Paris, most of whom were both anti-Communist and anti-Saigon, characterized the 1967 election as an American improvisation, an opportunist move to clothe with legality an essentially dictatorial military regime. The election victors were adjudged devoid of long-range objectives for the achievement of peace and the rebuilding of the country.[119]

Vietnamese student reaction as of the middle sixties was a mixture of mounting frustration and limited expressions of idealism. Well-meaning vacationers tried to assist in token fashion distressed villagers and slum dwellers to achieve minimal living standards, while others sought to bridge over the rifts separating hostile religious communities. A more characteristic response was the growing disillusionment and hostility directed toward corrupt and power-hungry officials.[120] Meanwhile, the classrooms of the University of Saigon were jammed with 26,500 matriculants, far exceeding the institution's resources in either faculty or books. Other university centers at Saigon (one of them founded by Thieu himself in 1967), at Hué, and at Dalat were only slightly less crowded. Students generally were more interested in draft evasion and antigovernment demonstrations than in serious study.[121]

Concurrent developments at the peasant edge of the social spectrum were illustrated by an American eye-witness description of the havoc wrought by a three-week search-and-destroy operation staged by American forces some 310 miles from Saigon along the upcoast highway. American naval guns, artillery, and bombers were directed against three hamlets who were suspected of harboring Vietcong. Around one thousand houses were destroyed, one hundred civilians killed and several times that number injured, and a total of five thousand destitute refugees created. Nearby paddy fields were desolated by bomb craters, and all palm tree orchards were destroyed. Prompt retirement from the area by attacking American forces left the Vietcong agents free to return and to press effectively their propaganda line among survivors that the American imperialists and their Saigon lackies cared nothing for the village people. The net political result was an increase of Vietcong recruits and supporters within the region.[122]

The Vietcong's efforts to enlist villager cooperation were usually far more effective than were Saigon's. Their policy was to respect the peasants' property, to cancel their tax and rental obligations, and to encourage the exercise of local leadership. By comparison, Saigon's troops violated property rights and failed to provide security from rebel attack, while the government reneged on land reform and denigrated local leadership. In the hard choice that many villagers had to make between the dire risks of siding with the Vietcong and the dangers from the predatory ARVN, the country people generally, according to a Rand Corporation study made in 1968, accorded a higher level of respect and cooperation to the Vietcong.[123] Communism itself had relatively little to do with determining popular preferences. The tactics of the NLF were geared to the realization of national goals, greater social mobility, land reform, and justice for all. Informed observers estimated that 75 percent of the Vietcong supporters were influenced primarily by personal and family considerations; 20 percent because of nationalist factors; and a mere 5 percent because of Communist ideology.[124]

It is understandable why informed American officials, including Ambassador Bunker, doubted the ability of the Saigon government to compete politically with the NLF in any popularly responsive coalition government. International volunteer personnel declared flatly in September 1967 that American relations with the Vietnamese people had deteriorated to the point of negating any chance for positive response. American advisory personnel, whether military or civilian, were assigned for only one year and usually failed to develop in so short a time any genuine understanding of the people they were supposed to serve. The cultural rift was widened by the enormous differences in standards of living and by the demoralizing relations generated through troop contacts with the people both in battle and on leave. Furthermore, refugee villagers experienced difficulty in finding rapport with urban groups.

The Washington View at the End of 1967

In the face of the rising chorus of criticism from the United States and abroad, Washington apologists argued that the war had not been lost and made the most of what gains could be claimed in the staging of elections and in the pacification program. The fact that some 80 percent of the eligible voters had participated in the September elections was proclaimed as providing a firm base for the authority of the government. Saigon's control over the population had reportedly increased from the previously exaggerated 55 percent in 1966 to 68 percent in 1967. The kill ratio was described as running ten to one

571

against the Communists. Thus Saigon authority was being consolidated, while the opposing forces, their morale fading and their number allegedly reduced to no more than 223,000 troops, were said to be quite incapable of initiating any major military action. Light was beginning to show at the end of the tunnel. Washington officials indicated that some American troops withdrawals could be anticipated in the foreseeable future.[125]

The barriers to a realistic policy evaluation centered mainly in Washington. American military leadership could not admit, without loss of prestige, that a small force of "faceless" Oriental peasants could successfully resist near-saturation bombing attacks, plus the pressure exerted on the ground by more than a half-million elite American troops and other allied contingents. Navy and air force leaders saw in the war an opportunity to demonstrate their own service's capabilities in the presence of ground army difficulties.[126]

Meanwhile, the State Department had measurably abdicated its responsibility to direct American foreign policy in the face of Pentagon intrusions and the dominating personality in the White House. Long-time students of Southeast Asian affairs in the State Department staff and the Foreign Service, not to mention academia, were denied opportunity for any meaningful expression of their critical views. Secretary of State Dean Rusk persisted in characterizing the problem in oversimplified terms as "aggression from the North," ignoring the serious internal divisions within South Vietnamese society and the popular rejection of the military successors of Ngo Dinh Diem. Still neglected in Washington were the possibilities of exploiting noticeable differences between Hanoi's declared position regarding neutralization and unification, and that of the National Liberation Front, as well as the growing rift between Moscow and Peking.

Washington also faced several domestic political considerations impinging on the outcome of the Vietnam War, which were in essential conflict with each other. The first was characterized as "the inherent dynamic" within the governmental context behind the quest to achieve a military decision. Any administration despairing of an early negotiated settlement would be inclined to accede to inevitable pressure for continuing the escalation of military effort and resources. The second factor was the inescapable political demand to achieve some kind of "solution" before the presidential elections of November, 1968. A third was the relentless polarization of popular opinion between the patriotic majority, who called for support of the boys at the fighting front, and a highly articulate dissenting minority, who were critical of the war. Youthful protesters, subject to draft call, were denied any effective means of influencing policy except through overt protest or civil disobedience[127] These three considerations provided the inevitable political context for the political developments of 1968-69.

1. Don Luce and John Sommer, *Vietnam, the Unheard Voices* (Ithaca, 1969), pp. 39-47.

2. John T. McAlister, *Viet Nam, the Origins of Revolution* (New York, 1969), pp. 351-52.

3. I. Milton Sacks, "Restructuring Government in South Vietnam," *Asian Survey* 7 (August 1967): 515-26; Robert Shaplen, *The Lost Revolution* (New York, 1966), pp. 213-24.

4. Shaplen, *op. cit.*, pp. 213-58, 269-312.

5. Gerald Hickey, *Village in Vietnam* (New Haven, 1964).

6. Shaplen, *op. cit.*, pp. 213-24, 227-36; Luce and Sommer, *op. cit.*, pp. 49-52.

7. Neil Sheehan et al., *The Pentagon Papers* (New York, 1971), pp. 283-85.

8. *Ibid.*, pp. 234-70.

9. *Ibid.*, pp. 274-76. (General Taylor to McNamara, January 20, 1964).

10. *Ibid.*, pp. 277-83 (McNamara to Johnson, March 16, 1964).

11. *Ibid.*, pp. 234-70 (Sheehan's account of the post-Diem situation).

12. *Ibid.*, pp. 285-86 (Johnson to Lodge, March 20, 1964).

13. Shaplen, *op. cit.*, pp. 235-48. Minh was reportedly a favorite of McNamara.

14. *Pentagon Papers*, pp. 244-50, 338-39.

15. *Ibid.*, pp. 286-88.

16. *Ibid.*, pp. 253-54.

17. *Ibid.*, pp. 257-58; Shaplen, *op. cit.*, pp. 235-48.

18. *Pentagon Papers*, pp. 288-89.

19. *Ibid.*, pp. 258-67.

20. Joseph Buttinger, *Vietnam, A Political History* (New York, 1968), p. 498.

21. *Pentagon Papers*, pp. 289-91.

22. *Ibid.*, pp. 294-98.

23. *Ibid.*, pp. 291-94 (August 10, 1964).

24. *Ibid.*, pp. 346-51 (August 18, 1964).
25. Buttinger, *op. cit.*, pp. 248-84.
26. *Pentagon Papers*, pp. 354-55 (August 26, 1964).
27. *Ibid.*, pp. 355-57 (John McNaughton, September 3, 1964).
28. *Ibid.*, pp. 357-60.
29. *Ibid.*, pp. 365-68.
30. *Ibid.*, pp. 333-37.
31. *Ibid.*, The author participated in a student conference at West Point in early December, 1964, where Academy faculty representatives worked persistently to obtain approval of proposed bombing forays against North Vietnam.
32. *Ibid.*, pp. 419-23.
33. *Ibid.*, pp. 325-26.
34. *Ibid.*, pp. 429-31.
35. *Ibid.*, pp. 379-81.
36. *Ibid.*, p. 342.
37. *Ibid.*, pp. 391-93.
38. *Ibid.*, pp. 443-46.
39. *Ibid.*, pp. 401-07.
40. *Ibid.*, pp. 440-41 (McCone, CIA).
41. *Ibid.*, pp. 432-40 (McNaughton).
42. *Ibid.*, pp. 446-47.
43. Shaplen, *op. cit.*, pp. 287-328, 341-47.
44. *Pentagon Papers.* pp. 413-17, 462-68.
45. *Ibid.*, pp. 449-54.
46. *Ibid.*, pp. 491-98 (January 9, 1966).
47. For the full texts, see George M. Kahin and John W. Lewis, *The United States and Vietnam* (Ithaca, 1967), pp. 403-07.
48. James Reston, "Where Did We Go Wrong?", *New York Times*, November 21, 1965; *ibid.*, "The Quiet Disaster," *New York Times*, December 1, 1965.
49. See Appendix 13 in Kahin and Lewis, *op. cit.*, pp. 422-29.
50. James Reston, "The Rising Brutality," *New York Times*, September 5, 1965; *ibid.*, "Where Did We Go Wrong?" *New York Times*, November 21, 1965.
51. Luce and Sommer, *op. cit.*, pp. 53-58, 118-19.
52. McAlister, *op. cit.*, pp. 3-5.
53. Luce and Sommer, *op. cit.*, pp. 6-14.
54. Jean Lacouture, *Ho Chi Minh: A Political Biography* (New York, 1968).
55. See McAlister, *op. cit.*, pp. 3-5.
56. Nguyen Thai, "The Two Vietnams and China," *The Harvard Review* 2 (1963): 26-32.
57. *FEER*, June 21, 1966, pp. 434-35.
58. *FEER, 1968 Yearbook*, pp. 36-37.
59. McAlister, *op. cit.*, pp. ix-xi.
60. Luce and Sommer, *op. cit.*, pp. 145-65.
61. McAlister, *op. cit.*, p. 196.
62. Luce and Sommers, *op. cit.*, pp. 153-59.
63. *Ibid.*, pp. 182-85.
64. *Ibid.*, pp. 169-80.
65. *FEER*, March 10, 1966, p. 463; and April 14, 1966, pp. 113-16.
66. Luce and Sommer, *op. cit.*, pp. 94-104.
67. *Ibid.*, p. 11.
68. Shaplen, *op. cit.*, pp. 328-32.
69. Charles Keyes, *Report to USOM/V* (Washington, March 1, 1968).

70. Charles A. Joiner, "The Ubiquity of the Administrative Role in Counterinsurgency," *Asian Survey* 7 (August, 1967): 540-44.

71. *Ibid.*, "South Vietnam: Political, Military, and Constitutional Arenas in Nation Building," *Asian Survey* 8 (January, 1968): 58-71.

72. *New York Times*, January 2, 1966.

73. F. Nivolon, "Who's on Top?" *FEER*, March 24, 1966, p. 555.

74. Tom Wicker, "Peace Bid Pressed," *New York Times*, February 8, 1966.

75. Oral statements by State Department officers in attendance at Honolulu; see also, Keesing, *op. cit.*, pp. 89-67.

76. *FEER*, March 24, 1966, pp. 555-58.

77. Neil Sheehan, "Saigon Parley," *New York Times*, April 13, 1966.

78. *Ibid.*, "Anti-Americanism Grows in Vietnam," *New York Times*, April 24, 1966; see also Keeting, *op. cit.*, pp. 89-97.

79. *Pentagon Papers*, pp. 499-500.

80. Sheehan, *op. cit.*, *New York Times*, April 13, 1966; Luce and Sommer, *op. cit.*, 119-37.

81. Keesing, *op. cit.*, pp. 93-106; *FEER*, June 16, 1966, p. 515.

82. Luce and Sommer, *op. cit.*, pp. 135-37.

83. *New York Times*, April 3, 1966.

84. *Ibid.*, May 18, 1966.

85. *Ibid.*, April 23, 1966.

86. *Ibid.*, January 20, 1967; *FEER*, March 18, 1966, pp. 494-96.

87. *New York Times*, September 3 and 9, 1966.

88. *Ibid.*, September 16, 1966.

89. *Ibid.*, September 22, 1966.

90. James Reston, "Manila Conference," *New York Times*, October 2, 1966.

91. Charles Mohr, "Saigon Plans a Major Appeal to Vietcong Leaders to Defect," *New York Times*, October 25, 1966.

92. *New York Times*, October 26 and November 2, 1966.

93. *Ibid.*, Charles Mohr's comments on Manila Conference.

94. *Pentagon Papers*, pp. 500-09.

95. *Ibid.*, pp. 542-51.

96. *Ibid.*, pp. 552-53.

97. *Ibid.*, pp. 553-55, 577-85.

98. *Ibid.*, pp. 567, 569

99. *Ibid.*, pp. 535-41.

100. John C. Donnell, "Pacification Reassessed," *Asian Survey* 7 (August 1967): 567-70.

101. Tom Buckley, "Pacification Reported Stalled in Vietnam's I Corps Region," *New York Times*, May 24, 1967.

102. *New York Times*, June 4, 1966.

103. Donnell, *op. cit.*, pp. 570-76.

104. *New York Times*, September 8, 1967.

105. I. Milton Sacks, "Restructuring Government," *Asian Survey* 7 (August 1967): 517-20.

106. *New York Times*, June 7, 1966.

107. Sacks, *op. cit.*, pp. 520-26.

108. Joiner, "The Ubiquity," *op. cit.*, pp. 540-54.

109. Tom Wicker, "Whose Skin is on the Wall?" *New York Times*, June 4, 1967.

110. Kahin and Lewis, *op. cit.*, pp. 257-69; McAlister, *op. cit.*, pp. 359-63.

111. See Tran Van Dinh "Buddhism—Road to Vietnam Nationalism," *New York Times* for Sept 27, 1966. Dinh was the father of Mme. Nhu. See also May 27, 1967.

112. Sacks, *op. cit.*, p. 526.

113. Luce and Sommer, *op. cit.*, pp. 58-61; Kahin and Lewis, *op. cit.*, pp. 258-69; Joiner, "South Vietnam," *Asian Survey* 8 (January 1968); 58-68.

114. Buttinger, *op. cit.*, p. 480.

115. Joiner, "Politics in South Vietnam," *Current History* 54 (January 1968); 35-41, 50-52.

116. *Ibid.*, "South Vietnam," *Asian Survey* 8 (January 1968): 58-62.

117. *FEER*, April 13, 1969, p. 43.

118. Luce and Sommer, *op. cit.*, pp. 303-15; *FEER*, July 3, 1969, p. 75.

119. *FEER*, March 6, 1969, pp. 17-18.

120. Luce and Sommer, *op. cit.*, pp. 242-64.

121. *Bangkok Post*, July 30, 1967.

122. Neil Sheehan, "Unnoted Victims: Vietnam's Peasants," *New York Times*, February 15, 1966.

123. *New York Times*, January 22, 1970, p. 12: Ithiel DeSola Pool, "Political Alternatives to the Vietcong," *Asian Survey* 7 (August 1967): 555-60.

124. Luce and Sommer provide supporting evidence in Chapters 9, 10, and 13 in *Vietnam, the Unheard Voices*.

125. This mood is summarized by Buttinger, *op. cit.*, pp. 489-96.

126. For a discussion of this issue, see David M. Shoup, "The New American Militarism," *Atlantic Monthly* (April 1969): 51-56. A more popular discussion is available in *Newsweek*, January 20, 1967.

127. See a letter to the editor of the *New York Times* by James C. Thomson Jr., a former employee of the Joint Chiefs of Staff, May 24, 1967.

XV

TET, DE-ESCALATION,
PEACE MOVES, AND
VIETNAMIZATION, 1968–69

The surprise that the Tet offensive of early February 1968 conveyed to American officials may be appreciated by reference to the following optimistic statement that had just appeared in General Westmoreland's year-end report. It was completed on January 27, only four days before the Lunar New Year date:

> Interdiction of the enemy's logistics train . . . by our indispensable air efforts has imposed significant difficulties on him. In many areas, the enemy has been driven away from the population centers; in others, he has been compelled to disperse and evade contact, thus nullifying much of his potential. The year ended with the enemy increasingly resorting to desperation tactics to achieve military/psychological victory, and he has experienced only failure in these attempts.[1]

The widely dispersed attacks on government positions that began on the night of January 31 were indeed desperate undertakings, but they carried an identifiable rationale and came very near succeeding. They demonstrated, among other things, the woeful inadequacy of American intelligence sources and the vulnerability of supposedly firmly held government centers. They influenced Washington to re-examine carefully American objectives and tactics and led to the refusal of requested troop reinforcements and to the replacement of General Westmoreland. Bombing raids above the twentieth parallel were discontinued, and President Johnson withdrew from the presidential contest in a move to facilitate peace negotiations. Within the United States, antiwar resistance gained momentum among draft-eligible youth and within liberal circles generally.

Communist Motivation and Planning

A number of basic considerations prompted the Communist side to stage the Lunar New Year offensive. Hanoi's victory plans—which involved progression from defensive harassment, to a posture of equality of challenge, and then to the final disintegration of enemy resistance —had stalled substantially short of the third phase. U.S. bombing of the North had reduced the volume of available consumer goods and stimulated black-market operations. Hanoi's dependence on China for food, small arms, munitions, and labor to keep open transportation facilities to the border had disquieting overtones. Peking's counsel to continue guerrilla resistance indefinitely, coupled with its promise of ultimate rescue, "using all weapons and . . . frontiers," carried ominous suggestions for Hanoi.[2]

Orthodox Communist leaders in North Vietnam were also unhappy over NLF advocacy of international neutrality and an indefinite postponement of unification. The NLF fashioned its propaganda program to attract support from all enemies of the Saigon regime. Affiliated groups included the Voice of the Intellectuals; the Committee for a Self-sufficient Economy, associations for the protection of national culture and for student autonomy; and a variety of reform advocates. A Czech visitor to Hanoi in late December 1967 reported disquietingly via the Prague press that the South's Liberation Front spokesmen were even advocating unorthodox peasant ownership of land, private participation in economic development, and a general amnesty for major elements of the Saigon government's civil service.[3] Could the Hanoi-directed cadres in the South maintain an orthodox Marxist line in competition with the ideologically diluted peace sentiment spreading in the South? Difficulties were being encountered in blending the young Northern reinforcements into the depleted ranks of veteran Vietcong guerrilla battalions.[4]

Moscow itself reportedly shared Hanoi's concern over the material and political risks involved should the American bombing of North Vietnam continue indefinitely. Deteriorating Soviet relations with China added to the tension. In early 1967, therefore, the Russian advisers to Hanoi proposed shifting to the tactic of "negotiating while fighting" as a possible means of bringing an end to the American bombing forays against the North. While accepting the Soviet proposal, Hanoi decided for psychological as well as military reasons to try to improve conditions for negotiations by exerting a maximum effort militarily, using all available resources.[5]

Hanoi's plan to attack directly both military installations and urban centers in the South was conveyed to NFL representatives at a conference held in April 1967. The initial move would be to pin down substantial numbers of American troops by staging attacks near DMZ border posts and in coastal cities adjacent to major installations. The second phase would involve attacks against Saigon and several score provincial and district centers. Many of the seventy thousand Vietcong troops assigned to attack Saigon would function as infiltration units, with smaller concentrations directed against other centers. Once such operations had demonstrated the inability of the police and the ARVN forces to protect urban centers long considered secure, the third and, it was hoped, final stage of revolution could conceivably get underway. The immediate objective would be to provoke popular risings and mass defections among the ARVN troops. The eventual goal would be replacement of Saigon's authority by a coalition regime dominated by the National Liberation Front apparatus. Depending on the outcome, a fourth round

579

of attacks could be launched later in the spring. If phase three should fail completely, the resistance effort could still revert to guerrilla tactics and await a more favorable opportunity in the future. Whether or not successful militarily, the move would conceivably assist in halting bombing operations and in initiating peace negotiations.[6] The daring proposal was acclaimed, with obvious exaggeration, by Ho Chi Minh as potentially one of the great battle plans of all history.

The Tet Offensive

The Communist offensive was timed to coincide with the widely publicized truce arrangement scheduled to start in late January 1968, at the beginning of the Lunar New Year holiday. Half of South Vietnam's armed forces were expected to be on leave at the time. Vietcong infiltrators dressed in civilian clothes would mingle with the preholiday traffic entering the towns. An initial diversionary attack was to be launched in the early hours of January 30 in the Second Corps area midway between Saigon and the seventeenth parallel. Operations within Saigon and Hué began twenty-four hours later. The Saigon police force, under the direction of General Nguyen Ngoc Loan, was forewarned and took some precautionary measures, but no effective defensive preparations were made by the army. American officers could not believe that anything so mad as a deliberate attempt to seize Saigon was really in prospect.

The attack on Saigon was carefully planned. Commando groups of Vietcong infiltrated the city, proceeding to designated points of rendezvous where arms and detailed directions were on deposit for their use. Some units operated as suicide squads. Selected targets within the city included the Presidential Palace, the government's radio station (seized and destroyed), the American Embassy (invaded), the headquarters of both the Joint General Staff and of the navy, the main Saigon prison, the race course, and the nearby Tan Son Nhut airfield. A particularly daring move involved an attempt by twelve men to seize the naval depot, situated on the river, where success might have permitted the ferrying of two waiting battalions of Vietcong troops into the very heart of the city. The threatening attack on the airfield got so far as the runway itself, to be turned back in the nick of time by American units arriving in the early morning via a bridge the invaders had neglected to destroy.[7]

Militarily, the attacks on Saigon were too thinly spread and too poorly coordinated to achieve their maximum goals. Efforts to supply and reinforce isolated units were ineffective, and several direct assaults by full Vietcong battalions endeavoring to split the city were repulsed. The planners were also mistaken in their expectation that the ARVN and the Saigon police would fall apart under stress of attack and that a popular rising would ensue. The desire of the people for peace and their hostile attitude toward the junta government at Saigon did not generate any overt pro-Vietcong response. General Loan's police forces conducted themselves with particular bravery, and the arrival of outside reinforcements turned the tide. Nevertheless, severe fighting in the Cholon section of the metropolitan area continued for seven days, inflicting severe damage on urban property. The Vietcong counted an estimated twelve thousand dead, compared to a reported one thousand for the defenders. The psychological impact was nevertheless devastating. One observer summed it up as follows:

> The fact that the Communists were able to infiltrate so many men and weapons without being detected revealed an astonishing amount of successful covert planning and organization, and that an effective underground was in existence.[8]

The simultaneous Tet attack on Hué was a serious and tragic affair. The Hué defenses collapsed at the outset largely because the mayor, Lieutenant-Colonel Phan Van Koa, although clearly warned, made no serious move to block the Vietminh occupation. Koa himself reportedly went into hiding for six days, leaving the city's government without leadership. His attitude reflected what one observer described as Hué's "close-knit, almost incestuous atmosphere of local maneuver and intrigue," which had previously characterized the abortive Struggle Movement of 1966. Hué's prevailing anti-Saigon and anti-American sentiments made preliminary infiltration and occupation by the invaders surprisingly easy.

The subsequent forcible dislodgement of the tenacious Communist occupation forces from the Citadel section of the city was a gruesome three-week operation. As soon as the monsoon clouds lifted, American troops countered with concentrated artillery fire and bombing attacks. The imposing eighteenth-century fortifications planned by French engineers in Gia Long's time were reduced to rubble. Civilian deaths numbered some four thousand (half the civilian total from all the Tet fighting), many of whom were victims of American fire power. The Communists themselves resorted to deliberate terrorist methods at the end of the siege, resulting in the fanatical execution of hundreds of civilians. Ninety thousand residents of Hué were left homeless, and morale of the population was shattered.

Both the Communist invaders and the counterattacking American forces alienated Hué residents beyond the possibility of early reconciliation. Local inhabitants who had trusted the Communists overmuch were bitterly disillusioned, but the devastation wrought by American artillery cancelled out any positive acceptance of the American presence. Amid the rubble and the graves of the dead, the demoralized survivors actually resorted to looting and profiteering on the sale of American-supplied relief contributions.[9]

A total of thirty-four provincial capitals and sixty-four district towns of South Vietnam were attacked during the Tet Communist offensive, the latter by rocket and mortar fire. An estimated seventy thousand urban residences were destroyed, mainly by artillery fire and bombings, which increased the refugee population by five to six hundred thousand. Damage to public buildings and to textile and other industrial installations was estimated at $175 million.[10] Around two hundred American planes were destroyed on the ground, and approximately four times that number were damaged. So gloomy did the situation appear for a while in Saigon that gold imports, which had been coming in regularly from France via Vientiane to soak up the surplus dollars, came to a complete halt.[11] Urban youth for the first time began to defect to the rebels in considerable numbers. In the face of popular hostility and apathy, ultimate allied military victory became clearly impossible.[12]

Washington's Decision to De-escalate

Washington's receipt of the shocking news of the Tet offensive brought to a crisis the long-smoldering argument between high-level intelligence agencies (CIA, Pentagon, and State) and the service chiefs within the Defense Department. Only a portion of the story can be assayed because documentary sources from State Department archives are not available for examination. It is known that Under-Secretary Ball gained influence and that Secretary Rusk, by March 5, reversed his previously registered opposition to bombing limitations. The contest developed between the newly appointed Defense Secretary Clark Clifford, successor to McNamara and supported by civilian leaders within the Pentagon, and the Chiefs of Staff. The professional interests and operational responsibilities of the military services involved considerations not shared by their more detached civilian opponents, including especially the military's resentment over having been obliged, for political reasons, to wage a limited war in Vietnam. Such sentiments were clearly reflected in the views of fifteen retired army and navy leaders published in March 1968. The group demanded: (1) a full declaration of war against Hanoi; (2) closing of the Haiphong port and an invasion of North

Vietnam, (3) warnings to Peking and Moscow that continued efforts to arm the enemy would constitute an overt act of war against the United States; and (4) the cashiering or impeachment of all U.S. public officials whose loyalty was considered to be compromised.[13]

The first reaction of the Joint Chiefs of Staff to the news from Saigon was to insist on sending to South Vietnam whatever reinforcements were immediately available. They also renewed demands for greater freedom in the choice of bombing sites and pressed the president to call up the National Guard as a step toward full mobilization.[14] The eventual request from General Westmoreland was for 206,750 troop reinforcements, plus permission to hire 12,000 additional Vietnamese civilians to relieve American personnel for combat duties. The demand for relaxation of bombing controls was early discarded, and the obvious political liabilities connected with mobilizing the National Guard in an election year vetoed any prospect of meeting Westmoreland's full request.[15] The task of reviewing military policy was assigned to the new secretary of defense, who took over the post on March 1. Clark Clifford was a long-time friend of President Johnson and had previously been a supporter of the war.

The principal arguments advanced by the CIA and other intelligence advisers were by no means new, but the post-Tet context made them more compelling. As presently led and motivated, the argument ran, the Saigon armies could not pacify the country, and the addition of two hundred thousand American troops would not alter the situation materially. A continued war of attrition would surely destroy South Vietnam and generate increasing world criticism of the American role. Bombing of the North had already reached the point of diminishing returns. The preferred alternative policy was to scale down the fighting, establish secure control over selected densely populated areas, and buy time to improve the capabilities of ARVN forces and the Saigon government. The proposal to expand and strengthen the South Vietnamese army received strong support from Ambassador Bunker. Secretary Rusk also came to Clifford's support by suggesting on March 5 the discontinuance of bombing above the twentieth parallel and concentration on selected battle zone areas.[16]

President Johnson was shocked and the Chiefs of Staff angered by Secretary Clifford's recommendations. Reacting negatively, the president on March 13 decided to dispatch forty thousand reinforcements and to call up approximately one hundred thousand reserves. On that same day, Senator Eugene McCarthy won his anti-war campaign victory in the New Hampshire Democratic primary, and three days later Robert Kennedy announced his own candidacy for the Democratic nomination.[17] The President still refused to "tuck tail" and repudiate America's commitments to Saigon. But when U.N. Ambassador Goldberg submitted a private memorandum to the White House advocating a bombing halt, the president requested on March 22 that he confer about the matter. On the same day, General Westmoreland was relieved of his command and asked to return to the Washington post of Army Chief of Staff. At a conference staged at Clark Field in the Philippines, Defense Department officials later trimmed the reinforcement requests to the politically manageable levels of ten thousand additional combat forces and thirteen thousand for support area service. Plans to reduce bombing operations below the twentieth parallel were formulated as a move calculated to improve the chances for opening peace negotiations.[18] The general deescalation policy was later approved by an advisory group of thirteen elder statesmen, who were assembled at the State Department on March 25.

The final White House announcement on March 31 of the decision to curtail the bombing and to seek a basis for negotiation was accompanied by the president's unexpected declaration that he was withdrawing from the presidential race in order to facilitate the peace effort. Military resentment over the bombing curtailment was apparently reflected in the immediate intensification of air operations up to the twentieth parallel, a seemingly gratuitous move that offended proponents of the new policy.[19]

Post-Tet Developments in South Vietnam

General Westmoreland's successor at Saigon, General Creighton Abrams, adopted a pragmatic approach. His immediate hope was to improve the fighting power of the locally recruited defense militia, some of whom had demonstrated genuine concern during Tet to defend their neighborhoods and relatives. Problems connected with improving the combat effectiveness of the regular ARVN forces were more difficult. The units assigned to the Saigon area were selected not to combat the Vietcong, but rather to protect the Thieu regime against any hostile coup attempts initiated by rival officers.[20] Contingents posted to regions distant from their homes had long been subject to debilitating rates of desertion, sometimes reaching 60 percent annually. Better disciplined ARVN divisions stationed next to the DMZ line in the First Corps area encountered chronic difficulty in replacing losses from illness and combat with recruits equally capable of disciplined control.

Relations with the rural population continued to be bad. Exposed villagers feared and hated the poorly disciplined and often thieving ARVN forces. Rather than create more refugees, Saigon's forces normally made little distinction between civilians and belligerents found in captured villages previously under Vietcong control. American forces themselves adopted similar tactics at Mylai.[21] Korean officers, when suffering sniper fire or other harassment in occupied villages, followed the practice of arbitrarily executing villagers selected by lot until the attacks ceased.[22] The extensive material destruction of villages, orchards, and paddy fields, mainly by bombing and artillery fire, aggravated the disintegration of social and cultural values in crowded refugee centers and urban slums. A worthy ruler in the Confucianist tradition, who would restore some measure of harmony between Heaven and Earth, was nowhere in evidence. President Thieu's labored political gestures contributed little to authenticate his government's exercise of power.

586

A major precaution taken by President Thieu was to remove all supporters of Vice-President Ky from strategically important posts. A Dai Viet leader was named assistant to the president. In May 1968 Thieu installed the former chief of state, Tran Van Huong of Saigon, as premier in place of Nguyen Van Loc, who was pro-Ky. Also pushed aside was General Nguyen Ngoc Loan, the hero of the defense of Saigon and a friend of Ky. Premier Huong's appointment was supported by American advisers as a move designed to broaden the political base of the government. In actuality, President Thieu afforded Huong very little room for maneuver in his own right. The four army corps commanders were all loyal to Thieu.[23]

Ky's angry response, delivered before two thousand Defense Department officials on May 22, 1968, indicated that he was prepared to resort to blood and fire to rid South Vietnam of traitors, particularly those in the service of "foreign powers." He affirmed that South Vietnam had no leader comparable in stature to Ho Chi Minh and Vo Nguyen Giap because "there exists a band of slaves among the leaders of our country." Ky pledged qualified support to Premier Huong "as long as he stays anti-Communist and tries to do good things for the country".[24]

The Initiation of Peace Negotiations

Hanoi responded to President Johnson on April 3 with an offer to participate in peace negotiations if American attacks on North Vietnam ceased, while otherwise continuing aggressive tactics. In early May, Communist forces launched a new series of operations within the Mekong delta and in the First and Second Corps areas in upper South Vietnam. Saigon claimed that eleven thousand attackers were killed. The NLF also installed Liberation committees in all Vietcong-held villages, while Hanoi projected a new organization called the Alliance of National Democratic and Peace Forces of Vietnam in an apparent effort to supplement the Vietcong's NLF.

By June 1968 the doctrinaire Marxist, Truong Chinh, had attained a measure of ideological ascendency at Hanoi. He revived the Maoist idea of waging a protracted guerrilla war, now that Le Duan's and Giap's Tet effort to seek a quick military decision had failed. The revised program would conserve resources and gain time to revolutionize the masses more thoroughly, while influencing the NLF to adhere to more orthodox Communist standards.[25] The new Communist political offensive in South Vietnam, launched in the early fall of 1968, included the organization of a Movement to Study for Peace and a proposed Peace Cabinet. The popular response to Hanoi's continuing effort was minimal, and the final phase of the 1968 offensive faded out. By the end of the year the standard political objective of most of the Vietcong cadres had reverted to the assassination of Allied revolutionary development teams who had been sent back into the villages, usually in ten-man units.[26]

The war had reached a stalemate. American saturation bombing in selected areas of South Vietnam produced meager results politically. In the Mekong delta, helicopter fire, gunboat attacks, and artillery bombardment were directed against centers that had long been under Vietcong control. Results were minimal, however, for residents of delta communities demonstrated fantastic recuperative power. Vietcong troops in the region were recruited from a local peasant population that continued to be stubbornly anti-Saigon.[27] The morale of the Saigon forces suffered from their antagonistic relations with Korean and American allies, who discounted the ARVN soldierly performance. Americans in particular regarded the Saigon forces as corrupt, cowardly, and lazy.[28]

President Johnson's eight months of pre-election efforts accomplished very little toward formulating a basis for peace negotiations. President Thieu was a principal barrier, for he resented the pressure exerted by Washington and maintained his stubborn resistance until almost the end of October.[29] His final grudging consent to the halting of all bombing operations and to his own participation in the projected Paris negotiations was generally unpopular in official Saigon circles.[30] Johnson's inability to obtain earlier acquiescence in the arrangement clearly contributed to the narrow defeat suffered by his Democratic candidate, Senator Hubert Humphrey. Distrust between the Vietnamese participants was reflected in the subsequent protocol problems. The shape of the negotiating table and seating arrangements developed into a formidable contest. Little or no progress was made in the waning months of Johnson's incumbency. President Nixon inherited no easy task.

Reforming Efforts of the Early Months of 1969

In the absence of access to the essential documents relating to post-1968 Vietnam, the serious student of the period must admit that no really authentic history can be prepared. Available documents include only those that the interested parties chose to release, while secondhand comments of newspaper reporters and unofficial observers can be discounted as incomplete and probably biased in interpretation. The historian's own viewpoint must also be taken into account in any careful assessment of a variety of interpretations. But the fact that the results can be only approximately correct does not cancel out the urgent need for some effort at detached investigation. The alternative is to leave the story to polemicists on both sides.

At the outset the new president subscribed in large measure to the traditional view of elite Washington that the problem in Vietnam was Communist inspired. If armed aggression were permitted to succeed in Vietnam, the freedom of other states in Southeast Asia and throughout the world would be jeopardized as confidence in America's commitments evaporated. The new secretary of state, William Rogers, was more inclined to solicit briefings from informed departmental experts than Dean Rusk had ever been, but the open-minded George Ball was no longer under-secretary, and the real direction of major foreign policy decisions shifted to the White House. The new defense secretary,

589

Melvin Laird, was less inclined than either McNamara or Clifford had been to challenge the Washington military establishment, and the military was not ready to concede that enemy forces in Indochina were beyond its ability to subdue.

Some new efforts were initiated, as will be indicated shortly, to improve Saigon's governmental and military performance, but in the absence of vigorous presidential initiative, no concerted effort was made to re-examine either the premises or the objectives behind America's involvement in Southeast Asia. There is little evidence that the collected *Pentagon Papers* were studied at all. The massive staff structure at both the State Department and the Pentagon was dominated by an inertia of massive proportions. Ball later stated the unmet need succinctly:

> To justify our expanding commitment of force, we have continually restated our objectives in increasingly strident terms, while at the same time exaggerating the political costs of extricating ourselves from a situation which large numbers of people find totally unacceptable. . . . Alarmist predictions are a form of self-indulgence which we can no longer afford. Instead, the major thrust of our policy should be to restore a more rational perspective.[31]

The most urgent problem American negotiators faced in the early months of 1969 was to persuade the three Vietnamese antagonists to negotiate at all. The argument over the shape of the negotiating table was indicative of the difficulties involved. Hanoi's stance was particularly rigid. It would denigrate the so-called American puppet regime at Saigon to the same level as the secondary NLF delegation at Paris; it flatly refused to equate the legitimacy of its own quarter-century involvement in the Vietnamese struggle for independence and unification with an American intervention carried on half way around the world in contravention of the Geneva agreement of 1954. North Vietnam would not agree to withdraw its troop assistance and supply services for the Vietcong as long as the American presence continued to bolster the unpopular Saigon regime.[32] Although NLF spokesmen at Paris diverged somewhat from Hanoi's policy with respect to the character of a possible successor government in the South and in the proposed schedule for unification, they were in full agreement in rejecting the claims of the Saigon junta.[33] Whereas Communist-side spokesmen agreed to welcome all proponents of peace, neutrality, and independence, regardless of political affiliations, to participate in an interim coalition government, they firmly refused to deal with the military triumvirate of Thieu, Ky, and Khiem.[34]

American efforts to get negotiations under way were persistent but discouragingly unsuccessful. It was not until early April that President Thieu even agreed to permit Saigon's representatives· at Paris to talk directly with the NLF delegation. Quite unconvincingly, Thieu also echoed at the time Washington's concern to achieve a reconciliation among all of the people of South Vietnam.[35] The first formal proposal from Vietcong spokesmen came on May 8, 1969. It asked that the Vietnamese people be permitted to fashion a provisional coalition government dedicated to basic democratic rights and representing all political elements interested in promoting peace, independence, neutrality, and social accord. Once operative, such a government should plan for a special election covering all of South Vietnam.

President Nixon's qualifiedly approving reply, delivered on May 14, was designed to encourage further discussion. He supported the idea of Vietnamese efforts for political self-determination and would favor the participation of all who would agree to forego the use of force and violence. He also proposed that an international body be designated to supervise the withdrawal of foreign troops from South Vietnam, Laos, and Cambodia and to arrange for the election of a widely representative government in Saigon.[36]

Although the vernacular press of Saigon at the outset praised President Nixon's proposals, the official reaction was violently critical. President Thieu resented the suggestion that special elections would be required prior to the constitutionally authorized date in October 1971, when his own four-year term would expire. This apparently unanticipated disagreement with Thieu necessitated hurried American efforts to reach an accommodation. Secretary of State Rogers presided over a special Saigon conference on May 16 and 17, but came up with the disappointingly equivocal statement that "the question of possible special elections was entirely open to negotiations between Saigon and the NL Front." Hanoi and the NLF replied that President Nixon's proposals merited careful consideration, but concluded that continued American support of the Thieu regime precluded achieving any progress at the Paris talks.[37]

Three weeks later, at Midway Island, President Nixon talked with Thieu in person. The resulting communiqué reviewed previous commitments made by both sides. In alleged support of the principle of self-determination, the statement rejected all attempts to impose on South Vietnam any particular system of government, including any coalition regime that did not accord with the wishes of the people. With obvious reluctance, Thieu conceded that the May 8 proposals of the NFL were worthy of discussion and agreed to accept the outcome of free elections held under international supervision. He also agreed to permit an increasing exercise of local self-government within South Vietnam and a redistribution of land titles. On his side, President Nixon pledged American cooperation for a full decade following the end of strife in realizing development plans for both South and North Vietnam.[38] Lost in the bickering and verbiage was any real effort to bring together moderate elements of the South interested primarily in the attainment of peace.

Meanwhile, the NLF endeavored to strengthen its own claim to de facto political status by staging a three-day conference in South Vietnam attended by some eighty delegates, who claimed to form a Provisional Government. Officers selected to head the alleged government were all Southerners. The list included prominent lawyers, professors, architects, and other representatives of the ingelligentsia, many of whom had non-Communist records.[39] The announcement also indicated that prominent exiles currently living abroad would appropriately be included in the eventual peace coalition government. This proposal was a wide departure from any pattern of Hanoi domination.

The objectives defined by the NLF's Provisional Government were not designed to further the progress of negotiations at Paris, but rather to attract support from non-Communist opponents of Saigon. They proposed: (1) to overthrow the puppet government at Saigon and to defeat the American plans to Vietnamize the war; (2) to free political prisoners jailed by Saigon and to grant protection to collaborators on both sides from reprisals and recriminations once peace was restored; (3) to oppose foreign monopoly capital but to safeguard private ownership of the means of production "within limits set by the state"; and (4) to re-establish normal relations with North Vietnam covering personal travel, correspondence, residence, trade, and cultural intercourse. Eventual unification would be accomplished "step by step, by peaceful means, through mutual discussions, without constraint."[40] Evident here was the contrasting effort of the NLF leadership to make accomodation with other dissident groups within South Vietnam and the Saigon government's contrasting lack of concerted effort to reach any accomodation with peace-oriented groups in the South.

Abortive Efforts to Liberalize the Saigon Government

Accompanying Washington's moves to establish an operative basis for the conduct of peace negotiations at Paris were concerted American efforts to make the Saigon government more efficient and representative. The method selected was direct executive action on the part of Premier Tran Van Huong, who had been a virtual nonentity politically during the previous year. The avowed objectives were to improve administrative performance and to broaden the popular base of the Saigon regime. Under Washington's encouragement, Premier Huong, in early March 1969, invited into his cabinet a number of technically competent and trustworthy civilian administrators. They would replace, for the most part, factionally motivated army officers. The proposed new roster included a number of competent men who had no specific party affiliation, plus several anti-Diem Buddhists and selected leaders of the Dai Viet Nationalists and the Hoa Hao sect. Only one of the personal followers of the president was included, General Tran Thien Khiem. He had suffered a kind of political exile under Khanh and Ky (1964–67), when he served as ambassador to Washington and Taipei. The move was a poorly disguised effort to expand the authority of the premier at the expense of the president. It could also conceivably improve the climate for peace negotiations on both sides of the table at Paris.

President Thieu's reaction was sharply negative. As a countermove, he organized his own six-party coalition group within the Assembly. The emerging National Socialist Democratic Front (NSDF) included representatives from such widely disparate groups as the Dai Viet Revolutionaries, the pre-1946 pro-Kuomintang Quoc Dan Dong, the Greater Union Force (Catholic) faction, a surviving fragment of the Can Lao (Ngo Dinh Nhu) Humanitarian Socialist party, the Hoa Hao Social Democratic party, and Thieu's own Social Revolutionary party. The designated political groups had attracted almost half the votes cast in the 1967 election, but the NSDF espoused no articulate objectives and developed no plan of cooperation apart from acting on signal as the spokesmen for President Thieu. The president also made an unsuccessful effort to group all opposition elements within the Assembly into a manageable National Movement, to be headed by the moderate Dr. Nguyen Ngoc Huy, then a member of the Paris negotiation team. A more substantial political move on Thieu's part was to expand the role of General Khiem. In addition to his position as minister of interior under Huong, Khiem was named to the additional posts of deputy premier and minister of pacification.[41]

594

Opposition elements within the Parliament Assembly were headed by Tran Ngoc Lieng's Progressive Forces Alliance and in the Senate by Major General Tran Van Don's Peoples National Salvationist Front. Lieng served as legal counsel for the imprisoned presidential candidate Dzu and also for Thich Thein Minh. Don had been associated with General Duong Van Minh in the 1963 coup and had once served as foreign minister. The various Buddhist factions, almost unrepresented in the Assembly and all hostile to Thieu, were themselves divided factionally. The monk Thich Thein Minh was still in jail, and the forthright Thich Tri Quang refused to cooperate with either General Don or Assemblyman Lieng. A substantial fraction of the Can Lao party also opposed the president. The frustrated Vice-President Ky, his office denied both responsibility and funds, sponsored the Peoples Anti-Communist Front. Only a few of the dissident assemblymen, backed by student demonstrators, dared advocate peace negotiations with the NLF and Hanoi.[42]

Once this confused political arena was thrown open to controversy, party feuding intensified. A series of unsuccessful assassination attempts were made, one of them against Premier Huong himself. President Thieu announced publicly on May 25 that if the Americans should decide to withdraw or should conclude an overhasty peace settlement, his own supporters were prepared to organize guerrilla resistance to continue the anti-Communist struggle.[43] As another part of his public relations effort, the president began to devote one day a week to mingling with the people in civilian garb. On June 9 his six-party NSDF group suggested that Huong should retire voluntarily as premier in favor of some other person of greater ability and firmness.[44]

During the two months of political deadlock that ensued, a number of other voices were raised blaming Premier Huong for widespread corruption and inadequate revenues, deficiencies that the new cabinet was designed to correct. In July opponents of the president countered by publicizing the embarrassing fact that Thieu's executive entourage was found to be infiltrated by more than two score Viet-

595

cong spies. One held the rank of a deputy minister; another served in the office of general secretary to the president; a large number were active in the agency set up to screen Vietcong defectors.

Under such circumstances, Premier Huong's American-sponsored cabinet reform proposal ran firmly aground. Leaked reports that American pressure was behind the effort weighed negatively against it. Most of the invited party leaders refused to be included within the new cabinet, with General Khiem as a noteworthy exception. During July the cabinet reform issue became more directly involved with the continuing American effort to promote the holding of special Assembly elections as a means of facilitating the Paris negotiations. The election proposal was particularly unpopular among incumbent assemblymen, whose privileged positions, including recently voted salaries of one hundred thousand *piasters* a month, were directly threatened.

The character of the continuing pressure exerted by American advisers in support of the special election plan as a necessary part of peace negotiation preparations, can be assessed in approximate fashion by examining the successive statements issued by President Thieu. Acting with obvious reluctance, he announced on July 11 his plan for selecting the special election commission. It would include representatives of all political parties, even including members of the National Liberation Front who would agree to repudiate Communism. All participants must also renounce violence as a political weapon and pledge to accept the results of the elections, which would be held following the withdrawal of all foreign troops. Party candidates would enjoy equal opportunity to campaign and to post observers at polling places. The elections themselves would be held under supervision of an international body, once the timing and the modality had been agreed upon "by the two sides." Nine days later under similar American pressure Thieu explicitly agreed to engage in direct discussions with representatives of North Vietnam and the NLF about problems of peace and reunification.[45]

Whereas the Communist side indicated genuine interest in discussing Thieu's conciliatory July proposals, the proposals aroused a storm of anti-American criticism in Saigon. A majority of the Senate agreed that the president had gone too far in complying with American wishes, and representative spokesmen of the assembly cautioned him against making any more such blunders. In a speech delivered before National Defense College personnel, Ky waxed virulently anti-American. He threatened to lead a coup if the proposed plans were pursued. Three of the six parties that Thieu had lined up to support his own government policies expressed their open opposition to the election commission proposal. Thieu himself commented: "Now we can say to our Allies: 'If you want to abandon us, do it. . . . We have gone as far as we can or should go in opening the door to negotiations which would bring peace'."[46]

The unpublicized but sustained American effort to promote both organizational and policy reforms in the Saigon regime and to broaden its base of support for peace negotiations had come to a standstill by the end of July 1969. Washington had repeatedly extracted from President Thieu periodic verbal accomodations to essential reform requirements, but never his sincere commitment to their implementation. Thieu obviously entertained no intention of qualifying his political or military position in the interest of peace. If Washington authorities were unwilling to threaten the ultimate alternative of withdrawing all economic and military support from the repressive Saigon junta, American advisers were in no position to compete effectively with the diplomatic and political maneuvering of the ruling group. The only peacefully inclined South Vietnamese groups free to speak their mind without restraint were the Paris exiles, who had themselves run out on the game. They called persistently for a cease-fire, for free elections, and for the eventual neutralization of their country, with or without the participation of the existing Saigon government. But there were grounds to suspect that the result could well be chaos rather then peace. Other leading critics of the Thieu regime, like Assemblyman Tran Ngoc Lieng, were obviously wide of the mark in their sweeping accusations of early 1969 that the most formidable barrier to peace was "the adamant and overpowering American political, military, and economic support for the Thieu regime."[47]

In any case, the peace negotiations had reached an impasse by August 1969. The demeanor of all of the negotiating parties at Paris became increasingly unconciliatory, so that repeated delineation of irreconcilable positions became both meaningless and futile. The crux of the problem was the inveterate hostility between the two South Vietnamese factions. Within Saigon, Washington abandoned its efforts to promote governmental reforms and began to concentrate on the alternative Vietnamization program.

Transition to Complete Military Rule at Saigon

By the end of July more than half of the assemblymen of the Lower House had joined the opposition to Premier Huong. The final confrontation came on August 5, when Huong advanced a concrete proposal to enlarge the cabinet to twenty-four members, three-fourths of whom would be assigned posts as administrative technicians rather than political leaders. During the ensuing two-week deadlock, when governmental functions virtually came to a halt, most of those whom Huong asked to enter the new government declined his invitation. On August 21 he and his entire cabinet resigned.[48]

On September 2 General Khiem assumed the post of premier in addition to his other cabinet responsibilities. Twenty-two of his expanded thirty-one-member cabinet were new faces. Notably absent was a single supporter of Vice-President Ky or any person previously approached by Premier Huong. All efforts to achieve political coalescence and to mobilize popular support for the government were abandoned in favor of imposed factional army control. Thieu designated an entirely new Council of Notables as his official advisory body. The elected National Assembly was thoroughly discredited and in no position to challenge presidential control, partly because the salaried members had a continuing stake in keeping their jobs. The Supreme Court yielded to executive pressure to concede that the president could exercise the power of budgetary controls.[49]

Regardless of what might happen at Paris and whether or not U.S. troops were withdrawn, the army faction led by Thieu and Khiem was preparing to fight to maintain control over South Vietnam. Premier Khiem's declared policy was still tailored to please American ears. He emphasized the need to improve the army and the police in cooperation with the American-sponsored Vietnamization program. He paid lip service to the search for peace "in accordance with national traditions." He would promote security within the countryside, implement the long-promised land reform law, and impose essential austerity measures on governmental expenditures. Both democracy and the peace negotiations were dead.

Vice-President Ky's strongly negative reaction to Khiem's elevation as premier was indicated in an interview address delivered before an applauding group of younger army officers at the Dalat Academy. It was reported as follows: "If the new Government tried to make a coalition with the Communists, there would be a *coup* within ten days. . . . Thieu cannot afford any more concessions. . . . If we don't make a revolution, someone else will. . . . If Thieu does nothing, then I will speak out. . . . The future of our country is in our hands—yours and mine. We cannot afford to have our destiny in the hands of dirty politicians. . . . No country including the United States can determine our future for us. . . . I would even be ready to . . . come back among you tomorrow if you want me to do so."[50]

The opinions of informed observers were not encouraging. A Hong Kong editor commented perceptively that with Khiem's accession as premier, the United States had become host to a political parasite, with America bearing all the burden but unable to exercise any real influence over the situation.[51] James Reston in the *New York Times* asked how President Nixon, who now backed the generals who were unalterably opposed to setting up a more representative regime, could ever expect to ascertain what the wishes of the South Vietnamese people really were. He continued:

> There cannot be free and fair elections for all of the divided and tormented factions in South Vietnam under the Thieu Government, which puts its leading political opponents in jail. . . . The dilemma can be reduced to a single formula: No coalition, no elections; no genuine test of the will of the people, and no peace.[52]

Developments in the Pacification Program

Despite the dismal record of the grounded Paris negotiations and the abortive efforts to make the Saigon regime more responsive to popular wishes, some substantial pacification gains were realized in 1969. The tempo of fighting on both sides declined sharply. The tide of refugees, which had reached its high point in the fall of 1968, began to recede moderately. During the course of 1969, an estimated half-million inhabitants of refugee camps, especially in the central Annam area, were resettled as agriculturalists on previously vacated lands. The operation included the transplanting of entire montagnard communities under the sponsorship of several American Operation Cooperation Centers. In Saigon and other crowded urban centers that had been heavily damaged or destroyed in 1968, some fifty thousand houses were rebuilt by the end of 1969. Road transport, rice shipments to the cities, water supplies, and electricity services were all improved. Few of the millions of the squatters in crowded Saigon returned to the countryside. They preferred for the time being to subsist on the artificial war-time prosperity created by the American presence, which afforded them a livelihood, legitimate or otherwise.[53]

Civilian attrition resulting from search-and-destroy operations against Vietcong cadres continued to take a heavy toll of lives, houses, paddy fields, and fruit trees. Survivors still had to flee to refugee camps. Although the level of fighting declined in the devastated areas, the "liberated peoples" understandably entertained little affection for either the ARVN or the Americans.[54] Seasoned press observers concluded that positive gains were not significant in terms of achieving defined objectives. American advisers usually did not comprehend the Vietnamese point of view, partly because of the rapid turnover of personnel assigned to the pacification program.[55] Such tragic incidents as the killing of women and children at Mylai and elsewhere in 1968 were parts of the larger problem. A British commentator from Hong Kong made the following relevant comment:

> For the G.I. in Vietnam . . . the war makes little sense; it has no obvious connection with America's national interest; it seems impossible to win on the battlefield, and it has done little to create a strong, free society in the South, which could provide a viable alternative to Communist domination. A war fought for lost ideals must sour the souls of the men conscripted to defend South Vietnam from external aggression, in which they find the foe so difficult to distinguish from a friend. . . . The American people must ask themselves . . . whether a war which can reduce men on both sides to the level of animals can realistically be regarded as a crusade to defend those values for which American civilization stands.[56]

Vietnamization and Nixon's November 3 Speech

President Nixon's policy to Vietnamize the war was first avowed during the spring of 1969. It involved the continuing but unscheduled withdrawal of American ground combat troops and the systematic strengthening of ARVN forces. From the beginning the proposal was far from popular at Saigon. The political context of the Vietnamization proposal changed during the summer following the virtual abandonment of hope for progress in the peace negotiations and in broadening the political base of the Saigon government.

Washingon's acquiescence in the militarization of Thieu's government in August 1969 involved the complete alienation of moderate peace advocates within the Assembly and of potentially cooperative elements within the leadership of the NLF Provisional government, most of whom were conscious of their Southern identity and not committed to doctrinaire Communism. The Vietnamization program not only implied approval of the military suppression of any peace sentiment, but also the abandonment of deep-seated demands for revolutionary social change, long denied by the French, by Diem, and by successor governments at Saigon. Opponents of the war and of the military junta were left little recourse for redress of grievances outside the dimensions of the Communist-directed rebellion.[57]

President Nixon's noteworthy November 3, 1969, speech was directed toward two critical situations, one growing out of the recent antiwar moratorium demonstration in Washington and the other concerned with a serious political crisis emerging in late October in Saigon. The president declared that his program of Vietnamization was the only feasible alternative to an abrupt American withdrawal from South Vietnam, which would betray long-standing commitments to the peoples affected and would precipitate a blood bath of incalculable dimensions. An American retreat from Southeast Asia would allegedly cancel existing restraints on the reckless endeavors of great powers intent on world conquest. Nixon affirmed that the successful termination of the Vietnam War was "the last hope for peace and freedom of millions of people about to be suffocated by the forces of totalitarianism." If Hanoi should attempt to take advantage of the staged withdrawal of American combat forces so as to threaten the safety of supporting troops remaining in the country, the president promised to take appropriate but undefined countermeasures.[58]

The speech also discounted the prospects of a negotiated settlement. Nixon cited Ho Chi Minh's alleged rejection of a letter sent to Hanoi on July 15, in his reply
dated August 25, just two weeks before Ho's death. As
subsequently disclosed, Ho's reply had affirmed North
Vietnam's desire for "a real peace with independence
and . . . freedom." He argued that the United States
would have to agree to withdraw its troops and to "respect
the right of the population of the South and of the Vietnamese nation to dispose of themselves without foreign
interference." Ho concluded that "with good will on both
sides, we might arrive at common efforts . . . in
finding a correct solution." Critics of the president's
interpretation questioned whether, by any balanced evaluation of purpose and character, the American-supported
Thieu-Khiem regime was not as great a barrier to
peace negotiations as was Hanoi.[59]

President Nixon concluded his address with an emotion-
laden denunciation of the "vocal minority" in the United
States who were, he said, ready to court defeat, humiliation, and disaster, and the massacre of Asian friends in
order to gain their ends.[60] The president's temporary
success in quieting American protests had no observable
effect on bringing the war to an end. Neither the Hanoi
nor the NLF representatives in Paris saw any point in
seeking a cease-fire in South Vietnam without an unequivocal promise of the withdrawal of the half-million
allied troops assigned to support the unacceptable government at Saigon.[61]

Press comments on the president's policy statement
noted that the limited dichotomy he posed between immediate withdrawal and total support of the Saigon regime
did not begin to exhaust the available alternatives. The
policies pursued by Washington during the preceding
year, with something less than full determination, had
allegedly proved the contrary. The early retirement of
Ambassador Lodge as head of the futile Paris peace
negotiation team signaled the virtual abandonment of
hope for progress toward a settlement. Some reporters

commented that a case could be made for complete American withdrawal by arguing that the United States had already honored its commitment to help defend South Vietnam.[62] On the other hand, an indefinite American commitment to provide support troops, money, and supplies for an ARVN force of one million men, very poorly led and badly motivated, was declared militarily bankrupt. Press comment concluded that unconditional American support of a military government that imprisoned its non-Communist critics, including elected members of the National Assembly, had itself demonstrated minimal concern for freedom against totalitarian rule.[63]

Problems of Vietnamization

The task of improving the discipline and performance of the ARVN forces as part of the Vietnamization program was critically important, but the plan also carried ominous political overtones. The admittedly superior fighting performance of the North Vietnamese troops and their Southern Vietcong allies was clearly attributable to better leadership and motivation. The ARVN problem lay presumably at the very top: Saigon's two score French-trained generals, admirals, and air marshals formed an exclusive club to which new members were seldom admitted. Lower ranking officers of the ARVN were drawn from well-to-do urban families who were able to finance their sons' education through high school. The more attractive army posts were usually available via personal or family connections or through direct purchase. As long as the castelike officer system remained unaltered, spot improvement in the discipline, equipment, and training of ARVN troops could achieve little improvement in combat performance. The ARVN forces often fought bravely in defense of a locality or population with which they were familiar, but seldom otherwise. The heavy desertions were attributable to homesickness, poor pay, bad living conditions, war weariness, and bad officering.[64] One Vietnamese officer-critic remarked, "What we need is not peace, but a social revolution."[65]

The anticipated economic impact of Vietnamization was also disturbing. The continuance of large-scale American financial aid was an integral part of the labored agreement reached between Saigon and Washington during 1969. Determining the nature and dimensions of this aid was an enormously complicated problem, which became the subject of a lively debate. Because ARVN would be adding a full hundred thousand men to its total of one million, Washington's military costs for 1970-71 would diminish little as the result of the gradual recall of American combat forces. American withdrawal from rear areas would in time sharply reduce dollar spending, which had provided during 1968-69 some 80 percent of the foreign exchange earned by the Saigon government. Even if peace should be restored, the cost of security maintenance and the provision of housing, food, medical care, and refugee settlement would continue to be high. Also in question was whether the Saigon economy could absorb the vast sums required to pay government and military costs without encountering disastrous inflation. The consumer price increment for 1969 was 35 percent despite an improved rice harvest and better food delivery to urban centers. But time was running out economically in South Vietnam.[66]

Completely lacking in the developing Vietnamization program was any concerted effort to seek a compromise settlement between non-Communist opponents of the war on the one hand and moderate elements of the Provisional Government on the other. A policy to bolster the power of the military rulers of Saigon and to expand a predatory and ineffective ARVN was not calculated to attract support from Saigon's opposition elements or to persuade the NLF to compromise.[67]

Saigon's Political Crisis of Late 1969.

Directly prior to President Nixon's speech of November 3, the Thieu-Khiem regime had encountered serious opposition from within the reconvened Saigon Assembly. Assemblymen Huynh Van Tu and Than Ngoc Chau echoed the demand, made by the exiled Pham The Truc in the previous

605

May, that Washington abandon its Vietnamization program and instead withdraw all support from the unrepresentative Thieu government in order to force a change.[68] In the Senate, Ton That Din and ex-General Tran Van Don, leader of the National Salvation Front, acted as spokesmen for the popular leader, General Duong Van Minh (Big Minh), now returned from Thailand exile. They proposed the convening of a national body representing non-Communist political elements.[69] Other opposition leaders within the Assembly included spokesmen for the Viet Front (Hoa Hao), the Citizens of all Faiths (Buddhist and Catholic), the Popular Front (led by the Francophobe Phan Khac Suu), and the so-called Progressive National Movement led by Lieng and Huy.[70] These several groups failed to coalesce, due in part to the vigilance of Thieu's espionage system and the possibility the dissenters faced of joining the other five thousand political prisoners in jail.[71] Their agreed demand that Washington pressure Thieu to end the fighting was vetoed by the U.S. military command at Saigon and Ambassador Bunker, who saw little to be gained from renewing the pressure on Saigon authorities in view of the collapse of the Huong government the previous August.[72] The opposition's effort was six months late.

In late October 1969 President Thieu was forced unavoidably to face the long-deferred problem of the government's deteriorating financial situation. Acting by executive decree, without consulting the National Assembly at all, Thieu imposed heavy customs duties on approximately one thousand luxury imports, accompanying the action by a request that the Assembly grant him still broader executive taxation authority. The financial situation was indeed grave, for Saigon had been spending, since the inauguration of the Vietnamization military build-up, around three *piasters* for every two in receipts. Saigon's proposed 1970 budget of 232 billion *piasters* contemplated a 100-billion-*piaster* deficit, even with anticipated American contributions.[73]

The consequences of the shock treatment employed by President Thieu were difficult to withstand both economically and politically. The price of gasoline doubled immediately, and that of most luxury imports tripled. The customs levies for refrigerators, for example, increased from 100 percent of dealer value to 300 percent; for television sets, from 75 percent to 225 percent; and the purchase price of a small auto jumped from $4000 to a prohibitive $19,000. The prices of imported foods, drugs, machinery, and paper were similarly affected.[74] Such tax increments were aimed primarily at the very well-to-do, who were generously represented in the National Assembly. The black-market rate for the dollar rose sharply from 200 *piasters* to 300, compared to the official rate of 80 *piasters* to the dollar and the free rate of 118. An immediate 17 percent rise occurred in the price of rice, levelling off at 20 percent by December.[75] Popular resentment over price inflation, anger within the Assembly over President Thieu's refusal to consult it on financial matters, and Thieu's efforts to suppress free discussion added up to a threatening crisis.

President Thieu tried to relieve the tension, on October 29, by granting clemency to some 310 political prisoners. Those released included the respected Buddhist monk Thich Thein Minh, who had been serving a sentence of three years solitary confinement imposed in March 1969. Clemency was later extended to some 1,245 other prisoners, including many suspects being held for trial plus an assortment of Vietcong-connected detainees (mainly women and children).[76]

On October 31, the sixth anniversary of the overthrow of Ngo Dinh Diem, Thieu made an impassioned radio and television effort to enlist popular support. He pledged to save the country from Communist domination and promised to surrender the presidency if the day should come when his policies were clearly opposed by a majority of the people. National pride and honor demanded that the Vietnamese people make sacrifices for their freedom, Thieu said; they must cease being beggars and learn to depend on themselves. At the conclusion of the fifty-minute address, the president was reportedly in tears.[77]

Following the president's public appeal, the popular General Duong Van Minh issued a call on November 2 for the assembling of a national convention, representing all non-Communist factions, to ascertain the real wishes of the people. The convention would be empowered to debate policy questions, to select a more representative government, and to consider needed revisions of the constitution. Big Minh also promised to do everything he could to promote national unity and to bring an end to the war.[78] These proposals were subsequently amplified in a three-page manifesto issued on November 15, which called for an immediate referendum to ascertain the popular will with respect to measures needed to make the government stronger and more representative. Affirming that a large majority of the people (estimated at 70 percent) could accept neither the Saigon government nor the Vietcong, Minh proposed to ask the American allies "to step into the background . . . and to let Vietnamese negotiate directly with Vietnamese."[79]

Opposition elements within the National Assembly responded affirmatively to Minh. Eleven members of the House, led by Tran Ngoc Chau, circulated a petition calling for a nationwide referendum to test the popularity of President Thieu. During the course of a concurrent three-day Senate hearing in review of government policy, Senator Tran Van Don, backed by a coterie of angry colleagues, denounced Thieu roundly as an autocrat.[80] Such was the climate of opposition developing at Saigon in early November 1969.

Response and Repression

President Nixon's address of November 3, as previously indicated, was designed not only to counter rising criticism in the United States but also to bolster the authority of the harassed Thieu government at Saigon. The speech had been cleared with Thieu prior to its delivery, and once delivered the South Vietnamese president promptly acclaimed it as "one of the most important and greatest" ever to come from Washington. He added: "The people of Vietnam want nothing more than gradually to take over the responsibility to preserve their independence and freedom." In contrast, the reaction of Thieu's critics within the National Assembly and among the Buddhist community in particular was one of complete dismay, for Nixon's unqualified support of the Thieu regime, like the endorsement accorded to General Ky by President Johnson at Honolulu in 1966, encouraged Saigon authorities to deal singly and summarily with domestic critics, whether in the press, the Assembly, or within the army itself.

In contrast to the apologetic tone of his October 31 speech, Thieu now moved with ruthless confidence to purge his critics. He closed down Saigon's leading newspapers, reshuffled army commands, and silenced his legally privileged opponents within the elected Assembly.[81] The president's exasperation was clearly reflected in the epithets he levelled at his critics later in November: imbeciles, cowards, dogs, traitors.[82] By mid-December his public denunciations had assumed an almost hourly cadence, punctuated regularly by Catholic-sponsored, anti-Communist demonstrations staged throughout the country. Thieu attacked opposition politicians, press and civil service critics, and rival army factions. When a dozen privileged assemblymen openly accused the president of planning to set up an illegal military dictatorship, Saigon's police permitted an allegedly spontaneous Saturday mob to break down the doors of the Assembly and reduce the premises to a shambles. Subsequent Assembly debates protesting the move developed such violent dimensions that fifty opposition members stalked out on one occasion. A woman assembly member even drew a gun. Twenty out of the forty senators in attendance at the Monday session blamed the president himself for instigating the mob outrage.[83]

President Thieu then denounced three assemblymen as overt Communist agents: Pham The Truc, an exile of the previous May; Huynh Van Tu, recently fled under

609

military threat; and the still-resident Tran Ngoc Chau. After failing to obtain the two-thirds vote of the Assembly required to impeach the three and to initiate criminal proceedings (the vote was 76 in a total of 135), Thieu shifted to cajolery, bribery, and intimidation to obtain the needed 102 signatures (a three-fourths majority) on a petition to cancel the privileged immunity of the offenders. Assemblymen were given no opportunity to challenge ostensibly forged signatures, and no debate was permitted on the floor of the Assembly. Three additional newspapers were shut down in December, bringing the total to 39 since April 1968.[84]

Tran Ngoc Chau refused to flee Saigon and took refuge for four days in the Assembly building. In late February police broke into the hall, seized the defiant Chau, and incidentally accorded rough treatment to press representatives who were present. Chau was summarily convicted of treason by two successive military tribunals and sentenced to ten years imprisonment at hard labor.

Chau's case attracted wide attention. As a former army colonel, he had served successively as a province chief in the Mekong delta, as mayor of Danang, and as a top official in the American revolutionary development program during 1966–67. In connection with his effective cooperation with American intelligence agencies, Chau had made a number of contacts between 1965 and 1969 with his brother, Tran Ngoc Hien, who was aligned with the Vietminh. Hien had been captured by Saigon police in April 1969 and later convicted as a Communist spy. According to Thieu, Chau's treasonable offense was that he had failed to report to the Saigon authorities his successive contacts with his brother, which were nevertheless fully known to the American embassy and to intelligence services. Neither the CIA nor the embassy came to Chau's defense, although American protests did presumably bring about a review of his first trial. All the newspapers still free to publish gave his story sympathetic coverage.

Chau's seizure and imprisonment took a heavy psychological toll. It left relations between the American intelligence apparatus and the Saigon authorities in complete disarray. It destroyed the dignity and independence of the elected assembly and dealt the final blow to all constitutional guarantees. Senator Pham Nam Sach, chairman of the Senate Judiciary Committee, commented that the Chau case had put "a flame into the opposition that had been building for a long time."[85] Big Minh kept discreetly quiet, and Senator Tran Van Don departed for Europe during the final phases of the episode.

The situation was reminiscent of 1963. President Thieu moved to guard against the possibility of a military coup by reshuffling army leadership. Three ARVN commanders in the delta were replaced, along with four province chiefs and ten other key administrative figures (all allegedly pro-Ky men). Trusted commanders from the capital area were reassigned to the crucial Second Corps region, below Danang, while young colonels replaced older generals in areas vulnerable to heavy enemy attack.[86] Thieu was almost as isolated politically as Diem had been in 1963.

President Thieu's annual address to the nation, televised on January 9, hailed the positive achievements of 1969 in areas of pacification and reconstruction. He also expressed confidence that the Communists would be completely defeated within the course of two or three years. Since the Communists had allegedly rejected his offers to hold free elections and to negotiate a cease-fire, he insisted that there remained for South Vietnam no middle way, only survival or death. Thieu thus left no room whatever for opponents like Generals Tran Van Don and Duong Van Minh, who would try to stand apart from the struggle as outsiders, hoping to mediate a settlement.[87] Thieu later affirmed that all advocates of a coalition government (such as Don) or of rapid withdrawal of American troops (Minh) were traitors working to accomplish the Communist goal of overthrowing the Saigon government. Thieu's own acquiescence with further American withdrawal plans, he explained, would be conditioned on U.S. fulfillment of Saigon's needs for military equipment, essential supplies, and funds, including provision

611

for improved living conditions for ARVN soldiers and their families.[88] If Thieu's conditions were met, it could be anticipated that the privileged military leadership would probably remain quiet, but at the cost of permanently grounding the Paris peace talks and forestalling a change of governmental leadership.[89]

The alternative to the Nixon policy of indefinite support of the vulnerable Thieu military dictatorship was eloquently stated by President Kingman Brewster of Yale during the October 1969 moratorium effort:

> Let us admit that it is not easy to stop short of victory in a cause in which so many have fallen. . . . Let us simply say that we cannot tolerate the abuse of their memory as a justification for continuation of the killing and dying at the behest of a corrupt Saigon government, which rejects both democracy and peace. . . . Let us admit that it is not easy to abandon the anonymous masses of South Vietnam who have relied upon us. Let us say simply that their interests as well as ours can no longer be served by the perpetuation of terror and death. . . . Let us say simply and proudly that our ability to keep the peace . . . requires above all that America once again become a symbol of decency and hope, fully deserving the trust and respect of all mankind.[90]

1. Robert Shaplen, *Time Out of Hand* (New York, 1969), pp. 392–96.
2. *Ibid.*, pp. 399–402.
3. *FEER*, December 7, 1967, pp. 437–40.
4. Shaplen, *op. cit.*, pp. 400–402, 419–23.
5. *Ibid.*, pp. 399–402.
6. *Ibid.*, pp. 396–99.
7. *Ibid.*, pp. 402–9.
8. *Ibid.*, pp. 405, 411, 415.
9. *Ibid.*, pp. 412–14.
10. *Ibid.*, p. 402.
11. *FEER*, April 13, 1969, p. 43-45.
12. Joseph Buttinger, *Vietnam, a Political History* (New York, 1968), pp. 504–50.
13. *Congressional Record*, October 23, 1969, p. E8797.
14. *Pentagon Papers* (1971), 594-600. The story is also told by Townsend Hoopes, then under-secretary of the Air Force, in his *The Limits of Intervention, An Inside Account of How the Johnson Policy of Escalation in Vietnam Was Reversed* (New York, 1969). Dissenters included CIA spokesmen Warnke (McNaughton's successor), Nitze, and Vance.

15. *Pentagon Papers*, pp. 615–21.
16. *Ibid.*, pp. 601–94.
17. *New York Times*, March 6, 1968.
18. *Pentagon Papers*, pp. 607–12.
19. *New York Times*, March 7, 1968.
20. Shaplen, *op. cit.*, p. 416.
21. *FEER*, April 24, 1969, pp. 246-48; Don Luce and John Sommer, *Vietnam, the Unheard Voices* (Ithaca, 1969), pp. 316-21.
22. Robert Smith in the *New York Times* of January 22, 1970 cites a suppressed report by A. Terry Rombo of Human Science Research, Inc., which was confirmed by the testimony of veterans.
23. *New York Times*, November 19, 1969; Luce and Sommer, *op. cit.*, pp. 389, 430.
24. *New York Times*, May 25, 1968; *Rangoon Guardian*, May 24, 1968.
25. Shaplen, *op. cit.*, pp. 428-29.
26. *Ibid.*, pp. 423-28.
27. *New York Times*, April 15, 1969.
28. *Ibid.*, May 25, 1969.
29. Shaplen, *op. cit.*, p. 450.
30. *FEER*, November 28, 1968, pp. 474-75.
31. George W. Ball, "We Should De-escalate the Importance of Vietnam," *New York Times Magazine*, December 21, 1969.
32. Max Frankel, "Paris Impasse; Each Blames Other," *New York Times*, November 25, 1969.
33. *FEER*, December 12, 1968, pp. 653–56.
34. Charles A. Joiner, "South Vietnam: the Politics of Peace," *Asian Survey* 9 (February 1969): 138-41.
35. *New York Times*, April 15, 1969.
36. *Ibid.*, May 9 and 15, 1969.
37. *Ibid.*, May 16, 17, and 21, 1969.
38. *Ibid.*, June 9, 1969.
39. See the *New York Times* for June 11, 12, and 13, 1969. The NLF president, Huynh Tan Phat, was a professional architect; the advisory council head, Nguyen Huu Tho, was a lawyer who had been jailed by Diem; the top Alliance official was a non-Communist lawyer named Trinh Dinh Thao; and one of the three vice-presidents, Nguyen Van Kiet, had once taught French literature at Saigon University.
40. *New York Times*, May 27 and June 12, 1969.
41. *New York Times*, March 26, April 3, and May 26, 1969.
42. Joiner, *op. cit.*, pp. 141-48.
43. *New York Times*, May 26, 1969.
44. Tom Wicker, "The Wrong Horse in Saigon," *New York Times*, June 19, 1969.
45. *New York Times*, July 12 and 21, 1969.
46. *Ibid.*, July 27 and 31, 1969; *FEER*, July 31, 1969, pp. 280–83.
47. *FEER*, March 20, 1969, pp. 17–18.
48. *New York Times*, August 3, 14, and 22, 1969.
49. *Ibid.*, August 19, 1969; *FEER*, September 4, 1969, p. 595.
50. *New York Times*, August 24, 26, September 7, 24, and 26, 1969.
51. *FEER*, September 4, 1969, p. 595.
52. *New York Times*, September 24, 1969.
53. See *FEER, 1970 Yearbook*, pp. 275–76; *New York Times*, February 12, 14, and 16, 1970.

54. Tom Buckley, "What's Life Like in Vietcong Territory?" *New York Times*, November 23, 1969, pp. 48–49, 136–40.

55. Shaplen, *op. cit.*, pp. 441–50.

56. *FEER*, December 4, 1969, p. 483.

57. See Shaplen, *op. cit.*, pp. 433–35.

58. *New York Times*, November 5 and 9, 1969.

59. *Ibid.*, November 5, 1969.

60. *Ibid.*, December 3, 1969.

61. Max Frankel, "Paris Impasse." *New York Times*, November 25, 1969.

62. Tom Wicker's comment on the Nixon speech, *New York Times*, November 9, 1969.

63. Luce and Sommer's earlier indictments of the Saigon regime (*op. cit.*, pp. 303-13) were authenticated by events of late 1969 and early 1970.

64. B. Brummond Ayres, Jr., "South Vietnam Soldier, Still Untested," *New York Times*, November 21, 1969.

65. Tom Buckley, "The ARVN is Bigger and Better, But—" *New York Times Magazine*, October 12, 1969, pp. 35, 122-32.

66. *New York Times*, January 27 and March 13, 1970.

67. See Alexander I. George and John William Lewis, "A Plan for a Progressive Cease-Fire in Vietnam," *New York Times*, January 17, 1970.

68. Phan The Truc's widely circulated report was dated May 30, 1969.

69. *FEER, 1970 Yearbook*, p. 274; *New York Times*, February 1, 1970.

70. Terrence Smith, "Splintered Opposition in South Vietnam Just Meets and Confers," *New York Times*, October 25, 1969.

71. *Ibid.*, quoting Nguyen Quoc Xung, a Vietcong leader.

72. *FEER*, January 15, 1970, p. 13.

73. *New York Times*, October 25, 1969; *FEER, 1970 Yearbook*, pp. 277-80.

74. *New York Times*, October 25, 1969.

75. Terrence Smith, "Austerity Chokes Vietnam Business," *New York Times*, October 31, 1969; see *ibid.*, January 19, 1970.

76. *New York Times*, October 30 and 31, 1969.

77. Terrence Smith, "Thieu in Tears, Asks Sacrifices," *New York Times*, November 1, 1969.

78. *Ibid.*, November 3, 1969.

79. *Ibid.*, November 14, 15, 1969.

80. Terrence Smith, "Nixon's Impact; Thieu is Helped in a Tight Spot," *New York Times*, November 10, 1969.

81. *Ibid.*, November 5, 22, and December 16, 1969.

82. *FEER*, January 22, 1970, p. 3.

83. *New York Times*, December 19 and 21, 1969.

84. Terrence Smith, "For Thieu, 1969 was a Good Year," *New York Times*, January 3, 1970.

85. *New York Times*, December 4, 1969, February 7, 11, and 17, 1970.

86. *Ibid.*, January 21, 1970.

87. *Ibid.*, January 9, 10, 1970.

88. Tom Wicker, "In the Nation: Talking Tough in Saigon," *New York Times*, January 13, 1970.

89. Arthur Dommen, "Vietnamese War Again Reaching Watershed Point, Such as in 1963," *New York Times*, November 30, 1969.

90. Anthony Lewis, "A Thoughtful Answer to Hard Questions," *New York Times*, October 17, 1969.

XVI

TRENDS AND
DEVELOPMENTS IN
THE EARLY SEVENTIES

It is manifestly impossible to undertake any definitive consideration of developments in Southeast Asia during the early seventies based on fragmentary press reports, and yet the events were so significant that they cannot be ignored. Three observable trends can be identified as intrinsically significant, and they will provide a meaningful theme for tentative discussion. The first was the seemingly relentless drift in the direction of military rule, which managed in some measure to encompass by late 1972 almost every state in the region. Malaysia and Singapore were the principal exceptions, but even there democratic constitutional principles were losing ground in the obvious trend toward single-party rule and the curtailment of freedom of political activity. The circumstances and results attending the exercise of arbitrary rule varied widely from country to country, but authoritarian methods became almost epidemic in their incidence.

A second major development not unassociated with factors contributing to the first was the intensification of military operations within the bounds of prewar French Indochina and the consequent subordination of democratic norms to power considerations. Warfare engulfed virtually all of Cambodia and Laos, as well as the two Vietnams.

Thailand continued as a peripheral participant. Bombing operations on an accelerated scale encompassed the entire area of conflict, including for a time all sections of North Vietnam. This phenomenon emerged as a by-product of the discouraging efforts to negotiate peace terms at Paris and to the growing American concern to Vietnamize the war and withdraw American ground forces.

A third major development was discernible by 1970–71 in the progressive efforts to diversify diplomatic alignments, within the context of the changing pattern of American relations with China and the Soviet Union. Apart from areas where military operations occupied center stage, economic patterns continued little changed from the situation of the late 1960s. This chapter will attempt to indicate some of the salient developments, on a country-by-country basis, relating to these three major trends. The principal sources for the material in this chapter are the *New York Times*, the *Far Eastern Economic Review* (Hong Kong), and *Asian Survey*.

The Continuance of Military Rule in Thailand

The approval of the long-prepared constitution in Thailand in June 1968 and the elections for the new Assembly in early 1969 were in part the result of a widely shared desire to broaden the basis of political power and in part designed to make the government more respectable before world opinion. Important elements in the ruling army clique—General Praphat Charusatien's faction in particular—were opposed to the new constitution from the outset. As head of the army and minister of interior, General Praphat appeared to be the most likely successor to Premier Marshal Thanom Kittikachorn, who had occupied the post since 1963 and who would reach the retirement age of sixty in 1971. The abrupt end of the constitutional regime in mid-November 1971 was due to the cabinet's resentment of the elected Assembly's immediate gesture of opposition to army rule by decree. Also observable was an erosion of the long-held assumption that the country's status in world opinion, and in the eyes of America in particular, called for Bangkok's paying some measure of deference to democratic standards. The convenient excuse of the new self-appointed National Revolutionary Council for reverting to army dictatorship was the allegedly growing threat of Communist rebellion. Personal rivalries and foreign policy considerations were also involved in the revival of authoritarian rule.

The principal international development to which the Bangkok authorities were obliged to respond in early 1970 was the near collapse of the post-Sihanouk government of Cambodia and the growing threat of expanding Vietnamese control—whether Northern or Southern—over the country. (This situation will be described in more detail later in the chapter.) General Praphat's initial reaction as head of the Thai army was to propose overt intervention in the interest of Thailand's security. The cabinet as a whole adopted a more cautious approach. The specific proposal that eventually emerged from consultations with General Lon Nol of Cambodia and U.S. spokesmen involved the training and equipping by the CIA of some two thousand or more Khmer Serei troops resident in Thailand for anti-Communist military service in neighboring Battambang and Siemreap. This sort of thing had been done earlier on a smaller scale. The United States at the time was training a similar force of Cambodian residents of the Mekong Delta of South Vietnam for anti-Communist duty. When it became evident to Thai officials that the United States was prepared to finance only a portion of the total costs involved, Bangkok lost interest in the proposal. Meanwhile, Thai forces occupied the long-disputed Preah Vihear temple site and otherwise conducted patrol activities along the Cambodian frontier. It also became obvious at the time that Cambodians in general, including members of the Lon Nol regime, were opposed to any direct Thai intervention. The observable cooling off of American-Thai military collaboration following the abortive consultations over Cambodian defense did not interfere with the continuing CIA enlistment of some five to six thousand Thai volunteers for service in Laos.

The changing international situation gave Foreign Minister Thanat Khoman the opportunity to proceed with his proposals for diplomatic rapprochement in the direction of Eastern Europe and China. With qualified support from the Premier, Thanat reverted to the traditional tactic of cultivating relations with both antagonists in the world contest. Faced with the prospect of eventual American withdrawal from Southeast Asia, which he ostensibly favored, Thanat proposed publicly that a Thai trade mission be sent to the USSR and that diplomatic relations be established with Yugoslavia. When Washington failed in early 1971 to respond affirmatively to Thai demands for additional military aid for use in Laos, Thanat suggested, presumably as a kind of blackmail, that if Americans contemplated repudiating their commitments to defend Thailand, he would solicit an alternative agreement with the Russians. Near the end of 1970, the Thai foreign minister also made an indirect approach to the Chinese representatives in Paris. For this purpose, he expedited the journey of the long-exiled Luang Pridi from Peking to Paris by issuing him a regular Thai passport. The eventual suggestion that Bangkok might lift the ban on trade with China was favorably received at Peking. By late 1970 and early 1971, Thanat's diplomatic vagaries, however intended, had generated considerable uneasiness within Bangkok army circles.

The emerging confusion over Thailand's foreign policy alignments served to aggravate differences relating to domestic politics. General Praphat and his spokesmen in the government denounced the foreign minister's proposals as a sell-out to Communist enslavement, much to the embarrassment of Premier Thanom Kittikachorn. The premier and Praphat had been in disagreement over the approval of the constitution during the elections of 1969 and more recently over the role the Assembly itself should be permitted to play. Under an arranged compromise, the several identifiable party groups represented within the Assembly were forbidden to organize and vote as disciplined political units, thereby ensuring that Praphat's extensive personal influence over the one-third Independent membership could wield the balance of power. A specific challenge developed in July 1970, when the opposition in the Assembly fell only one vote short of challenging the cabinet's decree calling for increases of some 20 percent in gasoline and cement taxes and 100 percent increments on a variety of consumer imports. Thanom attempted to conciliate by reducing the level of taxes on several items, but more differences arose later over the army's flat veto of proposed Assembly legislation to permit a semblance of collective bargaining by labor associations covering long-existing economic grievances.

The widening rift between Thanat and Praphat became so serious in mid-1970 that the foreign minister advanced his candidacy for a vacancy in the World Court, a move which came to nothing. Throughout the remainder of 1970 and into 1971, General Praphat and Premier Thanom Kittikachorn continued their ostensible collaboration, but not unconditionally or for an indefinite period of time. The Praphat faction within the Assembly managed to exclude the participation of opposition Democrat party members from budgetary committee hearings, a move so blatant that the angered director of the budget resigned. The Promoj brothers, Seni and Kukrit, both members of the Democrat party, denounced the army's abuse of its political power, but few others had the courage to do so. The days of constitutional government were obviously numbered.

Repudiation of the 1968 Constitution

Events leading to the abrupt repudiation on November 17, 1971, of Thailand's three-year-old constitution included the imposition of rigorous curbs on the public press. On the occasion of the strictly circumscribed visit of American Vice-President Spiro Agnew during the first week of

619

September, four Bangkok papers adopted a complete blackout of news covering the visit as a means of passively protesting impending press regulations. The government responded angrily with radio and television announcements to the effect that no news relating to student unrest, public opposition to government policies, prison breaks, suicides, or other types of information damaging to security and morals would be permitted. The threatened penalty would be closure of the offending paper and the confiscation of its plant. Appeals protesting such closures would be processed by officials and prosecutors responsible for enforcing the decree.

Immediately following Agnew's visit, General Praphat, acting contrary to solicited American pacification counsel, attacked Meo and Yao tribesmen of north Thailand who were protesting the government's resettlement program, using bombers and napalm derived from American sources. Such repressive acts simply aggravated peasant discontent with the government's chronic failure to provide essential water facilities and meet pressing health, education, and transportation needs. Finally, the one-candidate victory of General Nguyen Van Thieu in the long-awaited presidential election in South Vietnam helped set the emerging tone of complete army defiance of democratic constitutional principles in Bangkok.

The Thai authorities also faced increasingly serious economic and budgetary problems. One of them concerned the unfavorable balance in foreign trade and the consequent decline in available foreign exchange. American expenditures in the construction of airfields, roads, and port facilities had declined sharply since 1969, involving the discharge of a large proportion of the forty-five thousand Thai workers previously employed. During the interim, the government had moved to restrict the issuance of work-permit visas for foreigners and to regulate to its own advantage the operations of foreign airlines, traders, and investors. In the agricultural sector, the government's long-time policy of holding down the domestic price of rice to forestall worker demands for

620

higher wages, while at the same time collecting high taxes from licensed rice exporters, had come under critical review. Peasants lacked both the funds and the incentive to increase rice output, and all employees, including teachers and civil servants as well as wage laborers, found living costs rising faster than income. The government invariably stigmatized all protests, whether consumer or employee, as Communist inspired, although authorities were not unaware that widely shared grievances if unrelieved could become politically dangerous. Any form of organized public protest over mounting living costs or official abuse of privilege was completely forbidden, whether it came from within the elected Assembly, itself essentially conservative, or from the now-shackled press.

The immediate occasion for the November 17 coup was an attempt on the part of the Assembly's Budget Scrutiny Committee to alter moderately the Council's budget proposals. The outcome was the abrupt issuance of a decree abolishing the existing constitution, dissolving the Assembly, disbanding the cabinet, and instituting martial law, in the Sarit fashion of 1958. The action was allegedly designed to counter the machinations of the China-supported Thailand Patriotic Front, although the Front's association with the Assembly membership was far from clear. The army pledged to protect Thailand's king and people from Communist insurrection, student riots, strikes, terrorism, subversion, and parliamentary obstruction and abuse of democratic privilege, all presumably combined in the same nefarious package. The authors explicitly disclaimed any threat to American airfields. The National Executive Council that emerged from the coup included seven high-ranking military leaders, headed as before by Thanom and Praphat, plus two civilians, one of them Pote Sarasin, a supporter of the premier, and the other a Praphat supporter. The principal loser (aside from Thanat) was Police Chief Prasert, whose post Praphat had taken over in October.

The coup reflected a variety of international considerations, including the growing opposition of the army elite to America's Asian policy, especially the progressive military withdrawal from Vietnam and the admission of Thailand's enemy, China, to the United Nations. Another factor was official displeasure over the exercise of American influence domestically, which purportedly had encouraged the Assembly to abuse its power and to impede governmental operations. Under the changing political and international circumstances, the army elite felt justified in reverting to traditional authoritarian methods in both the definition and the defense of the national interest. Within the course of the week following the coup, the disputed budget was approved, public criticism was suppressed, and a revised criminal code was implemented. The imagined subversive threat was thus contained.

A new actor on Bangkok's political scene was Colonel Narong Kittikachorn, the son of Thanom and the son-in-law of Praphat. As the presumptive heir apparent of his relatives in the army elite, Narong embarked on a publicity campaign in late 1971 and 1972 comparable to that launched by General Sarit in 1957. In his frequent public appearances, Narong posed as a proponent of land reform, a friend of the students, an opponent of military conscription, and an enemy of the drug traffic and brothels. He managed to develop a moderate reputation for public welfare concern, but he was careful not to challenge the coup itself.

Expressions of opposition to the coup were generally timid, poorly coordinated, and therefore ineffective. In March 1972 three former members of the Assembly brought suit against Premier Thanom in criminal court, charging violation of the constitution and rebellion against the state. The three were promptly arrested and sentenced without trial to seven to ten years imprisonment. Bangkok was placed under military alert.

The most moving protest came from the respected economist, Puey Ungphakorn, formerly head of the Bank of Thailand and dean of the economics faculty of Thammasat University in Bangkok. With Rockefeller Foundation aid,

Dr. Puey had thoroughly modernized his faculty during the late sixties. Employing his Free Thai wartime pseudonym and writing from his post at Cambridge University, he drafted a letter to "Brother Thamnu," which circulated widely in Bangkok. Puey challenged the cancellation of Thailand's long-awaited democratic constitution, which had afforded freedom of expression and the opportunity to achieve through peaceful means the needed changes in governmental policy and thus to relieve increasing tensions. He expressed pride and confidence in both the intelligence and social concern of the Thai youth, who treasured Thailand's widely proclaimed democratic ideals and had hoped to share in the development of their country. Puey concluded by asking Brother Thamnu to restore the constitution by the end of 1972. Active student support for Dr. Puey's appeal was deferred to 1973.

After the Bangkok Coup

The early months of 1972 witnessed more deterioration than improvement in terrorist and subversive activities. Police jeeps were ambushed in southern Thailand and in the Tak and Nan provinces to the north, while hill tribesmen became more restive and aggressive. Several American airfields were attacked, with planes damaged on the ground.

In some respects, however, the elimination of parliamentary controls facilitated the implementation of the five-year economic development program. The abolition of premium payments by rice exporters increased substantially the volume of overseas sales, which were also augmented by growing maize shipments to Taiwan and Japan. Continued restriction of imports helped reduce the trade balance deficit, which had reached $608 million in 1970 and $495 million in 1971. Valued help came from International Banking agencies, from an economic assistance consultative group, as well as from Japan and the United States. Electrification plans were designed for the Chiengrai region in the extreme north, along with a proposal to construct an oil pipeline across the Kra isthmus that would function under international auspices. But much of the old order persisted. A contract was reportedly let in early 1972 to an American firm for the construction of an additional major airport to serve military needs in the Bangkok area. It involved the payment of one billion *baht* ($50 million) to the Thai government in compensation for American operational rights over a period of twenty years. All business negotiations with the Thai government continued to call for the services of experienced agents as go-betweens.

The first year of restored martial law witnessed more activity than progress. Some 313 decrees and orders were issued, covering a wide variety of topics, but unemployment increased steadily as did consumer prices and governmental corruption. General Praphat assumed full control of policing operations, while the premier acted as his own foreign minister and policy consultant. The National Executive Council issued a new law covering alien businesses in early December 1972, which was intended to end all alien-majority ownership of an extended category of business operations within two years, an arrangement that could conceivably prove profitable to stragetically placed officials. The list included agriculture, estates, accounting and law, architecture, construction, advertising, and brokerage. Other areas of economic activity could be made available to aliens only by special permission, while required work permits for individual immigrants would be issued by the Labor Department. Meanwhile, Thanom had agreed that a Thai table-tennis team could visit China, accompanied by an official Chinese-speaking trade expert. On the basis of the latter's report, the premier later agreed to the opening of trade relations with China.

A limited constitutional adjustment was initiated in early December 1972 with the promulgation of an interim constitution. The gesture followed the pattern set by Marshal Sarit in 1959 in authorizing the designation of an appointed consultative assembly, but it differed in the provision that a special committee, to be selected later, would be assigned the task of drafting a permanent constitution. The new Assembly included 299 members, 200 of them to be chosen from the ranks of the armed services. Accordingly, on December 18, National Executive Council Chairman Thanom became Premier Thanom by formal authorization of the king, the document being countersigned by the president of the new Assembly, General Siri Siriyothin, who was one of the few persons carried over from the 1971 Assembly. The interim constitution specified that approval of any permanent constitution would require a two-thirds approval by the new Assembly, which left the armed services in full control. As could be anticipated, the new royally appointed cabinet was similar in make-up to the disbanded National Executive Council. A significant change was the addition of a retired naval admiral, who was designated minister of communications. Some 30 naval personnel were also included in the Assembly, a new departure. The interim constitution reserved for the premier and cabinet all initiatory legislative authority in revenue, budgetary, and financial matters.

Accompanying the news of the transfer to interim constitutional rule on December 17 was Thanom's public acceptance of the American proposal to shift the headquarters of the United States Military Assistance Command, Southeast Asia, to Nakhon Phanom air base, located in northeastern Thailand, 380 miles from Bangkok and 8 miles from the border of Laos. Five other American-built airfields in Thailand, which from 1969 to 1971 had been in the process of evacuation, were reoccupied in full strength by 1972 as a result of the continuing transfer of forces from South Vietnam. During Vice-President Agnew's closely guarded visit to Bangkok on February 3, 1973, he reportedly renewed American pledges to continue support of the Thai government, both economically and militarily.

But despite such pledges, the Thanom-Praphat army dictatorship was destined to disappear during the course of 1973 as student protest mounted.

Burma Continues as Uusal

The promise held out in late 1969 of the development of a less rigidly repressive pattern on the part of the Burma government (for example, three-day travel visas, the five-day Asian games, hints at constitutional reform) failed to materialize in 1970. Socialist objectives and military authority took precedence over evidences of relaxed controls and greater personal freedom. Faintly symbolic of an abandonment of Marxian terminology was the substitution of the word *Myanma* (Burman) for "People's" in the names of several governmental projects. The rigidly Marxist General Tin Pe was officially retired in November 1970, presumably for personal reasons, but the move was suggestive at the time of a possible shift in ideological alignment within the army command. His replacement as minister of national solidarity, social welfare, and resettlement was Brigadier Thaung Dan, previously minister of information and culture. A new army-officer favorite of Ne Win emerged in the person of Brigadier San Yu, the minister of finance, who was reported to be of Chinese birth.

The slight increase in tourist traffic in 1970 did little to relieve economic deterioration, mainly because there were few entertainment facilities provided. Visitors to the Asian games discovered that Rangoon's taxis barely held together, and they also witnessed a riot among the spectators at a boxing match occasioned by the cornering of 80 percent of the tickets by black marketeers. University graduates, with no job openings available, understandably had little enthusiasm for becoming anonymous cogs in an inefficiently administered state-development program that promised them no reward for leadership abilities or imagination.

Little or no effective opposition to the Ne Win regime

could be mounted from within the government, from the Burman population generally, or from non-Communist rebel forces assembled along sections of the Thailand border. Not all of the dissident Karens would cooperate with Burman revolutionaries, and ex-Premier Nu was himself not prepared to collaborate with Communists. Nu's indiscreet suggestion that he might solicit Chinese aid backfired in favor of Ne Win, who characterized his rival as a power-minded maniac fingering Buddhist beads while joining hands with Burma's traditional enemies. The Tenasserim insurrectionists later distributed pamphlets in favor of the "lawfully elected government of Premier Nu," but they made only minor physical penetrations in the Sittang Valley region south of Toungoo and via seaborne raids on a delta township. Selectively targeted attacks were registered in Rangoon and Pegu. The widespread opposition to Ne Win simply could not be coordinated and it lacked the means of forcible resistance in any case. Sooner or later, Ne Win's continuing ill health and the game of musical chairs played by the Rangoon army elite might produce a change of leadership, but Nu's prospects appeared discouraging. He reportedly abandoned the rebel cause in 1972.

Reform of Party and Administrative Structure

Long-promised changes in the governmental structure were slow in coming. The first National Congress of the Burma Socialist Program party (BSPP) was convened at Rangoon in June 1971. It included representatives selected from local units of the Workers and Peasants Councils (Soviets), in addition to the regular BSPP leadership. The principal actions taken by the Congress were to increase the number of full members of the party to some seventy-three thousand and to expand the candidate list to more than a quarter-million names. The suggested modulation from military to "democratic" control was more apparent than real, since the armed services representatives in the BSPP still outnumbered civilians by

627

some forty-two to thirty-one thousand. The Congress also authorized the convening of a Constitutional Commission to prepare a formal document that would presumably become operative in 1974.

Ne Win's appointee as head of the Commission was Colonel (later Brigadier) San Yu. The body was obliged to function within the narrowly defined limits of orthodox Socialist Democratic principles. The new Burma was envisaged as a strictly unitary state, with no federalization, no communal representation, and no toleration of political factionalism or ideological vagaries. Citizenship status would be homogeneous throughout the countryside, with no second Chamber of Nationalities to represent minority interests.

Little happened until early 1972. The first ostensible move away from overt military control, in March 1972, involved the simultaneous resignations of high army commissions, starting with Ne Win himself, now premier, and including twelve of the fifteen military members of his cabinet. The remaining three who kept their commissions headed up the several branches of the armed services. The first draft of the new constitution was completed shortly thereafter and was distributed widely by government representatives who solicited critical comments, which, it is reported, numbered in the thousands. A second draft was ready by the end of the year. It was scheduled to be approved by the BSPP and later to be presented for acceptance by national referendum. The regime took few chances constitutionally.

Meanwhile, substantial changes were being attempted in the administrative structure of the government. The traditionally important district commissioner units and the coordinating Central Secretariat were both abolished in mid-1972. A new hierarchy of security and administrative committees would be substituted at various levels of government, composed of representative civil servants, Workers and Peasants Council members, selected professional and technical servants of the government, as well as members of the ever-present military, police,

628

and the BSPP. Under the proposed constitution, the membership of these several levels of committees would be elected by local constituencies. Administrative duties would be entrusted to functional (nonpolicy) departments, directorships, and cabinet ministers responsible for carrying out particular government programs.

Later in 1972 the traditional court system of expert, legally trained personnel was largely replaced by amateur People's Courts, to be composed of laymen selected for thirty-day duty periods by three-man judicial committees representing the BSPP and the local Peasants and Workers Councils. The new security and administrative committee structure would combine both judicial and administrative authority. Policies would still be determined within the BSPP. The only concessions made to bourgeois considerations were provisions for improved wage scales for officials; efforts to increase foreign exchange holdings (which fell to an all-time low of $52 million in 1972); and plans to expand training programs for skilled workers. Presumably as part of such reforming efforts, the two generals previously occupying the posts of labor and industrial minister and home minister—both of them long-time associates of Premier Ne Win—were retired for alleged incompetency in November 1972.

Economic Doldrums

The economic situation continued to be discouraging for both production and trade. Some minor increments were realized in timber output, but the only substantial gains were registered in oil. Offshore drilling had begun in February 1972 at five spots in the Gulf of Martaban under the direction of an American firm, Reading and Bates, and financed by a $10-million Japanese loan. One such operation struck a high-pressure gas pocket, and the ensuing explosion destroyed the large operating platform. The oil and gas potential was also clearly present in the southward extensions of the Arakan Yoma and its offshore projections. To turn to agriculture, the total

629

cultivated area by 1972 extended beyond the prewar limits, but per-unit rice production was low and the milled rice of poor quality, with little available for export in the face of the 50 percent increase in population since 1940. Overseas trade fell in 1971–72 to 37 percent of what it had been in 1961–62.

Government-run industry suffered from poor management, shortages of raw materials, and deteriorating machinery. The crucially important textile industry was a case in point. Many of the state-run cotton mills (increased in number from six to twenty-one since 1967) were idle for lack of fiber. Only a fraction of the needed fertilizers and pesticides were available to the cotton cultivators, so that output per acre was less than 60 percent of expected yield. Production was further discouraged because the manufacturers were permitted to sell cotton only to state purchasing agencies, at prices far below the scarcity value of the fiber. The cooperative distributing agencies for consumer needs, which had replaced the People's Stores in mid-1972, proved equally inefficient. An escalation of black-market prices for both rice and cooking oil developed in December 1972, which impelled the government to imprison more than five hundred large-scale urban dealers who were found in possession of hoarded stocks. Prices of cloth and various imported consumer items doubled during 1972. Burma's current four-year development plan was faltering badly.

One of the most difficult areas of government control concerned the northeastern frontiers adjacent to China, Laos, and Thailand. Since the Burmese *kyat* was nearly worthless in such areas, trade with Laos and Thailand for consumer needs could be conducted only by bartering gems or by dealing with the rapacious opium "kings" who dominated the processing and foreign sale of drugs. Rangoon's contacts with most population centers in the eastern Shan States were by air service to scattered landing strips. Burman Communist rebels still controlled the northern Shan State borders with China (Hsenwei, Kutkai, and Namkham) and the upper Salween Valley, where drug exports were also used to obtain needed arms and consumer supplies.

Burma was affected, as were many of its neighbors, by the changing power relationships in Eastern Asia. China posed the most important problem. The Bangladesh independence crisis in 1971–72, for example, witnessed the direct clash of Soviet and Chinese interests, with Burma tending to take on increasing importance strategically. Ne Win turned the situation to Burma's advantage by complying with Peking's request in early 1972 to assist in evacuating Chinese consular personnel from Dacca by air. He obtained, in return, the unspent portion (between $50 and $60 million) of China's $84-million loan of the pre-1967 period. Meanwhile, Soviet relations with Burma were deliberately muted by Ne Win, so as to give Peking no grounds for believing that he was part of the feared Russian encircling movement. Thus security concerns, national unity objectives, and ideological considerations continued to take precedence over economic development and expansion of political freedom in Burma.

Economic Recovery in Post-Sukarno Indonesia

General Suharto's Indonesian government faced extremely difficult problems as successor to the flamboyant Sukarno regime, with its cumulative neglect of economic problems, coupled with the aftermath of the bloodletting that followed the abortive coup of 1965. The state treasury was hopelessly bankrupt, incapable of servicing the vast $1.7-billion debt due to foreign government creditors. The country was also unable to attract the requisite traditional capital investments and loans, public and private, that conditioned the recovery program. The official unemployment figures ran around 12 to 15 percent in 1969, not counting part-time workers and the poverty-level salaried class, including the civil service. Efforts to curb inflation by cutting down on government expenditures and consumer imports served at the outset to aggravate unemployment and economic stagnation, as

631

both agricultural and industrial expansion plans ran aground. Public dissatisfaction found expression in various forms, including student demonstrations in January 1970 over increased bus fares and fuel prices, plus complaints over the widespread abuse of authority by impoverished government officials, including the police and the military. The reported 6 percent increase in the GNP in 1970 was deceptive, because the 1969 base was low and increases were attributable in large measure to the growing output of capital-intensive industries, which did little to reduce unemployment or prices.

On the positive side was Suharto's continued support of able civilian cabinet ministers who were struggling to cope with the situation. They took seriously the unexciting but salutary proposals of World Bank officials and other financial advisers, while Suharto himself utilized army disciplinary authority to provide essential public needs and to curb some of the abuse of official power.

By April 1970 Ministers Sumitro and Malik, with the assistance of a Dutch mediator, had worked out a formula for handling the 40 percent of the public debt owing to creditors outside the Communist bloc. All unpaid interest obligations due prior to the date of the agreement were to be cancelled, and the principal of the several loans was made payable in thirty annual installments, with no interest due until 1985. Once the credit barriers had been thus removed, new loans were advanced by friendly governments ($600 million came from Japanese and American sources), and even larger sums were available subsequently from private corporations interested in oil and mineral exploration and in plantation development. For a time there was something like a stampede of investors, who were apparently concerned that they not lose out on resource development opportunities. Negotiation problems were frequently solved by the payment of generous bribes, but even then Indonesian negotiators were generally dilatory and lackadaisical and frequently failed to keep appointments and formal commitments. Nevertheless, by mid-1971 Indonesia had reversed the downward economic trend, halted the runaway inflation, and was on its way to recovery.

The Soviet Union and other Eastern European creditors responded slowly to the changing financial climate in Indonesia. But as holders of the remaining 60 percent of the country's outstanding public debt, they had little choice but to accept the repayment formula proposed by Western nations. Moscow included its huge $800-million debt in the general arrangement and also agreed to resume work on several abandoned aid projects in Western Java, which had been started under Sukarno. During 1970 Soviet purchases of rubber, coffee, tea, and other items available in Indonesia reached $20 million, and the pace of trade doubled in the first quarter of 1971. Russian embassy and consular staffs as well as cultural and trade missions were revitalized as part of the decision to restore association with the island empire. The formal agreement for resuming work on an unfinished fertilizer plant and a steel mill was signed in July 1971, and two teams of Soviet technicians arrived in Java for the purpose in early August. An accompanying Soviet offer to supply, on easy credit terms, spare parts for inoperative planes and other military equipment supplied by Moscow in the early sixties was declined by the still-suspicious Indonesian military command.

These arrangements with the USSR were largely the work of Foreign Minister Adam Malik, who had served as ambassador to Moscow from 1959 to 1962. Malik was less successful in his efforts to restore diplomatic relations with mainland China. He wanted to gain Peking's recognition of the Suharto government and to halt the transmission of hostile Indonesian-language propaganda from China attacking Suharto's "fascist military clique." Direct Indonesian representation in Peking had ceased in 1967, and subsequent handling of such relations by the Cambodian embassy had also lapsed with Sihanouk's ouster in early 1970. China's reaction to Malik's overtures was cold and unfriendly, and army associates within the cabinet were equally hostile to the idea. Memories of the coup of

633

1965 and the resulting pogrom inflicted on Indonesian Communists and their alleged Chinese collaborators were not easily erased. For the time being, Indonesian purchases of Chinese-manufactured bicycles, hand tools, and tea cups had to continue to be via Hong Kong and Singapore.

The Indonesian Elections of 1971

Indonesia's most significant political project scheduled for 1971 was the holding of general elections on July 3, the first such occasion in sixteen years. In view of the fact that the army regime was in complete control and obviously in a position to influence the outcome, some critics raised questions about the high cost of the operation (estimated at $50 million) and its political contribution regardless of cost. Of the 460 persons who would compose the membership of the newly chosen House of Representatives, a full 100 were to be reserved for appointment by President Suharto. Only the government was in a position to sponsor a full slate of candidates, to be selected from specifically delineated, functional economic and occupational groups, including civil servants, politicians, business and professional men, labor leaders, cultivators, and students. An important objective was to subordinate political factionalism based on religious commitments, political ideologies, or regional associations to more pragmatic considerations. The political confusion that had characterized the parliamentary process of the early 1950s would, it was hoped, be replaced by broad-based support of the government, which could approximate traditional consensus standards. The Communist party was barred from participation in the election, as were the former leaders of the Masjumi party. If official elections plans succeeded, General Suharto could expect to gain the cooperation of a socially competent representative body and also be assured of his own reelection as president by the same group in 1973. The election project was characteristically Indonesian in origin and motivation.

The government's active two months of preparations

and campaigning (May and June 1971) constituted a massively staged public relations exercise. Its purpose was to publicize the role of the proposed Secretariat of Functional Groups, or Sekber Golkar (from *golongan karya*, workers and professionals), who would be pledged to back the president's recovery and development programs on pragmatic grounds. Nine other parties were permitted participation, but opposition candidates were forbidden to criticize either the president or the government's previous performance.

Election preparations included the establishment of some 330,000 voting booths, all supplied with ballot boxes, distributed over the nearly 1,000 inhabited islands of the archipelago. Djakarta alone was equipped with 9,900 polling places. The 57 million eligible voters in a myriad of local council units were asked to select from the various slates of candidates persons who would in turn vote for district representatives, and they for provincial-level electors, who would finally select the members of the central House of Representatives. The indirect election system thus tended to follow the old *Volksraad* pattern, except that the basic suffrage was universal and the representation more generally distributed. All officials of the government, from minor civil servants to cabinet ministers, were expected to take an active role in supporting the Sekber Golkar candidates. The president himself remained theoretically above the level of controversy, as a kind of generally accepted symbol of authority. The armed forces were also barred from participation in the campaign, by virtue of the fact that their officer leadership would constitute the major fraction of the 100 members of the House to be nominated later by the president.

The campaigning and balloting were conducted in orderly fashion. The contending politicians took the effort far more seriously than did the voters, most of whom had very little at stake in the operation. The outcome was a more impressive victory for the Sekber Golkar slate than had been anticipated. It won 236 of the 360 contested seats, and almost 63 percent of the total vote. Only the

635

orthodox Nahdatul Ulama party (mainly Javanese) made a respectable opposition showing with 60 seats. The more modernist Permusi Muslim party, denied access to former Masjumi leadership, won only 23 seats, while the remnants of Sukarno's PNI, lacking civil service support, won only 20. This left a mere 21 seats for the other participating groups.

The election experiment did much to strengthen the government's credentials as being representative and socially concerned and promoted the ideas of political secularization and functional representation divorced from divisive religious and ideological commitments. Some observers hoped that it may also have contributed usefully over the long run to developing a basis for modulation away from arbitrary army control and toward a semblance of governmental responsibility to the popular will. Sekber Golkar with all its compromises probably carried more significance to the participants than did Ne Win's 1972 Congress of the Burma Socialist Program Party.

During the course of the ensuing year, the opposition parties were pressured by the government to organize into two federated groups, one religiously oriented and Muslim, and the other non-Muslim secularist, nationalist, and Christian. The Muslim Unity groups responded reluctantly to such federation pressure, but they had little choice but to comply. Opposition party organizations were forbidden to function politically below the district level between election contests.

The House of Representatives selected in 1971 made up only one-half of the comprehensive People's Deliberative Assembly, which eventually gathered in March 1973. The additions were widely representative of functional social groups. The Assembly dutifully elected General Suharto to a second term as president, with Sultan Hamengku Buwono of Jogjakarta as the only Vice-Presidential candidate. The army continued very much in control of political activities. The Golkar majority within the House of Representatives operated politically at three levels. One was the area of security, in which task it enjoyed support from the armed forces organization; the second was improving relations with the village population. Finally, the Golkar majority served to generate ideas, which the government could accept or ignore at its discretion.

Official corruption continued rampant, especially within the State Oil Corporation and other government-controlled enterprises. Government ineptitude and possible collusion with rice brokers were partly responsible for development of serious rice shortages in later 1972. These and other grievances were not permitted to be the subject of public discussion. Political activity and social modernization were limited to the dimensions that the dominant Armed Forces Command would approve. But order was maintained, and basic economic development was proceeding.

Indonesia's Postelection Developments

One of the encouraging results of the election was the ensuing reshuffling of cabinet posts in the direction of increased participation by younger civilian personnel, especially in the economic areas of the administration. An economist, Widjojo, was assigned to development planning. Professors Mohammed Sadli and Subroto were designated minister of labor and head of cooperatives and transmigration services, respectively. Dr. Emil Salimin was put in charge of administrative reform. As a result, only four generals and one air vice-marshal remained in top cabinet posts. General Suharto continued to act as undisputed head of the government, and the military still constituted the ultimate sanction of authority —a kind of indispensable residuum of responsibility for national unity and economic growth. Apologists could argue that the political party system had failed under test and that professional standards were gradually developing within the army, including a more articulate conceptualization of its proper governmental role. In Indonesia as elsewhere, the army command would be loath to surrender

637

the perquisites of power, but contrary to the situation in Burma, the high command at Djakarta did see the need to enlist competent civilian assistance in economic planning and general administrative control.

The government's effective curbing of inflation in 1971–72 made possible a dramatic increase in bank deposits and a corresponding expansion of lending capacity at acceptable rates of interest. The level of savings doubled annually. Chinese business interests from Singapore, Malaysia, and Hong Kong were encouraged to invest in new labor-intensive enterprises. Cooperative efforts in agriculture boosted rice production from twelve to almost fifteen million tons annually. Major oil, gas, and mineral explorations proceeded under general government supervision, while substantial Japanese loans were obtained, in return for promises of ten-year oil deliveries, for revival of the Assahan Dam project and oil promotion in Sumatra. Other plans called for harbor construction, pipeline facilities, and water reservoirs in Western Java.

The five-year program to be initiated in 1973 called for concentration on industrial expansion and other efforts to promote employment opportunities. The plan recognized explicitly that Indonesia must continue to attract outside capital and technical assistance while endeavoring to maintain its regional identity and to avoid becoming a pawn in the chess game of the world powers. Oil production was Indonesia's major resource. It made up 40 percent of current exports, and the country's proved reserves constituted some 80 percent of the Pacific area's total. Other potential new sources of international exchange were timber production and tourism, the latter expanding at a rate of more than 25 percent a year and including mainly Java, Bali, and Eastern Island cruises. The most intractable problems were the need to alleviate overpopulation in Java and to boost per-capita income, thus broadening the tax base.

In matters of foreign policy, Indonesia played an active role in the sessions of ASEAN and in efforts to end the Vietnam War. In November 1972 the government accepted a place on the international commission selected to supervise the cease-fire in Vietnam. Army leadership within the government continued to oppose Adam Malik's efforts to reach accomodation with China. Indonesia's representative to the United Nations voted against the admission of China, on the ground that Peking's Indonesian-language radio propaganda continued to use exiled Communist spokesmen to attack the Suharto government and to encourage subversive activities by residents. Djakarta mistrusted the nonalignment policies advocated by its Southeast Asian neighbors as being essentially pro-Communist in their effect. On the occasion of the sessions of the People's Consultative Assembly in March 1973, Suharto insisted that Communist subversion still persisted both in Java and in Kalimantan and that improved relations with China depended on Peking's demonstration of a more genuinely friendly attitude.

Cooperative efforts with Malaysia produced an agreement instituting a five-year transition period to achieve a standard system of spelling for the *Bahasa Malay* lingua franca. The two also advanced territorial claims over the shallow Straits of Malacca as far out as twelve miles offshore. They avoided challenging directly the assumption of the great powers that the straits still constituted an international waterway "for innocent passage." The issue arose after Japan proposed that international action was needed to provide navigational aids in the form of radar buoys for particularly congested stretches of the straits. Extensive dredging operations were also needed to facilitate the passage of heavy draft oil tankers, mainly Japanese. Adam Malik eventually moderated his position on the territorial waters claim by considering it in the context of world relations rather than as a parochial or nationalist issue.

Although Indonesian leadership during the early seventies was itself not in full agreement on all important matters and was far from achieving national consensus, it had substantial accomplishments to its credit. Djakarta had placed essential economic needs above partisan factionalism;

it had achieved a semblance of popular cooperation without resort to arbitrary coercion, except where Communist subversion was involved; it had maintained the political primacy of Java while at the same time respecting the interests of the Outer Islands. Religious partisanship was still a major political problem, as was overpopulation, but the government had gained time to permit the consideration of more urgent issues in an atmosphere of adjustment and moderation.

Malaysia and Singapore, 1970

The first anniversary of the May 13, 1969, riots found Malaysia's population relatively quiet and seemingly reconciled to the cautious policy being followed by the ad hoc National Operations Council. No sensible person wanted to risk renewal of violence by permitting premature public discussion of controversial racial issues. The passion had cooled somewhat, even though the causes of friction still remained officially unresolved. The non-Malay Democratic Action party and the Party Rakyat were not represented at all in the Council, but the total body was far less nationalistic than were the partisans of the Pan Malay Islamic party (PMIP), which continued to stress the pre-eminence of the Malay language and the Islamic religion and the preservation of traditional Malay political privileges. Unemployed Malay and Chinese youth continued their explosive, mutually antagonistic mood; both were hostile, for different reasons, to the Council's moderate policy.

The prospect of Tengku Abdul Rahman's replacement by Tun Razak as premier, scheduled for September 1970, appeared at first to be likely to reduce the prestige of the Kuala Lumpur government and to postpone any prospect for early return to the electoral system. The deferred elections held in Sarawak and Sabah in July 1970 were somewhat less than reassuring to the Alliance party leadership. The proposed Alliance grouping in Sarawak disintegrated when the Sarawak Nationalist party refused to agree, as had been expected, to collaborate with the Bumiputra (Workers) party of Dato Rahman Yakub. The latter then worked out a coalition with the Leftist Chinese Sarawak United Peoples party (SUPP) to gain joint control over the provincial government. Yong, the Chinese head of SUPP, was later invited to participate in the central cabinet as an ethnic regional representative, thus establishing a new pattern for Alliance support. Meanwhile, in Sabah, the wealthy leader of the United Sabah National Organization, Tun Mustapha, agreed to deliver all of the area's assigned central seats to Alliance candidates as compensation for his own enjoyment of personal domination within the state government. The adjustments worked out within the two Borneo states demonstrated that the enjoyment of political power was more important than ideological or ethnic considerations and that the UMNO leadership could also profit by adopting a more flexible stance.

The still-popular Tengku stepped down as premier on September 21, 1970, partly because the changing political climate appeared better suited to the more earthy tactics of Razak, who assumed office on the same day. Tun Abdul Razak, the nephew of the Tengku, was not of princely origin but had served as deputy prime minister under the Tengku and since May 1969 had been director of the National Operations Council. Although not liked by some non-Malays, Razak was in a strong position as leader of the UMNO to solicit the support of moderate Malay opposition groups. He could also act more independently of the Chinese and Indian elements of the Alliance coalition, both of whom were threatened with political disintegration. A variety of coalition arrangements emerged in time, facilitating UMNO cooperation with disparate political groups in the northern tier of states in Western Malaysia, as well as in Sarawak and Sabah.

The first dramatic move made by the new premier was to reconvene the elected Parliament on February 20, 1971, thus ending twenty-one months of emergency Council rule. He insisted, however, on the immediate acceptance of a constitutional amendment outlawing as seditious all

641

public discussion, both within and outside of Parliament, of topics likely to arouse racial antagonisms or to cast distrust on the intentions of the government. At the same time, the essential provisions of the 1957 constitution regarding Malay privileges were not subject to parliamentary review. Razak proposed a second five-year development plan setting forth dual objectives. Economic expansion, projected hopefully at the rate of 6.5 percent per annum, was to be tempered by the primary objectives of balanced growth and an end of economic segregation along ethnic lines. The primary emphasis on more equitable distribution of income was intended to relieve poverty wherever it was found. The new plan would involve a larger measure of government initiative and control than had been the case heretofore.

Under Razak's political leadership, the UMNO attracted increasing indigenous support, while the faction-ridden MCA and MIC fragments of the Alliance coalition were scrambling to survive. The Malay Chinese Association was threatened first by an abortive effort of younger Chinese to capture control and later by opposition from the already factionalized Pan-Malaysian Chinese Guilds Association. The Chinese constituency was also divided by language dialect differences. The Teochieu-speaking groups dominated trade; the Hokkiens monopolized the rubber job market, while Cantonese, Hakka, and mandarin-speaking elements were otherwise employed. Defections from non-Malay political bodies developed from personal rivalries and general loss of morale, affording Razak considerably more political flexibility than Rahman had enjoyed prior to 1961. The new premier gained stature as a state leader with the passage of time, even though many administrative and economic problems awaited solution.

The world market for Malaysian rubber, tin, and iron ore was temporarily down, and the resulting losses could be made good only in part by increased agriculture production and manufacturing. If the five-year plan to double industrial output by 1975 was to be realized, government loans and private capital would have to be attracted from abroad. Suggested quota arrangements with respect to enterprise ownership or required employment of young Malays influenced Chinese employers to drag their feet in compliance. Among rival youth groups communal relations remained abrasive, with no prospect in sight for racial integration. Meanwhile, the Kuala Lumpur government encouraged expanded trade with China but held back on establishing diplomatic relations until Peking agreed to halt its alleged encouragement of Communist rebels operating along the Thailand border. Unlike Indonesia and Singapore, Malaysia favored, as early as 1970, the admission of mainland China to the United Nations.

A substantial psychological factor in the foreign relations picture was the conclusion of the Commonwealth Defense Agreement in April 1971, to become operative in November. The agreement actually provided little more than symbolic protection for Malaysia and Singapore. In case either of the two was threatened by overt attack from the outside, the other three participants—Britain, Australia, and New Zealand—agreed to consult with them over what defense measures could be undertaken jointly or separately. The British forces to be stationed in the area would consist of one infantry battalion, an air reconnaissance force, six surface naval vessels, and one submarine; smaller forces were to be provided by Australia and New Zealand. The limited measure of confidence generated initially by the agreement was gradually dissipated by the prospective withdrawal of American forces from South Vietnam.

In order to meet the threat of internal rebellion, which was not covered by the agreement, Malaysia undertook to expand its armed forces from eighteen to twenty-seven battalions and to acquire a Sabre jet squadron from Australia. Meanwhile the government adopted officially a neutralized and nonaligned policy similar to that espoused by Indonesia. Efforts would continue to achieve a larger measure of regional solidarity to restrict great power involvement, both economic and strategic, within the area. In terms of trade and technical assistance (flood control

643

and mining needs), Razak solicited aid from the USSR. He visited Eastern Europe personally in September 1972 and even managed to arrange a talk at Vienna with the resident Chinese ambassador. Foreign policy movement was in evidence, but the pace was cautiously slow.

By way of summary, Malaysia's escape from the blight of military rule that engulfed most of her Southeast Asian neighbors, coupled with the continued enjoyment of economic and political stability and the recovery of a qualified measure of democratic government, set it apart from other states in the region. These accomplishments may be attributable in part to the country's experience of a more complete transferral of administrative institutions from the preceding colonial regime, and to the fact that these inherited institutional patterns were not static. For six years prior to 1962, a British-directed Development Administrative Unit explored the problem of adjustments needed to meet the government's expanding duties and problems. This approach was continued after 1969 by Tun Razak's Implementation Coordinative Executive Agency, focusing attention on the dynamics of the communal problem and contributing to the increasing effectiveness of governmental efforts to promote cooperation to achieve agreed goals. Malaysia was also assisted in the task by the presence of a viable economic environment that afforded a wider margin of error and a broader time frame than most of its neighbors enjoyed. The inherent strength of the surviving Malaysian administrative structure, itself in the process of further adaptations, contributed materially to maintaining order under civilian control and to the eventual salvaging of some aspects of democratic freedom.

Singapore, 1970–72

The perennial question of whether the tiny island state of Singapore was a viable national entity seemed to merit a qualified affirmative answer in 1972. It was obviously so in economic affairs, which moved forward under full

644

throttle. The GNP was expanding at the phenomenal rate of 14 percent per annum, and per-capita income attained some $1,200 (U.S.), a remarkably high level for the region. Industrial expansion focused on shipbuilding and repair facilities, on oil and gas exploration and refineries, and on improved communications, financial resources, and technology. Industrial gains were supplemented by trade promotion and tourism, combined with hotel and apartment construction. Investment capital came from Japan, America, and Hong Kong for the most part, in response to vigorous solicitation. Unemployment shrank to minimal levels, and more than 70,000 workers were attracted from nearby Malaysia. The substantial trade deficit incurred by the entrepôt was made good by income from services.

The encouraging economic performance was not without substantial vulnerabilities, however. The process involved increasing dependence on external markets, the dangers of overinvestment and continuing price inflation, labor shortages and overcrowding, plus increasing social strain associated with the strenuous industrial tempo. Competition with enormous outside corporations involved some prospect that Singapore might become, over the long run, a neocolonialist outpost of multinational economic imperialism. Cultural evidence of such a trend was the growing preference for the use of English over both Malay and Chinese languages. All-out concern for maximum economic gain involved the prospect of diminishing humanitarian concern for the victims of the hectic pursuit of profits.

Most observers would have to concede that Premier Lee Kuan Yew had little alternative, however, granted Singapore's limited resources and markets, and none could deny the premier's positive accomplishments, governmental as well as economic. When the issue was put to popular test in the elections of September 2, 1972, the government's Political Action party won all sixty-five Assembly seats, eight of them without contest. The combined opposition parties gained only 31 percent of the total votes. Such tangible issues as higher wages, expanding educational opportunities, better technology and skills, and expanding business activity left the Socialists and the national identity advocates with little to say in reply.

Even so, the convincing election triumph produced more concern than confidence on the part of its architect, the premier. Overprosperous Singapore was inherently vulnerable as an orphaned Chinese island in a Malaysian sea. It was jealously regarded by both immediate neighbors and dependent for security on a far-from-convincing Commonwealth defense commitment. Following the election, Premier Lee exhibited an almost morbid concern about the motivation and the financing of the opposition. He demanded that all opposing party groups open their books to disclose the sources of any substantial contribution received during the course of the campaign. The possibility of outside political intervention in Singapore's affairs prompted his proposal of a constitutional amendment in late 1972 that would require that any future proposal for federation or incorporation be approved by a two-thirds majority plebiscite. At the same time, he expressed strong resentment of any form of criticism from the press, considering it by implication inspired by enemies of the country. Lee also shifted the emphasis of his foreign policy to a strong advocacy of America's continuing economic and strategic presence in Southeast Asia, reflecting his complete lack of confidence in both non-alignment tactics and Commonwealth cooperation.

Singapore's growing sense of international isolation was reflected in a variety of other policy decisions. Lee took note of Malaysia's and Indonesia's assertions of territorial claims extending twelve miles offshore, but he gave no approval of the idea. The talk of building a pipeline or shipment canal across the Thailand isthmus constituted potential threat to Singapore's commercial status. Currency identity with Malaysia was abandoned as was joint control over the peninsular airlines. Despite Singapore's increasing trade and growing volume of investments in Indonesia ($300 million) and increasing trade, the island government published no commercial statistics that might reveal the extent of illicit smuggling trade from scattered Indonesian ports. All announcements with reference to possible changing regional diplomatic relations with mainland China were discreetly left to Malaysia and Indonesia. Singapore was legally independent and prosperous, but still highly vulnerable and somewhat less than free.

Before leaving the former British Malayan area, a brief word needs to be said about Brunei. The tiny north Borneo state continued under British foreign policy control, with Gurkha garrison protection. With new sources of offshore oil and gas under constant development, Brunei's young sultan enjoyed more income than he could wisely spend, while the growing population of 136,000 paid no taxes. Brunei boasted expanding education and a new Malay-language college, a huge new mosque, two paved roads, increased water distribution facilities, and an impressive Winston Churchill museum. This wealthy survival of the colonial empire joined the company of Hong Kong—and some might suggest Singapore, also—as an anachronistic reminder of a bygone age. The possibility of developing oil and gas production adjacent to island groups in the center of the South China Sea attracted China's attention in late 1973.

The Philippines: Postelection Unrest, 1969-70.

Observers of the Manila scene found little in the aftermath of the Philippines election of 1969 to bolster their faith in the democratic process. President Marcos' impressive election victory was attributable in part to the plodding ineffectiveness of his conservative opponent, Osmeña. It also owed a great deal to the president's overgenerous distribution of "public works contributions" in $500 units to the heads of the many barrios he visited. Within a period of nine months the country's money supply increased some 24 percent, with inevitable inflationary consequences. Consumer prices rose from 40 to 66 percent, varying by categories, in a situation com-

647

plicated by flagrant banking and smuggling irregularities. The polling booths were properly supervised, but election violence claimed around one hundred lives.

The reelected president was widely blamed for rising prices and utility costs and for favoritism shown to misbehaving party cronies. He was also asked to explain his own annual income of some eleven times his presidential salary of $15,000. Marcos' subsequent proposal to dedicate his estimated $125-million fortune to a charitable Marcos Foundation aroused more criticism than praise. Serious-minded citizens doubted the wisdom of entrusting to Marcos the supervision of the authorized Constitutional Convention, scheduled to convene in June 1971. Revolutionary agitators attacked the allegedly fatuous confidence that Filipinos exhibited in constitutional reform.

The discouraged public mood was impressively dramatized by the following prayer delivered by Father Ortiz, president of the Ateneo de Manila, on the occasion of Marcos' State of the Nation message in February 1970:

> Oh God, we bring the growing fears, the dying hopes, the perished longings and expectations of a people who . . . walk through unsafe streets of their cities or roam through the Huk infested barrio lanes of Central Luzon, or stare at the dwindling goods and rising prices in the market stalls—who now know that salvation, political or economic, . . . can only come . . . from the people themselves firmly united under Your Divine Providence to stand for their rights, whether at the polls, in the marketplace, or at the barricades. . . . To have lost our political innocence . . . is also for a free people to stand on the trembling edge of revolution.

Student rioting, starting in January 1970, was first directed against the Presidential Palace. It took on a Maoist flavor in February, when the American embassy and U.S. business corporations became the targets. The disorder subsided after a time, only to erupt again several months later, when several students were killed by the police. The Marcos regime, while continuing to enjoy the advantages derived from American security installations, solicited nationalist support by calling loudly for the revision of American treaties. Marcos also bargained with the Japanese for prestigious claims to sovereignty over adjacent ocean areas. He eventually proposed developing relations with China and the USSR.

Lack of confidence in the existing party system was reflected during the course of the year in the revitalization of a number of religiopolitical factional groups that functioned as protective associations. Examples were the *Iglesia ni Christi*, a highly integrated but opportunistic organization, and the more constructive Free Farmers Association. Both groups were critical of the landlord-politico establishment and its governmental allies.

Expressions of opposition to the existing order could not be dismissed as insignificant, but it was unclear exactly what they signified. The outbreaks were, for the most part, a bit too overt and vocal to suggest any deep-seated revolutionary objectives and intentions. Filipinos cherished very much their periodic election fiestas and their freedom to voice dissent. Political and economic reforms were long overdue, and their actual realization might require resort to extralegal measures. A democratic government incapable of redressing popular grievances, both economic and political, was judged hardly worthy of respect. But overt revolution did not appear inevitable.

Economic prospects improved in 1970 as a result of an 18 percent leap in export earnings consequent on an effective devaluation of the *peso* at a floating rate of 6.4 to the dollar, compared to the earlier fixed rate of 3.9 to one. The favorable balance of payments was assisted by increases in rice production. Loans from U.S. commercial banks were repaid, and a balanced budget emerged, although unemployment remained high, fed by the 3.5 percent annual increase in population. A measure of encouragement was also derived from the successful staging on November 10, 1970, of elections for the Constituent Assembly. The well-conducted campaign was "issue-centered," with political partisanship playing a minor role. Among the 320 elected delegates were several former presidents of the Republic, a number of high-level judges and cabinet members, senators and assemblymen, and many young candidates and others representing a great variety of views. Father Ortiz of the Ateneo was among the group. The Committee on Elections performed admirably. Whether or not such a heterogeneous group could arrive at any agreement with respect to needed constitutional changes was to become a major problem of 1971–72. The demonstrated concern for constitutional adjustments and periodic elections held out some measure of hope.

Rising Tensions in 1970–71.

The tensions arising from the normal incidence of political infighting within the Manila government, accompanied by uninhibited press criticism, student demonstrations, and occasional terrorist violence, were aggravated in mid-1970 by the outbreak of strife in Eastern and Southern Mindanao. The controversy centered on the newly issued land titles granted to arriving Christian settlers from more crowded islands to the north and was destined to persist into 1973. Religious fanaticism added heat to the controversy. Muslim resistance modulated from initial efforts at extortion and intimidation to armed conflict. Communist agents from the Maoist-oriented New People's Army undertook to exploit the situation for revolutionary ends. At the outset, government spokesmen attempted, quite unconvincingly, to attribute the principal blame to unnamed Malaysian student provocateurs, allegedly trained in the Arab Republic, but alternative accusations against the Communists and their China connection took priority in the end.

Allegations of revived Communist activity were not entirely fictitious, although its limited magnitude did not in any way threaten the authority of the government. The older Huk peasant organization was disintegrating internally, especially following the killing by government agents in October 1970 of two outstanding leaders, one of them the son of Luis Taruc, Pedro by name. The New People's Communist Army group was not limited to a peasant constituency or to any locality. It derived part of its leadership and its newly acquired arms from the defection during 1970 of a number of lower-level army officers, particularly a Lieutenant Corpuz, alias Dencio. This embarrassing development provided the occasion for President Marcos to conduct a substantial purge of allegedly useless or undesirable elements of the upper-level army command, and to select as his secretary of defense a staunch civilian supporter, Ponce Enrile. The dismissals included eighteen generals, twenty colonels, and thirteen lieutenant colonels. China was officially blamed for the continuing export of national liberation, although Foreign Minister Romulo did substitute at this juncture the use of the more respectful term "People's Republic" rather than the opprobrious "Red China" when referring to mainland China. Marcos also decried the prospect of possible admission of China to the United Nations and complained that Washington had not consulted Manila regarding the changing American policy.

The 320 elected delegates to the Constitutional Convention assembled at the Manila Hotel in June 1971 to undertake the task of constitutional revision. The orientation of the delegate groups was essentially conservative, but leaders of both major parties were included, along with independent intellectuals and clergy, and even a few of the socialistically inclined. Politics were really never far away from the convention sessions. One of the group's first actions was to reject by a narrow margin the seemingly gratuitous proposal that Marcos and his wife be barred from the presidential candidacy in 1973. A consensus gradually developed that it would be desirable to shift to a parliamentary system, presumably as a means of controlling more effectively the power of the executive.

It was not until July 1972 that the preliminary constitutional draft was completed and publicized in a context of heightened political tension. Student demonstrations at the University had erupted in early 1971, eliciting an official threat that the incipient state of rebellion might call for martial law. Vice-President Fernando Lopez subsequently bolted to the Liberal party and began espousing a pro-American policy calculated to enlist financial support from sympathetic sugar interests and oil prospectors. Marcos appeared to be losing his influence and control.

Political controversy came to a focus during the off-year election campaign to fill eight Senate vacancies in the late summer of 1971. Marcos attempted to exploit the alleged Communist threat, while Liberal party spokesmen stressed rising prices, government corruption, unemployment, and growing popular disorder. Marcos accused the Liberal party secretary, Aquino, of deliberately aiding Communist subversion. An alleged abortive attempt to kidnap government leaders, highly publicized, was followed on August 21 by the explosion of two bombs in the middle of a major Liberal party meeting, attended by top party leaders and all eight senatorial candidates. The explosions killed nine persons and injured ninety others, including several of the candidates (one seriously) and two party leaders. No explanation of the episode was forthcoming, and no arrests were made. The president blamed his favorite culprits, the Communists, and exploited the tragic incident by suspending the writ of habeas corpus. One Maoist youth who was unconnected with the bombing was nevertheless arrested. The total casualties suffered during the course of the four months campaign were more than 200 killed (40 of them on election day), and some 250 wounded. The Liberal party captured six of the eight senatorial seats. By early 1972, President Marcos began addressing political audiences behind a bullet-proof enclosure, with the area barricaded against incursions by hostile demonstrators. By this time, he had adjusted to the changing international scene by advocating diplomatic recognition of both China and the Soviet Union.

The embarrassments of the Manila government were aggravated by successive crop failures, due initially to

652

plant diseases and pests and compounded in mid-1972 by a series of savage typhoons. The flooding was the worst in the history of the Islands. During 1971 the food price index rose by 25 percent; it soared by 37 percent in July 1972. The emergency relief program was less than adequate because of the usual administrative difficulties.

The initial report of the Constitutional Convention, presented in July 1972, reflected the growing popular unrest. It recommended shifting to a parliamentary system of government and supported a previous Supreme Court decision declaring illegal all American acquisition of lands in the Islands since 1946. The definition was broad enough to cover timber licenses, oil leases, and franchises covering public services. The new ruling left uncertain whether American firms and other alien interests could legally deal with state corporations, with actual owners of real estate, or through artificial corporations representing pension funds or other assets. In any case, American property rights acquired since 1946 were definitely liable to formal termination by 1974. In August 1972 the Supreme Court ruled that American and other alien firms that complied with the required reduction to a maximum of 40 percent foreign ownership of stock would also be barred from employing alien management personnel. Such rulings carried wide national appeal, but they displeased Filipino sugar interests and threatened to block official plans to encourage the expansion of timber and oil development efforts. Relevant issues had been posed by the brilliant Maoist author Sison in his *Philippine Society and Revolution* in 1970. He argued that continued official collaboration with both indigenous feudalism and expanding American economic imperialism made revolution unavoidable. Marcos tried to answer the argument in his own *Today's Revolution: Democracy*, which concluded that martial law might be the only means for realizing the necessary drastic changes, while at the same time serving to defend the state against Communism.

It was within this highly charged context that Marcos moved to exploit the proposed transition to parliamentary control as a means of legalizing and perpetuating his power. By resorting to the expedient of martial law, a possible legal recourse under the existing presidential constitution, he would be able to alter the proposed constitution materially and to qualify as prime minister under the new system. At the same time, he moved to enlist army support and American acquiescence by publicizing real or imagined threats of Communist subversion. The current orgy of stealing, kidnapping, and attempted assassinations would provide useful background justification. Once in control, Marcos could advance corrective assurance covering the future status of American investments and trade. It was noteworthy that budget revisions in August 1972 provided more funds for the army than it had ever anticipated.

Martial Law

Marcos' declaration of martial law on September 23 was issued with the full support of the army under Defense Secretary Enrile. It involved the closing down of eight prominent newspapers and the prohibition of nongovernment editorial comment by radio and television. Among those jailed were eleven critics of the president from the Constitutional Convention; the Liberal party secretary, Aquino; three provincial governors, thirty-six mayors; sixteen newspaper publishers and columnists; and four members of the adjourned Congress—plus around one hundred distrusted members of the Manila police. Although selected individuals were released from time to time, the number of persons detained by the end of 1972 had risen to around six thousand.

The justification advanced was cleverly devised. The president proposed to halt the spread of violence and crime and to counter the irresponsible attacks of hostile politicians. To law and order appeals he added a promise of implementing land reforms, long blocked by the conservative Congress. He dismissed a number of objectionable minor court judges, along with 450 notoriously corrupt internal revenue and customs officials. Altogether around 150,000 civil servants lost their jobs by early November. The president and his civilian cabinet exercised firm control over army leadership and they continued to pay deference to constitutional formalities. Strikes were banned, and private citizens who owned handguns were ordered to surrender them. More than 30,000 guns were reportedly collected during October and several times that number thereafter. The government assumed control over public utilities, railways, and airlines, as well as all means of public communication.

Apart from those people who were dismissed or imprisoned, the initial public reaction to martial law was, on balance, favorable. Public order was restored and crime sharply curbed. Few mourned what was assumed to be a temporary dismissal of the politically-obsessed Assembly, which had often shown itself to be irresponsible, self-seeking, and extravagant. Exercising full control, Marcos might be able to carry through his announced plans to distribute 1.5 million hectares of land in units of 5 hectares (12 acres) to more than 700,000 tenant farmers. The lands would be purchasable over 15 years, with annual payments amounting to only 25 percent of the normal crop output. Marcos also promised seeds and fertilizers; he assigned army engineers to public works construction, reduced electricity rates, and raised the pay of the army. With a cooperative army and an able and responsible civilian cabinet, it might conceivably be possible to demonstrate the truth that freedom must be responsibly exercized, and that democracy could be more than a political scramble for wealth and power. Few observers were fully confident that such hopes were real, but most felt it might be well to wait and see, taking advantage of the welcome discipline and order while it lasted. Press censorship would surely be relaxed in time, and some political freedom restored. It was nevertheless patently obvious that very much was at stake in the Marcos gamble, including a possible end to free political institutions, the provoking of widespread rebellion as a consequence of his abuse of power, and the destruction of the national

655

identity of the Philippines as the one symbol of Christianized civilization and democracy in the Orient.

The new regime's conciliatory economic policies with respect to alien investments aroused mixed reactions. In an obvious bid for American support, Marcos postponed the punitive application of both the Supreme Court and the Constitutional Convention rulings challenging the legality of American property holdings and forbidding alien corporations the right to select their own management personnel. The arrested Convention members and escapees included a number of the most vocal anti-American nationalists. The president explained that all alien business and development operations were indeed legally liable to government takeover, but that existing property titles would continue valid as regards the alternative claims of private Filipino owners until any such overt governmental action was taken. A great deal of property was at stake, including alien places of business, trading operations involving bulk imports, oil exploration leases and refineries, automobile production, and other industries, plus fruit and rubber plantations. Marcos was saying that alien interests were not subject to automatic legal liquidation and that for the time being existing contracts and titles would be regarded as valid. Oil development contracts, for example, if negotiated with the state as the formal owner, could be substituted for the older form of property leases.

A threat was clearly implied. If alien business interests or governments should decide to incur the risks involved in opposing dictatorial rule and espousing the cause of democratic freedom, they would be immediately vulnerable under the Marcos doctrine. By late November popular support for martial law had begun to waver, mainly because the promised relaxation of repressive measures failed to materialize. Only a few selected detainees were being released, and press restrictions were rigidly maintained, with great profit in advertising revenue going to the few cooperative publishers. Matters could not be allowed to drift indefinitely.

The New Constitution

On November 29 the Convention delegates formally approved the new draft constitution, including with it the cumulative decrees that Marcos had issued under the authority of martial law. The favorable decision was probably influenced by the accompanying action to include within the contemplated five-hundred-member interim National Assembly all members of the Convention who favored the new order, in addition to former senators and congressmen who decided to cooperate. A national plebiscite was scheduled for January 18, which would afford opportunity for the people to approve or to reject the new constitutional arrangement. As head of the martial law authority, President Marcos would be the permanent arbiter of the proper time to implement the proposed parliamentary system.

In early December a massive publicity campaign was launched to help ensure a favorable result from the plebiscite. Government agencies enlisted the cooperation of business leaders, police and military personnel, and school teachers, taking full advantage of the official monopoly of all available radio and press facilities, as well. But even if the new constitution should fail to be approved, martial law would still persist. In a minimal gesture of fairness, Secretary Tatad of the Information Ministry released from custody fifteen selected dissenters, including six newsmen, three delegates to the previous Convention, three mayors, two public prosecutors, and one radical student leader. All releasees were nevertheless required to keep the police informed as to their whereabouts.

Public criticism of the proposed plebiscite waxed increasingly caustic. The mood of the most violent dissenters was reflected in an attack on the president's wife, Imelda Marcos, by a knife-wielding assailant on December 7, during a government-sponsored rally in Manila. Serious injuries to her arms and hand resulted. Although obliged

at the outset to restrict their campaigning to hand-distrib-
uted mimeographed sheets, the opposition became increasingly articulate and vehement during the ensuing
holiday season. Criticism centered on the new constitution
itself, as well as associated presidential decrees (especially denials of free speech and the concessions made
to American business interests), plus the arbitrary and
illegal methods employed to authenticate the new order by
a rigged plebiscite. Groups of prominent citizens filed
suits before the Supreme Court seeking injunctions to halt
implementation of the new constitutional system. The most
prestigious group of petitioners was headed by a Harvard-trained lawyer and one-time supporter of Magsaysay,
Senator Lorenzo Tanada.

Marcos replied to the rising chorus of protest by allegations that enemies of the state were fomenting confusion and subversion. Finally, on January 8, he announced
abandonment of both the plebiscite plans and the proposed
convening of the interim Assembly. Then followed, from
January 10 to 15, the hurried mobilization by government
agencies of an estimated thirty-five thousand opinion-
sampling "citizen's assemblies," to whom the government's proposals were explained and approval requested
via a show of hands. Following public announcement of
the widespread affirmative reaction, a so-called Congress
of Citizen Assemblymen, two thousand strong and carefully
selected, was convened at the Presidential Palace. It
accorded prompt approval of the November 29 and January
8 decisions, recommended a possible seven-year continuance of martial law, and suggested the official proclamation
of an overt counterrevolution if circumstances warranted.
The president responded by saluting the allegedly spontaneous
democratic response of the citizen's assemblies and by officially proclaiming the implementation of the new constitutional system. The pronouncement halted for the time
being all Supreme Court hearings on the several pending
petitions. Under the projected regulations, all judges,
including those of the Supreme Court, were removable
at the president's discretion. For the time being and for

the indefinite future, Marcos assumed the right to exercise the combined powers of president, leader of the martial law regime, and prospective premier—if and when the new constitution was made operative.

The Supreme Court eventually reconvened in mid-February to consider four new protest actions. One of them involved the accusation of five senators that President Marcos had acted illegally in locking the doors of the Congress to prevent the constitutionally authorized convening of the legislative body on January 22. Others challenged the entire sequence of the president's usurpation of authority. In view of the fact that Marcos enjoyed full backing of both police and army, no one expected to obtain remedial action from the Court. One litigant characterized the several forlorn protests as the "last hurrah" for Philippine democracy. The Court ruled on April 2, 1973, by a six to four vote that the new constitution was legally in force.

Although virtually all informed observers recognized that the charade of constitutional manipulation by Marcos was a transparent device to legalize his dictatorship, not all reactions were negative. Some Filipinos still professed to find in the new regime encouraging signs of order and eventual public acquiescence, coupled with improved efficiency and concern for public welfare. Reactions also differed in Manila business circles and in Washington. Although the State Department was officially silent, staff opinion reflected dismay over the obvious fact that the course Marcos had pursued went far beyond any legitimate concern to end crime, corruption, and political extremism. It was, in fact, more likely to aggravate such problems in the long run. The Defense Department, with its eyes on Clark Field and the Subic Bay Naval Station, warned against "rocking the boat" and interfering in Philippines politics.

The American business community at Manila was strongly favorable to Marcos. Americans owned around $1 billion worth of investments in the Islands, and United States banks held debtor obligations amounting to some $950 million more. Particularly encouraging to alien business interests was the possible emergence of restored order and encouragement of foreign investor activity. The new Oil Exploration Development Bill proposed by Marcos would open the door for offshore explorations presumably on a par with opportunities available in Indonesia. It seemed likely, furthermore, that American property holdings after 1974 would be challenged only in agricultural lands, where Filipino wealth was concentrated. As of early 1973, investors were hesitant to move forward until clearer evidence was available that the regime was indeed stabilized, even though anticipations were reportedly high.

No amount of scholarly endeavor to maintain detachment in relating the dismal story of the denouement of Philippines democracy can avoid posing the question of what America's priorities in Southeast Asia really were. The alternative issue of human freedom versus dictatorship was movingly dramatized in late August 1973, when the long-time imprisoned liberal party leader Benigno Aquino was brought to trial before a military tribunal for alleged subversion. The accused denounced the trial as a charade, refused legal counsel, and cited the fact that Mr. Marcos had assumed by decree the power to reverse any decision which the tribunal might see fit to render. Aquino's statement to the court ran in part as follows:

> I have decided not to participate in these proceedings: first, because this ritual is an unconscionable mockery; and second, because every part of my being . . . is against any form of dictatorship. I agree that we must have public order and national discipline, if the country is to move ahead. But. . . . discipline without justice is merely another name for oppression. . . . In all humility, I say it is a rare privilege to share with the Motherland her bondage, her anguish, her every pain and suffering. . . .
>
> Mr. President, Honorable Members of this Commission, I fully realize the consequences of my decision. You have your duties to perform; I have my sad fate to meet. I have chosen to follow my conscience and to accept the tyrant's verdict. May God have mercy on all of us.

660

The shocked court recessed for forty-eight hours, then for a week, and was finally suspended indefinitely while the case was remanded by the president to a special panel for reexamination.

XVII

DEVELOPMENTS IN
INDOCHINA SINCE 1969

Post-1969 Cambodia
The Fall of Norodom Sihanouk

The political and military misfortunes that overtook
Cambodia in the early 1970s were in part the outgrowth
of cumulative problems associated with Prince Norodom
Sihanouk's torturous diplomatic balancing act of the
previous quarter-century. They also owed something to
the increasingly aggressive policy pursued by the new
Nixon administration at Washington in an effort to end
Sihanouk's equivocation. Distrusting, as Sihanouk did,
both his Vietnamese and Thai neighbors, who refused to
give iron-clad guarantees covering Cambodia's existing
frontiers, he undertook persistently to balance off the
contending forces affecting the country's independence.
A major policy objective was to isolate the hostile activities of the relatively small group of Khmer Rouge operating in the Elephant Mountains to the southwest of Phnom
Penh from the also Communist-supported, anti-Saigon
operations of the Vietminh and Vietcong forces occupying
the eastern South Vietnamese border areas. It was partly
to avoid embarrassing Peking and the Vietminh that
Sihanouk refused to accept the offer of American assistance against the Khmer Rouge by the so-called
Khmer Serai forces enlisted and trained by CIA agents
from among Cambodian residents across the Thai border.

Sihanouk's labored efforts during the middle sixties to cultivate friendly relations with Peking were designed to enlist Chinese influence as a means of checking possibly hostile moves on the part of both Communist factions. The tactic involved winking at the abuse of sanctuary privileges by both the Vietminh and Vietcong armies to the east of the lower Mekong River. Sihanouk's government also connived at the use of Cambodia's southern seaport facilities of Sihanoukville by Chinese and Soviet munition ships and the cooperating trucking services from the port to border sanctuary points of Cochin-China adjacent to Communist-occupied areas. Cumulative evidence of the mounting violations of Cambodian neutrality was submitted to Phnom Penh by United States intelligence services in early 1969.

Political leaders within Phnom Penh, including Sihanouk himself, were aware as early as 1967 that if the war continued, the tactics being pursued could threaten the integrity of Cambodia. In 1967 Sihanouk protested the openly pro-Maoist activities of the Cambodian-Chinese Friendship Association, as well as Peking's continuing support of the Khmer Rouge dissidents in the Elephant Mountain area. He also objected to the enlistment by the Vietminh of the services of Khmer Leou (Lao) montagnard contingents living in northeastern Cambodia. Supporting the growing concern of the army and other politically informed elements within the capital was the increasing popular unrest arising from the deteriorating economic situation. The serious decline of overseas trade was complicated by bad harvests, diminishing state revenues, and rising prices.

It was under these circumstances, during the summer of 1969, that the United States regained a measure of its pre-1962 influence at the Cambodian capital. President Nixon managed by July to satisfy Sihanouk's demands for border guarantees, so that diplomatic relations could be restored in August. The event was simultaneous with the elevation of General Lon Nol and Prince Sirik Matak as leaders in the new Cambodian cabinet. Although the returning American embassy assumed a distinctly low pos-

663

ture, the evidences of policy realignment multiplied. Numerous aspects of the faltering state socialization program were abandoned in favor of economic development along more orthodox lines outlined by the International Monetary Fund and the World Bank. By the end of the year Premier Lon Nol had closed down twenty-eight government-operated enterprises and began offering guarantees to prospective foreign investors against the threat of future nationalization. Negotiations were also pushed with Pan American Airways for the expansion of tourist trade, focusing on the monuments at Angkor.

Prince Sihanouk went along reluctantly with the change of course, still confident that his personal popularity and his virtually indispensable role as political leader and chief of state, backed by supporting provincial governors and police, would see him through the political crisis. Opposition developed within a number of disparate elite circles, including the rival Sisowath royalist faction; top army officers hungry for the perquisites of power; student opponents of royalty per se; nationalists resenting Vietnamese intrusions; and a majority of the elected Assembly. Aware of the growing opposition but mistakenly assuming that his political enemies would not dare depose him, Sihanouk departed for Europe in January 1970. The trip was made presumably for reasons of health, but also to initiate diplomatic efforts at both Moscow and Peking to obtain guarantees against Communist intrusions in violation of Cambodia's independence and presumably to counteract the growing influence of the United States. Although Lon Nol's moves accorded with Washington's objective to eliminate the Cambodian sanctuary nuisance, evidence is lacking that any detailed scenario of the tactics to achieve such ends had been worked out.

Following Sihanouk's departure, vocal criticism of the prince rapidly increased, and events developed an impetus of their own. A gratuitously provocative move occurred on March 11, when a Phnom Penh mob of some ten thousand demonstrators reportedly led by several score civilian-garbed soldier *provocateurs* attacked the local

Hanoi and Vietcong National Liberation Front embassies, with the police nowhere in evidence. On the following day, Premier Lon Nol coupled his formal apologies with arbitrary and impossible demands that all Vietminh and Vietcong forces withdraw from the country by March 15. Confused Hanoi and NLF spokesmen suggested negotiation of differences, but to no end. Instead of returning immediately to Phnom Penh on hearing of the riots, Prince Sihanouk proceeded with his plans to visit Moscow and Peking in an attempt to negotiate, as on previous occasions, for relief from Vietnamese intrusions into Cambodia. On March 18 a majority of the Assembly voted to bar the prince's return, elevating Cheng Heng, the chairman of the Assembly, to be his replacement as chief of state. The entire Assembly fell in line on March 22. Meanwhile, Saigon authorities moved to restore diplomatic relations with Phnom Penh.

The improvised character of Premier Lon Nol's program was suggested by his excessive concern from the outset to discredit the expelled chief of state as a playboy, a corruptionist, and a power-hungry publicity seeker. An angry reaction against these attacks developed in provincial areas, where the people still revered the popular prince. Bus convoys of protesters from Kompong Cham and elsewhere converged on the capital and had to be turned back by gunfire. Lon Nol's government then tried to divert attention by instigating renewed mob violence, this time directed against Vietnamese residents in Phnom Penh and vicinity (many of them Christians), whom he accused of collaborating with the Vietcong. Whether deliberately planned or not, a wholesale massacre of Vietnamese occurred in mid-April, and the river downstream became clogged with the dead bodies of the victims. The exodus of some two hundred thousand survivors to South Vietnam continued into August 1970. Another slaughter of Vietnamese civilians by Cambodian troops occurred later at Prasaut in the Parrot's Beak border area.

These well-publicized events outraged the Vietnamese people, North and South, and helped dissipate any inclination or hope Hanoi may have entertained of coming to terms with the Lon Nol government. Forewarned by spies and by several mid-April unilateral ARVN invasions of Cambodian border areas from Cochin-China, the Vietminh withdrew troops from the border sanctuaries and began fraternizing with the disaffected populations of northern Cambodian villages and towns. The efforts achieved remarkable success. By early May the hopes once entertained that the Lon Nol regime, assisted from South Vietnam could expel the Vietnamese forces and revitalize the country's economy, gave place to speculation as to how long or even whether Cambodia could survive as a national entity. Phnom Penh's thirty-thousand-man regular army was amateurish and lacked morale, training, and weapons. Meanwhile, the value of the *riel* dropped 30 percent in five weeks.

Whereas Soviet policy toward the exiled Sihanouk was decidedly reserved from the outset, the prince received a hearty welcome when he and his family eventually arrived at Peking. On April 27 he attended a four-sided conference held at Hanoi, with both Russian and Chinese representatives present. Perhaps the most significant development was Premier Pham Van Dong's reported assurance to Sihanouk that Hanoi, in the end, would respect Cambodia's frontiers. Moscow subsequently agreed to make good Hanoi's losses in military supplies sustained during border raids. The Soviet embassy at Phnom Penh nevertheless remained open. In mid-July Prince Sihanouk was convicted in absentia of treason in a three-day trial by a Phnom Penh court in a far-from-impressive prosecution performance.

The War in Cambodia

Warfare in Cambodia attained tragic proportions, extending far beyond the bounds foreseen by its allied sponsors. Sound military considerations could be cited in support of the decision to eliminate the border sanctuaries, but the long-term implications of the action were not fully appreciated. As late as April 20, President Nixon associated his expectation of a favorable outcome in Cambodia with the announcement that one hundred and fifty thousand American troops would be withdrawn from South Vietnam within the ensuing year. Unilateral moves across the border by ARVN forces began during the final week of April, with somewhat discouraging results. Pressed by American army leadership, Nixon abandoned his initial mood of confidence to announce on April 30 that American ground forces would also participate in the invasion. The action would be a limited, two-months operation designed to destroy enemy military supplies and headquarters establishments in the border sanctuaries. The move was defended as a necessary contribution to the successful execution of the espoused Vietnamization program; it was designed to ensure the safety of American troops and to avoid a decline in America's world influence. Neither the American Congress nor the Lon Nol government was consulted at the time.

During the ensuing two months, the invading allied forces destroyed substantial quantities of enemy food supplies and some military stores of Chinese origin, but they overran no headquarters and encountered few Vietminh troops. Instead of withdrawing from Cambodia under the combined pinch of Lon Nol's forces and invaders from South Vietnam, the Hanoi forces moved westward into Cambodia proper as part of their plan to collaborate with Cambodian rebels who were hostile to Lon Nol. The South Vietnam forces were particularly unwelcome because of their wanton looting of captured Cambodian villages and towns and their overbearing attitude toward the inferior Cambodian government forces. American air and logistic support contributed substantially to the operations of ARVN troops, a portion of whom, under General Do Cao Tri of the Third Corps, gave a creditable military performance. American bombing attacks were later directed against enemy operations far removed from the border sanctuaries, and U.S. ground troops entering Cambodia further to the north encountered minimal resistance.

Although Thai army units were widely deployed along the western Cambodian frontier, they did not become directly involved in the invasion. Bangkok's leaders bided their time, being in no mood to undertake any rescue mission within the neighboring state, which they had so long disdained, unless and until the United States agreed to pay the full costs. The Thai were accordingly taunted by the Saigon leaders for their alleged venality and lack of confidence. The American-sponsored Khmer Serai force resumed limited operations against the Khmer Rouge inside Cambodia. A somewhat larger Serai contingent from Cochin-China numbering around two thousand men was also organized to collaborate with the ARVN forces. Saigon spokesmen objected sharply to this move, however, because the Khmer Serai were better paid than their own troops. The regular Cambodian army, expanded substantially beyond its original size of thirty thousand men but lacking training and discipline, proved to be no match for the occupying Vietminh and Vietcong forces. The principal concern of the latter was to cultivate the support of the indigenous pro-Sihanouk villagers and they were assisted in the task after August 1 by regular radio broadcasts by Prince Sihanouk himself speaking from Peking. The American bombing raids tended to drive an increasing number of peasants over to the pro-Vietminh side.

Following the withdrawal of American ground forces from Cambodia by July 1, the early optimism of Phnom Penh gave way to disappointment and resignation. The protective charms and amulets carried into conflict by all Cambodian troops proved woefully ineffective. Increasing dissatisfaction over Lon Nol's fumbling administrative performance was reflected in the debates of the National Assembly. All high school and university classes were dismissed to stimulate army enlistment and to curb student protests. Elaborately staged ceremonies involving military salutes, palace uniforms, marching school children with flags and bands—all reminiscent of Sihanouk's earlier public relations performances—did little to improve morale. The newly drafted republican constitution attracted very little attention.

By early 1971 popular apathy was so widespread that a twelve-man Vietminh cadre managed to penetrate the city's principal airport and wreak havoc on planes and hangars. For a time Phnom Penh was virtually isolated, and economic activities throughout much of the countryside ground to a halt. Vietnamese forces at this juncture evinced no intention to attack the capital itself, being content to weaken morale and to politicize the peasantry. Premier Lon Nol eventually collapsed physically under the mounting strain, suffering a severe stroke on February 8, 1971. Prince Sirik Matak of the rival Sisowath branch of the royal family took over temporarily as chief executive.

The Problem of Governmental Leadership

The deficit of competent political and administrative leadership at Phnom Penh, which became increasingly acute following Lon Nol's stroke, was aggravated by the near collapse of the economy. The amount of money in circulation had more than doubled between 1967 and 1971, with the result that prices of consumer goods multiplied. The government treasury deficit of $230 million in 1970 approximately doubled in 1971, adding to the inflationary spiral. The exchange rate for the *riel* rose from the official 54 to the dollar to 250 in the black market. Plantation operations ceased, as did production by newly developed industries, including cement, paper, lumber, textiles, and oil refineries. Exports fell to a mere $14 million in 1971. Periodic roadblocks interrupted shipments of rice to the capital area, and only occasional truck convoys managed to get through from the port of Kampong Som.

Conditions within the capital reached a point of semi-anarchy following General Lon Nol's departure for medical treatment in Hawaii on March 1. The badly paid troops and police raided city markets and restaurants (mainly Chinese owned) and appropriated automobiles as needed.

669

Higher-ranking army officers profited personally from their handling of American funds for troop payments, which covered an estimated fifty to eighty thousand more men than were actually in the armed forces. Sandbags and wire barricades appeared within the crowded capital, associated with nightly curfews and an all-pervasive fear. Lon Nol returned from Hawaii on April 12, still far from recovered from his stroke and also suffering from diabetes and high blood pressure.

Not until May 3, when Prince Sirik Matak was formally named executive head of the government, was some clarification of administrative responsibilities achieved. Sirik had served as vice-president of the Council of Ministries since July 1970. He was a competent administrator but, as a relic of royalty, unpopular with both the army and the ruling political elite. Although largely incapacitated by continuing illness, Lon Nol continued to serve as titular premier and chief of state, mainly because no generally acceptable person was available to take his place. Sirik's rivals included the president of the General Assembly, In Tam, and the irresponsible younger brother of the premier, Lon Non. Non had risen to prominence as head of the Khmer Serai contingent recruited from Cochin-China from which post he derived ample personal income. So limited was the competition for leadership that the World War II anti-French nationalist newsman, Son Ngoc Thanh, was eventually included in the government.

This makeshift government arrangement persisted for a full year, with Sirik Matak able to exercise only limited authority in the absence of support from the partly incapacitated premier. Government control extended little beyond a fifty-mile radius from the capital. The country outside remained largely in the hands of rebels—partly Khmer Rouge, who repeatedly interrupted the highway to the seaport, and partly the Vietminh-sponsored, pro-Sihanouk opposition. The two rebel factions did not cooperate fully. In December 1971, for example, open strife developed between the Khmer Rouge and the Vietminh occupants of Angkor Wat when the former accused the latter of damaging the art treasures at the site. Historic tradition here demonstrated more vitality than did ideological Communist ties. Perhaps the greatest loss incurred was the enforced abandonment of the restoration efforts within the monument grounds that had previously been conducted by the Frenchman Groslier.

A major political crisis developed in Phnom Penh in early March 1972, when the long-delayed republican constitution came up for adoption. When Lon Nol attempted to alter the document to strengthen the president's powers, the Constituent Assembly refused to go along. After a week-long crisis, Lon Nol dismissed the body, named himself the first president, and appointed as premier, foreign minister and presidential adviser the politically emasculated Son Ngoc Thanh. (Five earlier nominees to whom he had offered the post had rejected the premiership because Lon Nol refused to give assurances concerning the conduct of elections and the role of the cabinet.) With a single exception, all of the new seventeen-member cabinet were personal followers of Lon Nol. As a former leader in the Khmer Serai, Son was recognized as safely anti-Communist and anti-Sihanouk, but he was rather eccentric and lacked administrative experience. The principal objection raised against the now-excluded Sirik Matak was that he was an unrepentant royalist who lacked sympathy with democratic goals.

Elections for the Assembly under the new constitution were eventually staged in August 1972, the first held since 1966. Both of the principal opposition parties—Sirik's Republican and In Tam's Democratic groups—were denied any possible chance of victory by Lon Nol's gerrymandering tactics, and both accordingly withdrew from the contest. This left the field to the president's own Socio-Republican party, with his younger brother, Lon Non, playing a prominent role. A phony People's Party, sponsored by a Lon Nol army officer, provided the only resistance. The official party won every seat in the new Assembly. An assassination attempt on Son Ngoc Thanh's life occurred during the course of the campaign.

The only real issue raised during the election was a complaint over the five-fold rise in the price of rice since 1970. One week after the election, a band of riotous young army personnel attacked the stall keepers, mainly Chinese, of Phnom Penh's central marketplace, reducing the place to a shambles. Shortly thereafter, a veritable rice panic developed at the capital, following a rebel blocking of road transportation from Battambang. The resulting 40 percent price increase within a single week was due in part to collaboration between bribe-taking officials and Chinese merchants who were out to recover their bribery costs. The rice panic eased only after United States planes brought in some ten thousand tons to relieve the critical shortage.

A cabinet reshuffling followed in October in response to American pressure on Lon Nol to select a vice-president who would serve as a kind of heir apparent, and also to broaden the political base of his cabinet by including experienced opposition party leaders. Son Ngoc Thanh was asked to resign in favor of the secretary-general of the victorious Socio-Republican party, Hang Thun Hak. As a former participant in the Khmer Serai under Lon Non, the new premier was expected to counter the growing popular support for Prince Sihanouk and to persuade dissident Cambodian factions to abandon all affiliations with the Communists. Nine of the sixteen cabinet members were carried over from Son's group, the most important change being the selection of Lon Non to head the key anti-Communist government agencies. No vice-president was named, and the followers of Sirik Matak and In Tam were ignored. In Tam led the rising chorus of civilian protest against army rule, which found expression not only in the press but within the ranks of the Buddhist monk community. Lon Nol's response on October 10 was to proclaim a state of emergency, which stifled criticism; he refused to "play the game of democracy and freedom" any longer in wartime. Henceforth, the president would take over all parliamentary functions, legislating by decree.

Washington's response to the Lon Nol coup was to renew the customary American pledge to support the Cambodian people in their efforts to defend themselves against Communist enemies, while insisting that the president use his decree power to curb inflation. The requisite measures included higher import taxes on luxuries, stringent credit controls, and a devaluation of the *riel* in relation to the dollar, plus some relaxation of press restrictions. A Hong Kong press report of late 1972 described the situation at Phnom Penh as one of hopeless disunity and spreading chaos. Wholesale extortion was practiced officially on the highways; a 20 percent surcharge was collected for all government services; higher officers within the army pocketed the pay provided for an admitted phantom army.

It was difficult for observers to envisage a feasible substitute for the increasingly ineffective and unpopular regime of the Lon brothers as of early 1973. For Cambodian traditionalists, including most of the country's peasants, a strong sense of nostalgia developed for the good old days before March 1970. Even among elitists and students, antiroyalist sentiments began to wane. All Cambodian nationalists, including the army and the Khmer Rouge, wanted their country cleared of foreign troops and interference, its border secured and neutralized, its independence preserved. But Lon Non's dominant army faction rejected collaboration with the allegedly treasonous followers of In Tam and Sirik Matak, while the Khmer Rouge continued to be hostile to Prince Sihanouk personally, despite Peking's efforts to bring the two Cambodian rebel groups together. Lon Nol indicated for a time that he might be willing to legalize the Khmer Rouge but refused to have any dealings with Sihanouk's followers.

The shifting·world power alignments at the time added to the confusion. When a Sihanouk delegation visited Moscow in late 1972, the Communist party functionary who received them pledged continuing support for the patriotic forces of Cambodia, but the Soviet government refused to recognize Sihanouk's government-in-exile located in Peking. In Phnom

Penh the Soviet ambassador reportedly favored a possible return of Sihanouk, but not under Chinese auspices. Meanwhile, Peking's reorientation with Washington raised doubts in Sihanouk's camp as to the dependability of his support from China. And in Cambodia rebel Khmer units hostile to Lon Nol were closing ranks and taking over most of the fighting, resisting the efforts of the gradually departing Vietminh forces to take back weapons they had previously supplied.

Under the circumstances, United States policy to protect the Cambodian people also became equivocal and uncertain. Having to deal with an incompetent and unrepresentative government and an impotent army incapable of making war or peace, and having no recourse save resort to destructive air raids to assist its ally, Washington had few acceptable options. Continued assistance to Lon Nol's government appeared very likely to expand the rebellion in the long run. Particularly disturbing was Lon Non's growing domination of the government, including what remained of the elected Assembly. Continued American pressure, including Vice-President Agnew's visit on February 1, 1973, influenced Lon Nol to invite In Tam to become a special counselor to the office of president, presumably in time to take the place of Premier Hang Thun Hak. An associated move on March 5 to nominate Sirik Matak as vice-president was flatly vetoed by Lon Non. Sirik had made his acceptance conditional on Lon Nol's curbing the powers of his brother.

Events began to take direction in mid-March, following a month-long teachers' strike at the capital protesting inadequate salaries and rising prices. Lon Nol's angry response on March 17 was to disrupt the strikers' meeting by hand grenade attacks and to imprison protesting spokesmen. On the same day a bomber attack was made on the President's Palace by a lone royalist sympathizer. Characterizing the two developments as expressions of a royalist-Communist plot, the president declared a state of unqualified national emergency, suspending all civil liberties. Hundreds of suspects were arrested and all criticism suppressed. Lon Nol published at the time the contents of a telegram of sympathy sent by President Nixon congratulating him on his escape from attempted assassination and expressing admiration for the courage and steadfastness of the Cambodian people under Lon Nol's leadership. The telegram also conveyed assurances of continuing American support.

Lon Nol's assertion of complete dictatorial control was apparently the signal for launching the first concerted attack on Phnom Penh by rebel Cambodian groups. The attacking forces included few if any organized Vietminh units. All approaches to the city were cut, and only the employment of massive bombing attacks from American airplane bases in Thailand saved the regime from imminent collapse. It was not surprising under the circumstances that negotiations for the complete withdrawal of Vietnam forces from Cambodia initiated by the faltering Lon Nol government ran completely aground. The controversy developed progressively into a civil war waged between rival Cambodian factions, while, except for cadre services, the Vietminh returned to their main concern with South Vietnam.

North Vietnam, 1969–70

Hanoi's relations with non-Communists in South Vietnam suffered an irreparable loss with the death of Ho Chi Minh in September 1969. As no other Vietnamese leader did, Ho commanded respect as a dedicated patriot. Nor could any of his disciples match his effectiveness in soliciting continuing Soviet and Chinese cooperation in support of his country's military and economic efforts to survive. His passing also left unresolved important differences within Hanoi's own leadership. There was disagreement with respect to acceptable standards of Communist orthodoxy and regimentation and on the feasibility of conducting prolonged guerrilla warfare in South Vietnam. Hanoi also continued not to be in full agreement with the provisional NLF regime over the character of an eventual coalition government for the South and the terms of Vietnam's unification, where Ho's presence would have helped. Radio reports from Hanoi suggested other unresolved problems relating to incentives for enhanced production, party discipline, war weariness, and flagging popular morale.

Despite these problems, North Vietnam continued to function effectively and to absorb the drain of supplying one hundred and fifty thousand men annually for military operations in the south, few of whom ever returned. The Vietminh forces enjoyed no alien manpower assistance, except what could be recruited locally from the Pathet Lao, the Vietcong, and the pro-Sihanouk Cambodians. Visitors to Hanoi found the city orderly and well policed, its people apparently content to use bicycles instead of the motorbike and limousine transportation of Saigon, and resigned to an indefinite continuation of the nationalist struggle. Deeply rooted social traditions deriving from two millennia of civilized living contributed more to the population's disciplined capacity to survive than did a mere two decades of Communist indoctrination.

Hanoi's major diplomatic problem was to maintain an acceptable balance between Soviet and Chinese influence. Only the Soviet Union could provide sophisticated weaponry and industrial equipment, while China could help with small arms, consumer needs, and food. Peking was extremely sensitive to the Southeast Asian aspects of its threatened encirclement by both Soviet and American bases around China's perimeter. Differences also developed over the Cambodian situation after Sihanouk took up residence in exile at Peking, which strengthened China's influence with both Hanoi and the NLF. But North Vietnamese leaders continued to be wary of possible dominance by their neighbor to the north. Negotiations were begun with Bangkok in 1970 over the repatriation of Vietnamese refugees in northeastern Thailand, dating from the French war. Hanoi's objectives included as always ending the U.S. bombing of Laos from Thai bases.

Immediately following Ho's death and into 1970, control

at Hanoi gravitated toward the orthodox Communist Truong Chinh, who maintained that top priority be given to building a disciplined socialist state along Maoist lines and that party members must demonstrate their selfless dedication to collectivist goals and must enlist the cooperation of the masses. By contrast, the pro-Soviet, South Vietnam-born Le Duan was more pragmatic. He and General Giap were bent on winning the war and were prepared to make incentive concessions to both workers and peasants to improve economic production and to curb black-market operations. Events in Cambodia following the downfall of Sihanouk in early 1970 tended to play into Chinh's hands, since for the time being any early prospect of a military victory in South Vietnam was postponed. Increased emphasis in North Vietnam was placed on economic recovery efforts to make good the damages suffered during the course of the American bombing operations from 1965 to 1968.

South Vietnam, 1970–71

The principal losers in the changing military situation of 1970 were the Vietcong forces, who were largely dependent on support from Vietnamese-populated areas in the South and who suffered from reduced military assistance from the Vietminh. The National Liberation Front spokesmen at Paris expressed the forlorn hope that some more moderate leader like General Duong Van Minh, recently returned from years of exile in Thailand, might succeed to control in Saigon and make possible the initiation of genuine peace negotiations. Some such change might become possible in the forthcoming Legislative Assembly and presidential elections scheduled for 1971.

Peace negotiations at Paris came to a standstill. Not only were the North Vietnamese spokesmen unresponsive and formal, but the Saigon representatives resented American efforts to engage in private exchanges with spokesmen for Hanoi. Generally speaking, both the Vietnamization program and the military diversion into Cambodia tended

677

to strengthen the position of President Thieu and the Saigon army command. The only countertrend was the election of the entire anti-Thieu, Buddhist slate of ten senatorial candidates out of a total of thirty for the off-year elections of 1969. Even so, the members of both the Senate and the National Assembly, remembering the fate of Tran Ngoc Chau and other critics in 1970, were understandably hesitant to voice their critical opinions. Chau was sentenced by an army tribunal to ten years at hard labor, and the civilian court's reversal of the decision was ignored by Thieu.

Challenge came mainly from religious groups. Early in 1970 several Catholic bishops published an open letter addressed to President Thieu advocating a cease-fire, serious peace negotiation efforts, revival of freedom of communication with the North, and plans for early reunification. Father Hoang Quynh sponsored a supporting demonstration in Saigon, calling openly for the replacement of Thieu by a leader of recognized integrity, presumably Duong Van Minh. But other Catholics remembered that Big Minh had helped overthrow Ngo Dinh Diem, and many of them tended to side with the president in opposing suggestions that special elections or a referendum covering negotiation policies be held before 1971. Buddhist protests during 1970 included a forty-eight-hour hunger strike in May and two immolations (one monk and one nun) in June. Antigovernment Buddhists occupied the National Pagoda briefly in May, only to be driven out by government-sponsored mobs, which left four dead and fifty injured.

Student protests against the Thieu government were also widespread during 1970, but largely futile. They staged a general boycott of classes following the incarceration of twenty-one student leaders in March. This was followed by a disabled veteran's attack against the bewildered Saigon police that was designed to protest dramatically their shabby treatment by the government. The move may have been instigated by General Ky. Students found another opportunity for protest in April, when news came of the anti-Vietnamese pogrom at Phom Penh. On this occasion Thieu closed down all schools in Saigon and imposed a strict curfew. One fringe group of students indicated sympathy for the Vietcong, while the vast majority became anti-American. Student frustration verged on despair.

Rival army leaders tried to make political capital out of their respective roles in connection with the war in Cambodia. Vice-President Ky, when assigned in May to repatriate Vietnamese refugees from Phnom Penh, attempted presumptuously to function as a kind of military viceroy. He was promptly replaced in the task by the regular foreign minister, General Tran Van Lam. General Do Cao Tri, the able Third Corps commander in the Parrot's Beak area, made sure that his own military activities were well advertised by ever-present cameramen. Tri's political pretensions were deflated by subsequent exposure within the Assembly of his flagrantly corrupt activities, topped off by the arrest of his uncle who was about to depart by plane for Hong Kong with four suitcases full of $700,000 in checks and bank notes. Tri died in a helicopter crash in early 1971. Duong Van Minh attracted some attention by proposing meanwhile that America's Vietnamization policy be extended to include political and economic affairs. His declared objective was to support a government capable of reflecting the views of the major religious constituencies. Thieu resisted American pressure for early ARVN withdrawal from Cambodia and asked for an additional $200 million to defray related military expenditures.

The Cambodian diversion and the consequent decline of military strife within South Vietnam strengthened governmental control and improved ARVN morale, but South Vietnamese relations with American and Korean troops did not improve. The respective allied intelligence agencies, all infiltrated with double and triple agents (U.S.-ARVN-Vietcong), continued to distrust each other. Well-to-do Vietnamese deposited their wealth abroad and paid fantastic sums to join exiled compatriots in France. South Vietnam's exports declined in 1969 to a mere $20 million, compared to $775 million in imports. Half of the revenue deficit was made good by forcing American personnel to spend their dollar pay at the exchange rate of 118 *piasters* per dollar, whereas the black market brought three times that number. But after all American aid was taken into account, the government's revenue deficit for 1970 was some $460 million. Land reform efforts came to a halt because of lack of funds and the breakdown of administering agencies. Washington's Vietnamization policy included the continued financing of the bankrupt Thieu regime.

The Elections of 1971

The South Vietnamese general elections for the National Assembly (scheduled for late August) and for the presidency (scheduled for early October 1971) held out, at best, little promise of resolving the political problems that plagued the country. Discontent with the government's performances was widespread, but complaints were also directed against landlords, rival politicians, partisan religious groups, the Americans, war leaders, and Communist rebels, as well as against Thieu himself. Factionalism was aggravated by the officially enforced absence of political organization. President Thieu's own efforts in 1969 to develop a supporting party coalition had faltered badly, so that he continued to be dependent as heretofore on the backing of certain disreputable remnants of the Diemist *Can Lao* Catholic faction, plus nepotist and army backing. More important was the president's control over the police and the mass media and his political and financial backing from Washington and the American Embassy. Under the circumstances, Thieu did not hesitate to manipulate the election laws and otherwise to embarrass all of his political opponents. He continued to deal with most of his individual critics either by police suppression or by bribery.

There was much diversity of political opinion within South Vietnam, relating in part to regional differences, which also cut across Buddhist, Catholic, and other religious and nationalist groupings. Antiwar sentiment was itself

680

divided over such issues as future relations with the National Liberation Front and North Vietnam. Worker organizations, minority Khmer and Chinese residents in Cochin-China, and the various sects all entertained distinct points of view. Under such circumstances and in the absence of sponsoring party organizations, the members of the National Assembly usually demonstrated little commitment to particular constituencies or issues, and much less to meeting the tangible economic needs of the nonelite electorate. Under normal conditions, assemblymen put their personal interests first, since a successful political career called for them to make accomodation with the existing power structure. Frances Fitzgerald (*Fire in the Lake*, p. 408) reported: "After all these years of war, the Saigon government remained a network of cliques held together by American subsidies, a group of people without a coherent political orientation bent on their own separate survival." It is not surprising that Assembly activities attracted correspondingly little interest on the part of the general electorate.

The prospects for making the executive arm of the government responsible to the people's will was even less promising than was the case for the legislature. Thieu's enormous personal stake in the outcome of the impending elections prompted the assumption that he would use every device at his command—legal or arbitrary—to influence the results. Only two serious rivals presented themselves: the former premier of 1963, General Duong Van Minh, and the vice-president, Air Marshal Nguyen Cao Ky. A possible third candidate, General Tran Van Don, a Minh supporter and ex-senator, made an abortive effort to revive the regulative Military Council of post-Diem times. Minh attracted substantial popular support by advocating that all proponents of peace, including individual Vietcong dissidents, should assist in establishing a more representative government for South Vietnam and work toward eventual unification with the North. Ky preferred to attack Thieu directly and spoke out not too convincingly about his own new-found desire for a military truce and a shift of priorities to economic recovery and an end of corruption. The electorate in general, when interviewed, reflected widespread war weariness along with fear of Communist domination. They would all cast their ballots because the police would later check the appropriate notches in their identity cards, but few expressed any faith in the alien electoral process.

President Thieu responded to his rivals by denouncing all proponents of peace as being prepared to grant politically to Communist enemies the victory they had failed to achieve by fighting. He declared such persons liable to charges of treasonable collusion with the enemy. In an effort to restrict the field of opposition candidates, Thieu made an abortive effort in December 1970 to secure legislative approval of a new election law. It would require all candidates for the presidency to obtain formal endorsement by at least 40 legislators (in a total of 197), or by 100 provincial or city councilors (in a total of 554) in order to qualify. All such endorsements would have to be officially authenticated. The measure passed the House, but the Senate struck out the endorsement provision as both politically and constitutionally objectionable. The proposal lapsed for the time being, but it was destined to be revived six months later.

The political campaign was interrupted by the much-publicized ARVN invasion of central Laos, which started on February 8, 1971, and continued for some 45 days. It involved more than 20,000 ground troops, assisted by an uncounted number of American-piloted helicopters. The objective was to capture the Communist supply center of Tchepone and to disrupt traffic proceeding down the Ho Chin Minh trail. The operation was designed to reduce the movement of military stores destined for use in Cambodia and South Vietnam and to assist the progress of the Vietnamization program both physically and psychologically. It was also intended to bolster the stature of President Thieu as military leader and as presidential candidate. American ground forces cleared the way to the Laotian border, where the Vietnamese forces took over. The confidence of the government was reflected in the fact that it had already authorized composition of a new victory song to celebrate the capture of Tchepone. The going was rough, and it was March 7 before the crossroads center was occupied, mainly by troops flown in by helicopter. The delayed release of the victory song via government radio was followed several weeks later by the staging of an elaborately prepared victory parade at Hué, celebrating the army's alleged heroic performance in Laos. Saigon claimed 13,800 North Vietnamese killed, 15,000 trucks rendered inoperable, and 176,000 tons of munitions destroyed, all of which figures were fantastically exaggerated.

Thieu's public relations ploy turned to mockery when it became evident in time that the invaders had been routed and forced into headlong retreat, accomplished with the help of a massive helicopter rescue operation. The humiliating episode not only discredited Thieu's role as military leader; it challenged directly the feasibility of the Vietnamization program. Vice-President Ky ridiculed the victory celebrations with biting sarcasm and denounced the helmsman of the sinking South Vietnam ship as unfaithful, disloyal, and dishonest. Ky also castigated the existing government as benefiting only the rich and the powerful while victimizing the soldiers, the honest civil servants, and the peasants. The more reticent General Minh continued to solicit the support of peace advocates (especially the dissident Buddhists), opposing any coalition government that would imply surrender of South Vietnam to Communist demands.

Forced sharply on the defensive by the attacks of Vice-President Ky, Thieu revived his previously rejected election law in early June, now designed explicitly to deny candidacy to his rival. The move precipitated a mild riot in the Assembly involving thrown furniture, drawn revolvers, and grenade threats. A standing vote on the proposal was taken by the Assembly on June 3 under strong presidential pressure, and the law was passed by 101 votes to 27, a majority sufficient to override a Senate veto.

Opponents charged bribery and miscount, as well as the unconstitutionality of the move. President Thieu delayed his final approval of the measure until June 3, the last permissible day. Meanwhile, he began actively to solicit his own endorsements within both designated groups, garnering approximately 100 legislative supporters, and an estimated 200 to 400 provincial councilor officials, many of the latter his own appointees.

Although both Ky and Minh denounced the election law, they had no choice but to try to qualify under its provisions. Few assemblymen would risk endorsing Ky under the circumstances, and he also had little influence within the provincial bureaucracy. All of his suspected sympathizers within the cabinet and the high army command were demoted, and the few assemblymen who did speak were harassed by the police. When Van Minh managed in the end to obtain his 44 Assembly sponsors, there were not enough left to sponsor Ky, taking account of Thieu's endorsements. It was well into July before Ky was able to come up with the names of 114 provincial sponsors. He selected as his vice-presidential running mate a 34-year-old North Vietnam-born Catholic.

But the crucial test was still to come. Ky's designated endorsers were immediately subjected to scrutiny by provincial election officials, who managed to validate by the end of July only twenty-nine of the total. Meanwhile Ky charged Thieu in an open letter with intimidation of his own provincial sponsors and with exerting pressure on the reviewing committees. He hinted vaguely that an attempted coup was possible. On August 5, two days after the deadline for filing all candidacies, the Supreme Court ruled that Ky had failed to qualify. Big Minh proceeded to announce his own candidacy, naming a Buddhist running mate, and registered substantial reservations about his continuing in the contest unless changes were made. Shortly thereafter Ambassador Bunker left for a ten-day conference in Washington. He returned to Saigon on August 19.

During the interim President Thieu began to campaign

684

in earnest. As part of his effort, he distributed in mid-August an estimated one hundred thousand twelve-by-fourteen-inch frameable portraits of himself to provincial officials, who were ordered to distribute them advantageously among the population. The portraits were copies of a 1970 picture, printed at considerable expense in the Philippines.

On the day following Ambassador Bunker's return to Saigon he held a long conference with Duong Van Minh, after which the angry general withdrew his candidacy. On the next day a hastily assembled Supreme Court session, extending far into the night, announced its reversal of the August 5 decision and issued a new declaration on August 21 authenticating Ky's eligibility as a presidential candidate. Mr. Bunker's hectic series of weekend sessions with Minh and Ky, urging them both to remain in the race, came to naught. On August 23 Vice-President Ky rejected the belated action of the court. Both he and Minh denounced the election as a farcical charade. American hopes that a fair and meaningful election could be held to strengthen the political stature of the Saigon government were thus hopelessly dashed.

The National Assembly elections proceeded as scheduled on August 29. Some 1,300 individual candidates ran for 152 seats. All of them were obliged to pay an advance deposit of 50,000 *piasters* ($190) subject to forfeit if they failed to poll a minimum percentage of their district vote. Many irregularities were reported, and two-thirds of the incumbent candidates failed of re-election. Such rejection reflected, among other things, a lack of popular respect for the assemblymen who had voted themselves annual salaries amounting to $400 a month for their limited 90-day service in the legislature. Since party organizations were generally lacking, only the easily identified Buddhist candidates, all anti-Thieu, managed to stage some gains. The qualifications of a number of would-be candidates were rejected. When 106 rejectees entered an appeal petition, the Central Election Council on July 29 acted to validate 65 of the number.

The voting on August 29 was widespread because it was virtually compulsory, but little popular interest was exhibited. Official nominees came through with fewer than the two-thirds majority that the president had hoped for, but the outcome made little difference. When the voting blocs within the new Assembly eventually coalesced in December 1971, 20 alleged opposition members defected to the government side, and only 33 (two-thirds of whom were Buddhist partisans) affiliated explicitly with the opposition People's Social Bloc.

The meaningless presidential election was duly scheduled for October 3 at Thieu's insistence. U.S. civilian officials were unhappy over the propaganda windfall the event provided for Communist partisans and for American opponents of the Saigon regime. The official American military interpretation was that Ky and Minh had withdrawn from the contest rather than face the humiliation of certain defeat. On September 22 a senate debate was held in Saigon on a resolution to postpone the election, and no member was found who was willing to defend the policy of President Thieu. The resolution was unanimously approved, but to no avail. Thieu replied by urging everyone to vote as a gesture of popular respect for the constitution. Those who wished to vote against him could do so by mutilating their ballots. Thieu's election move was in reality an act of defiance not only of his own political enemies at home and abroad, but also of America's presumptuous advisory role at a time when Washington itself was moving to open direct communication with Communist China. Presidential control over the elective process, the army, the governmental bureaucracy, and American financial resources completed the pattern of personal dictatorship.

Continuity and Change in Laos

Many aspects of the situation in Laos as of 1969 persisted into the early 1970s with little significant change. King Savang Vatthana occupied his palace in the royal city

of Luang Prabang, still revered by virtually all sections
of the Laos population. He constituted a kind of sacred
symbol standing above the raging civil war and the massive
military intrusions from the outside. The premier, Prince
Souvanna Phouma, continued as head of the Vientiane
government partly because he was in the center of the
political spectrum and also because he was the only acceptable official recipient of essential American financial
assistance. He lacked organized mass support and was
under constant attack by the Sananikone-Boun Oum conservative faction for his so-called neutralist stance, but he
was nevertheless indispensable. Pathet Lao representatives
continued to occupy their prominently located legation site
in Vientiane, and the premier maintained a somewhat
desultory communication with his half-brother, Souphanouvong, at the rebel capital at Sam Neua. The territory under
genuine or nominal Vientiane control dwindled progressively,
from an estimated 40 percent in 1969 to some 25 percent
or less in 1972, but still contained around two-thirds of
the population. Chinese workmen extended their road construction effort in northwestern Laos down to the Mekong
River terminus at Muang Pak Beng, but no one appeared
particularly alarmed about it.

Except for continuing subsistence farming operations in
regions not involved in military operations or bombing
attacks, the economy was prostrate. The major portion
of state revenues came from customs levies on American-
financed imports, plus direct dollar contributions expended
at official rates of exchange for AID grants, soldiers'
pay, and military costs generally. The wealthy Phoui Sananikone faction long continued to profit from the purchase of
duty-free imports at regular dollar-*kip* rates of exchange,
including radios, air conditioners, and motor vehicles,
which they then smuggled back for sale at full market
value in neighboring Thailand. This source of income was
somewhat curtailed following the *kip* devaluation in
August 1971, when the official rate was raised to 600 to
the dollar and the commercial rate to 840.

An alternative irregular source of revenue was the

internal traffic and export of opium and heroin originating along the Shan States border of Burma. The operation was headed by General Ouane Rathikone, army commander of the area directly affected, until his forced retirement in July 1971. Also reportedly participating in the traffic was General Vang Pao, commander of the thirty-thousand-man tribal army (Meo and Yao) maintained by the CIA. A portion of the profits from opium helped support the families of refugee victims of the war. A considerable fraction of the medicines brought in with American funds for use by the hapless refugees continued as before to end up in the black market, to the profit of the dispensing officials.

A bank crisis in November 1971 prompted a temporary experiment with higher import taxes, but it resulted mainly in wholesale smuggling abetted by official collusion. A policy shift in May 1972 to a more simplified and lower tax structure, combined with freer access to foreign exchange, increased the volume of legal imports but brought in little revenue. Price inflation continued at around 30 percent annually, and nothing happened to close the enormous gap between wealth and poverty. Prospects for an early modulation to a self-sustaining economy, even if peace should be restored, were remote.

The annual rhythm of military activity also continued much the same. With Vietminh support, the Pathet Lao army of forty to fifty thousand men (largely Meo) staged their regular offensive starting in the New Year dry season. Such attacks were necessarily broken off with the start of the rainy season in late May, which reduced support roads to a quagmire of mud. The counterattack of government forces and of American-sponsored tribal contingents usually began in August, near the end of the rains when the Pathet Lao was weakest. The operations were made possible by American logistical services and by bombing raids, plus the use of "volunteer" Thai artillery units. The counterattacks eventually ran aground before the end of the year, and the annual pattern would then be repeated. The net seasonal gains of the two sides were roughly equal at first, but by 1971 they began to favor the rebel army. Part of the reason was that excessive dependence on American bomber support tended to weaken the already faltering morale of the government's ground forces, who usually elected to withdraw rather than to defend their positions in close-order combat.

An American observer described the Laos battlefield scene in March 1970 as follows:

> Laotian boys in their teens are dying in uniforms too big for them. Uncounted thousands of fatherless families shuffle in rags about the country as permanent flotsam of war. . . . It is generally conceded that airpower cannot be decisive in Laos. Its use makes North Vietnam ground advances costly . . . , but they keep advancing, and supplies keep moving. . . . Informed Laotians . . . believed that the war must be stopped if Laos is to live, free or unfree.

The refugee problem in both government-occupied areas and those controlled by the Pathet Lao became steadily worse. Approximately 40 percent of American refugee-aid funds, as of 1970, went to some 100,000 persons from the families of soldiers in Vang Pao's Clandestine Army. An estimated 80,000 new refugees were added to the previous total of 280,000 during the 10 months of intensified bombing activity of the Pathet Lao country from July 1971 to May 1972.

One observable change in the government related to the gradual introduction of new personnel. As acting defense minister, Prince Sisouk na Champassak undertook on August 1, 1971, to reassign the five regional army commands to younger, nonpolitical army officers, who would presumably be more willing to take orders from Vientiane. General Abhay of the capital area and the previously mentioned General Oune Rathikone proved to be particularly difficult to move. Sisouk explained that he was trying to prevent the country's degeneration into a decentralized warlord system of government. It was also noted that periodic Assembly elections continued to attract widespread popular participation, with the electorate usually voting against distrusted incumbents. (In January 1972, for example, two-thirds of the older member candidates suffered defeat.) But the newly elected members quickly fell in line, like the older group, under Sananikone's pervasive influence, to support his perennial demand that Souvanna Phouma abandon his neutralist policy.

Early in 1970 the pro-Communist forces overran the Plain of Jars above Vientiane and captured several important allied installations to the south and west. The morale of the Royal Laotian troops virtually collapsed, and Souvanna Phouma talked of retirement. But instead of attempting to capture Luang Prabang and Vientiane, both highly vulnerable, the Hanoi-Pathet Lao leaders were content with renewing their efforts to negotiate a cessation of American bombing operations throughout Laos, including along the Ho Chi Minh trail. Vientiane forces recovered much of the lost ground later in the year, due in part to Vietminh military diversions in Cambodia.

The South Vietnamese invasion of Laos as far as Tchepone, in February and March of 1971, involved territories entirely outside Vientiane's control and therefore afforded some temporary relief from the usual early-in-the-year enemy offensive in the north. Following the repulse of the ARVN thrust on Tchepone, the Vietminh moved to consolidate their control over southern Laos, centering power at Pak Sone in the Bolovens Plateau. The ARVN invasion of 1971 nevertheless carried forbidding connotations for Vientiane, as Souvanna Phouma was quick to point out. It compromised seriously his basic objections to the presence of alien North Vietnamese troops within the country. Defense Minister Sisouk na Champassak explained that inviting Thai and South Vietnamese troops to join in the defense of Laos would only make the country a battleground and thus destroy the nation. Although Vientiane's neutrality was already under challenge by the presence of Thai volunteers and Thailand-based American bombers, Sisouk insisted that the policy must be preserved as long as Hanoi-directed forces did not imperil the Laos-controlled left bank of the Mekong River.

A massive Vietminh-Pathet Lao attack on areas to the

690

north of Vientiane was launched in late months of 1971. The important allied base of Long Tieng was defended at the time by Royal Lao forces and by a Thai artillery unit, while a Meo Clandestine Army contingent under General Vang Pao was airlifted to the northeast corner of the Plain of Jars to cut enemy supply lines. Long Tieng fell in February 1972 when the commanding Lao general and other high-level officers abandoned their troops in the field and took off for Savannakhet in commandeered army trucks. Half of the defending soldiers, including the Thai contingent, fled without a fight, and the remainder retreated with the CIA to new headquarters westward at Ban Xon and later to Vang Vieng midway on Route 13 between Vientiane and Luang Prabang. Hanoi's victory at Long Tieng coincided with President Nixon's arrival in Peking. Route 13 was cut off north of Vang Vieng by the Communist forces, thus isolating Luang Prabang by road. Vang Vieng lacked a paved landing strip, but was otherwise defensible.

By early 1972 little was left of the authority of the Laotian government except along the Mekong River itself. In late 1972 a mortar-rocket attack by Communist forces on the river town of Thakhek, located opposite the American air base of Nakhon Phanom, precipitated the flight of two-thirds of the civilian population and most of the town's defenders, but the Communist forces refrained from occupying the place.

The virtual military collapse of the Vientiane government, which led eventually to an agreement between Vientiane and Sam Neu in early 1973 to permit 50 percent Pathet Lao participation in the government, left a number of questions unanswered. Why were the tribal Pathet Lao forces so much more effective than the better-armed and airplane-supported royal troops? Was Hanoi's primary aim to conquer Laos behind the veneer of Pathet Lao collaboration as a means of extending Communist control and facilitating attack on Saigon?

Obviously the North Vietnamese two-thirds of the army that captured Long Tieng was far more potent than were its Pathet Lao allies, but the latter were probably something more than a puppet army. From the beginning of the anti-French struggle in 1946, the Vietminh leadership had made persistent efforts to enlist the willing cooperation of the non-Vietnamese border hill peoples. The Hanoi authorities afforded tribal leaders both training and administrative experience not only in military operations, but also in governmental matters and economic activities. The Pathet Lao administration at Sam Neua functioned under Vietnamese authority and direction and contributed to realizing Hanoi's essential objectives, which included border security, guaranteed access down the Ho Chi Minh trail to South Vietnam and Cambodia, and the development of an essentially congenial regime within Laos, such as Prince Souphanouvong and his associates could provide. Communism itself had little apparent relevance to the achievement of such ends and carried even less meaning to hill tribesmen in the Pathet Lao camp. By contrast, American and Thai support of the conservative Mekong Valley Lao elite, long-time enemies of the tribesmen, coupled with the devastating American bombing attacks on rebel centers, served to strengthen Pathet Lao links with Hanoi.

In whatever territorial or governmental configuration the country of Laos may conceivably survive the military ordeal, relations with Hanoi will inevitably constitute an important conditioning factor. It must nevertheless be recalled that Prince Souphanouvong and other rebel leaders have repeatedly affirmed their political and cultural allegiance to Luang Prabang and to King Savang Vatthana in particular. Caught between more powerful neighbors, and with much of its territorial domain, as delineated by French colonialist boundaries, lost beyond recovery, the only chance Laos and its people may have to survive is as a neutralized Buddhist buffer kingdom. Such has been the apparent objective to which both Souvanna Phouma and his half-brother Souphanouvong have been long committed. A new coalition government was eventually to be established in 1973.

692

Hanoi's 1972 Offensive across the DMZ

While it is not possible within the confines of this study (already overlong) to include a discussion of the complicated worldwide peace negotiation efforts of the Washington authorities as they affected the Indochina conflict, some attention must be accorded to events within South Vietnam that accompanied the peace effort. The principal development was the massive North Vietnamese military offensive mounted across the demilitarized zone in late March of 1972. It was essentially a Hanoi-planned undertaking, initiated in spite of an economy that was degenerating, especially in terms of consumer needs. The people of Tonkin at the time suffered from an influenza epidemic and had experienced severe flooding in both 1971 and 1972. Consumer goods industries continued to be poorly managed and had recovered only meagerly from the damage and dislocations caused by the bombing attacks of 1965–68. The dubious gamble across the DMZ was apparently instigated by General Giap and the military party and owed little to outside instigation.

The fact that the move was possible at all underscores the differences between Hanoi's general frame of mind and that of Saigon in terms of morale and self-discipline. A published *Congressional Record* report of the observations of an American vistor in 1970 contrasted Hanoi's oxcart and bicycle society, orderly and singleminded, with the motorbike and limousine confusion of crowded Saigon, disorderly, dirty, and hopelessly corrupt. The reporter commented, "The foreign presence in Hanoi is almost invisible [whereas] in Saigon it is overwhelming. . . . Hanoi is poor but honest. . . . Saigon is sodden with corruption." A *New York Times* report of January was in the same vein: "North Vietnam is a state of mind. The people just don't care that the war is hurting them. They won't give up their idea of independence, and this means driving out the Americans."

In the atmosphere of March 1972, the motivation for the attack appears to have been two-fold. The first goal was

693

to discredit the Vietnamization program, the ARVN army itself, and President Thieu and to occasion the collapse of all three. The second was to afford opportunity for the Vietcong rebels in South Vietnam to revive their faltering control over large sections of the Mekong delta and sections of central Annam.

The situation in the South during the early months of 1972 had appeared to be moving toward more stable governmental control. The supply-starved Vietcong guerrillas were far less in evidence; rice cultivation was beginning to recover; the power of the president seemed unassailable. In January 1972 Thieu had purged one-fourth of his provincial chiefs and had dismissed eleven high army commanders. In February he flatly prohibited the debarkation of returning airbound General Nguyen Chanh Thi, who had been exiled in Washington for the six years since his clash with Premier Ky in 1966. In early March the president's brother was assigned the long-term task of organizing an official party around a nucleus of provincial councilors and chiefs, several score army officers, and the head of the national police. The move reflected the president's response to his growing isolation from other non-Communist political elements within most population centers of the country. For the time being, rising discontent over America's pro-Thieu role and the growing unemployment problem consequent on the withdrawal of American personnel appeared to be fairly well contained.

The North Vietnamese invasion of the DMZ, starting on March 29, was regarded at first in the South as a desperate tactical gamble. The situation worsened within the ensuing month, until it constituted a serious threat to the survival of the Thieu regime. The provincial capital of Quang-tri fell to the invaders by default, when the officers in charge of the defense fled by helicopter to Hué. Leaderless soldiers stampeded down the connecting highway accompanied by a host of refugees, including an estimated seven-eighths of the provincial population. A massive employment of American airpower prevented a debacle, gaining time for fresh divisions of ARVN forces to arrive from the south to stabilize the situation.

Following the fall of Quang-tri in early May, President Thieu moved politically to establish dictatorial control. On May 8 he requested legislative approval of a proposal for a six-month period of rule by decree. Three days later ho imposed martial law. When the Senate in early June rejected the initially approved House bill granting decree powers, a second measure was passed by the House limiting arbitrary presidential authority to matters connected to the war and to the economy. When this measure also ran aground in the Senate on June 27, it was passed arbitrarily and unanimously by a rump session, meeting late at night after the debate had been officially postponed and all opponents had left the hall. In a subsequent move to curb growing dissent, the president in September closed down fourteen leading newspapers in Saigon along with fifteen leading periodical publications. The action came because the publishers failed to post a required $50,000 bond, which would be subject to forfeit if a newly decreed code outlawing criticism of both the government and the armed services was violated, with offending editors liable to imprisonment. Only one opposition newspaper managed to post the bond. One editor's concluding remark ran: "Our country of wasted land is being engulfed in darkness."

The invasion from the North fell substantially short of its major objective of demoralizing the government's entire defense system, however, although it did materially change the situation in areas of the Annamite highlands and in much of the Mekong delta. Guerrilla groups associated with the National Liberation Front were able to emerge from their long-time hiding to re-establish co-operative contacts with local community defenders. Whereas government control of the countryside had been improving noticeably until early May, by late July the situation was deteriorating alarmingly. NLF cadres had returned to many communities, and other groups that resisted Vietcong control cut off their connections with central authority. Because of this and other political reasons, the president on August 22 moved secretly to abolish the authority of the country's eleven thousand hamlet centers to elect their own chiefs. The move ended a six-year ruling that had

695

been designed to enlist village cooperation with the government. It was made without consulting United States officials at Saigon.

During the latter months of 1972, the character of the popular rebellion in South Vietnam began to change. Opponents of Saigon of whatever political commitment began to exercise greater freedom in local situations, which frequently involved agreements between pro- and anti-Communist elements to avoid hostile confrontations. Defecting members of former NLF contingents who were now prepared to fight off any Vietcong assault, also exhibited little or no respect for ARVN forces or unwelcome Saigon officials.

At the end of President Thieu's six months of rule by decree, he announced the formal organization of his New Democratic party, which his brother had long been preparing. In a decree delivered on the very last day of the rule-by-decree period, Thieu announced a new election law, requiring that all of South Vietnam's twenty-four recognized political groups, on pain of forced dissolution, must establish village-based party organizations capable of attracting at least 20 percent of the total vote in any national election in the future. The terms of the decree automatically limited the number of legalized parties to a maximum of four and eliminated all regionally or religiously centered expressions of political dissent. Government-selected hamlet chiefs constituted an additional barrier. Striking similarities with the concluding period of the Diem regime were suggestively obvious. The civil struggle within South Vietnam could no longer be identified as a struggle for or against Communism.

Press observers from both Hong Kong and America reported in mid-1972 a sharp increase in anti-American sentiment among the South Vietnamese. Intellectuals complained that their venting of dissenting political opinion amounted to nothing as long as the United States continued to back President Thieu financially and politically. Benjamin Cherry of the *FEER* of Hong Kong (later excluded from Saigon) reported that the South Vietnamese population as a whole hated the Americans, despised Thieu, and feared the results of an alternative Communist victory. Many of his informants harbored secret admiration for the dedicated spirit of the leadership of the NLF. Cherry concluded: "War weariness, the feeling that the Vietnamese are pawns of an American game over which they have no control, and constant repression have combined . . . to destroy the spirit of the people." These views were largely authenticated by a *New York Times* reporter who indicated that the progressive militarization of the population under the Vietnamization program had served mainly to increase President Thieu's capacity to repress all indications of dissent. Any protester could be accused of being pro-Communist and thereby become liable to arrest, torture, and indefinite confinement. Political protest itself had become a childish pretense under circumstances where society as a whole was threatened with complete disintegration and moral collapse. A complainant was quoted as follows: "We have come to despise ourselves and our nationality, and the more revulsion we feel, the more we excuse ourselves on the ground that we cannot survive in such a system without participating in it."

Epilogue

The ending of direct American involvement in the Indochina fighting came in January, 1973, more than four years after the initiation of the largely abortive Paris peace negotiations. The period witnessed the engulfment of both Cambodia and Laos in peripheral aspects of the Vietnamese conflict, involving massive destruction in both countries from American bombing operations. American frustration over the failure of Hanoi to respond to the progressive withdrawal of U.S. ground combat forces culminated during the final months of 1972 in a revival of attacks on North Vietnam, including the mining of coastal waters and harbors—a risk made acceptable only by reason of American rapprochement with both Peking and Moscow—and in the savage bombing of all of Tonkin

697

in December. The limited peace settlement signed by Henry Kissinger and Le Duc Tho at Paris in January 1973 covered arrangements for the repatriation of American prisoners of war in return for complete U.S. withdrawal from Indochina, but it did nothing to end the fighting in South Vietnam and Cambodia and provided for the establishment of no popularly acceptable government at Saigon. Major political concessions to the Pathet Lao side made possible the eventual emergence of a shaky coalition government for Laos at Vientiane, and brought a welcome end to the futile bloodletting and bomber forays.

Despite the alleged peace settlements, all three governments, at Saigon, Phnom Penh, and Vientiane, were still dependent for survival on continuing substantial American financial and material assistance, with the continuance of the Lon Nol regime in grave doubt. Aside from the fact that the alleged explanation of the problems encountered by post-colonial Indochina in terms of a worldwide struggle between the Communist conspiracy and the champions of political freedom was no longer tenable, very little positive contribution had been made by two decades of American political and military intervention. The peoples directly involved, both indigenous and American, had paid a terrible price during the course of the ordeal, not only in loss of life, material devastation, and social disintegration, but in political confusion and animosity.

Most informed observers would agree that Southeast Asia is too important economically and strategically to be permitted to degenerate into stagnation and chaos. The region's potential for oil production, minerals, and food forbids its abandonment. Whatever progress may be feasible in terms of voluntary regional cooperation in matters of health, education, cultural exchange, and economic development, it seems clear that some kind of neutralizing security arrangement will have to be provided with assistance from the outside. Peace must be established within the area, and safeguards afforded against outside intrusions. The debilitating cost of armaments and devastating effects of modern military operations, as

698

demonstrated in Indochina, are clearly beyond the capacity of Southeast Asia to withstand. The peoples involved can achieve some meaningful national identification by revitalizing cultural resources—in the areas of religion, social cohesion, literature, architecture, carving and sculpture, painting, and the dance—deriving from their long-civilized past. The validity of their experienced value judgments and their genius for self-expression may also contribute ethical and social alternatives to an outside modernized world enamored of greed for material possessions and the exercise of power.

No simplistic formula can possibly encompass the manifold problems of Southeast Asian independence, and no solutions can be found without an achievement of a much more thoroughgoing understanding of the situation than currently prevails in world capitals. Southeast Asia must certainly continue to be the concern of intelligent and concerned newsmen, who have provided virtually all of the sources available for the concluding chapters of this study. Serious scholarship must also endeavor to interpret the facts that are now available. A definitive history attempted twenty years hence will be too late.

BIBLIOGRAPHICAL GUIDES AND SUGGESTED READINGS

FORMAL BIBLIOGRAPHIES

Carnell, Francis, *The Politics of New States: a Select Annotated Bibliography with Special Reference to the Commonwealth.* London, 1961.

Eggan, Fred and Evett Hester, *Selected Bibliography of the Philippines: Topically Arranged and Annotated.* New Haven, 1956.

Fisher, Mary J., *Cambodia: An Annotated Bibliography of its History, Geography, Politics, and Economy Since 1954.* Cambridge, Mass., 1967.

Hay, Stephen N., *A Guide to Books on Southeast Asian History, 1961-1966.* Santa Barbara, 1969.

Hobbs, Cecil C. (et al.), *Indochina: a Bibliography of the Land and People.* Washington, 1950.

Jumper, Roy, *Bibliography of the Political and Administrative History of Vietnam.* Saigon, 1962.

Lian The and Paul van der Veur, *Treasures and Trivia: Doctoral Dissertations on Southeast Asia.* Athens, Ohio, 1968.

Kennedy, Raymond, *Bibliography of Indonesian Peoples and Cultures.* New Haven, 1962.

Mason, John Brown, and H. Carroll Parrish, *Thailand Bibliography.* Gainesville, Fla., 1958.

Pelzer, Karl J., *Selected Bibliography on the Geography of Southeast Asia.* 3 vols., New Haven, 1949-56.

Thrombley, Woodworth G. and William Siffin, *Thailand Politics, Economy, and Social-Cultural Setting. A Selected Guide to the Literature.* Bloomington, Indiana, 1972.

Trager, Frank N., *Annotated Bibliography on Burma.* New Haven, 1956.

Tregonning, K. G., *Southeast Asia: a Critical Bibliography.* Tucson, Arizona, 1969.

TREATMENTS OF SOUTHEAST ASIA AS A WHOLE

Badgley, John, *Asian Development: Problems and Prognosis.* New York, 1971.

Benda, Harry J., *Continuity and Change in Southeast Asia: Collected Journal Articles.* Yale University Southeast Asia Studies Monograph Series No. 18, 1972.

Braibanti, Ralph, (ed.), *Asian Bureaucratic Systems Emergent from the British Imperial Tradition.* Durham, N. Carolina, 1966.

700

BIBLIOGRAPHY

Butwell, Richard, *Southeast Asia Today-and Tomorrow: Problems of Political Development.* New York, Praeger, 1969.

Deutsch, Karl W., *Nationalism and Social Communication.* Cambridge, Mass., 1966.

Devillers, Philippe (et al.), *L'Asie du Sud-Est.* 2 vols. Paris, 1970.

Emerson, Rupert, *From Empire to Nation: The Rise of Self-Assertion of Asian and African Peoples.* Boston, 1960.

———, *Representative Government in Southeast Asia.* Cambridge, Mass., 1955.

Fifield, Russell, *Southeast Asia in United States Policy.* New York, 1963.

Fitzgerald, C. P. *The Third China.* Melbourne, 1965.

Geertz, Clifford (ed.), *Old Societies and New States. The Quest for Modernity in Asia and Africa.* New York, 1963.

Golay, Frank (et al.), *Underdevelopment and Economic Nationalism in Southeast Asia.* Ithaca, 1969.

Hla Myint, *Southeast Asia's Economy; Development Policies in the 1970s.* New York, Penguin, 1972.

Hunter, Guy, *Southeast Asia: Race, Culture, and Nation.* Oxford Press, 1966.

Jacoby, Erich H., *Agrarian Unrest in Southeast Asia.* New York, 1961.

Johnson, John II. (ed.), *The Role of the Military in Underdeveloped Countries.* Princeton, 1962.

Kahin, George McT. (ed.), *Governments and Politics in Southeast Asia.* Ithaca, 1964.

Landon, Kenneth P., *Southeast Asia, Crossroads of Religion.* Chicago, 1949.

Leifer, Michael, *Dilemma of Statehood in Southeast Asia.* Vancouver, 1972.

Levi, Werner, *The Challenge of World Politics in South and Southeast Asia.* Englewood Cliffs, 1968.

McGee, T. G., *The Southeast Asian City.* London, 1967.

Myrdal, Gunnar, *Asian Drama: an Inquiry into the Poverty of Nations.* 3 vols. New York, 1968.

Shaplen, Robert, *Time Out of Hand: Revolution and Reaction in Southeast Asia.* New York, 1969.

Silvert, K. H., *Expectant Peoples, Nationalism and Development.* New York, 1963.

Thayer, Philip W., *Nationalism and Progress in Free Asia.* Baltimore, 1956.

Thompson, Virginia and Richard Adloff, *Minority Problems in Southeast Asia.* Stanford, 1955.

———, *The Left Wing in Southeast Asia.* New York, 1950.

Tilman, Robert O. (ed.), *Man State, and Society in Contemporary Southeast Asia.* New York, 1969.

Trager, Frank N. (ed.), *Marxism in Southeast Asia: a Study of Four Countries.* Stanford, 1959.

Wertheim, W. F., *East-West Parallels.* The Hague, 1965.

701

Country by Country Selections

BURMA

Badgley, John, *Politics Among Burmans*. Athens. Ohio, 1970.
Butwell, Richard, *U Nu of Burma*. Stanford, 1963.
Cady, John F., *A History of Modern Burma*. Ithaca, 1958.
Maung Maung, *Aung San of Burma*. The Hague, 1962.
———, *Burma and General Ne Win*. New York, 1969.
Nash, Manning, *The Golden Road to Modernity. Village Life in Contemporary Burma*. New York, 1965.
Pye, Lucian, *Politics, Personality, and Nation Building: Burma's Search for Identity*. New Haven, 1962.
Sarkisyanz, E., *Buddhist Backgrounds of the Burmese Revolution*. The Hague, 1965.
Silverstein, Josef, *The Political Legacy of Aung San*. Cornell Data Paper no. 86, Ithaca, 1972.
Smith, Donald Eugene, *Religion and Politics in Burma*. Princton, 1965.
Spiro, Melford E., *Buddhism and Society: A Great Tradition and its Burmese Vicissitudes*. New York, 1970.
———, *Burmese Supernaturalism*. Englewood Cliffs, 1967.
Tinker, Hugh, *The Union of Burma*. London. 1959.
Trager, Frank N. *Burma: From Kingdom to Republic*. New York, 1966
Trager, Helen G., *We the Burmese: Voices from Burma*. New York, 1969.
Walinsky, Louis, *Economic Development in Burma, 1951-1960*. New York, 1962.
Johnstone, William C., *Burma's Foreign Policy, a Study in Neutralization*. Cambridge, Mass., 1963.

CAMBODIA

Armstrong, John, *Sihanouk Speaks*. New York, 1964.
Chandler, David P., *The Land and People of Cambodia*. Philadelphia, 1972.
Kirk, Donald, *Wider War: The Struggle for Cambodia*. New York, 1971.
Leifer, Michael, *Cambodia: The Search for Security*. New York, 1967.
Poole, Peter A., *Cambodia's Quest for Survival*. New York, 1969.
Smith, R. M., *Cambodia's Foreign Policy*. Ithaca, 1965.
Steinberg, David J., *Cambodia*. New Haven, 1959.
Willmott, W. E., *The Political Structure of the Chinese Community in Cambodia*. New York, 1970.

INDONESIA

Dahm, Bernard, *History of Indonesia in the Twentieth Century*, translated by P. S. Falla. New York, 1971.
———, *Sukarno and the Struggle for Indonesian Independence*, with foreword by Harry Benda. Ithaca, 1969.

702

BIBLIOGRAPHY

Feith, Herbert, *The Decline of Constitutional Democracy in Indonesia*. Ithaca, 1962.

——, and Lance Castle (eds.), *Indonesian Political Thinking, 1945-1965*. Ithaca, 1970.

Geertz, Clifford, *Agricultural Involution*. Berkeley, 1963.

——, *The Religion of Java*. Glencoe, Ill., 1960.

Hanna, Willard A., *Bung Karno's Indonesia*. New York, 1960.

Higgins, Benjamin, *Indonesia's Economic Stabilization and Development*. Institute of Pacific Relations, 1957.

——, Benjamin and Jean, *Indonesia: Crisis of the Millstones*. Princeton, 1963.

Hindley, Donald, *The Communist Party of Indonesia, 1951-1963*. Berkeley, 1964.

Jones, Howard Palfrey, *Indonesia: the Possible Dream*. New York, 1971.

Kahin, George McT., *Nationalism and Revolution in Indonesia*. Ithaca, 1952.

Legge, J. D., *Central Authority and Regional Autonomy in Indonesia: a Study in Local Administration, 1950-1960*. Ithaca, 1961.

——, *Sukarno: a Political Biography*. London, 1972

Lev, Daniel S., *The Transition to Guided Democracy: Indonesian Politics, 1957-1959*. Ithaca, 1966.

McVey, Ruth (ed.), *Indonesia*. New Haven, 1953.

——, *The Rise of Indonesian Communism*. Ithaca, 1965.

Paauw, Douglas S., *Financing Economic Development: the Indonesian Case*. Glencoe, Ill., 1960.

Selosomardjan, *Social Status in Jogjakarta*. Ithaca, 1962.

Smail, John. R. W., *Bandung in the Early Revolution, 1945-46: a Study in the Social History of the Indonesian Revolution*. Ithaca, 1964.

Tan, T. K., *Sukarno's Guided Indonesia*. Brisbane, 1967.

Taylor, Alastir M., *Indonesian Independence and the United Nations*. Ithaca, 1960.

Van der Kroef, Justus Maria. *Indonesia After Sukarno*. Vancouver, 1971.

Van Nieuwenhuijze, C.A.O., *Aspects of Islam in Post-Colonial Indonesia*. The Hague, 1958.

Wehl, David, *The Birth of Indonesia*. London, 1948.

Wertheim, W. F., *Indonesian Society in Transition*. The Hague, 1959.

Willmott, Donald Earl, *The Chinese of Semarang: A Changing Minority Community in Indonesia*. Ithaca, 1960.

——, *The National Status of the Chinese in Indonesia, 1900-1958*. Ithaca, 1960.

Wolf, Charles Jr., *The Indonesian Story*. New York, 1948.

LAOS

Adams, Nina and Alfred W. McCoy (eds.), *Laos: War and Revolution*. New York, 1970.

Champassak, Sisouk Na, *Storm Over Laos*. New York, 1961.

Dommen, Arthur J., *Conflict in Laos: The Politics of Neutralization*. New York, 1971.

Halpern, Joel, *The Economy and Society of Laos*. New Haven, 1964.

——, *Government, Politics, and Social Structure in Laos*. New Haven, 1964.

Langer, Paul F. and Joseph J. Zasloff, *North Vietnam and the Pathet Lao: Partners in the Struggle for Laos*. Cambridge, Mass., 1969.

BIBLIOGRAPHY

Le Bar, Frank and Adrienne Suddard, *Laos*. New Haven, 1951.
McCoy, Alfred W. (ed.), *The Politics of Heroin in Southeast Asia*. New York, 1972.
Meeker, Oden, *The Little World of Laos*. New York, 1959.
Toye, Hugh, *Laos: Buffer State or Battleground*. Oxford, 1948.

MALAYSIA AND SINGAPORE

Barberm Noel, *The War of the Running Dogs. The Malayan Emergency, 1948-1960*. New York, 1972.
Fletcher, Nancy McHenry, *The Separation of Singapore from Malaysia*. Cornell Data Paper No. 173, 1969.
Gullick, J. M., *Malaya*. London, 1963.
Hanna, W. A., *The Formation of Malaysia, New Factor in World Politics*. New York, 1964.
Hanrahan, Gene Z., *The Communist Struggle in Malaya*. Kuala Lumpur, 1971.
Josey, Alex, *Lee Kuan Yew*. Singapore, 1968.
Leigh, Michael, *The Chinese Community in Sarawak, a Study in Communal Relations*. Singapore, 1964.
Miller, Harry, *Prince and Premier: a Biography of Tunku Abdul Rahman*. London, 1959.
Milne, R. S., *Government and Politics in Malaysia*. Boston, 1967.
Ness, Gayle, *Bureaucracy and Rural Development in Malaysia*. Berkeley, 1967.
Purcell, Victor, *The Chinese in Malaya*. London, 1948 and 1967.
Pye, Lucian, *Guerrilla Communism in Malaysia; its Social and Political Meaning*. Princeton, 1956
Ratnam, K. J., *Communalism and the Political Process in Malaya*. Kuala Lumpur, 1963.
Silcock, T. H., and E. K. Fisk (eds.), *The Political Economy of Independent Malaya*. Canberra, 1963.
Tilman, Robert O., *Bureaucratic Transition in Malaya*. London, 1964.
Wang Gungwu, ed., *Malaysia: A Survey*. New York, 1964.

THE PHILIPPINES

Averch, H. A., F. H. Denton, and J. E. Koehler, *A Crisis in Ambiguity: Political and Economic Development in the Philippines*. Santa Monica, 1970.
Costa, Horacio de la, *Asia and the Philippines*. Manila, 1965.
———, *The Background of Nationalism*. Manila, 1965.
Golay, Frank H., *The Philippines: Public Policy and National Economic Development*. Ithaca, 1961.
——— (ed.), *The United States and the Philippines*. Englewood Cliffs, for the American Assembly, 1966.
Lachia, Eduardo, *Huk: Philippine Agrarian Society in Revolt*. Manila, 1971.
Pomeroy, William J., *The Forest: a Personal Record of the Huk Guerrilla Struggle in the Philippines*. New York, 1963.
Spencer, Joseph E., *Land and People in the Philippines*. Berkeley, 1954.

BIBLIOGRAPHY

Starner, Frances L., *Magsaysay and the Philippine Peasantry: the Agrarian Impact on Philippines Politics, 1953-56.* Berkeley, 1961.
Taruc, Luis, *Born of the People.* New York, 1953.
Taylor, George E., *The Philippines and the United States: Problems of Partnership.* Englewood Cliffs, 1966.

THAILAND

Coughlin, R. J., *Double Identity: the Chinese in Modern Thailand.* Hong Kong, 1960.
Darling, Frank C., *Thailand and the United States.* Washington, 1965.
Fistiè, Pierre, *L'Evolution de la Thailande contemporaine.* Paris, 1967.
Jacobs, Norman, *Modernization Without Development: Thailand as an Asian Case Study.* New York, 1971.
Neuchterlein, Donald E., *Thailand and the Struggle for Southeast Asia.* Ithaca, 1965.
Phillips, H. P., *Thai Personality. The Pattern of Interpersonal Behavior in the Village of Bang Chan.* Berkeley, 1965.
Riggs, Fred, *Thailand: Modernization of a Bureaucratic Polity.* Honolulu, 1966.
Siffin, William J., *The Thai Bureaucracy: Institutional Change and Development.* Honolulu, 1966.
Silcock, T. H. (ed.) *Thailand, Social and Economic Studies in Development.* Canberra, 1967.
Skinner, William G., *Chinese Society in Thailand; an Analytic History.* Ithaca, 1957
Wilson, David, *Politics in Thailand.* Ithaca, 1962.
, *The United States and the Future of Thailand.* New York, 1970.

VIETNAM: THE END OF COLONIALISM

Buttinger, Joseph, *A Dragon Defiant: A Short History of Vietnam.* New York, 1972.
Chaffard, Georges, *Les Deux Guerres du Vietnam: de Valluy à Westmoreland.* Paris, 1971.
Chesneaux, Jean, Georges Boudarel, and Daniel Hemery, *Tradition et Revolution au Vietnam* Paris, 1971.
Devillers, Philippe, *Vietnamese Nationalism and French Policies.* New York, 1953.
Fall, Bernard, *Hell in a Very Small Place.* Philadelphia, 1967.
, *Street Without Joy: Indochina at War, 1940-1954.* Harrisburg, Pa., 1961.
Hammer, Ellen, *The Struggle for Vietnam.* Stanford, 1954.
Honey, P. J., *Genesis of a Tragedy: the Historical Background to the Vietnam War.* London, 1968.
Lacouture, Jean, *Vietnam Between Two Truces.* London, 1966.
Lancaster, Donald, *The Emancipation of French Indochina,* New York, 1961.
McAlister, John T., *Vietnam: the Origins of Revolution.* New York, 1969.
, and Paul Mus, *The Vietnamese and their Revolution.* New York, 1970.
Smith, Ralph, *Vietnam and the West.* Ithaca, 1971.

BIBLIOGRAPHY

VIETNAM: THE COMMUNIST REGIME IN THE NORTH.

Chaliand, Gérard, *The Peasants of North Vietnam.* Paris, 1968, Baltimore, 1969.
Fall, Bernard, *Ho Chi Minh on Revolution: Selected Writings, 1920-1966.* New York, 1967.
Hoang Van Chi, *From Colonialism to Communism, A Case Study of North Vietnam.* London, 1964.
Honey, P. J., *Communism in North Vietnam. Its Role in the Sino-Soviet Dispute.* Cambridge, 1963.
——, ed., *North Vietnam Today.* New York, 1962.
Lacouture, Jean, *Ho Chi Minh: A Political Biography.* New York, 1968.
Neumann-Hoditz, Reinhold, *Portrait of Ho Chi Minh: an Illustrated Biography.* New York, 1972.
O'Neill, Robert J., *General Giap: Politician and Strategist.* Cassel, Australia, 1970.
Van Dyke, Jon M., *North Vietnam's Strategy for Survivial.* Palo Alto, 1972.
Zagoria, Donald, *Vietnam Triangle: Moscow, Peking, Hanoi.* New York, 1967.

VIETNAM: THE AMERICAN MILITARY INTERVENTION.

Department of State, *Aggression from the North: the Record of North Vietnam's Campaign to Conquer South Vietnam.* Publication no. 7893. Washington, 1965.
Falk, Richard A. (ed.), *The Vietnam War and International Law, volume 3: The Widening Context.* Princeton, 1972.
Halberstam, David, *The Best and the Brightest.* New York, 1972.
Hilsman, Roger, *To Move a Nation: The Politics of Foreign Policy in the Administration of John F. Kennedy.* Toronto, 1967.
Hoopes, Townsend, *The Limits of Intervention, An Inside Account of How the Johnson Policy of Escalation in Vietnam was Reversed.* New York, 1969.
Kahin, George McTurnan and John W. Lewis, *The United States and Vietnam.* New York, 1969.
Lyn, Peter, *War and Peace in Southeast Asia.* London, 1969. Chatham House.
Manning, Robert and Michael Janeway, *Who We Are: An annotated Chronicle of the United States and Vietnam.* Boston, 1969.
Neil Sheehan et al., *The Pentagon Papers.* New York Times, Bantam books, 1971.
Zasloff, Joseph J. and Allan E. Goodman (eds.), *Indochina in Conflict: a Political Assessment.* Boston, 1972.

VIETNAM: THE SOUTH IN WARTIME

Bloodgood, Dennis, *An Eye for the Dragon: Southeast Asia Observed, 1954-70.* New York, 1970.
Fitzgerald, Frances, *Fire in the Lake: The Vietnamese and the Americans in Vietnam.* Boston and Toronto, 1972.
Hickey, Gerald, *Village in Vietnam.* New Haven, 1964.
Luce. D. and John Sommers, *Vietnam- the Unheard Voices.* Ithaca, 1969.

706

BIBLIOGRAPHY

Nhat Hanh, Thich, *Vietnam: Lotus in a Sea of Fire*. New York, 1967.
Osbourne, Milton, *Strategic Hamlets in South Vietnam*. Cornell Data Paper no.
55, 1965.
Pike, Douglas, *The Viet Cong. The Organization and Techniques of the National
Liberation Front of South Vietnam*. Cambridge, M.I.T. Press, 1966.
    , *War, Peace, and the Viet Cong: A Current Analysis of Communist Strategy
in Vietnam*. Cambridge, M.I.T. Press, 1969.
Scigliano, Robert G., *South Vietnam: Nation Under Stress*. Boston, 1963.
Shaplen, Robert, *The Lost Revolution*. New York, 1965.
Warner, Dennis, *The Last Confucian*. New York, 1966.

INDEX

715

2-100